Outlooks
and Insights

A READER FOR COLLEGE WRITERS

Third Edition

Edited by PAUL ESCHHOLZ
and ALFRED ROSA
University of Vermont

Outlooks
and Insights

A READER FOR COLLEGE WRITERS
Third Edition

St. Martin's Press / New York

Senior editor: Mark Gallaher
Development editor: Cathy Pusateri
Managing editor: Patricia Mansfield
Project editor: Beverly Hinton Beers
Production supervisor: Alan Fischer
Photo researcher: Inge King
Cover design: Jeannette Jacobs
Cover photo: Ursula Kreis

For information, write:
St. Martin's Press, Inc.
175 Fifth Avenue
New York, NY 10010

ISBN: 0-312-03171-8

Photo Credits

Private Lives: Jean-Claude Lejeune
Family and Friends: Gale Zucker / Stock, Boston
Men and Women: Susan Van Etten / The Picture Cube
Campus Life: Martha Stewart / The Picture Cube
Language in America: Jean-Claude Lejeune / Stock, Boston
Culture and Pop Culture: Wide World Photos
Nature and Science: Lionel Delevingne / Stock, Boston
The Individual and Society: M. E. Warren / Photo Researchers

Preface

The third edition of *Outlooks and Insights*, like the first two editions, is an exciting yet practical and classroom-tested solution to an old problem: how best to use readings to help students improve their writing. Most teachers of writing, and indeed most writers, would agree that reading supports writing in many ways. A fine essay can serve as an example of masterful writing, and also of mature thought and insight; such examples can give inexperienced writers a sense of what is possible and inspire them to aim high. An essay can also provide students with information and ideas for use in their writing, or it may stimulate them to pursue new lines of inquiry and to write on new topics of their own. And, of course, an essay can illustrate the effective use of rhetorical strategies and techniques. The readings collected here will serve all of these familiar purposes. But *Outlooks and Insights* has an additional dimension: It provides students with explicit guidance—through discussion, examples, and exercises—in reading well and in using their reading in their writing.

This guidance is provided, first of all, in our introduction, "On Reading and Writing." Here we offer well-grounded, sympathetic, and practical instruction to students on how to become more active and accurate readers and how to turn what they read to effective use in their compositions. We acknowledge that different people respond differently to the same text, and also that one reader may use different reading strategies at different times according to his or her particular purpose in reading the piece. But we also insist that any interpretation of a text should be supported by evidence drawn from the words on the page, so that diverse readers can find common ground for discussion and agreement. To this end we offer criteria and a set of questions designed to help students respond fully to what they read and to help them distinguish between a purely personal response and a reasoned understanding.

Many students are unaware of the choices they have available to them when they are required to write about something they have read. To help them better understand these options, "On Reading and Writing" offers not only advice but full-length examples of three different kinds of papers that composition students are frequently required to write: the paper that analyzes a reading, the expository or argumentative essay on a topic derived from the reading, and the personal experience essay. All three essays were written in response to the same selection, George Orwell's "A Hanging." The first analyzes some aspects of Orwell's rhetoric, showing how he uses certain details to support his thesis. The second argues in support of capital punishment, engaging Orwell's topic but taking an independent position on it. The third recounts a personal experience in which the student writer discovered her own aptitude for thoughtless cruelty. Taken together, these compositions suggest the wide range of original responses that are possible in college writing assignments.

The heart of any anthology is, of course, the selections it contains. The readings in this new edition of *Outlooks and Insights* are both numerous and fresh. We have chosen 81 essays, 11 short stories, and 6 poems, offering instructors a large variety of options for making individual assignments and for organizing the course. The readings are grouped in eight large thematic units, beginning with themes of personal experiences and relationships, continuing with such aspects of our lives as education, work, language, and nature, and finally arriving at considerations of contemporary social issues and ethical questions. As in the second edition, we have focused subsections within each large thematic unit. These subsections are designed to concentrate classroom discussion and student writing on well-defined issues, concerns, and questions. For example, in the thematic unit "Campus Life" we have the subsections "The Aims of Education," "Teaching and Testing," and "Campus Issues of the 1990s," and in "Language in America" we have "Media and Advertising," "Prejudice and Sexism," and "Language and Propaganda." The selections in each subsection play off one another and encourage stimulating debate and controversy in the classroom and help to both focus and direct student writing. Because we've used these selections in our own classrooms, we know that each subsection provides a manageable and balanced assignment for a college composition class.

There are 58 new readings in this edition. Each has been chosen to be challenging but not baffling, and we have sought not only to appeal to students' interests and concerns but to broaden them. The selections are a mixture of the new and the familiar—familiar to composition instructors, that is, for few freshmen will have read even such durable pieces as E. B. White's "Once More to the Lake," Annie Dillard's "Sight into Insight," and George Orwell's "Politics and the English Language," essays that have earned their places in the small canon of essential readings for composition classes. We have been particularly careful to choose readings that are provocative or have an argumentative bent and that contain information that students can use to effect in their own writing.

Most of the essays in *Outlooks and Insights* were written in the last decade or two, but we have seasoned them with a few selections from classic authors—Jefferson, Hawthorne, Emerson, Dickinson. In most sections we have also included a poem and a story which we think can be used effectively in a composition course; any writer can learn from the meticulously sustained irony of Auden's "The Unknown Citizen" as well as from Gregory's "Shame," from the controlled and modulated prose style of a

Welty or Bambara story as well as from that of a Thomas or Didion essay. The questions and writing suggestions for the stories and poems are much like those supplied for the essays, with minimal attention to questions of literary form. At the end of "On Reading and Writing," however, we do alert students to some important generic differences, so that they will not read stories and poems in exactly the same way they read essays.

The questions and writing topics supplied for each selection further develop and exploit the advice and instruction given in "On Reading and Writing." The study questions about each essay, story, and poem, like the general questions in the introduction, help students to test and increase their understanding of what they have read, and may also help them gather material for analytical papers. The assignments, which are called "Writing Topics," focus the students' attention on the central issues and questions of the thematic units. Often we use these topics to generate classroom discussion and debate before we ask our students to write. We find that such discussions coax students to develop their own lines of thinking and to articulate clearly their views on a specific issue. The writing topics suggest ways that students may use a reading in their writing, and they are designed to elicit results ranging from autobiographical essays to research papers.

Each thematic section begins with a picture and several epigraphs which highlight the issues of that section. These materials, particularly the epigraphs, may find use in their own right as objects of discussion and as sources of writing assignments. Each selection is provided with a biographical headnote which sets the piece in the context of the author's work and where necessary supplies information about the author's original audience and purpose. To make *Outlooks and Insights* still more flexible and useful, there is a rhetorical table of contents that classifies the selections by type and by principle of organization, as well as a glossary that will help students understand rhetorical and literary terms in the questions without having to refer to other sources.

In working on the third edition of *Outlooks and Insights* we have benefited inestimably from the observations and suggestions of our fellow teachers from across the country: Iska Alter, Hofstra University; Deborah Asher, Union County College; Anne G. Atkinson, Oakton Community College: Keith Aubrey, Spokane Community College; Virginia Bishop, Essex Community College; Virginia A. Book, University of Nebraska; Dolores Bradley, Oakton Community College; Patricia H. Burns, Syracuse University; Rosemary Buteau, DePaul University; Lenore Cassesse, Hofstra University; William Clarke, Cypress College; Greta Cohan, Westchester Community College; Jean Cook, Bard College; Ron Dwelle, Grand Valley State University; Charles Elwert, University of Illinois at Chicago; Ruth Federman, Syracuse University; Margaret W. Franke, Northern New Mexico Community College; Lawrence B. Fuller, Bloomsburg University; Judith Harway, University of Wisconsin—Milwaukee; Claire Garcia, University of Denver; Michelle Garofolo, Modesto Junior College; Francine Hallcom, California State University—Northridge; Doris R. Hamer, Southeast Missouri State University; Richard J. Hawkey, Hofstra University; Richard Henze, Colorado State University; Thomas M. Kitts, St. John's University; Vivian Klein, Guilford College; John H. Knight, Fort Hays State University; Philip Korth, Michigan State University; Abraham Kotin, Los Angeles Valley College; Karen Krall, Temple University; Ali Lang-Smith, Southeastern Massachusetts University; Ruth Lupul, Los Angeles Pierce College; Mark Mabrito, University of Illinois at Chicago; Richard C. Mangnall, College of the Sequoias; Desmond F. McCarthy, Brandeis University; Michael McIntire, Los Angeles Pierce College; Rachel H. Moore, Baylor University; Muriel Myers, California State University—Los Angeles; Kathleen Nickerson, St. Clair County Community College; Catherine Noonan, University of Wisconsin—Milwaukee; Hildegard L. Owens, Essex Community College; Martha Pacelli, University of Illinois at Chicago; Sharon Pohlner, Essex Community College; Margaret Proctor, Grand Valley State University; Nancy Rayl, Cypress College; Dennis M. Read, Denison University; Barbara Rodman, Colorado State University; Catherine Sadow, Boston University; Carol Severino, University of Illinois at Chicago; Henry Sikorski, Hofstra University; M. Noel Sipple, Northern Virginia Community College; Craig Sirles, DePaul University; Ariel Slothower, San Jose State University; Elizabeth Stein, California State University—Fullerton; Louise M. Stone, Bloomsburg University; John Tagg, Palomar College; Sharon Thomas, Michigan State University; Joanne E. Walsh, Temple University; Nancy Woodard, Delta College; Linda Woodson, University of Texas at San Antonio; and William Zanghi, California State University—Los Angeles.

We are grateful to our editors at St. Martin's Press—Mark Gallaher, Cathy Pusateri, and Beverly Hinton Beers—for their insightful assistance and encouragement. Our colleagues at the University of Vermont helped us by assigning George Orwell's "A Hanging" to their composition classes and providing us with student papers for the introduction "On Reading and Writing." Finally, we want particularly to acknowledge the contribution of our students, who teach us something new every day.

Paul Eschholz
Alfred Rosa

Contents

6.   Culture and Pop Culture

7.   Nature and Science

8.   The Individual and Society   669

Rhetorical Table of Contents

The selections in *Outlooks and Insights* are arranged in eight sections according to their themes. The following contents, which is certainly not exhaustive, first classifies many of the essays according to the rhetorical strategies they exemplify. It then classifies selections by genre—e.g., public documents and speeches, poems, and short stories.

Argument and Persuasion

Cause and Effect

Comparison and Contrast

Definition

Description

Division and Classification

Illustration

Narration

Process Analysis

Public Documents and Speeches

Poems

Short Stories

Outlooks
and Insights

A READER FOR COLLEGE WRITERS

Third Edition

Introduction: On Reading and Writing

People read for many different reasons, and they read in different ways as well. They may read for enjoyment, or to improve themselves, or to gather information, or to obtain an education or do a job; sometimes their reading benefits them in several ways at once, and in ways they did not expect. Sometimes they read with painstaking care, while at other times they may skip and skim, or even begin reading in the middle or at the end, all depending on what they are reading and what they want from it. But whatever the reason and whatever the method, reading is most rewarding when it is done actively, in a thoughtful spirit and with an inquiring mind.

Many people believe that the right way to read is passively, taking in what they read and storing it away for later use. But this kind of reading is seldom either fulfilling or useful. Unless you bring to bear on your reading what you know and believe, testing what you read and allowing it to test you, you will seldom find the experience particularly rewarding, and you may have some trouble even remembering much of what you have read. Active reading is like conversation: You give as well as take. You examine and question the author's claims, you remember and ponder ideas and information that relate to your reading, you even laugh at the jokes—at least the good ones. By responding so fully, you are taking possession of what you read, making it your own and getting it ready for use—in discussions with your friends, classmates, and teachers, for example, or in writing of your own.

Unquestionably, one of the benefits of active reading is that it can help you become a better writer. Reading can provide you with information and ideas for use in your writing, and often with subjects to write about. Moreover, it can provide you with examples to learn from. Writing is a skill that can be learned, like playing tennis or playing the piano, and one of the best ways to improve your writing is by observing how accomplished writers get their results. As you read you can see for yourself what a writer's strategies are, analyze how they work, and then adapt them to your own writing purposes. By experiencing and discussing the ideas and techniques of many different writers and incorporating them into your writing, you can develop your writing skills and explore the dimensions of your own personal style.

In using *Outlooks and Insights*, you will learn to read as a writer. To read as a writer, you must be able to discover what is going on in any essay, to figure out the writer's reasons for shaping the essay in a particular way, to decide whether the result works well or poorly—and why. Like writing itself, analytical reading is a skill that takes time to acquire. But the skill is necessary if you are to understand the craft of a piece of writing. Perhaps the most important reason to master the skills of analytical reading is that, for everything you write, you will be your own first reader and critic. How well you are able to analyze your own drafts will powerfully affect how well you revise them; and revising well is crucial to writing well. So reading others' writings analytically is useful and important practice.

Outlooks and Insights is a reader for writers, as the subtitle says. The selections in this book can entertain you, inform you, and even contribute to your self-awareness and understanding of the world around you. The writers included here are among the most skillful of their time, many of them well known and widely published. From their work you can learn important and useful writing strategies and skills. Most are contemporary, writing on issues of our own day for readers like us, but some great writers of the past are here as well. The idealism of a Henry David Thoreau, the moral indignation of an Elizabeth Cady Stanton, the noble vision of a Martin Luther King, Jr. continue to move readers despite the intervening years.

Outlooks and Insights is an anthology of writings arranged according to their subjects and themes. The first of its eight sections includes narratives and discussions of personal experiences and relationships, while the following sections broaden to increasingly wide frames of reference, finally arriving at themes concerning our society and, ultimately, all humanity. Each section begins with several aphorisms that highlight the issues addressed and serve as topics for thought, discussion, and writing. Within each section, every piece has its own brief introduction providing information about the author and often about the selection's original purpose and audience. After each piece comes "Questions for Study and Discussion," an aid to active reading. These questions ask you to analyze what you have just read to discover, or rediscover, important points about its content and its writing. In addition, each selection has two or more "Writing Topics."

Although intended primarily to stimulate writing, these suggested writing topics may be used as a starting point for your own thoughts or for class discussion.

Getting the Most Out of What You Read

What does it mean, to understand a piece of writing—an essay, for example? It means, of course, that you comprehend all the words in it. It also means that you have enough background knowledge to grasp its subject matter; a discussion of Brownian motion would mean little to someone who knew no physics, nor would an analysis of Elizabethan metrics enlighten someone unfamiliar with sixteenth-century English poetry. You have only understood the essay if you have grasped it as a whole, so that you can summarize and explain its chief points in your own words and show what each part contributes to the whole.

As you read, you absorb the essay part by part. You cannot "read" the whole all at once, as you can take in a building or a face, but must hold most of the essay in your memory and form your impression of it bit by bit as you read. How this works—what the mind does—is not fully understood, and different readers may well have different ways of doing it. That could be yet another reason why a single piece can evoke so many diverse responses. But there are some guidelines that can help you achieve an understanding of what you read.

UNDERSTANDING THE PARTS OF AN ESSAY

As you progress through an essay, word by word and sentence by sentence, keep the following guidelines in mind to help you think critically about what you are reading:

- *Make sure you understand what each word means. If a word is new to you and the context does not make its meaning clear, don't guess—look it up.*

- *Stay sensitive to connotations, the associations words carry with them. The words* falsehood *and* fib *mean about the same thing, but they convey quite different attitudes and feelings.*

- *Watch for allusions and try to interpret them. If the author refers to "the patience of Job," you don't really understand the passage unless you know how patient Job was. If you don't understand the allusion, check standard reference works such as dictionaries, encyclopedias, and books of quotations, or ask someone you think might know the answer.*

- *Be on the alert for key words and ideas. The two often go together. Key words in this introduction, for example, are* reading *and* writing; *their repetition points up the key idea that these activities are really inseparable and mutually beneficial. A key idea within an essay is normally developed at some length in one or more paragraphs, and it may be stated directly at the beginning or end of a paragraph.*

- *Be a critical thinker. Use your knowledge and your common sense to test what you read. Is each "fact" true, as far as you know (or can find out)? Is the author's reasoning logical?*

- *Interpret figures of speech. When George Orwell speaks of a writer who "turns as it were instinctively to long words and exhausted idioms, like a cuttlefish squirting out ink," you must not only know or find out what a cuttlefish is but also find out how and why it squirts ink and judge how well the image expresses the author's idea.*

- *Pay attention to where you are in the essay. Note where the introduction ends and the body of the essay begins, and where the body gives way to the conclusion. Note where the author turns, let us say, from personal narrative to a series of arguments, or where those arguments are succeeded by refutation of other people's views. And be on the alert for the point at which you discover what the essay is really about—the point where it "makes its move," like a chess player going on the attack or a basketball forward streaking toward the basket. Often the essay's purpose and main idea are clear from the beginning, but sometimes the author withholds or even conceals them until much later.*

UNDERSTANDING THE WHOLE ESSAY

As you read, you are constantly creating and recreating your idea of the essay as a whole. At the end you will have reached some conclusions about it. Here, again, are some points to keep in mind while reading:

- *Look for the main idea of the essay—what is often called the* thesis. *Sometimes the main idea is directly stated, either in the introduction or later on; sometimes it is not stated but can be inferred from the essay as a whole. Define the thesis of an essay as narrowly and specifically as you can while still taking the whole of the essay into account.*

- *Determine the author's purpose. Is it to persuade you to a point of view? To explain a subject to you? The author may directly state his or her purpose, or it may be clearly implied by the thesis.*

- *Analyze the relation between the whole and its parts. How does the main idea of each paragraph relate to the thesis? Does the information supplied in the body of the essay support the thesis—make it more persuasive or easier to understand? Does the author ever seem to get away from the main point, and if so why?*

- *Be sure that the author's thinking is both reasonable and complete. Has the author left out any information that you think might be relevant to the thesis? Does he or she fail to consider any important views—including perhaps your own view? Does the author assume anything without supporting the assumption or even stating it? How important are the omissions—do they lessen the clarity or the persuasiveness of the essay?*

- *Evaluate the essay. Whether or not you like the essay or agree with it is important, but don't stop there; ask yourself why. Test its reasoning for errors and omissions. Test its explanation for clarity and completeness. Consider the author's style, whether it is suitable to the subject, agreeable or powerful in itself, and consistently maintained. In short, assess all the strengths and weaknesses.*

Some Tips and Techniques for Reading an Essay

Each essay offers its own distinctive challenges and rewards, but there are some reading techniques that you can use successfully with all of them in your quest for understanding. Here are some tips on reading.

Prepare Yourself. Before you plunge into reading the essay itself, form some expectations of it. Ponder the title: What does it tell you about the essay's subject matter? About its tone? Think about the author: Have you read anything else by him or her? If so, what do you know about the author's attitudes and style that may help prepare you now? If any materials accompany the essay, like the introductions in *Outlooks and Insights*, read them. These preparations will help you put yourself into an alert, ready frame of mind.

Read and Reread. You should read the selection at least twice, no matter how long or short it is. Very few essays yield their full meaning on first reading, and their full meaning is what you should be aiming to extract.

The first reading is for getting acquainted with the essay and forming your first impressions of it. The essay will offer you information, ideas, and arguments you did not expect, and as you read you will find yourself continually modifying your sense of its purpose, its strategy, and sometimes even what it is about or what point it is intended to make. (This is especially true when the author delays stating the thesis—or makes no thesis statement at all.) Only when you have finished your first reading can you be confident that you have then really begun to understand the piece as a whole.

The second reading is quite different from the first. You will know what the essay is about, where it is going, and how it gets there; now you can relate the parts more accurately to the whole. You can work at the difficult passages to make sure you fully understand what they mean. You can test your first impressions against the words on the page, developing and deepening your sense of the essay's core meaning—or possibly changing your mind about it. And as a writer, you can now pay special attention to the author's purpose and means of achieving that purpose, looking for features of organization and style that you can learn from and adapt to your own work.

Ask Yourself Questions. As you probe the essay, focus your attention by asking yourself some basic questions about it. Here are some you may find useful:

1. Do I like the essay or not? What, for me, are the most interesting parts of it? What parts do I find least interesting or hardest to understand?

2. What is the essay's main idea? What are the chief supporting ideas, and how do they relate to the main idea?

3. What is the author's attitude toward the essay's subject? What is the author's purpose? What readers was the author apparently writing for, and what is his or her attitude toward them? How am I part of the intended audience—if I am?

4. How is the essay structured? How does its organization relate to its main idea and to the author's purpose?

5. Can I follow the essay's line of reasoning? Is its logic valid, however complex, or are there mistakes and fallacies? If the reasoning is flawed, how much damage does this do to the essay's effect?

6. Does the author supply enough information to support the essay's ideas, and enough details to make its description precise? Is all of the information relevant and, as far as I know, accurate? Are all of the details convincing? What does the author leave out, and how do these omissions affect my response to the essay?

7. What are the essay's basic, underlying assumptions? Which are stated and which are left unspoken? Are they acceptable, or do I challenge them? If I do, and I am right, how does this affect the essay's main idea?

8. Do all the elements of the essay relate, directly or indirectly, to its main idea? Can I explain how they relate? If any do not, what other purposes do they serve, if any?

9. Where do I place this essay in the context of my other reading? In the context of my life and thought? What further thoughts, and further reading, does it incite me to? Would I recommend it to anyone else to read? To whom, and why?

Each selection in *Outlooks and Insights* is followed by a set of questions, similar to the ones just suggested but usually more specific, which should help you in your effort to understand the piece. All of these questions work best when you try to answer them as fully as you can, remembering and considering many details from the selection to support your answers. Most of the questions are variations on these three basic ones: "What's going on here?" and "Why?" and "What do I think about it?"

Make Notes. Keep a pencil in hand and use it. Some readers like to write in their books, putting notes and signals to themselves in the margins and underlining key passages; others keep notebooks and jot their responses down there.

There is no all-purpose, universal method for annotating a text; what you write will depend on the details of the work at hand and how you respond. But you may find these tips useful:

- *Keep track of your responses. Jot down ideas that come to mind whether or not they seem directly relevant to what you are reading. If you think of a fact or example that supports the author's ideas, or disproves them, make a note. If a passage impresses or amuses you, set if off with an exclamation point in the margin. Converse with the text. Write yes or no or why? or so what? in response to the author's ideas and arguments.*

- *Mark words or passages you don't understand at first reading. A question mark in the margin may do the job, or you may want to circle words or phrases in the text. During the second reading you can look up the words and allusions and puzzle out the more difficult passages.*

- *Mark key points. Underline or star the main idea, or write it down in your notebook. Mark off the selection into its main sections, so that you can better see the essay's organization and understand the sequence of the author's thoughts.*

When annotating your text, don't be timid. Mark up your book as much as you please. Above all, don't let annotating become burdensome; it's an aid, not a chore. A word or phrase will often serve as well as a sentence. You may want to delay much of your annotating until your second reading, so that the first reading can be fast and free.

Using Your Reading in the Writing Process

What does analytical reading have to do with your own writing? Reading is not simply an end in itself; it is also a means to help you become a better writer. In *Outlooks and Insights* we are concerned with both the content and the form of an essay—that is, with what an essay has to say and with the strategies used to say it. All readers pay attention to content, to the substance of what an author is saying. Far fewer, however, notice the strategies that authors use to organize their writing, to make it understandable and effective. Yet using these strategies is an essential element of the writer's craft, an element that must be mastered if one is to write well.

There is nothing difficult about the strategies themselves. When you want to tell a story about being unemployed, for example, you naturally use the strategy called *narration*. When you want to show the differences between families in the 1940s and families today, you naturally *compare and contrast* representative families of the two eras. When you want to explain how toxins enter the food chain, you fall automatically into the strategy called *process analysis*. And when you want to determine the reasons for the disaster at the Chernobyl nuclear plant, you use *cause and effect analysis*. These and other strategies are ways we think about the world and our experiences in it and come to an understanding of them. What makes them sometimes seem difficult, especially in writing, is that most people use them more or less unconsciously, with little awareness that they're doing so. Critical thinking, especially in writing, does not come from simply using these structures—everyone does that—but from using them with purpose and thoughtfulness.

At the simplest level, reading can provide you with information and ideas both to give authority to your writing and to enliven it. Moreover, your reading often provides you with subjects to write about. For example, one of our students, after reading James Rachels's "Active and Passive Euthanasia" (p. 771), wrote an essay analyzing the strengths and weaknesses of the author's argument. Another student read Charlotte Perkins Gilman's short story "The Yellow Wallpaper" (p. 721) and used it as a springboard to her essay defining "anxiety." In a more subtle way, analytical reading can increase your awareness of how the writing of others affects you, and thus make you more sensitive to how your own writing will affect your readers. If you've ever been irritated by an article that makes an outrageous claim without a shred of supporting evidence, you might be more likely to back up your own claims more carefully. If you've been delighted by a happy turn of phrase or absorbed by a new idea, you might be less inclined to feed your own readers on clichés and platitudes. You will begin to consider in more detail how your own readers are likely to respond.

Analytical reading of the kind you'll be encouraged to do in this text will help you master important strategies of critical thinking and writing that you can use very specifically throughout the writing process. During the early stages of your writing you will need to focus on the large issues of choosing a subject, gathering information, planning the strategies suited to your purpose, and organizing your ideas. As you move from a first draft through further revisions, your concerns will begin to narrow. In conference with your instructor you may discover a faulty beginning or ending, or realize that your tone is inappropriate, or see that the various parts of your essay are not quite connected, or notice awkward repetitions in your choice of words and phrases. Analytical reading can lead you to solutions for such problems at every stage of your writing, from selecting a subject to revising and editing your final draft.

Reading George Orwell's "A Hanging": A Case Study

Some writers, and some essays, become classics—people continue to read them for decades or centuries. Such a writer is George Orwell, the

English author best known for his novel *1984*, a vivid and terrifying evocation of life in a totalitarian state. But that was his last major work. One of his first works was an essay, "A Hanging," which he wrote in 1931 (he was then twenty-eight) about one of his experiences as a police official in Burma, where he had served from 1922 to 1927. "A Hanging" was published in *The Adelphi*, a socialist literary magazine whose readers would have been sympathetic to Orwell's attitudes.

As you read "A Hanging," note your own questions and responses in the margins or in your notebook. At the end of the essay you will find one reader's notes to which you can compare your responses.

A Hanging

GEORGE ORWELL

It was in Burma, a sodden morning of the rains. A sickly light, like yellow tinfoil, was slanting over the high walls into the jail yard. We were waiting outside the condemned cells, a row of sheds fronted with double bars, like small animal cages. Each cell measured about ten feet by ten and was quite bare within except for a plank bed and a pot for drinking water. In some of them brown silent men were squatting at the inner bars, with their blankets draped around them. These were the condemned men, due to be hanged within the next week or two. 1

One prisoner had been brought out of his cell. He was a Hindu, a puny wisp of a man, with a shaven head and vague liquid eyes. He had a thick, sprouting moustache, absurdly too big for his body, rather like the moustache of a comic man on the films. Six tall Indian warders were guarding him and getting him ready for the gallows. Two of them stood by with rifles and fixed bayonets, while the others handcuffed him, passed a chain through his handcuffs and fixed it to their belts, and lashed his arms right to his sides. They crowded very close about him, with their hands always on him in a careful, caressing grip as though all the while feeling him to make sure he was there. It was like men handling a fish which is still alive and may jump back into the water. But he stood quite unresisting, yielding his arms limply to the ropes, as though he hardly noticed what was happening. 2

Eight o'clock struck and a bugle call, desolately thin in the wet air, floated from the distant barracks. The superintendent of the jail, who was standing apart from the rest of us, moodily prodding the gravel with his stick, raised his head at the sound. He was an army doctor, with a gray toothbrush moustache and a gruff voice. "For God's sake hurry up, Francis," he said irritably. "The man ought to have been dead by this time. Aren't you ready yet?" 3

Francis, the head jailer, a fat Dravidian in a white drill suit and gold spectacles, waved his black hand. "Yes sir, yes sir," he bubbled. "All iss satisfactorily prepared. The hangman iss waiting. We shall proceed." 4

"Well, quick march, then. The prisoners can't get their breakfast till   5
this job's over."

We set out for the gallows. Two warders marched on either side of   6
the prisoner, with their rifles at the slope; two others marched close
against him, gripping him by arm and shoulder, as though at once
pushing and supporting him. The rest of us, magistrates and the like,
followed behind. Suddenly, when we had gone ten yards, the procession
stopped short without any order or warning. A dreadful thing had
happened—a dog, come goodness knows whence, had appeared in the
yard. It came bounding among us with a loud volley of barks, and leapt
round us wagging its whole body, wild with glee at finding so many
human beings together. It was a large woolly dog, half Airedale, half
pariah. For a moment it pranced round us, and then, before anyone could
stop it, it had made a dash for the prisoner and, jumping up, tried to lick
his face. Everyone stood aghast, too taken aback even to grab at the dog.

"Who let that bloody brute in here?" said the superintendent   7
angrily. "Catch it, somone!"

A warder, detached from the escort, charged clumsily after the dog,   8
but it danced and gamboled just out of his reach, taking everything as
part of the game. A young Eurasian jailer picked up a handful of gravel
and tried to stone the dog away, but it dodged the stones and came after
us again. Its yaps echoed from the jail walls. The prisoner, in the grasp of
the two warders, looked on incuriously, as though this was another
formality of the hanging. It was several minutes before someone managed
to catch the dog. Then we put my handkerchief through its collar and
moved off once more, with the dog still straining and whimpering.

It was about forty yards to the gallows. I watched the bare brown   9
back of the prisoner marching in front of me. He walked clumsily with his
bound arms, but quite steadily, with that bobbing gait of the Indian who
never straightens his knees. At each step his muscles slid neatly into
place, the lock of hair on his scalp danced up and down, his feet printed
themselves on the wet gravel. And once, in spite of the men who gripped
him by each shoulder, he stepped slightly aside to avoid a puddle on the
path.

It is curious, but till that moment I had never realized what it means   10
to destroy a healthy, conscious man. When I saw the prisoner step aside to
avoid the puddle I saw the mystery, the unspeakable wrongness, of cutting
a life short when it is in full tide. This man was not dying, he was alive just
as we are alive. All the organs of his body were working—bowels digesting
food, skin renewing itself, nails growing, tissues forming—all toiling away
in solemn foolery. His nails would still be growing when he stood on the
drop, when he was falling through the air with a tenth of a second to live.
His eyes saw the yellow gravel and the gray walls, and his brain still
remembered, foresaw, reasoned—reasoned even about puddles. He and
we were a party of men walking together, seeing, hearing, feeling, understanding the same world; and in two minutes, with a sudden snap, one of
us would be gone—one mind less, one world less.

The gallows stood in a small yard, separate from the main grounds   11
of the prison, and overgrown with tall prickly weeds. It was a brick

erection like three sides of a shed, with planking on top, and above that two beams and a crossbar with the rope dangling. The hangman, a gray-haired convict in the white uniform of the prison, was waiting beside his machine. He greeted us with a servile crouch as we entered. At a word from Francis the two warders, gripping the prisoner more closely than ever, half led half pushed him to the gallows and helped him clumsily up the ladder. Then the hangman climbed up and fixed the rope round the prisoner's neck.

We stood waiting, five yards away. The warders had formed in a rough circle round the gallows. And then, when the noose was fixed, the prisoner began crying out to his god. It was a high, reiterated cry of "Ram! Ram! Ram! Ram!"[1] not urgent and fearful like a prayer or cry for help, but steady, rhythmical, almost like the tolling of a bell. The dog answered the sound with a whine. The hangman, still standing on the gallows, produced a small cotton bag like a flour bag and drew it down over the prisoner's face. But the sound, muffled by the cloth, still persisted, over and over again: "Ram! Ram! Ram! Ram! Ram!"

The hangman climbed down and stood ready, holding the lever. Minutes seemed to pass. The steady, muffled crying from the prisoner went on and on, "Ram! Ram! Ram!" never faltering for an instant. The superintendent, his head on his chest, was slowly poking the ground with his stick; perhaps he was counting the cries, allowing the prisoner a fixed number—fifty, perhaps, or a hundred. Everyone had changed color. The Indians had gone gray like bad coffee, and one or two of the bayonets were wavering. We looked at the lashed, hooded man on the drop, and listened to his cries—each cry another second of life; the same thought was in all our minds: oh, kill him quickly, get it over, stop that abominable noise!

Suddenly the superintendent made up his mind. Throwing up his head he made a swift motion with his stick. "Chalo!"[2] he shouted almost fiercely.

There was a clanking noise, and then dead silence. The prisoner had vanished, and the rope was twisting on itself. I let go of the dog, and it galloped immediately to the back of the gallows; but when it got there it stopped short, barked, and then retreated into a corner of the yard, where it stood among the weeds, looking timorously out at us. We went round the gallows to inspect the prisoner's body. He was dangling with his toes pointed straight downward, very slowly revolving, as dead as a stone.

The superintendent reached out with his stick and poked the bare brown body: it oscillated slightly. *"He's all right,"* said the superintendent. He backed out from under the gallows, and blew out a deep breath. The moody look had gone out of his face quite suddenly. He glanced at his wrist watch. "Eight minutes past eight. Well, that's all for this morning, thank God."

---

[1] In the Hindu religion, Rama is the incarnation of the god Vishnu.

[2] *"Let go,"* in Hindi.

The warders unfixed bayonets and marched away. The dog, sobered   17
and conscious of having misbehaved itself, slipped after them. We walked
out of the gallows yard, past the condemned cells with their waiting
prisoners, into the big central yard of the prison. The convicts, under the
command of warders armed with lathis,[3] were already receiving their
breakfast. They squatted in long rows, each man holding a tin pannikin,
while two warders with buckets marched round ladling out rice; it seemed
quite a homely, jolly scene, after the hanging. An enormous relief had
come upon us now that the job was done. One felt an impulse to sing, to
break into a run, to snigger. All at once everyone began chattering gaily.

The Eurasian boy walking beside me nodded toward the way we had   18
come, with a knowing smile: "Do you know, sir, our friend [he meant the
dead man] when he heard his appeal had been dismissed, he pissed on the
floor of his cell. From fright. Kindly take one of my cigarettes, sir. Do you
not admire my new silver case, sir? From the boxwalah, two rupees eight
annas.[4] Classy European style."

Several people laughed—at what, nobody seemed certain.   19

Francis was walking by the superintendent, talking garrulously: 20
"Well, sir, all hass passed off with the utmost satisfactoriness. It was all
finished—flick! like that. It iss not always so—oah, no! I have known cases
where the doctor was obliged to go beneath the gallows and pull the
prissoner's legs to ensure decease. Most disagreeable!"

"Wriggling about, eh? That's bad," said the superintendent.   21

"Ach, sir, it iss worse when they become refractory! One man, I   22
recall, clung to the bars of hiss cage when we went to take him out. You
will scarcely credit, sir, that it took six warders to dislodge him, three
pulling at each leg. We reasoned with him. 'My dear fellow,' we said,
'think of all the pain and trouble you are causing to us!' But no, he would
not listen! Ach, he wass very troublesome!"

I found that I was laughing quite loudly. Everyone was laughing.   23
Even the superintendent grinned in a tolerant way. "You'd better all come
out and have a drink," he said quite genially. "I've got a bottle of whisky
in the car. We could do with it."

We went through the big double gates of the prison into the road.   24
"Pulling at his legs!" exclaimed a Burmese magistrate suddenly, and burst
into a loud chuckling. We all began laughing again. At that moment
Francis' anecdote seemed extraordinarily funny. We all had a drink
together, native and European alike, quite amicably. The dead man was a
hundred yards away.

One Reader's Notes

Here are the notes one reader made in his notebook during and after
his first reading of "A Hanging." They include personal comments, queries

---

[3] Wooden batons.

[4] Indian currency worth less that 50 cents. *Boxwalah:* in Hindi, a seller of boxes.

concerning the meaning of words and details, and some reflections on the piece and its subject. The numbers in parentheses indicate which paragraphs the notes refer to.

NOTES MADE DURING THE READING

(2) puny prisoner, 6 tall guards, handcuffs, rope, chains. handled "like a fish"—cells like animal cages. suggests prisoner thought less than human.

(4) natives do dirty work, Brits stand around supervising. what's a Dravidian?

(6) dog—half Airedale, half pariah, like prison staff a mixture of Brits and natives. prisoner its favorite person. why? pet?

(10) main idea (?): "I saw the mystery, the unspeakable wrongness, of cutting a life short when it is in full tide."

But what was the man's crime? might have been a murderer or terrorist. Does O. mean that *all* cap. pun. is wrong?

Dog incident—dog recog. prisoner's humanity, behaves naturally, O. claims the execution is unnatural.

(11) hangman a convict, not an official. yard overgrown—significance?

(12) what god is Ram? prisoner a Hindu.

(13) why everyone transfixed? more than surprise? "kill him quickly"—selfish.

(15) the dog again. What was O. doing there anyway? all he does is hold dog. observer from P.D.?

(17) what's a lathi? or lathis? dog "conscious of having misbehaved"—how does O. know?

(18) prisoner afraid before, found courage to face death—humanizes him. what's a boxwalah?

Anticlimax from here on. prisoners impassive, officials near hysteria. again, why such a big deal, if they do executions often (other condemned men there). take O's word that this time was different. laughing it off, life goes on, etc.

(24) Euros and natives on same side, against prisoners. still nothing about dead man's crime, but can't have been so bad given everyone's reactions—? nobody says it's what he deserved.

NOTES MADE AFTER FINISHING THE READING

did this really happen? seems too pat, with dog and all, and O. hanging around doing nothing instead of whatever he usually did. Could have happened, maybe that's enough.

no argument against cap. pun., just personal insight from personal experience. can't make laws that way. no reasons pro or con except O. thinks it unnatural, with dog's behavior as the proof.

form—chron. narration, no gaps or flashbacks. intro para 1, sets scene. climax: the hanging. conclusion starts para 17 (?), winds story down. style clear, direct, not fancy, strong words, lots of detail and color, etc. good writing obviously, but he doesn't persuade me about cap. pun.

Looking over this reader's shoulder, you can see that he gets increasingly skeptical about Orwell's thesis statement, and you may guess that he himself supports capital punishment—or at least sees some point in it. The reader has noted a good deal of what Orwell put into the essay, such as who does what at the prison; perhaps on the second reading he will get more out of the essay's concluding paragraphs, which are skimmed over in his notes. And the reader has also noticed some of the things Orwell left out, such as the nature of the prisoner's offense. He has begun to find relations between the details and the whole, notably by thinking about the significance of the dog's behavior. All in all, he has made a good beginning at understanding "A Hanging."

From Reading to Writing

In many college courses you will be required to discuss your reading in some writing of your own. In composition courses, such writing assignments often take these forms:

1. An analysis of the reading's content, form, or both.
2. An original composition on the topic of the reading, or on a related topic.
3. An original composition on a topic of your choice, inspired in some way by the reading but not bound by its subject matter.

Which kind of paper you write may be specified by your instructor, or the choice may be left to you.

Three Student Essays in Response to George Orwell's "A Hanging"

In the following pages you will find an analytical essay, an argumentative essay, and a narrative essay; each is a response to Orwell's "A Hanging" and each is typical of how students write for their composition courses.

An Analytical Essay

When you write an analysis of something you have read, your purpose is to show that you have understood the work and to help your readers increase their understanding of it, too. You do this by drawing attention to aspects of its meaning, structure, and style that are important but not obvious. Such an analysis grows directly out of your reading, and more specifically out of the notes you made during your first and subsequent readings of the text.

When planning your analytical paper, start by considering what point you most want to make—what your thesis will be. If you can think of several possible theses for your paper, and you often will be able to, select the one that seems to you the most important—and that you think you can support and defend most strongly and effectively using evidence from the piece you are writing about. Many different theses would be possible for an analytical paper about Orwell's "A Hanging." Here are a few:

> In "A Hanging," George Orwell *carefully selects details to persuade us that capital punishment is wrong.*
>
> "A Hanging" *reveals how thoroughly the British had imposed their laws, customs, and values on colonial Burma.*
>
> *Though "A Hanging" appeals powerfully to the emotions, it does not make a reasoned argument against capital punishment.*
>
> In "A Hanging," George Orwell *employs metaphor, personification, and dialogue to express man's inhumanity to other men.*

This last is the thesis of the student paper that follows, "The Disgrace of Man."

Think, too, about your audience. Who will read your paper? Will they know the work you are analyzing? If not, then you need to supply enough information about the work so that your readers can understand you. But if you expect your essay to be read by your instructor and classmates, and if it is about an assigned reading, you can usually assume that they know the work and need no summary of it, though they may need clear reminders of specific details and passages that you analyze closely and that may have escaped their attention.

Students writing papers for their courses have a special problem: What can they say that their readers, especially their instructors, do not already know? This is a problem all writers face, including instructors themselves when writing professional articles, and the answer is always the same: Write honestly about what you see in the work and what you think about it. Since all readers respond differently to the same text, any one of them—including you—may notice details or draw conclusions that others miss. Teachers may be experienced, knowledgeable readers, but they do not know everything. Some might not have noticed that Orwell excludes from "A Hanging" any hint of the prisoner's crime, yet this omission is important because it reinforces Orwell's main point: Capital punishment is always wrong, no matter what the circumstances. And even if you think you have no such discoveries to offer, your individual point of view and response to the text will lend your writing originality and interest. As the poet James

Stephens once wrote, "Originality does not consist in saying what no one has ever said before, but in saying exactly what you think yourself."

The following student essay, "The Disgrace of Man," is original in Stephens's sense, and the student has also discovered something in "A Hanging" that other readers might well have missed, something about Orwell's way of telling his story that contributes, subtly but significantly, to its effect.

The Disgrace of Man

George Orwell's "A Hanging" graphically depicts the execution of a prisoner in a way that expresses a universal tragedy. He artfully employs metaphor, personification, and dialogue to indicate man's inhumanity toward other men, and to prompt the reader's sympathy and self-examination.

Orwell uses simile and metaphor to show that the prisoner is treated more like an animal than like a human being. The cells of the condemned men, "a row of sheds . . . quite bare within," are "like small animal cages." The warders grip the prisoner "like men handling a fish." Though they refer to the prisoner as "the man" or "our friend," the other characters view him as less than human. Even his cry resounds like the "tolling of a bell" rather than a human "prayer or cry for help," and after he is dead the superintendent pokes at the body with a stick. These details direct the reader's attention to the lack of human concern for the condemned prisoner.

In contrast, Orwell emphasizes the "wrongness of cutting a life short" by representing the parts of the prisoner's body as taking on human behavior. He describes the lock of hair "dancing" on the man's scalp, his feet "printing themselves" on the gravel, all his organs "toiling away" like a team of laborers at some collective project. In personifying these bodily features, Orwell forces the reader to see the prisoner's vitality, his humanity. The reader, in turn, associates each bodily part with himself; he becomes highly aware of the frailty of life. As the author focuses on how easily these actions can be stopped, in any human being, "with a sudden snap," the reader feels the "wrongness" of the hanging as if his own life were threatened.

In addition to creating this sense of unmistakable life, Orwell uses the dog as a standard for evaluating the characters' appreciation of human life. The dog loves people—he is "wild with glee to find so many human beings together"—and the person he loves the most is the prisoner, who has been treated as less than human by the jail attendants. When the prisoner starts to pray, the other people are silent, but the dog answers "with a whine." Even after the hanging, the dog runs directly to the gallows to see the prisoner again. The reader is forced to reflect on his own reaction: Which is more shocking, the dog's actions or the observers' cold response?

Finally, Orwell refers to the characters' nationalities to stress that this insensitivity extends to all nationalities and races. The hanging takes place in Burma, in a jail run by a European army doctor and a native of southern India. The warders are also Indians, and the hangman is actually a fellow prisoner. The author calls attention to each of these participants and implies that each one of them might have halted the brutal proceedings. He was there too and could have intervened when he suddenly realized that killing the prisoner would be wrong. Yet the "formality of the hanging" goes on.

As he reflects on the meaning of suddenly destroying human life, Orwell emphasizes the similarities among all men, regardless of nationality. Before the hanging, they are "seeing, hearing, feeling, understanding the same world," and afterward there would be "one mind less, one world less." Such feelings do not affect the other characters, who think of the hanging not as killing but as a job to be done, a job made unpleasant by those reminders (the incident of the dog, the prisoner's praying) that they are dealing with a human being. Orwell uses dialogue to show how selfish and callous the observers are. Though they have different accents—the superintendent's "for God's sake hurry up," the Dravidian's "It was all finished"—they think and feel the same. Their words, such as "*He's* all right," show that they are more concerned about their own lives than the one they are destroying.

Although George Orwell sets his story in Burma, his point is universal; although he deals with capital punishment, he implies other questions of life and death. We are all faced with issues such as capital punishment, abortion, and euthanasia, and sometimes we find ourselves directly involved, as Orwell did. "A Hanging" urges us to examine ourselves and to take very seriously the value of a human life.

Most teachers would consider "The Disgrace of Man" a fine student essay. It is well organized, stating its thesis early, supporting it effectively, and sticking to the point. The discussion is clear and coherent, and it is firmly based on Orwell's text—the student author has understood the core meaning of "A Hanging." She has also noticed many details that express Orwell's attitude toward the hanging and toward his imperial colleagues, and she has interpreted them so that her readers can plainly see how those details contribute to the total effect of "A Hanging." How many would have observed that Orwell actually personifies the parts of the prisoner's body? How many, having noticed it, would have grasped the relation of this detail to Orwell's point? That's accurate, active reading.

An Argumentative Essay

Perhaps you recall the annotations of "A Hanging" on pages 13–14. The writer of those notes was attentive to the meaning of the text, but as he read he found himself disagreeing with Orwell's view that taking human life is always unspeakably wrong. He might have gone on to analyze "A Hanging," as he was obviously capable of doing, but he did not. Instead, given the opportunity to choose his own topic, he decided to present his own views on Orwell's subject: capital punishment.

The writer began by exploring the topic, jotting down notes on what he knew and believed. He also went to the library to look up recent research into the effects of capital punishment, but found that authorities still cannot agree on whether the death penalty deters crime or protects society, so his efforts led only to a few sentences in his first paragraph. Why go to so much trouble for a short writing assignment? Evidently the writer cared enough about his topic to want to do it justice, not just for the assignment's sake but for his own. As the English philosopher John Stuart Mill wrote, "If the cultivation of the understanding consists in one thing more than in another, it is surely in learning the grounds of one's own opinions." The author of "For Capital Punishment" knew what he believed, and he used the occasion of a writing assignment to work out a rationale for that belief.

For Capital Punishment

The debate on capital punishment goes on and on. Does the death penalty deter people from committing murder? Does it protect us from criminals who would murder again if they were returned to society? These questions have not yet been answered beyond any doubt, and maybe they never will be. But is the death penalty cruel and unnatural? This is a different kind of question, having to do with the nature of the punishment itself, and it can be answered. I think the answer is no, and that capital punishment has a place in a civilized society. I also feel that it should be imposed as the penalty for the worst crimes.

In the United States this is a constitutional issue, because the Bill of Rights does not allow cruel and unusual punishment. The Supreme Court has interpreted these words not to include capital punishment, and there is a basis in the Constitution for their decision: The fifth amendment says that "no person shall . . . be deprived of life, liberty, or property, without due process of law," which means that a person can be deprived of life if due process has been observed. The Court did find some years ago that the death penalty was being imposed much more often on poor black people than on any others, and suspended capital punishment throughout the nation because due process was obviously *not* being observed, but when the Court considered that that situation had been corrected it permitted executions to resume in 1977 with the death of Gary Gilmore.

But beyond the constitutionality of capital punishment there is the deeper question of whether it is morally wrong. We accept some punishments as just, while others seem barbaric. The difference, I think, has to do with what the condemned man is made to suffer. The lightest punishments take away some of his money or restrict his freedom of movement in society; some examples are fines, probation, and work-release programs. Then there are punishments that remove the criminal from society, such as imprisonment and deportation. The kind of punishment we do not accept, though it is still used in some countries, is the kind that is meant to do physical harm: beating, maiming, torture. The death penalty is a special case. It removes criminals from society permanently and economically, but it also involves physical harm. It is in the balance between these two effects, I think, that we can find out whether capital punishment is morally acceptable.

If we condemned people to death because we wanted them to suffer, you would expect that methods of execution would have been made more painful and frightening over the years. Instead, the opposite has happened. Traitors used to be tortured to death before screaming mobs, but now the condemned man dies in private as painlessly as possible; Texas now uses chemical injections that are apparently almost painless. It must be, then, that the reason for execution is not physical harm but removal from society, which is a widely accepted purpose for judicial punishment.

But why, then, would not life imprisonment serve the same purpose just as well? There are two main reasons why it does not. First, "life imprisonment" does not mean what it says; most lifers are considered for parole after fifteen years or less, even monsters like Charles Manson and Sirhan Sirhan. It's true that these two have not been released, but they might be at any time their California parole board changes its mind. So life imprisonment does not insure that the worst criminals will be removed from society permanently. Second, as long as a criminal stays in prison he is a burden on the very society he has offended against, costing society tens of thousands of dollars each year to keep him secure and healthy. There is also a real question in my mind whether caging a prisoner for life, if it actually is for life, is any more merciful than putting him to death. The conditions in American prisons, where the inmates are often brutalized and degraded by each other and even by their guards, must often seem a "fate worse than death."

Most nations of the world, and most states in the United States, have legalized capital punishment and used it for many years. They—we—are not bloodthirsty monsters, but ordinary people seeking safety and justice under the law. Maybe the time will come when the death penalty is no longer needed or wanted, and then it will be abolished. But that time is not yet here.

The writer of "For Capital Punishment" has taken on a large subject, on which many books have been and many more will be written. When discussing a controversial topic of wide interest, many people tend to parrot back uncritically the opinions they have read and heard, which is easy to do but does not add much to what everyone knows. This writer has escaped that temptation and thought his subject through, in the process working out reasoned and partly original arguments of his own to support his view. His discussion is clear and well organized; he states his thesis at the end of the first paragraph and supports it with evidence and reasoning throughout the paper. Of course many reasonable people will disagree with his support of capital punishment, just as he disagrees with Orwell's opposition to it. But most composition teachers, even those who do not share this writer's views, would consider "For Capital Punishment" a good student paper.

A Narrative Essay

In "A Hanging," George Orwell writes about an incident that brought him to an important insight. The author of the following essay did the same. Reading Orwell brought back to mind a childhood experience that had made her aware of the potential for thoughtless violence that lies within us all. Part of Orwell's influence on her is revealed by her choice of subject—the heedless killing of three helpless nestlings. But she also follows Orwell in her choice of a writing strategy; like him she narrates a personal experience that illustrates a general moral principle.

Killing for Fun

Every summer my family returns to our ancestral home, which is in a community where the same families have lived generation after generation. There are tennis courts, a golf course, boats, and other occupations to help pass the long, hot days. This all sounds very enjoyable, and it usually was, but sometimes it got very boring. Spending every summer with the same gang and doing the same things, under the same grown-ups' noses, began to seem dull, and by the time I was thirteen I was ready to experience the thrill of the forbidden.

One afternoon in July, I was supposed to sail in some races with my best friend Mitchell, but the air was so thick and heavy that we decided not to go. We sat around his house all day, waiting for his brother to bring back the family power boat so that we could water ski. Thinking back to that summer, I remember how frustrated and irritable we were, our pent-up energy ready to explode. We roamed his house searching for something—anything—to do, but we only succeeded in making one mess after another and angering his mother. Finally we hit on something. We were eating lunch on Mitchell's back porch when we both noticed his father's rifle propped in a corner.

Now Mitchell's father had often warned all of us that his rifle was strictly off limits. The rifle itself was not very dangerous, as it was only an air gun that shot small pellets, but he was afraid of its being misused and hurting someone. He himself used it to scare off stray dogs and was usually very careful to put it away, but for some reason on that particular day he had forgotten. We decided that it would be fun to take the rifle out in the nearby woods and shoot at whatever we found there.

We had to be very careful not to be seen by the borough residents as they all knew us. For most parents, kids heading for the woods meant trouble. So Mitchell and I sneaked out of his house with the gun and went slinking through some old horse stables on our way to the woods. By the time we arrived at the edge of the woods we felt like spies. There was a caretaker's cottage there, and the caretaker was forever on the lookout for what he thought were troublesome kids. When we successfully passed the cottage our spirits were high, as we had gotten safely through the danger zone on the way to our forbidden project.

As we went into the woods we began to find some animals and birds to use as targets, but try as we might, we could not hit anything. Our pellets seemed to disappear in flight, not even giving us the satisfaction of hitting a tree and making a noise. Our mission was not succeeding, and we decided to look for an easier target.

Finally we startled a mother bird, who flew away leaving her nest behind. We thought the nest would make a fine target, stationary as it was and with live creatures inside. We took turns shooting at it in an attempt to knock it out of the tree, intoxicated with our power and carried away by the thrill of it all. Mitchell was the one to knock it down. It tottered, and after a little rustling a small object fell out, and the nest followed, landing upside down.

Mitchell ran up and excitedly turned it over. The sight was horribly repulsive. Underneath lay three naked pink corpses, staring up at us silently with wide dark eyes and wide, underdeveloped, faintly yellow beaks. They looked as if they had been savagely strangled one by one, except for the small pellet holes in each tiny body. A few feet away a slight movement caught my eye. The object that had fallen first was a fourth baby bird. It has survived the shooting and the fall and was flopping around, mutilated as it was. I poked Mitchell, who was staring at the massacre underneath the nest, and directed his attention to the desperately flapping pink lump a few feet away.

I could see that Mitchell was repulsed by the sight, but being a thirteen-year-old boy he refused to show it. He made an attempt to maintain a hunter's attitude, and fiercely drove pellet after pellet into the injured bird. We tried to joke about it, and as soon as we were out of sight of the nest we broke into hysterically uncontrollable laughter, trying to avoid thinking about what we had done. On the way home we avoided talking about it, and I felt relieved to part company with Mitchell when we got home.

That incident shocked me into thinking about the results of my actions. Mitchell and I were not inhuman monsters, determined to massacre baby birds; we were just bored kids looking for an adventure and not thinking about the consequences. I wonder how much unhappiness and even crime comes from young people acting selfishly and thoughtlessly, out for a thrill. If they had to see the suffering they cause, they would surely think harder before they act.

The author of "Killing for Fun" tells her story well. She describes her experience vividly, with much closely observed detail, and builds suspense to hold her readers' attention. What makes "Killing for Fun" not just a story but a personal essay is the last paragraph, where she turns her experience into an observation about life. The observation may not be brand new, but then it needn't be—few important truths are. George Orwell was certainly not the first to oppose capital punishment. In both narrative essays it is the authors' personal experiences, honestly and precisely recounted, that gives their general observations force.

These three essays, each different from the other two and from Orwell's, illustrate but a few of the many ways different people can respond to their reading and use their responses in their writing. Each paper also shows how a student, working under the limitations of an assigned reading and a specific writing assignment, can create an interesting and original piece of writing by analyzing the reading carefully, or exploring his or her own beliefs, or drawing on personal experience. Each of the selections in *Outlooks and Insights* provides you with opportunities to do the same.

Some Notes on Fiction and Poetry

The poems and short stories in *Outlooks and Insights* explore many of the same themes the essays do, and can serve your writing purposes in similar ways. A story or a poem may give you ideas for your writing; and even though you may never write poetry or fiction, you can still learn much about structure and style from reading literature. These selections will be most useful to you, however, if you know about the basic elements of fiction and poetry. The following pages provide a brief, highly selective introduction to some of their most important qualities and forms.

READING SHORT STORIES

Short stories look much like essays, and the two forms are similar in other ways as well. Both are written in prose; some essays, like nearly all stories, are narratives; both may contain dialogue. And certainly a reader can learn from fiction as well as from nonfiction about the ways other people think, feel, and behave, and how they deal with ethical problems. But stories also differ from essays in fundamental respects, and call for different expectations and responses from their readers.

Though a short story may incorporate materials from real life, including places and even characters and incidents, it is essentially the product of the author's imagination. Eudora Welty says that she got the idea for her short story "A Worn Path" (page 131) from watching an old woman walking slowly across a winter country landscape, but that the rest of the story was pure invention. In an essay, on the other hand, we expect the events and characters to be rendered accurately from real life. Part of the force of George Orwell's "A Hanging" comes from our belief that he is reporting a personal experience—that he did indeed attend a hanging at which the events he narrates actually took place.

Both essays and stories can make points about life, but each type does so differently. An essay normally states its main idea or *thesis* openly and explains or argues that idea at length in a direct and orderly way. A story, however, does not tell—it shows. Its main idea, called its *theme*, is not so much discussed as embodied in the characters and action, and is seldom presented openly—each reader has to discover a story's theme for himself or herself. As Eudora Welty puts it, "A narrative line is in its deeper sense . . . the tracing out of a meaning"—which is the story's theme. Theme is not the same as subject. The subject of "A Worn Path" is an old woman's long, wearying trip to town to get medicine for her ill grandson—a trip which she has made many times before and will make again. The story's theme, however, is the general observation it illustrates and embodies. Different readers may put the theme of "A Worn Path" into different words. Welty says it this way: "The habit of love cuts through confusion and stumbles or contrives its way out of difficulty, it remembers the way even when it forgets, for a dumbfounded moment, its reason for being." This is the story's true meaning and encompasses all of its details, right down to the path itself, worn by the old woman's often-repeated errand of love. As this suggests, a story's theme reveals the unity of the whole work—or can even be said to give the work its unity.

Most short stories have other elements in common which are seldom found in nonfiction writing. The action in a short story, called its *plot*, typically unfolds in a pattern consisting of a series of stages that can be diagrammed in this way:

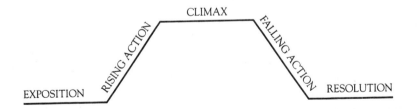

The *exposition* sets the scene, describes the situation, and begins to introduce some of the characters. The *rising action* (sometimes called the *complication*) sets the characters into conflict—with each other or within themselves—and the conflict rises in tension and complexity. At the *climax* the tension and complexity reach their peak, and the central character takes an action or undergoes an experience that is the turning point of the story.

After the climax comes the *falling action*, in which the tension slackens and the story moves toward its conclusion. The end of the story is the *resolution*, in which the conflict of the plot gives way to a new stability. "A Worn Path" follows this pattern. Its exposition consists of the first two paragraphs. The rising action, beginning in paragraph 3, builds to a climax when Phoenix meets the hunter. After the falling action, in which she makes her way into town, the resolution begins in paragraph 70 when she arrives at the doctor's office. These conventions of plot have served countless writers for more than two thousand years with no loss in effectiveness and vitality, and still provide the structure for novels, short stories, plays—even movies and television dramas.

How we take in the events of the plot is determined by the author's use of a narrative *point of view*. Sometimes the story is told by one of the characters, as in Isaac Bashevis Singer's "Gimpel the Fool" (p. 49). This is called *first person point of view* because the narrator often uses the first person pronoun *I*. When the story is told by a narrator standing somewhere outside the events of the story, this is called *third person point of view* because the narrator uses the third person pronouns *he, she*, and *they*. "A Worn Path" is told from the third person point of view; the narrator, like a movie camera's eye, tracks old Phoenix Jackson all the way to town, reporting on her doings from outside the story.

The third person point of view has two main forms: *omniscient* and *limited*. If the narrator tells us what all the characters are doing, wherever they are, and even what they are thinking and feeling, the author is using the third person omniscient point of view. An example is Nathaniel Hawthorne's "The Birth-Mark" (p. 654). In "A Worn Path," on the other hand, the narrator tells us only what Phoenix Jackson does, says, hears, and sees; we can only infer what the characters are thinking from what they say and do.

READING POEMS

Almost anything can be subject matter for poetry, and the range of poetic styles and forms is enormous: Henry Reed's "Naming of Parts" (p. 513), for example, uses poetic devices such as metaphor and juxtaposition, while Robert Frost's "The Road Not Taken" (p. 107) seems as plain as prose. But even the plainest poetry should never be read merely to understand its message, for that would be to ignore the special delights and the special kinds of meaning which only poetry can convey.

Let's look at one poem as an active reader would, trying to respond not only to its literal meaning but also to its special qualities as a poem. The poem is by William Shakespeare:

That time of year thou may'st in me behold
When yellow leaves, or none, or few, do hang
Upon those boughs which shake against the cold,
Bare ruined choirs where late the sweet birds sang.
In me thou seest the twilight of such day   5
As after sunset fadeth in the west,
Which by and by black night doth take away,
Death's second self that seals up all in rest.
In me thou seest the glowing of such fire   10
That on the ashes of his youth doth lie,
As the deathbed whereon it must expire,
Consumed with that which it was nourished by.
   This thou perceiv'st, which makes thy love more strong,
   To love that well which thou must leave ere long.

     One of the first things a reader would notice about this poem is that it conveys its meaning in a special way. The speaker of the poem says, in effect, that he is old, but he only tells us so indirectly. He compares his time of life with a season, a time of day, and a stage in the life of a fire, and these three images evoke our own experience so that we understand what he means. In autumn the days grow shorter and colder, at twilight the day's heat and light are going fast, and the embers of a dying fire grow dimmer and cooler with every minute; so too with advancing age, when the vigor and passions of earlier years have faded and death is soon to come. The images also reinforce each other, each describing a natural process that cannot be avoided or stopped and evoking the same progression from warmth to cold, from light to dark. And there is a progression from one image to the next: Autumn, a span of months and days, is succeeded by twilight, a matter of an hour or less, and last comes fire, which can rise and go out in a few minutes. This speeding up of time prepares for the last line's suggestion that death will come "ere long." Images such as these, which occur only occasionally in prose, can often be a poem's chief means of conveying its meaning.

     Another resource which prose writers use sparingly but which is vital to poetry is the *sound* of the language—its vowels and consonants, and the rhythms of words and phrases. Tradition has it that poetry began as song, and poets often choose their words not only to convey meaning but to make a kind of music through planned patterns of verbal sounds. To hear and appreciate that music to the fullest, it's a good idea to read a poem aloud, listening for those patterns. And even if you can't read aloud (for example, if you are in a library reading room or on the bus), try to "hear" the poem in your imagination.

Even on first reading "That Time of Year" you probably noticed that Shakespeare has written his poem with not only its sense but its sound in mind. The rhythm is regular, as each of the fourteen lines has exactly ten syllables, and those syllables alternate regularly between weak and strong stress: "That *time* of *year* thou *may'st* in *me* be*hold.*" Shakespeare's skill is such that to achieve this musical effect he never needs to sacrifice clarity, and indeed he rarely departs from natural phrasing. There is evidence, too, that Shakespeare has coordinated the vowel and consonant sounds of his poem. For one thing, he rhymes his lines in a complex but regular pattern. For another, two particular consonants, *l* and *s*, recur throughout the poem. They are most conspicuous in phrases like "second *self* that *seals*" (line 8) and "*leave ere long*" (line 14), which are examples of alliteration, but on closer examination you will find that one or both sounds appear, usually more than once, in each line of the poem, and help to give it its special music.

Shakespeare's use of rhyme deserves special attention, because it fits perfectly the meaning and even the grammar of his poem. Each of the three images is expressed in a single sentence that takes up four lines, and those lines are rhymed in an interlocking pattern that makes the image, and the sentence, seem all the more self-contained. The arrival of a new image brings the beginning not only of a new sentence but also of a new and different set of rhymes. The last two lines of the poem are not an image but a direct statement, and they have a rhyme pattern of their own using *strong* and *long*. Some readers may even notice in this last rhyme a distant echo of *hang* and *sang* from the beginning of the poem.

Shakespeare's rhyme scheme fits the meaning of his poem so closely that you might think he had invented both as part of the same creative act. In fact this is not so. He wrote 153 other poems in exactly the same form, which is sometimes called the Shakespearean sonnet in his honor. Moreover, Shakespeare did not invent the form, which had existed for forty years and been used by many poets before he took it up. Here we have a strange thing: Maybe the form itself gave Shakespeare ideas for poems, or at least set him challenges that heated rather than cooled his imagination. How versatile the sonnet form was in Shakespeare's hands you can see from the following, which has exactly the same structure as "That Time of Year" but a very different theme:

My mistress' eyes are nothing like the sun;
Coral is far more red than her lips' red;
If snow be white, why then her breasts are dun;
If hairs be wires, black wires grow on her head.
I have seen roses damasked, red and white,
But no such roses see I in her cheeks;
And in some perfumes is there more delight

5

Than in the breath that from my mistress reeks.
I love to hear her speak; yet well I know
That music hath a far more pleasing sound: 10
I grant I never saw a goddess go;
My mistress, when she walks, treads on the ground.
    And yet, by heaven, I think my love as rare
    As any she belied with false compare.

1 *Private Lives*

Our entire life, with our fine moral code and our precious freedom, consists ultimately in accepting ourselves as we are.
JEAN ANOUILH

It's pretty hard to tell what does bring happiness. Poverty and wealth have both failed.
KIN HUBBARD

A Sense of Self

DICK GREGORY

Dick Gregory was one of the angry African-American comics who emerged at the beginning of the 1960s who, as entertainers, could speak of racial injustice to audiences that would not listen to other African-American leaders. A contemporary of Martin Luther King, Jr., and Malcolm X, Gregory played a significant part in the civil rights movement of the sixties with his comedy, his political advocacy, and his writing. His books include *From the Back of the Bus* (1962) and *Nigger* (1964). After having lost a tremendous amount of weight, Gregory has in recent years turned to counseling people whose lives are threatened by obesity. His experimental approaches to diet, weight, and self-esteem have received much public notice, and he has written *Dick Gregory's Natural Diet for Folks Who Eat: Cookin' with Mother Nature*.

Gregory's childhood was hard. He was born in the Depression year of 1932 in the segregated state of Missouri, and grew up burdened by deprivations of all kinds. The following excerpt from his autobiography, *nigger*, gives a hint of what his early years were like, describing a childhood experience that made him aware of how other saw him—and of the meaning of shame.

Shame

     I never learned hate at home, or shame. I had to go to school for that. I was about seven years old when I got my first big lesson. I was in love with a little girl named Helene Tucker, a light-complected little girl with pigtails and nice manners. She was always clean and she was smart in school. I think I went to school then mostly to look at her. I brushed my hair and even got me a little old handkerchief. It was a lady's handkerchief, but I didn't want Helene to see me wipe my nose on my hand. The pipes were frozen again, there was no water in the house, but I washed my socks and shirt every night. I'd get a pot, and go over to Mister Ben's grocery store, and stick my pot down into his soda machine. Scoop out some chopped ice. By evening the ice melted to water for washing. I got sick a lot that winter because the fire would go out at night before the clothes were dry. In the morning I'd put them on, wet or dry, because they were the only clothes I had.

Everybody's got a Helene Tucker, a symbol of everything you want. I   2
loved her for her goodness, her cleanness, her popularity. She'd walk down my street and my brothers and sisters would yell, "Here comes Helene," and I'd rub my tennis sneakers on the back of my pants and wish my hair wasn't so nappy and the white folks' shirt fit me better. I'd run out on the street. If I knew my place and didn't come too close, she'd wink at me and say hello. That was a good feeling. Sometimes I'd follow her all the way home, and shovel the snow off her walk and try to make friends with her Momma and her aunts. I'd drop money on her stoop late at night on my way back from shining shoes in the taverns. And she had a Daddy, and he had a good job. He was a paper hanger.

I guess I would have gotten over Helene by summertime, but some-   3
thing happened in that classroom that made her face hang in front of me for the next twenty-two years. When I played the drums in high school it was for Helene and when I broke track records in college it was for Helene and when I started standing behind microphones and heard applause I wished Helene could hear it too. It wasn't until I was twenty-nine years old and married and making money that I finally got her out of my system. Helene was sitting in that classroom when I learned to be ashamed of myself.

It was on a Thursday. I was sitting in the back of the room, in a seat   4
with a chalk circle drawn around it. The idiot's seat, the troublemaker's seat.

The teacher thought I was stupid. Couldn't spell, couldn't read,   5
couldn't do arithmetic. Just stupid. Teachers were never interested in finding out that you couldn't concentrate because you were so hungry, because you hadn't had any breakfast. All you could think about was noontime, would it ever come? Maybe you could sneak into the cloakroom and steal a bite of some kid's lunch out of a coat pocket. A bite of something. Paste. You can't really make a meal of paste, or put it on bread for a sandwich, but sometimes I'd scoop a few spoonfuls out of the big paste jar in the back of the room. Pregnant people get strange tastes. I was pregnant with poverty. Pregnant with dirt and pregnant with smells that made people turn away, pregnant with cold and pregnant with shoes that were never bought for me, pregnant with five other people in my bed and no Daddy in the next room, and pregnant with hunger. Paste doesn't taste too bad when you're hungry.

The teacher thought I was a troublemaker. All she saw from the front   6
of the room was a little black boy who squirmed in his idiot's seat and made

noises and poked the kids around him. I guess she couldn't see a kid who made noises because he wanted someone to know he was there.

It was on a Thursday, the day before the Negro payday. The eagle 7
always flew on Friday. The teacher was asking each student how much his father would give to the Community Chest. On Friday night, each kid would get the money from his father, and on Monday he would bring it to the school. I decided I was going to buy a Daddy right then. I had money in my pocket from shining shoes and selling papers, and whatever Helene Tucker pledged for her Daddy I was going to top it. And I'd hand the money right in. I wasn't going to wait to Monday to buy me a Daddy.

I was shaking, scared to death. The teacher opened her book and 8
started calling out names alphabetically.

"Helene Tucker?" 9

"My Daddy said he'd give two dollars and fifty cents." 10

That's very nice, Helene. Very, very nice indeed." 11

That made me feel pretty good. It wouldn't take too much to top that. 12
I had almost three dollars in dimes and quarters in my pocket. I stuck my hand in my pocket and held onto the money, waiting for her to call my name. But the teacher closed her book after she called everybody else in the class.

I stood up and raised my hand. 13

"What is it now?" 14

"You forgot me?" 15

She turned toward the blackboard. "I don't have time to be playing 16
with you, Richard."

"My Daddy said he'd . . ." 17

"Sit down, Richard, you're disturbing the class." 18

"My Daddy said he'd give . . . fifteen dollars." 19

She turned around and looked mad. "We are collecting this money for 20
you and your kind, Richard Gregory. If your Daddy can give fifteen dollars you have no business being on relief."

"I got it right now, I got it right now, my Daddy gave it to me to turn 21
in today, my Daddy said . . ."

"And furthermore," she said, looking right at me, her nostrils getting 22
big and her lips getting thin and her eyes opening wide. "We know you don't have a Daddy."

Helene Tucker turned around, her eyes full of tears. She felt sorry for 23
me. Then I couldn't see her too well because I was crying, too.

"Sit down, Richard." 24

And I always thought the teacher kind of liked me. She always picked 25
me to wash the blackboard on Friday, after school. That was a big thrill, it made me feel important. If I didn't wash it, come Monday the school might not function right.

"Where are you going, Richard?" 26

I walked out of school that day, and for a long time I didn't go back   27
very often. There was shame there.

Now there was shame everywhere. It seemed like the whole world had   28
been inside that classroom, everyone has heard what the teacher had said,
everyone had turned around and felt sorry for me. There was shame in
going to the Worthy Boys Annual Christmas Dinner for you and your kind,
because everyone knew what a worthy boy was. Why couldn't they just call
it the Boys Annual Dinner, why'd they have to give it a name? There was
shame in wearing the brown and orange and white plaid mackinaw the
welfare gave to 3,000 boys. Why'd it have to be the same for everybody so
when you walked down the street the people could see you were on relief? It
was a nice warm mackinaw and it had a hood, and my Momma beat me
and called me a little rat when she found out I stuffed it in the bottom of a
pail full of garbage way over on Cottage Street. There was shame in running
over to Mister Ben's at the end of the day and asking for his rotten peaches,
there was shame in asking Mrs. Simmons for a spoonful of sugar, there was
shame in running out to meet the relief truck. I hated that truck, full of food
for you and your kind. I ran into the house and hid when it came. And then
I started to sneak through alleys, to take the long way home so the people
going into White's Eat Shop wouldn't see me. Yeah, the whole world heard
the teacher that day, we all know you don't have a Daddy.

It lasted for a while, this kind of numbness. I spent a lot of time feeling   29
sorry for myself. And then one day I met this wino in a restaurant. I'd been
out hustling all day, shining shoes, selling newspapers, and I had googobs of
money in my pocket. Bought me a bowl of chili for fifteen cents, and a
cheeseburger for fifteen cents, and a Pepsi for five cents, and a piece of
chocolate cake for ten cents. That was a good meal. I was eating when this
old wino came in. I love winos because they never hurt anyone but
themselves.

The old wino sat down at the counter and ordered twenty-six cents   30
worth of food. He ate it like he really enjoyed it. When the owner, Mister
Williams, asked him to pay the check, the old wino didn't lie or go through
his pocket like he suddenly found a hole.

He just said: "Don't have no money."   31

The owner yelled: "Why in hell you come in here and eat my food if   32
you don't have no money? That food cost me money."

Mister Williams jumped over the counter and knocked the wino off   33
his stool and beat him over the head with a pop bottle. Then he stepped
back and watched the wino bleed. Then he kicked him. And he kicked him
again.

I looked at the wino with blood all over his face and I went over.   34
"Leave him alone, Mister Williams. I'll pay the twenty-six cents."

The wino got up, slowly, pulling himself up to the stool, then up to the   35
counter, holding on for a minute until his legs stopped shaking so bad. He

looked at me with pure hate. "Keep your twenty-six cents. You don't have to pay, not now. I just finished paying for it."

He started to walk out, and as he passed me, he reached down and touched my shoulder. "Thanks, sonny, but it's too late now. Why didn't you pay before?"   36

I was pretty sick about that. I waited too long to help another man.   37

Questions for Study and Discussion

1. What does Gregory mean by *shame*? What precisely was he ashamed of, and what in particular did he learn from the incident at school?

2. What is the teacher's attitude toward Gregory? Consider her own words and actions as well as Gregory's opinion in arriving at your answer.

3 What role does money play in Gregory's narrative? How does it relate to his sense of shame?

4 Gregory's use of details—his description of Helene Tucker's manners or his plaid mackinaw, for example—does more than merely make his narrative vivid and interesting. Cite several other specific details he gives, and consider the effect each has on your response to the story.

5. What effect does Gregory's repetition of the word *shame* have on you? Does Gregory repeat any other words or phases? If so, with what effect?

Writing Topics

1. Write an essay in which you describe an event in your life that made you sharply aware of how other people see you. How did you feel—surprised, ashamed, angry, proud, or something else? Why? Do you still feel the same way?

2. Social institutions and organizations help to shape our self-esteem, as they did with Dick Gregory. In an essay, discuss the effect one such institution or organization has had on you. How did it influence you? Did it help or hinder you in developing a positive image of yourself?

3. Gregory's work with overweight people has not been restricted to diet, but has included improving their self-esteem. Write an essay in which you explore the relationship between appearance (such as dress, behavior, weight, height, hairstyle) and self-image. It may be useful to discuss those factors that affect self-image with your friends before you begin to write.

GEORGE ORWELL

George Orwell (1903–1950) was one of the most brilliant social critics of our times. He was born in Bengal, India, but grew up in England and received a traditional education at the prestigious school of Eton. Instead of going on to a university, he joined the civil service and was sent to Burma at nineteen as an assistant superintendent of police. Disillusioned with British imperialism, Orwell resigned in 1929 and began a decade of studying social and political issues firsthand and then writing about them in such works as *Down and Out in Paris and London* (1933) and *The Road to Wigan Pier* (1937). His most famous books are *Animal Farm* (1945), a satire on the Russian Revolution, and *1984* (1949), a chilling novel set in an imagined totalitarian state of the future.

"Shooting an Elephant" was published in the British magazine *New Writing* in 1936. Hitler, Mussolini, and Stalin were in power, building the "younger empires" Orwell refers to in his second paragraph, and the old British Empire was soon to decline, as Orwell predicted. In this essay, Orwell tells of a time when, in a position of authority, he found himself compelled to act against his convictions.

Shooting an Elephant

In Moulmein, in lower Burma, I was hated by large numbers of people—the only time in my life that I have been important enough for this to happen to me. I was sub-divisional police officer of the town, and in an aimless, petty kind of way anti-European feeling was very bitter. No one had the guts to raise a riot, but if a European woman went through the bazaars alone somebody would probably spit betel juice over her dress. As a police officer I was an obvious target and was baited whenever it seemed safe to do so. When a nimble Burman tripped me up on the football field and the referee (another Burman) looked the other way, the crowd yelled with hideous laughter. This happened more than once. In the end the sneering yellow faces of young men that met me everywhere, the insults hooted after me when I was at a safe distance, got badly on my nerves. The young Buddhist priests were the worst of all. There were several thousands of them in the town and none of them seemed to have anything to do except stand on street corners and jeer at Europeans.

All this was perplexing and upsetting. For at that time I had already   2
made up my mind that imperialism was an evil thing and the sooner I
chucked up my job and got out of it the better. Theoretically—and secretly,
of course—I was all for the Burmese and all against their oppressors, the
British. As for the job I was doing, I hated it more bitterly than I can
perhaps make clear. In a job like that you see the dirty work of Empire at
close quarters. The wretched prisoners huddling in the stinking cages of the
lock-ups, the gray, cowed faces of the long-term convicts, the scarred
buttocks of the men who had been flogged with bamboos—all these oppressed me with an intolerable sense of guilt. But I could get nothing into
perspective. I was young and ill educated and I had had to think out my
problems in the utter silence that is imposed on every Englishman in the
East. I did not even know that the British Empire is dying, still less did I
know that it is a great deal better than the younger empires that are going to
supplant it. All I knew was that I was stuck between my hatred of the
empire I served and my rage against the evil-spirited little beasts who tried
to make my job impossible. With one part of my mind I thought of the
British Raj as an unbreakable tyranny, as something clamped down, in
saecula saeculorum, upon the will of prostrate peoples; with another part I
thought that the greatest joy in the world would be to drive a bayonet into a
Buddhist priest's guts.[1] Feelings like these are the normal by-products of
imperialism; ask any Anglo-Indian official, if you can catch him off duty.

One day something happened which in a roundabout way was en-   3
lightening. It was a tiny incident in itself, but it gave me a better glimpse
than I had had before of the real nature of imperialism—the real motives for
which despotic governments act. Early one morning the sub-inspector at a
police station the other end of the town rang me up on the 'phone and said
that an elephant was ravaging the bazaar. Would I please come and do
something about it? I did not know what I could do, but I wanted to see
what was happening and I got on a pony and started out. I took my rifle, an
old .44 Winchester and much too small to kill an elephant, but I
thought the noise might be useful *in terrorem*. Various Burmans stopped me
on the way and told me about the elephant's doings. It was not, of course, a
wild elephant, but a tame one which had gone "must."[2] It had been chained
up, as tame elephants always are when their attack of "must" is due, but on
the previous night it had broken its chain and escaped. Its mahout, the only
person who could manage it when it was in that state, had set out in
pursuit, but had taken the wrong direction and was now twelve hours'
journey away, and in the morning the elephant had suddenly reappeared in

---

[1]Raj: rule, especially in India. *Saecula saeculorum*: from time immemorial.

[2]That is, gone into an uncontrollable frenzy.

the town. The Burmese population had no weapons and were quite helpless against it. It had already destroyed somebody's bamboo hut, killed a cow and raided some fruit-stalls and devoured the stock; also it had met the municipal rubbish van and, when the driver jumped out and took to his heels, had turned the van over and inflicted violences upon it.

The Burmese sub-inspector and some Indian constables were waiting   4
for me in the quarter where that elephant had been seen. It was a very poor quarter, a labyrinth of squalid bamboo huts, thatched with palm-leaf, winding all over a steep hillside. I remember that it was a cloudy, stuffy morning at the beginning of the rains. We began questioning the people as to where the elephant had gone and, as usual, failed to get any definite information. That is invariably the case in the East; a story always sounds clear enough at a distance, but the nearer you get to the scene of events the vaguer it becomes. Some of the people said that the elephant had gone in one direction, some said that he had gone in another, some professed not even to have heard of any elephant. I had almost made up my mind that the whole story was a pack of lies, when we heard yells a little distance away. There was a loud, scandalized cry of "Go away, child! Go away this instant!" and an old woman with a switch in her hand came round the corner of a hut, violently shooing away a crowd of naked children. Some more women followed, clicking their tongues and exclaiming; evidently there was something that the children ought not to have seen. I rounded the hut and saw a man's dead body sprawling in the mud. He was an Indian, a black Dravidian coolie, almost naked, and he could not have been dead many minutes. The people said that the elephant had come suddenly upon him round the corner of the hut, caught him with its trunk, put its foot on his back and ground him into the earth. This was the rainy season and the ground was soft, and his face had scored a trench a foot deep and a couple of yards long. He was lying on his belly with arms crucified and head sharply twisted to one side. His face was coated with mud, the eyes wide open, the teeth bared and grinning with an expression of unendurable agony. (Never tell me, by the way, that the dead look peaceful. Most of the corpses I have seen looked devilish.) The friction of the great beast's foot had stripped the skin from his back as neatly as one skins a rabbit. As soon as I saw the dead man I sent an orderly to a friend's house nearby to borrow an elephant rifle. I had already sent back the pony, not wanting it to go mad with fright and throw me if it smelt the elephant.

The orderly came back in a few minutes with a rifle and five car-   5
tridges, and meanwhile some Burmans had arrived and told us that the elephant was in the paddy fields below, only a few hundred yards away. As I started forward practically the whole population of the quarter flocked out of the houses and followed me. They had seen the rifle and were all shouting excitedly that I was going to shoot the elephant. They had not shown much interest in the elephant when he was merely ravaging their

homes, but it was different now that he was going to be shot. It was a bit of fun to them, as it would be to an English crowd; besides they wanted the meat. It made me vaguely uneasy. I had no intention of shooting the elephant—I had merely sent for the rifle to defend myself if necessary—and it is always unnerving to have a crowd following you. I marched down the hill, looking and feeling a fool, with the rifle over my shoulder and an ever-growing army of people jostling at my heels. At the bottom, when you got away from the huts, there was a metalled road and beyond that a miry waste of paddy fields a thousand yards across, not yet ploughed but soggy from the first rains and dotted with coarse grass. The elephant was standing eight yards from the road, his left side toward us. He took not the slightest notice of the crowd's approach. He was tearing up bunches of grass, beating them against his knees to clean them, and stuffing them into his mouth.

I had halted on the road. As soon as I saw the elephant I knew with   6 perfect certainty that I ought not to shoot him. It is a serious matter to shoot a working elephant—it is comparable to destroying a huge and costly piece of machinery—and obviously one ought not to do it if it can possibly be avoided. And at that distance, peacefully eating, the elephant looked no more dangerous than a cow. I thought then and I think now that his attack of "must" was already passing off; in which case he would merely wander harmlessly about until the mahout came back and caught him. Moreover, I did not in the least want to shoot him. I decided that I would watch him for a little while to make sure that he did not turn savage again, and then go home.

But at that moment I glanced round at the crowd that had followed   7 me. It was an immense crowd, two thousand at the least and growing every minute. It blocked the road for a long distance on either side. I looked at the sea of yellow faces above the garish clothes—faces all happy and excited over this bit of fun, all certain that the elephant was going to be shot. They were watching me as they would watch a conjurer about to perform a trick. They did not like me, but with the magical rifle in my hands I was momentarily worth watching. And suddenly I realized that I should have to shoot the elephant after all. The people expected it of me and I had got to do it; I could feel their two thousand wills pressing me forward, irresistibly. And it was at this moment, as I stood there with the rifle in my hands, that I first grasped the hollowness, the futility of the white man's dominion in the East. Here was I, the white man with his gun, standing in front of the unarmed native crowd—seemingly the leading actor of the piece; but in reality I was only an absurd puppet pushed to and fro by the will of those yellow faces behind. I perceived in this moment that when the white man turns tyrant it is his own freedom that he destroys. He becomes a sort of hollow, posing dummy, the conventionalized figure of a sahib. For it is the condition of his rule that he shall spend his life in trying to impress the "natives," and so in every crisis he has got to do what the "natives" expect of him. He wears a mask, and his face grows to fit it. I had got to shoot the elephant. I had committed myself to doing it when I sent for the rifle. A sahib has got to act like a sahib; he has got to appear resolute, to know his own mind and do definite things. To come all that way, rifle in hand, with two thousand people marching at my heels, and then to trail feebly away, having done nothing—no, that was impossible. The crowd would laugh at me. And my whole life, every white man's life in the East, was one long struggle not to be laughed at.

But I did not want to shoot the elephant. I watched him beating his   8 bunch of grass against his knees with that preoccupied grandmotherly air that elephants have. It seemed to me that it would be murder to shoot him. At that age I was not squeamish about killing animals, but I had never shot an elephant and never wanted to. (Somehow it always seems worse to kill a *large* animal.) Besides, there was the beast's owner to be considered. Alive, the elephant was worth at least a hundred pounds; dead, he would only be worth the value of his tusks, five pounds, possibly.[3] But I had got to act quickly. I turned to some experienced-looking Burmans who had been there when we arrived, and asked them how the elephant had been behaving. They all said the same thing; he took no notice of you if you left him alone, but he might charge if you went too close to him.

It was perfectly clear to me what I ought to do. I ought to walk up to   9 within, say, twenty-five yards of the elephant and test his behavior. If he charged, I could shoot; if he took no notice of me, it would be safe to leave him until the mahout came back. But also I knew that I was going to do no such thing. I was a poor shot with a rifle and the ground was soft mud into which one would sink at every step. If the elephant charged and I missed him, I should have about as much chance as a toad under a steam-roller. But even then I was not thinking particularly of my own skin, only of the watchful yellow faces behind. For at that moment, with the crowd watching me, I was not afraid in the ordinary sense, as I would have been if I had been alone. A white man mustn't be frightened in front of "natives"; and so, in general, he isn't frightened. The sole thought in my mind was that if anything went wrong those two thousand Burmans would see me pursued, caught, trampled on, and reduced to a grinning corpse like that Indian up the hill. And if that happened it was quite probable that some of them would laugh. That would never do. There was only one alternative. I shoved the cartridges into the magazine and lay down on the road to get a better aim.

The crowd grew very still, and a deep, low, happy sigh, as of people   10 who see the theater curtain go up at last, breathed from innumerable throats. They were going to have their bit of fun after all. The rifle was a

---

[3]The British pound would have been worth $5.00 at the time.

beautiful German thing with cross-hair sights. I did not then know that in shooting an elephant one would shoot to cut an imaginary bar running from ear-hole to ear-hole. I ought, therefore, as the elephant was sideways on, to have aimed straight at his ear-hole; actually I aimed several inches in front of this, thinking the brain would be further forward.

When I pulled the trigger I did not hear the bang or feel the kick—one never does when a shot goes home—but I heard the devilish roar of glee that went up from the crowd. In that instant, in too short a time, one would have thought, even for the bullet to get there, a mysterious, terrible change had come over the elephant. He neither stirred nor fell, but every line of his body had altered. He looked suddenly stricken, shrunken, immensely old, as though the frightful impact of the bullet had paralyzed him without knocking him down. At last, after what seemed a long time—it might have been five seconds, I dare say—he sagged flabbily to his knees. His mouth slobbered. An enormous senility seemed to have settled upon him. One could have imagined him thousands of years old. I fired again into the same spot. At the second shot he did not collapse but climbed with desperate slowness to his feet and stood weakly upright, with legs sagging and head drooping. I fired a third time. That was the shot that did for him. You could see the agony of it jolt his whole body and knock the last remnant of strength from his legs. But in falling he seemed for a moment to rise, for as his hind legs collapsed beneath him he seemed to tower upward like a huge rock toppling, his trunk reaching skyward like a tree. He trumpeted, for the first and only time. And then down he came, his belly toward me, with a crash that seemed to shake the ground even where I lay.

I got up. The Burmans were already racing past me across the mud. It was obvious that the elephant would never rise again, but he was not dead. He was breathing very rhythmically with long rattling gasps, his great mound of a side painfully rising and falling. His mouth was wide open—I could see far down into caverns of pale pink throat. I waited a long time for him to die, but his breathing did not weaken. Finally, I fired two remaining shots into the spot where I thought his heart must be. The thick blood welled out of him like red velvet, but still he did not die. His body did not even jerk when the shots hit him, the tortured breathing continued without a pause. He was dying, very slowly and in great agony, but in some world remote from me where not even a bullet could damage him further. I felt that I had got to put an end to that dreadful noise. It seemed dreadful to see the great beast lying there, powerless to move and yet powerless to die, and not even to be able to finish him. I sent back for my small rifle and poured shot after shot into his heart and down his throat. They seemed to make no impression. The tortured gasps continued as steadily as the ticking of a clock.

In the end I could not stand it any longer and went away. I heard later that it took him half an hour to die. Burmans were bringing dahs[4] and baskets even before I left, and I was told they had stripped his body almost to the bones by the afternoon.

Afterwards, of course, there were endless discussions about the shoot-   14
ing of the elephant. The owner was furious, but he was only an Indian and could do nothing. Besides, legally I had done the right thing, for a mad elephant has to be killed, like a mad dog, if its owner fails to control it. Among the Europeans opinion was divided. The older men said I was right, the younger men said it was a damn shame to shoot an elephant for killing a coolie, because an elephant was worth more than any damn Coringhee coolie. And afterwards I was very glad that the coolie had been killed; it put me legally in the right and it gave me a sufficient pretext for shooting the elephant. I often wondered whether any of the others grasped that I had done it solely to avoid looking a fool.

Questions for Study and Discussion

1. Why is the setting of this narrative significant? What is imperialism, and what does Orwell's essay say about it?

2. Why, according to Orwell, did he shoot the elephant? Do you find his interpretation convincing? Why, or why not?

3. What do you think was Orwell's purpose in telling this story? Cite evidence from the essay that indicates to you that purpose. Does he accomplish his purpose?

4. What part of the essay struck you most strongly? The shooting itself? Orwell's feelings? The descriptions of the Burmans and their behavior? Or something else? Can you identify anything about Orwell's prose that enhances the impact of that passage? Explain.

5. What is Orwell doing in the final paragraph? How does that paragraph affect your response to the whole essay?

Writing Topics

1. Consider situations in which you have been a leader, like Orwell, or part of a crowd, like the Burmans. As a leader, what was your attitude toward your followers? As a follower, what did you feel toward your leader? From these experiences, what conclusions can you draw? Write an essay about the relationship between leaders and followers.

2. Tell of a situation in which you felt compelled to act against your convictions. What arguments can justify your action? How much freedom of choice did you actually have, and what were the limits on your freedom? On

---

[4] Heavy knives.

what basis can you refuse to subordinate your convictions to others', or to society's?

3. Orwell has shown one of the ironies of imperialism, that colonial officers are ruled by those they govern, or, to put it another way, that the rulers are ruled by the ruled. What are some other criticisms of imperialism? Using library sources, write an essay on the differing views of imperialism, from the perspective of the imperial power and from that of the people subject to the power.

ZORA NEALE HURSTON

Zora Neale Hurston (1903–1960) was raised in the rural South and grew up to become one of the stars of the Harlem Renaissance. Her work as an anthropologist, folklorist, and novelist has centered on maintaining and sharing her cultural heritage. Her works include a collection of folktales, numerous short stories and magazine articles, an autobiography, and five novels, most notable among them her masterwork, *Their Eyes Were Watching God*.

In the following essay, taken from *I Love Myself When I Am Laughing*, Hurston expresses an enthusiastic pride in having grown up "colored" in a white world.

How It Feels to Be Colored Me

I am colored but I offer nothing in the way of extenuating circum- 1
stances except the fact that I am the only Negro in the United States whose grandfather on the mother's side was *not* an Indian chief.

I remember the very day that I became colored. Up to my thirteenth 2
year I lived in the little Negro town of Eatonville, Florida. It is exclusively a colored town. The only white people I knew passed through the town going to or coming from Orlando. The native whites rode dusty horses, the Northern tourists chugged down the sandy village road in automobiles. The town knew the Southerners and never stopped cane chewing when they passed. But the Northerners were something else again. They were peered at cautiously from behind curtains by the timid. The more venturesome would come out on the porch to watch them go past and got just as much pleasure out of the tourists as the tourists got out of the village.

The front porch might seem a daring place for the rest of the town, 3
but it was a gallery seat for me. My favorite place was atop the gate-post. Proscenium box for a born first-nighter. Not only did I enjoy the show, but I didn't mind the actors knowing that I liked it. I usually spoke to them in passing. I'd wave at them and when they returned my salute, I would say something like this: "Howdy-do-well-I-thank-you-where-you-goin'?" Usually automobile or the horse paused at this, and after a queer exchange of compliments, I would probably "go a piece of the way" with them, as we say in farthest Florida. If one of my family happened to come to the front in

time to see me, of course negotiations would be rudely broken off. But even so, it is clear that I was the first "welcome-to-our-state" Floridian, and I hope the Miami Chamber of Commerce will please take notice.

During this period, white people differed from colored to me only in that they rode through town and never lived there. They liked to hear me "speak pieces" and sing and wanted to see me dance the parse-me-la, and gave me generously of their small silver for doing these things, which seemed strange to me for I wanted to do them so much that I needed bribing to stop. Only they didn't know it. The colored people gave no dimes. They deplored any joyful tendencies in me, but I was their Zora nevertheless. I belonged to them, to the nearby hotels, to the county—everybody's Zora.

But changes came in the family when I was thirteen, and I was sent to school in Jacksonville. I left Eatonville, the town of the oleanders, as Zora. When I disembarked from the river-boat at Jacksonville, she was no more. It seemed that I had suffered a sea change. I was not Zora of Orange County any more, I was now a little colored girl. I found it out in certain ways. In my heart as well as in the mirror, I became a fast brown—warranted not to rub nor run.

But I am not tragically colored. There is no great sorrow dammed up in my soul, nor lurking behind my eyes. I do not mind at all. I do not belong to the sobbing school of Negrohood who hold that nature somehow has given them a lowdown dirty deal and whose feelings are all hurt about it. Even in the helter-skelter skirmish that is my life, I have seen that the world is to the strong regardless of a little pigmentation more or less. No, I do not weep at the world—I am too busy sharpening my oyster knife.

Someone is always at my elbow reminding me that I am the grand-daughter of slaves. It fails to register depression with me. Slavery is sixty years in the past. The operation was successful and the patient is doing well, thank you. The terrible struggle that made me an American out of a potential slave said "On the line!" The Reconstruction said "Get set!"; and the generation before said "Go!" I am off to a flying start and I must not halt in the stretch to look behind and weep. Slavery is the price I paid for civilization, and the choice was not with me. It is a bully adventure and worth all that I have paid through my ancestors for it. No one on earth ever had a greater chance for glory. The world to be won and nothing to be lost. It is thrilling to think—to know that for any act of mine, I shall get twice as much praise or twice as much blame. It is quite exciting to hold the center of the national stage, with the spectators not knowing whether to laugh or to weep.

The position of my white neighbor is much more difficult. No brown specter pulls up a chair beside me when I sit down to eat. No dark ghost thrusts its leg against mine in bed. The game of keeping what one has is never so exciting as the game of getting.

I do not always feel colored. Even now I often achieve the unconscious   9
Zora of Eatonville before the Hegira. I feel most colored when I am thrown
against a sharp white background.

For instance at Barnard. "Beside the waters of the Hudson" I feel my   10
race. Among the thousand white persons, I am a dark rock surged upon,
and overswept, but through it all, I remain myself. When covered by the
waters, I am; and the ebb but reveals me again.

Sometimes it is the other way around. A white person is set down in   11
our midst, but the contrast is just as sharp for me. For instance, when I sit in
the drafty basement that is The New World Cabaret with a white person,
my color comes. We enter chatting about any little nothing that we have in
common and are seated by the jazz waiters. In the abrupt way that jazz
orchestras have, this one plunges into a number. It loses no time in
circumlocutions, but gets right down to business. It constricts the thorax
and splits the heart with its tempo and narcotic harmonies. This orchestra
grows rambunctious, rears on its hind legs and attacks the tonal veil with
primitive fury, rending it, clawing it until it breaks through to the jungle
beyond. I follow those heathen—follow them exultingly. I dance wildly
inside myself; I yell within, I whoop; I shake my assegai above my head, I
hurl it true to the mark *yeeeeooww*! I am in the jungle and living in the
jungle way. My face is painted red and yellow and my body is painted blue.
My pulse is throbbing like a war drum, I want to slaughter something—give
paid, give death to what, I do not know. But the piece ends. The men of the
orchestra wipe their lips and rest their fingers. I creep back slowly to the
veneer we call civilization with the last tone and find the white friend sitting
motionless in his seat, smoking calmly.

"Good music they have here," he remarks, drumming the table with   12
his fingertips.

Music. The great blobs of purple and red emotion have not touched   13
him. He has only heard what I felt. He is far away and I see him but dimly
across the ocean and the continent that have fallen between us. He is so
pale with his whiteness then and I am *so* colored.

At certain times I have no race, I am *me*. When I set my hat at a certain   14
angle and saunter down Seventh Avenue, Harlem City, feeling as snooty as
the lions in front of the Forty-Second Street Library, for instance. So far as my
feelings are concerned, Peggy Hopkins Joyce on the Boule Mich with her
gorgeous raiment, stately carriage, knees knocking together in a most
aristocratic manner, has nothing on me. The cosmic Zora emerges. I belong to
no race nor time. I am the eternal feminine with its string of beads.

I have no separate feeling about being an American citizen and   15
colored. I am merely a fragment of the Great Soul that surges within the
boundaries. My country, right or wrong.

Sometimes, I feel discriminated against, but it does not make me   16
angry. It merely astonishes me. How *can* any deny themselves the pleasure of
my company? It's beyond me.

But in the main, I feel like a brown bag of miscellany propped against a   17
wall. Against a wall in company with other bags, white, red and yellow.
Pour out the contents, and there is discovered a jumble of small things
priceless and worthless. A first-water diamond, an empty spool, bits of
broken glass, lengths of string, a key to a door long since crumbled away, a
rusty knife-blade, old shoes saved for a road that never was and never will
be, a nail bent under the weight of things too heavy for any nail, a dried
flower or two still a little fragrant. In your hand is the brown bag. On the
ground before you is the jumble it held—so much like the jumble in the
bags, could they be emptied, that all might be dumped in a single heap and
the bags refilled without altering the content of any greatly. A bit of colored
glass more or less would not matter. Perhaps that is how the Great Stuffer of
Bags filled them in the first place—who knows?

Questions for Study and Discussion

1. What does Hurston mean when she says she remembers the day she
became colored? How does she contrast her "colored" self with her "no race"
self?

2. Many African-American and other minority writers convey attitudes
ranging from rage, to despair, to resignation at the way that they are discriminated against by whites. Hurston is different. How would you characterize her
attitude? What does it tell you about the kind of person she is? What in
Hurston's choice of words and images led you to your conclusion?

3. In you own words, what are the "brown specter" and the "dark ghost"
that Hurston refers to in paragraph 8? How do these images relate to her
statement that "the game of keeping what one has is never so exciting as the
game of getting"? Do you agree or disagree with this statement? Explain.

4. What cultural stereotype does Hurston claim with pride in paragraph
11? What image of whites does it evoke? How does her contrasting of blacks and
whites strike you? Is it fair? Explain.

5. Hurston concludes her essay with an analogy. What is that analogy,
and how well does it work? What does it reveal to the reader about the author's
view of citizenship and humankind? Does her vision of humankind and citizenship strike you as realistic?

Writing Topics

1. Reread Dick Gregory's essay "Shame" in the beginning of this section.
Write an essay in which you discuss the ways his attitude toward being

"different" contrast with Hurston's. Note how the two authors use word choice and tone to convey their self-image.

2. Hurston grew up in a world in which most blacks were discriminated against and made to feel inferior to whites. What do you suppose were some of the influences that enabled Hurston to maintain such a positive self-image? Do you think these influences can counteract discrimination not only against race, but against sex, age, or some other trait perceived as limiting? In your essay be sure to discuss the ways in which certain influences can nurture or destroy a child's positive self-image.

3. Although Hurston has a positive attitude toward being "colored," she is nevertheless aware that not all blacks do. Think of some trait of yours such as race, national origin, sex, or a limiting physical condition that has been a concern in your life. Write an essay in which you reflect on this concern. To what extent have you been successful in maintaining a positive self-image in the face of discrimination and self-doubt?

Born in the small Polish town of Bilgoray, in 1904, Isaac Bashevis Singer grew up in the Jewish ghetto in Warsaw. His father was a rabbi of the mystical Hasidic sect, and Singer himself studied to become a rabbi. Instead he began a career as a writer with Warsaw's Yiddish newspaper, meanwhile writing short stories, novellas, and his first novel, *Satan in Goray* (1935). In 1935 he immigrated to New York, four years before Hitler invaded Poland. Though fluent in English, he has continued to write his fiction in Yiddish, saying: "In a figurative way, Yiddish is the wise and humble language of us all, the idiom of frightened and hopeful humanity." Singer was awarded the Nobel Prize for Literature in 1978.

In "Gimpel the Fool," first published in 1953 in Saul Bellow's translation from the Yiddish, Isaac Bashevis Singer explores the tension between faith and doubt. Gimpel is so willing to believe what others tell him that his neighbors think him a fool. Yet trust, the willingness to accept things on faith, is no less important to our public and private lives than our inclination to question and suspect. In the surprising conclusion, Gimpel completely changes his way of life, yet manages to maintain his trust of humankind.

Gimpel the Fool

I am Gimpel the fool. I don't think myself a fool. On the contrary. But that's what folks call me. They gave me the name while I was still in school. I had seven names in all: imbecile, donkey, flax-head, dope, glump, ninny, and fool. The last name stuck. What did my foolishness consist of? I was easy to take in. They said, "Gimple, you know the rabbi's wife has been brought to childbed?" So I skipped school. Well, it turned out to be a lie. How was I supposed to know? She hadn't had a big belly. But I never looked at her belly. Was that really so foolish? The gang laughed and hee-hawed, stomped and danced and chanted a good-night prayer. And instead of the raisins they give when a woman's lying in, they stuffed my hand full of goat turds. I was no weakling. If I slapped someone he'd see all the way to Cracow. But I'm really not a slugger by nature. I think to myself: Let it pass. So they take advantage of me.

I was coming home from school and heard a dog barking. I'm not   2
afraid of dogs, but of course I never want to start up with them. One of
them may be mad, and if he bites there's not a Tartar in the world who can
help you. So I made tracks. Then I looked around and saw the whole market
place wild with laughter. It was no dog at all but Wolf-Leib the Thief. How
was I supposed to know it was he? It sounded like a howling bitch.

When the pranksters and leg-pullers found that I was easy to fool,   3
every one of them tried his luck with me. "Gimpel, the Czar is coming to
Frampol; Gimpel, the moon fell down in Turbeen;[1] Gimpel, little Hodel
Furpiece found a treasure behind the bathhouse." And I like a golem[2]
believed everyone. In the first place, everything is possible, as it is written in
the Wisdom of the Fathers. I've forgotten just how. Second, I had to believe
when the whole town came down on me! If I ever dared to say, "Ah, you're
kidding!" there was trouble. People got angry. "What do you mean! You
want to call everyone a liar?" What was I to do? I believed them, and I hope
at least that did them some good.

I was an orphan. My grandfather who brought me up was already   4
bent toward the grave. So they turned me over to a baker, and what a time
they gave me there! Every woman or girl who came to bake a batch of
noodles had to fool me at least once. "Gimpel, there's a fair in heaven;
Gimpel, the rabbi gave birth to a calf in the seventh month; Gimple, a cow
flew over the roof and laid brass eggs." A student from the yeshiva[3] came
once to buy a roll, and he said, "You, Gimpel, while you stand here scraping
with your baker's shovel the Messiah has come. The dead have arisen."
"What do you mean?" I said. "I heard no one blowing the ram's horn!" He
said, "Are you deaf?" And all began to cry, "We heard it, we heard!" Then
in came Rietze the Candle-dipper and called out in her hoarse voice,
"Gimpel, your father and mother have stood up from the grave. They're
looking for you."

To tell the truth, I knew very well that nothing of the sort had   5
happened, but all the same, as folks were talking, I threw on my wool vest
and went out. Maybe something had happened. What did I stand to lose by
looking? Well, what a cat music went up! And then I took a vow to believe
nothing more. But that was no go either. They confused me so that I didn't
know the big end from the small.

I went to the rabbi to get some advice. He said, "It is written, better to   6
be a fool all your days than for one hour to be evil. You are not a fool. They
are the fools. For he who causes his neighbor to feel shame loses Paradise
himself." Nevertheless the rabbi's daughter took me in. As I left the

---

[1]Frampol and Turbeen are mythical towns in Singer's fiction.

[2]A slow-witted simpleton.

[3]In Europe, a rabbinical seminary.

rabbinical court she said, "Have you kissed the wall yet?" I said "No; what for?" She answered, "It's the law; you've got to do it after every visit." Well, there didn't seem to be any harm in it. And she burst out laughing. It was a fine trick. She put one over on me, all right.

I wanted to go off to another town, but then everyone got busy matchmaking, and they were after me so they nearly tore my coat tails off. They talked at me and talked until I got water on the ear. She was no chaste maiden, but they told me she was virgin pure. She had a limp, and they said it was deliberate, from coyness. She had a bastard, and they told me the child was her little brother. I cried, "You're wasting your time, I'll never marry that whore." But they said indignantly, "What a way to talk! Aren't you ashamed of yourself? We can take you to the rabbi and have you fined for giving her a bad name." I saw then that I wouldn't escape them so easily and I thought: They're set on making me their butt. But when you're married the husband's the master, and if that's all right with her it's agreeable to me too. Besides, you can't pass through life unscathed, nor expect to. 7

I went to her clay house, which was built on the sand, and the whole gang, hollering and chorusing, came after me. They acted like bear-baiters. When we came to the well they stopped all the same. They were afraid to start anything with Elka. Her mouth would open as if it were on a hinge, and she had a fierce tongue. I entered the house. Lines were strung from wall to wall and clothes were drying. Barefoot she stood by the tub, doing the wash. She was dressed in a worn hand-me-down gown of plush. She had her hair put up in braids and pinned across her head. It took my breath away, almost, the reek of it all. 8

Evidently she knew who I was. She took a look at me and said, "Look who's here! He's come, the drip. Grab a seat." 9

I told her all; I denied nothing. "Tell me the truth," I said, "are you really a virgin, and is that mischievous Yechiel actually your little brother? Don't be deceitful with me, for I'm an orphan." 10

"I'm an orphan myself," she answered, "and whoever tries to twist you up, may the end of his nose take a twist. But don't let them think they can take advantage of me. I want a dowry of fifty guilders, and let them take up a collection besides. Otherwise they can kiss my you-know-what." She was very plainspoken. I said, "It's the bride and not the groom who gives a dowry." Then she said, "Don't bargain with me. Either a flat 'yes' or a flat 'no'—Go back where you came from." 11

I thought: No bread will ever be baked from *this* dough. But ours is not a poor town. They consented to everything and proceeded with the wedding. It so happened that there was a dysentery epidemic at the time. The ceremony was held at the cemetery gates, near the little corpse-washing hut. The fellows got drunk. While the marriage contract was being drawn up I heard the most pious high rabbi ask, "Is the bride a widow or a divorced 12 woman?" And the sexton's wife answered for her, "Both a widow and divorced." It was a black moment for me. But what was I to do, run away from under the marriage canopy?

There was singing and dancing. An old granny danced opposite me, hugging a braided white *chalah*[4]. The master of revels made a "God'a mercy" in memory of the bride's parents. The schoolboys threw burrs, as on Tishe b'Av fast day.[5] There were a lot of gifts after the sermon: a noodle board, a kneading trough, a bucket, brooms, ladles, household articles galore. Then I took a look and saw two strapping young men carrying a crib. "What do we need this for?" I asked. So they said, "Don't rack your brains about it. It's all right, it'll come in handy." I realized I was going to be rooked. Take it another way though, what did I stand to lose? I reflected: I'll see what comes of it. A whole town can't go altogether crazy.

At night I came where my wife lay, but she wouldn't let me in. "Say, look here, is this what they married us for?" I said. And she said, "My monthly has come." "But yesterday they took you to the ritual bath, and that's afterward, isn't it supposed to be?" "Today isn't yesterday," said she, "and yesterday's not today. You can beat it if you don't like it." In short, I waited.

Not four months later she was in childbed. The townsfolk hid their laughter with their knuckles. But what could I do? She suffered intolerable pains and clawed at the walls. "Gimpel," she cried, I'm going. Forgive me." The house filled with women. They were boiling pans of water. The screams rose to the welkin.

The thing to do was to go to the House of Prayer to repeat Psalms, and that was what I did.

The townsfolk liked that, all right. I stood in a corner saying Psalms and prayers, and they shook their heads at me. "Pray, pray!" they told me. "Prayer never made any woman pregnant." One of the congregation put a straw to my mouth and said, "Hay for the cows." There was something to that too, by God!

She gave birth to a boy. Friday at the synagogue the sexton stood up before the Ark, pounded the reading table, and announced, "The wealthy Reb Gimpel invites the congregation to a feast in honor of the birth of a son." The whole House of Prayer rang with laughter. My face was flaming. But there was nothing I could do. After all, I *was* responsible for the circumcision honors and rituals.

Half the town came running. You couldn't wedge another soul in. Women brought peppered chick-peas, and there was a keg of beer from the tavern. I ate and drank as much as anyone, and they all congratulated me.

[4]Bread.

[5]A day of fasting and mourning commemorating the destruction of the Temple in Jerusalem.

Then there was a circumcision, and I named the boy after my father, may he rest in peace. When all were gone and I was left with my wife alone, she thrust her head through the bed-curtain and called me to her.

"Gimpel," said she, "why are you silent? Has your ship gone and sunk?" 20

"What shall I say?" I answered. "A fine thing you've done to me! If my mother had known of it she'd have died a second time." 21

She said, "Are you crazy, or what?" 22

"How can you make such a fool," I said, "of one who should be the lord and master?" 23

"What's the matter with you?" she said. "What have you taken it into your head to imagine?" 24

I saw that I must speak bluntly and openly. "Do you think this is the way to use an orphan?" I said. "You have borne a bastard." 25

She answered, "Drive this foolishness out of your head. The child is yours." 26

"How can he be mine?" I argued. "He was born seventeen weeks after the wedding." 27

She told me then that he was premature. I said, "Isn't he a little too premature?" She said, she had a grandmother who carried just as short a time and she resembled this grandmother of hers as one drop of water does another. She swore to it with such oaths that you would have believed a peasant at the fair if he had used them. To tell the plain truth, I didn't believe her; but when I talked it over next day with the schoolmaster he told me that the very same thing had happened to Adam and Eve. Two they went up to bed and four they descended. 28

"There isn't a women in the world who is not the granddaughter of Eve," he said. 29

That was how it was; they argued me dumb. But then, who really knows how such things are? 30

I began to forget my sorrow. I loved the child madly, and he loved me too. As soon as he saw me he'd wave his little hands and want me to pick him up, and when he was colicky I was the only one who could pacify him. I bought him a little bone teething ring and a little gilded cap. He was forever catching the evil eye from someone, and then I had to run to get one of those abracadabras for him that would get him out of it. I worked like an ox. You know how expenses go up when there's an infant in the house. I don't want to lie about it; I didn't dislike Elka either, for that matter. She swore at me and cursed, and I couldn't get enough of her. What strength she had! One of her looks could rob you of the power of speech. And her orations! Pitch and sulphur, that's what they were full of, and yet somehow also full of charm. I adored her every word. She gave me bloody wounds though. 31

In the evening I brought her a white loaf as well as a dark one, and also poppyseed rolls I baked myself. I thieved because of her and swiped everything I could lay hands on: macaroons, raisins, almonds, cakes. I hope 32

I may be forgiven for stealing from the Saturday pots the women left to warm in the baker's oven. I would take out scraps of meat, a chunk of pudding, a chicken leg or head, a piece of tripe, whatever I could nip quickly. She ate and became fat and handsome.

I had to sleep away from home all during the week, at the bakery. On Friday nights when I got home she always made an excuse of some sort. Either she had heartburn, or a stitch in the side, or hiccups, or headaches. You know what women's excuses are. I had a bitter time of it. It was rough. To add to it, this little brother of hers, the bastard, was growing bigger. He'd put lumps on me, and when I wanted to hit back she'd open her mouth and curse so powerfully I saw a green haze floating before my eyes. Ten times a day she threatened to divorce me. Another man in my place would have taken French leave and disappeared. But I'm the type that bears it and says nothing. What's one to do? Shoulders are from God, and burdens too.

One night there was a calamity in the bakery; the oven burst, and we almost had a fire. There was nothing to do but go home, so I went home. Let me, I thought, also taste the joy of sleeping in bed in midweek. I didn't want to wake the sleeping mite and tiptoed into the house. Coming in, it seemed to me that I heard not the snoring of one but, as it were, a double snore, one a thin enough snore and the other like the snoring of a slaughtered ox. Oh, I didn't like that! I didn't like it at all. I went up to the bed, and things suddenly turned black. Next to Elka lay a man's form. Another in my place would have made an uproar, and enough noise to rouse the whole town, but the thought occurred to me that I might wake the child. A little thing like that—why frighten a little swallow, I thought. All right then, I went back to the bakery and stretched out on a sack of flour and till morning I never shut an eye. I shivered as if I had had malaria. "Enough of being a donkey," I said to myself. "Gimpel isn't going to be a sucker all his life. There's a limit even to the foolishness of a fool like Gimpel."

In the morning I went to the rabbi to get advice, and it made a great commotion in the town. They sent the beadle for Elka right away. She came, carrying the child. And what do you think she did? She denied it, denied everything, bone and stone! "He's out of his head," she said. "I know nothing of dreams or divinations." They yelled at her, warned her, hammered on the table, but she stuck to her guns: it was a false accusation, she said.

The butchers and the horse-traders took her part. One of the lads from the slaughterhouse came by and said to me, "We've got our eye on you, you're a marked man." Meanwhile the child started to bear down and soiled itself. In the rabbinical court there was an Ark of the Covenant, and they couldn't allow that, so they sent Elka away.

I said to the rabbi, "What shall I do?"

"You must divorce her at once," said he.

"And what if she refuses?" I asked.

He said, "You must serve the divorce. That's all you'll have to do." 40

I said, "Well, all right, Rabbi. Let me think about it." 41

"There's nothing to think about," said he. "You mustn't remain under 42
the same roof with her."

"And what if she refuses?" I asked. 43

"Let her go, the harlot," said he, "and her brood of bastards with 44
her."

The verdict he gave was that I mustn't even cross her threshold— 45
never again, as long as I should live.

During the day it didn't bother me so much. I thought: It was bound 46
to happen, the abscess had to burst. But at night when I stretched out upon
the sacks I felt it all very bitterly. A longing took me, for her and for the
child. I wanted to be angry, but that's my misfortune exactly, I don't have it
in me to be really angry. In the first place—this was how my thoughts
went—there's bound to be a slip sometimes. You can't live without errors.
Probably that lad who was with her led her on and gave her presents and
what not, and women are often long on hair and short on sense, and so he
got around her. And then since she denies it so, maybe I was only seeing
things? Hallucinations do happen. You see a figure or a mannikin or
something, but when you come up closer it's nothing, there's not a thing
there. And if that's so, I'm doing her an injustice. And when I got so far in
my thoughts I started to weep. I sobbed so that I wet the flour where I lay. In
the morning I went to the rabbi and told him that I had made a mistake.
The rabbi wrote on with his quill, and he said that if that were so he would
have to reconsider the whole case. Until he had finished I wasn't to go near
my wife, but I might send her bread and money by messenger.

Nine months passed before all the rabbis could come to an agreement. 47
Letters went back and forth. I hadn't realized that there could be so much
erudition about a matter like this.

Meanwhile Elka gave birth to still another child, a girl this time. On 48
the Sabbath I went to the synagogue and invoked a blessing on her. They
called me up to the Torah[6] and I named the child for my mother-in-law—
may she rest in peace. The louts and loudmouths of the town who came into
the bakery gave me a going over. All Frampol refreshed its spirits because of
my trouble and grief. However, I resolved that I would always believe what I
was told. What's the good of *not* believing? Today it's your wife you don't
believe; tomorrow it's God Himself you won't take stock in.

By an apprentice who was her neighbor I sent her daily a corn or a 49
wheat loaf, or a piece of pastry, rolls or bagels, or, when I got the chance, a
slab of pudding, a slice of honeycake, or wedding strudel—whatever came

---

[6]The holy scriptures of the Jews, usually in a scroll. On special occasions a member of the
congregation is called upon to read from the scroll. It is considered a great honor.

my way. The apprentice was a goodhearted lad, and more than once he added something on his own. He had formerly annoyed me a lot, plucking my nose and digging me in the ribs, but when he started to be a visitor to my house he became kind and friendly, "Hey, you, Gimpel," he said to me, "you have a very decent little wife and two fine kids. You don't deserve them."

"But the things people say about her," I said.   50

"Well, they have long tongues," he said, "and nothing to do with them   51
but babble. Ignore it as you ignore the cold of last winter."

One day the rabbi sent for me and said, "Are you certain, Gimpel,   52
that you were wrong about your wife?"

I said, "I'm certain."   53

"Why, but look here! You yourself saw it."   54

"It must have been a shadow," I said.   55

"The shadow of what?"   56

"Just of one of the beams, I think"   57

"You can go home then. You owe thanks to the Yanover rabbi. He   58
found an obscure reference in Maimonides [7] that favored you."

I seized the rabbi's hand and kissed it.   59

I wanted to run home immediately. It's no small thing to be separated   60
for so long a time from wife and child. Then I reflected: I'd better go back to work now, and go home in the evening. I said nothing to anyone, although as far as my heart was concerned it was like one of the Holy Days. The women teased and twitted me as they did every day, but my thought was: Go on, with your loose talk. The truth is out, like the oil upon the water. Maimonides says it's right, and therefore, it is right!

At night, when I had covered the dough to let it rise, I took my share   61
of bread and a little sack of flour and started homeward. The moon was full and the stars were glistening, something to terrify the soul. I hurried onward, and before me darted a long shadow. It was winter, and a fresh snow had fallen. I had a mind to sing, but it was growing late and I didn't want to wake the householders. Then I felt like whistling, but I remembered that you don't whistle at night because it brings the demons out. So I was silent and walked as fast as I could.

Dogs in the Christian yards barked at me when I passed, but I   62
thought: Bark your teeth out! What are you but mere dogs? Whereas I am a man, the husband of a fine wife, the father of promising children.

As I approached the house my heart started to pound as though it   63
were the heart of a criminal. I felt no fear, but my heart went thump! thump! Well, no drawing back. I quietly lifted the latch and went in. Elka was asleep. I looked at the infant's cradle. The shutter was closed, but the

---

[7]Moses ben Maimon (1135–1204), Jewish philosopher and commentator on religious law.

moon forced its way through the cracks. I saw the newborn child's face and loved it as soon as I saw it—immediately—each tiny bone.

Then I came nearer to the bed. And what did I see but the apprentice lying there beside Elka. The moon went out all at once. It was utterly black, and I trembled. My teeth chattered. The bread fell from my hands, and my wife waked and said, "Who is that, ah?" 64

I muttered, "It's me." 65

"Gimpel?" she asked. "How come you're here? I thought it was forbidden." 66

"The rabbi said," I answered and shook as with a fever. 67

"Listen to me, Gimpel," she said, "go out to the shed and see if the goat's all right. It seems she's been sick." I have forgotten to say that we had a goat. When I heard she was unwell I went into the yard. The nannygoat was a good little creature. I had a nearly human feeling for her. 68

With hesitant steps I went up to the shed and opened the door. The goat stood there on her four feet. I felt her everywhere, drew her by the horns, examined her udders, and found nothing wrong. She had probably eaten too much bark. "Good night, little goat," I said. "Keep well." And the little beast answered with a "Maa" as though to thank me for the good will. 69

I went back. The apprentice had vanished. 70

"Where," I asked, "is the lad?" 71

"What lad?" my wife answered. 72

"What do you mean?" I said. "The apprentice. You were sleeping with him." 73

"The things I have dreamed this night and the night before," she said, "may they come true and lay you low, body and soul! An evil spirit has taken root in you and dazzles your sight." She screamed out, "You hateful creature! You moon calf! You spook! You uncouth man! Get out, or I'll scream all Frampol out of bed!" 74

Before I could move, her brother sprang out from behind the oven and struck me a blow on the back of the head. I thought he had broken my neck. I felt that something about me was deeply wrong, and I said, "Don't make a scandal. All that's needed now is that people should accuse me of raising spooks and *dybbuks*."[8] For that was what she had meant. "No one will touch bread of my baking." 75

In short, I somehow calmed her. 76

"Well," she said, "that's enough. Lie down, and be shattered by wheels." 77

Next morning I called the apprentice aside. "Listen here, brother!" I said. And so on and so forth. "What do you say?" He stared at me as though I had dropped from the roof or something. 78

---

[8]A demon.

"I swear," he said, "you'd better go to an herb doctor or some healer.   79
"I'm afraid you have a screw loose, but I'll hush it up for you." And that's
how the thing stood.

To make a long story short, I lived twenty years with my wife. She   80
bore me six children, four daughters and two sons. All kinds of things
happened, but I neither saw nor heard. I believed, and that's all. The rabbi
recently said to me, "Belief in itself is beneficial. It is written that a good
man lives by his faith."

Suddenly my wife took sick. It began with a trifle, a little growth upon   81
the breast. But she evidently was not destined to live long; she had no years.
I spent a fortune on her. I have forgotten to say that by this time I had a
bakery of my own and in Frampol was considered to be something of a rich
man. Daily the healer came, and every witch doctor in the neighborhood
was brought. They decided to use leeches, and after that to try cupping.
They even called a doctor from Lublin,[9] but it was too late. Before she died
she called me to her bed and said, "Forgive me, Gimpel."

I said, "What is there to forgive? You have been a good and faithful   82
wife."

"Woe, Gimpel!" she said. "It was ugly how I deceived you all these   83
years. I want to go clean to my Maker, so I have tell you that the children
are not yours."

If I had been clouted on the head with a piece of wood it couldn't have   84
bewildered me more.

"Whose are they?" I asked.   85

"I don't know," she said. "There were a lot . . . but they're not yours."   86
And as she spoke she tossed her head to the side, her eyes turned glassy, and
it was all up with Elka. On her whitened lips there remained a smile.

I imagined that, dead as she was, she was saying, "I deceived Gim-   87
pel. That was the meaning of my brief life."

One night, when the period of mourning was done, as I lay dreaming   88
on the flour sacks, there came the Spirit of Evil himself and said to me,
"Gimpel, why do you sleep?"

I said, "What should I be doing? Eating *kreplach*?[10]   89

"The whole world deceives you," he said, "and you ought to deceive   90
the world in your turn."

"How can I deceive all the world?" I asked him.   91

He answered, "You might accumulate a bucket of urine every day and   82
at night pour it into the dough. Let the sages of Frampol eat filth."

"What about the judgment in the world to come?" I said.   93

"There is no world to come," he said. "They've sold you a bill of goods   94

---

[9]A town in Poland.

[10]A dumpling.

and talked you into believing you carried a cat in your belly. What nonsense!"

"Well then," I said, "and is there a God?" 95

He answered, "There is no God, either." 96

"What," I said, "is there, then?" 97

"A thick mire." 98

He stood before my eyes with a goatish beard and horn, long-toothed 99
and with a tail. Hearing such words, I wanted to snatch him by the tail, but
I tumbled from the flour sacks and nearly broke a rib. Then it happened
that I had to answer the call of nature, and, passing, I saw the risen dough,
which seemed to say to me, "Do it!" In brief, I let myself be persuaded.

At dawn the apprentice came. We kneaded the bread, scattered 100
caraway seeds on it, and set it to bake. Then the apprentice went away, and
I was left sitting in the little trench of the oven, on a pile of rags. Well,
Gimpel, I thought, you've revenged yourself on them for all the shame
they've put on you. Outside the frost glittered, but it was warm beside the
oven. The flames heated my face. I bent my head and fell into a doze.

I saw in a dream, at once, Elka in her shroud. She called to me, "What 101
have you done, Gimpel?"

I said to her, "It's all your fault," and started to cry. 102

"You fool!" she said. "You fool! Because I was false is everything false 103
too? I never deceived anyone but myself. I'm paying for it all, Gimpel. They
spare you nothing here."

I looked at her face. It was black; I was startled and waked, and 104
remained sitting dumb. I sensed that everything hung in the balance. A
false step now and I'd lose Eternal Life. But God gave me His help. I seized a
long shovel and took out the loaves, carried them into the yard, and started
to dig a hole in the frozen earth.

My apprentice came back as I was doing it. "What are you doing, 105
boss?" he said, and grew pale as a corpse.

"I know what I'm doing," I said, and I buried it all before his very eyes. 106

Then I went home, took my hoard from its hiding place, and divided 107
it among the children. "I saw your mother tonight," I said. "She's turning
black, poor thing."

They were so astounded they couldn't speak a word. 108

"Be well," I said, "and forget that such a one as Gimpel ever existed." I 109
put on my short coat, a pair of boots, took the bag that held my prayer
shawl in one hand, my stock in the other, and kissed the *mezzuzah*.[11] When
people saw me in the street they were greatly surprised.

"Where are you going?" they said. 110

---

[11] A small oblong container affixed to the door jamb of devout Jews. It contains verses
from the Torah and is kissed each time a Jew passes through the door.

I answered, "Into the world." And so I departed from Frampol.   111

I wandered over the land, and good people did not neglect me. After   112
many years I became old and white; I heard a great deal, many lies and
falsehoods, but the longer I lived the more I understood that there were
really no lies. Whatever doesn't really happen is dreamed at night. It
happens to one if it doesn't happen to another, tomorrow if not today, or a
century hence if not next year. What difference can it make? Often I heard
tales of which I said, "Now this is a thing that cannot happen." But before a
year had elapsed I heard that it actually had come to pass somewhere.

Going from place to place, eating at strange tables, it often happens   113
that I spin yarns—improbable things that could never have happened—
about devils, magicians, windmills, and the like. The children run after me,
calling, "Grandfather, tell us a story." Sometimes they ask for particular
stories, and I try to please them. A fat young boy once said to me,
"Grandfather, it's the same story you told us before." The little rogue, he
was right.

So it is with dreams too. It is many years since I left Frampol, but as   114
soon as I shut my eyes I am there again. And whom do you think I see?
Elka. She is standing by the washtub, as at our first encounter, but her face
is shining and her eyes are as radiant as the eyes of a saint, and she speaks
outlandish words to me, strange things. When I wake I have forgotten it all.
But while the dream lasts I am comforted. She answers all my queries, and
what comes out is that all is right. I weep and implore, "Let me be with
you." And she consoles me and tells me to be patient. The time is nearer
than it is far. Sometimes she strokes and kisses me and weeps upon my face.
When I awaken I feel her lips and taste the salt of her tears.

No doubt the world is entirely an imaginary world, but it is only once   115
removed from the true world. At the door of the hotel where I lie, there
stands the plank on which the dead are taken away. The gravedigger Jew has
his spade ready. The grave waits and the worms are hungry; the shrouds are
prepared—I carry them in my beggar's sack. Another *schnorrer*[12] is waiting
to inherit my bed of straw. When the time comes I will go joyfully. Whatever
may be there, it will be real, without complication, without ridicule,
without deception. God be praised: there even Gimpel cannot be deceived.

Questions for Study and Discussion

1. Is Gimpel really a fool? What evidence do you find in the story that he
is, or is not? If he is not, why does he let himself be made to seem foolish?

2. Are the lies people tell Gimpel all of the same kind, or are there
differences?

---

[12]A beggar.

3. What does Gimpel's confession of thievery reveal about his character? What of his decision to defile the villagers' bread and his later change of mind?

4. Gimpel speaks of visions–of the devil, of his dead wife. How do you interpret these visions?

5. What is the turning point of the story? What does Gimpel give up, and why? What is his new purpose? How does his later life relate to his earlier life? What has Gimpel discovered about himself in the course of the story?

6. What is Singer's theme in this story? What does Gimpel mean in the last paragraph of the story when he talks about the imaginary world and the true world?

Writing Topics

1. Gimpel is often troubled by the relation between appearance and reality. Are things as they seem or is there an explanation which, though perhaps far from obvious, offers more of the truth? This question lies at the root of many personal, professional, and social dilemmas. Choose a topic that you think embodies the problem of appearance and reality and develop it in an essay, drawing on your experience and your reading for examples.

2. "Gimpel the Fool" is, at least in part, a story about how one should live. In this respect it is similar to "The Sermon on the Mount" in the Gospel according to Saint Matthew. In preparation for writing an essay on the philosophy of life presented in each work, read "The Sermon on the Mount." What do the two have in common? Where do they differ?

In Pursuit of Happiness

JOHN CIARDI

Poet, educator, editor, and critic, the late John Ciardi was born in Boston in 1916. After graduating from Tufts University and the University of Michigan, he taught for a number of years at Harvard and Rutgers universities and directed the summer Bread Loaf Writers' Conference. Ciardi has written several volumes of poetry, including *Homeward to America* and *From Time to Time*. The three volumes of his translation of *Dante's Divine Comedy—Inferno* (1954), *Purgatorio* (1961), and *Paradiso* (1970)—are among his finest achievements. Ciardi was for many years poetry editor for the *Saturday Review*. He died in 1986.

In this essay, first published in the *Saturday Review* in 1964, Ciardi, popularly known as a writer of the short essay, attempts to define *happiness*, a term he feels "will not sit still for easy definition."

Is Everybody Happy?

The right to pursue happiness is issued to Americans with their birth certificates, but no one seems quite sure which way it ran. It may be we are issued a hunting license but offered no game. Jonathan Swift seemed to think so when he attacked the idea of happiness as "the possession of being well-deceived," the felicity of being "a fool among knaves." For Swift saw society as Vanity Fair, the land of false goals.

It is, of course, un-American to think in terms of fools and knaves. We do, however, seem to be dedicated to the idea of buying our way to happiness. We shall all have made it to Heaven when we possess enough.

And at the same time the forces of American commercialism are hugely dedicated to making us deliberately unhappy. Advertising is one of our major industries, and advertising exists not to satisy desires but to create them—and to create them faster than any man's budget can satisfy them. For that matter, our whole economy is based on a dedicated insatiability. We are taught that to possess is to be happy, and then we are made to want. We are even told it is our duty to want. It was only a few years ago, to cite a single example, that car dealers across the country were flying banners that read "You Auto Buy Now." They were calling upon Americans, as an act approaching patriotism, to buy at once, with money they did not have, automobiles they did not really need, and which they would be required to grow tired of by the time next year's models were released.

Or look at any of the women's magazines. There, as Bernard DeVoto 4
once pointed out, advertising begins as poetry in the front pages and ends as pharmacopoeia and therapy in the back pages. The poetry of the front matter is the dream of perfect beauty. This is the baby skin that must be hers. These, the flawless teeth. This, the perfumed breath she must exhale. This, the sixteen-year-old figure she must display at forty, at fifty, at sixty, and forever.

Once past the vaguely uplifting fiction and feature articles, the reader 5
finds the other face of the dream in the back matter. This is the harness into which Mother must strap herself in order to display that perfect figure. These, the chin straps she must sleep in. This is the salve that restores all, this is her laxative, these are the tablets that melt away fat, these are the hormones of perpetual youth, these are the stockings that hide varicose veins.

Obviously no half-sane person can be completely persuaded either by 6
such poetry or by such pharmacopoeia and orthopedics. Yet someone is obviously trying to buy the dream as offered and spending billions every year in the attempt. Clearly the happiness-market is not running out of customers, but what is it trying to buy?

The idea "happiness," to be sure, will not sit still for easy definition: 7
the best one can do is to try to set some extremes to the idea and then work in toward the middle. To think of happiness as acquisitive and competitive will do to set the materialistic extreme. To think of it as the idea one senses in, say, a holy man of India will do to set the spiritual extreme. That holy man's idea of happiness is in needing nothing from outside himself. In wanting nothing, he lacks nothing. He sits immobile, rapt in contemplation, free even of his own body. Or nearly free of it. If devout admirers bring him food he eats it; if not, he starves indifferently. Why be concerned? What is physical is an illusion to him. Contemplation is his joy and he achieves it through a fantastically demanding discipline, the accomplishment of which is itself a joy within him.

Is he a happy man? Perhaps his happiness is only another sort of 8
illusion. But who can take it from him? And who will dare say it is more illusory than happiness on the installment plan?

But, perhaps because I am Western, I doubt such catatonic happiness, as I doubt the dreams of the happiness-market. What is certain is that his way of happiness would be torture to almost any Western man. Yet these extremes will still serve to frame the area within which all of us must find some sort of balance. Thoreau—a creature of both Eastern and Western thought—had his own firm sense of that balance. His aim was to save on the low levels in order to spend on the high.

Possession for its own sake or in competition with the rest of the neighborhood would have been Thoreau's idea of the low levels. The active discipline of heightening one's perception of what is enduring in nature would have been his idea of the high. What he saved from the low was time and effort he could spend on the high. Thoreau certainly disapproved of starvation, but he would put into feeding himself only as much effort as would keep him functioning for more important efforts.

Effort is the gist of it. There is no happiness except as we take on life-engaging difficulties. Short of the impossible, as Yeats put it, the satisfactions we get from a lifetime depend on how high we choose our difficulties. Robert Frost was thinking in something like the same terms when he spoke of "The pleasure of taking pains." The mortal flaw in the advertised version of happiness is in the fact that it purports to be effortless.

We demand difficulty even in our games. We demand it because without difficulty there can be no game. A game is a way of making something hard for the fun of it. The rules of the game are an arbitrary imposition of difficulty. When the spoilsport ruins the fun, he always does so by refusing to play by the rules. It is easier to win at chess if you are free, at your pleasure, to change the wholly arbitrary rules, but the fun is in winning within the rules. No difficulty, no fun.

The buyers and sellers at the happiness-market seem too often to have lost their sense of pleasure of difficulty. Heaven knows what they are playing, but it seems a dull game. And the Indian holy man seems dull to us, I suppose, because he seems to be refusing to play anything at all. The Western weakness may be in the illusion that happiness can be bought. Perhaps the Eastern weakness is in the idea that there is such a thing as perfect (and therefore static) happiness.

Happiness is never more than partial. There are no pure states of mankind. Whatever else happiness may be, it is neither in having nor in being, but in becoming. What the Founding Fathers declared for us as an inherent right, we should do well to remember, was not happiness but the *pursuit* of happiness. What they might have underlined, could they have foreseen the happiness-market, is the cardinal fact that happiness is in the pursuit itself, in the meaningful pursuit of what is life-engaging and life-revealing, which is to say, in the idea of *becoming*. A nation is not measured by what it possesses or wants to possess, but by what it wants to become.

By all means let the happiness-market sell us minor satisfactions and even minor follies so long as we keep them in scale and buy them out of spiritual change. I am no customer for either puritanism or asceticism. But drop any real spiritual capital at those bazaars, and what you come home to will be your own poorhouse.

Questions for Study and Discussion

1. How does Ciardi define *happiness*? Do you agree with his definition?

2. What does Ciardi mean when he says that "the forces of American commercialism are hugely dedicated to making us deliberately unhappy"? What evidence does he offer in support of his claim?

3. Ciardi feels that *happiness* is a difficult term to define. Do you agree? Why, or why not?

4. What is Ciardi's attitude toward materialistic happiness and spiritual happiness?

5. Ciardi coins the term "happiness-market" in this essay. Define the term. What are its connotations as Ciardi uses it?

6. What do you think Ciardi is trying to accomplish by using the quotation from Swift in paragraph 1 and the ones from Yeats and Frost in paragraph 11?

Writing Topics

1. What for you is happiness? Write an essay in which you define happiness, using examples from your own experience.

2. Ciardi believes that "there is no happiness except as we take on life-engaging difficulties." Write an essay in which you agree or disagree with Ciardi's position. Use specific examples to document your essay.

3. Write an essay in which you discuss your understanding of the American Dream and its relationship to happiness. Is it unrealistic to think that money can't buy at least a certain degree of happiness? Does material success preclude happiness?

NORMAN LEAR

Norman Lear, writer, producer, and director, was born in New Haven, Connecticut, on July 27, 1922. Lear studied at Emerson College for two years and then enlisted in the Air Force where he served with distinction during World War II. After the war, Lear started his long-time association with television and film as a comedy writer. During the 1960s he wrote and produced such films as *Divorce American Style* and *The Night They Raided Minsky's*. But it is as the creator of the classic television comedy series "All in the Family," "Maude," "Sanford and Sons," "The Jeffersons," "One Day at a Time," and "Hot L Baltimore" that Lear built his reputation as a social satirist.

In "Cashing in the Commonweal for the Commonwheel of Fortune" Lear criticizes what he calls "America's obsession with short-term success." By putting the modern corporation with its profit-statement mentality up on a pedestal, he fears we may be sacrificing our futures for today's gratification. An excerpt from a speech Lear delivered at the John F. Kennedy School at Harvard University in February 1987, this essay was first published in the *Washington Post* the following April.

In the following essay, Lear argues that our culture has traded in the long-term benefits of traditional values to reap the immediate satisfaction of short-term goals. According to Lear, this brand of thinking has made heroes of such men as Rambo, Ivan Boesky, Oliver North, and other "raiders" of the common good. He warns that unless we return to more traditional values of family and community and find our heroes among the people who work for the long-term benefit of the many, we are headed for cultural and moral extinction.

Cashing in the Commonweal for the Commonwheel of Fortune

The societal disease of our time, I am convinced, is America's obses- 1
sion with short-term success, its fixation with the proverbial bottom-line. "Give me a profit statement this quarter larger than the last, and everything else be damned!" That is today's predominant business ethic. It took root in the business community but has since spread beyond business and insinu- ated itself into the rest of our culture. In this climate, a quiet revolution in values has occurred, and it has not been for the better.

Short-term thinking, corrosive individualism, fixating on "economic   2
man" at the expense of the human spirit, has taken an alarming toll. I focus
on the business community for starters, not to make it a scapegoat—but
because I believe business has become a fountainhead of values in our
society.

If the church was the focal point for personal values and public mores   3
in medieval times, that role in our time has been assumed, unwittingly
perhaps, by the modern corporation.

For better or worse, traditional institutions such as the family, the   4
churches and education are no longer as influential in molding moral-
cultural values. There are, I suppose, dozens of reasons one could find: the
disruptions of urbanization; the alarming increase of single-parent households; the rise of the mass media, especially television; the dizzy mobility of
our car culture; the telecommunications revolution and the altered sense of
time and distance it has created. As traditional families have come under
stress and splintered, as education has come under siege, as churches and
synagogues have become less influential in daily life, the modern corporation with the help of the media has stepped into the breach.

Mythologist Joseph Campbell has said that in medieval times, when   5
one approached a city, one saw the cathedral and the castle. Now one sees
the soaring tower of commerce. People build their lives around these towers.
Communities take shape. Work skills are learned. Social relationships are
formed. Attitudes and aspirations are molded. A dense matrix of values
grow up around the towers of commerce and spread beyond.

Never before has the business of business been such a cultural preoc-   6
cupation. If media attention is any indication of popular interest—and it
is—today there is an unprecedented interest in business affairs. In recent
years, a dozen new business programs have burst forth on commercial
television, public television and cable. Americans once found their heroes,
for the most part, in Congress or the entertainment world or sports; now
more and more people find them in business: Lee Iacocca; T. Boone Pickens;
H. Ross Perot; Carl Icahn; until 10 minutes ago, Ivan Boesky; and until a
moment ago, Martin A. Siegel.

If you grant me the possibility that American business is the preemi-   7
nent force in shaping our culture and its values, what example are its
leaders setting? What attitudes and behavior do they endorse and foster?

The *Wall Street Journal* recently took an overview of the American   8
corporation and concluded: "Gone is talk of balanced, long-term growth;
impatient shareholders and well-heeled corporate raiders have seen to that.
Now anxious executives, fearing for their jobs or their companies, are
focusing their efforts on trimming operations and shuffling assets to improve near-term profits, often at the expense of both balance and growth."

There are no two-legged villains in this "get-while-the-getting-is-good"   9
atmosphere. Only victims. The villain is the climate which, like a house

with a leaking gas pipe, is certain to see us all dead in our sleep one day, never knowing what hit us.

Sociologist Daniel Bell has argued that in promoting an ethic of "materialistic hedonism," the free enterprise system tends to subvert the very values that help to sustain it. If American business insists upon defining itself solely in terms of its market share, profitability and stock price—if its short-term material goals are allowed to prevail over all else—then business tends to subvert the moral-cultural values that undergird the entire system, such values as social conscience, pride in one's work, commitment to one's community, loyalty to one's company—in short, a sense of the commonweal.

This ethic breeds in a climate where leadership everywhere—in business, Congress, federal agencies, state legislatures, organized labor, the universities—refuses, through greed or myopia or weakness, to make provisions for the future. And in this climate, with this kind of short-sighted leadership, we have been raising generations of children to believe that there is nothing between winning and losing. The notion that life has anything to do with succeeding at the level of doing one's best, or that some of life's richest rewards are not monetary, is lost to these kids in this short-term, bottom-line climate.

America has become a game show. Winning is all that matters. Cash prizes. Get rich quick. We are the captives of a culture that celebrates instant gratification and individual success no matter the larger costs. George Will, in his book *Statecraft as Soulcraft,* argues that the country's future is imperiled unless our leaders can cultivate in citizens a deeper commitment to the commonweal. Yet rather than heed that admonition, we are turning the commonweal into the Commonwheel of Fortune.

Take a look at the Commonwheel of Fortune gameboard. It's not unlike the Monopoly gameboard—but instead of real estate, we've got just about every major American corporation represented, all up for grabs. For you latecomers to the game, Owens Corning, NBC, Texaco and TWA are off the board now—but Goodyear, USX, Union Carbide and many more have been in play recently. With a little roll of the dice and the junk bonds the game is played with, just watch the raiding and merging and acquisitioning! What fun!

The game produced 14 new billionaires last year—not to mention what it's done for foreign investors who, with their yens and deutschemarks, have caught on to our national lack of concern for the future. We are now selling them America as cheaply, under the circumstances, as the Indians sold us Manhattan.

On the surface, we seem to have accepted the selling of America just as we seem to have accepted the fact that we no longer make the best automobiles, the best radios and stereos and television sets and compact discs; the fact is we hardly make any of these products by ourselves today where we once were responsible for most of them. We've accepted that without a whimper.

There is a psychic, spiritual dimension to these changes that cannot   16
be ignored. There is an open wound, a gash, on the American psyche that must be attended to.

Take the American motor car. Through all the years I was growing up,   17
it was the standard of the world. "Keeping up with the Joneses" in those years meant only one thing: You were either trading up the General Motors line, the Ford line or the Chrysler line. My dad was a GM man. He got as far as the Oldsmobile; one year he almost made it to the Buick. But caring about your motor car was the universal family vocation. The American motor car was the national, non-military symbol of America's macho—and one does not have to be a social scientist to know that when we lost that symbol, sometime in the past 25 years, it left a big dent in the American Dream.

The Big Three automakers failed to heed the handwriting on the wall   18
and refused to innovate, to build small fuel-efficient cars; refused to sacrifice a current quarterly profit statement to invest in the future and meet the threat of imports from abroad.

There is the ailing steel industry, which refused to modernize and   19
invest in its future. There are the labor unions in both industries, which fought only for added wages and benefits—and declined to fight to modernize and to protect their members' jobs in the long term. There is the U.S. consumer electronics industry, which surrendered the compact-disc technology to Japan and Holland, who were willing to make long-term investments in the fledgling technology.

There is a hurt and an emptiness and confusion in this nation to   20
which attention must be paid. There is fear and resentment, which makes Americans ripe for extremists who offer promises of easy salvation. It can exacerbate social tensions and result in an escalation of the kind of racism we have witnessed around the country recently.

If you agree with me that our culture has been weaned from a respect   21
for other values to the worshipping of money and success and the fruits of instant gratification—and that this is resulting in a spiritual and cultural crisis—what, then, do we do about it? How can we reclaim the commonweal from the mindless game show it has become?

We can start by recognizing that government has a major respon-   22
sibility here. I am a product of the free-enterprise system, and I cherish it. I am also a human being, and I cherish my humanity. But everything I know about human nature tells me we are innately selfish. We do look out for ourselves first. And then our family, our loved ones. Some of us, not enough, reach out beyond that. But when we, the people, talk about caring

for things that are ours—our water, our air, our safety, our protection from the myriad harmful things we reasonable good people are capable of doing to each other—we have to know we can only rely on our government! It is we, through government, who provide for the common welfare.

Business nurtures the conceit that its behavior is purely private—but   23
take one look at the largess it receives from the government: It once accounted for 29 percent of federal tax revenues; it is now down to 6 percent. Take a look, too, at the role of corporate political action committees and the cultural values that business fosters—and it is clear why government must play a more influential role in protecting the commonweal from the Commonwheel of Fortune.

This, again, is a climate we are seeking to change—and there are   24
thermostats that address that climate in every home, in every school, in every church, in every business in this country. We can start, perhaps, by establishing a new set of symbols and heroes. We have had Rambo and Oliver North and Ivan Boesky; corporate raiders and arbitrageurs; the "yuppie generation" and the culture of conspicuous consumption; we have had religious zealots who would abridge the First Amendment in the name of God and political extremists who would censor books and condone racism.

But we have also had, and more attention must be paid to, people like   25
Robert Hayes. An attorney with a top-flight New York law firm, he quit his lucrative job several years ago to start a new branch of legal practice: defending the rights of the homeless. His initiative inspired dozens of other such legal practices around the country.

Attention must be paid to Eugene Lang, a New York millionaire who,   26
while speaking at an elementary school graduation, spontaneously offered to pay for the college expenses of some sixth graders of an inner city school if they would study hard and not drop out of school. His example has caught on in other cities, where individuals and businesses "adopt" students to help them succeed.

And attention must be paid to Warren Buffett, the Nebraska chair-   27
man of Berkshire-Hathaway, who has seen to it that a part of every single dollar among the millions of dollars earmarked for shareholders goes to a charity or a cause selected by that shareholder in advance.

We need to rehabilitate the idea of public service; to set new ethical   28
standards for business; to harness the natural idealism of young people; and to encourage leadership everywhere to assume a greater burden of responsibility to lead. As I said, the villain here is the climate. It needs changing.

Plant in your mind, if you will, the close-up actions of a man, as in a   29
film. Savagely, he is cutting off the hands of another man. We are horrified; this action defies our understanding. Now pull back to examine the context, and learn that we are in a different culture—perhaps, but not necessarily, in an earlier time. Eyes can be gouged out here. Men are drawn and

quartered—sometimes for sheer entertainment. We don't accept, but we understand better now that first savage act. Its perpetrators were behaving in the context of their time and culture.

Now look at Martin A. Siegel and gang, arrested recently for insider   30
trading. A thief. Broke a trust. We don't understand. He was making $2 million. Why did he need another $7 million?

But let's pull back and see Siegel in the context of the culture I have   31
been describing, and we must ask: In some perverse way, doesn't his story speak for the '80s?

Isn't Siegel's story an example in microcosm of the perverted values of   32
our culture—where the making of money, not working hard, producing well, leaving something lasting behind—but the making of money has become the sole value?

The problem isn't Martin Siegel's alone. It is ours. We have found the   33
Holy Grail, and it is the Bottom Line.

Do we want it?   34

Must we continue cashing in the commonweal for the Commonwheel   35
of Fortune?

Questions for Study and Discussion

1. What is the author's thesis and where is it best stated?

2. Lear refers to Joseph Campbell's idea that the tallest building in a city defines the values of that city. Do you agree? Why or why not?

3. In your own words, describe what is wrong with the idea of working for short-term benefits? What values are traded or lost in this world view?

4. What kinds of examples does Lear use to support his thesis? Are they effective? Why or why not?

5. Lear suggests that we turn to government to save us from the business ethic that is sapping our strength as a country. Do you agree with him? What are the advantages and risks of depending on a government solution to the problem?

6. Lear argues that to be fully understood, the behavior of the individual must be viewed in the context of his or her societal values. In so saying, he indicts all of us by insisting that we take responsibility for society's problems. Do you agree with his assessment? Why or why not?

7. Who are the heroes of short-term gain? What do they have in common? What are the characteristics of the new heroes Lear calls for?

8. Lear ends his essay with a question. How would you answer it? How do you suppose most people you know would answer it?

Writing Topics

1. Historians claim that all the great nations have eventually lost their preeminence as a result of moral decay, overextending their resources, or simply

a kind of cultural entropy. They cite ancient Greece, Rome, and England as just a few obvious examples. Is the United States falling victim to this inevitable cycle, or can the country maintain preeminence by following the steps Lear suggests? In your opinion, how necessary is it that we maintain our world power?

2. Lear suggests some of the many areas in which our culture suffers the effects of short-term thinking. Drawing from his list or naming areas he may have left out, explain in more detail how short-term thinking has effected these areas.

ANNIE DILLARD

Annie Dillard was born in Pittsburgh and attended Hollins College. She now makes her home in Middletown, Connecticut, where she is writer in residence at Wesleyan University. A poet, journalist, and contributing editor to *Harper's* magazine, Dillard has written *Tickets for a Prayer Wheel* (1973), *Holy the Firm* (1977), *Teaching a Stone to Talk* (1982), *An American Childhood* (1988), and *A Writer's Life* (1989). In 1974 she published *Pilgrim at Tinker Creek*, a fascinating collection of natural observations for which she was awarded the Pulitzer Prize for nonfiction.

In the following selection from *Pilgrim at Tinker Creek*, Dillard uses a childhood activity or game to help her explain the happiness that can be derived from an active perception of the world around us.

Sight into Insight

When I was six or seven years old, growing up in Pittsburgh, I used to take a penny of my own and hide it for someone else to find. It was a curious compulsion; sadly, I've never been seized by it since. For some reason I always "hid" the penny along the same stretch of sidewalk up the street. I'd cradle it at the roots of a maple, say, or in a hold left by a chipped-off piece of sidewalk. Then I'd take a piece of chalk and, starting at either end of the block, draw huge arrows leading up to the penny from both directions. After I learned to write I labeled the arrows "SURPRISE AHEAD" or "MONEY THIS WAY." I was greatly excited, during all this arrowdrawing, at the thought of the first lucky passerby who would receive in this way, regardless of merit, a free gift from the universe. But I never lurked about. I'd go straight home and not give the matter another thought, until, some months later, I would be gripped by the impulse to hide another penny.

There are lots of things to see, unwrapped gifts and free surprises. The world is fairly studded and strewn with pennies cast broadside from a generous hand. But—and this is the point—who gets excited by a mere penny? If you follow one arrow, if you crouch motionless on a bank to watch a tremulous ripple thrill on the water, and are rewarded by the sight of a muskrat kit paddling from its den, will you count that sight a chip of copper only, and go your rueful way? It is very dire poverty indeed for a man to be so malnourished and fatigued that he won't stoop to pick up a penny. But if you cultivate a healthy poverty and simplicity, so that finding a penny will make your day, then, since the world is in fact planted in pennies, you have with your poverty bought a lifetime of days. What you see is what you get.

Unfortunately, nature is very much a now-you-see-it, now-you-don't affair. A fish flashes, then dissolves in the water before my eyes like so much salt. Deer apparently ascend bodily into heaven: the brightest oriole fades into leaves. These disappearances stun me into stillness and concentration; they say of nature that it conceals with a grand nonchalance, and they say of vision that it is a deliberate gift, the revelation of a dancer who for my eyes only flings away her seven veils.

For nature does reveal as well as conceal; now-you-don't-see-it, now-you-do. For a week this September migrating red-winged blackbirds were feeding heavily down by Tinker Creek at the back of the house. One day I went out to investigate the racket; I walked up to a tree, an Osage orange, and a hundred birds flew away. They simply materialized out of the tree. I saw a tree, then a whisk of color, then a tree again. I walked closer and another hundred blackbirds took flight. Not a branch, not a twig budged: the birds were apparently weightless as well as invisible. Or, it was as if the leaves of the Osage orange had been freed from a spell in the form of red-winged blackbirds; they flew from the tree, caught my eye in the sky, and vanished. When I looked again at the tree, the leaves had reassembled as if nothing had happened. Finally I walked directly to the trunk of the tree and a final hundred, the real diehards, appeared, spread, and vanished. How could so many hide in the tree without my seeing them? The Osage orange, unruffled, looked just as it had looked from the house, when three hundred red-winged blackbirds cried from its crown. I looked upstream where they flew, and they were gone. Searching, I couldn't spot one. I wandered upstream to force them to play their hand, but they'd crossed the creek and scattered. One show to a customer. These appearances catch at my throat; they are the free gifts, the bright coppers at the roots of trees.

It's all a matter of keeping my eyes open. Nature is like one of those line drawings that are puzzles for children: Can you find hidden in the tree a duck, a house, a boy, a bucket, a giraffe, and a boot? Specialists can find the most incredibly hidden things. A book I read when I was young recommended an easy way to find caterpillars: you simply find some fresh caterpillar droppings, look up, and there's your caterpillar. More recently an author advised me to set my mind at ease about those piles of cut stems on the ground in grassy fields. Field mice make them; they cut the grass down by degrees to reach the seeds at the head. It seems that when the grass is tightly packed, as in a field of ripe grain, the blade won't topple at a single cut through the stem; instead, the cut stem simply drops vertically, held in the crush of grain. The mouse severs the bottom again and again, the stem keeps dropping an inch at a time, and finally the head is low enough for the mouse to reach the seeds. Meanwhile the mouse is positively littering the field with its little piles of cut stems into which, presumably, the author is constantly stumbling.

If I can't see these minutiae, I still try to keep my eyes open. I'm always   6
on the lookout for ant lion traps in sandy soil, monarch pupae near
milkweed, skipper larvae in locust leaves. These things are utterly common,
and I've not seen one. I bang on hollow trees near water, but so far no flying
squirrels have appeared. In flat country I watch every sunset in hopes of
seeing the green ray. The green ray is a seldom-seen streak of light that rises
from the sun like a spurting fountain at the moment of sunset; it throbs into
the sky for two seconds and disappears. One more reason to keep my eyes
open. A photography professor at the University of Florida just happened
to see a bird die in midflight; it jerked, died, dropped, and smashed on the
ground.

I squint at the wind because I read Stewart Edward White: "I have   7
always maintained that if you looked closely enough you could *see* the
wind—the dim, hardly-made-out, find débris fleeing high in the air." White
was an excellent observer, and devoted an entire chapter of *The Mountains*
to the subject of seeing deer. "As soon as you can forget the naturally
obvious and construct an artificial obvious, then you too will see deer."

But the artificial obvious is hard to see. My eyes account for less than   8
1 percent of the weight of my head; I'm bony and dense; I see what I expect.
I just don't know what the lover knows; I can't see the artificial obvious that
those in the know construct. The herpetologist asks the native, "Are there
snakes in that ravine?" "No, sir." And the herpetologist comes home with,
yessir, three bags full. Are there butterflies on that mountain? Are the
bluets in bloom? Are there arrowheads here, or fossil ferns in the shale?

Peeping through my keyhole I see within the range of only about 30   9
percent of light that comes from the sun; the rest is infrared and some little
ultraviolet, perfectly apparent to many animals, but invisible to me. A
nightmare network of ganglia, charged and firing without my knowledge,
cuts and splices what I do see, editing it for my brain. Donald E. Carr points
out that the sense impressions of one-celled animals are *not* edited for the
brain: "This is philosophically interesting in a rather mournful way, since it
means that only the simplest animals perceive the universe as it is."

A fog that won't burn away drifts and flows across my field of vision.   10
When you see fog move against a backdrop of deep pines, you don't see the
fog itself, but streaks of clearness floating across the air in dark shreds. So I
see only tatters of clearness through a pervading obscurity. I can't distinguish the fog from the overcast sky; I can't be sure if the light is direct or
reflected. Everywhere darkness and the presence of the unseen appalls. We
estimate now that only one atom dances alone in every cubic meter of
intergalactic space. I blink and squint. What planet or power yanks Halley's
Comet out of orbit? We haven't seen it yet; it's a question of distance,
density, and the pallor of reflected light. We rock, cradled in the swaddling
band of darkness. Even the simple darkness of night whispers suggestions to
the mind. This summer, in August, I stayed at the creek too late.

Questions for Study and Discussion

1. Dillard seems to be teaching us something she has learned from her experiences as a naturalist. What exactly is her lesson?

2. Dillard uses the analogy of hidden pennies to make her point. Explain how her analogy works. How effective did you find the analogy? Does the analogy seem at all contrived?

3 Dillard uses two clichés: "what you see is what you get" and "now-you-see-it, now-you-don't." Are these clichés used thoughtlessly? What do you suppose her purpose is in using them?

4. What does Dillard mean when she asks us to "cultivate a healthy poverty and simplicity"?

5. Dillard uses a number of examples from the natural world to illustrate her point. How would you characterize these examples? Why does she develop one more than others?

Writing Topics

1. Write an essay in which you describe several of the "unwrapped gifts" that nature has given you and try to explain the meaning that each had for you. How have they added to your satisfaction and personal happiness?

2. Dillard's essay addressed a theme that has been a concern of writers and naturalists throughout the ages. Consider, for example, the following poem by William Wordsworth.

The World Is Too Much with Us

The world is too much with us; late and soon,
Getting and spending, we lay waste our powers:
Little we see in Nature that is ours;
We have given our hearts away, a sordid boon!
This Sea that bares her bosom to the moon;   5
The winds that will be howling at all hours,
And are up-gathered now like sleeping flowers;
For this, for everything, we are out of tune;
It moves us not.—Great God! I'd rather be
A Pagan suckled in a creed outworn;   10
So might I, standing on this pleasant lea,
Have glimpses that would make me less forlorn;
Have sight of Proteus rising from the sea;
Or hear old Triton blow his wreathèd horn.

Write an essay in which you talk about our relationship to nature. What are the obstacles in contemporary life that prevent us from truly seeing nature and receiving the benefits of the natural world?

EMILY DICKINSON

Emily Dickinson (1830–1886), hailed as one of the greatest American poets, was born in Amherst, Massachusetts, into a Calvinist household. Her father was a lawyer prominent in civic affairs, affording her the opportunity to meet many of the history-making personalities of the day. Nevertheless, by the time she was thirty, Dickinson had become a virtual recluse in her father's home. She renounced her family's religion, yet continued to mourn the loss of the spiritual refuge it offered. This tension in her own nature likened her to such contemporary poets as Ralph Waldo Emerson and Henry David Thoreau, who perceived a universe at once beautiful and cold and saw its fulfillment in the reconciling of those dualities.

In "Success is counted sweetest," Dickinson suggests that success is sweeter to one who yearns for it than to one who has attained it.

Success is counted sweetest

Success is counted sweetest
By those who ne'er succeed.
To comprehend a nectar
Requires sorest need.

Not one of all the purple Host   5
Who took the Flag today
Can tell the definition
So clear of Victory

As he defeated—dying—
On whose forbidden ear   10
The distant strains of triumph
Burst agonized and clear!

Questions for Study and Discussion

1. In her poem, Dickinson makes the point that success is sweeter for those who yearn for it than it is for those who achieve it. However, she never

Reprinted by permission of the publishers and the Trustees of Amherst College for *The Poems of Emily Dickinson*, Thomas H. Johnson, ed., Cambridge, Mass.: The Belknap Press of Harvard University Press, copyright 1951, © 1955, 1979, 1983 by the President and Fellows of Harvard College.

explains why she believes that this is true. Do you agree with her central idea? Why or why not? What other feelings or goals, if any, could be substituted for "success" in Dickinson's poem?

2. In the second stanza, Dickinson uses the example of the battlefield to illustrate her theme. What do you think of her example? Does it make her point in a way you can understand? What other examples of her central idea can you think of from your own experience or observation?

3. How would you describe Dickinson's tone in this poem? Is she resigned, angry, defiant, or something else? How well does her tone suit her meaning?

Writing Topics

1. Like the Brontë sisters and Elizabeth Barrett Browning, Dickinson was a woman who never ventured very far from home, nor did she experience much of the drama of life firsthand. Yet they all produced works of uncommon depth of emotion and complexity. What does this suggest to you about the nature of their art? How does the possibility of writing what we have not known relate to "Success is counted sweetest"? In an essay discuss how it is possible for writers to capture the extremes of pleasure or pain that have not been experienced firsthand.

2. Think of a goal you have attained and another goal that you have not been able to reach. Write an essay in which you compare and contrast your feelings about the two experiences. How was the contemplation of success sweeter than its achievement? How was it more bitter?

KATE CHOPIN

Kate O'Flaherty Chopin (1851–1904) was born in St. Louis, Missouri, of Creole-Irish descent. After her marriage she lived in Louisiana where she acquired the intimate knowledge of Creole-Cajun culture that provided the impetus for much of her writing and earned her a reputation as a local colorist. However, her first novel, *The Awakening* (1899), generated scorn and outrage for its explicit depiction of a southern woman's sexual awakening. Only recently has Chopin been recognized for her literary talent and independence of style and feeling. Besides the novel, her works include two collections of her short fiction, *Bayou Folk* (1894) and *A Night in Acadie* (1897).

"The Story of an Hour" describes the tragic consequences of a woman's feelings of unexpected joy at the news of her husband's death.

The Story of an Hour

Knowing that Mrs. Mallard was afflicted with a heart trouble, great care was taken to break to her as gently as possible the news of her husband's death. 1

It was her sister Josephine who told her, in broken sentences; veiled hints that revealed in half concealing. Her husband's friend Richards was there, too, near her. It was he who had been in the newspaper office when intelligence of the railroad disaster was received, with Brently Mallard's name leading the list of "killed." He had only taken the time to assure himself of its truth by a second telegram, and had hastened to forestall any less careful, less tender friend in bearing the sad message. 2

She did not hear the story as many women have heard the same, with a paralyzed inability to accept its significance. She wept at once, with sudden, wild abandonment, in her sister's arms. When the storm of grief had spent itself she went away to her room alone. She would have no one follow her. 3

There stood, facing the open window, a comfortable, roomy armchair. Into this she sank, pressed down by a physical exhaustion that haunted her body and seemed to reach into her soul. 4

She could see in the open square before her house the tops of trees that were all aquiver with the new spring life. The delicious breath of rain was in the air. In the street below a peddler was crying his wares. The notes of a distant song which some one was singing reached her faintly, and countless sparrows were twittering in the eaves. 5

There were patches of blue sky showing here and there through the clouds that had met and piled one above the other in the west facing her window. 6

She sat with her head thrown back upon the cushion of the chair, quite motionless, except when a sob came up into her throat and shook her, as a child who has cried itself to sleep continues to sob in its dreams.

She was young, with a fair, calm face, whose lines bespoke repression and even a certain strength. But now there was a dull stare in her eyes, whose gaze was fixed away off yonder on one of those patches of blue sky. It was not a glance of reflection, but rather indicated a suspension of intelligent thought.

There was something coming to her and she was waiting for it, fearfully. What was it? She did not know; it was too subtle and elusive to name. But she felt it, creeping out of the sky, reaching toward her through the sounds, the scents, the color that filled the air.

Now her bosom rose and fell tumultuously. She was beginning to recognize this thing that was approaching to possess her, and she was striving to beat it back with her will—as powerless as her two white slender hands would have been.

When she abandoned herself a little whispered word escaped her slightly parted lips. She said it over and over under her breath: "free, free, free!" The vacant stare and the look of terror that had followed it went from her eyes. They stayed keen and bright. Her pulses beat fast, and the coursing blood warmed and relaxed every inch of her body.

She did not stop to ask if it were or were not a monstrous joy that held her. A clear and exalted perception enabled her to dismiss the suggestion as trivial.

She knew that she would weep again when she saw the kind, tender hands folded in death; the face that had never looked save with love upon her, fixed and gray and dead. But she saw beyond that bitter moment a long procession of years to come that would belong to her absolutely. And she opened and spread her arms out to them in welcome.

There would be no one to live for her during those coming years; she would live for herself. There would be no powerful will bending hers in that blind persistence with which men and women believe they have a right to impose a private will upon a fellow-creature. A kind intention or a cruel intention made the act seem no less a crime as she looked upon it in that brief moment of illumination.

And yet she had loved him—sometimes. Often she had not. What did it matter! What could love, the unsolved mystery, count for in face of this possession of self-assertion which she suddenly recognized as the strongest impulse of her being!

"Free! Body and soul free!" she kept whispering.

Josephine was kneeling before the closed door with her lips to the keyhole, imploring for admission. "Louise, open the door! I beg; open the door—you will make yourself ill. What are you doing, Louise? For heaven's sake open the door."

"Go away. I am not making myself ill." No; she was drinking in a very   18
elixir of life through that open window.

Her fancy was running riot along those days ahead of her. Spring   19
days, and summer days, and all sorts of days that would be her own. She
breathed a quick prayer that life might be long. It was only yesterday she
had thought with a shudder that life might be long.

She arose at length and opened the door to her sister's importunities.   20
There was a feverish triumph in her eyes, and she carried herself unwittingly like a goddess of Victory. She clasped her sister's waist, and together
they descended the stairs. Richards stood waiting for them at the bottom.

Some one was opening the front door with a latchkey. It was Brently   21
Mallard who entered, a little travel-stained, composedly carrying his grip-
sack and umbrella. He had been far from the scene of accident, and did not
even know there had been one. He stood amazed at Josephine's piercing cry;
at Richards' quick motion to screen him from the view of his wife.

But Richards was too late.   22

When the doctors came they said she had died of heart disease—of joy   23
that kills.

Questions for Study and Discussion

1. What assumption do Mrs. Mallard's relatives and friends make about
her feelings toward her husband? How would you describe her true feelings?
What evidence does the author give to bring you to your conclusion?

2. Chopin uses language to create a sensual expression for her feelings.
Choose examples of this sensuality from the text and explain the senses they
appeal to and in what way. How do these impressions add or detract from the
story?

3. Why do you suppose Mrs. Mallard fights her feeling of freedom,
however briefly?

4. Chopin could have written an essay detailing the sense of oppression
some women feel within the confines of marriage, yet she chose a narrative
form. What advantages does Chopin gain in her use of the narrative?

5. For most of the story we know the heroine of the tale only as "Mrs.
Mallard." Why has the author chosen not to mention her first name sooner?
How does this omission suit the point of the story?

6. What is the final irony of Chopin's story?

7. The entire action of this story takes place in an hour. Why has the
author selected this title for her story? What is the significance of the short
period?

Writing Topics

1. Chopin's story describes feelings of oppression and near-hatred of a
spouse that might be hard for a college student to comprehend, especially in a

time when women are moving closer to controlling their own destinies. The fact is that Chopin, writing in the late 1890s, was a staunch feminist who used the story form to eloquently and poignantly describe the life and feelings of wives during that era.

Write an essay describing how you reacted to this story. Do you think that women of the 1990s experience the same kinds of feelings toward their husbands?

2. Toward the end of the story, Chopin describes Mrs. Mallard's feelings of love and hate toward her husband. Is it possible to love and hate someone at the same time? In an essay, recall a close relationship you have been in that encompassed both these feelings.

Turning Points

LANGSTON HUGHES

Langston Hughes was born in 1902 in Joplin, Missouri, and though he began writing poetry at an early age, he was at first unable to get his work published and supported himself by traveling about the country, doing whatever work he could find. He was working as a busboy when his poetry was discovered in 1925 by Vachel Lindsay, a famous poet of the time. A year later Hughes published his first book of poems, *The Weary Blues*, and entered Lincoln University in Pennsylvania. He graduated in 1929 and set about making his way as a writer. Hughes's work focuses on African-American life, often incorporating dialect and jazz rhythms. His writings include novels, plays, and a popular series of newspaper sketches, but his reputation rests most solidly on his poems. Much of his finest poetry has been collected as *Selected Poems* (1959). He died in 1967.

In this selection taken from his autobiography, *The Big Sea*, Hughes narrates his experiences at a church revival meeting he attended when he was twelve years old.

Salvation

I was saved from sin when I was going on thirteen. But not really   1
saved. It happened like this. There was a big revival at my Auntie Reed's church. Every night for weeks there had been much preaching, singing, praying, and shouting, and some very hardened sinners had been brought to Christ, and the membership of the church had grown by leaps and bounds. Then just before the revival ended, they held a special meeting for children, "to bring the young lambs to the fold." My aunt spoke of it for days ahead. That night I was escorted to the front row and placed on the mourners' bench with all the other young sinners, who had not yet been brought to Jesus.

My aunt told me that when you were saved you saw a light, and   2
something happened to you inside! And Jesus came into your life! And God
was with you from then on! She said you could see and hear and feel Jesus in
your soul. I believed her. I have heard a great many old people say the same
thing and it seemed to me they ought to know. So I sat there calmly in the
hot, crowded church, waiting for Jesus to come to me.

The preacher preached a wonderful rhythmical sermon, all moans and   3
shouts and lonely cries and dire pictures of hell, and then he sang a song
about the ninety and nine safe in the fold, but one little lamb was left out in
the cold. Then he said: "Won't you come? Won't you come to Jesus? Young
lambs, won't you come?" And he held out his arms to all us young sinners
there on the mourners' bench. And the little girls cried. And some of them
jumped up and went to Jesus right away. But most of us just sat there.

A great many old people came and knelt around us and prayed, old   4
women with jet-black faces and braided hair, old men with work-gnarled
hands. And the church sang a song about the lower lights are burning,
some poor sinners to be saved. And the whole building rocked with prayer
and song.

Still I kept waiting to *see* Jesus.   5

Finally all the young people had gone to the alter and were saved, but   6
one boy and me. He was a rounder's son named Westley. Westley and I were
surrounded by sisters and deacons praying. It was very hot in the church,
and getting late now. Finally Westley said to me in a whisper: "God damn!
I'm tired o' sitting here. Let's get up and be saved." So he got up and was
saved.

Then I was left all alone on the mourners' bench. My aunt came and   7
knelt at my knees and cried, while prayers and songs swirled all around me
in the little church. The whole congregation prayed for me alone, in a
mighty wail of moans and voices. And I kept waiting serenely for Jesus,
waiting, waiting—but he didn't come. I wanted to see him, but nothing
happened to me. Nothing! I wanted something to happen to me, but
nothing happened.

I heard the songs and the minister saying: "Why don't you come? My   8
dear child, why don't you come to Jesus? Jesus is waiting for you. He wants
you. Why don't you come? Sister Reed, what is this child's name?"

"Langston," my aunt sobbed.   9

"Langston, why don't you come? Why don't you come and be saved?   10
Oh, Lamb of God! Why don't you come?"

Now it was really getting late. I began to be ashamed of myself,   11
holding everything up so long. I began to wonder what God thought about
Westley, who certainly hadn't seen Jesus either, but who was now sitting
proudly on the platform, swinging his knickerbockered legs and grinning
down at me, surrounded by deacons and old women on their knees praying.
God had not struck Westley dead for taking his name in vain or for lying in

the temple. So I decided that maybe to save further trouble, I'd better lie, too, and say that Jesus had come, and get up and be saved.

So I got up. 12

Suddenly the whole room broke into a sea of shouting, as they saw me 13
rise. Waves of rejoicing swept the place. Women leaped in the air. My aunt threw her arms around me. The minister took me by the hand and led me to the platform.

When things quieted down, in a hushed silence, punctuated by a few 14
ecstatic "Amens," all the new young lambs were blessed in the name of God. Then joyous singing filled the room.

That night, for the last time in my life but one—for I was a big boy 15
twelve years old—I cried. I cried, in bed alone, and couldn't stop. I buried my head under the quilts, but my aunt heard me. She woke up and told my uncle I was crying because the Holy Ghost had come into my life, and because I had seen Jesus. But I was really crying because I couldn't bear to tell her that I had lied, that I had deceived everybody in the church, that I hadn't seen Jesus, and that now I didn't believe there was a Jesus any more, since he didn't come to help me.

Questions for Study and Discussion

1. Why does the young Langston expect to be saved at the revival meeting? Once the children are in church, what appeals are made to them to encourage them to seek salvation?

2. Trace the various pressures working on Hughes that lead to his decision to "get up and be saved." What important realization finally convinces him to lie about being saved?

3. Even though Hughes's account of the events at the revival is at points humorous, the experience was nonetheless painful for him. Why does he cry on the night of his "salvation"? Why does his aunt think he is crying? What significance is there in the disparity between their views?

4. What paradox or apparent contradiction does Hughes present in the first two sentences of the narrative? Why do you suppose he uses this device?

5. What is the function of the third sentence, "It happened like this"?

6. Hughes consciously varies the structure and length of his sentences to create different effects. What effect does he create through the short sentences in paragraphs 2 and 3 and the long sentence that concludes the final paragraph? How do the short, one-sentence paragraphs aid him in telling his story?

7. Although Hughes tells most of his story himself, he allows Auntie Reed, the minister, and Westley to speak for themselves. What does Hughes gain by having his characters speak for themselves?

8. How does Hughes's choice of words help to establish a realistic atmosphere for a religious revival meeting? Does he use any traditional religious figures of speech?

9. Why does Hughes italicize the word *see* in paragraph 5? What do you think he means by *see*? What do you think his aunt means by *see*? Explain.

Writing Topics

1. Like the young Langston Hughes, we sometimes find ourselves in situations in which, for the sake of conformity, we do things we do not believe in. Consider one such experience you have had. What is it about human nature that makes us occasionally act in ways that contradict our inner feelings?

2. In the end of his essay Langston Hughes suffers alone. He cannot bring himself to talk about his dilemma with other people. Why can it be so difficult to seek the help of others? Consider examples from your experience and what you have seen and read about other people.

3. Sometimes the little, insignificant, seemingly trivial experiences in our daily lives can provide the material for narratives that reveal something about ourselves and the world we live in. Select one seemingly trivial event in your life, and write an essay in which you narrate that experience and explain its significance.

JOAN DIDION

Essayist, novelist, and journalist, Joan Didion was born in Sacramento in 1934 and educated at the University of California at Berkeley. She often writes on aspects of life in California and in the West. She has written for a wide spectrum of magazines, from *Mademoiselle* to the *National Review*, and her essays have been collected in *Slouching Towards Bethlehem* (1969), *The White Album* (1979), and *Salvador* (1983). Her novels include *Run River* (1963), *Play It As It Lays* (1971), and *A Book of Common Prayer* (1977). And in 1987 she published *Miami*, a portrait of a city.

This selection, taken from her highly acclaimed collection of essays *Slouching Towards Bethlehem*, first appeared in the *Saturday Evening Post*. Didion recalls the experience of going home to her parents' house with her adopted daughter, Quintana, for the child's first birthday.

On Going Home

I am home for my daughter's first birthday. By "home" I do not mean the house in Los Angeles where my husband and I and the baby live, but the place where my family is, in the Central Valley of California. It is a vital although troublesome distinction. My husband likes my family but is uneasy in their house, because once there I fall into their ways, which are difficult, oblique, deliberately inarticulate, not my husband's ways. We live in dusty houses ("D-U-S-T," he once wrote with his finger on surfaces all over the house, but no one noticed it) filled with mementos quite without value to him (what could the Canton dessert plates mean to him? how could he have known about the assay scales, why should he care if he did know?), and we appear to talk exclusively about people we know who have been committed to mental hospitals, about people we know who have been booked on drunk-driving charges, and about property, particularly about property, land, price per acre, and C-2 zoning and assessments and freeway access. My brother does not understand my husband's inability to perceive the advantage in the rather common real-estate transaction known as "sale-leaseback," and my husband in turn does not understand why so many of the people he hears about in my father's house have recently been committed to mental hospitals or booked on drunk-driving charges. Nor does he understand that when we talk about sale-leasebacks and right-of-way condemnations we are talking in code about the things we like best, the yellow fields and the cottonwoods and the rivers rising and falling and the mountain roads closing when the heavy snow comes in. We miss each other's points, have another drink and regard the fire. My brother refers to my husband, in his presence, as "Joan's husband." Marriage is the classic betrayal.

Or perhaps it is not any more. Sometimes I think that those of us who are now in our thirties were born into the last generation to carry the burden of "home," to find in family life the source of all tension and drama. I had by all objective accounts a "normal" and a "happy" family situation, and yet I was almost thirty years old before I could talk to my family on the telephone without crying after I had hung up. We did not fight. Nothing was wrong. And yet some nameless anxiety colored the emotional charges between me and the place that I came from. The question of whether or not you could go home again was a very real part of the sentimental and largely literary baggage with which we left home in the fifties; I suspect that it is irrelevant to the children born of the fragmentation after World War II. A few weeks ago in a San Francisco bar I saw a pretty young girl on crystal take off her clothes and dance for the cash prize in an "amateur-topless" contest. There was no particular sense of moment about this, none of the effect of romantic degradation, of "dark journey," for which my generation strived so assiduously. What sense could that girl possibly make of, say, *Long Day's Journey into Night?* Who is beside the point?

That I am trapped in this particular irrelevancy is never more apparent to me than when I am home. Paralyzed by the neurotic lassitude engendered by meeting one's past at every turn, around every corner, inside every cupboard, I go aimlessly from room to room. I decide to meet it head-on and clean out a drawer, and I spread the contents on the bed. A bathing suit I wore the summer I was seventeen. A letter of rejection from *The Nation*, an aerial photograph of the site for a shopping center my father did not build in 1954. Three teacups hand-painted with cabbage roses and signed "E.M.," my grandmother's initials. There is no final solution for letters of rejection from *The Nation* and teacups hand-painted in 1900. Nor is there any answer to snapshots of one's grandfather as a young man on skis, surveying around Donner Pass in the year 1910. I smooth out the snapshot and look into his face, and do and do not see my own. I close the drawer, and have another cup of coffee with my mother. We get along very well, veterans of a guerrilla war we never understood.

Days pass. I see no one. I come to dread my husband's evening call, not only because he is full of news of what by now seems to me our remote life in Los Angeles, people he has seen, letters which require attention, but because he asks me what I have been doing, suggests uneasily that I get out, drive to San Francisco or Berkeley. Instead I drive across the river to a family graveyard. It has been vandalized since my last visit and the monuments are broken, overturned in the dry grass. Because I once saw a rattlesnake in the grass I stay in the car and listen to a country-and-Western station. Later I drive with my father to a ranch he has in the foothills. The man who runs his cattle on it asks us to the roundup, a week from Sunday, and although I know that I will be in Los Angeles I say, in the oblique way my family talks, that I will come. Once home I mention the broken monuments in the graveyard. My mother shrugs.

I go to visit my great-aunts. A few of them think now that I am my cousin, or their daughter who died young. We recall an anecdote about a relative last seen in 1948, and they ask if I still like living in New York City. I have lived in Los Angeles for three years, but I say that I do. The baby is offered a horehound drop, and I am slipped a dollar bill "to buy a treat." Questions trail off, answers are abandoned, the baby plays with the dust motes in a shaft of afternoon sun. 5

It is time for the baby's birthday party: a white cake, strawberry-marshmallow ice cream, a bottle of champagne saved from another party. In the evening, after she has gone to sleep, I kneel beside the crib and touch her face, where it is pressed against the slats, with mine. She is an open and trusting child, unprepared for and unaccustomed to the ambushes of family life, and perhaps it is just as well that I can offer her little of that life. I would like to give her more. I would like to promise her that she will grow up with a sense of her cousins and of rivers and of her great-grandmother's teacups, would like to pledge her a picnic on a river with fried chicken and her hair uncombed, would like to give her *home* for her birthday, but we live differently now and I can promise her nothing like that. I give her a xylophone and a sundress from Madeira, and promise to tell her a funny story. 6

Questions for Study and Discussion

1. What does Didion mean by *home*? Why does she say that the distinction between her house in Los Angeles and her family's place in the Central Valley of California is "vital although troublesome"?

2. What are Didion's attitudes toward home? Are they in any way contradictory? Explain.

3. What does Didion mean when she says, "Marriage is the classic betrayal"? Explain.

4. Eugene O'Neill's *Long Day's Journey into Night* is an autobiographical domestic tragedy which, as Didion correctly implies, finds "in family life the source of all tension and drama." Why does Didion feel that the pretty young girl who dances in the "amateur-topless" contest would have difficulty making any sense of this play?

5. What details does the author use to support her feelings of being "paralyzed by the neurotic lassitude engendered by meeting one's past at every

turn"? What does she mean when she says of her relationship with her mother, "We get along very well, veterans of a guerrilla war we never understood"?

6. Why do you think Didion gives her daughter a xylophone and a sundress from Madeira for her birthday? What else would she have liked to give her? Why does she feel that she could not make a promise "like that"?

7. Good narrative tells when an action happened, where it happened, and to whom it happened. Where does Didion give us this information?

8. In the context of this essay, comment on the appropriateness of each of the following substitutions for Didion's diction. Which word is better in each case? Why?

   a. *important* for *vital* (1)
   b. *bothersome* for *troublesome* (1)
   c. *dirty* for *dusty* (1)
   d. *heirlooms* for *mementos* (1)
   e. *argue* for *fight* (2)
   f. *uncertainty* for *fragmentation* (2)
   g. *immoblilized* for *paralyzed* (3)
   h. *fear* for *dread* (4)
   i. *obscure* for *oblique* (1, 4)
   j. *outing* for *picnic* (6)

Writing Topics

1. Drawing on your own experience of home life, do you think that Didion is correct when she says that "those of us who are now in our thirties were born into the last generation to carry the burden of 'home,' to find in family life the source of all tension and drama"? Write a brief narrative which conveys what home is like for you.

2. In "On Going Home" Didion honestly confronts her feelings about her parents, her husband, her child and the passage of time. In attempting not to deceive herself she gains a measure of what might be called self-respect, or self-understanding. How and why do people deceive themselves? Why is self-deception so difficult to overcome? Finally, what does it mean to have self-respect? Write an essay in which you develop your answers to these questions.

3. In another essay from *Slouching Towards Bethlehem*, Didion defines character as "the willingness to accept responsibility for one's own life." Is that what character means to you? If so, develop the definition into an essay of your own. If not, write an essay explaining what you think character really is.

E. B. WHITE

Master essayist, storyteller, and poet, Elwyn Brooks White (1899–1985) was born in Mount Vernon, New York, lived some years in New York City, and for many years made his home on a salt-water farm in Maine. After studying at Cornell University, he joined the staff of *The New Yorker* in 1926, where he wrote essays, editorials, anonymous fillers, and even cartoon captions that helped to establish the magazine's and his own reputation for witty and graceful prose. A selection of his essays is available in *The Essays of E. B. White* (1977). He is the author of the classic children's stories *Stuart Little* (1945) and *Charlotte's Web* (1952), and he revised William Strunk's celebrated work *The Elements of Style* several times beginning in 1959. "Once More to the Lake," first published in *Harper's* in 1941, is a loving account of a trip White took with his son to the site of his own childhood vacations.

Once More to the Lake

One summer, along about 1904, my father rented a camp on a lake in Maine and took us all there for the month of August. We all got ringworm from some kittens and had to rub Pond's Extract on our arms and legs night and morning, and my father rolled over in a canoe with all his clothes on; but outside of that the vacation was a success and from then on none of us ever thought there was any place in the world like that lake in Maine. We returned summer after summer—always on August 1st for one month. I have since become a salt-water man, but sometimes in summer there are days when the restlessness of the tides and the fearful cold of the sea water and the incessant wind which blows across the afternoon and into the evening make me wish for the placidity of a lake in the woods. A few weeks ago this feeling got so strong I bought myself a couple of bass hooks and a spinner and returned to the lake where we used to go, for a week's fishing and to revisit old haunts.

I took along my son, who had never had any fresh water up his nose and who had seen lily pads only from train windows. On the journey over to the lake I began to wonder what it would be like. I wondered how time would have marred this unique, this holy spot—the coves and streams, the hills that the sun set behind, the camps and the paths behind the camps. I was sure that the tarred road would have found it out and I wondered in what other ways it would be desolated. It is strange how much you can remember about places like that once you allow your mind to return into the grooves which lead back. You remember one thing, and that suddenly reminds you of another thing. I guess I remembered clearest of all the early mornings, when the lake was cool and motionless, remembered how the bedroom smelled of the lumber it was made of and of the wet woods whose scent entered through the screen. The partitions in the camp were thin and did not extend clear to the top of the rooms, and as I was always the first up I would dress softly so as not to wake the others, and sneak out into the sweet outdoors and start out in the canoe, keeping close along the shore in the long shadows of the pines. I remembered being very careful never to rub my paddle against the gunwale for fear of disturbing the stillness of the cathedral.

The lake had never been what you would call a wild lake. There were   3
cottages sprinkled around the shores, and it was in farming country although the shores of the lake were quite heavily wooded. Some of the cottages were owned by nearby farmers, and you would live at the shore and eat your meals at the farmhouse. That's what our family did. But although it wasn't wild, it was a fairly large and undisturbed lake and there were places in it which, to a child at least, seemed infinitely remote and primeval.

I was right about the tar: it led to within half a mile of the shore. But   4
when I got back there, with my boy, and we settled into a camp near a farmhouse and into the kind of summertime I had known, I could tell that it was going to be pretty much the same as it had been before—I knew it, lying in bed the first morning, smelling the bedroom and hearing the boy sneak quietly out and go off along the shore in a boat. I began to sustain the illusion that he was I, and therefore, by simple transposition, that I was my father. This sensation persisted, kept cropping up all the time we were there. It was not an entirely new feeling, but in this setting it grew much stronger. I seemed to be living a dual existence. I would be in the middle of some simple act, I would be picking up a bait box or laying down a table fork, or I would be saying something, and suddenly it would be not I but my father who was saying the words and making the gesture. It gave me a creepy sensation.

We went fishing the first morning. I felt the same damp moss covering   5
the worms in the bait can, and saw the dragonfly alight on the tip of my rod as it hovered a few inches from the surface of the water. It was the arrival of this fly that convinced me beyond any doubt that everything was as it always had been, that the years were a mirage and there had been no years. The small waves were the same, chucking the rowboat under the chin as we fished at anchor, and the boat was the same boat, the same color green and the ribs broken in the same places, and under the floor-boards the same freshwater leavings and débris—the dead helgramite, the wisps of moss, the rusty discarded fishhook, the dried blood from yesterday's catch. We stared

silently at the tips of our rods, at the dragonflies that came and went. I lowered the tip of mine into the water, tentatively, pensively dislodging the fly, which darted two feet away, poised, darted two feet back, and came to rest again a little farther up the rod. There had been no years between the ducking of this dragonfly and the other one—the one that was part of memory. I looked at the boy, who was silently watching his fly, and it was my hands that held his rod, my eyes watching. I felt dizzy and didn't know which rod I was at the end of.

We caught two bass, hauling them in briskly as though they were   6
mackerel, pulling them over the side of the boat in a businesslike manner without any landing net, and stunning them with a blow on the back of the head. When we got back for a swim before lunch, the lake was exactly where we had left it, the same number of inches from the dock, and there was only the merest suggestion of a breeze. This seemed an utterly enchanted sea, this lake you could leave to its own devices for a few hours and come back to, and find that it had not stirred, this constant and trustworthy body of water. In the shallows, the dark, water-soaked sticks and twigs, smooth and old, were undulating in clusters on the bottom against the clean ribbed sand, and the track of the mussel was plain. A school of minnows swam by, each minnow with its small individual shadow, doubling the attendance, so clear and sharp in the sunlight. Some of the other campers were in swimming, along the shore, one of them with a cake of soap, and the water felt thin and clear and unsubstantial. Over the years there had been this person with the cake of soap, this cultist, and here he was. There had been no years.

Up to the farmhouse to dinner through the teeming, dusty field, the   7
road under our sneakers was only a two-track road. The middle track was missing, the one with the marks of the hooves and the splotches of dried, flaky manure. There had always been three tracks to choose from in choosing which track to walk in; now the choice was narrowed down to two. For a moment I missed terribly the middle alternative. But the way led past the tennis court, and something about the way it lay there in the sun reassured me; the tape had loosened along the backline, the alleys were green with plantains and other weeds, and the net (installed in June and removed in September) sagged in the dry noon, and the whole place steamed with midday heat and hunger and emptiness. There was a choice of pie for dessert, and one was blueberry and one was apple, and the waitresses were the same country girls, there having been no passage of time, only the illusion of it as in a dropped curtain—the waitresses were still fifteen; their hair had been washed, that was the only difference—they had been to the movies and seen the pretty girls with the clean hair.

Summertime, oh summertime, pattern of life indelible, the fade-proof   8
lake, the woods unshatterable, the pasture with the sweetfern and the juniper forever and ever, summer without end; this was the background,

and the life along the shore was the design, the cottages with their innocent and tranquil design, their tiny docks with the flagpole and the American flag floating against the white clouds in the blue sky, the little paths over the roots of the trees leading from camp to camp and the paths leading back to the outhouses and the can of lime for sprinkling, and at the souvenir counters at the store the miniature birch-bark canoes and the post cards that showed things looking a little better than they looked. This was the American family at play, escaping the city heat, wondering whether the newcomers in the camp at the head of the cove were "common" or "nice," wondering whether it was true that the people who drove up for Sunday dinner at the farmhouse were turned away because there wasn't enough chicken.

It seemed to me, as I kept remembering all this, that those times and those summers had been infinitely precious and worth saving. There had been jollity and peace and goodness. The arriving (at the beginning of August) had been so big a business in itself, at the railway station the farm wagon drawn up, the first smell of the pine-laden air, the first glimpse of the smiling farmer, and the great importance of the trunks and your father's enormous authority in such matters, and the feel of the wagon under you for the long ten-mile haul, and at the top of the last long hill catching the first view of the lake after eleven months of not seeing this cherished body of water. The shouts and cries of the other campers when they saw you, and the trunks to be unpacked, to give up their rich burden. (Arriving was less exciting nowadays, when you sneaked up in your car and parked it under a tree near the camp and took out the bags and in five minutes it was all over, no fuss, no loud wonderful fuss about trunks.)

Peace and goodness and jollity. The only thing that was wrong now, really, was the sound of the place, an unfamiliar nervous sound of the outboard motors. This was the note that jarred, the one thing that would sometimes break the illusion and set the years moving. In those other summertimes all motors were inboard; and when they were at a little distance, the noise they made was a sedative, an ingredient of summer sleep. They were one-cylinder and two-cylinder engines, and some were make-and-break and some were jump-spark, but they all made a sleepy sound across the lake. The one-lungers throbbed and fluttered, and the twin-cylinder ones purred and purred, and that was a quiet sound too. But now the campers all had outboards. In the daytime, in the hot mornings, these motors made a petulant, irritable sound; at night, in the still evening when the afterglow lit the water, they whined about one's ears like mosquitoes. My boy loved our rented outboard, and his great desire was to achieve singlehanded mastery over it, and authority, and he soon learned the trick of choking it a little (but not too much), and the adjustment of the needle valve. Watching him I would remember the things you could do with the old one-cylinder engine with the heavy flywheel, how you could have it eating out of your hand if you got really close to it spiritually. Motor boats in those days didn't have clutches, and you would make a landing by shutting off the motor at the proper time and coasting in with a dead rudder. But there was a way of reversing them, if you learned the trick, by cutting the switch and putting it on again exactly on the final dying revolution of the flywheel, so that it would kick back against compression and begin reversing. Approaching a dock in a strong following breeze, it was difficult to slow up sufficiently by the ordinary coasting method, and if a boy felt he had complete mastery over his motor, he was tempted to keep it running beyond its time and then reverse it a few feet from the dock. It took a cool nerve, because if you threw the switch a twentieth of a second too soon you could catch the flywheel when it still had speed enough to go up past center, and the boat would leap ahead, charging bull-fashion at the dock.

We had a good week at the camp. The bass were biting well and the 11 sun shone endlessly, day after day. We would be tired at night and lie down in the accumulated heat of the little bedrooms after the long hot day and the breeze would stir almost imperceptibly outside and the smell of the swamp drift in through the rusty screens. Sleep would come easily and in the morning the red squirrel would be on the roof tapping out his gay routine. I kept remembering everything, lying in bed in the mornings—the small steamboat that had a long rounded stern like the lip of a Ubangi,[1] and how quietly she ran on the moonlight sails, when the older boys played their mandolins and the girls sang and we ate doughnuts dipped in sugar, and how sweet the music was on the water in the shining night, and what it had felt like to think about girls then. After breakfast we would go up to the store and the things were in the same place—the minnows in a bottle, the plugs and spinners disarranged and pawed over by the youngsters from the boys' camp, the fig newtons and the Beeman's gum. Outside, the road was tarred and cars stood in front of the store. Inside, all was just as it had always been, except there was more Coca-Cola and not so much Moxie and root beer and birch beer and sarsaparilla. We would walk out with a bottle of pop apiece and sometimes the pop would backfire up our noses and hurt. We explored the streams, quietly, where the turtles slid off the sunny logs and dug their way into the soft bottom; and we lay on the town wharf and fed worms to the tame bass. Everywhere we went I had trouble making out which was I, the one walking at my side, the one walking in my pants.

One afternoon while we were there at that lake a thunderstorm came 12 up. It was like the revival of an old melodrama that I had seen long ago with childish awe. The second-act climax of the drama of the electrical disturbance over a lake in America had not changed in any important respect.

------

[1] A member of an African tribe whose lower lip is stretched around a wooden, platelike disk.

This was the big scene, still the big scene. The whole thing was so familiar, the first feeling of oppression and heat and a general air around camp of not wanting to go very far away. In midafternoon (it was all the same) a curious darkening of the sky, and a lull in everything that had made life tick; and then the way the boats suddenly swung the other way at their moorings with the coming of a breeze out of the new quarter, and the premonitory rumble. Then the kettle drum, then the snare and then the bass drum and cymbals, then crackling light against the dark, and the gods grinning and licking their chops in the hills. Afterward the calm, the rain steadily rustling in the calm lake, the return of light and hope and spirits, and the campers running out in joy and relief to go swimming in the rain, their bright cries perpetuating the deathless joke about how they were getting simply drenched, and the children screaming with delight at the new sensation of bathing in the rain, and the joke about getting drenched linking the generations in a strong indestructible chain. And the comedian who waded in carrying an umbrella.

When the others went swimming my son said he was going in too. He   13
pulled his dripping trunks from the line where they had hung all through the shower, and wrung them out. Languidly, and with no thought of going in, I watched him, his hard little body, skinny and bare, saw him wince slightly as he pulled up around his vitals the small, soggy, icy garment. As he buckled the swollen belt suddenly my groin felt the chill of death.

Questions for Study and Discussion

1. The first three paragraphs introduce White's essay. Taken together, how do they prepare for what follows? What does each paragraph contribute?

2. White returns to the lake wondering whether it will be as he remembers it from his childhood vacations. What remains the same? What significance does White attach to the changes in the road, the waitresses, and the outboard motorboats?

3. In paragraph 4 White tells us, "I began to sustain the illusion that [my son] was I, and therefore, by simple transposition, that I was my father." What first prompts this "illusion"? Where else does White refer to it? How does it affect your understanding of what the week at the lake means to White?

4. In paragraph 12 White describes a late afternoon thunderstorm at the lake. How does White organize his description? What does the metaphor of the old melodrama contribute to that description?

5. What is the tone of this essay, and what does it reveal about White's attitude toward his experience? Has he undergone a process of self-discovery? Give examples to support your answer.

6. The closing sentence takes many readers by surprise. Why did White feel the "chill of death"? Has he prepared for this surprise earlier in the essay? If so, where?

Writing Topics

1. Have you ever returned to a place you once knew well but have not seen in years—a house or a city where you once lived, a school you once attended, a favorite vacation spot? What memories did the visit bring back? Did you, like White, find that little had changed and feel that time had stood still, or were there many changes? If possible, you might make such a visit, to reflect on what has happened to the place—and to you—since you were last there.

2. What, for you, is the ideal vacation? Where would you go and what would you do? What do you hope and expect that a good vacation will do for you?

3. Write an essay in which you discuss death and when you first became aware of your own mortality.

JEAN SHEPHERD

Actor, radio announcer, humorist, and writer, Jean Shepherd was born in 1929 in Chicago. As an actor he has had four one-man shows and has appeared in off-Broadway plays, and as an announcer he has worked for radio stations in Cincinnati, Philadelphia, and New York. Shepherd has also contributed columns to the *Village Voice* (1960–1967) and to *Car and Driver* (1968–1977), as well as prize-winning fiction to *Playboy*. His published works include *The America of George Ade* (1961); *In God We Trust: All Others Pay Cash* (1967); *Wanda Hickey's Night of Golden Memories and Other Disasters* (1972); *The Ferrari in the Bedroom* (1973); *The Phantom of the Open Hearth* (1977); and *A Fistful of Fig Newtons* (1981).

In the following essay, Shepherd takes us along as he relives a not-so-easily forgotten blind date. In telling his story he displays his considerable talent for evoking a sense of drama, pathos, and humor.

The Endless Streetcar Ride into the Night, and the Tinfoil Noose

Mewling, puking babes. That's the way we all start. Damply clinging   1
to someone's shoulder, burping weakly, clawing our way into life. *All* of us. Then gradually, surely, we begin to divide into two streams, all marching together up that long yellow brick road of life, but on opposite sides of the street. One crowd goes on to become the Official people, peering out at us from television screens; magazine covers. They are forever appearing in newsreels, carrying attaché cases, surrounded by banks of microphones while the world waits for their decisions and statements. And the rest of us go on to become . . . just us.

They are the Prime Ministers, the Presidents, Cabinet members,   2
Stars, dynamic molders of the Universe, while we remain forever the onlookers, the applauders of their real lives.

Forever down in the dark dungeons of our souls we ask ourselves: 3

"How did they get away from me? When did I make that first misstep   4
that took me forever to the wrong side of the street, to become eternally part of the accursed, anonymous Audience?"

It seems like one minute we're all playing around back of the garage,   5
kicking tin cans and yelling at girls, and the next instant you find yourself

doomed to exist as an office boy in the Mail Room of Life, while another ex-mewling, puking babe sends down Dicta, says "No comment" to the Press, and lives a real, genuine *Life* on the screen of the world.

Countless sufferers at this hour are spending billions of dollars and endless man hours lying on analysts' couches, trying to pinpoint the exact moment that they stepped off the track and into the bushes forever.   6

It all hinges on one sinister reality that is rarely mentioned, no doubt due to its implacable, irreversible inevitability. These decisions cannot be changed, no matter how many brightly cheerful, buoyantly optimistic books on HOW TO ACHIEVE A RICHER, FULLER, MORE BOUNTIFUL LIFE or SEVEN MAGIC GOLDEN KEYS TO INSTANT DYNAMIC SUCCESS or THE SECRET OF HOW TO BECOME A BILLIONAIRE we read, or how many classes are attended for instruction in handshaking, back slapping, grinning, and making After-Dinner speeches. Joseph Stalin was not a Dale Carnegie graduate. He went all the way. It is an unpleasant truth that is swallowed, if at all, like a rancid, bitter pill. A star is a star; a numberless cipher is a numberless cipher.   7

Even more eerie a fact is that the Great Divide is rarely a matter of talent or personality. Or even luck. Adolf Hitler had a notoriously weak handshake. His smile was, if anything, a vapid mockery. But inevitably his star zoomed higher and higher. Cinema luminaries of the first order are rarely blessed with even the modicum of Talent, and often their physical beauty leaves much to be desired. What is the difference between Us and Them, We and They, the Big Ones and the great, teeming rabble?   8

There are about four times in a man's life, or a woman's, too, for that matter, when unexpectedly, from out of the darkness, the blazing carbon lamp, the cosmic searchlight of Truth shines full upon them. It is how we react to those moments that forever seals our fate. One crowd simply puts on its sunglasses, lights another cigar, and heads for the nearest plush French restaurant in the jazziest section of town, sits down and orders a drink, and ignores the whole thing. While we, the Doomed, caught in the brilliant glare of illumination, see ourselves inescapably for what we are, and from that day on skulk in the weeds, hoping no one else will spot us.   9

Those moments happen when we are least able to fend them off. I caught the first one full in the face when I was fourteen. The fourteenth summer is a magic one for all kids. You have just slid out of the pupa stage, leaving your old baby skin behind, and have not yet become a grizzled, hardened, tax-paying beetle. At fourteen you are made of cellophane. You curl easily and everyone can see through you.   10

When I was fourteen, Life was flowing through me in a deep, rich torrent of Castoria. How did I know that the first rocks were just ahead, and I was about to have my keel ripped out on the reef? Sometimes you feel as though you are alone in a rented rowboat, bailing like mad in the darkness with a leaky bailing can. It is important to know that there are at   11 least two billion other ciphers in the same boat, bailing with the same leaky can. They all think they are alone and are crossed with an evil star. They are right.

I'm fourteen years old, in my sophomore year at high school. One day   12
Schwartz, my purported best friend, sidled up to me edgily outside of school while we were waiting on the steps to come in after lunch. He proceeded to outline his plan:

"Helen's old man won't let me take her out on a date on Saturday   13
night unless I get a date for her girlfriend. A double date. The old coot figures, I guess, that if there are four of us there won't be no monkey business. Well, how about it? Do you want to go on a blind date with this chick? I never seen her."

Well. For years I had this principle—absolutely *no* blind dates. I was a   14
man of perception and taste, and life was short. But there is a time in your life when you have to stop taking and begin to give just a little. For the first time the warmth of sweet Human Charity brought the roses to my cheeks. After all, Schwartz was my friend. It was little enough to do, have a blind date with some no doubt skinny, pimply girl for your best friend. I would do it for Schwartz. He would do as much for me.

"Okay. Okay, Schwartz."   15

Then followed the usual ribald remarks, feckless boasting, and dirty   16
jokes about dates in general and girls in particular. It was decided that next Saturday we would go all the way. I had a morning paper route at the time, and my life savings stood at about $1.80. I was all set to blow it on one big night.

I will never forget that particular Saturday as long as I live. The air   17
was as soft as the finest of spun silk. The scent of lilacs hung heavy. The catalpa trees rustled in the early evening breeze from off the Lake. The inner Me itched in that nameless way, that indescribable way that only the fourteen-year-old Male fully knows.

All that afternoon I had carefully gone over my wardrobe to select the   18
proper symphony of sartorial brilliance. That night I set out wearing my magnificent electric blue sport coat, whose shoulders were so wide that they hung out over my frame like vast, drooping eaves, so wide I had difficulty going through an ordinary door head-on. The electric blue sport coat that draped voluminously almost to my knees, its wide lapels flapping sound-lessly in the slightest breeze. My pleated gray flannel slacks began just below my breastbone and indeed chafed my armpits. High-belted, cascading down finally to grasp my ankles in a vise-like grip. My tie, indeed one of my most prized possessions, had been a gift from my Aunt Glenn upon the state occasion of graduation from eighth grade. It was of a beautiful silky fabric, silvery pearly colored, four inches wide at the fulcrum, and of such a length to endanger occasionally my zipper in moments of haste. Hand-painted upon it was a magnificent blood-red snail.

I had spent fully two hours carefully arranging and rearranging my   19
great mop of wavy hair, into which I had rubbed fully a pound and a half of
Greasy Kid Stuff.

Helen and Schwartz waited on the corner under the streetlight at the   20
streetcar stop near Junie Jo's home. Her name was Junie Jo Prewitt. I won't
forget it quickly, although she has, no doubt, forgotten mine. I walked down
the dark street alone, past houses set back off the street, through the
darkness, past privet hedges, under elm trees, through air rich and ripe with
promise. Her house stood back from the street even farther than the others.
It sort of crouched in the darkness, looking out at me, kneeling. Pregnant
with Girldom. A real Girlfriend house.

The first faint touch of nervousness filtered through the marrow of my   21
skullbone as I knocked on the door of the screen-enclosed porch. No
answer. I knocked again, louder. Through the murky screens I could see
faint lights in the house itself. Still no answer. Then I found a small doorbell
button buried in the sash. I pressed. From far off in the bowels of the house I
heard two chimes "Bong" politely. It sure didn't sound like our doorbell.
We had a real ripper that went off like a broken buzz saw, more of a
BRRRAAAAKKK than a muffled Bong. This was a rich people's doorbell.

The door opened and there stood a real, genuine, gold-plated Father: 22
potbelly, underwear shirt, suspenders, and all.

"Well?" he asked.   23

For one blinding moment of embarrassment I couldn't remember her   24
name. After all, she was a blind date. I couldn't just say:

"I'm here to pick up some girl."   25

He turned back into the house and hollered: 26

"JUNIE JO! SOME KID'S HERE!"   27

"Heh, heh. . . ." I countered.   28

He led me into the living room. It was an itchy house, sticky stucco   29
walls of a dull orange color, and all over the floor this Oriental rug with the
design crawling around, making loops and sworls. I sat on an overstuffed
chair covered in stiff green mohair that scratched even through my slacks.
Little twisty bridge lamps stood everywhere. I instantly began to sweat
down the back of my clean white shirt. Like I said, it was a very itchy house.
It had little lamps sticking out of the walls that looked like phony candles,
with phony glass orange flames. The rug started moaning to itself.

I sat on the edge of the chair and tried to talk to this Father. He was a   30
Cub fan. We struggled under water for what seemed like an hour and a half,
when suddenly I heard someone coming down the stairs. First the feet; then
those legs, and there she was. She was magnificent! The greatest-looking girl
I ever saw in my life! I have hit the double jackpot! And on a blind date!
Great Scot!

My senses actually reeled as I clutched the arm of that bilge-green   31
chair for support. Junie Jo Prewitt made Cleopatra look like a Girl Scout!

Five minutes later we are sitting in the streetcar, heading toward the   32
bowling alley. I am sitting next to the most fantastic creation in the
Feminine department known to Western man. There are the four of us in
that long, yellow-lit streetcar. No one else was aboard; just us four. I,
naturally, being a trained gentleman, sat on the aisle to protect her from
candy wrappers and cigar butts and such. Directly ahead of me, also on the
aisle, sat Schwartz, his arm already flung affectionately in a death grip
around Helen's neck as we boomed and rattled through the night.

I casually flung my right foot up onto my left knee so that she could   33
see my crepe-soled, perforated, wind-toed, Scotch bluchers with the two-
toned laces. I started to work my famous charm on her. Casually, with my
practiced offhand, cynical, cutting sardonic humor I told her about how my
Old Man had cracked the block in the Oldsmobile, how the White Sox
were going to have a good year this year, how my kid brother wet his pants
when he saw a snake, how I figured it was going to rain, what a great guy
Schwartz was, what a good second baseman I was, how I figured I might go
out for football. On and on I rolled, like Old Man River, pausing significantly for her to pick up the conversation. Nothing.

Ahead of us Schwartz and Helen were almost indistinguishable one   34
from the other. They giggled, bit each other's ears, whispered, clasped
hands, and in general made me itch even more.

From time to time Junie Jo would bend forward stiffly from the waist   35
and say something I could never quite catch into Helen's right ear.

I told her my great story of the time that Uncle Carl lost his false teeth   36
down the airshaft. Still nothing. Out of the corner of my eye I could see that
she had her coat collar turned up, hiding most of her face as she sat silently,
looking forward past Helen Weathers into nothingness.

I told her about this old lady on my paper route who chews tobacco   37
and roller skates in the backyard every morning. I still couldn't get through
to her. Casually I inched my right arm up over the back of the seat behind
her shoulders. The acid test. She leaned forward, avoiding my arm, and
stayed that way.

"Heh, heh, heh. . . ."   38

As nonchalantly as I could, I retrieved it, battling a giant cramp in my   39
right shoulder blade. I sat in silence for a few seconds, sweating heavily as
ahead Schwartz and Helen are going at it hot and heavy.

It was then that I became aware of someone saying something to me. It   40
was an empty car. There was no one else but us. I glanced around, and there
it was. Above us a line of car cards looked down on the empty streetcar.
One was speaking directly to me, to me alone.

DO YOU OFFEND?

Do I *offend*?!   41

With no warning, from up near the front of the car where the   42
motorman is steering I see this thing coming down the aisle directly toward

This examination copy of

Outlooks and Insights
A READER FOR COLLEGE WRITERS
Third Edition
Edited by Paul Eschholz and Alfred Rosa

is sent to you with the compliments of
your St. Martin's Press representative.

Your comments on our books help us estimate printing requirements, assist us in preparing revisions, and guide us in shaping future books to your needs. Will you please take a moment to fill out and return this postpaid card?

☐ you may quote me for advertising purposes
☐ I have adopted this book for _____ semester, 19 _____ .
☐ I am seriously considering it.

Date _____

Comments

Name _____ Department _____
School _____ Phone Number ( ) _____
City _____ State _____ Zip _____

Course Title _____ Enrollment _____
Present Text _____
Do you plan to change texts this year?   Yes ☐   No ☐   When is your decision due? _____
Is your text decision   individual ☐   committee ☐   department ☐
If committee or department, please list others involved _____

BUSINESS REPLY MAIL

FIRST CLASS MAIL   PERMIT NO. 14   LAVALLETTE, NJ

POSTAGE WILL BE PAID BY ADDRESSEE

St. Martin's Press, Inc.

P.O. Box 36

Lavallette, NJ 08735-9988

me. It's coming closer and closer. I can't escape it. It's this blinding, fantastic, brilliant, screaming blue light. I am spread-eagled in it. There's a pin sticking through my thorax. I see it all now.

I AM THE BLIND DATE!   43

ME!!   44

I'M the one they're being nice to!   45

I'm suddenly getting fatter, more itchy. My new shoes are like bowling   46
balls with laces; thick, rubber-crepe bowling balls. My great tie that Aunt
Glenn gave me is two feet wide, hanging down to the floor like some crinkly
tinfoil noose. My beautiful hand-painted snail is seven feet high, sitting up
on my shoulder, burping. Great Scot! It is all clear to me in the searing
white light of Truth. My friend Schwartz, I can see him saying to Junie Jo:

"I got this crummy fat friend who never has a date. Let's give him a   47
break and. . . ."

I AM THE BLIND DATE!   48

They are being nice to *me!* She is the one who is out on a Blind Date.   49
A Blind Date that didn't make it.

In the seat ahead, the merriment rose to a crescendo. Helen tittered;   50
Schwartz cackled. The marble statue next to me stared gloomily out into
the darkness as our streetcar rattled on. The ride went on and on.

I AM THE BLIND DATE!   51

I didn't say much the rest of the night. There wasn't much to be said.   52

Questions for Study and Discussion

1. Shepherd develops his long narrative to illustrate his point about turning points in life. What exactly is his point, and where is it stated? In what way is the blind date episode a moment of truth?
2. Where does Shepherd's narrative begin?
3. What distinction does Shepherd draw between "Official people" and "just us"? Do you agree with his assessment? Explain.
4. For whom has Shepherd written this essay? How do you know?
5. What event triggers the narrator's moment of insight?
6. Explain Shepherd's title. What is the "tinfoil noose"?
7. What do you know of the narrator from the story he tells? What do you learn of his appearance? His personality?
8. To what extent does Shepherd use figurative language in his essay? Cite several examples of metaphors and similes. What do these figures add to his style?

Writing Topics

1. Shepherd believes that people on average experience four moments of truth in a lifetime. Moreover, he states that "it is how we react to those

moments that forever seals our fate." From your own experiences, recount one such moment in your life and how you dealt with it. In retrospect, how do you think you handled the situation?

2. Write an essay in which you argue for or against Shepherd's assertion that "Official people" are insensitive to or can simply ignore moments of truth.

ROBERT FROST

Robert Frost (1874–1963) was born in San Francisco but moved with his family to Massachusetts when he was eleven, and he became a New Englander through and through. He attended Dartmouth and Harvard briefly, spent some time as a millworker and schoolteacher, and in 1900 moved to a farm in New Hampshire, where he lived most of the rest of his life. From 1912 to 1915 he lived in England, where he published two books of poems that brought him his first critical recognition. He returned to the United States a popular poet and soon became a highly influential one. He taught at Amherst, Dartmouth, Harvard, and the University of Michigan and was awarded several Pulitzer Prizes as well as numerous honors. Among his most celebrated poems are "The Tuft of Flowers" (1913), "Birches" (1916), and "Fire and Ice" (1923); they can be found in *The Poetry of Robert Frost* (1969).

   Completed in 1916, "The Road Not Taken" has become a cultural symbol of the difficulty and consequences of making a choice in life. Ostensibly about the choice between two roads that diverge in the woods, the poem, of course, implies much more. As Frost himself said, "I'm always saying something that's just the edge of something more."

The Road Not Taken

Two roads diverged in a yellow wood,
And sorry I could not travel both
And be one traveler, long I stood
And looked down one as far as I could
To where it bent in the undergrowth;   5

Then took the other, as just as fair,
And having perhaps the better claim,
Because it was grassy and wanted wear;
Though as for that the passing there
Had worn them really about the same,   10

And both that morning equally lay
In leaves no step had trodden black.
Oh, I kept the first for another day!

Yet knowing how way leads on to way,
I doubted if I should ever come back.   15

I shall be telling this with a sigh
Somewhere ages and ages hence:
Two roads diverged in a wood, and I—
I took the one less traveled by,
And that has made all the difference.   20

Questions for Study and Discussion

1. Why did the speaker in the poem make the decision that he did? Was it a difficult choice to make? What things did the speaker consider when making his decision?

2. Can the speaker in the poem really tell that he made the right decision? Explain.

3. Metaphorically, what do the roads and the yellow wood signify?

4. What, if anything, does Frost's poem reveal about turning points, those significant decisions that alter the course of our lives?

Writing Topics

1. Compare the sentiments expressed in Frost's twenty-line poem to those expressed in Langston Hughes's autobiographical essay "Salvation" (pp. 85–87). In what ways are they similar; in what ways different?

2. By the time you enter college you have been exposed to poetry and have formed an opinion about it—you either like it, dislike it, or are merely indifferent to it. What is it in poetry, or your own attitudes, that causes you to respond to it as you do?

3. Write an essay in which you examine a choice or decision you made some time ago. Would you make the same choice again? What do you know now that you didn't know then?

2 *Family and Friends*

Love makes the ego lose itself in the object it loves, and yet at the same time it wants to have the object as its own. This is a contradiction, and a great tragedy of life.

D. T. SUZUKI

God gives us relatives; thank God, we can choose our friends.

ADDISON MIZNER

It is . . . astonishing that, under the circumstances, marriage is still legally allowed. If nearly half of anything else ended so disastrously, the government would surely ban it immediately.

LIONEL TIGER

Family Ties

S. I. HAYAKAWA

He has been president of San Francisco State College and a U.S. senator, but Samuel Ichiyé Hayakawa has been most influential as a scholar and teacher of general semantics, the study of the meanings of words and how they influence our lives. Born in Vancouver, Canada, in 1906, Hayakawa attended the University of Manitoba, McGill University, and the University of Wisconsin before beginning a career as a professor of English. Since then he has written several books, including *Language in Thought and Action* (1941), which has been widely used as a textbook. Hayakawa has also written many articles on a wide range of social and personal issues, making frequent reference to the use of general semantics in everyday life.

This is one of those articles. It was written for *McCall's* magazine. Some of his readers were no doubt faced with the same dilemma as the Hayakawas, whose son Mark was born with Down's syndrome, a form of retardation. What happened next, and why, is the subject of "Our Son Mark."

Our Son Mark

It was a terrible blow for us to discover that we had brought a retarded   1
child into the world. My wife and I had had no previous acquaintance with the problems of retardation—not even with the words to discuss it. Only such words as imbecile, idiot, and moron came to mind. And the prevailing opinion was that such a child must be "put away," to live out his life in an institution.

Mark was born with Down's syndrome, popularly known as mongol-   2
ism. The prognosis for his ever reaching anything approaching normality was hopeless. Medical authorities advised us that he would show some mental development, but the progress would be painfully slow and he would never reach an adolescent's mental age. We could do nothing about it, they

said. They sympathetically but firmly advised us to find a private institution that would take him. To get him into a public institution, they said,
would require a waiting period of five years. To keep him at home for this
length of time, they warned, would have a disastrous effect on our family.

That was twenty-seven years ago. In that time, Mark has never been
"put away." He has lived at home. The only institution he sees regularly is
the workshop he attends, a special workshop for retarded adults. He is as
much a part of the family as his mother, his older brother, his younger sister,
his father, or our longtime housekeeper and friend, Daisy Rosebourgh.

Mark has contributed to our stability and serenity. His retardation
has brought us grief, but we did not go on dwelling on what might have
been, and we have been rewarded by finding much good in things the way
they are. From the beginning, we have enjoyed Mark for his delightful self.
He has never seemed like a burden. He was an "easy" baby, quiet, friendly,
and passive; but he needed a baby's care for a long time. It was easy to be
patient with him, although I must say that some of his stages, such as his
love of making chaos, as we called it, by pulling all the books he could reach
off the shelves, lasted much longer than normal children's.

Mark seems more capable of accepting things as they are than his
immediate relatives; his mental limitation has given him a capacity for
contentment, a focus on the present moment, which is often enviable. His
world may be circumscribed, but it is a happy and bright one. His enjoyment of simple experiences—swimming, food, birthday candles, sports-car
rides, and cuddly cats—has that directness and intensity so many philosophers recommend to all of us.

Mark's contentment has been a happy contribution to our family, and
the challenge of communicating with him, of doing things we can all enjoy,
has drawn the family together. And seeing Mark's communicative processes
develop in slow motion has taught me much about the process in all
children.

Fortunately Mark was born at a time when a whole generation of
parents of retarded children had begun to question the accepted dogmas
about retardation. Whatever they were told by their physicians about their
children, parents began to ask: "Is that so? Let's see." For what is meant by
"retarded child"? There are different kinds of retardation. Retarded child
No. 1 is not retarded child No. 2, or 3, or 4. Down's syndrome is one
condition, while brain damage is something else. There are different degrees
of retardation, just as there are different kinds of brain damage. No two
retarded children are exactly alike in all respects. Institutional care *does*
turn out to be the best answer for some kinds of retarded children or some
family situations. The point is that one observes and reacts to the *specific*
case and circumstances rather than to the generalization.

This sort of attitude has helped public understanding of the nature
and problems of retardation to become much deeper and more widespread.
It's hard to believe now that it was "definitely known" twenty years ago that

institutionalization was the "only way." We were told that a retarded child could not be kept at home because "it would not be fair to the other children." The family would not be able to stand the stress. "Everybody" believed these things and repeated them, to comfort and guide the parents of the retarded.

We did not, of course, lightly disregard the well-meant advice of university neurologists and their social-worker teams, for they had had much experience and we were new at this shattering experience. But our general semantics, or our parental feelings, made us aware that their reaction to Mark was to a generalization, while to us he was an individual. They might have a valid generalization about statistical stresses on statistical families, but they knew virtually nothing about our particular family and its evaluative processes.   9

Mark was eight months old before we were told he was retarded. Of course we had known that he was slower than the average child in smiling, in sitting up, in responding to others around him. Having had one child who was extraordinarily ahead of such schedules, we simply thought that Mark was at the other end of the average range.   10

In the course of his baby checkups, at home and while traveling, we had seen three different pediatricians. None of them gave us the slightest indication that all was not well. Perhaps they were made uncertain by the fact that Mark, with his part Japanese parentage, had a right to have "mongolian" features. Or perhaps this news is as hard for a pediatrician to tell as it is for parents to hear, and they kept putting off the job of telling us. Finally, Mark's doctor did suggest a neurologist, indicating what his fears were, and made an appointment.   11

It was Marge who bore the brunt of the first diagnosis and accompanying advice, given at the university hospital at a time when I had to be out of town. Stunned and crushed, she was told: "Your husband is a professional man. You can't keep a child like this at home."   12

"But he lives on love," she protested.   13

"Don't your other children live on love, too?" the social worker asked.   14

Grief-stricken as she was, my wife was still able to recognize a non sequitur. One does not lessen the love for one's children by dividing it among several.   15

"What can I read to find out more about his condition and how to take care of him?" Marge asked.   16

"You can't get help from a book," answered the social worker. "You must put him away."   17

Today this sounds like dialogue from the Dark Ages. And it *was* the Dark Ages. Today professional advice runs generally in the opposite direction: "Keep your retarded child at home if it's at all possible."   18

It was parents who led the way: They organized into parents' groups; they pointed out the need for preschools, schools, diagnostic centers, work-training centers, and sheltered workshops to serve the children who were   19 being cared for at home; they worked to get these services, which are now being provided in increasing numbers. But the needs are a long way from being fully met.

Yet even now the cost in money—not to mention the cost in human terms—is much less if the child is kept at home than if he is sent to the institutions in which children are put away. And many of the retarded are living useful and independent lives, which would never have been thought possible for them.

But for us at that time, as for other parents who were unknowingly pioneering new ways for the retarded, it was a matter of going along from day to day, learning, observing, and saying, "Let's see."

There was one more frightening hurdle for our family to get over. On that traumatic day Marge got the diagnosis, the doctor told her that it was too risky for us to have any more children, that there was a fifty percent chance of our having another mongoloid child. In those days, nothing was known of the cause of mongolism. There were many theories. Now, at least, it is known to be caused by the presence of an extra chromosome, a fault of cell division. But the question "Why does it happen?" had not yet been answered.

Today, genetic counseling is available to guide parents as to the probabilities of recurrence on a scientific basis. We were flying blind. With the help of a doctor friend, we plunged into medical books and discovered that the doctor who gave us the advice was flying just as blind as we were. No evidence could be found for the fifty percent odds. Although there did seem to be some danger of recurrence, we estimated that the probabilities were with us. We took the risk and won.

Our daughter, Wynne, is now twenty-five. She started as Mark's baby sister, passed him in every way, and really helped bring him up. The fact that she had a retarded brother must have contributed at least something to the fact that she is at once delightfully playful and mature, observant, and understanding. She has a fine relationship with her two brothers.

Both Wynne and Alan, Mark's older brother, have participated, with patience and delight, in Mark's development. They have shown remarkable ingenuity in instructing and amusing him. On one occasion, when Mark was not drinking his milk, Alan called him to his place at the table and said, "I'm a service station. What kind of car are you?" Mark, quickly entering into the make-believe, said, "Pord."

Alan: "Shall I fill her up?"
Mark: "Yes."
Alan: "Ethyl or regular?"
Mark: "Reg'lar."
Alan (bringing the glass to Mark's mouth): "Here you are."
When Mark finished his glass of milk, Alan asked him, "Do you want your windshield cleaned?" Then, taking a napkin, he rubbed it briskly

across Mark's face, while Mark grinned with delight. This routine became a regular game for many weeks.

Alan and Wynne interpret and explain Mark to their friends, but never once have I heard them apologize for him or deprecate him. It is almost as if they judge the quality of other people by how they react to Mark. They think he is "great," and expect their friends to think so too.

Their affection and understanding were shown when Wynne flew to Oregon with Mark to visit Alan and his wife, Cynthea, who went to college there. Wynne described the whole reunion as "tremendous" and especially enjoyed Mark's delight in the trip.

"He was great on the plane," she recalls. "He didn't cause any trouble except that he rang the bell for the stewardess a couple of times when he didn't need anything. He was so great that I was going to send him back on the plane alone. He would have enjoyed that." But she didn't, finally, because she didn't trust others to be able to understand his speech or to know how to treat him without her there to give them clues.

Mark looks reasonably normal. He is small for his age (about five feet tall) and childlike. Anyone who is aware of these matters would recognize in him some of the characteristic symptomatic features, but they are not extreme. His almost incomprehensible speech, which few besides his family and teachers can understand, is his most obvious sign of retardation.

Mark fortunately does not notice any stares of curiosity he may attract. To imagine how one looks in the eyes of others takes a level of awareness that appears to be beyond him. Hence he is extremely direct and totally without self-consciousness.

I have seen him come into our living room, walk up to a woman he has never seen before, and kiss her in response to a genuinely friendly greeting. Since few of us are accustomed to such directness of expression—especially the expression of affection—the people to whom this has happened are deeply moved.

Like other children, Mark responds to the evaluation of others. In our family, he is accepted just as he is. Because others have always treated him as an individual, a valued individual, he feels good about himself, and, consequently, he is good to live with. In every situation between parent and child or between children, evaluations are involved—and these interact on each other. Certainly, having Mark at home has helped us be more aware and be more flexible in our evaluations.

This kind of sensitivity must have carried over into relations between the two normal children, because I cannot remember a single real fight or a really nasty incident between Alan and Wynne. It's as if their readiness to try to understand Mark extended into a general method of dealing with people. And I think Marge and I found the same thing happening to us, so that we became more understanding with Alan and Wynne than we might otherwise have been. If we had time and patience for Mark, why not for the children who were quick and able? We knew we could do serious damage to Mark by expecting too much of him and being disappointed. But how easy it is to expect too much of bright children and how quickly they feel your disappointment! Seeing Mark's slow, slow progress certainly gave us real appreciation of the marvelous perception and quick learning processes of the other two, so that all we had to do was open our eyes and our ears, and listen and enjoy them.

I don't want to sound as if we were never impatient or obtuse as   40
parents. We were, of course. But parents need to be accepted as they are, too. And I think our children—bless their hearts—were reasonably able to do so.

With Mark, it was easy to feel surprise and delight at any of his   41
accomplishments. He cannot read and will never be able to. But he can pick out on request almost any record from his huge collection—Fleetwood Mac, or the Rolling Stones, or Christmas carols—because he knows so well what each record looks like. Once we were discussing the forthcoming marriage of some friends of ours, and Mark disappeared into his playroom to bring out, a few minutes later, a record with the song "A House, a Car, and a Wedding Ring."

His love of music enables him to figure out how to operate almost any   42
record changer or hi-fi set. He never tries to force a piece of machinery because he cannot figure out how it works, as brighter people often do. And in a strange hotel room, with a TV set of unknown make, it is Mark—not Marge or I—who figures out how to turn it on and get a clear picture. As Alan once remarked: "Mark may be retarded, but he's not stupid!"

Of course, it has not all been easy—but when has easiness been the   43
test of the value of anything? To us, the difficult problems that must be faced in the future only emphasize the value of Mark as a person.

What does that future hold for Mark?   44

He will never be able to be independent; he will always have to live in   45
a protected environment. His below-50 IQ reflects the fact that he cannot cope with unfamiliar situations.

Like most parents of the retarded, we are concentrating on providing   46
financial security for Mark in the future, and fortunately we expect to be able to achieve this. Alan and his wife and Wynne have all offered to be guardians for Mark. It is wonderful to know they feel this way. But we hope that Mark can find a happy place in one of the new residence homes for the retarded.

The residence home is something new and promising and it fills an   47
enormous need. It is somewhat like a club, or a family, with a house-mother or manager. The residents share the work around the house, go out to work if they can, share in recreation and companionship. Away from their families, who may be overprotective and not aware of how much the retarded can do for themselves (are we not guilty of this, too!), they are able to live more fully as adults.

An indication that there is still much need for public education about 48
the retarded here in California is that there has been difficulty in renting
decent houses for this kind of home. Prospective neighbors have objected.
In some ways the Dark Ages are still with us; there are still fear and hostility
where the retarded are concerned.

Is Mark able to work? Perhaps. He thrives on routine and enjoys 49
things others despise, like clearing the table and loading the dishwasher. To
Mark, it's fun. It has been hard to develop in him the idea of work, which to
so many of us is "doing what you don't want to do because you have to." We
don't know yet if he could work in a restaurant loading a dishwasher. In
school, he learned jobs like sorting and stacking scrap wood and operating a
delightful machine that swoops the string around and ties up a bundle of
wood to be sold in the supermarket. That's fun, too.

He is now in a sheltered workshop where he can get the kind—the one 50
kind—of pleasure he doesn't have much chance for. That's the pleasure of
contributing something productive and useful to the outside world. He does
various kinds of assembling jobs, packaging, sorting, and simple machine
operations. He enjoys getting a paycheck and cashing it at the bank. He
cannot count, but he takes pride in reaching for the check in a restaurant
and pulling out his wallet. And when we thank him for dinner, he glows
with pleasure.

It's a strange thing to say, and I am a little startled to find myself 51
saying it, but often I feel that I wouldn't have had Mark any different.

Questions for Study and Discussion

1. The Hayakawas were warned that Mark, if kept at home, would have a
"disastrous effect" on the family. Why? What effect did Mark actually have on
his parents, his brother, and his sister?

2. What do you believe was Hayakawa's purpose in writing this essay?
Apart from what the essay says about Mark, and about Down's syndrome, what
important point does it make?

3. How did the Hayakawas' sensitivity to the uses and misuses of language affect their responses to professional advice about Mark?

4. Several times Hayakawa refers to the Dark Ages. What were the Dark
Ages? Why are they relevant to Hayakawa's account?

5. Are there any suggestions in this essay that the Hayakawas may at
times have found Mark's behavior irritating, or worse? How does this affect
your response to the essay?

Writing Topics

1. Sometimes it is wise to accept and follow expert advice. At other times
it may be necessary to disregard such advice and make one's own decision. Have

you or another member of your family ever deliberately gone against an authoritative opinion? Recount the episode, and say whether on reflection you think the decision was a good one.

2. What is now known about Down's syndrome—its cause, its treatment, its risks?

3. According to many books, magazine articles, and television documentaries, the American family is "in trouble." Do you agree? What exactly does such a statement mean to you? Is it a meaningful statement at all?

ANTHONY BRANDT

Anthony Brandt was born in Cranford, New Jersey, in 1936 and studied at Princeton and Columbia. After a brief career in business, he became a freelance writer and has contributed essays and poems to such magazines as the *Atlantic Monthly, Prairie Schooner,* and the *New York Quarterly.* He published *Reality Police: The Experience of Insanity in America* in 1975 and is presently at work on a book about the American dream, which he says will attempt to define that dream and trace its origins and development.

As a young boy, Brandt was forced to watch his beloved grandmother slowly lose her grip on reality and gradually slide into senility. Thirty years later his mother, too, has had to be consigned to a nursing home, no longer able to take care of herself. In the following memoir, first published in the *Atlantic Monthly,* Brandt describes the two cases and what they have meant to him.

My Grandmother: A Rite of Passage

Some things that happen to us can't be borne, with the paradoxical result that we carry them on our backs the rest of our lives. I have been half obsessed for almost thirty years with the death of my grandmother. I should say with her dying: with the long and terrible changes that came at the worst time for a boy of twelve and thirteen, going through his own difficult changes. It felt like and perhaps was the equivalent of a puberty rite: dark, frightening, aboriginal, an obscure emotional exchange between old and young. It has become part of my character.

I grew up in New Jersey in a suburban town where my brother still lives and practices law. One might best describe it as quiet, protected, and green; it was no preparation for death. Tall, graceful elm trees lined both sides of the street where we lived. My father's brother-in-law, a contractor, built our house; we moved into it a year after I was born. My grandmother and grandfather (my mother's parents; they were the only grandparents who mattered) lived up the street "on the hill"; it wasn't much of a hill, the terrain in that part of New Jersey being what it is, but we could ride our sleds down the street after it snowed, and that was hilly enough.

Our family lived, or seemed to a young boy to live, in very stable, very ordinary patterns. My father commuted to New York every day, taking the Jersey Central Railroad, riding in cars that had windows you could open, getting off the train in Jersey City and taking a ferry to Manhattan. He held the same job in the same company for more than thirty years. The son of Swedish immigrants, he was a funny man who could wiggle his ears without raising his eyebrows and made up the most dreadful puns. When he wasn't being funny he was quiet, the newspaper his shield and companion, or the *Saturday Evening Post*, which he brought home without fail every Wednesday evening, or *Life*, which he brought home Fridays. It was hard to break through the quiet and the humor, and after he died my mother said, as much puzzled as disturbed, that she hardly knew him at all.

She, the backbone of the family, was fierce, stern, the kind of person who can cow you with a glance. My brother and I, and my cousins, were all a little in awe of her. The ruling passion in her life was to protect her family; she lived in a set of concentric circles, sons and husband the closest, then nieces, nephews, brothers, parents, then more distant relatives, and outside that a few friends, very few. No one and nothing else existed for her; she had no interest in politics, art, history, or even the price of eggs. "Fierce" is the best word for her, or single-minded. In those days (I was born in 1936) polio was every parent's bugbear; she, to keep my brother and me away from places where the disease was supposed to be communicated, particularly swimming pools, took us every summer for the entire summer to the Jersey shore, first to her parents' cottage, later to a little cottage she and my father bought. She did that even though it meant being separated from my father for nearly three months, having nobody to talk to, having to handle my brother and me on her own. She hated it, she told us years later, but she did it: fiercely. Or there's the story of one of my cousins who got pregnant when she was sixteen or seventeen; my mother took her into our house, managed somehow to hide her condition from the neighbors, then, after the birth, arranged privately to have the child adopted by a family the doctor recommended, all this being done without consulting the proper authorities, and for the rest of her life never told a single person how she made these arrangements or where she had placed the child. She was a genuine primitive, like some tough old peasant woman. Yet her name was Grace, her nickname Bunny; if you saw through the fierceness, you understood that it was a version of love.

Her mother, my grandmother, seemed anything but fierce. One of our weekly routines was Sunday dinner at their house on the hill, some five or six houses from ours. When I was very young, before World War II, the house had a mansard roof, a barn in the back, lots of yard space, lots of rooms inside, and a cherry tree. I thought it was a palace. Actually it was rather small, and became smaller when my grandmother insisted on tearing down the mansard roof and replacing it with a conventional peaked roof; the house lost three attic rooms in the process. Sunday dinner was invariably roast beef or chicken or leg of lamb with mashed potatoes and vegetables, standard American fare but cooked by my grandparents' Polish maid, Josephine, not by my grandmother. Josephine made wonderful pies in an old cast-iron coal stove and used to let me tie her with string to the kitchen sink. My grandfather was a gentle man who smoked a pipe, had a bristly reddish moustache, and always seemed to wind up paying everybody else's debts in the family; my mother worshipped him. There were usually lots of uncles at these meals, and they were a playful bunch. I have a very early memory of two of them tossing me back and forth between them, and another of the youngest, whose name was Don, carrying me on his shoulders into the surf. I also remember my grandmother presiding at these meals. She was gray-haired and benign.

Later they sold that house. My benign grandmother, I've been told since, was in fact a restless, unsatisfied woman; changing the roof line, moving from house to house, were her ways of expressing that dissatisfaction. In the next house, I think it was, my grandfather died; my grandmother moved again, then again, and then to a house down the street, at the bottom of the hill this time, and there I got to know her better. I was nine or ten years old. She let me throw a tennis ball against the side of the house for hours at a time; the noise must have been terribly aggravating. She cooked lunch for me and used to make pancakes the size of dinner plates, and corn fritters. She also made me a whole set of yarn figures a few inches long, rolling yarn around her hand, taking the roll and tying off arms, legs, and a head, then sewing a face onto the head with black thread. I played with these and an odd assortment of hand-me-down toy soldiers for long afternoons, setting up wars, football games, contests of all kinds, and designating particular yarn figures as customary heroes. Together we played a spelling game: I'd be on the floor playing with the yarn figures, she'd be writing a letter and ask me how to spell "appreciate" (it was always that word), and I'd spell it for her while she pretended to be impressed with my spelling ability and I pretended that she hadn't asked me to spell that same word a dozen times before. I was good, too, at helping her find her glasses. 6

One scene at this house stands out. My uncle Bob came home from the war and the whole family, his young wife, other uncles, my mother and father and brother and I, gathered at the house to meet him, and he came in wearing his captain's uniform and looking to me, I swear it, like a handsome young god. In fact he was an ordinary man who spent the rest of his life selling insurance. He had been in New Guinea, a ground officer in the Air Corps, and the story I remember is of the native who came into his tent one day and took a great deal of interest in the scissors my uncle was using. The native asked in pidgin English what my uncle would require for the scissors in trade, and he jokingly said, well, how about a tentful of bananas. Sure enough, several days later two or three hundred natives came out of the jungle, huge bunches of bananas on their shoulders, and filled my uncle's tent. 7

Things went on this way for I don't know how long, maybe two years, maybe three. I don't want to describe it as idyllic. Youth has its problems. But this old woman who could never find her glasses was wonderful to me, a 8 grandmother in the true likeness of one, and I couldn't understand the changes when they came. She moved again, against all advice, this time to a big, bare apartment on the other side of town. She was gradually becoming irritable and difficult, not much fun to be around. There were no more spelling games; she stopped writing letters. Because she moved I saw her less often, and her home could no longer be a haven for me. She neglected it, too; it grew dirtier and dirtier, until my mother eventually had to do her cleaning for her.

Then she began to see things that weren't there. A branch in the back yard became a woman, I remember, who apparently wasn't fully clothed, and a man was doing something to her, something unspeakable. She developed diabetes and my mother learned to give her insulin shots, but she wouldn't stop eating candy, the worst thing for her, and the diabetes got worse. Her face began to change, to slacken, to lose its shape and character. I didn't understand these things; arteriosclerosis, hardening of the arteries, whatever the explanation, it was only words. What I noticed was that her white hair was getting thinner and harder to control, that she herself seemed to be shrinking even as I grew, that when she looked at me I wasn't sure it was me she was seeing anymore.

After a few months of this, we brought her to live with us. My mother was determined to take care of her, and certain family pressures were brought to bear too. That private man my father didn't like the idea at all, but he said nothing, which was his way. And she was put in my brother's bedroom over the garage, my brother moving in with me. It was a small house, six rooms and a basement, much too small for what we had to face.

What we had to face was a rapid deterioration into senile dementia and the rise from beneath the surface of this smiling, kindly, white-haired old lady of something truly ugly. Whenever she was awake she called for attention, calling, calling a hundred times a day. Restless as always, she picked the bedclothes off, tore holes in sheets and pillows, took off her nightclothes and sat naked talking to herself. She hallucinated more and more frequently, addressing her dead husband, a dead brother, scolding, shouting at their apparitions. She became incontinent and smeared feces on herself, the furniture, the walls. And always calling—"Bunny, where are you? Bunny, I want you!"—scolding, demanding; she could seldom remember what she wanted when my mother came. It became an important event when she fell asleep; to make sure she stayed asleep the radio was kept off, the four of us tiptoed around the house, and when I went out to close the garage door, directly under her window (it was an overhead door and had to be pulled down), I did it so slowly and carefully, half an inch at a time, that it sometimes took me a full fifteen minutes to get it down.

That my mother endured this for six months is a testimony to her strength and determination, but it was really beyond her and almost destroyed her health. My grandmother didn't often sleep through the night;

she would wake up, yell, cry, a creature of disorder, a living *memento mori*,[1] and my mother would have to tend to her. The house began to smell in spite of all my mother's efforts to keep my grandmother's room clean. My father, his peace gone, brooded in his chair behind his newspaper. My brother and I fought for *Lebensraum*,[2] each of us trying to grow up in his own way. People avoided us. My uncles were living elsewhere—Miami, Cleveland, Delaware. My grandmother's two surviving sisters, who lived about ten blocks away, never came to see her. Everybody seemed to sense that something obscene was happening, and stayed away. Terrified, I stayed away, too. I heard my grandmother constantly, but in the six months she lived with us I think I went into her room only once. That was as my mother wished it. She was a nightmare, naked and filthy without warning.

After six months, at my father's insistence, after a night nurse had been hired and left, after my mother had reached her limits and beyond, my parents started looking for a nursing home, anyplace they could put her. It became a family scandal; the two sisters were outraged that my mother would consider putting her own mother in a home, there were telephone calls back and forth between them and my uncles, but of course the sisters had never come to see her themselves, and my mother never forgave them. One of my uncles finally came from Cleveland, saw what was happening, and that day they put my grandmother in a car and drove her off to the nearest state mental hospital. They brought her back the same day; desperate as they were, they couldn't leave her in hell. At last, when it had come time to go to the shore, they found a nursing home in the middle of the Pine Barrens, miles from anywhere, and kept her there for a while. That, too, proving unsatisfactory, they put her in a small nursing home in western New Jersey, about two hours away by car. We made the drive every Sunday for the next six months, until my grandmother finally died. I always waited in the car while my mother visited her. At the funeral I refused to go into the room for one last look at the body. I was afraid of her still. The whole thing had been a subtle act of violence, a violation of the sensibilities, made all the worse by the fact that I knew it wasn't really her fault, that she was a victim of biology, of life itself. Hard knowledge for a boy just turned fourteen. She became the color of all my expectations.

Life is savage, then, and even character is insecure. Call no man happy until he be dead, said the Greek lawgiver Solon. But what would a wise man say to this? In that same town in New Jersey, that town I have long since abandoned as too flat and too good to be true, my mother, thirty years older now, weighing in at ninety-two pounds, incontinent, her

13

14

---

[1]A remembrance of death, usually a work of art with symbols of death or mortality, such as a skull.

[2]Living space, room for growth, development, or the like.

white hair wild about her head, sits strapped into a chair in another nursing home talking incoherently to her fellow patients and working her hands at the figures she thinks she sees moving around on the floor. It's enough to make stones weep to see this fierce, strong woman, who paid her dues, surely, ten times over, reduced to this.

Yet she is *cheerful*. This son comes to see her and she quite literally babbles with delight, introduces him (as her father, her husband—the connections are burnt out) to the aides, tells him endless stories that don't make any sense at all, and *shines*, shines with a clear light that must be her soul. Care and bitterness vanish in her presence. Helpless, the victim of numerous tiny strokes—"shower strokes," the doctors call them—that are gradually destroying her brain, she has somehow achieved a radiant serenity that accepts everything that happens and incorporates and transforms it.

Is there a lesson in this? Is some pattern larger than life working itself out; is this some kind of poetic justice on display, a mother balancing a grandmother, gods demonstrating reasons beyond our comprehension? It was a bitter thing to put her into that place, reeking of disinfectant, full of senile, dying old people, and I used to hate to visit her there, but as she has deteriorated she has also by sheer force of example managed to change my attitude. If she can be reconciled to all this, why can't I? It doesn't last very long, but after I've seen her, talked to her for half an hour, helped feed her, stroked her hair, I walk away amazed, as if I had been witness to a miracle.

Questions for Study and Discussion

1. What, for Brandt, is the meaning of his experiences with his grandmother and mother? How have those experiences affected his attitude toward life?

2. A "rite of passage" is a ritual associated with an important change in one's life. Brandt finds an analogy between his experiences with his grandmother and the frightening ritual in primitive societies by which the elders formally initiate the young into adulthood. How are Brandt's experiences like an initiation? How do they differ?

3. Are there any other "rites of passage" (besides Brandt's own) in the essay? Who changes, and how? What rituals, if any, are involved?

4. How much time passes between the onset of the grandmother's senility and her death? How does Brandt indicate this passage of time? As you read, did you feel that events were moving more quickly or slowly than that? Why do you suppose Brandt handles time the way he does?

5. What part of this essay struck you most forcefully? Examine the writing of that passage. Can you identify any specific elements that seem to affect the total impact of the passage?

6. Brandt writes in paragraph 13, "The whole thing had been a subtle act of violence, a violation of the sensibilities." What does he mean? You may find it helpful to look up the word *sensibility* in your desk dictionary.

Writing Topics

1. Anthony Brandt describes his grandmother as an elderly, loving, playful companion. What have your grandparents been to you? What do you think a grandparent's role should be?

2. Old age may be a time of great achievement, as the cellist Pablo Casals or the artist Georgia O'Keeffe demonstrated, or it may bring senility, as with Anthony Brandt's grandmother. What is your conception of old age? Describe the people you know, or know about, who are examples of that conception.

WILLIAM ALLEN WHITE

William Allen White (1868–1944) was born in Emporia, Kansas, and studied law at Kansas State University. In 1895 he bought the *Emporia Gazette*, which he edited until his death, earning it and himself nationwide fame for his attention to grass-roots political opinion. A liberal Republican, White opposed industrialization in favor of small-town values.

Among his works of fiction are the short story "In Our Town" (1906) and the novel *A Certain Rich Man* (1909). His other works include biographies of Woodrow Wilson (1924) and Calvin Coolidge (1925 and 1938), and two collections of his newspaper writings, *The Editor and His People* (1924) and *Forty Years on Main Street* (1937). "Mary White" is the eulogy White wrote for his daughter Mary, after her untimely death at the age of seventeen in 1921.

Mary White

The Associated Press reports carrying the news of Mary White's death 1 declared that it came as the result of a fall from a horse. How she would have hooted at that! She never fell from a horse in her life. Horses have fallen on her and with her—"I'm always trying to hold 'em in my lap," she used to say. But she was proud of few things, and one was that she could ride anything that had four legs and hair. Her death resulted not from a fall, but from a blow on the head which fractured her skull, and the blow came from the limb of an overhanging tree on the parking.

The last hour of her life was typical of its happiness. She came home 2 from a day's work at school, topped off by a hard grind with the copy on the High School Annual, and felt that a ride would refresh her. She climbed into her khakis, chattering to her mother about the work she was doing, and hurried to get her horse and be out on the dirt roads for the country air and radiant green fields of the spring. As she rode through the town on an easy gallop she kept waving at passers-by. She knew everyone in town. For a decade the little figure with the long pigtail and the red hair ribbon has been familiar on the streets of Emporia, and she got in the way of speaking to those who nodded at her. She passed the Kerrs, walking the horse, in front of the Normal Library, and waved at them; passed another friend a few hundred feet further on, and waved at her. The horse was walking and as she turned into North Merchant Street she took off her cowboy hat, and the horse swung into a lope. She passed the Tripletts and waved her cowboy hat at them, still moving gaily north on Merchant Street. A Gazette carrier passed—a High School boy friend—and she waved at him, but with her bridle hand; the horse veered quickly; plunged into the parking where the low-hanging limb faced her, and, while she still looked back waving, the blow came. But she did not fall from the horse; she slipped off, dazed a bit, staggered and fell in a faint. She never quite recovered consciousness.

But she did not fall from the horse, neither was she riding fast. A year 3 or so ago she used to go like the wind. But that habit was broken, and she used the horse to get into the open to get fresh, hard exercise, and to work off a certain surplus energy that welled up in her and needed a physical outlet. That need has been in her heart for years. It was back of the impulse that kept the dauntless, little brown-clad figure on the streets and country roads of this community and built into a strong, muscular body what had been a frail and sickly frame during the first years of her life. But the riding gave her more than a body. It released a gay and hardy soul. She was the happiest thing in the world. And she was happy because she was enlarging her horizon. She came to know all sorts and conditions of men; Charley O'Brien, the traffic cop, was one of her best friends. W. L. Holtz, the Latin teacher, was another. Tom O'Connor, farmer-politician, and Rev. J. H. J. Rice, preacher and police judge, and Frank Beach, music master, were her special friends, and all the girls, black and white, above the track and below the track, in Pepville and Stringtown, were among her acquaintances. And she brought home riotous stories of her adventures. She loved to rollick; persiflage was her natural expression at home. Her humor was a continual bubble of joy. She seemed to think in hyperbole and metaphor. She was mischievous without malice, as full of faults as an old shoe. No angel was Mary White, but an easy girl to live with, for she never nursed a grouch five minutes in her life.

With all her eagerness for the out-of-doors she loved books. On her 4 table when she left her room were a book by Conrad, one by Galsworthy, *Creative Chemistry* by E. E. Slossom, and a Kipling book. She read Mark Twain, Dickens and Kipling before she was ten—all of their writings. Wells and Arnold Bennett particularly amused and diverted her. She was entered as a student in Wellesley in 1922; was assistant editor of the High School Annual this year, and in line for election to the editorship of the Annual next year. She was a member of the executive committee of the High School YWCA.

Within the last two years she had begun to be moved by an ambition 5 to draw. She began as most children do by scribbling in her school books, funny pictures. She bought cartoon magazines and took a course—rather casually, naturally, for she was, after all, a child with no strong purpose— and this year she tasted the first fruits of success by having her pictures accepted by the High School Annual. But the thrill of delight she got when Mr. Ecord, of the Normal Annual, asked her to do the cartooning for that book this spring was too beautiful for words. She fell to her work with all her enthusiastic heart. Her drawings were accepted, and her pride—always repressed by a lively sense of the ridiculousness of the figure she was cutting—was a really gorgeous thing to see. No successful artist ever drank a deeper draught of satisfaction than she took from the little fame her work was getting among her school-fellows. In her glory, she almost forgot her horse—but never her car.

For she used the car as a jitney bus. It was her social life. She never had a "party" in all her nearly seventeen years—wouldn't have one; but she never drove a block in the car in her life that she didn't begin to fill the car with pickups! Everybody rode with Mary White—white and black, old and young, rich and poor, men and women. She liked nothing better than to fill the car full of long-legged High School boys and an occasional girl, and parade the town. She never had a "date," nor went to a dance, except once with her brother, Bill, and the "boy proposition" didn't interest her—yet. But young people—great spring-breaking, varnish-cracking, fender-bending, door-sagging, carloads of "kids" gave her great pleasure. Her zests were keen. But the most fun she ever had in her life was acting as chairman of the committee that got up the big turkey dinner for the poor folks at the county home; scores of pies, gallons of slaw; jam, cakes, preserves, oranges and a wilderness of turkey were loaded in the car and taken to the county home. And, being of a practical turn of mind, she risked her own Christmas dinner by staying to see that the poor folks actually got it all. Not that she was a cynic; she disliked to tempt folks. While there she found a blind colored uncle, very old, who could do nothing but make rag rugs, and she rustled up from her school friends rags enough to keep him busy for a season. The last engagement she tried to make was to take the guests at the county home out for a car ride. And the last endeavor of her life was to try to get a rest room for colored girls in the High School. She found one girl reading in the toilet, because there was no better place for a colored girl to loaf, and it inflamed her sense of injustice and she became a nagging harpy to those who, she thought, could remedy the evil. The poor she had always with her, and was glad of it. She hungered and thirsted for righteousness; and was the most impious creature in the world. She joined the Congregational Church without consulting her parents; not particularly for her soul's good. She never had a thrill of piety in her life, and would have hooted at a "testimony." But even as a little child she felt the church was an agency for helping people to more of life's abundance, and she wanted to help. She never wanted help for herself. Clothes meant little to her. It was a fight to get a new rig on her; but eventually a harder fight to get it off. She never wore a jewel and had no ring but her High School class ring, and never asked for anything but a wrist watch. She refused to have her hair up;

though she was nearly seventeen. "Mother," she protested, "you don't know how much I get by with, in my braided pigtails, that I could not with my hair up." Above every other passion of her life was her passion not to grow up, to be a child. The tom-boy in her, which was big, seemed to loathe to be put away forever in skirts. She was a Peter Pan, who refused to grow up.

Her funeral yesterday at the Congregational Church was as she would   7
have wished it; no singing, no flowers save the big bunch of red roses from her brother Bill's Harvard classmen—Heavens, how proud that would have made her! And the red roses from the Gazette force—in vases at her head and feet. A short prayer, Paul's beautiful essay on "Love" from the Thirteenth Chapter of First Corinthians, some remarks about her democratic spirit by her friend, John H. J. Rice, pastor and police judge, which she would have deprecated if she could, a prayer sent down for her by her friend, Carl Nau, and opening the service the slow, poignant movement from Beethoven's Moonlight Sonata, which she loved, and closing the service a cutting from the joyously melancholy first movement of Tschaikowski's Pathetic Symphony, which she liked to hear in certain moods on the phonograph; then the Lord's Prayer by her friends in the High School.

That was all.   8

For her pall-bearers only her friends were chosen: her Latin teacher,   9
W. L. Holtz; her High School principal, Rice Brown; her doctor, Frank Foncannon; her friend, W. W. Finney; her pal at the Gazette office, Walter Hughes; and her brother, Bill. It would have made her smile to know that her friend, Charley O'Brien, the traffic cop, had been transferred from Sixth and Commercial to the corner near the church to direct her friends who came to bid her good-by.

A rift in the clouds on a gray day threw a shaft of sunlight upon her   10
coffin as her nervous, energetic little body sank to its last sleep. But the soul of her, the glowing, gorgeous, fervent soul of her, surely was flaming in eager joy upon some other dawn.

Questions for Study and Discussion

1. White uses the third person to tell of his daughter's last day alive. To some this might seem impersonal or inappropriate for a father. Why do you think he uses this point of view? What is gained or lost by White's use of the third person in his obituary for his daughter?

2. White says happiness described his daughter Mary's life. What kinds of examples does he include to give the reader an accurate picture of his daughter's life? How does he use verbs and adjectives to enhance the description?

3. White says the last hour of his daughter's life was typical of her whole life. In one or two sentences, how would you describe her life?

4. White never expresses his exact feelings for Mary, yet the reader is left with no doubts as to his love for her. How does White manage to convey to the reader his attitude toward his daughter without stating it directly?

5. In reading about Mary, we also learn about her surroundings. Paying attention to the details White includes in his description of Mary's life, what do you learn about the rest of her family, her neighbors, and the period when this piece was written?

6. The poignancy of an obituary such as White's lies in its capturing either the uniqueness or the universality of the life of the young person who has died. In your opinion, does White describe a girl who is similar to or very different from other girls her age? Explain.

Writing Topics

1. Try writing a description of someone you care very much about without expressing your feelings directly. Use examples, active verbs, and concrete nouns to make the person come alive for the reader.

2. Think about the aspects of your life—the activities, the friends, and the attitudes—that best describe you. Then in an essay try to convey to the reader the essential you.

EUDORA WELTY

The American South has brought forth more than its share of fine writers, and Eudora Welty holds an honored place among them. She was born in 1909 in Jackson, Mississippi, and that is where she has lived for most of her life. Her father was president of an insurance company, and she was able to go away to the University of Wisconsin and then to take a postgraduate course in advertising at Columbia University's business school. During the Great Depression, jobs in advertising were scarce, so Welty returned home to Jackson and began to write. Her published works include many short stories, now available as her *Collected Stories* (1980), five novels, and a collection of her essays, *The Eye of the Story* (1975). Welty's *One Writer's Beginnings* (1987) recounts the events in childhood that influenced her development as a writer. In "A Worn Path" we meet one of Welty's memorable characters, old Phoenix Jackson, on her way to town on a vital errand.

A Worn Path

It was December—a bright frozen day in the early morning. Far out in the country there was an old Negro woman with her head tied in a red rag, coming along a path through the pinewoods. Her name was Phoenix Jackson. She was very old and small and she walked slowly in the dark pine shadows, moving a little from side to side in her steps, with the balanced heaviness and lightness of a pendulum in a grandfather clock. She carried a thin, small cane made from an umbrella, and with this she kept tapping the frozen earth in front of her. This made a grave and persistent noise in the still air, that seemed meditative like the chirping of a solitary little bird. 1

She wore a dark striped dress reaching down to her shoe tops, and an equally long apron of bleached sugar sacks, with a full pocket: all near and tidy, but every time she took a step she might have fallen over her shoelaces, which dragged from her unlaced shoes. She looked straight ahead. Her eyes were blue with age. Her skin had a pattern all its own of numberless branching wrinkles and as though a whole little tree stood in the middle of her forehead, but a golden color ran underneath, and the two knobs of her cheeks were illumined by a yellow burning under the dark. Under the red rag her hair came down on her neck in the frailest of ringlets, still black, and with an odor like copper. 2

Now and then there was a quivering in the thicket. Old Phoenix said, 3
"Out of my way, all you foxes, owls, beetles, jack rabbits, coons and wild
animals! . . . Keep out from under these feet, little bob-whites. . . . Keep the
big wild hogs out of my path. Don't let none of those come running my
direction. I got a long way." Under her small black-freckled hand her cane,
limber as a buggy whip, would switch at the brush as if to rouse up any
hiding things.

On she went. The woods were deep and still. The sun made the pine 4
needles almost too bright to look at, up where the wind rocked. The cones
dropped as light as feathers. Down in the hollow was the mourning dove—it
was not too late for him.

The path ran up a hill. "Seem like there is chains about my feet, time I 5
get this far," she said, in the voice of argument old people keep to use with
themselves. "Something always take a hold of me on this hill—pleads I
should stay."

After she got to the top she turned and gave a full, severe look behind 6
her where she had come. "Up through pines," she said at length. "Now
down through oaks."

Her eyes opened their widest, and she started down gently. But before 7
she got to the bottom of the hill a bush caught her dress.

Her fingers were busy and intent, but her skirts were full and long, 8
so that before she could pull them free in one place they were caught
in another. It was not possible to allow the dress to tear. "I in the
thorny bush," she said. "Thorns, you doing your appointed work. Never
want to let folks pass, no sir. Old eyes thought you was a pretty little green
bush."

Finally, trembling all over, she stood free, and after a moment dared to 9
stoop for her cane.

"Sun so high!" she cried, leaning back and looking, while the thick 10
tears went over her eyes. "The time getting all gone here."

At the foot of this hill was a place where a log was laid across the 11
creek.

"Now comes the trial," said Phoenix. 12

Putting her right foot out, she mounted the log and shut her eyes. 13
Lifting her skirt, leveling her cane fiercely before her, like a festival figure in
some parade, she began to march across. Then she opened her eyes and she
was safe on the other side.

"I wasn't as old as I thought," she said. 14

But she sat down to rest. She spread her skirts on the bank around her 15
and folded her hands over her knees. Upon above her was a tree in a pearly
cloud of mistletoe. She did not dare to close her eyes, and when a little boy
brought her a plate with a slice of marble-cake on it she spoke to him. "That
would be acceptable," she said. But when she went to take it there was just
her own hand in the air.

So she left that tree, and had to go through a barbed-wire fence. There
she had to creep and crawl, spreading her knees and stretching her fingers
like a baby trying to climb the steps. But she talked loudly to herself: she
could not let her dress be torn now, so late in the day, and she could not pay
for having her arm or her leg sawed off if she got caught fast where she was. 16

At last she was safe through the fence and risen up out in the clearing.
Big dead trees, like black men with one arm, were standing in the purple
stalks of the withered cotton field. There sat a buzzard. 17

"Who you watching?" 18

In the furrow she made her way along. 19

"Glad this not the season for bulls," she said, looking sideways, "and
the good Lord made his snakes to curl up and sleep in the winter. A
pleasure I don't see no two-headed snake coming around that tree, where it
come once. It took a while to get by him, back in the summer." 20

She passed through the old cotton and went into a field of dead corn.
It whispered and shook and was taller than her head. "Through the maze
now," she said, for there was no path. 21

Then there was something tall, black, and skinny there, moving
before her. 22

At first she took it for a man. It could have been a man dancing in the
field. But she stood still and listened, and it did not make a sound. It was as
silent as a ghost. 23

"Ghost," she said sharply, "who be you the ghost of? For I have heard
of nary death close by." 24

But there was no answer—only the ragged dancing in the wind. 25

She shut her eyes, reached out her hand, and touched a sleeve. She
found a coat and inside that an emptiness, cold as ice. 26

"You scarecrow," she said. Her face lighted. "I ought to be shut up for
good," she said with laughter. "My senses is gone. I too old. I the oldest
people I ever know. Dance, old scarecrow," she said, "while I dancing with
you." 27

She kicked her foot over the furrow, and with mouth drawn down,
shook her head once or twice in a little strutting way. Some husks blew
down and whirled in streamers about her skirts. 28

Then she went on, parting her way from side to side with the cane,
through the whispering field. At last she came to the end, to a wagon track
where the silver grass blew between the red ruts. The quail were walking
around like pullets, seeming all dainty and unseen. 29

"Walk pretty," she said. "This the easy place. This the easy going." 30

She followed the track, swaying through the quiet bare fields, through
the little strings of trees silver in their dead leaves, past cabins silver from
weather, with the doors and windows boarded shut, all like old women
under a spell sitting there. "I walking in their sleep," she said, nodding her
head vigorously. 31

In a ravine she went where a spring was silently flowing through a 32 hollow log. Old Phoenix bent and drank. "Sweetgum makes the water sweet," she said, and drank more. "Nobody know who made this well, for it was here when I was born."

The track crossed a swampy part where the moss hung as white as lace 33 from every limb. "Sleep on, alligators, and blow your bubbles." Then the track went into the road.

Deep, deep the road went down between the high green-colored 34 banks. Overhead the live-oaks met, and it was as dark as a cave.

A black dog with a lolling tongue came up out of the weeds by the 35 ditch. She was meditating, and not ready, and when he came at her she only hit him a little with her cane. Over she went in the ditch, like a little puff of milkweed.

Down there, her senses drifted away. A dream visited her, and she 36 reached her hand up, but nothing reached down and gave her a pull. So she lay there and presently went to talking. "Old woman," she said to herself, "that black dog came up out of the weeds to stall you off, and now there he sitting on his fine tail, smiling at you."

A white man finally came along and found her—a hunter, a young 37 man, with his dog on a chain.

"Well, Granny!" he laughed. "What are you doing there?" 38

"Lying on my back like a June-bug waiting to be turned over, mister," 39 she said, reaching up her hand.

He lifted her up, gave her a swing in the air, and set her down. 40 "Anything broken, Granny?"

"No sir, them old dead weeds is springy enough," said Phoenix, when 41 she had got her breath. "I thank you for your trouble."

"Where do you live, Granny?" he asked, while the two dogs were 42 growling at each other.

"Away back yonder, sir, behind the ridge. You can't even see it from 43 here."

"On your way home?" 44

"No sir, I going to town." 45

"Why, that's too far! That's as far as I walked when I come out myself, 46 and I get something for my trouble." He patted the stuffed bag he carried, and there hung down a little closed claw. It was one of the bob-whites, with its beak hooked bitterly to show it was dead. "Now you go on home, Granny!"

"I bound to go to town, mister," said Phoenix. "The time come 47 around."

He gave another laugh, filling the whole landscape. "I know you odd 48 colored people! Wouldn't miss going to town to see Santa Claus!"

But something held old Phoenix very still. The deep lines in her face 49 went into a fierce and different radiation. Without warning, she had seen with her own eyes a flashing nickel fall out of the man's pocket onto the ground.

"How old are you, Granny?" he was saying.   50

"There is no telling, mister," she said, "no telling."

Then she gave a little cry and clapped her hands and said, "Git on away   52 from here, dog! Look! Look at that dog!" She laughed as if in admiration. "He ain't scared of nobody. He a big black dog." She whispered, "Sic him!"

"Watch me get rid of that cur," said the man. "Sic him, Pete! Sic him!"   53

Phoenix heard the dogs fighting, and heard the man running and   54 throwing sticks. She even heard a gunshot. But she was slowly bending forward by that time, further and further forward, the lids stretched down over her eyes, as if she were doing this in her sleep. Her chin was lowered almost to her knees. The yellow palm of her hand came out from the fold of her apron. Her fingers slid down and along the ground under the piece of money with the grace and care they would have in lifting an egg from under a setting hen. Then she slowly straightened up, she stood erect, and the nickel was in her apron pocket. A bird flew by. Her lips moved. "God watching me the whole time. I come to stealing."

The man came back, and his own dog panted about them. "Well I   55 scared him off that time," he said, and then he laughed and lifted his gun and pointed it at Phoenix.

She stood straight and faced him.   56

"Doesn't the gun scare you?" he said, still pointing it.   57

"No, sir, I seen plenty go off closer by, in my day, and for less than   58 what I done," she said, holding utterly still.

He smiled, and shouldered the gun. "Well, Granny," he said, "you   59 must be a hundred years old, and scared of nothing. I'd give you a dime if I had any money with me. But you take my advice and stay home, and nothing will happen to you."

"I bound to go on my way, mister," said Phoenix. She inclined her   60 head in the red rag. Then they went in different directions, but she could hear the gun shooting again and again over the hill.

She walked on. The shadows hung from the oak trees to the road like   61 curtains. Then she smelled wood-smoke, and smelled the river, and she saw a steeple and the cabins on their steep steps. Dozens of little black children whirled around her. There ahead was Natchez shining. Bells were ringing. She walked on.

In the paved city it was Christmas time. There were red and green   62 electric lights strung and crisscrossed everywhere, and all turned on in the daytime. Old Phoenix would have been lost if she had not distrusted her eyesight and depended on her feet to know where to take her.

She paused quietly on the sidewalk where people were passing by. A   63 lady came along in the crowd, carrying an armful of red, green, and silver-wrapped presents; she gave off perfume like the red roses in hot summer, and Phoenix stopped her.

"Please, missy, will you lace up my shoe?" She held up her foot. 64

"What do you want, Grandma?" 65

"See my shoe," said Phoenix. "Do all right for out in the country, but 66 wouldn't look right to go in a big building."

"Stand still then, Grandma," said the lady. She put her packages 67 down on the sidewalk beside her and laced and tied both shoes tightly.

"Can't lace 'em with a cane," said Phoenix. "Thank you, missy. I 68 doesn't mind asking a nice lady to tie up my shoe, when I gets out on the street."

Moving slowly and from side to side, she went into the big building, 69 and into a tower of steps, where she walked up and around and around until her feet knew to stop.

She entered a door, and there she saw nailed up on the wall the 70 document that had been stamped with the gold seal and framed in the gold frame, which matched the dream that was hung up in her head.

"Here I be," she said. There was a fixed and ceremonial stiffness over 71 her body.

"A charity case, I suppose," said an attendant who sat at the desk 72 before her.

But Phoenix only looked above her head. There was sweat on her face, 73 the wrinkles in her skin shone like a bright net.

"Speak up, Grandma," the woman said. "What's your name? We must 74 have your history, you know. Have you been here before? What seems to be the trouble with you?"

Old Phoenix only gave a twitch to her face as if a fly were bothering 75 her.

"Are you deaf?" cried the attendant. 76

But then the nurse came in. 77

"Oh, that's just old Aunt Phoenix," she said. "She doesn't come for 78 herself—she has a little grandson. She makes these trips just as regular as clockwork. She lives away back off the Old Natchez Trace." She bent down. "Well, Aunt Phoenix, why don't you just take a seat? We won't keep you standing after your long trip." She pointed.

The old woman sat down, bolt upright in the chair. 79

"Now, how is the boy?" asked the nurse. 80

Old Phoenix did not speak. 81

"I said, how is the boy?" 82

But Phoenix only waited and stared ahead, her face very solemn and 83 withdrawn into rigidity.

"Is his throat any better?" asked the nurse. "Aunt Phoenix, don't you 84 hear me? Is your grandson's throat any better since the last time you came for the medicine?"

With her hands on her knees, the old woman waited, silent, erect, and motionless, just as if she were in armor. 85

"You mustn't take up our time this way, Aunt Phoenix," the nurse said. "Tell us quickly about your grandson, and get it over. He isn't dead, is he?" 86

At last there came a flicker and then a flame of comprehension across her face, and she spoke. 87

"My grandson. It was my memory had left me. There I sat and forgot why I made my long trip." 88

"Forgot?" The nurse frowned. "After you came so far?" 89

Then Phoenix was like an old woman begging a dignified forgiveness for waking up frightened in the night. "I never did go to school, I was too old at the Surrender," she said in a soft voice. "I'm an old woman without an education. It was my memory fail me. My little grandson, he is just the same, and I forgot it in the coming." 90

"Throat never heals, does it?" said the nurse, speaking in a loud, sure voice to old Phoenix. By now she had a card with something written on it, a little list. "Yes. Swallowed lye. When was it?—January—two-three years ago—" 91

Phoenix spoke unasked now. "No, missy, he not dead, he just the same. Every little while his throat begin to close up again, and he not able to swallow. He not get his breath. He not able to help himself. So the time come around, and I go on another trip for the soothing medicine." 92

"All right. The doctor said as long as you came to get it, you could have it," said the nurse. "But it's an obstinate case." 93

"My little grandson, he sit up there in the house all wrapped up, waiting by himself," Phoenix went on. "We is the only two left in the world. He suffer and it don't seem to put him back at all. He got a sweet look. He going to last. He wear a little patch quilt and peep out holding his mouth open like a little bird. I remembers so plain now. I not going to forget him again, no, the whole enduring time. I could tell him from all the others in creation." 94

"All right." The nurse was trying to hush her now. She brought her bottle of medicine. "Charity," she said, making a check mark in a book. 95

Old Phoenix held the bottle close to her eyes, and then carefully put it into her pocket. 96

"I thank you," she said. 97

"It's Christmas time, Grandma," said the attendant. "Could I give you a few pennies out of my purse?" 98

"Five pennies is a nickel," said Phoenix stiffly. 99

"Here's a nickel," said the attendant. 100

Phoenix rose carefully and held out her hand. She received the nickel   101
and then fished the other nickel out of her pocket and laid it beside the new
one. She stared at her palm closely, with her head on one side.

Then she gave a tap with her cane on the floor.   102

"This is what come to me to do," she said. "I going to the store and   103
buy my child a little windmill they sells, made out of paper. He going to find
it hard to believe there such a thing in the world. I'll march myself back
where he waiting, holding it straight up in this hand."

She lifted her free hand, gave a little nod, turned around, and walked   104
out of the doctor's office. Then her slow step began on the stairs, going
down.

Questions for Study and Discussion

1. Why is Old Phoenix going to Natchez? Who does she tell, and why?

2. What obstacles does Phoenix meet on the way? How, emotionally, does
she cope with those obstacles? What does this reveal about her character?

3. How does Phoenix get the money she plans to spend at the end of the
story? What will she be bringing home to her grandson? What is the significance
of this gift?

4. What is the nature of the relationship between Phoenix and her
grandson?

5. In paragraph 90 Phoenix says, "I never did go to school, I was too old
at the Surrender." What does this mean?

6. Welty uses many figurative comparisons in this story—for example,
"Over she went in the ditch, like a little puff of milkweed." Collect some other
examples of metaphor and simile, and explain what each means. Do all of them
have something in common? If so, what significance do you find in that?

7. What does the title of the story mean to you? Does it have any
metaphorical meaning? Explain.

8. After reading this story, many people have asked: "Is Phoenix Jackson's grandson really dead?" Did this question occur to you? Is an answer to this
question important to an understanding of Welty's story? Explain.

Writing Topics

1. Write a character sketch of an old person you know well. If you like,
you can organize your sketch by showing your subject engaged in some typical
activity.

2. Family obligations can be tiresome chores, or willing acts of love, or
even both. What family obligations do you have—or do others have toward
you? How do you feel about these obligations? Write an essay in which you
explain your thoughts on these obligations.

3. Though brought up in a time and place where racial discrimination and hatred were widespread, Eudora Welty writes of Phoenix Jackson with understanding and love. Is this typical of her? Read some of her other works—perhaps the story "Powerhouse" or the essay "A Pageant of Birds"—and then write an essay in which you assess the image of African-Americans in her work.

The Troubled
American Family

MARGARET MEAD

With the publication of *Coming of Age in Samoa* in 1928, Margaret Mead
(1901–1978) began a career that would establish her as one of the world's leading
cultural anthropologists. During her lifetime she studied in various fields—family
structures, primitive societies, ecology, cultural traditions, and mental health. She
was curator of ethnology at the American Museum of Natural History and director
of Columbia University's Research on Contemporary Cultures. After she retired,
she became a contributing editor for *Redbook*, where the following article appeared
in 1977. In this essay she examines the problems besetting the contemporary
American family. Despite the grim picture she paints, Mead remains essentially
optimistic. She believes that we can help each other make the family viable for
ourselves and future generations.

Can the American Family Survive?

All over the United States, families are in trouble. It is true that there 1
are many contented homes where parents are living in harmony and raising
their children responsibly, and with enjoyment in which the children share.
Two out of three American households are homes in which a wife and
husband live together, and almost seven out of ten children are born to
parents living together in their first marriage.

However, though reassuring, these figures are deceptive. A great many 2
of the married couples have already lived through one divorce. And a very
large number of the children in families still intact will have to face the

141

disruption of their parents' marriage in the future. The numbers increase every year.

It is also true that the hazards are much greater for some families than for others. Very young couples, the poorly educated, those with few skills and a low income, Blacks and members of other minority groups—particularly if they live in big cities—all these are in danger of becoming high-risk families for whose children a family breakdown is disastrous.   3

But no group, whatever its status and resources, is exempt. This in itself poses a threat to all families, especially those with young children. For how can children feel secure when their friends in other families so like their own are conspicuously lost and unhappy? In one way or another we all are drawn into the orbit of families in trouble.   4

Surely it is time for us to look squarely at the problems that beset families and to ask what must be done to make family life more viable, not only for ourselves now but also in prospect for all the children growing up who will have to take responsibility for the next generation.   5

The Grim Picture

There are those today—as at various times in the past—who doubt that the family can survive, and some who believe it should not survive. Indeed, the contemporary picture is grim enough.   6

- *Many young marriages entered into with love and high hopes collapse before the first baby is weaned. The very young parents, on whom the whole burden of survival rests, cannot make it entirely on their own, and they give up.*   7

- *Families that include several children break up and the children are uprooted from the only security they have known. Some children of divorce, perhaps the majority, will grow up as stepchildren in homes that, however loving, they no longer dare to trust fully. Many—far too many—will grow up in single-parent homes. Still others will be moved, rootless as rolling stones, from foster family to foster family until at last they begin a rootless life on their own.*   8

- *In some states a family with a male breadwinner cannot obtain welfare, and some fathers, unable to provide adequately for their children, desert them so that the mothers can apply for public assistance. And growing numbers of mothers, fearful of being deserted, are leaving their young families while, as they hope and believe, they still have a chance to make a different life for themselves.*   9

- *As divorce figures have soared—today the proportion of those currently divorced is more than half again as high as in 1960, and it is predicted that one in three young women in this generation will be divorced—Americans have accepted as a truism the myth that from the mistakes made in their first marriage women and men learn how to do it better the second time around.*   10

Sometimes it does work. But a large proportion of those who have resorted to divorce once choose this as the easier solution again and again. Easily dashed hopes become more easily dashed.

- *At the same time, many working parents, both of whom are trying hard to care for and keep together the family they have chosen to bring into being, find that there is no place at all where their children can be cared for safely and gently and responsibly during the long hours of their own necessary absence at their jobs. They have no relatives nearby and there is neither a daycare center nor afterschool care for their active youngsters. Whatever solution they find, their children are likely to suffer.* 11

The Bitter Consequences

The consequences, direct and indirect, are clear. Thousands of young   12
couples are living together in some arrangement and are wholly dependent on their private, personal commitment to each other for the survival of their relationship. In the years from 1970 to 1975 the number of single persons in the 25-to-34-year age group has increased by half. Some couples living together have repudiated marriage as a binding social relationship and have rejected the family as an institution. Others are delaying marriage because they are not sure of themselves or each other; still others are simply responding to what they have experienced of troubled family life and the effects of divorce.

At the end of the life span there are the ever-growing numbers of   13
women and men, especially women, who have outlived their slender family relationships. They have nowhere to turn, no one to depend on but strangers in public institutions. Unwittingly we have provided the kind of assistance that, particularly in cities, almost guarantees such isolated and helpless old people will become the prey of social vultures.

And at all stages of their adult life, demands are made increasingly on   14
women to earn their living in the working world. Although we prefer to interpret this as an expression of women's wish to fulfill themselves, to have the rights that go with money earned and to be valued as persons, the majority of women who work outside their homes do so because they must. It is striking that ever since the 1950s a larger proportion of married women with children than of married but childless women have entered the labor force. According to recent estimates some 14 million women with children—four out of ten mothers of children under six years of age and more than half of all mothers of school-age children—are working, the great majority of them in full-time jobs.

A large proportion of these working women are the sole support of   15
their families. Some 10 million children—more than one in six—are living with only one parent, generally with the mother. This number has doubled since 1960.

The majority of these women and their children live below the   16
poverty level, the level at which the most minimal needs can be met. Too
often the women, particularly the younger ones, having little education and
few skills, are at the bottom of the paid work force. Though they and their
children are in great need, they are among those least able to demand and
obtain what they require merely to survive decently, in good health and
with some hope for the future.

But the consequences of family trouble are most desperate as they   17
affect children. Every year, all over the country, over 1 million adolescents,
nowadays principally girls, run away from home because they have found
life with their families insupportable. Some do not run very far and in the
end a great many come home again, but by no means all of them. And we
hear about only a handful whose terrifying experiences or whose death
happens to come into public view.

In homes where there is no one to watch over them, elementary   18
school children are discovering the obliterating effects of alcohol; a growing
number have become hard-case alcoholics in their early teens. Other young
girls and boys, wanderers in the streets, have become the victims of corruption and sordid sex. The youngsters who vent their rage and desperation on
others by means of violent crimes are no less social victims than are the girls
and boys who are mindlessly corrupted by the adults who prey on them.

Perhaps the most alarming symptom of all is the vast increase in child   19
abuse, which, although it goes virtually unreported in some groups, is not
limited to any one group in our population. What seems to be happening is
that frantic mothers and fathers, stepparents or the temporary mates of
parents turn on the children they do not know how to care for, and beat
them—often in a desperate, inarticulate hope that someone will hear their
cries and somehow bring help. We know this, but although many organizations have been set up to help these children and their parents, many adults
do not know what is needed or how to ask for assistance or whom they may
expect a response from.

And finally there are the children who end their own lives in absolute   20
despair. Suicide is now third among the causes of death for youngsters 15 to
19 years old.

What Has Gone Wrong?

In recent years, various explanations have been suggested for the   21
breakdown of family life.

Blame has been placed on the vast movement of Americans from rural   22
areas and small towns to the big cities and on the continual, restless surge of
people from one part of the country to another, so that millions of families,
living in the midst of strangers, lack any continuity in their life-style and
any real support for their values and expectations.

Others have emphasized the effects of unemployment and under- 23
employment among Blacks and other minority groups, which make their
families peculiarly vulnerable in life crises that are exacerbated by economic
uncertainty. This is particularly the case where the policies of welfare
agencies penalize the family that is poor but intact in favor of the single-
parent family.

There is also the generation gap, particularly acute today, when 24
parents and their adolescent children experience the world in such very
different ways. The world in which the parents grew up is vanishing,
unknown to their children except by hearsay. The world into which adolescents are growing is in many ways unknown to both generations—and
neither can help the other very much to understand it.

Then there is our obvious failure to provide for the children and 25
young people whom we do not succeed in educating, who are in deep
trouble and who may be totally abandoned. We have not come to grips with
the problems of hard drugs. We allow the courts that deal with juveniles to
become so overloaded that little of the social protection they were intended
to provide is possible. We consistently underfund and understaff the institutions into which we cram children in need of re-education and physical and
psychological rehabilitation, as if all that concerned us was to get them—
and keep them—out of our sight.

Other kinds of explanations also have been offered. 26

There are many people who, knowing little about child development, 27
have placed the principal blame on what they call "permissiveness"—on the
relaxing of parental discipline to include the child as a small partner in the
process of growing up. Those people say that children are "spoiled," that
they lack "respect" for their parents or that they have not learned to obey
the religious prohibitions that were taught to their parents, and that all the
troubles plaguing family life have followed.

Women's Liberation, too, has come in for a share of the blame. It is 28
said that in seeking self-fulfillment, women are neglecting their homes and
children and are undermining men's authority and men's sense of responsibility. The collapse of the family is seen as the inevitable consequence.

Those who attribute the difficulties of troubled families to any single 29
cause, whether or not it is related to reality, also tend to advocate panaceas,
each of which—they say—should restore stability to the traditional family
or, alternatively, supplant the family. Universal day care from birth, communal living, group marriage, contract marriage and open marriage all have
their advocates.

Each such proposal fastens on some trouble point in the modern 30
family—the lack of adequate facilities to care for the children of working
mothers, for example, or marital infidelity, which, it is argued, would be
eliminated by being institutionalized. Others, realizing the disastrous effects
of poverty on family life, have advocated bringing the income of every
family up to a level at which decent living is possible. Certainly this must be

one of our immediate aims. But it is wholly unrealistic to suppose that all else that has gone wrong will automatically right itself if the one—but very complex—problem of poverty is eliminated.

A Look at Alternatives

Is there, in fact, any viable alternative to the family as a setting in which children can be successfully reared to become capable and responsible adults, relating to one another and a new generation of children as well as to the world around them? Or should we aim at some wholly new social invention? 31

Revolutionaries have occasionally attempted to abolish the family, or at least to limit its strength by such measures as arranging for marriages without binding force or for rearing children in different kinds of collectives. But as far as we know, in the long run such efforts have never worked out satisfactorily. 32

The Soviet Union, for instance, long ago turned away from the flexible, impermanent unions and collective child-care ideals of the early revolutionary days and now heavily emphasizes the values of a stable family life. In Israel the kibbutz, with its children's house and carefully planned, limited contact between parents and children, is losing out to social forms in which the family is both stronger and more closely knit. In Scandinavian countries, where the standards of child care are very high, serious efforts have been made to provide a viable situation for unmarried mothers and the children they have chosen to bring up alone; but there are disturbing indices of trouble, expressed, for example, in widespread alcoholism and a high rate of suicide. 33

Experience suggests that we would do better to look in other directions. Two approaches may be rewarding. First we can look at other kinds of societies—primitive societies, peasant societies and traditional complex but unindustrialized societies (prerevolutionary China, for example)—to discover whether there are ways in which families are organized that occur in all societies. This can give us some idea of needs that must be satisfied for families to survive and prosper. 34

Second we can ask whether the problems that are besetting American families are unique or are instead characteristic of families wherever modern industrialization, a sophisticated technology and urban living are drawing people into a new kind of civilization. Placing our own difficulties within a wider context can perhaps help us to assess what our priorities must be as we attempt to develop new forms of stability in keeping with contemporary expressions of human needs. 35

Looking at human behavior with all that we know—and can infer—about the life of our human species from earliest times, we have to realize 36 that the family, as an association between a man and a woman and the children she bears, has been universal. As far as we know, both primitive "group" marriage and primitive matriarchy are daydreams—or nightmares, depending on one's point of view—without basis in historical reality. On the contrary, the evidence indicates that the couple, together with their children, biological or adopted, are everywhere at the core of human societies, even though this "little family" (as the Chinese called the nuclear family) may be embedded in joint families, extended families of great size, clans, manorial systems, courts, harems or other institutions that elaborate on kin and marital relations.

Almost up to the present, women on the whole have kept close to home and domestic tasks because of the demands of pregnancy and the nursing of infants, the rearing of children and the care of the disabled and the elderly. They have been concerned primarily with the conservation of intimate values and human relations from one generation to another over immense reaches of time. In contrast, men have performed tasks that require freer movement over greater distances, more intense physical effort and exposure to greater immediate danger; and everywhere men have developed the formal institutions of public life and the values on which these are based. However differently organized, the tasks of women and men have been complementary, mutually supportive. And where either the family or the wider social institutions have broken down, the society as a whole has been endangered. 37

In fact, almost everywhere in the world today societies *are* endangered. The difficulties that beset families in the United States are by no means unique. Families are in trouble everywhere in a world in which change—kind of change that in many cases we ourselves proudly initiated—has been massive and rapid, and innovations have proliferated with only the most superficial concern for their effect on human lives and the earth itself. One difference between the United States and many other countries is that, caring so much about progress, Americans have moved faster. But we may also have arrived sooner at a turning point at which it becomes crucial to redefine what we most value and where we are headed. 38

Looking to the past does not mean that we should return to the past or that we can undo the experiences that have brought us where we are now. The past can provide us only with a base for judging what threatens sound family life and for considering whether our social planning is realistic and inclusive enough. Looking to the past is not a way of binding ourselves but of increasing our awareness, so that we are freer to find new solutions in keeping with our deepest human needs. 39

So the question is not whether women should be forced back into their homes or should have an equal say with men in the world's affairs. We urgently need to draw on the talents women have to offer. Nor is there any question whether men should be deprived of a more intimate family role. 40

We have made a small beginning by giving men a larger share in parenting, and I believe that men and children have been enriched by it.

What we need to be sure of is that areas of caretaking associated in the   41
past with families do not simply drop out of our awareness so that basic human needs go unmet. All the evidence indicates that this is where our greatest difficulties lie. The troubles that plague American families and families all over the industrialized world are symptomatic of the breakdown of the responsible relationship between families and the larger communities of which they are part.

For a long time we have worked hard at isolating the individual family.   42
This has increased the mobility of individuals; and by encouraging young families to break away from the older generation and the home community, we have been able to speed up the acceptance of change and the rapid spread of innovative behavior. But at the same time we have burdened every small family with tremendous responsibilities once shared within three generations and among a large number of people—the nurturing of small children, the emergence of adolescents into adulthood, the care of the sick and disabled and the protection of the aged. What we have failed to realize is that even as we have separated the single family from the larger society, we have expected each couple to take on a range of obligations that traditionally have been shared within a larger family and a wider community.

So all over the world there are millions of families left alone, as it were,   43
each in its own box—parents faced with the specter of what may happen if either one gets sick, children fearful that their parents may end their quarrels with divorce, and empty-handed old people without any role in the life of the next generation.

Then, having pared down to almost nothing the relationship between   44
families and the community, when families get into trouble because they cannot accomplish the impossible we turn their problems over to impersonal social agencies, which can act only in a fragmented way because they are limited to patchwork programs that often are too late to accomplish what is most needed.

Individuals and families do get some kind of help, but what they learn   45
and what those who work hard within the framework of social agencies convey, even as they try to help, is that families should be able to care for themselves.

What Can We Do?

Can we restore family stability? Can we establish new bonds between   46
families and communities? Perhaps most important of all, can we move to a firm belief that living in a family is worth a great effort? Can we move to a

new expectation that by making the effort, families can endure? Obviously the process is circular. Both optimism and action are needed.

We shall have to distinguish between the things that must be done at once and the relations between families and communities that can be built up only over time. We shall have to accept willingly the cost of what must be done, realizing that whatever we do ultimately will be less costly than our present sorry attempts to cope with breakdown and disaster. And we shall have to care for the failures too.

In the immediate future we shall have to support every piece of Federal legislation through which adequate help can be provided for families, both single-parent families and intact poor families, so that they can live decently and safely and prepare their children for another kind of life.

We shall have to support Federal programs for day care after-school care for the children of working mothers and working parents, and for facilities where in a crisis parents can safely leave their small children for brief periods; for centers where the elderly can be cared for without being isolated from the rest of the world; for housing for young families and older people in communities where they can actually interact as friendly grandparents and grandchildren might; and for a national health program that is concerned not with fleecing the Government but with health care. And we must support the plea of Vice-President Walter F. Mondale, who, as chairman of the Senate Subcommittee on Children and Youth, called for "family impact" statements requiring Government agencies to account for what a proposed policy would do for families—make them worse off or better able to take care of their needs.

Government-funded programs need not be patchwork, as likely to destroy as to save. We need to realize that problems related to family and community life—problems besetting education, housing, nutrition, health care, child care, to name just a few—are interlocked. To solve them, we need awareness of detail combined with concern for the whole, and a wise use of tax dollars to accomplish our aims.

A great deal depends on how we see what is done—whether we value it because we are paying for it and because we realize that the protection given families in need is a protection for all families, including our own. Committing ourselves to programs of care—instead of dissociating ourselves from every effort—is one step in the direction of reestablishing family ties with the community. But this will happen only if we accept the idea that each of us, as part of a community, shares in the responsibility for everyone, and thereby benefits from what is done.

The changes that are needed cannot be accomplished by Federal legislation alone. Over a longer time we must support the design and building of communities in which there is housing for three generations, for the fortunate and the unfortunate, and for people of many backgrounds. Such communities can become central in the development of the necessary support system for families. But it will take time to build such communities, and we cannot afford just to wait and hope they will happen.

Meanwhile we must act to interrupt the runaway belief that marriages   53
must fail, that parents and children can't help but be out of communication, that the family as an institution is altogether in disarray. There still are far more marriages that succeed than ones that fail; there are more parents and children who live in trust and learn from one another than ones who are out of touch; there are more people who care about the future than we acknowledge.

What we need, I think, is nationwide discussion—in magazines, in   54
newspapers, on television panel shows and before Congressional committees—of how people who are happily married can help those who are not, how people who are fortunate can help those who are not and how people who have too little to do can help those who are burdened by too much.

Out of such discussions can come a heightened awareness and perhaps   55
some actual help, but above all, fresh thought about what must be done and the determination to begin to do it.

It is true that all over the United States families are in trouble.   56
Realizing this should not make us cynical about the family. It should start us working for a new version of the family that is appropriate to the contemporary world.

Questions for Study and Discussion

1. What types of families, according to Mead, are more prone to breakdown? Why do you suppose this is true? What effect does this breakdown have on the children of so-called secure families?

2. In paragraph 6 Mead draws a grim picture of the contemporary American family. In her analysis of the situation what does she see as the major effects on adults? On children?

3. What for Mead is the "most alarming symptom" of family trouble? What explanation does she offer for why it occurs so often?

4. What according to Mead are the explanations that have been suggested for the breakdown of family life? Which ones do you find most plausible?

5. Mead suggests that it is sometimes helpful to look to the past. Does she advocate returning to the past? Explain.

6. What does Mead mean when she states in paragraph 41, "The troubles that plague American families and families all over the industrialized world are symptomatic of the breakdown of the responsible relationship between families and the larger communities of which they are part"?

7. Paragraphs 1–5 introduce Mead's essay. What would be gained or lost had Mead combined these paragraphs into a single paragraph?

8. What solutions to the problem of family breakdown does Mead offer? Do you agree with her on any of these solutions? Wouldn't the dissolution of the family structure be a much easier solution? Does Mead see this as a viable alternative?

Writing Topics

1. Write an essay in which you argue for one or more innovative alternatives to the family as a traditional social unit.

2. Write an essay in which you explore the importance of family for you. What benefits do you derive from your family? What do you give your family in return? Do you think the American family is in trouble? Why or why not?

GEORGE GALLUP, JR.

George Gallup, Jr., is president of the Gallup Poll, the well-known public opinion poll. Born in 1930 in Evanston, Illinois, Gallup graduated from Princeton University and has been director of the Princeton Religion Research Center. Apart from his research work, Gallup has published numerous articles on politics, religion, and other contemporary issues. His books include *America's Search for Faith* (1980) with David Poling, *My Kid on Drugs?* (1981) with Art Linkletter, and *Adventures in Immortality* (1982) and *Forecast 2000* (1985), both with William Proctor.

In the following selection from *Forecast 2000*, Gallup explores the cultural forces that are changing the American family and, based on the results of several opinion polls, predicts that it will someday disappear.

The Faltering Family

In a recent Sunday school class in a United Methodist Church in the 1 Northeast, a group of eight- to-ten-year-olds were in a deep discussion with their two teachers. When asked to choose which of ten stated possibilities they most feared happening, their response was unanimous. All the children most dreaded a divorce between their parents.

Later, as the teachers, a man and a woman in their late thirties, 2 reflected on the lesson, they both agreed they'd been shocked at the response. When they were the same age as their students, they said, the possibility of their parents being divorced never entered their heads. Yet in just one generation, children seemed to feel much less security in their family ties.

Nor is the experience of these two Sunday school teachers an isolated 3 one. Psychiatrists revealed in one recent newspaper investigation that the fears of children definitely do change in different periods; and in recent times, divorce has become one of the most frequently mentioned anxieties. In one case, for example, a four-year-old insisted that his father rather than his mother walk him to nursery school each day. The reason? He said many of his friends had "no daddy living at home, and I'm scared that will happen to me" (*The New York Times*, May 2, 1983).

In line with such reports, our opinion leaders expressed great concern 4 about the present and future status of the American family. In the poll 33 percent of the responses listed decline in family structure, divorce, and other family-oriented concerns as one of the five major problems facing the nation today. And 26 percent of the responses included such family difficulties as one of the five major problems for the United States in the year 2000.

Historical and sociological trends add strong support to these expressions of concern. For example, today about one marriage in every two ends in divorce. Moreover, the situation seems to be getting worse, rather than better. In 1962, the number of divorces was 2.2 per 1,000 people, according to the National Center for Health Statistics. By 1982, the figure had jumped to 5.1 divorces per 1,000 people—a rate that had more than doubled in two decades.

One common concern expressed about the rise in divorces and decline in stability of the family is that the family unit has traditionally been a key factor in transmitting stable cultural and moral values from generation to generation. Various studies have shown that educational and religious institutions often can have only a limited impact on children without strong family support.

Even grandparents are contributing to the divorce statistics. One recent study revealed that about 100,000 people over the age of fifty-five get divorced in the United States each year. These divorces are usually initiated by men who face retirement, and the relationships being ended are those that have endured for thirty years or more (*The New York Times Magazine*, December 19, 1982).

What are the pressures that have emerged in the past twenty years that cause long-standing family bonds to be broken?

Many now agree that the sexual revolution of the 1960s worked a profound change on our society's family values and personal relationships. Certainly, the seeds of upheaval were present before that critical decade. But a major change that occurred in the mid-sixties was an explicit widespread rejection of the common values about sexual and family relationships that most Americans in the past had held up as an ideal.

We're just beginning to sort through all the changes in social standards that have occurred. Here are some of the major pressures that have contributed to those changes:

Pressure One: Alternative Lifestyles

Twenty years ago, the typical American family was depicted as a man and woman who were married to each other and who produced children (usually two) and lived happily ever after. This was the pattern that young people expected to follow in order to become "full" or "normal" members of society. Of course, some people have always chosen a different route—

remaining single, taking many partners, or living with a member of their own sex. But they were always considered somewhat odd, and outside the social order of the traditional family.

In the last two decades, this picture has changed dramatically. In addition to the proliferation of single people through divorce, we also have these developments: 12

- *Gay men and women have petitioned the courts for the right to marry each other and to adopt children. These demands are being given serious considera-tion, and there may even be a trend of sorts in this direction. For example, the National Association of Social Workers is increasingly supporting full adop-tion rights for gay people* (The New York Times, January 10, 1983).

- *Many heterosexual single adults have been permitted to adopt children and set up single-parent families. So being unattached no longer excludes people from the joys of parenthood.*

- *Some women have deliberately chosen to bear children out of wedlock and raise them alone. In the past, many of these children would have been given up for adoption, but no longer.*

  A most unusual case involved an unmarried psychologist, Dr. Afton Blake, who recently gave birth after being artificially inseminated with sperm from a sperm bank to which Nobel Prize winners had contributed (The New York Times, September 6, 1983).

- *In a recent Gallup Youth Poll, 64 percent of the teenagers questioned said that they hoped their lives would be different from those of their parents. This included having more money, pursuing a different kind of profession, living in a different area, having more free time—and staying single longer.*

  Most surveys show increasing numbers of unmarried couples living together. Also, there are periodic reports of experiments in communal living, "open marriages," and other such arrangements. Although the more radical approaches to relationships tend to come and go and never seem to attract large numbers of people, the practice of living together without getting married seems to be something that's here to stay. The law is beginning to respond to these arrangements with awards for "palimony"—compensation for long-term unmarried partners in a relationship. But the legal and social status of unmarried people who live together is still quite uncertain—especially as far as any children of the union are concerned.

- *Increasing numbers of married couples are choosing to remain childless. Planned Parenthood has even established workshops for couples to assist them in making this decision* (Los Angeles Herald-Examiner, November 27, 1979).

So clearly, a situation has arisen during the last twenty years in which traditional values are no longer as important. Also, a wide variety of alternatives to the traditional family have arisen. Individuals may feel that old-fashioned marriage is just one of many options.   13

Pressure Two: Sexual Morality

The changes in attitudes toward sexual morality have changed as 14
dramatically in the last two decades as the alternatives to traditional
marriage. Hear what a widely used college textbook, published in 1953, said
about premarital sex:

> The arguments against premarital coitus outweigh those in its favor.
> Except for the matter of temporary physical pleasure, all arguments about
> gains tend to be highly theoretical, while the risks and unpleasant con-
> sequences tend to be in equal degree highly practical . . .
>
> The promiscuity of young men is certainly poor preparation for marital
> fidelity and successful family life. For girls it is currently no better and
> sometimes leads still further to the physical and psychological shock of
> abortion or the more prolonged suffering of bearing an illegitimate child and
> giving it up to others. From the viewpoint of ethical and religious leaders, the
> spread of disease through unrestrained sex activities is far more than a health
> problem. They see it as undermining the dependable standards of character
> and the spiritual values that raise life to the level of the "good society."

(This comes from *Marriage and the Family* by Professor Ray E. Baber of
Pomona College, California, which was part of the McGraw-Hill Series in
Sociology and Anthropology and required reading for some college
courses.)

Clearly, attitudes have changed a great deal in just three decades. 15
Teenagers have accepted the idea of premarital sex as the norm. In one
recent national poll, 52 percent of girls and 66 percent of boys favored
having sexual relations in their teens. Ironically, however, 46 percent of the
teenagers thought that virginity in their future marital partner was fairly
important. Youngsters, in other words, display some confusion about what
they want to do sexually, and what they expect from a future mate.

But of course, only part of the problem of defining sexual standards 16
lies with young people and premarital sex. The strong emphasis on achieving an active and rewarding sex life has probably played some role in
encouraging many husbands and wives into rejecting monogamy. Here's
some of the evidence that's been accumulating:

- *Half of the men in a recent nationwide study admitted cheating on their wives*
  (Pensacola Journal, *May 30, 1978).*

- *Psychiatrists today say they see more patients who are thinking about having
  an extramarital affair and who wonder if it would harm their marriage* (New
  York Post, *November 18, 1976).*

- *A psychiatrist at the Albert Einstein College of Medicine says, "In my
  practice I have been particularly struck by how many women have been able
  to use an affair to raise their consciousness and their confidence."*

So the desire for unrestrained sex now tends to take a place among 17
other more traditional priorities, and this can be expected to continue to
exert strong pressure on marriage relationships.

Pressure Three: The Economy

The number of married women working outside the home has been 18
increasing steadily, and most of these women are working out of economic
necessity. As a result, neither spouse may have time to concentrate on the
nurturing of the children or of the marriage relationship.

One mother we interviewed in New Jersey told us about her feelings 19
when she was forced to work full time in a library after her husband lost his
job.

"It's the idea that I have no choice that really bothers me," she said. "I 20
have to work, or we won't eat or have a roof over our heads. I didn't mind
working part-time just to have extra money. I suppose that it's selfish, but I
hate having to work every day and then to come home, fix dinner, and have
to start doing housework. Both my husband and I were raised in traditional
families, where the father went to work and the mother stayed home and
took care of the children. [My husband] would never think of cooking or
doing housework. I've raised my boys the same way, and now I'm paying for
it. Sometimes, I almost hate my husband, even though I know it's not his
fault."

Unfortunately, such pressures probably won't ease in the future. Even 21
if the economy improves and the number of unemployed workers decreases,
few women are likely to give up their jobs. Economists agree that working-
class women who have become breadwinners during a recession can be
expected to remain in the work force. One reason is that many unemployed
men aren't going to get their old jobs back, even when the economy
improves.

"To the extent that [the men] may have to take lower-paying service 22
jobs, their families will need a second income," says Michelle Brandman,
associate economist at Chase Econometrics. "The trend to two paycheck
families as a means of maintaining family income is going to continue" (*The
Wall Street Journal*, December 8, 1982).

In addition to the pressures of unemployment, the cost of having, 23
rearing, and educating children is steadily going up. Researchers have found
that middle-class families with two children *think* they're spending only
about 15 percent of their income on their children. Usually, though, they
actually spend about 40 percent of their money on them. To put the cost in
dollars and cents, if you had a baby in 1977, the estimated cost of raising
that child to the age of eighteen will be $85,000, and that figure has of

course been on the rise for babies born since then (*New York Daily News,* July 24, 1977).

Another important factor that promises to keep both spouses working full time in the future is the attitude of today's teenagers toward these issues. They're not so much concerned about global issues like overpopulation as they are about the high cost of living. Both boys and girls place a lot of emphasis on having enough money so that they can go out and do things. Consequently, most teenage girls surveyed say they expect to pursue careers, even after they get married.   24

So it would seem that by the year 2000 we can expect to see more working mothers in the United States. The woman who doesn't hold down any sort of outside job but stays at home to care for her children represents a small percentage of wives today. By the end of the century, with a few exceptions here and there, she may well have become a part of America's quaint past.   25

As women have joined the work force in response to economic needs, one result has been increased emotional strains on the marriage and family relationships. But there's another set of pressures that has encouraged women to pursue careers. That's the power of feminist philosophy to permeate attitudes in grassroots America during the past couple of decades.   26

Pressure Four: Grassroots Feminist Philosophy

Many women may not agree with the most radical expressions of feminist philosophy that have arisen in the past decade or so. But most younger women—and indeed, a majority of women in the United States—tend to agree with most of the objectives that even the radical feminist groups have been trying to achieve. The basic feminist philosophy has filtered down to the grass roots, and young boys and girls are growing up with feminist assumptions that may have been foreign to their parents and grandparents.   27

For example, child care and housework are no longer regarded strictly as "women's work" by the young people we've polled. Also, according to the Gallup Youth Poll, most teenage girls want to go to college and pursue a career. Moreover, they expect to marry later in life and to continue working after they're married. Another poll, conducted by *The New York Times* and CBS News, revealed that only 2 percent of the youngest age group interviewed—that is, those eighteen to twenty-nine years old—preferred "traditional marriage." By this, they meant a marriage in which the husband is exclusively a provider and the wife is exclusively a homemaker and mother.   28

If these young people continue to hold views similar to these into later 29
life, it's likely that the changes that are occurring today in the traditional
family structure will continue. For one thing, more day-care centers for
children will have to be established. Consequently, the rearing of children
will no longer be regarded as solely the responsibility of the family, but will
become a community or institutional responsibility.

But while such developments may lessen the strain on mothers and 30
fathers, they may also weaken the bonds that hold families together. Among
other things, it may become psychologically easier to get a divorce if a
person is not getting along with a spouse, because the divorcing spouses will
believe it's less likely that the lives of the children will be disrupted.

So the concept of broadening the rights of women vis-à-vis their 31
husbands and families has certainly encouraged women to enter the working world in greater numbers. They're also more inclined to seek a personal
identity that isn't tied up so much in their homelife.

These grassroots feminist forces have brought greater benefits to 32
many, but at the same time they've often worked against traditional family
ties, and we remain uncertain about what is going to replace them. Feminists may argue that the traditional family caused its own demise—or else
why would supposedly content wives and daughters have worked so hard to
transform it? Whatever its theories, though, feminism is still a factor that, in
its present form, appears to exert a destabilizing influence on many traditional familial relationships among husbands, wives, and children.

As things stand now, our family lives are in a state of flux and will 33
probably continue to be out of balance until the year 2000. The pressures
we've discussed will continue to have an impact on our family lives in future
years. But at the same time, counterforces, which tend to drive families
back together again, are also at work.

One of these factors is a traditionalist strain in the large majority of 34
American women. The vast majority of women in this country—74
percent—continue to view marriage with children as the most interesting
and satisfying life for them personally, according to a Gallup Poll for the
White House Conference on Families released in June, 1980.

Another force supporting family life is the attitude of American 35
teenagers toward divorce. According to a recent Gallup Youth Poll, 55
percent feel that divorces are too easy to get today. Also, they're concerned
about the high rate of divorce, and they want to have enduring marriages
themselves. But at the same time—in a response that reflects the confusion
of many adult Americans on this subject—67 percent of the teens in this
same poll say it's right to get a divorce if a couple doesn't get along together.
In other words, they place little importance on trying to improve or salvage
a relationship that has run into serious trouble.

There's a similar ambivalence in the experts we polled. As we've seen, 33 percent of them consider family problems as a top concern today, and 26 percent think these problems will be a big difficulty in the year 2000. But ironically, less than 3 percent suggest that strengthening family relationships is an important consideration in planning for the future! It's obvious, then, that we're confused and ambivalent in our feelings about marriage and the family. Most people know instinctively, without having to read a poll or a book, that happiness and satisfaction in life are rooted largely in the quality of our personal relationships. Furthermore, the most important of those relationships usually begin at home. So one of the greatest challenges we face before the year 2000, both as a nation and as individuals, is how to make our all-important family ties strong and healthy. It's only upon such a firm personal foundation that we can hope to venture forth and grapple effectively with more public problems.

Questions for Study and Discussion

1. Gallup begins his essay with an anecdote. Why did he choose this beginning? What does it reveal to the reader about Gallup's attitude toward his subject? Where else in the essay does he express his attitude toward the weakening of the American family?

2. Gallup points out that more and more women work outside the home. Why does he believe this life-style change is permanent?

3. What is the two-pronged effect that Gallup says the grassroots feminist philosophy has had on the American home? Do you agree with him? Why or why not?

4. What counterforces does Gallup say are working to drive the family back together? In your opinion, are they as powerful as the destabilizing factors? Explain.

5. Gallup lists four major pressures that he says have contributed to the weakening of the American family. But what are the several effects of these pressures? Which effects are stated directly? Which are implied?

6. What are the different kinds of evidence Gallup uses to document and describe each of the pressures he names? Are some more effective than others? Explain.

7. What attitudes among teenagers and adults reflect a cultural ambivalence toward marriage and the family?

Writing Topics

1. At the end of his essay, Gallup suggests that strengthening the American family is one of the "greatest challenges we face before the year 2000." However, he does not offer any suggestions about how to stabilize family ties. In

an essay discuss your views on strengthening the family. Should we even try? If so, what means might we use? Keep in mind the difficulty of resolving the needs of the family with the needs of the individual as Gallup has presented them.

2. Think of someone—you, someone in your family, or one of your friends—who has chosen one of the alternative life-styles Gallup mentions. What have been the effects, for good or for bad, on you, your family, or your friends? In what ways has the choice worked to strengthen or weaken relationships?

MICHAEL REESE AND PAMELA ABRAMSON

In the last few years, the spread of AIDS has heightened public awareness of the homosexual life-style. Nevertheless, most parents still react with anger and denial at the news of their child's homosexuality. In the following selection, Michael Reese and Pamela Abramson chronicle the reactions of each member of the Chronister family to just such news. And while the parents' negative reaction to their son Kelly's homosexuality may be expected, what is surprising is that Kelly also experienced feelings of guilt, shame, and anxiety. The story, which is at once objective and sensitive, first ran as a cover story for a January 1986 issue of *Newsweek*.

Homosexuality: One Family's Affair

It was the hardest question she'd ever had to ask. "Are you gay?" Joan   1
Chronister finally blurted out to her son, Kelly, who was fidgeting at the other end of the sofa. When he begrudgingly, almost bitterly, replied yes, Joan immediately felt her tears and disgust dissolve into detachment. After 22 years of nursing him through mumps and measles, tending his cuts and bruises and applauding his football feats and straight-A report cards, Joan suddenly saw her son as a stranger. *He's my child*, she thought as he walked out the door. *And I don't even know him.*

That afternoon Joan sat and sobbed, unsure whether she was crying   2
for Kelly or the family's dashed expectations. He had been named after K. O. Kelly, Brenda Starr's rough-and-tough comic-strip boyfriend, because his father wanted him to be "tough as hell." But expectations die hard, and if Paul Chronister was disappointed that Kelly hadn't always been his idea of tough, it was nothing compared with the betrayal he felt when he learned his son was homosexual. It was, he says bitterly, like "the son I knew had died, and a new one was born." Four years have passed, and the Chronisters are still trying to cope with that jarring midlife adjustment. It's been both an individual and a family struggle—and has coincided with the nation's heightened awareness of homosexuality because of the AIDS health crisis. What the Chronisters have learned is that there is no easy way for an American family to confront homosexuality. Joan has taped a saying to her

refrigerator door to remind herself of that. "Be into acceptance," it says. "Not understanding."

The Chronisters' entire notion of homosexuality had been shaped by   3
stereotypes: effeminate men with limp wrists. But Kelly wasn't like that. His preppy good looks, athletic prowess and All-American demeanor never foretold that today, at 26, he would be living with his lover, Randy Ponce, in a fashionable brownstone in a gay enclave of northwestern Portland, Ore. It's just 15 miles south of his parents' tidy ranch house in Vancouver, Wash., but it might as well be a foreign country. Though Joan was raised in a tolerant rural Canadian family and Paul broke early from his own Pentecostal upbringing, they have remained conservative in their social values— clinging to tenets that took them from being penniless newlyweds to life as owners of three successful pizza franchises in Washington state.

Paul was proud of his own aggressive instincts in business but thought   4
them lacking in his son. "If we could just get him to be a little meaner," Paul would say, "he could go as far as he wanted to go." That wasn't Kelly. He could be competitive, playing a hard game of street hockey or starring as first-string tackle on his high-school football team. But he was always hardest on himself, a perfectionist who still remembers a B in seventh-grade science as a crushing defeat. Even at home Kelly was almost *too* good, always eager to fix dinners and do the laundry. "Odd that a teen-age boy wants to help his mom," Joan remembers thinking. Both she and Paul came to regard Kelly's perfectionism as his greatest fault. "Everyone is looking for the perfect kid," sighs Paul. "Then you have one and you wish they'd be a little bit ornery."

On the Fringe

Kelly saw his perfectionism as a way of hiding from himself and from   5
others. By always being the teacher's pet, by being a hustler in football practice and by being a fringe member of many social groups but the leader of none, Kelly managed to mask his insecurities. Despite his achievements, he had long felt himself an outsider, separate from his peers. He remembers vague sexual feelings as early as the age of seven, when he would linger in the boys' showers after swimming lessons. When his feelings blossomed in his early teens, Kelly had no point of reference and no one he felt comfortable talking to. The only person he even suspected might be gay was a coach whom all the other boys laughed at when they caught him eyeing them in the showers. And though Kelly knew he was only looking for guys when he peeked at his father's girlie magazines, it confused him when he once saw a pornographic picture of a man putting on nylons. "That isn't me," he thought.

It was easier for Kelly to know what he wasn't. He wasn't comfortable   6
when his football buddies told faggot jokes; he knew he might betray

himself by not laughing, so he even told a few himself. He wasn't able to join in their postgame drinking and picking-up-girls sprees: he was afraid that if he got drunk the truth might slip out. Most of all, he wasn't interested in girls. He came up with lame excuses for those bold enough to ask him out. When that failed, he made up an imaginary girlfriend who lived out of town and to whom he loudly professed he would always remain loyal.

At home, Kelly's cover-ups were just as elaborate. He refused to ask his parents to buy him a coat and tie for his senior yearbook photo session because he was afraid they would expect him to wear the new clothes to a dance or on a date. Then, when his father inevitably asked why he wasn't going to the senior prom, Kelly could shrug and say he had nothing to wear. The ruse seemed to work. His parents never suspected that their son might be homosexual. That was something entirely beyond their realm of experience; Kelly, they assured each other, was simply shy and would "come out of his shell" in college. But Kelly knew all along that he was postponing the crisis. He saw college as his only escape.

After a few months at Eastern Washington University near Spokane, Kelly began to feel despair. There was no one on campus he even remotely thought might be gay. Then one fall day Kelly found himself on the athletic field staring at another student; the young man returned Kelly's stare, came over and struck up a conversation. That night Kelly agonized over the overture: *Maybe he's gay. Maybe it'll finally happen.* But Kelly still wasn't sure, even when they met again the next day on the athletic field and exchanged an awkward touch. Finally, a few weeks later, they moved into a private music room, where Kelly listened for hours while his friend played the piano. There Kelly had his first sexual experience with another man.

It left him scared, happy but even more confused than before. "What's going to happen to me? What kind of a life will I have?" he kept asking himself between encounters with his friend that continued sporadically for the next four years. "Why do I feel this way?" There were few places to turn for answers. At that time the gay community at Eastern Washington was virtually invisible. There was not—as there is now—a Gay Students' Union nor places that openly offered counseling to gay students. His sexual contact throughout college was restricted to that single relationship. Kelly channeled his energy into his business studies and long, lonely bicycle rides along the wheat fields near campus. He sometimes rode a hundred miles a day, as if just by pedaling hard enough and fast enough he could push away his feelings.

Knowing what he now knew about himself, Kelly couldn't face long family visits or summers working for his father at the pizza parlor. Instead, he moved from the dorms into an apartment of his own, immersed himself in classes and timidly continued his sexual education. He went to the campus bookstore, furtively browsing through gay psychology texts he was too afraid to buy. Through the mail he ordered a "gay guide" of Spokane but couldn't work up the nerve to go into the three gay bars that were listed. Finally, one Thanksgiving, he imploded. After fixing himself Cornish game hen, mashed potatoes, gravy and pumpkin pie, he went for a long walk in the snow. *I know what I am*, he thought, *but why me? Why was I dealt this?* He began to cry. *I'm alone*, he sobbed, *and it's because I'm gay that I'm alone.*

Kelly's fear of rejection meant he could share his secret with no one, especially not his family. When his parents called and teased him about girls, he always responded with a curt "Leave me alone." That's just Kelly's way, they told themselves, glad that at least he seemed to be doing well in school. And when he graduated with high honors in business management, they proudly drove the six hours to Spokane thinking their son's future was made—that surely a wife and grandchildren would soon follow. But Paul never made it to the ceremonies. After suffering chest pains, he was rushed by air ambulance back to Portland for open-heart surgery. Kelly, who had made no firm postgraduation plans, suddenly found himself back in Vancouver watching TV and helping to run the pizza parlors.

He could stand it only for so long. Soon he was back on his bicycle— speeding across the river to Portland, a gay-bar guide tucked in his back pocket. Still too scared to go inside, Kelly usually ended up alone in some shopping-mall restaurant, drinking coffee. That's where he met David, whom Kelly, despite his apprehension, accompanied to his first gay bar, The Rafters. It was not at all what he had imagined. Instead of being dark and ominous, it was bright and friendly; instead of aging drag queens and tough guys in leather, the bar was filled with good-looking young men dancing and having a good time. *They're just average Joes!* Kelly thought. *Guys just like me.*

Kelly didn't feel that way about David, who was loud, flamboyant and sissified in his dress—not at all the sort Kelly wanted his parents to meet. Or did he? To this day, Kelly isn't sure whether he wasn't trying to make a statement the one time he brought David home—or whether he really wanted to slip him out before Joan, eager to meet the first friend Kelly had brought home in years, confronted them at the front door. Joan took one look and went pale. "Oh, my God," she said to Paul after they had left. "That boy with Kelly is queer."

A Secret Search

She tried to make sense of it. She looked back on Kelly's mood swings, his long, unexplained bike rides into Portland and his almost giddy excitement about going to a Halloween party; that wasn't like Kelly, especially staying out all night with the excuse he'd had too much to drink. But Joan needed proof. Shaking with guilt and apprehension, she steamed open a letter, and searched through his dresser drawers, where she found a scrap of paper. Written on it was the title of a book: "Young, Gay and Proud." "He's queer! He's queer!" she screamed, running hysterically into the arms of her husband, who held her and tried to tell her it was going to be OK.

When Joan confronted Kelly the next day, Paul decided to get "the hell out of the house." Unable to face Kelly or more of Joan's tears, Paul beat a hasty overnight retreat to one of his pizza parlors; he felt he needed to be alone with his anger, sadness and confusion. He tried not to place blame, but the thoughts came anyway: "Jesus, Joan was more domineering than I was." He felt anger toward Kelly: "He can't cope with the ladies. He's taking the easy way out." He wondered whether they should send him to a psychiatrist: "You have a flat tire, you fix it." Finally, alone in a motel room, Paul broke down and cried, an uncharacteristic release for a man who always held everything inside. But it didn't help: that night Paul suffered a mild heart attack. 15

With Paul sick and uneager to talk about Kelly, Joan had no one to share her own quandary. Finally she looked in the Yellow Pages under "H" for homosexuals and then under "G," where she found a listing for a gay-crisis hot line. She was trembling when she picked up the phone, and her voice cracked when she first heard herself say the words out loud: "My son is gay." The hot line put her in touch with another mother, who listened to Joan's story and promised to send her a pamphlet about a support group for friends and parents of gay people. She invited Joan to a Gay Men's Chorus Christmas performance. Joan, accompanied by Kelly's older sister, Rhonda, was overwhelmed to see hundreds of gay men, so many of them just like Kelly. She asked them questions: "Where do you work?" "Where do you live?" "Do your parents accept you?" But most of all she kept asking, "Are you happy?" 16

Icy Stares

Joan realized she'd been closed off from Kelly's world and she wanted to make up for lost time. But she had to do it on her own. Paul was in retreat, refusing to talk about it or even to acknowledge Kelly when he came home to pick up some of his possessions; he had moved in with a man in Portland. Kelly continued to keep his mother at arm's length; their phone calls and visits consisted of monosyllables and icy stares. Finally, while Paul slumped silently in his chair in the family room, Joan attended a monthly support-group meeting. It took her months to choke out the words: "I'm Joan Chronister and I have a gay son." 17

She listened and learned, quickly realizing that Kelly was not going to change and that no one was to blame. She started manning the hot line and joining excursions to Portland's gay bars. She talked with all kinds of 18 people—from drag queens and lesbians to other parents of gays—and if she couldn't completely understand, at least she was beginning to accept. One June day she attended Portland's Gay Pride Day parade. As she watched the curious crowd go by, Joan noticed a lone man holding a sign, "Parents and Friends of Lesbians and Gay Men." Overcome with emotion, she stepped out into the street and joined him.

Paul never marched or went to a support-group meeting. Instead, he 19 stayed at home and hoped time would work its wonders. For a while he thought Kelly might come home lisping and limp-wristed; when he didn't, Paul breathed a sigh of relief and decided it was enough to accept what he'd accepted that first night in his motel room: that as much as he hated Kelly's homosexuality, he could never close the door on his own son. He still doesn't want to know what Kelly's gay life and friends are like, or to imagine what he does inside his bedroom. Joan's transformation into self-proclaimed gay-rights activist sometimes creates a strain. "I don't want to hash it over all the time," says Paul. "But she has the need, an exceptional need."

Stable Relationship

It's also hard on Kelly, who is still trying to find a comfortable way to 20 express his sexuality. He's come a long way since he and a boyfriend showed up at Rhonda's wedding wearing identical blazers and pink shirts. Now Kelly tries to make a softer statement by inviting his parents to dinner and letting his relationship with Randy speak for itself. They met more than two years ago through a mutual friend; they found they shared a distaste for the bar scene and a desire for a stable relationship. Since then they've exchanged identical gold rings, furnished a home together and worked side by side at a suburban Portland video store; with their joint savings account, they now plan to go back to college and maybe start a business. And if Paul still can't bring himself to refer to Randy as his son's "lover," Kelly understands. He knows by the way his father teases and firmly shakes Randy's hand that Paul is, in his own way, making an effort to accept them both.

It is problematic whether the fractures Kelly's homosexuality have 21 opened in the Chronister family will ever completely heal. Paul continues to struggle with his inner anguish and could not bring himself to accompany his wife to the Portland Gay Pride Day parade, where she spoke last June ("My name is Joan Chronister and I'm proud my child is homosexual"). Joan for her part blames her husband for not being more understanding. Both are trying to reach some sort of common ground between themselves.

And for Kelly there remains detachment from his parents and uncer- 22 tainty about the future. He was all of 10 when the gay-rights movement was born with the 1969 Stonewall Inn riot. And though he has never been inside a bathhouse or slipped into the boozy world of obsessive sex, he knows that AIDS—not cries of liberation—is the historical force shaping his generation of gay men. He hears evangelists call the epidemic divine retribution for crimes against nature and he fears the political backlash that might come. But he has no illusions about changing society—or changing himself. Says Kelly, "It's part of my being."

Questions for Study and Discussion

1. When Kelly's mother learned of her son's homosexuality she said, "he's my child. And I don't even know him." His father said, "the son I knew had died, and a new one was born." Based on comments they made later, what do you suppose they meant by these remarks?

2. Why was it easier for Kelly when he was young, to know what he "wasn't" rather than what he "was"?

3. Although Kelly is a homosexual, he harbored many stereotypical attitudes of his own against gay men. What were some of these stereotypes? What were some of the "truths" he learned about gay men?

4. What devices did Kelly employ to hide his insecurities from himself and from others?

5. How was the anguish of Kelly's homosexuality similar for him and for his parents? How was it different? How has each of them chosen to deal with it? How realistic do you think their various choices are?

6. The title suggests that the authors will present the attitudes of each member of the Chronister family. What of the authors' attitudes toward their subjects? Do the authors' tones vary from section to section as they deal with different members of the family? Do they present one or another of the family members more favorably? Cite examples of diction and tone to support your answer.

7. The members of the Chronister family ask themselves many questions. What are some of these questions? Why do you suppose they are left unanswered? Choose one or two and answer them yourself.

Writing Topics

1. After reading about the Chronister family, how would you describe each of them? How do you feel about each of them? Is any one more or less sympathetic? What reasons can you offer for your opinion?

2. Imagine that you have to tell your parents something about yourself that you expect they will find deeply disturbing, such as that you are gay, or marrying someone they will object to, or changing your religion. In an essay describe how you would tell them. How do you think they would receive the news?

JOHN UPDIKE

John Updike was born in 1932 in Shillington, Pennsylvania, a small town where his father taught high school. Updike attended Harvard University where he became editor of the famed undergraduate humor magazine *The Harvard Lampoon*. Later he spent a year at Oxford University in England. Since graduation he has published many short stories, novels, and poems—often in *The New Yorker*—many of which draw on his middle-class upbringing for their characters and situations. Updike is best known for his novels, among them *The Centaur* (1963), recipient of the National Book Award, and *Rabbit Is Rich* (1982), which earned him the Pulitzer Prize, the American Book Award, and the National Book Critics Award.

"Separating" tells the story of a middle-aged man and his family who agonize separately and together over his decision to leave his wife for another woman.

Separating

The day was fair. Brilliant. All that June the weather had mocked the Maples' internal misery with solid sunlight—golden shafts and cascades of green in which their conversations had wormed unseeing, their sad murmuring selves the only stain in Nature. Usually by this time of the year they had acquired tans; but when they met their elder daughter's plane on her return from a year in England they were almost as pale as she, though Judith was too dazzled by the sunny opulent jumble of her native land to notice. They did not spoil her homecoming by telling her immediately. Wait a few days, let her recover from jet lag, had been one of their formulations, in that string of gray dialogues—over coffee, over cocktails, over Cointreau—that had shaped the strategy of their dissolution, while the earth performed its annual stunt of renewal unnoticed beyond their closed windows. Richard had thought to leave at Easter; Joan had insisted they wait until the four children were at last assembled, with all exams passed and ceremonies attended, and the bauble of summer to console them. So he had drudged away, in love, in dread, repairing screens, getting the mowers sharpened, rolling and patching their new tennis court. 1

The court, clay, had come through its first winter pitted and wind-swept bare of redcoat. Years ago the Maples had observed how often, among their friends, divorce followed a dramatic home improvement, as if the 2 marriage were making one last effort to live; their own worst crisis had come amid the plaster dust and exposed plumbing of a kitchen renovation. Yet, a summer ago, as canary-yellow bulldozers gaily churned a grassy, daisy-dotted knoll into a muddy plateau, and a crew of pigtailed young men raked and tamped clay into a plane, this transformation did not strike them as ominous, but festive in its impudence; their marriage could rend the earth for fun. The next spring, waking each day at dawn to a sliding sensation as if the bed were being tipped, Richard found the barren tennis court— its net and tapes still rolled in the barn—an environment congruous with his mood of purposeful desolation, and the crumbling of handfuls of clay into cracks and holes (dogs had frolicked on the court in a thaw; rivulets had eroded trenches) an activity suitably elemental and interminable. In his sealed heart he hoped the day would never come.

Now it was here. A Friday. Judith was re-acclimated; all four children were assembled, before jobs and camps and visits again scattered them. Joan thought they should be told one by one. Richard was for making an announcement at the table. She said, "I think just making an announcement is a cop-out. They'll start quarrelling and playing to each other instead of focusing. They're each individuals, you know, not just some corporate obstacle to your freedom."

"O.K., O.K. I agree." Joan's plan was exact. That evening, they were giving Judith a belated welcome-home dinner, of lobster and champagne. Then, the party over, they, the two of them, who nineteen years before would push her in a baby carriage along Fifth Avenue to Washington Square, were to walk her out of the house to the bridge across the salt creek, and tell her, swearing her to secrecy. Then Richard Jr., who was going directly from work to a rock concert in Boston, would be told, either late when he returned on the train or early Saturday morning before he went off to his job; he was seventeen and employed as one of a golf-course maintenance crew. Then the two younger children, John and Margaret, could, as the morning wore on, be informed.

"Mopped up, as it were," Richard said.

"Do you have any better plan? That leaves you the rest of Saturday to answer any questions, pack, and make your wonderful departure."

"No," he said, meaning he had no better plan, and agreed to hers, though to him it showed an edge of false order, a hidden plea for control, like Joan's long chore lists and financial accountings and, in the days when he first knew her, her too-copious lecture notes. Her plan turned one hurdle for him into four—four knife-sharp walls, each with a sheer blind drop on the other side.

All spring he had moved through a world of insides and outsides, of barriers and partitions. He and Joan stood as a thin barrier between the children and the truth. Each moment was a partition, with the past on one side and the future on the other, a future containing this unthinkable now.

Beyond four knifelike walls a new life for him waited vaguely. His skull cupped a secret, a white face, a face both frightened and soothing, both strange and known, that he wanted to shield from tears, which he felt all about him, solid as the sunlight. So haunted, he had become obsessed with battening down the house against his absence, replacing screens and sash cords, hinges and latches—a Houdini making things snug before his escape.

The lock. He had still to replace a lock on one of the doors of the   9 screened porch. The task, like most such, proved more difficult than he had imagined. The old lock, aluminum frozen by corrosion, had been deliberately rendered obsolete by manufacturers. Three hardware stores had nothing that even approximately matched the mortised hole its removal (surprisingly easy) left. Another hole had to be gouged, with bits too small and saws too big, and the old hole fitted with a block of wood—the chisels dull, the saw rusty, his fingers thick with lack of sleep. The sun poured down, beyond the porch, on the world of neglect. The bushes already needed pruning, the windward side of the house was shedding flakes of paint, rain would get in when he was gone, insects, rot, death. His family, all those he would lose, filtered through the edges of his awareness as he struggled with screw holes, splinters, opaque instructions, minutiae of metal.

Judith sat on the porch, a princess returned from exile. She regaled   10 them with stories of fuel shortages, of bomb scares in the Underground, of Pakistani workmen loudly lusting after her as she walked past on her way to dance school. Joan came and went, in and out of the house, calmer than she should have been, praising his struggles with the lock as if this were one more and not the last of their long succession of shared chores. The younger of his sons for a few minutes held the rickety screen door while his father clumsily hammered and chiseled, each blow a kind of sob in Richard's ears. His younger daughter, having been at a slumber party, slept on the porch hammock through all the noise—heavy and pink, trusting and forsaken. Time, like the sunlight, continued relentlessly; the sunlight slowly slanted. Today was one of the longest days. The lock clicked, worked. He was through. He had a drink; he drank it on the porch, listening to his daughter. "It was so sweet," she was saying, "during the worst of it, how all the butchers and bakery shops kept open by candlelight. They're all so plucky and cute. From the papers, things sounded so much worse here— people shooting people in gas lines, and everybody freezing."

Richard asked her, "Do you still want to live in England forever?"   11 *Forever*: the concept, now a reality upon him, pressed and scratched at the back of his throat.

"No," Judith confessed, turning her oval face to him, its eyes still   12 childishly far apart, but the lips set as over something succulent and satisfactory. "I was anxious to come home. I'm an American." She was a woman. They had raised her; he and Joan had endured together to raise her, alone of the four. The others had still some raising left in them. Yet it was the thought of telling Judith—the image of her, their first baby, walking between them arm in arm to the bridge—that broke him. The partition between his face and the tears broke. Richard sat down to the celebratory meal with the back of his throat aching; the champagne, the lobster seemed phases of sunshine; he saw them and tasted them though tears. He blinked, swallowed, croakily joked about hay fever. The tears would not stop leaking through; they came not through a hole that could be plugged but through a permeable spot in a membrane, steadily, purely, endlessly, fruitfully. They became, his tears, a shield for himself against these others—their faces, the fact of their assembly, a last time as innocents, at a table where he sat the last time as head. Tears dropped from his nose as he broke the lobster's back; salt flavored his champagne as he sipped it; the raw clench at the back of his throat was delicious. He could not help himself.

His children tried to ignore his tears. Judith, on his right, lit a cigarette, gazed upward in the direction of her too energetic, too sophisticated exhalation; on her other side, John earnestly bent his face to the extraction of the last morsels—legs, tail segments—from the scarlet corpse. Joan, at the opposite end of the table, glanced at him surprised, her reproach displaced by a quick grimace, of forgiveness, or of salute to his superior gift of strategy. Between them, Margaret, no longer called Bean, thirteen and large for her age, gazed from the other side of his pane of tears as if into a shopwindow at something she coveted—at her father, a crystalline heap of splinters and memories. It was not she, however, but John who, in the kitchen, as they cleared the plates and carapaces away, asked Joan the question: *"Why is Daddy crying?"*

Richard heard the question but not the murmured answer. Then he heard Bean cry, "Oh, no-oh!"—the faintly dramatized exclamation of one who had long expected it.

John returned to the table carrying a bowl of salad. He nodded tersely at his father and his lips shaped the conspiratorial words "She told."

"Told what?" Richard asked aloud, insanely.

The boy sat down as if to rebuke his father's distraction with the example of his own good manners. He said quietly, "The separation."

Joan and Margaret returned; the child, in Richard's twisted vision, seemed diminished in size, and relieved, relieved to have had the bogieman at last proved real. He called out to her—the distances at the table had grown immense—"You knew, you always knew," but the clenching at the back of his throat prevented him from making sense of it. From afar he heard Joan talking, levelly, sensibly, reciting what they had prepared: it was a separation for the summer, an experiment. She and Daddy both agreed it would be good for them; they needed space and time to think; they liked each other but did not make each other happy enough, somehow.

Judith, imitating her mother's factual tone, but in her youth off-key, too cool, said, "I think it's silly. You should either live together or get divorced."

Richard's crying, like a wave that has crested and crashed, had   20
become tumultuous; but it was overtopped by another tumult, for John,
who had been so reserved, now grew larger and larger at the table. Perhaps
his younger sister's being credited with knowing set him off. "Why didn't
you *tell* us?" he asked, in a large round voice quite unlike his own. "You
should have *told* us you weren't getting along."

Richard was startled into attempting to force words through his tears.   21
"We *do* get along, that's the trouble, so it doesn't show even to us—" *That we
do not love each other* was the rest of the sentence; he couldn't finish it.

Joan finished for him, in her style. "And we've always, *especially*, loved   22
our children."

John was not mollified. "What do you care about *us?*" he boomed.   23
"We're just little things you *had*." His sisters' laughing forced a laugh from
him, which he turned hard and parodistic: "Ha, ha, *ha*." Richard and Joan
realized simultaneously that the child was drunk, on Judith's homecoming
champagne. Feeling bound to keep the center of the stage, John took a
cigarette from Judith's pack, poked it into his mouth, let it hang from his
lower lip, and squinted like a gangster.

"You're not little things we had," Richard called to him. "You're the   24
whole point. But you're grown. Or almost."

The boy was lighting matches. Instead of holding them to his cigarette   25
(for they had never seen him smoke; being "good" had been his way of
setting himself apart), he held them to his mother's face, closer and closer,
for her to blow out. Then he lit the whole folder—a hiss and then a torch,
held against his mother's face. Prismed by tears, the flame filled Richard's
vision; he didn't know how it was extinguished. He heard Margaret say,
"Oh stop showing off," and saw John, in response, break the cigarette in
two and put the halves entirely into his mouth and chew, sticking out his
tongue to display the shreds to his sister.

Joan talked to him, reasoning—a fountain of reasons, unintelligible.   26
"Talked about it for years . . . our children must help us . . . Daddy and I
both want . . ." As the boy listened, he carefully wadded a paper napkin
into the leaves of his salad, fashioned a ball of paper and lettuce, and
popped it into his mouth, looking around the table for the expected
laughter. None came. Judith said, "Be mature," and dismissed a plume of
smoke.

Richard got up from this stifling table and led the boy outside.   27
Though the house was in twilight, the outdoors still brimmed with light,
the lovely waste light of high summer. Both laughing, he supervised John's
spitting out the lettuce and paper and tobacco into the pachysandra. He
took him by the hand—a square gritty hand, but for its softness a man's.
Yet, it held on. They ran together up into the field, past the tennis court.
The raw banking left by the bulldozers was dotted with daisies. Past the
court and a flat stretch where they used to play family baseball stood a soft

green rise glorious in the sun, each weed and species of grass distinct as illumination on parchment. "I'm sorry, so sorry," Richard cried. "You were the only one who ever tried to help me with all the goddam jobs around this place."

Sobbing, safe within his tears and the champagne, John explained, "It's not just the separation, it's the whole crummy year. I *hate* that school, you can't make any friends, the history teacher's a scud." 28

They sat on the crest of the rise, shaking and warm from their tears but easier in their voices, and Richard tried to focus on the child's sad year—the weekdays long with homework, the weekends spent in his room with model airplanes, while his parents murmured down below, nursing their separation. How selfish, how blind, Richard thought; his eyes felt scoured. He told his son, "We'll think about getting you transferred. Life's too short to be miserable." 29

They had said what they could, but did not want the moment to heal, and talked on, about the school, about the tennis court, whether it would ever again be as good as it had been that first summer. They walked to inspect it and pressed a few more tapes more firmly down. A little stiltedly, perhaps trying now to make too much of the moment, Richard led the boy to the spot in the field where the view was best, of the metallic blue river, the emerald marsh, the scattered islands velvety with shadow in the low light, the white bits of beach far away. "See," he said. "It goes on being beautiful. It'll be here tomorrow." 30

"I know," John answered, impatiently. The moment had closed. 31

Back in the house, the others had opened some white wine, the champagne being drunk, and still sat at the table, the three females, gossiping. Where Joan sat had become the head. She turned, showing him a tearless face, and asked, "All right?" 32

"We're fine," he said, resenting it, though relieved, that the party went on without him. 33

In bed she explained, "I couldn't cry I guess because I cried so much all spring. It really wasn't fair. It's your idea, and you made it look as though I was kicking you out." 34

"I'm sorry," he said. "I couldn't stop. I wanted to but couldn't." 35

"You *didn't* want to. You loved it. You were having your way, making a general announcement." 36

"I love having it over," he admitted. "God, those kids were great. So brave and funny." John, returned to the house, had settled to a model airplane in his room and kept shouting down to them, "I'm O.K. No sweat." "And the way," Richard went on, cozy in his relief, "they never questioned the reasons we gave. No thought of a third person. Not even Judith." 37

"That *was* touching," Joan said. 38

He gave her a hug. "You were great too. Very reassuring to everybody. Thank you." Guiltily, he realized he did not feel separated.   39

"You still have Dickie to do," she told him. These words set before   40
him a black mountain in the darkness; its cold breath, its near weight affected his chest. Of the four children, his elder son was most nearly his conscience. Joan did not need to add, "That's one piece of your dirty work I won't do for you."

"I know. I'll do it. You go to sleep."   41

Within minutes, her breathing slowed, became oblivious and deep. It   42
was quarter to midnight. Dickie's train from the concert would come in at one-fourteen. Richard set the alarm for one. He had slept atrociously for weeks. But whenever he closed his lids some glimpse of the last hours scorched them—Judith exhaling toward the ceiling in a kind of aversion, Bean's mute staring, the sunstruck growth in the field where he and John had rested. The mountain before him moved closer, moved within him; he was huge, momentous. The ache at the back of his throat felt stale. His wife slept as if slain beside him. When, exasperated by his hot lids, his crowded heart, he rose from bed and dressed, she awoke enough to turn over. He told her then, "Joan, if I could undo it all, I would."

"Where would you begin?" she asked. There was no place. Giving him   43
courage, she was always giving him courage. He put on shoes without socks in the dark. The children were breathing in their rooms, the downstairs was hollow. In their confusion they had left lights burning. He turned off all but one, the kitchen overhead. The car started. He had hoped it wouldn't. He met only moonlight on the road; it seemed a diaphanous companion, flickering in the leaves along the roadside, haunting his rearview mirror like a pursuer, melting under his headlights. The center of town, not quite deserted, was eerie at this hour. A young cop in uniform kept company with a gang of T-shirted kids on the steps of the bank. Across from the railroad station, several bars kept open. Customers, mostly young, passed in and out of the warm night, savoring summer's novelty. Voices shouted from cars as they passed; an immense conversation seemed in progress. Richard parked and in his weariness put his head on the passenger seat, out of the commotion and wheeling lights. It was as when, in the movies, an assassin grimly carries his mission through the jostle of a carnival—except the movies cannot show the precipitous, palpable slope you cling to within. You cannot climb back down; you can only fall. The synthetic fabric of the car seat, warmed by his cheek, confided to him an ancient, distant scent of vanilla.

A train whistle caused him to lift his head. It was on time; he had   44
hoped it would be late. The slender drawgates descended. The bell of approach tingled happily. The great metal body, horizontally fluted, rocked to a stop, and sleepy teen-agers disembarked, his son among them. Dickie did not show surprise that his father was meeting him at this terrible hour. He sauntered to the car with two friends, both taller than he. He said "Hi"

to his father and took the passenger's seat with an exhausted promptness that expressed gratitude. The friends got in the back, and Richard was grateful; a few more minutes' postponement would be won by driving them home.

He asked, "How was the concert?" 45

"Groovy," one boy said from the back seat. 46

"It bit," the other said. 47

"It was O.K.," Dickie said, moderate by nature, so reasonable that in 48 his childhood the unreason of the world had given him headaches, stomach aches, nausea. When the second friend had been dropped off at his dark house, the boy blurted, "Dad, my eyes are killing me with hay fever! I'm out there cutting that mothering grass all day!"

"Do we still have those drops?" 49

"They didn't do any good last summer." 50

"They might this." Richard swung a U-turn on the empty street. The 51 drive home took a few minutes. The mountain was here, in his throat. "Richard," he said, and felt the boy, slumped and rubbing his eyes, go tense at his tone, "I didn't come to meet you just to make your life easier. I came because your mother and I have some news for you, and you're a hard man to get ahold of these days. It's sad news."

"That's O.K." The reassurance came out soft, but quick, as if released 52 from the tip of a spring.

Richard had feared that his tears would return and choke him, but 53 the boy's manliness set an example, and his voice issued forth steady and dry. "It's sad news, but it needn't be tragic news, at least for you. It should have no practical effect on your life, though it's bound to have an emotional effect. You'll work at your job and go back to school in September. Your mother and I are really proud of what you're making of your life; we don't want that to change at all."

"Yeah," the boy said lightly, on the intake of his breath, holding 54 himself up. They turned the corner; the church they went to loomed like a gutted fort. The home of the woman Richard hoped to marry stood across the green. Her bedroom light burned.

"Your mother and I," he said, "have decided to separate. For the 55 summer. Nothing legal, no divorce yet. We want to see how it feels. For some years now, we haven't been doing enough for each other, making each other as happy as we should be. Have you sensed that?"

"No," the boy said. It was an honest, unemotional answer: true or 56 false in a quiz.

Glad for the factual basis, Richard pursued, even garrulously, the 57 details. His apartment across town, his utter accessibility, the split vacation arrangements, the advantages to the children, the added mobility and variety of the summer. Dickie listened, absorbing. "Do the others know?"

"Yes." 58

"How did they take it?" 59

"The girls pretty calmly. John flipped out; he shouted and ate a 60
cigarette and made a salad out of his napkin and told us how much he
hated school."

His brother chuckled. "He did?" 61

"Yeah. The school issue was more upsetting for him than Mom and 62
me. He seemed to feel better for having exploded."

"He did?" The repetition was the first sign that he was stunned. 63

"Yes. Dickie, I want to tell you something. This last hour, waiting for 64
your train to get in, has been about the worst of my life. I hate this. *Hate* it.
My father would have died before doing it to me." He felt immensely
lighter, saying this. He had dumped the mountain on the boy. They were
home. Moving swiftly as a shadow, Dickie was out of the car, through the
bright kitchen. Richard called after him, "Want a glass of milk or anything?"

"No thanks." 65

"Want us to call the course tomorrow and say you're too sick to work?" 66

"No, that's all right." The answer was faint, delivered at the door to 67
his room; Richard listened for the slam that went with a tantrum. The door
closed normally, gently. The sound was sickening.

Joan had sunk into that first deep trough of sleep and was slow to 68
awake. Richard had to repeat, "I told him."

"What did he say?" 69

"Nothing much. Could you say goodnight to him? Please." 70

She left their room, without putting on a bathrobe. He sluggishly 71
changed back into his pajamas and walked down the hall. Dickie was
already in bed, Joan was sitting beside him, and the boy's bedside clock
radio was murmuring music. When she stood, an inexplicable light—the
moon—outlined her body through the nightie. Richard sat on the warm
place she had indented on the child's narrow mattress. He asked him, "Do
you want the radio on like that?"

"It always is." 72

"Doesn't it keep you awake? It would me." 73

"No." 74

"Are you sleepy?" 75

"Yeah." 76

"Good. Sure you want to get up and go to work? You've had a big 77
night."

"I want to go." 78

Away at school this winter he had learned for the first time that you 79
can go short of sleep and live. As an infant he had slept with an immobile,
sweating intensity that had alarmed his babysitters. In adolescence he had
often been the first of the four children to go to bed. Even now, he would go

slack in the middle of a television show, his sprawled legs hairy and brown. "O.K. Good boy. Dickie, listen. I love you so much, I never knew how much until now. No matter how this works out, I'll always be with you. Really."

Richard bent to kiss an averted face but his son, sinewy, turned and   80
with wet cheeks embraced him and gave him a kiss, on the lips, passionate as a woman's. In his father's ear he moaned one word, the crucial, intelligent word: "Why?"

Why. It was a whistle of wind in a crack, a knife thrust, a window   81
thrown open on emptiness. The white face was gone, the darkness was featureless. Richard had forgotten why.

Questions for Study and Discussion

1. From the things the father says and his family's reactions to him, the reader can draw a portrait of the man. How do you think he would describe himself? How would you describe him?

2. Updike refers to the "other woman" only twice in a fairly long story. Why do you suppose she plays so small a role in his narrative? What would have been the effect of knowing more about her?

3. Each of the Maple children reacts very differently to their father's plan to leave home. How does Updike characterize each child? Does he clearly differentiate each from the others for the reader? Explain.

4. Richard and Joan tell their children that the fact that they "get along" concealed the truth (even from themselves) that they no longer loved each other. What clues, if any, does Updike offer the reader of the trouble in the Maples' relationship? How are the problems in the marriage played out in the ways each of them handles telling the children of their breakup?

5. How would you characterize the Maples family? Is it very different from or similar to most families you know? Cite passages from the story that typify the family's relationship.

6. What are the chief issues for the different members of the Maple's family as they contemplate the separation? In what ways do you think the separation might have been different for the parents if they had not had children? Would it have been any less difficult? Would other issues have become more important? Explain.

7. At the end of Updike's story his eldest son asks him a tearful, wrenching question. Why has the father dreaded it? Why do you suppose he is unable to answer it? Given what you know about the man, how would you answer it for him?

Writing Topics

1. Updike's story, although it conveys the feelings of every member of the Maples family, is told from the point of view of the father. Write a similar story

in which you present a child's point of view. What are some of the chief concerns of children facing the breakup of their family? How do parents seem to children under these circumstances?

2. Choose a family crisis other than divorce, such as a house fire, the death of a family member, the loss of a job, or a forced relocation. Write a short story from one person's point of view while being sure to convey the concerns of other members of the family.

What Are Friends?

MARGARET MEAD AND RHODA METRAUX

Margaret Mead (1901–1978) was a noted educator, anthropologist, and author. Educated at Barnard College and Columbia University, she was for many years a professor of anthropology at Columbia. She spent much of her life studying foreign societies and became an expert in such fields as family structure, mental health, drugs, environmental problems, and women's roles in society. Her best-known books include *Coming of Age in Samoa* (1928), *Male and Female* (1949), *The Study of Culture at a Distance* (1953), and *Childhood in Contemporary Cultures* (1955). Rhoda Metraux was born in 1914 and is also an anthropologist. She was educated at Vassar, Yale, and Columbia. Metraux first met Mead while working at the American Museum of Natural History. A contributor to anthropological journals, Metraux collaborated with Mead on *A Way of Seeing* (1970), from which the following selection was taken. As you read this essay, notice the way the authors use examples both to define friendship and to point out the way different cultures regard friendship.

On Friendship

Few Americans stay put for a lifetime. We move from town to city to suburb, from high school to college in a different state, from a job in one region to a better job elsewhere, from the home where we raise our children to the home where we plan to live in retirement. With each move we are forever making new friends, who become part of our new life at that time.

For many of us the summer is a special time for forming new friendships. Today millions of Americans vacation abroad, and they go not only to see new sights but also—in those places where they do not feel too

---

strange—with the hope of meeting new people. No one really expects a vacation trip to produce a close friend. But surely the beginning of a friendship is possible? Surely in every country people value friendship?

They do. The difficulty when strangers from two countries meet is not   3
a lack of appreciation of friendship, but different expectations about what constitutes friendship and how it comes into being. In those European countries that Americans are most likely to visit, friendship is quite sharply distinguished from other, more casual relations, and is differently related to family life. For a Frenchman, a German or an Englishman friendship is usually more particularized and carries a heavier burden of commitment.

But as we use the word, "friend" can be applied to a wide range of   4
relationships—to someone one has known for a few weeks in a new place, to a close business associate, to a childhood playmate, to a man or woman, to a trusted confidant. There are real differences among these relations for Americans—a friendship may be superficial, casual, situational or deep and enduring. But to a European, who sees only our surface behavior, the differences are not clear.

As they see it, people known and accepted temporarily, casually, flow   5
in and out of Americans' homes with little ceremony and often with little personal commitment. They may be parents of the children's friends, house guests of neighbors, members of a committee, business associates from another town or even another country. Coming as a guest into an American home, the European visitor finds no visible landmarks. The atmosphere is relaxed. Most people, old and young, are called by first names.

Who, then, is a friend?   6

Even simple translation from one language to another is difficult. "You   7
see," a Frenchman explains, "if I were to say to you in French, 'This is my good friend,' that person would not be as close to me as someone about whom I say only, 'This is my friend.' Anyone about whom I have to say *more* is really less."

In France, as in many European countries, friends generally are of the   8
same sex, and friendship is seen as basically a relationship between men. Frenchwomen laugh at the idea that "women can't be friends," but they also admit sometimes that for women "it's a different thing." And many French people doubt the possibility of a friendship between a man and a woman. There is also a kind of relationship within a group—men and women who have worked together for a long time, who may be very close, sharing great loyalty and warmth of feeling. They may call one another *copains*—a word that in English becomes "friends" but has more the feeling of "pals" or "buddies." In French eyes this is not friendship, although two members of such a group may well be friends.

For the French, friendship is a one-to-one relationship that demands a   9
keen awareness of the other person's intellect, temperament and particular interests. A friend is someone who draws out your own best qualities, with

whom you sparkle and become more of whatever the friendship draws upon. Your political philosophy assumes more depth, appreciation of a play becomes sharper, taste in food or wine is accentuated, enjoyment of a sport is intensified.

And French friendships are compartmentalized. A man may play 10 chess with a friend for thirty years without knowing his political opinions, or he may talk politics with him for as long a time without knowing about his personal life. Different friends fill different niches in each person's life. These friendships are not made part of family life. A friend is not expected to spend evenings being nice to children or courteous to a deaf grand- mother. These duties, also serious and enjoined, are primarily for relatives. Men who are friends may meet in a café. Intellectual friends may meet in larger groups for evenings of conversation. Working people may meet at the little *bistro* where they drink and talk, far from the family. Marriage does not affect such friendships; wives do not have to be taken into account.

In the past in France, friendships of this kind seldom were open to any 11 but intellectual women. Since some women's lives centered on their homes, their warmest relations with other women often went back to their girl- hood. The special relationship of friendship is based on what the French value most—on the mind, on compatibility of outlook, on vivid awareness of some chosen area of life.

Friendship heightens the sense of each person's individuality. Other 12 relationships commanding as great loyalty and devotion have a different meaning. In World War II the first resistance groups formed in Paris were built on the foundation of *les copains*. But significantly, as time went on these little groups, whose lives rested in one another's hands, called them- selves "families." Where each had a total responsibility for all, it was kinship ties that provided the model. And even today such ties, crossing every line of class and personal interest, remain binding on the survivors of these small, secret bands.

In Germany, in contrast with France, friendship is much more articu- 13 lately a matter of feeling. Adolescents, boys and girls, form deeply senti- mental attachments, walk and talk together—not so much to polish their wits as to share their hopes and fears and dreams, to form a common front against the world of school and family and to join in a kind of mutual discovery of each other's and their own inner life. Within the family, the closest relationship over a lifetime is between brothers and sisters. Outside the family, men and women find in their closest friends of the same sex the devotion of a sister, the loyalty of a brother. Appropriately, in Germany friends usually are brought into the family. Children call their father's and their mother's friends "uncle" and "aunt." Between French friends, who have chosen each other for the congeniality of their point of view, lively disagreement and sharpness of argument are the breath of *life*. But for Germans, whose friendships are based on mutuality of feeling, deep disagreement on any subject that matters to both is regarded as a tragedy. Like ties of kinship, ties of friendship are meant to be irrevocably binding. Young Germans who come to the United States have great difficulty in establishing such friendships with Americans. We view friendship more tentatively, subject to changes in intensity as people move, change their jobs, marry, or discover new interests.

English friendships follow still a different pattern. Their basis is   14
shared activity. Activities at different stages of life may be of very different kinds—discovering a common interest in school, serving together in the armed forces, taking part in a foreign mission, staying in the same country house during a crisis. In the midst of the activity, whatever it may be, people fall into step—sometimes two men or two women, sometimes two couples, sometimes three people—and find that they walk or play a game or tell stories or serve on a tiresome and exacting committee with the same easy anticipation of what each will do day by day or in some critical situation. Americans who have made English friends comment that, even years later, "you can take up just where you left off." Meeting after a long interval, friends are like a couple who begin to dance again when the orchestra strikes up after a pause. English friendships are formed outside the family circle, but they are not, as in Germany, contrapuntal to the family nor are they, as in France, separated from the family. And a break in an English friendship comes not necessarily as a result of some irreconcilable difference of viewpoint or feeling but instead as a result of misjudgment, where one friend seriously misjudges how the other will think or feel or act, so that suddenly they are out of step.

What, then, is friendship? Looking at these different styles, including   15
our own, each of which is related to a whole way of life, are there common elements? There is the recognition that friendship, in contrast with kinship, invokes freedom of choice. A friend is someone who chooses and is chosen. Related to this is the sense each friend gives the other of being a special individual, on whatever grounds this recognition is based. And between friends there is inevitably a kind of equality of give-and-take. The similarities make the bridge between societies possible, and the American's characteristic openness to different styles of relationship makes it possible for him to find new friends abroad with whom he feels at home.

Questions for Study and Discussion

1. How, according to Mead and Metraux, do Americans use the term *friend?* Do you agree with their sense of how the word is used? How does our use of the word differ from that of Europeans?
2. What is the authors' purpose in this essay—to tell a story, to explain, to persuade? How do you know?

3. What are the major differences between the way friends are viewed in France, Germany, and England? Do any of these differences surprise you? Explain.

4. What do Mead and Metraux see as the differences between "friendship" and "kinship"?

5. Why do Americans seem to be able to find new "friends" when traveling abroad?

Writing Topics

1. What are your expectations of a friendship? What does the term "best friend" mean to you? How has your conception of friendship changed as you've grown older? Present your responses to these three questions in an essay.

2. Is it possible for men and women to have friendships? What, if any, are the problems that could arise with such a relationship? Your essay may simply reflect on the issue, or it may take the form of an argument for or against the possibility of male-female friendships.

JUDITH VIORST

The American philosopher George Santayana once wrote, "Friendship is almost always the union of a part of one mind with a part of another; people are friends in spots." Judith Viorst would agree. In fact, in this essay, she goes further, mapping the different kinds of spots where her mind achieves union with her friends'. A professional writer, Viorst was born in 1936 and has marked off the periods of her life with books of light verse: *It's Hard to Be Hip over Thirty and Other Tragedies of Married Life* (1970); *How Did I Get to Be Forty and Other Atrocities* (1976). More recently, she's written *Love and Guilt and the Meaning of Life* (1984), *Necessary Losses* (1986), and *When Did I Stop Being Twenty and Other Injustices* (1987). She also writes books for children, has collaborated with her husband on a guide to the restaurants of Washington, D.C., and is a contributing editor at *Redbook*. As you read this essay, which first appeared in her regular column in *Redbook*, see whether your own friends fit into Viorst's categories.

Friends, Good Friends—and Such Good Friends

Women are friends, I once would have said, when they totally love and support and trust each other, and bare to each other the secrets of their souls, and run—no questions asked—to help each other, and tell harsh truths to each other (no, you can't wear that dress unless you lose ten pounds first) when harsh truths must be told. 1

Women are friends, I once would have said, when they share the same affection for Ingmar Bergman, plus train rides, cats, warm rain, charades, Camus, and hate with equal ardor Newark and Brussels sprouts and Lawrence Welk and camping. 2

In other words, I once would have said that a friend is a friend all the way, but now I believe that's a narrow point of view. For the friendships I have and the friendships I see are conducted at many levels of intensity, serve many different functions, meet different needs and range from those as all-the-way as the friendship of the soul sisters mentioned above to that of the most nonchalant and casual playmates. 3

Consider these varieties of friendship: 4

1. Convenience friends. These are women with whom, if our paths weren't crossing all the time, we'd have no particular reason to be friends: a next-door neighbor, a woman in our car pool, the mother of one of our 5

children's closest friends or maybe some mommy with whom we serve juice and cookies each week at the Glenwood Co-op Nursery.

Convenience friends are convenient indeed. They'll lend us their cups 6 and silverware for a party. They'll drive our kids to soccer when we're sick. They'll take us to pick up our car when we need a lift to the garage. They'll even take our cats when we go on vacation. As we will for them.

But we don't, with convenience friends, ever come too close or tell too 7 much; we maintain our public face and emotional distance. "Which means," says Elaine, "that I'll talk about being overweight but not about being depressed. Which means I'll admit being mad but not blind with rage. Which means that I might say that we're pinched this month but never that I'm worried sick over money."

But which doesn't mean that there isn't sufficient value to be found in 8 these friendships of mutual aid, in convenience friends.

2. Special-interest friends. These friendships aren't intimate, and they 9 needn't involve kids or silverware or cats. Their value lies in some interest jointly shared. And so we may have an office friend or a yoga friend or a tennis friend or a friend from the Women's Democratic Club.

"I've got one woman friend," says Joyce, "who likes, as I do, to take 10 psychology courses. Which makes it nice for me—and nice for her. It's fun to go with someone you know and it's fun to discuss what you've learned, driving back from the classes." And for the most part, she says, that's all they discuss.

"I'd say that what we're doing is *doing* together, not being together," 11 Suzanne says of her Tuesday-doubles friends. "It's mainly a tennis relationship, but we play together well. And I guess we all need to have a couple of playmates."

I agree. 12

My playmate is a shopping friend, a woman of marvelous taste, a 13 woman who knows exactly *where* to buy *what*, and furthermore is a woman who always knows beyond a doubt what one ought to be buying. I don't have the time to keep up with what's new in eyeshadow, hemlines and shoes and whether the smock look is in or finished already. But since (oh, shame!) I care a lot about eyeshadows, hemlines and shoes, and since I don't *want* to wear smocks if the smock look is finished, I'm very glad to have a shopping friend.

3. Historical friends. We all have a friend who knew us when . . . 14 maybe way back in Miss Meltzer's second grade, when our family lived in that three-room flat in Brooklyn, when our dad was out of work for seven months, when our brother Allie got in that fight where they had to call the police, when our sister married the endodontist from Yonkers and when, the morning after we lost our virginity, she was the first, the only, friend we told.

The years have gone by and we've gone separate ways and we've little   15
in common now, but we're still an intimate part of each other's past. And so
whenever we go to Detroit we always go to visit this friend of our girlhood.
Who knows how we looked before our teeth were straightened. Who knows
how we talked before our voice got un-Brooklyned. Who knows what we ate
before we learned about artichokes. And who, by her presence, puts us in
touch with an earlier part of ourself, a part of ourself it's important never to
lose.

"What this friend means to me and what I mean to her," says Grace,   16
"is having a sister without sibling rivalry. We know the texture of each
other's lives. She remembers my grandmother's cabbage soup. I remember
the way her uncle played the piano. There's simply no other friend who
remembers those things."

4. Crossroads friends. Like historical friends, our crossroads friends   17
are important for *what was*—for the friendship we shared at a crucial, now
past time of life. A time, perhaps, when we roomed in college together; or
worked as eager young singles in the Big City together; or went together, as
my friend Elizabeth and I did, through pregnancy, birth and that scary first
year of new motherhood.

Crossroads friends forge powerful links, links strong enough to endure   18
with not much more contact than once-a-year letters at Christmas. And out
of respect for those crossroads years, for those dramas and dreams we once
shared, we will always be friends.

5. Cross-generational friends. Historical friends and crossroads friends   19
seem to maintain a special kind of intimacy—dormant but always ready to
be revived—and though we may rarely meet, whenever we do connect, it's
personal and intense. Another kind of intimacy exists in the friendships
that form across generations in what one woman calls her daughter-mother
and her mother-daughter relationships.

Evelyn's friend is her mother's age—"but I share so much more than I   20
ever could with my mother"—a woman she talks to of music, of books and
of life. "What I get from her is the benefit of her experience. What she gets—
and enjoys—from me is a youthful perspective. It's a pleasure for both
of us."

I have in my own life a precious friend, a woman of 65 who has lived   21
very hard, who is wise, who listens well; who has been where I am and can
help me understand it; and who represents not only an ultimate ideal
mother to me but also the person I'd like to be when I grow up.

In our daughter role we tend to do more than our share of self-   22
revelation; in our mother role we tend to receive what's revealed. It's
another kind of pleasure—playing wise mother to a questing younger person. It's another very lovely kind of friendship.

6. Part-of-a-couple friends. Some of the women we call our friends we   23
never see alone—we see them as part of a couple at couples' parties. And

though we share interests in many things and respect each other's views, we aren't moved to deepen the relationship. Whatever the reason, a lack of time or—and this is more likely—a lack of chemistry, our friendship remains in the context of a group. But the fact that our feeling on seeing each other is always, "I'm *so* glad she's here" and the fact that we spend half the evening talking together says that this too, in its own way, counts as a friendship.

(Other part-of-a-couple friends are the friends that came with the   24
marriage, and some of these are friends we could live without. But sometimes, alas, she married our husband's best friend; and sometimes, alas, she *is* our husband's best friend. And so we find ourselves dealing with her, somewhat against our will, in a spirit of what I'll call *reluctant* friendship.)

7. Men who are friends. I wanted to write just of women friends, but   25
the women I've talked to won't let me—they say I must mention man-woman friendships too. For these friendships can be just as close and as dear as those that we form with women. Listen to Lucy's description of one such friendship:

"We've found we have things to talk about that are different from   26
what he talks about with my husband and different from what I talk about with his wife. So sometimes we call on the phone or meet for lunch. There are similar intellectual interests—we always pass on to each other the book that we love—but there's also something tender and caring too."

In a couple of crises, Lucy says, "he offered himself for talking and for   27
helping. And when someone died in his family he wanted me there. The sexual, flirty part of our friendship is very small—but *some* just enough to make it fun and different." She thinks—and I agree—that the sexual part, though small, is always *some*, is always there when a man and a woman are friends.

It's only in the past few years that I've made friends with men, in the   28
sense of a friendship that's *mine*, not just part of two couples. And achieving with them the ease and the trust I've found with women friends has value indeed. Under the dryer at home last week, putting on mascara and rouge, I comfortably sat and talked with a fellow named Peter. Peter, I finally decided, could handle the shock of me minus mascara under the dryer. Because we care for each other. Because we're friends.

There are medium friends, and pretty good friends, and very good   29
friends indeed, and these friendships are defined by their level of intimacy. And what we'll reveal at each of these levels of intimacy is calibrated with care. We might tell a medium friend, for example, that yesterday we had a fight with our husband. And we might tell a pretty good friend that this fight with our husband made us so mad that we slept on the couch. And we might tell a very good friend that the reason we got so mad in that fight that we slept on the couch had something to do with that girl who works in his office. But it's only to our very best friends that we're willing to tell all, to tell what's going on with that girl in his office.

The best of friends, I still believe, totally love and support and trust 30
each other, and bare to each other the secrets of their souls, and run—no
questions asked—to help each other, and tell harsh truths to each other
when they must be told.

But we needn't agree about everything (only 12-year-old girl friends 31
agree about *everything*) to tolerate each other's point of view. To accept
without judgment. To give and to take without ever keeping score. And to
be there, as I am for them and as they are for me, to comfort our sorrows, to
celebrate our joys.

Questions for Study and Discussion

1. In the opening paragraphs Viorst explains how she once would have
defined friendship. What definition might she have given? Why does she now
think differently?

2. What is Viorst's purpose in this essay? How does her extended list of
categories serve that purpose?

3. The readership of *Redbook*, where this essay first appeared, consists
largely of women between the ages of twenty-five and thirty-five. If Viorst had
been writing for an audience of young men, how might her categories have been
different? How might her examples have been different?

4. How does Viorst use quotation in her essay? Are her quotations
appropriate and credible?

5. Throughout the essay Viorst often uses the word *we*. Why do you
think she does this? Does it cause problems? If so, where?

6. What is the tone of this essay? Cite passages that show how Viorst
creates the tone.

Writing Topics

1. Some people would say that all the relationships Viorst describes are
forms of friendship. Others may feel that most are mere acquaintances, and
that true friendship is something different. Write an essay in which you explain
what your idea of friendship is. Illustrate your definition with examples from
your experience or your reading.

2. American society holds a much broader notion of friendship than
many other societies do, and Americans are quite quick to address each other
familiarly—using first names and not using titles, for example. Those who have
traveled or lived abroad invariably notice this, as do foreigners visiting the
United States. What do you think are the advantages of such "easy" friendship
and informality? What might the disadvantages be? Write an essay in which you
explain your views.

MARC FEIGEN FASTEAU

Marc Feigen Fasteau is a practicing lawyer in New York City with a specialty in sex-discrimination litigation. While at Harvard Law School he was the editor of the Harvard Law Review, and later he worked in government service in Washington, D.C., his birthplace. Fasteau is a frequent lecturer on topics ranging from sex-discrimination legislation to sexual stereotypes, and is the author of *The Male Machine* (1974). His articles have appeared in scholarly journals as well as in such popular magazines as *Ms.*

In *The Male Machine* Fasteau analyzes the stereotype of the American male and concludes that the prevailing stereotype has, in part, dehumanized American men. The following selection is an excerpt from *The Male Machine* in which Fasteau explains why friendships among men are seemingly unfeeling.

Friendships among Men

There is a long-standing myth in our society that the great friendships are between men. Forged through shared experience, male friendship is portrayed as the most unselfish, if not the highest form, of human relationship. The more traditionally masculine the shared experience from which it springs, the stronger and more profound the friendship is supposed to be. Going to war, weathering crises together at school or work, playing on the same athletic team, are some of the classic experiences out of which friendships between men are believed to grow.

By and large, men do prefer the company of other men, not only in their structured time but in the time they fill with optional, nonobligatory activity. They prefer to play games, drink, and talk, as well as work and fight together. Yet something is missing. Despite the time men spend together, their contact rarely goes beyond the external, a limitation which tends to make their friendships shallow and unsatisfying.

My own childhood memories are of doing things with my friends— playing games or sports, building walkie-talkies, going camping. Other people and my relationships to them were never legitimate subjects for attention. If someone liked me, it was an opaque, mysterious occurrence that bore no analysis. When I was slighted, I felt hurt. But relationships with people just happened. I certainly had feelings about my friends, but I can't remember a single instance of trying consciously to sort them out until I was well into college.

For most men this kind of shying away from the personal continues   4
into adult life. In conversations with each other, we hardly ever use ourselves as reference points. We talk about almost everything except how we ourselves are affected by people and events. Everything is discussed as though it were taking place out there somewhere, as though we had no more felt response to it than to the weather. Topics that can be treated in this detached, objective way become conversational mainstays. The few subjects which are fundamentally personal are shaped into discussions of abstract general questions. Even in an exchange about their reactions to liberated women—a topic of intensely personal interest—the tendency will be to talk in general, theoretical terms. Work, at least its objective aspects, is always a safe subject. Men also spend an incredible amount of time rehashing the great public issues of the day. Until early 1973, Vietnam was the work-horse topic. Then came Watergate. It doesn't seem to matter that we've all had a hundred similar conversations. We plunge in for another round, trying to come up with a new angle as much as to impress the others with what we know as to keep from being bored stiff.

Games play a central role in situations organized by men. I remember a weekend some years ago at the country house of a law-school classmate as a blur of softball, football, croquet, poker, and a dice-and-board game called Combat, with swimming thrown in on the side. As soon as one game ended, another began. Taken one at a time, these "activities" were fun, but the impression was inescapable that the host, and most of his guests, would do anything to stave off a lull in which they would be together without some impersonal focus for their attention. A snapshot of almost any men's club would show the same thing, 90 percent of the men engaged in some activity—ranging from backgammon to watching the tube—other than, or at least as an aid to, conversation.*

My composite memory of evenings spent with a friend at college and   6
later when we shared an apartment in Washington is of conversations punctuated by silences during which we would internally pass over any personal or emotional thoughts which had arisen and come back to the permitted track. When I couldn't get my mind off personal matters, I said very little. Talks with my father have always had the same tone. Respect for privacy was the rationale for our diffidence. His questions to me about how things were going at school or at work were asked as discreetly as he would have asked a friend about someone's commitment to a hospital for the criminally insane. Our conversations, when they touched these matters at

---

*Women may use games as a reason for getting together—bridge clubs, for example. But the show is more for the rest of the world—to indicate that they are doing *something*— and the games themselves are not the only means of communication.

all, to say nothing of more sensitive matters, would veer quickly back to safe topics of general interest.

In our popular literature, the archetypal hero embodying this personal muteness is the cowboy. The classic mold for the character was set in 1902 by Owen Wister's novel *The Virginian* where the author spelled out, with an explicitness that was never again necessary, the characteristics of his protagonist. Here's how it goes when two close friends the Virginian hasn't seen in some time take him out for a drink:

> All of them had seen rough days together, and they felt guilty with emotion.
> "It's hot weather," said Wiggin.
> "Hotter in Box Elder," said McLean. "My kid has started teething."
> Words ran dry again. They shifted their positions, looked in their glasses, read the labels on the bottles. They dropped a word now and then to the proprietor about his trade, and his ornaments.

One of the Virginian's duties is to assist at the hanging of an old friend as a horse thief. Afterward, for the first time in the book, he is visibly upset. The narrator puts his arm around the hero's shoulders and describes the Virginian's reaction:

> I had the sense to keep silent, and presently he shook my hand, not looking at me as he did so. He was always very shy of demonstration.

And, for explanation of such reticence, "As all men know, he also knew that many things should be done in this world in silence, and that talking about them is a mistake."

There are exceptions, but they only prove the rule.

One is the drunken confidence: "Bob, ole boy, I gotta tell ya—being divorced isn't so hot. . . . [and see, I'm too drunk to be held responsible for blurting it out]." Here, drink becomes an excuse for exchanging confidences and a device for periodically loosening the restraint against expressing a need for sympathy and support from other men—which may explain its importance as a male ritual. Marijuana fills a similar need.

Another exception is talking to a stranger—who may be either someone the speaker doesn't know or someone who isn't in the same social or business world. (Several black friends told me that they have been on the receiving end of personal confidences from white acquaintances that they were sure had not been shared with white friends.) In either case, men are willing to talk about themselves only to other men with whom they do not have to compete or whom they will not have to confront socially later.

Finally, there is the way men depend on women to facilitate certain conversations. The women in a mixed group are usually the ones who make the first personal reference, about themselves or others present. The men can then join in without having the onus of initiating a discussion of "personalities." Collectively, the men can "blame" the conversation on the women. They can also feel in these conversations that since they are talking "to" the women instead of "to" the men, they can be excused for deviating from the masculine norm. When the women leave, the tone and subject invariably shift away from the personal.

The effect of these constraints is to make it extraordinarily difficult for   12
men to really get to know each other. A psychotherapist who has conducted a lengthy series of encounter groups for men summed it up:

> With saddening regularity [the members of these groups] described how much they wanted to have closer, more satisfying relationships with other men: "I'd settle for having one really close man friend. I supposedly have some close men friends now. We play golf or go for a drink. We complain about our jobs and our wives. I care about them and they care about me. We even have some physical contact—I mean we may even give a hug on a big occasion. But it's not enough."

The sources of this stifling ban on self-disclosure, the reasons why men hide from each other, lie in the taboos and imperatives of the masculine stereotype.

To begin with, men are supposed to be functional, to spend their time   13
working or otherwise solving or thinking about how to solve problems. Personal reaction, how one feels about something, is considered dysfunctional, at best an irrelevant distraction from the expected objectivity. Only weak men, and women, talk about—i.e., "give in," to their feelings. "I group my friends in two ways," said a business executive:

> those who have made it and don't complain and those who haven't made it. And only the latter spend time talking to their wives about their problems and how bad their boss is and all that. The ones who concentrate more on communicating . . . are those who have realized that they aren't going to make it and therefore they have changed the focus of attention.

In a world which tells men they have to choose between expressiveness and manly strength, this characterization may be accurate. Most of the men who talk personally to other men *are* those whose problems have gotten the best of them, who simply can't help it. Men not driven to despair don't talk about themselves, so the idea that self-disclosure and expressiveness are associated with problems and weakness becomes a self-fulfilling prophecy.

Obsessive competitiveness also limits the range of communication in   14
male friendships. Competition is the principal mode by which men relate to each other—at one level because they don't know how else to make contact, but more basically because it is the way to demonstrate, to themselves and others, the key masculine qualities of unwavering toughness and the ability to dominate and control. The result is that they inject competition into situations which don't call for it.

In conversations, you must show that you know more about the   15
subject than the other man, or at least as much as he does. For example, I
have often engaged in a contest that could be called My Theory Tops Yours,
disguised as a serious exchange of ideas. The proof that it wasn't serious was
that I was willing to participate even when I was sure that the participants,
including myself, had nothing fresh to say. Convincing the other person—
victory—is the main objective, with control of the floor an important tactic.
Men tend to lecture at each other, insist that the discussion follow their
train of thought, and are often unwilling to listen. As one member of a
men's rap group said,

> When I was talking I used to feel that I had to be driving to a point, that it had
> to be rational and organized, that I had to persuade at all times, rather than
> exchange thoughts and ideas.

Even in casual conversation some men hold back unless they are absolutely
sure of what they are saying. They don't want to have to change a position
once they have taken it. It's "just like a woman" to change your mind, and,
more important, it is inconsistent with the approved masculine posture of
total independence.

Competition was at the heart of one of my closest friendships, now   16
defunct. There was a good deal of mutual liking and respect. We went out of
our way to spend time with each other and wanted to work together. We
both had "prospects" as "bright young men" and the same "liberal but
tough" point of view. We recognized this about each other, and this recognition was the basis of our respect and of our sense of equality. That we saw
each other as equals was important—our friendship was confirmed by the
reflection of one in the other. But our constant and all-encompassing
competition made this equality precarious and fragile. One way or another,
everything counted in the measuring process. We fought out our tennis
matches as though our lives depended on it. At poker, the two of us would
often play on for hours after the others had left. These *mano a mano* poker
marathons seem in retrospect especially revealing of the competitiveness of
the relationship: playing for small stakes, the essence of the game is in
outwitting, psychologically beating down the other player—the other skills
involved are negligible. Winning is the only pleasure, one that evaporates
quickly, a truth that struck me in inchoat form every time our game broke
up at four A.M. and I walked out the door with my five-dollar winnings, a
headache, and a sense of time wasted. Still, I did the same think the next
time. It was what we did together, and somehow it counted. Losing at tennis
could be balanced by winning at poker; at another level, his moving up in
the federal government by my getting on the *Harvard Law Review*.

This competitiveness feeds the most basic obstacle to openness be-   17
tween men, the inability to admit to being vulnerable. Real men, we learn
early, are not supposed to have doubts, hopes and ambitions which may not

be realized, things they don't (or even especially do) like about themselves, fears and disappointments. Such feelings and concerns, of course, are part of everyone's inner life, but a man must keep quiet about them. If others know how you really feel you can be hurt, and that in itself is incompatible with manhood. The inhibiting effect of this imperative is not limited to disclosures of major personal problems. Often men do not share even ordinary uncertainties and half-formulated plans of daily life with their friends. And when they do, they are careful to suggest that they already know how to proceed—that they are not really asking for help or under-standing but simply for particular bits of information. Either way, any doubts they have are presented as external, carefully characterized as having to do with the issue as distinct from the speaker. They are especially guarded about expressing concern or asking a question that would invite personal comment. It is almost impossible for men to simply exchange thoughts about matters involving them personally in a comfortable, non-crisis atmosphere. If a friend tells you of his concern that he and a colleague are always disagreeing, for example, he is likely to quickly supply his own explanation—something like "different professional backgrounds." The effect is to rule out observations or suggestions that do not fit within this already reconnoitered protective structure. You don't suggest, even if you believe it is true, that in fact the disagreements arise because he presents his ideas in a way which tends to provoke a hostile reaction. It would catch him off guard; it would be something he hadn't already thought of and accepted about himself and, for that reason, no matter how constructive and well-intentioned you might be, it would put you in control for the moment. He doesn't want that; he is afraid of losing your respect. So, sensing he feels that way, because you would yourself, you say something else. There is no real give-and-take.

It is hard for men to get angry at each other honestly. Anger between friends often means that one has hurt the other. Since the straightforward expression of anger in these situations involves an admission of vul-nerability, it is safer to stew silently or find an "objective" excuse for retaliation. Either way, trust is not fully restored. [18]

Men even try not to let it show when they feel good. We may report the reasons for our happiness, if they have to do with concrete accomplish-ments, but we try to do it with a straight face, as if to say, "Here's what happened, but it hasn't affected my grown-up unemotional equilibrium, and I am not asking for any kind of response." Happiness is a precarious, "childish" feeling, easy to shoot down. Others may find the event that triggers it trivial or incomprehensible, or even threatening to their own self-esteem—in the sense that if one man is up, another man is down. So we tend not to take the risk of expressing it. [19]

What is particularly difficult for men is seeking or accepting help from friends. I, for one, learned early that dependence was unacceptable. When I [20] was eight, I went to a summer camp I disliked. My parents visited me in the middle of the summer and, when it was time for them to leave, I wanted to go with them. They refused, and I yelled and screamed and was miserably unhappy for the rest of the day. That evening an older camper comforted me, sitting by my bed as I cried, patting me on the back soothingly and saying whatever it is that one says at times like that. He was in some way clumsy or funny-looking, and a few days later I joined a group of kids in cruelly making fun of him, an act which upset me, when I thought about it, for years. I can only explain it in terms of my feeling, as early as the age of eight, that by needing and accepting his help and comfort I had compromised myself, and took it out on him.

"You can't express dependence when you feel it," a corporate executive said, "because it's a kind of absolute. If you are loyal 90 percent of the time and disloyal 10 percent, would you be considered loyal? Well, the same happens with independence: you are either dependent or independent; you can't be both." "Feelings of dependence," another explained, "are identified with weakness or 'untoughness' and our culture doesn't accept those things in men." The result is that we either go it alone or "act out certain games or rituals to provoke the desired reaction in the other and have our needs satisfied without having to ask for anything." 21

Somewhat less obviously, the expression of affection also runs into emotional barriers growing out of the masculine stereotype. When I was in college, I was suddenly quite moved while attending a friend's wedding. The surge of feeling made me uncomfortable and self-conscious. There was nothing inherently difficult or, apart from the fact of being moved by a moment of tenderness, "unmasculine" about my reaction. I just did not know how to deal with or communicate what I felt. "I consider myself a sentimentalist," one man said, "and I think I am quite able to express my feelings. But the other day my wife described a friend of mine to some people as my best friend and I felt embarrassed when I heard her say it. 22

A major source of these inhibitions is the fear of being, of being thought, homosexual. Nothing is more frightening to a heterosexual man in our society. It threatens, at one stroke, to take away every vestige of his claim to a masculine identity—something like knocking out the foundations of a building—and to expose him to the ostracism, ranging from polite tolerance to violent revulsion, of his friends and colleagues. A man can be labeled as homosexual not just because of an overt sexual act but because of almost any sign of behavior which does not fit the masculine stereotype. The touching of another man, other than shaking hands or, under emotional stress, an arm around the shoulder, is taboo. Woman may kiss each other when they meet; men are uncomfortable when hugged even by close friends. Onlookers might misinterpret what they say, and more important, what would we think of ourselves if we feel a twinge of sensual pleasure from the embrace. 23

Direct verbal expressions of affection or tenderness are also something   24
that only homosexuals and women engage in. Between "real" men affection
had to be disguised in gruff, "you old son-of-a-bitch" style. Paradoxically, in
some instances, terms of endearment between men can be used as a ritual
badge of manhood, dangerous medicine safe only for the strong. The
flirting with homosexuality that characterizes the initiation rites of many
fraternities and men's clubs serves this purpose. Claude Brown wrote about
black life in New York City in the 1950s:

> The term ["baby"] had a hip ring to it. . . . It was like saying, "Man, look at
> me. I've got masculinity to spare. . . . I can say 'baby' to another cat and he
> can say 'baby' to me, and we can say it with strength in our voices." If you
> could say it, this meant that you really had to be sure of yourself, sure of your
> masculinity.

Fear of homosexuality does more than inhibit the physical display of
affection. One of the major recurring themes in the men's groups led by
psychotherapist Don Clark was:

> A large segment of my feelings about other men are unknown or distorted
> because I am afraid they might have something to do with homosexuality.
> Now I'm lonely for other men and don't know how to find what I want with
> them.

As Clark observes, "The specter of homosexuality seems to be the dragon at
the gateway to self-awareness, understanding, and acceptance of male-male
needs. If a man tries to pretend the dragon is not there by turning a blind
eye to erotic feelings for all other males, he also blinds himself to the rich
variety of feelings that are related."

The few situations in which men do acknowledge strong feelings of   25
affection and dependence toward other men are exceptions which prove the
rule. With "cop couples," for example, or combat soldier "buddies," intimacy and dependence are forced on the men by their work—they have to
ride in the patrol car or be in the same foxhole with somebody—and the
jobs themselves have such highly masculine images that the man can get
away with behavior that would be suspect under any other conditions.

Furthermore, even these combat-buddy relationships, when looked at   26
closely, turn out not to be particularly intimate or personal. Margaret Mead
has written:

> During the last war English observers were confused by the apparent contra-
> diction between American soldiers' emphasis on the buddy, so grievously
> exemplified in the break-downs that followed a buddy's death, and the results
> of detailed inquiry which showed how transitory these buddy relationships
> were. It was found that men actually accepted their buddies as derivatives
> from their outfit, and from accidents of association, rather than because of
> any special personality characteristics capable of ripening into friendship.

One effect of the fear of appearing to be homosexual is to reinforce the practice that two men rarely get together alone without a reason. I once called a friend to suggest that we have dinner together. "O.K.," he said. "What's up?" I felt uncomfortable telling him that I just wanted to talk, that there was no other reason for the invitation.

Men get together to conduct business, to drink, to play games and sports, to re-establish contact after long absences, to participate in heterosexual social occasions—circumstances in which neither person is responsible for actually wanting to see the other. Men are particularly comfortable seeing each other in groups. The group situation defuses any possible assumptions about the intensity of feeling between particular men and provides the safety of numbers—"All the guys are here." It makes personal communication, which requires a level of trust and mutual understanding not generally shared by all members of a group, more difficult and offers an excuse for avoiding this dangerous territory. And it provides what is most sought after in men's friendships: mutual reassurance of masculinity.

27

Questions for Study and Discussion

1. Why does Fasteau think that the belief that the great friendships are between men is a long-standing myth?

2. Why does Fasteau find male friendships "shallow and unsatisfying"?

3. Why do men tend to shy away from anything that smacks of the personal? How do they rationalize this behavior?

4. Why do games play such an important role in men's lives? What role do they play in women's lives?

5. In what types of situations do men become personal?

6. According to Fasteau, what effect does competition have on male friendships? Do you agree with his analysis? Explain.

7. Fasteau concludes his essay by stating that the group situation "provides what is most sought after in men's friendships: mutual reassurance of masculinity." Why do you suppose men need such reassurance? Do they seem to need it more today than in times past? Explain.

Writing Topics

1. Using your own experiences and observations write an essay in which you argue with Fasteau's position that "despite the time men spend together, their contact rarely goes beyond the external."

2. If you accept Fasteau's analysis of the "reasons why men hide from each other," what can be done to make more meaningful communication possible? Write an essay in which you propose some solutions.

BANESH HOFFMANN

Mathematician, physicist, author, and professor, Banesh Hoffmann was born in Richmond, England, in 1906. He earned his B.A. at Oxford and his Ph.D. at Princeton University. Hoffmann has served on the faculties of the University of Rochester, Queens College, and the Institute for Advanced Study at Princeton where he worked side-by-side with Albert Einstein. In collaboration with Einstein's personal secretary, Helen Dukas, he has written two highly praised biographical studies—*Albert Einstein: Creator and Rebel* (1973) and *Albert Einstein: The Human Side* (1979). Hoffmann has also authored *The Strange Story of the Quantum* (1959) and *The Tyranny of Testing* (1978).

In the following selection that first appeared in *Reader's Digest* and later in the anthology *Unforgettable Characters* (1980), Hoffmann describes the kind of man he found his colleague and friend Albert Einstein to be.

My Friend, Albert Einstein

He was one of the greatest scientists the world has ever known, yet if I had to convey the essence of Albert Einstein in a single work, I would choose *simplicity*. Perhaps an anecdote will help. Once, caught in a downpour, he took off his hat and held it under his coat. Asked why, he explained, with admirable logic, that the rain would damage the hat, but his hair would be none the worse for its wetting. This knack for going instinctively to the heart of a matter was the secret of his major scientific discoveries—this and his extraordinary feeling for beauty.

I first met Albert Einstein in 1935, at the famous Institute for Advanced Study in Princeton, N.J. He had been among the first to be invited to the Institute, and was offered *carte blanche* as to salary. To the director's dismay, Einstein asked for an impossible sum: it was far too *small*. The director had to plead with him to accept a larger salary.

I was in awe of Einstein, and hesitated before approaching him about some ideas I had been working on. When I finally knocked on his door, a gentle voice said, "Come"—with a rising inflection that made the single word both a welcome and a question. I entered his office and found him seated at a table, calculating and smoking his pipe. Dressed in ill-fitting clothes, his hair characteristically awry, he smiled a warm welcome. His utter naturalness at once set me at ease.

As I began to explain my ideas, he asked me to write the equations on 4 the blackboard so he could see how they developed. Then came the staggering—and altogether endearing—request: "Please go slowly. I do not understand things quickly." This from Einstein! He said it gently, and I laughed. From then on, all vestiges of fear were gone.

Einstein was born in 1879 in the German city of Ulm. He had been no 5 infant prodigy; indeed, he was so late in learning to speak that his parents feared he was a dullard. In school, though his teachers saw no special talent in him, the signs were already there. He taught himself calculus, for example, and his teachers seemed a little afraid of him because he asked questions they could not answer. At the age of 16, he asked himself whether a light wave would seem stationary if one ran abreast of it. From that innocent question would arise, ten years later, his theory of relativity.

Einstein failed his entrance examinations at the Swiss Federal Poly- 6 technic School, in Zurich, but was admitted a year later. There he went beyond his regular work to study the masterworks of physics on his own. Rejected when he applied for academic positions, he ultimately found work, in 1902, as a patent examiner in Berne, and there in 1905 his genius burst into fabulous flower.

Among the extraordinary things he produced in that memorable year 7 were his theory of relativity, with its famous offshoot, $E = mc^2$ (energy equals mass times the speed of light squared), and his quantum theory of light. These two theories were not only revolutionary, but seemingly contradictory: the former was intimately linked to the theory that light consists of waves, while the latter said it consists somehow of particles. Yet this unknown young man boldly proposed both at once—and he was right in both cases, though how he could have been is far too complex a story to tell here.

Collaborating with Einstein was an unforgettable experience. In 1937, 8 the Polish physicist Leopold Infeld and I asked if we could work with him. He was pleased with the proposal, since he had an idea about gravitation waiting to be worked out in detail. Thus we got to know not merely the man and the friend, but also the professional.

The intensity and depth of his concentration were fantastic. When 9 battling a recalcitrant problem, he worried it as an animal worries its prey. Often, when we found ourselves up against a seemingly insuperable diffi- culty, he would stand up, put his pipe on the table, and say in his quaint English, "I will a little tink" (he could not pronounce "th"). Then he would pace up and down, twirling a lock of his long, graying hair around his forefinger.

A dreamy, faraway and yet inward look would come over his face. 10 There was no appearance of concentration, no furrowing of the brow—only a placid inner communion. The minutes would pass, and then suddenly Einstein would stop pacing as his face relaxed into a gentle smile. He had found the solution to the problem. Sometimes it was so simple that Infeld and I could have kicked ourselves for not having thought of it. But the magic had been performed invisibly in the depths of Einstein's mind, by a process we could not fathom.

Although Einstein felt no need for religious ritual and belonged to no   11
formal religious group, he was the most deeply religious man I have known. He once said to me, "Ideas come from God," and one could hear the capital "G" in the reverence with which he pronounced the word. On the marble fireplace in the mathematics building at Princeton University is carved, in the original German, what one might call his scientific credo: "God is subtle, but he is not malicious." By this Einstein meant that scientists could expect to find their task difficult, but not hopeless: the Universe was a Universe of law, and God was not confusing us with deliberate paradoxes and contradictions.

Einstein was an accomplished amateur musician. We used to play   12
duets, he on the violin, I at the piano. One day he surprised me by saying Mozart was the greatest composer of all. Beethoven "created" his music, but the music of Mozart was of such purity and beauty one felt he had merely "found" it—that it had always existed as part of the inner beauty of the Universe, waiting to be revealed.

It was this very Mozartean simplicity that most characterized Ein-   13
stein's methods. His 1905 theory of relativity, for example, was built on just two simple assumptions. One is the so-called principle of relativity, which means, roughly speaking, that we cannot tell whether we are at rest or moving smoothly. The other assumption is that the speed of light is the same no matter what the speed of the object that produces it. You can see how reasonable this is if you think of agitating a stick in a lake to create waves. Whether you wiggle the stick from a stationary pier, or from a rushing speedboat, the waves, once generated, are on their own, and their speed has nothing to do with that of the stick.

Each of these assumptions, by itself, was so plausible as to seem   14
primitively obvious. But together they were in such violent conflict that a lesser man would have dropped one or the other and fled in panic. Einstein daringly kept both—and by so doing he revolutionized physics. For he demonstrated they could, after all, exist peacefully side by side, provided we gave up cherished beliefs about the nature of time.

Science is like a house of cards, with concepts like time and space at   15
the lowest level. Tampering with time brought most of the house tumbling down, and it was this that made Einstein's work so important—and contro-versial. At a conference in Princeton in honor of his 70th birthday, one of the speakers, a Nobel Prize-winner, tried to convey the magical quality of Einstein's achievement. Words failed him, and with a shrug of helplessness he pointed to his wristwatch, and said in tones of awed amazement, "It all

came from this." His very ineloquence made this the most eloquent tribute I have heard to Einstein's genius.

We think of Einstein as one concerned only with the deepest aspects of science. But he saw scientific principles in everyday things to which most of us would give barely a second thought. He once asked me if I had ever wondered why a man's feet will sink into either dry or completely submerged sand, while sand that is merely damp provides a firm surface. When I could not answer, he offered a simple explanation.

It depends, he pointed out, on *surface tension*, the elastic-skin effect of a liquid surface. This is what holds a drop together, or causes two small raindrops on a window pane to pull into one big drop the moment their surfaces touch.

When sand is damp, Einstein explained, there are tiny amounts of water between grains. The surface tensions of these tiny amounts of water pull all the grains together, and friction then makes them hard to budge. When the sand is dry, there is obviously no water between grains. If the sand is fully immersed, there is water between grains, but no water *surface* to pull them together.

This is not as important as relativity; yet there is no telling what seeming trifle will lead an Einstein to a major discovery. And the puzzle of the sand does give us an inkling of the power and elegance of his mind.

Einstein's work, performed quietly with pencil and paper, seemed remote from the turmoil of everyday life. But his ideas were so revolutionary they caused violent controversy and irrational anger. Indeed, in order to be able to award him a belated Nobel Prize, the selection committee had to avoid mentioning relativity, and pretend the prize was awarded primarily for his work on the quantum theory.

Political events upset the serenity of his life even more. When the Nazis came to power in Germany, his theories were officially declared false because they had been formulated by a Jew. His property was confiscated, and it is said a price was put on his head.

When scientists in the United States, fearful that the Nazis might develop an atomic bomb, sought to alert American authorities to the danger, they were scarcely heeded. In desperation, they drafted a letter which Einstein signed and sent directly to President Roosevelt. It was this act that led to the fateful decision to go all-out on the production of an atomic bomb—an endeavor in which Einstein took no active part. When he heard of the agony and destruction that his $E = mc^2$ had wrought, he was dismayed beyond measure, and from then on there was a look of ineffable sadness in his eyes.

There was something elusively whimsical about Einstein, It is illustrated by my favorite anecdote about him. In his first year in Princeton, on Christmas Eve, so the story goes, some children sang carols outside his house. Having finished, they knocked on his door and explained they were collecting money to buy Christmas presents. Einstein listened, then said, "Wait a moment." He put on his scarf and overcoat, and took his violin from its case. Then, joining the children as they went from door to door, he accompanied their singing of "Silent Night" on his violin.

How shall I sum up what it meant to have known Einstein and his works? Like the Nobel Prize-winner who pointed helplessly at his watch, I can find no adequate words. It was akin to the revelation of great art that lets one see what was formerly hidden. And when, for example, I walk on the sand of a lonely beach, I am reminded of his ceaseless search for cosmic simplicity—and the scene takes on a deeper, sadder beauty. 24

Questions for Study and Discussion

1. Hoffmann feels that the word *simplicity* captures the essence of Albert Einstein. What character traits does Hoffmann describe to substantiate this impression of Einstein?
2. What is Hoffmann's purpose in writing this essay? Is it stated or implied?
3. Hoffmann uses several anecdotes to develop his description of Einstein. How do these anecdotes describe Einstein in a way that statements of the author's impressions of the man could not? Refer to a few of the anecdotes to support your answer.
4. Hoffmann begins his essay by offering a personal impression of Einstein. Why do you suppose he chose this beginning? Would another beginning have been more effective? Why or why not?
5. What, for Hoffmann, was the secret of Einstein's major scientific discoveries? Explain.
6. In 1905 Einstein produced both his theory of relativity and his quantum theory of light. What is remarkable about the fact that both theories were advanced by the same man?
7. What is the meaning of the last line of Hoffmann's essay? How is it an effective ending for his description of Einstein?

Writing Topics

1. In describing the nature of Einstein's genius—that is, the apparent "simplicity" of his thinking—Hoffmann offers a possible definition for the essence of all genius. Consider some of the great thinkers you have read about and the means by which they have arrived at seemingly revolutionary ideas. Ask your fellow students if they have ever thought about what it is that distinguishes the genius from other thinkers. In an essay discuss the traits that geniuses have in common. How well does Hoffmann's definition of Einstein's genius apply to other thinkers?

2. Write a descriptive essay about a friend or relative whom you particularly admire. Keep in mind that your reader will not know that person. You must make him or her come to life through anecdotes, quotations, or some other means. In preparing to write, consider what distinguishes that person from other people you know. How and why is he or she special to you?

The exodus of women from the home to the workplace has not been accompanied by a new view of marriage and work that would make this transition smooth. Most workplaces have remained inflexible in the face of the changing needs of workers with families and most men have yet to really adapt to the changes in women.

ARLIE HOCHSCHILD

Doesn't popular psychology, brandishing the banner of Freud with more enthusiasm than knowledge, tell us, in effect, that any male who stays single is selfish or homosexual or mother-dominated and generally neurotic? and any unmarried female frustrated (or worse, not frustrated) and neurotic?

ERNEST VAN DEN HAAG

Gender Roles

SUSAN JACOBY

When Susan Jacoby became a newspaper reporter in 1963 at the age of seventeen, she had no intention of writing about "women's subjects." "To write about women was to write about trivia: charity balls, cake sales, and the like," she recalls. "I would have laughed at anyone who tried to tell me that one day I would believe the members of my own sex were important enough to write about." But times have changed. Although the old female stereotypes have not completely disappeared, many people have come to regard them as unfair and unacceptable. And Jacoby has, in fact, written extensively about women's subjects, often in the *New York Times* and *McCall's*. Many of these pieces have been collected in her book *The Possible She* (1979). In the following essay, originally published in the "Hers" column of the *Times* in 1978, Jacoby tells of two experiences when she felt mistreated because she was a woman and describes how she dealt with each situation.

Unfair Game

My friend and I, two women obviously engrossed in conversation, are 1 sitting at a corner table in the crowded Oak Room of the Plaza at ten o'clock on a Tuesday night. A man materializes and interrupts us with the snappy opening line, "A good woman is hard to find."

We say nothing, hoping he will disappear back into his bottle. But he 2 fancies himself as our genie and asks, "Are you visiting?" Still we say nothing. Finally my friend looks up and says, "We live here." She and I look at each other, the thread of our conversation snapped, our thoughts focused on how to get rid of this intruder. In a minute, if something isn't done, he will scrunch down next to me on the banquette and start offering to buy us drinks.

"Would you leave us alone, please," I say in a loud but reasonably 3 polite voice. He looks slightly offended but goes on with his bright social patter. I become more explicit. "We don't want to talk to you, we didn't ask you over here, and we want to be alone. Go away." This time he directs his full attention to me—and he is mad. "All right, all right, *excuse me.*" He pushes up the corners of his mouth in a Howdy Dowdy smile. "You ought to try smiling. You might even be pretty if you smiled once in a while."

At last the man leaves. He goes back to his buddy at the bar. I watch   4
them out of the corner of my eye, and he gestures angrily at me for at least fifteen minutes. When he passes our table on the way out of the room, this well-dressed, obviously affluent man mutters, "Good-bye, bitch," under his breath.

Why is this man calling me names? Because I have asserted my right to   5
sit at a table in a public place without being drawn into a sexual flirtation. Because he has been told, in no uncertain terms, that two attractive women prefer each other's company to his.

This sort of experience is an old story to any woman who travels,   6
eats, or drinks—for business or pleasure—without a male escort. In Holiday Inns and at the Plaza, on buses and airplanes, in tourist and first class, a woman is always thought to be looking for a man in addition to whatever else she may be doing. The man who barged in on us at the bar would never have broken into the conversation of two men, and it goes without saying that he wouldn't have imposed himself on a man and a woman who were having a drink. But two women at a table are an entirely different matter. Fair game.

This might be viewed as a relatively small flaw in the order of the   7
universe—something in a class with an airline losing luggage or a computer fouling up a bank statement. Except a computer doesn't foul up your bank account every month and an airline doesn't lose your suitcase every time you fly. But if you are an independent woman, you have to spend a certain amount of energy, day in and day out, in order to go about your business without being bothered by strange men.

On airplanes, I am a close-mouthed traveler. As soon as the "No   8
Smoking" sign is turned off, I usually pull some papers out of my briefcase and start working. Work helps me forget that I am scared of flying. When I am sitting next to a woman, she quickly realizes from my monosyllabic replies that I don't want to chat during the flight. Most men, though, are not content to be ignored.

Once I was flying from New York to San Antonio on a plane that was   9
scheduled to stop in Dallas. My seatmate was an advertising executive who kept questioning me about what I was doing and who remained undiscouraged by my terse replies until I ostentatiously covered myself with a blanket and shut my eyes. When the plane started its descent into Dallas, he made his move.

"You don't really have to get to San Antonio today, do you?"   10

"Yes."   11

"Come on, change your ticket. Spend the evening with me here. I'm   12
staying at a wonderful hotel, with a pool, we could go dancing . . ."

"No."   13

"Well, you can't blame a man for trying."   14

I do blame a man for trying in this situation—for suggesting that a   15
woman change her work and travel plans to spend a night with a perfect
stranger in whom she had displayed no personal interest. The "no personal
interest" is crucial; I wouldn't have blamed the man for trying if I had been
stroking his cheek and complaining about my dull social life.

There is a nice postscript to this story. Several months later, I was   16
walking my dog in Carl Schurz Park when I ran into my erstwhile seatmate,
who was taking a stroll with his wife and children. He recognized me, all
right, and was trying to avoid me when I went over and courteously
reintroduced myself. I reminded him that we had been on the same flight to
Dallas. "Oh yes," he said. "As I recall you were going on to somewhere
else." "San Antonio," I said. "I was in a hurry that day."

The code of feminine politeness, instilled in girlhood, is no help in   17
dealing with the unwanted approaches of strange men. Our mothers didn't
teach us to tell a man to get lost; they told us to smile and hint that we'd be
just delighted to spend time with the gentleman if we didn't have other
commitments. The man in the Oak Room bar would not be put off by a
demure lowering of eyelids; he has to be told, roughly and loudly, that his
presence was a nuisance.

Not that I am necessarily against men and women picking each other   18
up in public places. In most instances, a modicum of sensitivity will tell a
woman or a man whether someone is open to approaches.

Mistakes can easily be corrected by the kind of courtesy so many   19
people have abandoned since the "sexual revolution." One summer evening, I was whiling away a half hour in the outdoor bar of the Stanhope
Hotel. I was alone, dressed up, having a drink before going on to meet
someone in a restaurant. A man at the next table asked, "If you're not busy,
would you like to have a drink with me?" I told him I was sorry but I would
be leaving shortly. "Excuse me for disturbing you," he said, turning back to
his own drink. Simple courtesy. No insults and no hurt feelings.

One friend suggested that I might have avoided the incident in the   20
Oak Room by going to the Palm Court instead. It's true that the Palm Court
is a traditional meeting place for unescorted ladies. But I don't like violins
when I want to talk. And I wanted to sit in a large, comfortable leather
chair. Why should I have to hide among the potted palms to avoid men who
think I'm looking for something else?

Questions for Study and Discussion

1. What is the main point of Jacoby's essay? Where is it stated most directly? What was her purpose in writing this piece?

2. What solutions, if any, does Jacoby suggest for dealing with the problem she describes?

3. Jacoby complains about the code of feminine politeness. What exactly is this "code"? Does she seem constrained by it?

4. In paragraph 16, why does Jacoby say as her parting shot, "I was in a hurry that day"?

5. What is Jacoby's tone in this essay? How does she achieve this tone? Give several examples from the essay.

Writing Topics

1. Jacoby has written that this article drew a larger response than anything she has ever published. What kinds of responses do you imagine it drew from women? From men? How do you respond to this article? Compose a response as if you were going to send it to *The New York Times* or to Jacoby herself.

2. In one respect, the situations Jacoby describes have mainly to do with courtesy, with good and bad manners. Write an essay in which you define *courtesy*. What purpose does it serve? Should people be expected always to show consideration for others, or should they be free to say and do whatever they please? Why?

3. Write an essay on some aspect of dating. Why do people go on dates? What do people gain from dining together, or going to a movie together? How has dating changed since you started dating? How should one arrange a date with a stranger?

MIKE McGRADY

Born in New York City in 1933, Mike McGrady was educated at Yale University and spent a year as a Neiman Fellow at Harvard. He is a free-lance writer who has taken on many different assignments, from reporting to reviewing to ghostwriting. He has published several books, including *A Dove in Vietnam* (1968) and *The Kitchen Sink Papers—My Life as a Househusband* (1975). He is currently a restaurant critic for Long Island's *Newsday*.

The following essay, which first appeared in a 1976 issue of *Newsweek*, presents McGrady's views on the limitations of housework and offers a somewhat radical proposal.

Let 'em Eat Leftovers

Last year my wife and I traded roles. Every morning she went off to an   1
office and earned the money that paid the bills. I cooked and cleaned, picked up after three kids, went head-to-head with bargain-hunting shoppers, pleaded for a raise in allowance and lived the generally hellish life that half the human race accepts as its lot.

The year is over now but the memories won't go away. What is   2
guaranteed to stir them up is any of those Total Woman or Fascinating Womanhood people singing the praises of the happy housewife—that mythical woman who manages a spotless house, runs herd over half a dozen kids, whips up short-order culinary masterpieces, smells good and still finds time to read Great Books and study Japanese line engraving.

I never qualified. Never even came close. In fact, I never quite mas-   3
tered that most basic task, the cleaning of the house. Any job that requires six hours to do and can be undone in six minutes by one small child carrying a plate of crackers and a Monopoly set—this is not a job that will long capture my interest. After a year of such futility, I have arrived at a rule of thumb—if the debris accumulates to a point where small animals can be seen to be living there, it should be cleaned up, preferably by someone hired for the occasion.

Housekeeping was just one facet of the nightmare. I think back to a   4
long night spent matching up four dozen bachelor socks, all of them wool,

211

most of them gray. Running an all-hours taxi service for subteens. Growing older in orthodontists' waiting rooms. Pasting trading stamps into little booklets. Oh, the nightmare had as many aspects as there were hours in the day.

Empress of Domestic Arts

At the heart of my difficulty was this simple fact: for the past two decades I had been paid for my work. I had come to feel my time was valuable. Suddenly my sole payment was a weekly allowance given to me with considerable fanfare by my breadwinning wife. I began to see that as a trap, a many-stings-attached offering that barely survived a single session in the supermarket and never got me through a neighborhood poker game. 5

The pay was bad and the hours were long but what bothered me most was my own ineptitude, my inability to apply myself to the business of managing a home. No longer do I feel guilty about my failure as a homemaker. I would no more applaud the marvelously efficient and content house-wife than I would applaud the marvelously efficient and content elevator operator. The image strikes me as useful on several levels but the point is this: it is always someone else who goes up, someone else who gets off. 6

Some people seem to feel that the housewife's lot would be bettered if she were given a new title, one that takes into account the full range and complexity of her role, something along the lines of "household engineer" or, perhaps, "domestic scientist." Wonderful. You come and take care of my house and my kids and you can be the Empress of the Domestic Arts, the Maharanee of the Vacuum Cleaner. 7

Try a Little Neglect

A more intriguing suggestion is that husbands pay their wives salaries for housework. I suggested this to my wife and she said I don't make enough money to pay her to do that job again. Neither, according to her, does J. Paul Getty. I am coming to the feeling that this is a job that should not be done by any one person for love or for money. 8

This is not to put down the whole experience. By the end of the year, I had succeeded in organizing my time so that there were a few hours for the occasional book, the random round of golf. Then, too, it was a pleasure to be more than a weekend visitor in my kids' lives. While my wife and I are now willing to de-emphasize housekeeping, neither of us would cut back on 9 what some people call parenting and what I look at as the one solid reward in this belated and male motherhood of mine.

Of course, I had it easy—relatively easy anyway. This was my little experiment, not my destiny. There is a considerable difference between a year in prison and a life sentence. 10

It will be argued: well, *someone* has to do these things. Not necessarily. In the first place, some two can do most of these things. Secondly, I can think of no area in modern life that could more easily sustain a policy of benign neglect than the home. I'm arguing here in favor of letting the dust gather where it may; in favor of making greater use of slow cookers and nearby fish-and-chips stands; of abolishing, as far as possible, the position of unpaid servant in the family. 11

Many men surely will find this line of thought threatening. That's just as it should be. Few plantation owners were enthusiastic about the Emancipation Proclamation. What is more surprising is that these thoughts will prove equally threatening to many women. OK. Those females who demand the right to remain in service should not necessarily be discouraged— we all know how hard it is to find decent household help these days. 12

I suspect the real reason for many women's reluctance to break bonds is fear of the world that exists outside the home. They sense the enormous complexity of their husbands' lives, the tremendous skills required to head up a team of salesmen or to write cigarette commercials or to manufacture lawn fertilizer. The mind that feels these fears may be beyond the reach of change. It is another sort of mind, the mind that finds itself in constant rebellion against the limitations of housewifery, that concerns me more here. 13

The Life You Save

To this mind, this person, we should say: go ahead. There is a world out there, a whole planet of possibilities. The real danger is that you won't do it. If Guttenburg had been a housewife, I might be writing these words with a quill pen. And if Edison had been a housewife, you might be reading them by candlelight. 14

No escape is simple and a certain amount of toughness will be required. How do you do it? You might start by learning how to sweep things under the rug. You might have to stop pampering the rest of the family—let 'em eat leftovers. And be prepared for the opposition that will surely develop. Even the most loving family hates to lose that trusted servant, that faithful family retainer, that little old homemaker, you. No one enjoys it when the most marvelous appliance of them all breaks down. But if it will be any comfort to you, the life you save will surely be your own. 15

Questions for Study and Discussion

1. How does McGrady respond to the concept of "the happy housewife"? What does he think about "those Total Woman or Fascinating Womanhood people"?

2. What is so distressing about cleaning a house, as far as McGrady is concerned? What other aspects of being a homemaker are central to McGrady's dissatisfaction? Why does McGrady not feel guilty about being a bad homemaker?

3. What is the "one solid reward" McGrady sees in being a homemaker?

4. What, in McGrady's view, keeps some housewives from breaking free of their positions? What suggestions does he offer to those who *are* in rebellion?

5. In paragraph 7, McGrady writes, "Some people seem to feel that the housewife's lot would be bettered if she were given a new title, one that takes into account the full range and complexity of her role. . ." What is his opinion of this proposal? Do you agree with him? Why, or why not?

6. Who, do you suppose, is McGrady's audience? To what belief and/or action is he trying to persuade his audience? What, if anything, did you find particularly persuasive about this method of development?

7. Upon being informed that the poor people of France were without bread and starving, Marie Antoinette allegedly said, "Let them eat cake." The reply is now justly famous for its apparent callousness. Is McGrady's title callous? What connection does it bear to his essay?

8. McGrady's tone might be called sarcastic. Find at least three examples of sarcasm in his essay and describe your response. Has McGrady made his point effectively?

9. Does McGrady need the headings "Empress of Domestic Arts," "Try a Little Neglect," and "The Life You Save"? What effect do they have on you as a reader?

Writing Topics

1. Choose an editorial about a controversial issue from your local newspaper or from a national newsmagazine. First, outline the argument made in the editorial. Then, assume that you have been given equal space in the publication to present an opposing viewpoint. Consider the types of evidence you will need; then write a counterargument, trying as much as possible to respond to each point made in the editorial.

2. Write an essay in which you examine how traditional roles—husband as breadwinner, wife as homemaker—are giving way to other arrangements in many modern marriages.

NOEL PERRIN

Noel Perrin is a New Yorker by birth and has spent much of his life in the academic world, yet he is most widely known as an essayist on the demands and rewards of country life. He was born in 1927, attended Williams College, Duke University, and Cambridge University, England, and is now a professor of English at Dartmouth College in New Hampshire. He lives in neighboring Vermont and wrote about his home state in *Vermont in All Weathers* (1973). His country pieces, which he calls "essays of a sometime farmer," have been collected in *First Person Rural* (1978), *Second Person Rural* (1980), and *Third Person Rural* (1982).

In "The Androgynous Man," first published in the *New York Times* in 1984, Perrin addresses the restrictive roles that sexual stereotyping casts us into and the effects that these roles have on our personality and behavior. In keeping with the independent spirit of his other writings, he argues for freedom from such restrictive sex roles.

The Androgynous Man

The summer I was 16, I took a train from New York to Steamboat   1
Springs, Colo., where I was going to be assistant wrangler at a camp. The trip took three days, and since I was much too shy to talk to strangers, I had quite a lot of time for reading. I read all of *Gone With the Wind*. I read all of the interesting articles in a couple of magazines I had, and then I went back and read all the dull stuff. I also took all the quizzes, a thing of which magazines were fuller then than now.

The one that held my undivided attention was called "How Mascu-   2
line/Feminine Are You?" It consisted of a large number of inkblots. The reader was supposed to decide which of four objects each blot most resembled. The choices might be a cloud, a steam-engine, a caterpillar and a sofa.

When I finished the test, I was shocked to find that I was barely   3
masculine at all. On a scale of 1 to 10, I was about 1.2. Me, the horse wrangler? (And not just wrangler, either. That summer, I had to skin a couple of horses that died—the camp owner wanted the hides.)

The results of that test were so terrifying to me that for the first time   4
in my life I did a piece of original analysis. Having unlimited time on the train, I looked at the "masculine" answers over and over, trying to find what it was that distinguished real men from people like me—and eventually I

discovered two very simple patterns. It was "masculine" to think the blots looked like man-made objects, and "feminine" to think they looked like natural objects. It was masculine to think they looked like things capable of causing harm, and feminine to think of innocent things.

Even at 16, I had the sense to see that the compilers of the test were 5 using rather limited criteria—maleness and femaleness are both more complicated than that—and I breathed a hugh sigh of relief. I wasn't necessarily a wimp, after all.

That the test did reveal something other than the superficiality of its 6 makers I realized only many years later. What it revealed was that there is a large class of men and women both, to which I belong, who are essentially androgynous. That doesn't mean we're gay, or low in the appropriate hormones, or uncomfortable performing the jobs traditionally assigned our sexes. (A few years after that summer, I was leading troops in combat and, unfashionable as it now is to admit this, having a very good time. War is exciting. What a pity the 20th century went and spoiled it with high-tech weapons.)

What it does mean to be spiritually androgynous is a kind of freedom. 7 Men who are all-male, or he-man, or 100% red-blooded Americans, have a little biological set that causes them to be attracted to physical power, and probably also to dominance. Maybe even to watching football. I don't say this to criticize them. Completely masculine men are quite often wonderful people: good husbands, good (though sometimes overwhelming) fathers, good members of society. Furthermore, they are often so unself-consciously at ease in the world that other men seem to imitate them. They just aren't as free as androgynes. They pretty nearly have to be what they are; we have a range of choices open.

The sad part is that many of us never discover that. Men who are not 8 100% red-blooded Americans—say those who are only 75% red-blooded— often fail to notice their freedom. They are too busy trying to copy the he-men ever to realize that men, like women, come in a wide variety of acceptable types. Why this frantic imitation? My answer is mere speculation, but not casual. I have speculated on this for a long time.

Partly they're just envious of the he-man's unconscious ease. Mostly 9 they're terrified of finding that there may be something wrong with them deep down, some weakness at the heart. To avoid discovering that, they spend their lives acting out the role that the he-man naturally lives. Sad.

One thing that men owe to the women's movement is that this kind of 10 failure is less common than it used to be. In releasing themselves from the single ideal of the dependent woman, women have more or less incidentally released a lot of men from the single ideal of the dominant male. The one mistake the feminists have made, I think, is in supposing that all men need this release, or that the world would be a better place if all men achieved it. It wouldn't. It would just be duller.

So far I have been pretty vague about just what the freedom of the androgynous man is. Obviously it varies with the case. In the case I know best, my own, I can be quite specific. It has freed me most as a parent. I am, among other things, a fairly good natural mother. I like the nurturing role. It makes me feel good to see a child eat—and it turns me to mush to see a 4-year-old holding a glass with both small hands, in order to drink. I even enjoyed sewing patches on the knees of my daughter Amy's Dr. Dentons when she was at the crawling stage. All that pleasure I would have lost if I had made myself stick to the notion of the paternal role that I started with.

Or take a smaller and rather ridiculous example. I feel free to kiss cats. Until recently it never occurred to me that I would want to, though my daughters have been doing it all their lives. But my elder daughter is now 22, and in London. Of course, I get to look after her cat while she is gone. He's a big, handsome farm cat named Petrushka, very unsentimental though used from kittenhood to being kissed on the top of the head by Elizabeth. I've gotten very fond of him (he's the adventurous kind of cat who likes to climb hills with you), and one night I simply felt like kissing him on the top of the head, and did. Why did no one tell me sooner how silky cat fur is?

Then there's my relation to cars. I am completely unembarrassed by my inability to diagnose even minor problems in whatever object I happen to be driving, and don't have to make some insider's remark to mechanics to try to establish that I, too, am a "Man With His Machine."

The same ease extends to household maintenance. I do it, of course. Service people are expensive. But for the last decade my house has functioned better than it used to because I have had the aid of a volume called "Home Repairs Any Woman Can Do," which is pitched just right for people at my technical level. As a youth, I'd as soon have touched such a book as I would have become a transvestite. Even though common sense says there is really nothing sexual whatsoever about fixing sinks.

Or take public emotion. All my life I have easily been moved by certain kinds of voices. The actress Siobhan McKenna's, to take a notable case. Give her an emotional scene in a play, and within ten words my eyes are full of tears. In boyhood, my great dread was that someone might notice. I struggled manfully, you might say, to suppress this weakness. Now, of course, I don't see it as a weakness at all, but as a kind of fulfillment. I even suspect that the true he-men feel the same way, or one kind of them does, at least, and it's only the poor imitators who have to struggle to repress themselves.

Let me come back to the inkblots, with their assumption that masculine equates with machinery and science, and feminine with art and nature. I have no idea whether the right pronoun for God is He, She, or It. But this I'm pretty sure of. If God could somehow be induced to take that test, God would not come out macho and not feminismo, either, but right in the middle. Fellow androgynes, it's a nice thought.

Questions for Study and Discussion

1. What does Perrin mean by *androgyny*? Where does he present his definition? Why does he present it at that point? Is he using the term in the strict dictionary sense? Explain.

2. State Perrin's thesis in your own words. What do you think his purpose is in writing the essay?

3. What does Perrin believe are the benefits of androgyny? Are all his examples equally convincing to you? Explain.

4. Perrin's essay first appeared in a weekly column called "About Men." Do you think Perrin intended his essay primarily for male readers or readers of both sexes?

5. Explain the meaning of Perrin's last paragraph. How effective is it as a conclusion? Explain.

Writing Topics

1. Write an essay in which you establish your own definition of masculinity or femininity. What are its identifying characteristics? How does your definition differ, if at all, from prevailing stereotypes?

2. Using Perrin's essay as a model, recount experiences you have had in growing up in which gender roles have been a significant factor. For example, were there ever summer jobs you felt you could not apply for? Or, were you ever made to feel inadequate in certain athletic or social situations? How were you able to resolve the problem?

BOBBIE ANN MASON

Bobbie Ann Mason (1940–) grew up in western Kentucky, graduated from the University of Kentucky, and holds a Ph.D. in literature from the University of Connecticut. Her short stories have appeared in such distinguished magazines as *Vanity Fair*, the *New Yorker*, the *Atlantic Monthly*, and the *North American Review*. She is also the author of *Shiloh and Other Stories* (1982) and two novels, *In Country* (1985) and *Spence + Lila* (1988).

"Shiloh," which appeared in the October 20, 1980, issue of the *New Yorker*, explores the relationship of a husband and wife who are suddenly forced to spend all their time together.

Shiloh

Leroy Moffitt's wife, Norma Jean, is working on her pectorals. She lifts three-pound dumbbells to warm up, then progresses to a twenty-pound barbell. Standing with her legs apart, she reminds Leroy of Wonder Woman. 1

"I'd give anything if I could just get these muscles to where they're real hard," says Norma Jean. "Feel this arm. It's not as hard as the other one." 2

"That's 'cause you're right-handed," says Leroy, dodging as she swings the barbell in an arc. 3

"Do you think so?" 4

"Sure." 5

Leroy is a truckdriver. He injured his leg in a highway accident four months ago, and his physical therapy, which involves weights and a pulley, prompted Norma Jean to try building herself up. Now she is attending a body-building class. Leroy has been collecting temporary disability since his tractor-trailer jackknifed in Missouri, badly twisting his left leg in its socket. He has a steel pin in his hip. He will probably not be able to drive his rig again. It sits in the backyard, like a gigantic bird that has flown home to roost. Leroy has been home in Kentucky for three months, and his leg is almost healed, but the accident frightened him and he does not want to drive any more long hauls. He is not sure what to do next. In the meantime, he makes things from craft kits. He started by building a miniature log cabin from notched Popsicle sticks. He varnished it and placed it on the TV set, 6 where it remains. It reminds him of a rustic Nativity scene. Then he tried string art (sailing ships on black velvet), a macramé owl kit, a snap-together B-17 Flying Fortress, and a lamp made out of a model truck, with a light fixture screwed in the top of the cab. At first the kits were diversions, something to kill time, but now he is thinking about building a full-scale log house, and besides, Leroy has grown to appreciate how things are put together. He has begun to realize that in all the years he was on the road he never took time to examine anything. He was always flying past scenery.

"They won't let you build a log cabin in any of the new subdivisions," Norma Jean tells him.

"They will if I tell them it's for you," he says, teasing her. Ever since they were married, he has promised Norma Jean he would build her a new home one day. They have always rented, and the house they live in is small and nondescript. It does not even feel like a home, Leroy realizes now.

Norma Jean works at the Rexall drugstore, and she has acquired an amazing amount of information about cosmetics. When she explains to Leroy the three stages of complexion care, involving creams, toners, and moisturizers, he thinks happily of other petroleum products—axle grease, diesel fuel. This is a connection between him and Norma Jean. Since he has been home, he has felt unusually tender about his wife and guilty over his long absences. But he can't tell what she feels about him. Norma Jean has never complained about his traveling; she has never made hurt remarks, like calling his truck a "widow-maker." He is reasonably certain she has been faithful to him, but he wishes she would celebrate his permanent homecoming more happily. Norma Jean is often startled to find Leroy at home, and he thinks she seems a little disappointed about it. Perhaps he reminds her too much of the early days of their marriage, before he went on the road. They had a child who died as an infant, years ago. They never speak about their memories of Randy, which have almost faded, but now that Leroy is home all the time, they sometimes feel awkward around each other, and Leroy wonders if one of them should mention the child. He has the feeling that they are waking up out of a dream together—that they must create a new marriage, start afresh. They are lucky they are still married. Leroy has read that for most people losing a child destroys the marriage—or else he heard this on "Donahue." He can't always remember where he learns things anymore.

At Christmas, Leroy bought an electric organ for Norma Jean. She used to play the piano when she was in high school. "It don't leave you," she told him once. "It's like riding a bicycle."

The new instrument has so many keys and buttons that she was bewildered by it at first. She touched the keys tentatively, pushed some buttons, then pecked out "Chopsticks." It came out in an amplified fox-trot rhythm, with marimba sounds.

"It's an orchestra!" she cried.

The organ has a pecan-look finish and eighteen preset chords, with

7

8

9

10

11

12

13

optional flute, violin, trumpet, clarinet, and banjo accompaniments. Norma Jean mastered the organ almost immediately. At first she played Christmas songs. Then she bought *The Sixties Songbook* and learned every tune in it, adding variations to each with the rows of brightly colored buttons.

"I didn't like these old songs back then," she said. "But I have this crazy feeling I missed something." 14

"You didn't miss a thing," said Leroy. 15

Leroy liked to lie on the couch and smoke a joint and listen to Norma Jean play "Can't Take My Eyes Off You" and "I'll Be Back." He is back again. After fifteen years on the road, he is finally settling down with the woman he loves. She is still pretty. Her skin is flawless. Her frosted curls resemble pencil trimmings. 16

Now that Leroy has come home to stay, he notices how much the town has changed. Subdivisions are spreading across western Kentucky like an oil slick. The sign at the edge of town says "Pop: 11,500—only seven hundred more than it said twenty years ago. Leroy can't figure out who is living in all the new houses. The farmers who used to gather around the courthouse square on Saturday afternoons to play checkers and spit tobacco juice have gone. It has been years since Leroy has thought about the farmers, and they have disappeared without his noticing. 17

Leroy meets a kid named Stevie Hamilton in the parking lot at the shopping center. While they pretend to be strangers meeting over a stalled car, Stevie tosses an ounce of marijuana under the front seat of Leroy's car. Stevie is wearing orange jogging shoes and a T-shirt that says CHAT-TAHOOCHEE SUPER-RAT. His father is a prominent doctor who lives in one of the subdivisions in a new white-columned brick house that looks like a funeral parlor. In the phone book under his name there is a separate number, with the listing "Teenagers." 18

"Where do you get this stuff?" asks Leroy. "From your pappy?" 19

"That's for me to know and you to find out," Stevie says. He is slit-eyed and skinny. 20

"What else you got?" 21

"What you interested in?" 22

"Nothing special. Just wondered." 23

Leroy used to take speed on the road. Now he has to go slowly. He needs to be mellow. He leans back against the car and says, "I'm aiming to build me a log house, soon as I get time. My wife, though, I don't think she likes the idea." 24

"Well, let me know when you want me again," Stevie says. He has a cigarette in his cupped palm, as though sheltering it from the wind. He takes a long drag, then stomps it on the asphalt and slouches away. 25

Stevie's father was two years ahead of Leroy in high school. Leroy is thirty-four. He married Norma Jean when they were both eighteen, and 26 their child Randy was born a few months later, but he died at the age of four months and three days. He would be about Stevie's age now. Norma Jean and Leroy were at a drive-in, watching a double feature (*Dr. Strangelove* and *Lover Come Back*), and the baby was sleeping in the back seat. When the first movie ended, the baby was dead. It was the sudden infant death syndrome. Leroy remembers handing Randy to a nurse at the emergency room, as though he were offering her a large doll as a present. A dead baby feels like a sack of flour. "It just happens sometimes," said the doctor, in what Leroy always recalls as a nonchalant tone. Leroy can hardly remember the child anymore, but he still sees vividly a scene from *Dr. Strangelove* in which the president of the United States was talking in a folksy voice on the hot line to the Soviet premier about the bomber accidentally headed toward Russia. He was in the War Room, and the world map was lit up. Leroy remembers Norma Jean standing catatonically beside him in the hospital and himself thinking: Who is this strange girl? He had forgotten who she was. Now scientists are saying that crib death is caused by a virus. Nobody knows anything, Leroy thinks. The answers are always changing.

When Leroy gets home from the shopping center, Norma Jean's   27
mother, Mabel Beasley, is there. Until this year, Leroy has not realized how much time she spends with Norma Jean. When she visits, she inspects the closets and then the plants, informing Norma Jean when a plant is droopy or yellow. Mabel calls the plants "flowers," although there are never any blooms. She always notices if Norma Jean's laundry is piling up. Mabel is a short, overweight woman whose tight, brown-dyed curls look more like a wig than the actual wig she sometimes wears. Today she has brought Norma Jean an off-white dust ruffle she made for the bed; Mabel works in a custom-upholstery shop.

"This is the tenth one I made this year," Mabel says. "I got started and   28
couldn't stop."

"It's really pretty," says Norma Jean.   29

"Now we can hide things under the bed," says Leroy, who gets along   30
with his mother-in-law primarily by joking with her. Mabel has never really forgiven him for disgracing her by getting Norma Jean pregnant. When the baby died, she said that fate was mocking her.

"What's that thing?" Mabel said to Leroy in a loud voice, pointing to a   31
tangle of yarn on a piece of canvas.

Leroy holds it up for Mabel to see. "It's my needlepoint," he explains.   32
"This is a *Star Trek* pillow cover."

"That's what a woman would do," says Mabel. "Great day in the   33
morning!"

"All the big football players on TV do it," he says.   34

"Why, Leroy, you're always trying to fool me. I don't believe you for a   35
minute. You don't know what to do with yourself— that's the whole trouble. Sewing!"

"I'm aiming to build us a log house," says Leroy. "Soon as my plans 36
come."

"Like *heck* you are," says Norma Jean. She takes Leroy's needlepoint 37
and shoves it in a drawer. "You have to find a job first. Nobody can afford
to build now anyway."

Mabel straightens her girdle and says, "I still think before you get tied 38
down y'all ought to take a little run to Shiloh."

"One of these days, Mama," Norma Jean says impatiently. 39

Mabel is talking about Shiloh, Tennessee. For the past few years, she 40
has been urging Leroy and Norma Jean to visit the Civil War battleground
there. Mabel went there on her honeymoon—the only real trip she ever
took. Her husband died of a perforated ulcer when Norma Jean was ten, but
Mabel, who was accepted into the United Daughters of the Confederacy in
1975, is still preoccupied with going back to Shiloh.

"I've bèen to kingdom come and back in that truck out yonder," Leroy 41
says to Mabel, "but we never yet set foot in that battleground. Ain't that
something? How did I miss it?"

"It's not even that far," Mabel says. 42

After Mabel leaves, Norma Jean reads to Leroy from a list she has 43
made. "Things you could do," she announces. "You could get a job as a
guard at Union Carbide, where they'd let you set on a stool. You could get
on at the lumberyard. You could do a little carpenter work, if you want to
build so bad. You could—"

"I can't do something where I'd have to stand up all day." 44

"You ought to try standing up all day behind a cosmetics counter. It's 45
amazing that I have strong feet, coming from two parents that never had
strong feet at all." At the moment Norma Jean is holding on to the kitchen
counter, raising her knees one at a time as she talks. She is wearing two-
pound ankle weights.

"Don't worry," says Leroy. "I'll do something." 46

"You could truck calves to slaughter for somebody. You wouldn't have 47
to drive any big old truck for that."

"I'm going to build you this house," says Leroy. "I want to make you a 48
real home."

"I don't want to live in any log cabin." 49

"It's not a cabin. It's a house." 50

"I don't care. It looks like a cabin." 51

"You and me together could lift those logs. It's just like lifting weights." 52

Norma Jean doesn't answer. Under her breath, she is counting. Now 53
she is marching through the kitchen. She is doing goose steps.

Before his accident, when Leroy came home he used to stay in the 54
house with Norma Jean, watching TV in bed and playing cards. She would
cook fried chicken, picnic ham, chocolate pie—all his favorites. Now he is

home alone much of the time. In the mornings, Norma Jean disappears, leaving a cooling place in the bed. She eats a cereal called Body Buddies, and she leaves the bowl on the table, with the soggy tan balls floating in a milk puddle. He sees things about Norma Jean that he never realized before. When she chops onions, she stares off into a corner, as if she can't bear to look. She puts on her house slippers almost precisely at nine o'clock every evening and nudges her jogging shoes under the couch. She saves bread heels for the birds. Leroy watches the birds at the feeder. He notices the peculiar way goldfinches fly past the window. They close their wings, then fall, then spread their wings to catch and lift themselves. He wonders if they close their eyes when they fall. Norma Jean closes her eyes when they are in bed. She wants the lights turned out. Even then, he is sure she closes her eyes.

He goes for long drives around town. He tends to drive a car rather carelessly. Power steering and an automatic shift make a car feel so small and inconsequential that his body is hardly involved in the driving process. His injured leg stretches out comfortably. Once or twice he has almost hit something, but even the prospect of an accident seems minor in a car. He cruises the new subdivisions, feeling like a criminal rehearsing for a robbery. Norma Jean is probably right about a log house being inappropriate here in the new subdivisions. All the houses look grand and complicated. They depress him.

One day when Leroy comes home from a drive he finds Norma Jean in tears. She is in the kitchen making a potato and mushroom-soup casserole, with grated-cheese topping. She is crying because her mother caught her smoking.

"I didn't hear her coming. I was standing here puffing away pretty as you please," Norma Jean says, wiping her eyes.

"I knew it would happen sooner or later," says Leroy, putting his arm around her.

"She don't know the meaning of the word 'knock,'" says Norma Jean. "It's a wonder she hadn't caught me years ago."

"Think of it this way," Leroy says. "What if she caught me with a joint?"

"You better not let her!" Norma Jean shrieks. "I'm warning you, Leroy Moffitt!"

"I'm just kidding. Here, play me a tune. That'll help you relax."

Norma Jean puts the casserole in the oven and sets the timer. Then she plays a ragtime tune, with horns and banjo, as Leroy lights up a joint and lies on the couch, laughing to himself about Mabel's catching him at it. He thinks of Stevie Hamilton—a doctor's son pushing grass. Everything is funny. The whole town seem crazy and small. He is reminded of Virgil Mathis, a boastful policeman Leroy used to shoot pool with. Virgil recently led a drug bust in a back room at a bowling alley, where he seized ten thousand dollars' worth of marijuana. The newspaper had a picture of him holding up the bags of grass and grinning widely. Right now, Leroy can imagine Virgil breaking down the door and arresting him with a lungful of smoke. Virgil would probably have been alerted to the scene because of all the racket Norma Jean is making. Now she sounds like a hard-rock band. Norma Jean is terrific. When she switches to a Latin-rhythm version of "Sunshine Superman," Leroy hums along. Norma Jean's foot goes up and down, up and down.

"Well, what do you think?" Leroy says, when Norma Jean pauses to search through her music.

"What do I think about what?"

His mind has gone blank. Then he says, "I'll sell my rig and build us a house." That wasn't what he wanted to say. He wanted to know what she thought—what she *really* thought—about them.

"Don't start in on that again," says Norma Jean. She begins playing "Who'll Be the Next in Line?"

Leroy used to tell hitchhikers his whole life story—about his travels, his hometown, the baby. He would end with a question: "Well, what do you think?" It was just a rhetorical question. In time, he had the feeling that he'd been telling the same story over and over to the same hitchhikers. He quit talking to hitchhikers when he realized how his voice sounded—whining and self-pitying, like some teenage-tragedy song. Now Leroy has the sudden impulse to tell Norma Jean about himself, as if he had just met her. They have known each other so long they have forgotten a lot about each other. They could become reacquainted. But when the oven timer goes off and she runs to the kitchen, he forgets why he wants to do this.

The next day, Mabel drops by. It is Saturday and Norma Jean is cleaning. Leroy is studying the plans of his log house, which have finally come in the mail. He has them spread out on the table—big sheets of stiff blue paper, with diagrams and numbers printed in white. While Norma Jean runs the vacuum, Mabel drinks coffee. She sets her coffee cup on a blueprint.

"I'm just waiting for time to pass," she says to Leroy, drumming her fingers on the table.

As soon as Norma Jean switches off the vacuum, Mabel says in a loud voice, "Did you hear about the datsun dog that killed the baby?"

Norma Jean says, "The word is 'dachshund.'"

"They put the dog on trial. It chewed the baby's legs off. The mother was in the next room all the time." She raises her voice. "They thought it was neglect."

Norma Jean is holding her ears. Leroy manages to open the refrigerator and get some Diet Pepsi to offer Mabel. Mabel still has some coffee and she waves away the Pepsi.

"Datsuns are like that," Mabel says. "They're jealous dogs. They'll tear a place to pieces if you don't keep an eye on them."　75

"You better watch out what you're saying, Mabel," says Leroy.　76

"Well, facts is facts."　77

Leroy looks out the window at his rig. It is like a huge piece of furniture gathering dust in the backyard. Pretty soon it will be an antique. He hears the vacuum cleaner. Norma Jean seems to be cleaning the living room rug again.　78

Later, she says to Leroy, "She just said that about the baby because she caught me smoking. She's trying to pay me back."　79

"What are you talking about?" Leroy says, nervously shuffling blueprints.　80

"You know good and well," Norma Jean says. She is sitting in a kitchen chair with her feet up and her arms wrapped around her knees. She looks small and helpless. She says, "The very idea, her bringing up a subject like that! Saying it was neglect."　81

"She didn't mean that," Leroy says.　82

"She might not have *thought* she meant it. She always says things like that. You don't know how she goes on."　83

"But she didn't really mean it. She was just talking."　84

Leroy opens a king-sized bottle of beer and pours it into two glasses, dividing it carefully. He hands a glass to Norma Jean and she takes it from him mechanically. For a long time, they sit by the kitchen window watching the birds at the feeder.　85

Something is happening. Norma Jean is going to night school. She has graduated from her six-week body-building course and now she is taking an adult-education course in composition at Paducah Community College. She spends her evenings outlining paragraphs.　86

"First you have a topic sentence," she explains to Leroy. "Then you divide it up. Your secondary topic has to be connected to your primary topic."　87

To Leroy, this sounds intimidating. "I never was any good in English," he says.　88

"It makes a lot of sense."　89

"What are you doing this for, anyhow?"　90

She shrugs. "It's something to do." She stands up and lifts her dumbbells a few times.　91

"Driving a rig, nobody cared about my English."　92

"I'm not criticizing your English."　93

Norma Jean used to say, "If I lose ten minutes' sleep, I just drag all day." Now she stays up late, writing compositions. She got a B on her first paper—a how-to theme on soup-based casseroles. Recently Norma Jean has been cooking unusual foods—tacos, lasagna, Bombay chicken. She doesn't play the organ anymore, though her second paper was called "Why Music Is Important to Me." She sits at the kitchen table, concentrating on her　94 outlines, while Leroy plays with his log house plans, practicing with a set of Lincoln Logs. The thought of getting a truckload of notched, numbered logs scares him, and he wants to be prepared. As he and Norma Jean work together at the kitchen table, Leroy has the hopeful thought that they are sharing something, but he knows he is a fool to think this. Norma Jean is miles away. He knows he is going to lose her. Like Mabel, he is just waiting for time to pass.

One day, Mabel is there before Norma Jean gets home from work, and 95 Leroy finds himself confiding in her. Mabel, he realizes, must know Norma Jean better than he does.

"I don't know what's got into that girl," Mabel says. "She used to go 96 to bed with the chickens. Now you say she's up all hours. Plus her a-smoking. I like to died."

"I want to make her this beautiful home," Leroy says, indicating the 97 Lincoln Logs. "I don't think she even wants it. Maybe she was happier with me gone."

"She don't know what to make of you, coming home like this." 98

"Is that it?" 99

Mabel takes the roof off his Lincoln Log cabin. "You couldn't get *me* 100 in a log cabin," she says. "I was raised in one. It's no picnic, let me tell you."

"They're different now," says Leroy. 101

"I tell you what," Mabel says, smiling oddly at Leroy. 102

"What?" 103

"Take her on down to Shiloh. Y'all need to get out together, stir a 104 little. Her brain's all balled up over them books."

Leroy can see traces of Norma Jean's features in her mother's face. 105 Mabel's worn face has the texture of crinkled cotton, but suddenly she looks pretty. It occurs to Leroy that Mabel has been hinting all along that she wants them to take her with them to Shiloh.

"Let's all go Shiloh," he says. "You and me and her. Come Sunday." 106

Mabel throws up her hands in protest. "Oh, no, not me. Young folks 107 want to be by theirselves."

When Norma Jean comes in with groceries, Leroy says excitedly, 108 "Your mama here's been dying to go to Shiloh for thirty-five years. It's about time we went, don't you think?"

"I'm not going to butt in on anybody's second honeymoon," Mabel 109 says.

"Who's going on a honeymoon, for Christ's sake?" Norma Jean says 110 loudly.

"I never raised no daughter of mine to talk that-a-way," Mabel says. 111

"You ain't seen nothing yet," says Norma Jean. She starts putting 112 away boxes and cans, slamming cabinet doors.

"There's a log cabin at Shiloh, " Mabel says. "It was there during the 113 battle. There's bullet holes in it."

"When are you going to *shut up* about Shiloh, Mama?" asks Norma 114
Jean.

"I always thought Shiloh was the prettiest place, so full of history," 115
Mabel goes on. "I just hoped y'all could see it once before I die, so you could
tell me about it." Later, she whispers to Leroy, "You do what I said. A little
change is what she needs."

"Your name means 'the king,'" Norma Jean says to Leroy that eve- 116
ning. He is trying to get her to go to Shiloh, and she is reading a book about
another century.

"Well, I reckon I ought to be right proud." 117

"I guess so." 118

"Am I still king around here?" 119

Norma Jean flexes her biceps and feels them for hardness. "I'm not 120
fooling around with anybody, if that's what you mean," she says.

"Would you tell me if you were?" 121

"I don't know." 122

"What does *your* name mean?" 123

"It was Marilyn Monroe's real name." 124

"No kidding!" 125

"Norma comes from the Normans. They were invaders," she says. She 126
closes her book and looks hard at Leroy. "I'll go to Shiloh with you if you'll
stop staring at me."

On Sunday, Norma Jean packs a picnic and they go to Shiloh. To 127
Leroy's relief, Mabel says she does not want to come with them. Norma Jean
drives, and Leroy, sitting beside her, feels like some boring hitchhiker she
has picked up. He tries some conversation, but she answers him in monosyllables. At Shiloh, she drives aimlessly through the park, past bluffs and
trails and steep ravines. Shiloh is an immense place, and Leroy cannot see it
as a battleground. It is not what he expected. He thought it would look like
a golf course. Monuments are everywhere, showing through the thick
clusters of trees. Norma Jean passes the log cabin Mabel mentioned. It is
surrounded by tourists looking for bullet holes.

"That's not the kind of log house I've got in mind," says Leroy 128
apologetically.

"I know *that*." 129

"This is a pretty place. Your mama was right." 130

"It's O.K.," says Norma Jean. "Well, we've seen it. I hope she's 131
satisfied."

They burst out laughing together. 132

At the park museum, a movie on Shiloh is shown every half hour, but 133
they decide they don't want to see it. They buy a souvenir Confederate flag
for Mabel, and then they find a picnic spot near the cemetery. Norma Jean

has brought a picnic cooler, with pimiento sandwiches, soft drinks, and Yodels. Leroy eats a sandwich and then smokes a joint, hiding it behind the picnic cooler. Norma Jean has quit smoking altogether. She is picking cake crumbs from the cellophane wrapper, like a fussy bird.

Leroy says, "So the boys in gray ended up in Corinth. The Union soldiers zapped 'em finally. April 7, 1862." 134

They both know that he doesn't know any history. He is just talking about some of the historical plaques they have read. He feels awkward, like a boy on a date with an older girl. They are still just making conversation. 135

"Corinth is where Mama eloped to," says Norma Jean. 136

They sit in silence and stare at the cemetery for the Union dead and, beyond, at a tall cluster of trees. Campers are parked nearby, bumper to bumper, and small children in bright clothing are cavorting and squealing. Norma Jean wads up the cake wrapper and squeezes it tightly in her hand. Without looking at Leroy, she says, "I want to leave you." 137

Leroy takes a bottle of Coke out of the cooler and flips off the cap. He holds the bottle poised near his mouth but cannot remember to take a drink. Finally he says, "No, you don't." 138

"Yes, I do." 139

"I won't let you." 140

"You can't stop me." 141

"Don't do me that way." 142

Leroy knows Norma Jean will have her own way. "Didn't I promise to be home from now on?" he says. 143

"In some ways, a woman prefers a man who wanders," says Norma Jean. "That sounds crazy, I know." 144

"You're not crazy." 145

Leroy remembers to drink from his Coke. Then he says, "Yes, you *are* crazy. You and me could start over again. Right back at the beginning." 146

"We *have* started all over again," says Norma Jean. "And this is how it turned out." 147

"What did I do wrong?" 148

"Nothing." 149

"Is this one of those women's lib things?" Leroy asks. 150

"Don't be funny." 151

The cemetery, a green slope dotted with white markers, looks like a subdivision site. Leroy is trying to comprehend that his marriage is breaking up, but for some reason he is wondering about white slabs in a graveyard. 152

"Everything was fine till Mama caught me smoking," says Norma Jean, standing up. "That set something off." 153

"What are you talking about?" 154

"She won't leave me alone—*you* won't leave me alone." Norma Jean seems to be crying, but she is looking away from him. "I feel eighteen again. 155

I can't face that all over again." She start walking away. "No, it *wasn't* fine. I don't know what I'm saying. Forget it."

Leroy takes a lungful of smoke and closes his eyes as Norma Jean's words sink in. He tries to focus on the fact that thirty-five hundred soldiers died on the grounds around him. He can only think of that war as a board game with plastic soldiers. Leroy almost smiles, as he compares the Confederates' daring attack on the Union camps and Virgil Mathis's raid on the bowling alley. General Grant, drunk and furious, shoved the Southerners back to Corinth, where Mabel and Jet Beasley were married years later, when Mabel was still thin and good-looking. The next day, Mabel and Jet visited the battleground, and then Norma Jean was born, and then she married Leroy and they had a baby, which they lost, and now Leroy and Norma Jean are here at the same battleground. Leroy knows he is leaving out a lot. He is leaving out the insides of history. History was always just names and dates to him. It occurs to him that building a house out of logs is similarly empty—too simple. And the real inner workings of a marriage, like most of history, have escaped him. Now he sees that building a log house is the dumbest idea he could have had. It was clumsy of him to think Norma Jean would want a log house. It was a crazy idea. He'll have to think of something else, quickly. He will wad the blueprints into tights balls and fling them into the lake. Then he'll get moving again. He opens his eyes. Norma Jean has moved away and is walking through the cemetery, following a serpentine path.   156

Leroy gets up to follow his wife, but his good leg is asleep and his bad leg still hurts him. Norma Jean is far away, walking rapidly toward the bluff by the river, and he tries to hobble toward her. Some children run past him, screaming noisily. Norma Jean has reached the bluff, and she is looking out over the Tennessee River. Now she turns toward Leroy and waves her arms. Is she beckoning to him? She seems to be doing an exercise for her chest muscles. The sky is unusually pale—the color of the dust ruffle Mabel made for their bed.   157

Questions for Study and Discussion

1. Norma Jean becomes increasingly impatient and dissatisfied with Leroy as the story progresses. At the end of the story she says, "In some ways, a woman prefers a man who wanders." What does she mean by that? How does the remark help to explain the cause of her discontent? Do you think her discontent is simply the result of her husband's accident or is it the result of something else?

2. What details does the author include to ensure that the reader is aware that Norma Jean and Leroy are working-class people?

3. What kinds of evidence does Mason use to plot the steady decline in the relationship between Leroy and Norma Jean?

4. In a short story no character or detail can be superfluous. There simply isn't room for extras. What is the author's purpose in including Norma Jean's mother in the drama? Is she superfluous? Explain.

5. The battlefield at Shiloh is an important focal point for the characters in the story. What role does it play in the story? How is it important to Leroy, Norma Jean, and Mabel? What does its meaning to each character tell you about their relationship? Were you surprised when Norma Jean chose that place to announce her intention to leave Leroy?

6. When Norma Jean expresses her intention to leave Leroy, he asks "Is this one of those women's lib things?" She replies, "Don't be funny." What do his question and her answer reveal to the reader about Leroy's understanding of his wife and her understanding of herself? Is she a feminist?

7. What is Norma Jean doing at the end of the story when she waves her arms?

Writing Topics

1. Reread Kate Chopin's "Story of an Hour" (pp. 80–83), which, much like "Shiloh," tells the story of a woman facing unpleasant and unexpected feelings about her husband. How are the feelings of the two women similar? How do they differ? How have the two authors portrayed each woman's sense of frustration and despair? Do you sympathize more with one woman than the other? In an essay, explore these questions as well as the ways in which the eras in which the two women live affect both their attitudes toward their husbands and their options.

2. Norma Jean is a working-class woman experiencing the same anxieties and feelings of oppression described by the middle-class women who have led the feminist movement. However, it is possible that these attitudes will be expressed differently by blue-collar women who have not been educated into the philosophy and rhetoric of the movement. In an essay, explore the ways women from different economic backgrounds might be apt to express their feminist attitudes. If the women's movement has been a middle-class campaign, how is that campaign likely to change as it moves into the ranks? How will the issues differ, if at all, for women and men with less money and education?

Men and Women in the Workplace

GLORIA STEINEM

Gloria Steinem is a political activist, editor, lecturer, writer, and one of this country's leading feminists. She was born in Toledo, Ohio, in 1934 and graduated from Smith College in 1956. After college she traveled to India to study and then returned to New York, where she later helped to found two important magazines, *New York* and *Ms.* Steinem has published many articles and four books: *The Thousand Indias* (1957), *The Beach Book* (1963), *Outrageous Acts and Everyday Rebellions* (1983)—from which the following essay is taken—and *Marilyn* (1987).

In "The Importance of Work" Steinem argues that the standard answer that women give to the question of why they work, "Womenworkbecausewehaveto," is inadequate and a self-deception. Women should be able, she claims, to admit openly that they work because it is a human right and because it is an activity that is both natural and pleasurable.

The Importance of Work

Toward the end of the 1970s, the *Wall Street Journal* devoted an eight-page, front-page series to "the working woman"—that is, the influx of women into the paid-labor force—as the greatest change in American life since the Industrial Revolution. 1

Many women readers greeted both the news and the definition with cynicism. After all, women have always worked. If all the productive work of human maintenance that women do in the home were valued at its replacement cost, the gross national product of the United States would go up by 26 percent. It's just that we are now more likely than ever before to 2 leave our poorly rewarded, low-security, high-risk job of homemaking (though we're still trying to explain that it's a perfectly good one and that the problem is male society's refusal both to do it and to give it an economic value) for more secure, independent, and better-paid jobs outside the home.

Obviously, the real work revolution won't come until all productive   3
work is rewarded—including child rearing and other jobs done in the home—and men are integrated into so-called women's work as well as vice versa. But the radical change being touted by the *Journal* and other media is one part of that long integration process: the unprecedented flood of women into salaried jobs, that is, into the labor force as it has been male-defined and previously occupied by men. We are already more than 41 percent of it—the highest proportion in history. Given the fact that women also make up a whopping 69 percent of the "discouraged labor force" (that is, people who need jobs but don't get counted in the unemployment statistics because they've given up looking), plus an official female unemployment rate that is substantially higher than men's, it's clear that we could expand to become fully half of the national work force by 1990.

Faced with this determination of women to find a little independence   4
and to be paid and honored for our work, experts have rushed to ask: "Why?" It's a question rarely directed at male workers. Their basic motivations of survival and personal satisfaction are taken for granted. Indeed, men are regarded as "odd" and therefore subjects for sociological study and journalistic reports only when they *don't* have work, even if they are rich and don't need jobs or are poor and can't find them. Nonetheless, pollsters and sociologists have gone to great expense to prove that women work outside the home because of dire financial need, or if we persist despite the presence of a wage-earning male, out of some desire to buy "little extras" for our families, or even out of good old-fashioned penis envy."

Job interviewers and even our own families may still ask salaried   5
women the big "Why?" If we have small children at home or are in some job regarded as "men's work," the incidence of such questions increases. Condescending or accusatory versions of "What's a nice girl like you doing in a place like this?" have not disappeared from the workplace.

How do we answer these assumptions that we are "working" out of   6
some pressing or peculiar need? Do we feel okay about arguing that it's as natural for us to have salaried jobs as for our husbands—whether or not we have young children at home? Can we enjoy strong career ambitions without worrying about being thought "unfeminine"? When we confront men's growing resentment to women competing in the work force (often in the form of such guilt-producing accusations as "You're taking men's jobs away" or "You're damaging you children"), do we simply state that a decent job is a basic human right for everybody?

I'm afraid the answer is often no. As individuals and as a movement,   7
we tend to retreat into some version of a tactically questionable defense: "Womenworkbecausewehaveto." The phrase has become one word, one key

on the typewriter—an economic form of the socially "feminine" stance of passivity and self-sacrifice. Under attack, we still tend to present ourselves as creatures of economic necessity and familial devotion. "Womenworkbecausewehaveto" has become the easiest thing to say.

Like most truisms, this one is easy to prove with statistics. Economic need *is* the most consistent work motive—for women as well as men. In 1976, for instance, 43 percent of all women in the paid-labor force were single, widowed, separated, or divorced, and working to support themselves and their dependents. An additional 21 percent were married to men who had earned less than ten thousand dollars in the previous year, the minimum then required to support a family of four. In fact, if you take men's pensions, stocks, real estate, and various forms of accumulated wealth into account, a good statistical case can be made that there are more women who "have" to work (that is, who have neither the accumulated wealth, nor husbands whose work or wealth can support them for the rest of their lives) than there are men with the same need. If we were going to ask one group "Do you really need this job?" we should ask men.

But the first weakness of the whole "have to work" defense is its deceptiveness. Anyone who has ever experienced dehumanized life on welfare or any other confidence-shaking dependency knows that a paid job may be preferable to the dole, even when the handout is coming from a family member. Yet the will and self-confidence to work on one's own can diminish as dependency and fear increase. That may explain why—contrary to the "have to" rationale—wives of men who earn less than three thousand dollars a year are actually *less* likely to be employed than wives whose husbands make ten thousand dollars a year or more.

Furthermore, the greatest proportion of employed wives is found among families with a total household income of twenty-five to fifty thousand dollars a year. This is the statistical underpinning used by some sociologists to prove that women's work is mainly important for boosting families into the middle or upper middle class. Thus, women's incomes are largely used for buying "luxuries" and "little extras": a neat doublewhammy that renders us secondary within our families, and makes our jobs expendable in hard times. We may even go along with this interpretation (at least, up to the point of getting fired so a male can have our job). It preserves a husbandly ego-need to be seen as the primary breadwinner, and still allows us a safe "feminine" excuse for working.

But there are often rewards that we're not confessing. As noted in *The Two-Career Couple*, by Francine and Douglas Hall: "Women who hold jobs by choice, even blue-collar routine jobs, are more satisfied with their lives than are the full-time housewives."

In addition to personal satisfaction, there is also society's need for all its members' talents. Suppose that jobs were given out on only a "have to work" basis to both women and men—one job per household. It would be unthinkable to lose the unique abilities of, for instance, Eleanor Holmes

Norton, the distinguished chair of the Equal Employment Opportunity Commission. But would we then be forced to question the important work of her husband, Edward Norton, who is also a distinguished lawyer? Since men earn more than twice as much as women on the average, the wife in most households would be more likely to give up her job. Does that mean the nation could do as well without millions of its nurses, teachers, and secretaries? Or that the rare man who earns less than his wife should give up his job?

It was this kind of waste of human talents on a society-wide scale that   13
traumatized millions of unemployed or underemployed Americans during the Depression. Then, a one-job-per-household rule seemed somewhat justified, yet the concept was used to displace women workers only, create intolerable dependencies, and waste female talent that the country needed. That Depression experience, plus the energy and example of women who were finally allowed to work during the manpower shortage created by World War II, led Congress to reinterpret the meaning of the country's full-employment goal in its Economic Act of 1946. Full employment was officially defined as "the employment of those who want to work, without regard to whether their employment is, by some definition, necessary. This goal applies equally to men and to women." Since bad economic times are again creating a resentment of employed women—as well as creating more need for women to be employed—we need such a goal more than ever. Women are again being caught in a tragic double bind: We are required to be strong and then punished for our strength.

Clearly, anything less than government and popular commitment to   14
this 1946 definition of full employment will leave the less powerful groups, whoever they may be, in danger. Almost as important as the financial penalty paid by the powerless is the suffering that comes from being shut out of paid and recognized work. Without it, we lose much of our self-respect and our ability to prove that we are alive by making some difference in the world. That's just as true for the suburban woman as it is for the unemployed steel worker.

But it won't be easy to give up the passive defense of "weworkbecause-   15
wehaveto."

When a women who is struggling to support her children and grand-   16
children on welfare sees her neighbor working as a waitress, even though that neighbor's husband has a job, she may feel resentful; and the waitress (of course, not the waitress's husband) may feel guilty. Yet unless we establish the obligation to provide a job for everyone who is willing and able to work, that welfare woman may herself be penalized by policies that give out only one public-service job per household. She and her daughter will have to make a painful and divisive decision about which of them gets that precious job, and the whole household will have to survive on only one salary.

A job as a human right is a principle that applies to men as well as   17
women. But women have more cause to fight for it. The phenomenon of the
"working woman" has been held responsible for everything from an increase in male impotence (which turned out, incidentally, to be attributable
to medication for high blood pressure) to the rising cost of steak (which was
due to high energy costs and beef import restrictions, not women's refusal
to prepare the cheaper, slower-cooking cuts). Unless we see a job as part of
every citizen's right to autonomy and personal fulfillment, we will continue
to be vulnerable to someone else's idea of what "need" is, and whose "need"
counts the most.

In many ways, women who do not have to work for simple survival,   18
but who choose to do so nonetheless, are on the frontier of asserting this
right for all women. Those with well-to-do husbands are dangerously easy
for us to resent and put down. It's easier still to resent women from families
of inherited wealth, even though men generally control and benefit from
that wealth. (There is no Rockefeller Sisters Fund, no J. P. Morgan &
Daughters, and sons-in-law may be the ones who really sleep their way to
power.) But to prevent a woman whose husband or father is wealthy from
earning her own living, and from gaining the self-confidence that comes
with that ability, is to keep her needful of that unearned power and less
willing to disperse it. Moreover, it is to lose forever her unique talents.

Perhaps modern feminists have been guilty of a kind of reverse snob-   19
bism that keeps us from reaching out to the wives and daughters of wealthy
men; yet it was exactly such women who refused the restrictions of class and
financed the first wave of feminist revolution.

For most of us, however, "womenworkbecausewehaveto" is just true   20
enough to be seductive as a personal defense.

If we use it without also staking out the larger human right to a job,   21
however, we will never achieve that right. And we will always be subject to
the false argument that independence for women is a luxury affordable only
in good economic times. Alternatives to layoffs will not be explored,
acceptable unemployment will always be used to frighten those with jobs
into accepting low wages, and we will never remedy the real cost, both to
families and to the country, of dependent women and a massive loss of
talent.

Worst of all, we may never learn to find productive, honored work as a   22
natural part of ourselves and as one of life's basic pleasures.

Questions for Study and Discussion

1. In your own words, what is Gloria Steinem's thesis in this essay?
2. Why did many women readers greet the *Wall Street Journal's* definition
of "the working woman" with cynicism? What was Steinem's response?

3. Steinem states that many women use the "Womenworkbecausewe-haveto" defense when asked why they work. Why does Steinem believe they use this defense? Why does she object to it? And what does she gain from turning the sentence "Women work because we have to" into a single word? Explain.

4. How does Steinem dismiss the claim that women who enter the workplace are robbing men of their jobs and damaging their children?

5. What is Steinem's attitude toward women who work even though they don't need to financially? Does she believe they should be applauded or resented?

6. How is "full employment" defined in the Economic Recovery Act of 1946? Is it a definition that Steinem supports? How, according to Steinem, do attitudes toward working women change during bad economic times?

7. How does society benefit from the full employment of men and women? How do individuals benefit?

8. On the basis of Steinem's tone, diction, and evidence in the essay, would you characterize her as a persuasive writer?

9. For what audience do you believe Steinem intended her article? What assumptions does she make about her audience? Would this audience find her argument convincing? Would a different audience be persuaded as well? Explain.

Writing Topics

1. Steinem believes that "a decent job is a basic human right for everybody." Is such a position realistic? Does America have an obligation to provide such a job for every citizen? Write an essay in which you argue your position.

2. In preparation for an essay on working parents, analyze your own family situation. Did only one or both of your parents work outside the home? What was the effect on the fabric of your family life? Would you have preferred the alternative situation?

MARY MEBANE

Mary Mebane was born in 1933 in Durham, North Carolina. After earning her B.A. at North Carolina State College, she went on to receive her M.A. and Ph.D. from the University of North Carolina and to teach, most recently at the University of Wisconsin at Milwaukee. Her writing has appeared in *A Galaxy of Black Writers* and *The Eloquence of Protest*; her play *Take a Sad Song* was produced in 1975. She has published two widely acclaimed autobiographical books, *Mary* (1981) and *Mary, Wayfarer* (1983). About her own work Mebane has said, "My writings center on the black folk of the South, post-1960. It is my belief that the black folk are the most creative, viable people that America has produced. They just don't know it."

In "Summer Job," taken from *Mary*, Mebane describes the process of getting a job in a southern tobacco factory. And in so doing, she also introduces us to the plight of African-American women workers in the years preceding the Civil Rights Act of 1964.

Summer Job

It was summer 1949, and I needed a job. Everybody tried to "get on" at the tobacco factory during "green season," when lots of extra workers were hired to "work up" new tobacco—that is, process it for cigarettes. Some people made their chief money of the year during the ten-to-twelve-week green season. The factory paid more money than days work, so lots of women gladly left their housekeeping jobs and went to the factories. In Durham there were two major factories and several smaller ones. The major factories worked up tobacco, but they also made cigarettes and had a shipping department and research laboratories. The smaller factories mainly worked up tobacco for the larger ones, in Durham and in other cities. Of the two major factories in Durham, Liggett and Myers did relatively little hiring in green season; it had a stable year-round force and gave preference to its former workers during the season. My mother worked there. The American Tobacco Company, the other factory, hired a great many temporary workers.

I was told that my best bet was the American. I wasn't eighteen, but I was tall and stocky and could pass for older, and besides, they never asked to see your birth certificate; so, a few months short of my sixteenth birthday, I went to get work at the American, makers of Lucky Strike cigarettes and other brands. From the start, I knew that I wouldn't get a job on the "cigarette side." That was easy work, and I was told that mostly whites worked over there. I would get a chance on the belt on the "tobacco side." Several women in the neighborhood who had worked at the American during the green season instructed me about how to get on. I was told to get there early and stand on the sidewalk in front of the employment office and just as close as possible to it, so that when they came out to select workers I would be easily seen. Also I was told to say, if they asked me, that I had worked there before. Nobody ever checked the records. So, on the morning that hiring began for green season, I went to Durham.

I accompanied neighbors who had received postcards informing them   3
they could come to work. They left me outside while they went in. I was dismayed, for the whole street in front of the employment office was filled with black women. They crowded around the brick porch leading to the employment office; they were on the sidewalk; they overflowed the street and covered the sidewalk behind. They were directly in front of the office, spreading out fanwise in both directions from it. Nobody was allowed on the porch except those who already had cards.

A pudgy white man with a cigar in his mouth came and stood on the   4
porch and said, "All those who have cards, come forward." Those who had cards held them up over their heads and started pushing through the crowd. Sometimes they had to remonstrate with some stubborn woman who refused to give way: "Let me pass, please! Move out of my way!" Slowly the one blocking her path would grudgingly give ground. Others quickly surged forward, trying to fill the space that was left, taking advantage of the confusion to try to push even nearer the office. When the favored ones got in, there began the long wait for the man to come back and start selecting more "hands" from the crowd of women left standing there. The crowd continued to grow bigger by the minute as new arrivals came.

You could tell the veterans from the rookies by the way they were   5
dressed. The knowledgeable ones had their heads covered by kerchiefs, so that if they were hired, tobacco dust wouldn't get in their hair; they had on clean dresses that by now were faded and shapeless, so that if they were hired they wouldn't get tobacco dust and grime on their best clothes. Those who were trying for the first time had their hair freshly done and wore attractive dresses; they wanted to make a good impression. But the dresses couldn't be seen at the distance that many were standing from the employment office, and they were crumpled in the crush.

Some women looked as if they had large families; they looked tired   6
and anxious, but determined. Some looked single; they had on lipstick and eyebrow pencil, and some even wore black patent-leather pumps with stockings.

The morning passed and the sun got hotter; there was no shade on the   7
sidewalks or in the street. The street stayed full, except when trucks edged their way in and the crowd gave way slowly.

After a while, the pudgy white man with the big cigar came to the 8 door and stood and looked. Instantly the whole mass surged forward. The shorter ones tried to stand on tiptoe to be seen over the heads of their taller sisters. Hands shot up in the air, trying to make them notice them. Those at the front who'd gotten shoved against the brick porch shouted, "Stop pushing, stop pushing, ya'll! You're hurting me!"

Finally the pudgy man spoke, standing on the porch with his cigar in 9 his mouth. "Until ya'll stop pushing and shoving I'm not gonna hire none of ya'll." Then he stood for a moment to see what effect his words were having on the crowd. Sensing that they were having no discernible effect, the man went back inside, and the surge forward stopped for the time being.

The women stood and stood; the sun grew hotter. Some grew tired of 10 waiting: "I left my baby with a neighbor. I told her that if I didn't get on I'd be back before twelve. I gotta go." Others left saying that they were "tired of this mess." One woman said, "All ya'll might as well go home. He's got his number for today. Come back tomorrow when they'll know how many more they'll need." At that, even more women faded away. The mass shrunk, but it was still a mass.

Finally, shortly before noon, the pudgy man came quietly to the porch 11 and pointed quickly to two women standing close by. Before the crowd knew people were getting on, the two women were on the porch and in the hall, following him. The crowd surged forward but the man was gone. "What time is it?" someone said. "High noon" was the answer and everyone seemed to agree that there would be no more hiring until one or two o'clock, after lunch.

Some sat right down on the sidewalk up against the building and took 12 out their sandwiches. Others drifted away from the crowd and down to a nearby luncheonette for cold drinks and sandwiches. I had a tomato sandwich that had become soggy in the press and the heat. I went with some other women far down the street to sit on the grass and eat my sandwich. They talked in front of me as if I were grown, so I knew that I would have no trouble if I got hired. What they said was so interesting that the crowd was re-forming in front of the employment office in the hot, boiling sun before I knew it.

Word came over the grapevine that they needed some more helpers 13 and would hire some more today. This gave everybody courage, so the crowd grew calm. Then the pudgy man came again. He made an announcement: "Any shoving, any pushing, and there'll be no more hiring today." The women grew quiet. Those who had been impatient hadn't come back from lunch, leaving those who were determined to get on.

The man selected two more women; the crowd gave a little surge 14 forward, but nothing like the shoving and pushing of the morning. In another hour he came back for one more, and soon the word came over the grapevine that we might as well go home. The crowd started fading away, but not the diehards. They didn't believe the grapevine and were determined to stay to see what was going to happen. I had no choice; I was staying until the people I rode with got off from work. It was now three o'clock and we all had been standing in the sun since eight o'clock in the morning. When the neighbors I was waiting for came, they said, "Don't worry. You'll get on tomorrow." Besides, they would go in earlier now that they were on.

I lay in bed that night, too tired to do anything else, and thought   15
about the day. Hundreds of women had stood in the hot sun for seven or eight hours under really bad conditions. There was no bathroom, no drinking fountain, no place to sit down. Those who had to leave lost their place in line and, thus, their chance for a job. Why was this? Because they needed work and the factory didn't need them. The factory had more hands available than it could use. That is why they could treat the surplus as they chose, and there was nothing that the women could do about it.

The next day I was there early and standing in place by the steps   16
before the employment office opened. I recognized some of the faces from the day before, and there were some that looked new to me. The crowd stretched out as far as it had the previous day. The sun was already hot when the pudgy man came to the platform with his cigar in his mouth. "Anyone here with a card?" he called. A few women who hadn't come in yesterday came forward. He went back inside.

I was close enough to see into the hall inside and the glass-faced side of   17
the employment office. It was shut off from the hall by glass because it was air-conditioned. There was a man, so slim and shapely that he looked like a girl, who came to the door and watched as the pudgy man came back and stood over the crowd. He watched the crowd surge forward, and he stepped back a little as if all the energy would wash over him. It seemed to give him great satisfaction to see the sea of black women struggling forward, trying to get a job in his factory; he'd stand and watch for a while, then turn and go into the air-conditioned office. At first the women thought that he was going to do some of the hiring and they pressed close to him and looked up. But once they'd determined that he had nothing to do with the hiring, he ceased to exist for them and they paid him no more attention.

More and more women were hired; the pudgy man would point here   18
and there, then take them off. In an hour or so, he'd come back and hire one or two more. Lunch came and the crowd scattered. I'd brought a meat sandwich, hoping that it wouldn't get crumpled and soggy like my tomato sandwich the day before. I knew enough not to leave my good place near the porch, so I ate standing in the hot sun, along with the rest of the women who had good places. I had been listening to the crowd for two days, so now I knew the words and phrases that would make me sound like a veteran, and I employed them. Evidently nothing was wrong with what I said, for no one looked at me "funny."

Around two o'clock the pudgy man came back and his eye fell on me   19
and the woman standing beside me. He motioned us in. I was now a factory
hand.

The air-conditioning in the office chilled me after the heat of the   20
street as I gave the necessary information. I made up a birthday and nobody
questioned it. Then I was taken to a "line" on the first floor.

It was a cavernous room, long and tall. The man who led me there   21
called to the boss, who came over to tell me what to do, but the machinery
was so loud that I couldn't hear him and I was so startled by my new
surroundings that I didn't really concentrate on what he said. I was afraid to
take a deep breath, for the room was so cloudy with tobacco dust that
brown particles hung in the air. I held my breath as long as I could and then
took a deep breath. I started to cough and my eyes watered. I saw lots of
women and some men, each doing a task seemingly unrelated to the others',
but I knew that there must be a plan.

My job had something to do with a conveyor belt. It was shaped like a   22
child's sliding board, only it had a deep trough and it moved. Shredded
tobacco was on this belt—I think that it came from upstairs—and my job
was to sit by the belt and pick out the pieces whose stems was too large. I
tried to determine what kind of stem was too large, for the belt was
constantly moving, and obviously I couldn't pick out every single stem on
the belt. I looked at the others, but I couldn't see what method they were
using. I was in misery, for this was my first "public" job and I didn't want to
do badly on it. I did the best that I could, but soon the boss came and told
me he was going to put me on the belt upstairs. I was glad, for my back hurt
from bending over, trying to pick out stems. Maybe I could do better
upstairs.

The air was full of tobacco dust there, too, but not as much as it had   23
been downstairs; also, it was quieter. This belt moved horizontally, from
right to left; women stood parallel to it, two women facing each other on the
same side of the belt, with a barrel of tied tobacco leaves in front of them.
They worked in pairs, taking the tobacco from the barrel, the hogshead,
and putting it on the belt. The important thing, as my partner explained to
me, was to make sure that the tied ends faced me, for the belt was on its way
to the cutter and the machine would cut off the hard tied end—which
would not go into the making of cigarettes—while the leaves went another
way.

The job seemed easy enough as I picked up bundle after bundle of   24
tobacco and put it on the belt, careful to turn the knot end toward me so
that it would be placed right to go under the cutting machine. Gradually, as
we worked up our tobacco, I had to bend more, for as we emptied the
hogshead we had to stoop over to pick up the tobacco, then straighten up
and put it on the belt just right. Then I discovered the hard part of the job:
the belt kept moving at the same speed all the time and if the leaves were not

placed on the belt at the same tempo there would be a big gap where your bundle should have been. So that meant that when you got down lower, you had to bend down, get the tobacco, straighten up fast, make sure it was placed knot end toward you, place it on the belt, and bend down again. Soon you were bending down, up; down, up; down, up. All along the line, heads were bobbing—down, up; down, up—until you finished the barrel. Then you could rest until the men brought you another one.

To make sure that you kept the belt filled, there was a line boss, a little   25
blond man who looked scared most of the time. He'd walk up and down behind you, saying, "Put the tobacco on the belt, girls. Put the tobacco on the belt. Too many empty spaces, girls. Too many empty spaces." You'd be working away, when suddenly behind you'd hear this voice: "Put the tobacco on the belt, girls. Put the tobacco on the belt. No empty spaces, girls. No empty spaces." I noticed that no one paid him any mind. He could be standing right by the belt talking, and it was as if he were invisible. The line kept moving, and the women kept bending and putting tobacco on the belt.

Over him was the floor boss. He had charge of all the operations on   26
the floor. He was the line boss's boss, and the line boss was clearly afraid of him. Over the floor boss was the big boss, who seldom came on the floor unless there was real trouble. Most of the women had never seen him, but some had and said that he was mean as the devil.

I bent and straightened and bent and straightened and thought that   27
my back would break. Once in the afternoon I got a ten-minute break in the "house" (toilet). I went there and collapsed into a chair.

That evening on the way home I tried to talk cheerfully to my   28
neighbors about the new job. They were quite pleased that I had gotten on. That was the one thing that kept me from quitting. I didn't want to let them down by telling them that I found the work killing. So I made up my mind to stay, no matter what, for I knew it was a short season.

Questions for Study and Discussion

1. What expectations did Mebane have of work at the American Tobacco Company? How did she come to have these expectations? Mebane devotes the first two-thirds of her essay to the "hiring process." What would have been gained or lost has she shortened this drastically?

2. What jobs did Mebane perform once she was hired? What did she think about the work she performed?

3. Why did everybody seek work at the tobacco factories during the season? Why do you think the work force was made up mostly of women?

4. Mebane's narrative is built upon a series of contrasts. What contrasts did you notice? Explain how they help her convey her experiences.

5. After only one day, Mebane found the work in the factory "killing." Why did she decide not to quit?

6. Mebane uses a great number of details in her writing to give the reader an accurate sense of where she is and what's going on. Cite several instances of her use of details that impressed you and attempt to explain the effect they had on your understanding of her situation.

7. How does Mebane's narrative help her establish the time, place, and circumstances of her narrative? Cite several examples to document your points.

Writing Topics

1. Write an essay in which you describe the process of seeking summer employment. What steps are generally involved? Offer some tips or suggestions that would enhance a person's chances of getting a summer job.

2. Using your own experiences or observations of summer jobs, write an essay in which you discuss the major differences and similarities between summer work and full-time employment. Is a summer job a fair and accurate introduction to what full-time work is really like? Explain. Write an essay in which you talk about your first summer job. What impressed you the most? The least? What did you think of your fellow workers? Of the working conditions? The pay? Did the job in any way affect your attitude toward education? Did it, for example, make you want to stay in school, or give you a greater appreciation of what school was doing for you?

LEWIS THOMAS

Lewis Thomas was born in 1913 in New York and attended Princeton and the Harvard Medical School. Thomas has had a distinguished career as a physician, administrator, researcher, teacher, and writer. Having been affiliated with a number of institutions, including the Yale University Medical School, Thomas is currently president of the Memorial Sloan-Kettering Cancer Center. He began his writing career in 1971 with a series of essays for the *New England Journal of Medicine*; many of these were collected in *The Lives of a Cell: Notes of a Biology Watcher*, winner of a National Book Award in 1974. Two further collections of essays have followed: *The Medusa and the Snail: More Notes of a Biology Watcher* and *Late Night Thoughts on Listening to Mahler's Ninth Symphony*.

"Nurses" is a chapter from *The Youngest Science: Notes of a Medicine-Watcher* (1983), Thomas's personal account of the development of the medical profession in this century. Here he examines the ways in which nurses' roles have changed in the last forty years and helps us to realize that the nursing staff is what holds any hospital together.

Nurses

When my mother became a registered nurse at Roosevelt Hospital, in 1903, there was no question in anyone's mind about what nurses did as professionals. They did what the doctor ordered. The attending physician would arrive for his ward rounds in the early morning, and when he arrived at the ward office the head nurse would be waiting for him, ready to take his hat and coat, and his cane, and she would stand while he had his cup of tea before starting. Entering the ward, she would hold the door for him to go first, then his entourage of interns and medical students, then she followed. At each bedside, after he had conducted his examination and reviewed the patient's progress, he would tell the nurse what needed doing that day, and she would write it down on the part of the chart reserved for nursing notes. An hour or two later he would be gone from the ward, and the work of the rest of the day and the night to follow was the nurse's frenetic occupation. In addition to the stipulated orders, she had an endless list of routine things to do, all learned in her two years of nursing school: the beds had to be changed and made up with fresh sheets by an exact geometric design of folding and tucking impossible for anyone but a trained nurse; the patients had to be washed head to foot; bedpans had to be brought, used, emptied, and washed; temperatures had to be taken every four hours and meticulously recorded on the chart; enemas were to be given; urine and stool samples collected, labeled, and sent off to the laboratory; throughout the day and night, medications of all sorts, usually pills and various vegetable extracts and tinctures, had to be carried on trays from bed to bed. At most times of the year about half of the forty or so patients on the ward had typhoid fever, which meant that the nurse couldn't simply move from bed to bed in the performance of her duties; each typhoid case was screened from the other patients, and the nurse was required to put on a new gown and wash her hands in disinfectant before approaching the bedside. Patients with high fevers were sponged with cold alcohol at frequent intervals. The late-evening back rub was the rite of passage into sleep.

In addition to the routine, workaday schedule, the nurse was responsible for responding to all calls from the patients, and it was expected that she would do so on the run. Her rounds, scheduled as methodical progressions around the ward, were continually interrupted by these calls. It was up to her to evaluate each situation quickly: a sudden abdominal pain in a typhoid patient might signify intestinal perforation; the abrupt onset of weakness, thirst, and pallor meant intestinal hemorrhage; the coughing up of gross blood by a tuberculous patient was an emergency. Some of the calls came from neighboring patients on the way to recovery; patients on open wards always kept a close eye on each other: the man in the next bed might slip into coma or seem to be dying, or be indeed dead. For such emergencies the nurse had to get word immediately to the doctor on call, usually the intern assigned to the ward, who might be off in the outpatient department or working in the diagnostic laboratory (interns of that day did all the laboratory work themselves; technicians had not yet been invented) or in his room. Nurses were not allowed to give injections or to do such emergency procedures as spinal punctures or chest taps, but they were expected to know when such maneuvers were indicated and to be ready with appropriate trays of instruments when the intern arrived on the ward.

It was an exhausting business, but by my mother's accounts it was the most satisfying and rewarding kind of work. As a nurse she was a low person in the professional hierarchy, always running from place to place on orders from the doctors, subject as well to strict discipline from her own administrative superiors on the nursing staff, but none of this came through in her recollections. What she remembered was her usefulness.

Whenever my father talked to me about nurses and their work, he spoke with high regard for them as professionals. Although it was clear in his view that the task of the nurse was to do what the doctor told them to, it was also clear that he admired them for being able to do a lot of things he couldn't possibly do, had never been trained to do. On his own rounds later on, when he became an attending physician himself, he consulted the ward nurse for her opinion about problem cases and paid careful attention to her observations and chart notes. In his own days of intern training (perhaps partly under my mother's strong influence, I don't know) he developed a deep and lasting respect for the whole nursing profession.

I have spent all of my professional career in close association with, and close dependency on, nurses, and like many of my faculty colleagues, I've done a lot of worrying about the relationship between medicine and nursing. During most of this century the nursing profession has been having a hard time of it. It has been largely, although not entirely, an occupation for women, and sensitive issues of professional status, complicated by the special issue of the changing role of women in modern society, have led to a standoffish, often adversarial relationship between nurses and doctors. Already swamped by an increasing load of routine duties, nurses have been obliged to take on more and more purely administrative tasks: keeping the records in order; making sure the supplies are on hand for every sort of ward emergency; supervising the activities of the new paraprofessional group called LPNs (licensed practical nurses), who perform much of the bedside work once done by RNs (registered nurses); overseeing ward maids, porters, and cleaners; seeing to it that patients scheduled for X rays are on their way to the X-ray department on time. Therefore, they have to spend more of their time at desks in the ward office and less time at the bedsides. Too late maybe, the nurses have begun to realize that they are gradually being excluded from the one duty which had previously been their most important reward but which had been so taken for granted that nobody mentioned it in listing the duties of a nurse: close personal contact with patients. Along with everything else nurses did in the long day's work, making up for all the tough and sometimes demeaning jobs assigned to them, they had the matchless opportunity to be useful friends to great numbers of human beings in trouble. They listened to their patients all day long and through the night, they gave comfort and reassurance to the patients and their families, they got to know them as friends, they were depended on. To contemplate the loss of this part of their work has been the deepest worry for nurses at large, and for the faculties responsible for the curricula of the nation's new and expanding nursing schools. The issue lies at the center of the running argument between medical school and nursing school administrators, but it is never clearly stated. Nursing education has been upgraded in recent years. Almost all the former hospital schools, which took in highschool graduates and provided an RN certificate after two or three years, have been replaced by schools attached to colleges and universities, with a four-year curriculum leading simultaneously to a bachelor's degree and an RN certificate.

The doctors worry that nurses are trying to move away from their historical responsibilities to medicine (meaning, really, to the doctors' orders). The nurses assert that they are their own profession, responsible for their own standards, coequal colleagues with physicians, and they do not wish to become mere ward administrators or technicians (although some of them, carrying the new and prestigious title of "nurse practitioner," are being trained within nursing schools to perform some of the most complex technological responsibilities in hospital emergency rooms and intensive care units). The doctors claim that what the nurses really want is to become substitute psychiatrists. The nurses reply that they have unavoidable responsibilities for the mental health and wellbeing of their patients, and that these are different from the doctors' tasks. Eventually the arguments will work themselves out, and some sort of agreement will be reached, but if it is to be settled intelligently, some way will have to be found to preserve and strengthen the traditional and highly personal nurse-patient relationship.

I have had a fair amount of firsthand experience with the issue, having 7 been an apprehensive patient myself off and on over a three-year period on the wards of the hospital for which I work. I am one up on most of my physician friends because of this experience. I know some things they do not know about what nurses do.

One thing the nurses do is to hold the place together. It is an 8 astonishment, which every patient feels from time to time, observing the affairs of a large, complex hospital from the vantage point of his bed, that the whole institution doesn't fly to pieces. A hospital operates by the constant interplay of powerful forces essential for getting necessary things done, but always at odds with each other. The intern staff is an almost irresistible force in itself, learning medicine by doing medicine, assuming all the responsibility within reach, pushing against an immovable attending and administrative staff, and frequently at odds with the nurses. The attending physicians are individual entrepreneurs trying to run small cottage industries at each bedside. The diagnostic laboratories are feudal fiefdoms, prospering from the insatiable demands for their services from the interns and residents. The medical students are all over the place, learning as best they can and complaining that they are not, as they believe they should be, at the epicenter of everyone's concern. Each individual worker in the place, from the chiefs of surgery to the dieticians to the ward maids, porters, and elevator operators, lives and works in the conviction that the whole apparatus would come to a standstill without his or her individual contribution, and in one sense or another each of them is right.

My discovery, as a patient first on the medical service and later in 9 surgery, is that the institution is held together, *glued* together, enabled to function as an organism, by the nurses and by nobody else.

The nurses, the good ones anyway (and all the ones on my floor were 10 good), make it their business to know everything that is going on. They spot errors before errors can be launched. They know everything written on the chart. Most important of all, they know their patients as unique human beings, and they soon get to know the close relatives and friends. Because of this knowledge, they are quick to sense apprehensions and act on them.

The average sick person in a large hospital feels at risk of getting lost, with no identity left beyond a name and a string of numbers on a plastic wristband, in danger always of being whisked off on a litter to the wrong place to have the wrong procedure done, or worse still, *not* being whisked off at the right time. The attending physician or the house officer, on rounds and usually in a hurry, can murmur a few reassuring words on his way out the door, but it takes a confident, competent, and cheerful nurse, there all day long and in and out of the room on one chore or another through the night, to bolster one's confidence that the situation is indeed manageable and not about to get out of hand.

Knowing what I know, I am all for the nurses. If they are to continue   11
their professional feud with the doctors, if they want their professional status enhanced and their pay increased, if they infuriate the doctors by their claims to be equal professionals, if they ask for the moon, I am on their side.

Questions for Study and Discussion

1. What is Thomas's thesis, and where is it stated? Could it have been placed elsewhere? Explain.
2. What was nursing like when Thomas's mother was practicing? What is the profession like today? How does Thomas account for the changes?
3. In what ways is comparison and contrast a useful strategy for Thomas in accomplishing his purpose?
4. What job reward does Thomas believe nurses are missing out on today?
5. How has nursing education changed over the years? What effects have these changes had on the nursing profession and its relationship to the medical profession?
6. What specifically does Thomas mean when he says, "One thing the nurses do is to hold the place together"? Why does Thomas believe he has a better understanding of the role of nurses than his fellow physicians?
7. What influence did Thomas's father have on his view of nurses? Who influenced his father?

Writing Topics

1. Argue for or against the proposition that women are better suited than men to be nurses.
2. Explore the problem that a person encounters when he or she enters a profession largely dominated by the opposite sex—for example, men who choose to be elementary school teachers, nurses, or secretaries or women who choose to go into the clergy, engineering, or police work. Your essay should consider not only problems associated with the job, but also those concerned with education, training, and even the reactions of family and friends.

PATRICK FENTON

Patrick Fenton was born in Brooklyn in 1941, and at sixteen dropped out of school to go to work in a local factory before entering the army. After a two-year hitch in Germany, he went to work as an airport cargo handler at John F. Kennedy Airport in New York. At the same time he started to write articles for local publications. Eight years as a cargo handler proved to be too much. Fenton took a civil-service job and continued to work as a free-lance writer. He is now a free-lance writer and is working toward a college degree he began some years ago.

While working as a cargo handler for Seaboard World Airlines, Fenton wrote "Confessions of a Working Stiff," in which he tells us how he makes his living and how physically and spiritually debilitating such a job is. The essay was first published in the April 1975 issue of *New York* magazine.

Confessions of a Working Stiff

The Big Ben is hammering out its 5:45 alarm in the half-dark of another Tuesday morning. If I'm lucky, my car down in the street will kick over for me. I don't want to think about that now; all I want to do is roll over into the warm covers that hug my wife. I can hear the wind as it whistles up and down the sides of the building. Tuesday is always the worst day—it's the day the drudgery, boredom, and fatigue start all over again. I'm off from work on Sunday and Monday, so Tuesday is my blue Monday. 1

I make my living humping cargo for Seaboard World Airlines, one of the big international airlines at Kennedy Airport. They handle strictly all cargo. I was once told that one of the Rockefellers is the major stockholder for the airline, but I don't really think about that too much. I don't get paid to think. The big thing is to beat that race with the time clock every morning of your life so the airline will be happy. The worst thing a man could ever do is to make suggestions about building a better airline. They pay people $40,000 a year to come up with better ideas. It doesn't matter that these ideas never work; it's just that they get nervous when a guy from South Brooklyn or Ozone Park acts like he actually has a brain. 2

I throw a Myadec high-potency vitamin into my mouth to ward off one of the ten colds I get every year from humping mailbags out in the cold rain at Kennedy. A huge DC-8 stretch jet waits impatiently for the 8,000 3 pounds of mail that I will soon feed its empty belly. I wash the Myadec down with some orange juice and grab a brown bag filled with bologna and cheese. Inside the lunch bag there is sometimes a silly note from my wife that says, "I Love You—Guess Who?" It is all that keeps me going to a job that I hate.

I've been going there for seven years now and my job is still the same. It's weary work that makes a man feel used up and worn out. You push and you pull all day long with your back. You tie down pallets loaded with thousands of pounds of freight. You fill igloo-shaped containers with hundreds of boxes that look the same. If you're assigned to work the warehouse, it's really your hard luck. This is the job all the men hate most. You stack box upon box until the pallet resembles the exact shape of the inside of the plane. You get the same monotonous feeling an adult gets when he plays with a child's blocks. When you finish one pallet, you find another and start the whole dull process over again.

The airline pays me $192 a week for this. After they take out taxes and $5.81 for the pension, I go home with $142. Once a month they take out $10 for term life insurance, and $5.50 for union dues. The week they take out the life insurance is always the worst: I go home with $132. My job will never change. I will fill up the same igloos with the same boxes for the next 34 years of my life, I will hump the same mailbags into the belly of the plane, and push the same 8,000-pound pallets with my back. I will have to do this until I'm 65 years old. Then I'll be free, if I don't die of a heart attack before that, and the airline will let me retire.

In winter the warehouse is cold and damp. There is no heat. The large steel doors that line the warehouse walls stay open most of the day. In the cold months, wind, rain and snow blow across the floor. In the summer the warehouse becomes an oven. Dust and sand from the runways mix with the toxic fumes of fork lifts, leaving a dry, stale taste in your mouth. The high windows above the doors are covered with a thick, black dirt that kills the sun. The men work in shadows with the constant roar of jet engines blowing dangerously in their ears.

Working the warehouse is a tedious job that leaves a man's mind empty. If he's smart he will spend his days wool-gathering. He will think about pretty girls that he once knew, or some other daydream of warm, dry places where you never had a chill. The worst thing he can do is to think about his problems. If he starts to think about how he is going to pay the mortgage on the $30,000 home that he can't afford, it will bring him down. He will wonder why he comes to the cargo airline every morning of his life, and even on Christmas Day. He will start to wonder why he has to listen to the deafening sound of the jets as they rev up their engines. He will wonder why he crawls on his hands and knees, breaking his back a little more every day.

To keep kids in that great place in the country in the summer, that great place far away from Brooklyn and the South Bronx, he must work every hour of overtime that the airline offers him. If he never turns down an hour, if he works some 600 hours over, he can make about $15,000. To do this he must turn against himself, he must pray that the phone rings in the middle of the night, even though it's snowing out and he doesn't feel like working. He must hump cargo late into the night, eat meatball heroes for supper, drink coffee that starts to taste like oil, and then hope that his car starts when it's time to go home. If he gets sick—well, he better not think about that.

All over Long Island, Ozone Park, Brooklyn, and as far away as the Bronx, men stir in the early morning hours as a new day begins. Every morning is the same as the last. Some of the men drink beer for breakfast instead of coffee. Way out in Bay Shore a cargoman snaps open a can of Budweiser. It's 6 A.M., and he covers the top of the can with his thumb in order to keep down the loud hiss as the beer escapes. He doesn't want to awaken his children as they dream away the morning in the next room. Soon he will swing his Pinto wagon up onto the crowded Long Island Expressway and start the long ride to the job. As he slips the car out of the driveway he tucks another can of beer between his legs.   **9**

All the men have something in common: they hate the work they are doing and they drink a little too much. They come to work only to punch a timecard that has their last name on it. At the end of the week they will pick up a paycheck with their last name on it. They will never receive a bonus for a job well done, or even a party. At Christmastime a card from the president of the airline will arrive at each one of their houses. It will say Merry Christmas and have the president's name printed at the bottom of it. They know that the airline will be there long after they are dead. Nothing stops it. It runs non-stop, without sleep, through Christmas Day, New Year's Eve, Martin Luther King's birthday, even the deaths of Presidents.   **10**

It's seven in the morning and the day shift is starting to drift in. Huge tractors are backing up to the big-mouth doors of the warehouse. Cattle trucks bring in tons of beef to feed its insatiable appetite for cargo. Smoke-covered trailers with refrigerated units packed deep with green peppers sit with their diesel engines idling. Names like White, Mack, and Kenworth are welded to the front of their radiators, which hiss and moan from the overload. The men walk through the factory-type gates of the parking lot with their heads bowed, oblivious of the shuddering diesels that await them.   **11**

Once inside the warehouse they gather in groups of threes and fours like prisoners in an exercise yard. They stand in front of the two time clocks that hang below a window in the manager's office. They smoke and cough in the early morning hour as they await their work assignments. The manager, a nervous-looking man with a stomach that is starting to push out at his belt, walks out with the pink work sheets in his hand.   **12**

Eddie, a young Irishman with a mustache, has just bolted in through the door. The manager has his timecard in his hand, holding it so no one else can hit Eddie in. Eddie is four minutes late by the time clock. His name will now go down in the timekeeper's ledger. The manager hands the card to   **13** him with a "you'll be up in the office if you don't straighten out" look. Eddie takes the card, hits it in, and slowly takes his place with the rest of the men. He has been out till four in the morning drinking beer in the bars of Ozone Park; the time clock and the manager could blow up, for all he cares. "Jesus," he says to no one in particular, "I hope to Christ they don't put me in the warehouse this morning."

Over in another group, Kelly, a tall man wearing a navy knit hat, talks to the men. "You know, I almost didn't make it in this morning. I passed this green VW on the Belt Parkway. The girl driving it was singing. Jesus, I thought to myself, it must be great going somewhere at 6:30 in the morning that makes you want to sing." Kelly is smiling as he talks. "I often think, why the hell don't you keep on going, Kelly? Don't get off at the cargo exit, stay on. Go anywhere, even if it's only Brooklyn. Christ, if I was a single man I think I would do just that. Some morning I'd pass this damn place by and drive as far away as Riverhead. I don't know what I'd do when I got there—maybe I'd pick up a pound of beefsteak tomatoes from one of those roadside stands or something."   14

The men laugh at Kelly but they know he is serious. "I feel the same way sometimes," the man next to him says. "I find myself daydreaming a lot lately; this place drives you to do that. I get up in the morning and I just don't want to come to work. I get sick when I hit that parking lot. If it wasn't for the kids and the house I'd quit." The men then talk about how hard it is to get work on "the outside." They mention "outside" as if they were in a prison.   15

Each morning there is an Army-type roll call from the leads. The leads are foremen who must keep the men moving; if they don't, it could mean their jobs. At one time they had power over the men but as time went by the company took away their little bit of authority. They also lost the deep interest, even enjoyment, for the hard work they once did. As the cargo airline grew, it beat this out of them, leaving only apathy. The ramp area is located in the backyard of the warehouse. This is where the huge jets park to unload their 70,000-pound payloads. A crew of men fall in behind the ramp lead as he mopes out of the warehouse. His long face shows the hopelessness of another day.   16

A brutal rain has started to beat down on the oil-covered concrete of the ramp as the 306 screeches in off the runway. Its engines scream as they spit off sheets of rain and oil. Two of the men cover their ears as they run to put up a ladder to the front of the plane. The airline will give them ear covers only if they pay for half of them. A lot of the men never buy them. If they want, the airline will give them two little plugs free. The plugs don't work and hurt the inside of the ears.   17

The men will spend the rest of the day in the rain. Some of them will set up conveyor belts and trucks to unload the thousands of pounds of cargo that sit in the deep belly of the plane. Then they will feed the awkward bird until it is full and ready to fly again. They will crawl on their   18 hands and knees in its belly, counting and humping hundreds of mailbags. The rest of the men will work up topside on the plane, pushing 8,000-pound pallets with their backs. Like Egyptians building a pyramid, they will pull and push until the pallet finally gives in and moves like a massive stone sliding through sand. They don't complain too much; they know that when the airline comes up with a better system some of them will go.

The old-timers at the airline can't understand why the younger men   19
stay on. They know what the cargo airline can do to a man. It can work him hard but make him lazy at the same time. The work comes in spurts. Sometimes a man will be pushed for three hours of sweat, other times he will just stand around bored. It's not the hard work that breaks a man at the airline, it's the boredom of doing the same job over and over again.

At the end of the day the men start to move in off the ramp. The rain   20
is still beating down at their backs but they move slowly. Their faces are red and raw from the rain-soaked wind that has been snapping at them for eight hours. The harsh wind moves in from the direction of the city. From the ramp you can see the Manhattan skyline, gray- and blue-looking, as it peeks up from the west wall of the warehouse. There is nothing to block the winter weather as it rolls in like a storm across a prairie. They head down to the locker room, heads bowed, like a football team that never wins.

With the workday almost over, the men move between the narrow,   21
gray rows of lockers. Up on the dirty walls that surround the lockers someone has written a couple of four-letter words. There is no wit to the words; they just say the usual. As they strip off their wet gear the men seem to come alive.

"Hey, Arnie! You want to stay four hours? They're asking for over-   22
time down in Export," one of the men yells over the lockers.

Arnie is sitting about four rows over, taking off his heavy winter   23
clothing. He thinks about this for a second and yells back, "What will we be doing?"

"Working the meat trailer." This means that Arnie will be humping   24
huge sides of beef off rows of hooks for four hours. Blood will drip down onto his clothes as he struggles to the front of the trailer. Like most of the men, he needs the extra money, and knows that he should stay. He has Master Charge, Korvettes, Times Square Stores, and Abraham & Straus to pay.

"Nah, I'm not staying tonight. Not if it's working the meat trailer. Don   25
wanted to stop for a few beers at The Owl; maybe I'll stay tomorrow night."

It's four o'clock in the afternoon now—the men have twelve minutes   26
to go before they punch out. The airline has stopped for a few seconds as the men change shifts. Supervisors move frantically across the floor pushing the fresh lot of new men who have just started to come in. They hand out work sheets and yell orders: "Jack, get your men into their rain gear. Put three men in the bellies to finish off the 300 flight. Get someone on the pepper trailers, they've been here all morning."

The morning shift stands around the time clock with three minutes to go. Someone says that Kevin Delahunty has just been appointed to the Fire Department. Kevin, a young Irishman from Ozone Park, has been working the cargo airline for six years. Like most of the men, he has hated every minute of it. The men are openly proud of him as they reach out to shake his hand. Kevin has found a job on "the outside." "Ah, you'll be leaving soon," he tells Pat. "I never thought I'd get out of here either, but you'll see, you're going to make it." 27

The manager moves through the crowd handing out timecards and stops when he comes to Kevin. Someone told him Kevin is leaving. "Is that right, Delahunty? Well I guess we won't expect you in tomorrow, will we? Going to become a fireman, eh? That means you'll be jumping out of windows like a crazy man. Don't act like you did around here," he adds as he walks back to his office. 28

The time clock hits 4:12 and the men pour out of the warehouse. Kevin will never be back, but the rest of them will return in the morning to grind out another eight hours. Some of them will head straight home to the bills, screaming children, and a wife who tries to understand them. They'll have a Schaefer or two, then they'll settle down to a night of television. 29

Some of them will start to fill up the cargo bars that surround Kennedy Airport. They will head to places like Gaylor's on Rockaway Boulevard or The Dew Drop Inn down near Farmers Boulevard. They will drink deep glasses of whiskey and cold mugs of Budweiser. The Dew Drop has a honky-tonk mood of the Old West to it. The barmaid moves around like a modern-day Katie Elder. Like Brandy, she's a fine girl, but she can out-curse any cargoman. She wears a low-cut blouse that reveals most of her breasts. The jukebox will beat out some Country & Western as she says, "Ah, hell, you played my song." The cargomen will hoot and holler as she substitutes some of her own obscene lyrics. 30

They will drink late into the night, forgetting time clocks, Master Charge, First National City, Korvettes, mortgages, cars that don't start, and jet engines that hurt their ears. They will forget about damp, cold warehouses, winters that get longer and colder every year, minutes that drift by like hours, supervisors that harass, and the thought of growing old on a job they hate. At midnight they will fall dangerously into their cars and make their way up onto the Southern State Parkway. As they ride into the dark night of Long Island they will forget it all until 5:45 the next morning— when the Big Ben will start up the whole grind all over again. 31

Questions for Study and Discussion

1. What is Fenton's attitude toward the airline company he works for? What in particular does Fenton dislike about his job? What are the immediate

causes for his dissatisfaction? Why does he continue to work for the airline company?

2. Why, in your opinion, does the airline not do something to improve working conditions for its employees? Why does the airline company "get nervous when a guy from South Brooklyn or Ozone Park acts like he actually has a brain?"

3. What are "leads," and why does Fenton feel it is important to define and to discuss them?

4. For Fenton and his co-workers, working for the airline is a regimented, prison-like existence. How do Fenton's diction and imagery help to establish this motif?

5. Fenton uses concrete details and specific incidents to show rather than merely tell us how awful a job with the airline is. Identify several paragraphs that rely heavily on concrete detail and two or three revealing incidents that dramatize the plight of the workers. Explain how these passages make the cause-and-effect relationship that Fenton sees real for the reader.

6. Comment on the appropriateness of the following similes, which Fenton uses to describe the workers:

  a. "like prisoners in an exercise yard" (12)
  b. "like Egyptians building a pyramid" (18)
  c. "like a football team that never wins" (20)

7. In the title of his essay Fenton refers to himself as a "working stiff." What does he mean?

8. What is it, according to Fenton, that breaks a man at the airline?

Writing Topics

1. In "Confessions of a Working Stiff," Patrick Fenton discusses the reasons why he hates his job. Not all people, of course, dislike their work. In fact, many people derive considerable satisfaction from the work they do. In an essay, discuss the reasons why some jobs are more satisfying than others. Why is it possible for a job to be satisfying for one person and not for another?

2. You are a manager who supervises a crew of Patrick Fentons. What do you think you could do as a manager to address the problems he raises in his essay? Write an essay in which you make proposals for such changes, explain how they would work, and argue for their acceptance.

VICTOR FUCHS

Born in 1934 in New York City, Victor Fuchs is both a professor of economics at Stanford University and a research associate at the National Bureau of Economic Research. He was elected to the Institute of Medicine of the National Academy of Sciences and was appointed a Fellow of the American Academy of Arts and Sciences. His books include *Who Shall Live? Health, Economics and Social Choice* (1974), *How We Live: An Economic Perspective on Americans from Birth to Death* (1983), and *The Health Economy* (1986). He is also editor of *The Economics of Physician and Patient Behavior* and writes for professional journals. *Los Angeles Times* book critic Harry S. Ashmore says that Fuchs approaches issues of marriage, divorce, fertility, and education in "terms usually applied to the market-price, quantity, demand, supply, and the like. But he abandons the jargon, and tempers the dehumanizing effect, as he goes on to discuss the implications for public policy."

In the following selection from *How We Live*, Fuchs applies the same method of inquiry to the question of why mothers work outside the home. More surprising to readers than the reasons Fuchs says explain the growing number of working mothers may be the reasons he says do not.

Why Married Mothers Work

Among single women ages 25–44 four out five work for pay, and this 1 proportion has not changed since 1950. Divorced and separated women have also traditionally worked, and their participation rates (about 75 percent) have grown only slightly. The truly astonishing changes have taken place in the behavior of married women with children, as shown in Figure 1. . . .

Why has the participation of married mothers grown so *rapidly* and so 2 *steadily*? Popular discussions frequently attribute this growth to changes in attitudes that were stimulated by the feminist movement, but the time pattern portrayed in Figure 1 does not lend much support to this view. Betty Friedan's *The Feminine Mystique*, which is often credited with sparking the modern feminist movement, was published in 1963, long after the surge of married mothers into the labor force was under way. Moreover, there is no evidence of any sudden acceleration in response to this movement. Similarly, widespread public expressions of feminism *followed* rather

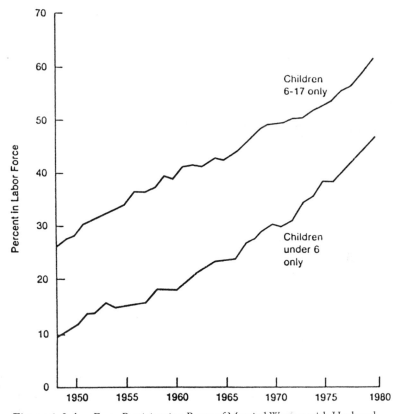

Figure 1. Labor Force Participation Rates of Married Women with Husband Present, by Presence and Age of Own Children, 1948–1980. (*Sources:* Employment and Training Administration, *Employment and Training Report of the President, 1980,* table B-4; idem, *Employment and Training Report of the President, 1981,* table B-7.)

than preceded the rise in the age of marriage and the fall in the birth rate. Divorce is the one variable whose change coincided with the burgeoning feminist movement, rising rapidly between 1965 and 1975. Thus, the feminist writings and discussion, valid as they may be in their own terms, will probably not be viewed by future historians as a basic cause of social change but primarily as a rationale and a rhetoric for changes that were already occurring for other reasons.

Government affirmative action programs are regarded by many as fostering female employment, but the timing again suggests that too much has been claimed for this explanation. These programs, which did not gain force until well into the 1960s, cannot explain the rapid rise in participation of married mothers in the 1950s—a rise that was even more rapid for older women with grown children. The timing of changes in the occupational distribution of employed married women is also contrary to what one would expect if the feminist movement or government affirmative action had a great deal of effect. The proportion who were in professional and technical occupations rose rapidly between 1948 and 1965, from 7.7 percent to 14.7 percent, but thereafter the rate of increase was more modest, only to 17.7 percent by 1979.

One of the most popular explanations for the two-earner family is that the wife's earnings are "needed to help make ends meet." This answer is the one most frequently given by women to survey researchers, and it receives some support from analytical studies that attempt to explain why, at any particular time, some wives work and some don't. There is a strong consensus among economists that, other things held constant, the higher the husband's income, the less likely it is that the wife will work for pay.

This explanation, however, does not contribute much to an understanding of changes over time. "Need," in an absolute sense, can hardly be the reason for the rapid rise in labor force participation of married mothers in the 1950s, when the real hourly earnings of their husbands were increasing at an unprecedented pace. Nathan Keyfitz observed that when women are asked why they work outside the home, they tend to reply that they need the money. "But," he writes, "the answer cannot be correct, since in earlier decades their husbands were earning less, presumably families needed money, and yet wives were content to stay home. Needing money is a universal, a constant, and a first rule of method is that one cannot explain a variable. . .with a constant."

One frequently mentioned but inadequately evaluated explanation for the surge of women into paid employment is the spread of time-saving household innovations such as clothes washers and dryers, frozen foods, and dishwashers. There is little doubt that it is easier to combine paid employment with home responsibilities now than it was fifty years ago, but it is not clear whether these time-saving innovations were the *cause* of the rise in female labor force participation or whether they were largely a *response* to meet a demand created by working women. Confusion about this point is most evident in comments that suggest that the rapid growth of supermarkets and fast-food outlets is a cause of women going to work. Similar time-saving organizations were tried at least sixty years ago, but with less success because the value of time was much lower then. The absence of supermarkets and fast-food eating places in low-income countries today also shows that their rapid growth in the United States is primarily a *result* of the rising value of time and the growth of women in the work force, not the reverse.

Within the economics profession the explanation that commands the widest consensus is that *higher wages* have attracted more married mothers into the labor force. This explanation is more firmly grounded in economic theory than many of the others and is reasonably consistent with observed behavior, both over time and among families at a given point in time. Ever since the pioneering work of Jacob Mincer, numerous cross-section analyses—studies that examine differences among individual families or groups of families—uniformly report that the probability of a wife's working is *positively* related to her potential wage rate, holding constant a spouse's education. This is the opposite of the previously noted *negative* effect of the husband's wage rate on the wife's labor force participation. . . .

In addition to higher wages, the rapid expansion of jobs in the service sector has contributed to the rise in female labor force participation (Fuchs 1968). The service industries (retail trade, financial service, education, health, personal services, public administration) have traditionally offered much greater employment opportunities for women than have mining, manufacturing, construction, and other branches of the industrial sector. For instance, 73 percent of nonfarm female employment was in the service sector in 1960, whereas the comparable figure for males was only 44 percent.

There are many reasons for this large differential. First, most occupations in the service sector do not place a premium on physical strength. Second, hours of work are frequently more flexible in service industries and there are many more opportunities for part-time work. Other things held constant, mothers of small children are more likely to be working in those metropolitan areas where there is large variation in the weekly hours of men (King). This variation is a good indicator of the existence of part-time employment opportunities, and women are much more likely than men to seek part-time employment. Third, service sector jobs are more likely to be located in or near residential areas, thus making them more attractive to women who bear large responsibilities for child care and homemaking.

The propensity of women to seek service sector employment is particularly relevant because it is this sector that has provided nearly all of the additional job opportunities in the U.S. economy since the end of World War II. Between 1947 and 1980 U.S. employment expanded by 39 million; the service sector provided 33 million of these additional jobs. To be sure, some of the growth of service employment is the *result* of the increase in female labor force participation rather than the cause (Fuchs). Families with working mothers are more likely to eat out, to send their children to nursery school, and to purchase a wide range of personal and professional services. This feedback effect, however, accounts for only a part of the growth of service employment. The major explanation is that rapid increases in output per worker in agriculture and industry cut the demand for labor in those sectors and shifted employment to services. A secondary reason is that consumer demand shifted slightly toward services in response to the growth of real income.

I conclude that the growth of real wages and the expansion of the service sector have been the most important reasons for the growth of female labor force participation. This participation, in turn, has had important effects on marriage, fertility, and divorce, but there is also some feedback from fertility and divorce to labor force participation. Better control of fertility makes a career in the labor market more promising to women, not only because of a reduction in the *number* of children but also because women now have better control over the *timing* of births. The increase in the *probability* of divorce contributes to the rise in female labor force participation because women recognize that complete commitment to home and husband can leave them in a perilous economic position if the marriage should dissolve. Alimony and child support payments are often inadequate, and are not paid at all in a large proportion of cases. An old song says that "diamonds are a girl's best friend," but today the ability to earn a good wage is likely to prove a more reliable asset.

Questions for Study and Discussion

1. Fuchs offers two basic reasons for the fact that more and more married mothers work outside the home. What are these reasons? Do you agree or disagree with his arguments? Can you think of any others?

2. What kinds of evidence does Fuchs use to document the trend he writes about? Is his evidence convincing? Why or why not?

3. Does Fuchs rely on logical, emotional, or some other kind of appeal to present his argument? Select examples of his diction and phrasing to support your answer.

4. What is the significance of the word *married* in Fuchs's argument? How does it relate to his overall thesis? What is that thesis and where is it stated? Why do you think he waits so long to state it?

5. In paragraphs 4 and 6 Fuchs debunks one of the commonly held beliefs as to the reason for the increase in the number of married women working outside the home. How well does he support his argument? How important are these two paragraphs to his overall argument?

6. Find the topic sentence in each of Fuchs's paragraphs. Where are they located? How well do these sentences provide a transition from one "cause" to another?

7. In offering his causal analysis, does Fuchs ever confuse the causes with the results of the trend of married women to work outside the home? Where does Fuchs discuss the danger of this confusion? What are the dangers?

8. Make a scratch outline of Fuchs's essay. How has he organized his material? What are the advantages and disadvantages to his method of organization?

Writing Topics

1. In several major corporations, as well as small companies, professional-level women have fought for and won the right to work flextime so they can

spend more hours at home with their children. They argue that they can do as good a job in 30 hours a week as in 40 if they are not worried about being away from their children for 8 hours a day. Some feminists say it will harm the movement to suggest that women with children are unable or unwilling to give full attention to executive-level responsibility. How do you respond to this debate? Using your own ideas and drawing on the information contained in Fuchs's article, write an essay in which you argue for or against a shortened work week for working mothers.

2. How has the college population on your campus changed over the past fifteen years? To what causes can these changes be attributed? Before writing, research your subject by speaking with college professors who have witnessed changing student behavior. In your research, be sure to consider some of the points Fuchs raises in his essay such as changing economic, social, and political realities.

Education is what survives when what has been learnt has been forgotten.

B. F. SKINNER

Most Americans do value education as a business asset, but not as the entrance into the joy of intellectual experience or acquaintance with the best that has been said and done in the past. They value it not as an experience, but as a tool.

W. H. P. FAUNCE

The Aims of Education

DAVID P. GARDNER

David P. Gardner was born in 1933 in Berkeley, California, and graduated from Brigham Young University. After a two-year stint in the army, he returned to the University of California, Berkeley, where he received his M.A. and Ph.D. His experience as a professor of higher education and as a university administrator prepared him for the presidency of the University of Utah. He is now the president of the University of California and has written widely on the purposes, functions, and problems of public education. In 1981 President Reagan appointed Gardner chairman of a commission to study the condition of public education in the United States. The commission published its report, *A Nation at Risk*, in 1983.

In the following excerpt from this report, Gardner and his fellow commission members sharply criticized certain trends in public education and called for a renewed emphasis on excellence.

A Nation at Risk

Our Nation is at risk. Our once unchallenged preeminence in commerce, industry, science and technological innovation is being overtaken by competitors throughout the world. This report is concerned with only one of the many causes and dimensions of the problem, but it is the one that undergirds American prosperity, security, and civility. We report to the American people that while we can take justifiable pride in what our schools and colleges have historically accomplished and contributed to the United States and the well-being of its people, the educational foundations of our society are presently being eroded by a rising tide of mediocrity that threatens our very future as a Nation and a people. What was unimaginable a generation ago has begun to occur—others are matching and surpassing our educational attainments.

If an unfriendly foreign power had attempted to impose on America the mediocre educational performance that exists today, we might well have viewed it as an act of war. As it stands, we have allowed this to happen to ourselves. We have even squandered the gains in student achievement made in the wake of the Sputnik challenge. Moreover, we have dismantled essential support systems which helped make those gains possible. We have, in effect, been committing an act of unthinking, unilateral educational disarmament.

Our society and its educational institutions seem to have lost sight of   3
the basic purposes of schooling, and of the high expectations and disciplined effort needed to attain them. This report, the result of 18 months of study, seeks to generate reform of our educational system in fundamental ways to renew the Nation's commitment to schools and colleges of high quality throughout the length and breadth of our land.

That we have compromised this commitment is, upon reflection,   4
hardly surprising, given the multitude of often conflicting demands we have placed on our Nation's schools and colleges. They are routinely called on to provide solutions to personal, social, and political problems that the home and other institutions either will not or cannot resolve. We must understand that these demands on our schools and colleges often exact an educational cost as well as a financial one.

On the occasion of the Commission's first meeting President Reagan   5
noted the central importance of education in American life when he said: "Certainly there are few areas of American life as important to our society, to our people, and to our families as our schools and colleges." This report, therefore, is as much an open letter to the American people as it is a report to the Secretary of Education. We are confident that the American people, properly informed, will do what is right for their children and for the generations to come.

The Risk

History is not kind to idlers. The time is long past when America's   6
destiny was assured simply by an abundance of natural resources and inexhaustible human enthusiasm and by our relative isolation from the malignant problems of older civilizations. The world is indeed one global village. We live among determined, well-educated, and strongly motivated competitors. We compete with them for international standing and markets, not only with products but also with the ideas of our laboratories and neighborhood workshops. America's position in the world may once have been reasonably secure with only a few exceptionally well-trained men and women. It is no longer.

The risk is not only that the Japanese make automobiles more effi-   7
ciently than Americans and have government subsidies for development and export. It is not just that the South Koreans recently built the world's most efficient steel mill, or that American machine tools, once the pride of the world, are being displaced by German products. It is also that these developments signify a redistribution of trained capability throughout the globe. Knowledge, learning, information, and skilled intelligence are the

new raw materials of international commerce and are today spreading throughout the world as vigorously as miracle drugs, synthetic fertilizers, and blue jeans did earlier. If only to keep and improve on the slim competitive edge we still retain in world markets, we must dedicate ourselves to the reform of our educational system for the benefit of all—old and young alike, affluent and poor, majority and minority. Learning is the indispensable investment required for success in the "information age" we are entering.

Our concern, however, goes well beyond matters such as industry and 8 commerce. It also includes the intellectual, moral, and spiritual strengths of our people which knit together the very fabric of our society. The people of the United States need to know that individuals in our society who do not possess the levels of skill, literacy, and training essential to this new era will be effectively disenfranchised, not simply from the material rewards that accompany competent performance, but also from the chance to participate fully in our national life. A high level of shared education is essential to a free, democratic society and to the fostering of a common culture, especially in a country that prides itself on pluralism and individual freedom.

For our country to function, citizens must be able to reach some 9 common understandings on complex issues, often on short notice and on the basis of conflicting or incomplete evidence. Education helps form these common understandings, a point Thomas Jefferson made long ago in his justly famous dictum:

> I know no safe depository of the ultimate powers of the society but the people themselves; and if we think them not enlightened enough to exercise their control with a wholesome discretion, the remedy is not to take it from them but to inform their discretion.

Part of what is at risk is the promise first made on this continent: All, 10 regardless of race or class or economic status, are entitled to a fair chance and to the tools for developing their individual powers of mind and spirit to the utmost. This promise means that all children by virtue of their own efforts, competently guided, can hope to attain the mature and informed judgment needed to secure gainful employment and to manage their own lives, thereby serving not only their own interests but also the progress of society itself.

Indicators of the Risk

The educational dimensions of the risk before us have been amply 11 documented in testimony received by the Commission. For example:

- *International comparisons of student achievement, completed a decade ago, reveal that on 19 academic tests American students were never first or second and, in comparison with other industrialized nations, were last seven times.*

- *Some 23 million American adults are functionally illiterate by the simplest tests of everyday reading, writing, and comprehension.*

- *About 13 percent of all 17-year-olds in the United States can be considered functionally illiterate. Functional illiteracy among minority youth may run as high as 40 percent.*

- *Average achievement of high school students on most standardized tests is now lower than 26 years ago when Sputnik was launched.*

- *Over half the population of gifted students do not match their tested ability with comparable achievement in school.*

- *The College Board's Scholastic Aptitude Tests (SAT) demonstrate a virtually unbroken decline from 1963 to 1980. Average verbal scores fell over 50 points and average mathematics scores dropped nearly 40 points.*

- *College Board achievement tests also reveal consistent declines in recent years in such subjects as physics and English.*

- *Both the number and proportion of students demonstrating superior achievement on the SATs (i.e., those with scores of 650 or higher) have also dramatically declined.*

- *Many 17-years-olds do not possess the "higher order" intellectual skills we should expect of them. Nearly 40 percent cannot draw inferences from written material; only one-fifth can write a persuasive essay; and only one-third can solve a mathematics problem requiring several steps.*

- *There was a steady decline in science achievement scores of U.S. 17-year-olds as measured by national assessments of science in 1969, 1973, and 1977.*

- *Between 1975 and 1980, remedial mathematics courses in public 4-year colleges increased by 72 percent and now constitute one-quarter of all mathematics courses taught in those institutions.*

- *Average tested achievement of students graduating from college is also lower.*

- *Business and military leaders complain that they are required to spend millions of dollars on costly remedial education and training programs in such basic skills as reading, writing, spelling, and computation. The Department of the Navy, for example, reported to the Commission that one-quarter of its recent recruits cannot read at the ninth grade level, the minimum needed simply to understand written safety instructions. Without remedial work they cannot even begin, much less complete, the sophisticated training essential in much of the modern military.*

These deficiencies come at a time when the demand for highly skilled workers in new fields is accelerating rapidly. For example: 12

- *Computers and computer-controlled equipment are penetrating every aspect of our lives—homes, factories, and offices.*

- *One estimate indicates that by the turn of the century millions of jobs will involve laser technology and robotics.*

- *Technology is radically transforming a host of other occupations. They include health care, medical science, energy production, food processing, construction, and the building, repair, and maintenance of sophisticated scientific, educational, military, and industrial equipment.*

Analysts examining these indicators of student performance and the   13
demands for new skills have made some chilling observations. Educational researcher Paul Hurd concluded at the end of a thorough national survey of student achievement that within the context of the modern scientific revolution, "We are raising a new generation of Americans that is scientifically and technologically illiterate." In a similar vein, John Slaughter, a former Director of the National Science Foundation, warned of "a growing chasm between a small scientific and technological elite and a citizenry ill-informed, indeed uninformed, on issues with a science component."

But the problem does not stop there, nor do all observers see it the   14
same way. Some worry that schools may emphasize such rudiments as reading and computation at the expense of other essential skills such as comprehension, analysis, solving problems, and drawing conclusions. Still others are concerned that an over-emphasis on technical and occupational skills will leave little time for studying the arts and humanities that so enrich daily life, help maintain civility, and develop a sense of community. Knowledge of the humanities, they maintain, must be harnessed to science and technology if the latter are to remain creative and humane, just as the humanities need to be informed by science and technology if they are to remain relevant to the human condition. Another analyst, Paul Copperman, has drawn a sobering conclusion. Until now, he has noted:

> Each generation of Americans has outstripped its parents in education, in literacy, and in economic attainment. For the first time in the history of our country, the educational skills of one generation will not surpass, will not equal, will not even approach, those of their parents.

It is important, of course, to recognize that *the average citizen* today is   15
better educated and more knowledgeable than the average citizen of a generation ago—more literate, and exposed to more mathematics, literature, and science. The positive impact of this fact on the well-being of our country and the lives of our people cannot be overstated. Nevertheless, *the average graduate* of our schools and colleges today is not as well-educated as the average graduate of 25 or 35 years ago, when a much smaller proportion of our population completed high school and college. The negative impact of this fact likewise cannot be overstated.

Hope and Frustration

Statistics and their interpretation by experts show only the surface   16
dimension of the difficulties we face. Beneath them lies a tension between hope and frustration that characterizes current attitudes about education at every level.

We have heard the voices of high school and college students, school   17
board members, and teachers; of leaders of industry, minority groups, and
higher education; of parents and State officials. We could hear the hope
evident in their commitment to quality education and in their descriptions
of outstanding programs and schools. We could also hear the intensity of
their frustration, a growing impatience with shoddiness in many walks of
American life, and the complaint that this shoddiness is too often reflected
in our schools and colleges. Their frustration threatens to overwhelm their
hope.

What lies behind this emerging national sense of frustration can be   18
described as both a dimming of personal expectations and the fear of losing
a shared vision for America.

On the personal level the student, the parent, and the caring teacher   19
all perceive that a basic promise is not being kept. More and more young
people emerge from high school ready neither for college nor for work. This
predicament becomes more acute as the knowledge base continues its rapid
expansion, the number of traditional jobs shrinks, and new jobs demand
greater sophistication and preparation.

On a broader scale, we sense that this undertone of frustration has   20
significant political implications, for it cuts across ages, generations, races,
and political and economic groups. We have come to understand that the
public will demand that educational and political leaders act forcefully and
effectively on these issues. Indeed, such demands have already appeared
and could well become a unifying national preoccupation. This unity,
however, can be achieved only if we avoid the unproductive tendency of
some to search for scapegoats among the victims, such as the beleaguered
teachers.

On the positive side is the significant movement by political and   21
educational leaders to search for solutions—so far centering largely on the
nearly desperate need for increased support for the teachers of mathematics
and science. This movement is but a start on what we believe is a larger and
more educationally encompassing need to improve teaching and learning in
fields such as English, history, geography, economics, and foreign languages.
We believe this movement must be broadened and directed toward reform
and excellence throughout education.

Excellence in Education

We define "excellence" to mean several related things. At the level of   22
the *individual learner*, it means performing on the boundary of individual
ability in ways that test and push back personal limits, in school and in the
workplace. Excellence characterizes a *school or college* that sets high expectations and goals for all learners, then tries in every way possible to help

students reach them. Excellence characterizes a *society* that has adopted these policies, for it will then be prepared through the education and skill of its people to respond to the challenges of a rapidly changing world. Our Nation's people and its schools and colleges must be committed to achieving excellence in all these senses.

We do not believe that a public commitment to excellence and educational reform must be made at the expense of a strong public commitment to the equitable treatment of our diverse population. The twin goals of equity and high-quality schooling have profound and practical meaning for our economy and society, and we cannot permit one to yield to the other either in principle or in practice. To do so would deny young people their chance to learn and live according to their aspirations and abilities. It also would lead to a generalized accommodation to mediocrity in our society on the one hand or the creation of an undemocratic elitism on the other.

Our goal must be to develop the talents of all to their fullest. Attaining that goal requires that we expect and assist all students to the limits of their capabilities. We should expect schools to have genuinely high standards rather than minimum ones, and parents to support and encourage their children to make the most of their talents and abilities.

The search for solutions to our educational problems must also include a commitment to life-long learning. The task of rebuilding our system of learning is enormous and must be properly understood and taken seriously: Although a million and a half new workers enter the economy each year from our schools and colleges, the adults working today will still make up about 75 percent of the workforce in the year 2000. These workers, and new entrants into the workforce, will need further education and retraining if they—and we as a Nation—are to thrive and prosper.

The Learning Society

In a world of ever-accelerating competition and change in the conditions of the workplace, of ever-greater danger, and of ever-larger opportunities for those prepared to meet them, educational reform should focus on the goal of creating a Learning Society. At the heart of such a society is the commitment to a set of values and to a system of education that affords all members the opportunity to stretch their minds to full capacity, from early childhood through adulthood, learning more as the world itself changes. Such a society has as a basic foundation the idea that education is important not only because of what it contributes to one's career goals but also because of the value it adds to the general quality of one's life, Also at the heart of the Learning Society are educational opportunities extending far beyond the traditional institutions of learning, our schools and colleges. They extend into homes and workplaces; into libraries, art galleries, museums, and science centers; indeed, into every place where the individual can develop and mature in work and in life. In our view, formal schooling in youth is the essential foundation for learning throughout one's life. But without life-long learning, one's skills will become rapidly dated.

In contrast to the ideal of the Learning Society, however, we find that for too many people education means doing the minimum work necessary for the moment, then coasting through life on what may have been learned in its first quarter. But this should not surprise us because we tend to express our educational standards and expectations largely in terms of "minimum requirements." And where there should be a coherent continuum of learning, we have none, but instead an often incoherent, outdated patchwork quilt. Many individual, sometimes heroic, examples of schools and colleges of great merit do exist. Our findings and testimony confirm the vitality of a number of notable schools and programs, but their very distinction stands out against a vast mass shaped by tensions and pressures that inhibit systematic academic and vocational achievement for the majority of students. In some metropolitan areas basic literacy has become the goal rather than the starting point. In some colleges maintaining enrollment is of greater day-to-day concern than maintaining rigorous academic standards. And the ideal of academic excellence as the primary goal of schooling seems to be fading across the board in American education.

Thus, we issue this call to all who care about America and its future: to parents and students; to teachers, administrators, and school board members; to colleges and industry; to union members and military leaders; to governors and State legislators; to the President; to members of Congress and other public officials; to members of learned and scientific societies; to the print and electronic media; to concerned citizens everywhere. America is at risk.

Questions for Study and Discussion

1. What is the main point that the commission is trying to get across in their report? What are the assumptions underlying their argument? In your opinion, do they have a valid point? Explain.

2. What exactly is the purpose of the commision's report?

3. What does Gardner mean when he refers to a "rising tide of mediocrity"? To the "Sputnik challenge"? To the "information age"?

4. The report states that our nation's schools are "routinely called on to provide solutions to personal, social, and political problems that the home and other institutions either will not or cannot resolve." From your own experience in high school, what types of programs and services do you think the commission is referring to? Do you believe that these programs and services should be the schools' responsibilities? Explain.

5. In paragraph 11, the commission summarizes what they call the "dimensions of the risk." How convincing do you find their documentation? Explain.

6. The commission concludes that "educational reform should focus on the goal of creating a Learning Society." What are the main characteristics of this Learning Society? Are the means already in place to achieve it? Explain.

7. How would you characterize the tone of the report? What in the diction of the report led you to this conclusion? Is the tone appropriate for both the subject of the report and the audience? Explain.

8. How does the commission define *excellence*? Is this definition helpful in the context of the report?

Writing Topics

1. Analyze and evaluate your high school in light of the commission's report. Then write a report pointing out both areas of excellence and areas that could be improved.

2. Write an essay in which you examine the relationship between individual motivations and academic challenges. How do we as a society encourage our young people to aspire to excellence? Which comes first, the motivation or the challenge? Explain.

3. In the past twenty years computers have begun what futurist and science fiction writer Arthur C. Clark calls "one of the swiftest and most momentous revolutions in the entire history of technology." How has this affected your life? Try to make your own educated guess as to how computers will affect the future.

NATHAN GLAZER

Nathan Glazer was born in New York City in 1923 and is currently a professor at Harvard University in the education and sociology departments. His publications include *The Lonely Crowd* and *Beyond the Melting Pot*. Glazer is also co-editor of the magazine *Public Interest*.

In the following essay, first published in *Daedalus* in 1984, Glazer presents his proposal for trimming education budgets by decreasing the bureaucracy in America's primary and secondary schools.

Some Very Modest Proposals for the Improvement of American Education

That we can do a great deal for the sorry state of American education with more money is generally accepted. Even apparently modest proposals will, however, cost a great deal of money. Consider something as simple as increasing the average compensation of American teachers—who are generally considered underpaid—by $2,000 a year each. The bill would come to five billion dollars a year. A similar figure is reached by the report of the highly qualified Twentieth Century Fund Task Force on Federal, Elementary, and Secondary Education Policy, which proposes fellowships and additional compensation for master teachers. Reducing class size 10 percent, or increasing the number of teachers by the same percentage, would cost another five billion dollars: With present-day federal deficits, these look like small sums, but since education is paid for almost entirely by states and local government, these modest proposals would lead to substantial and painful tax increases. (I leave aside for the moment the views of skeptics who believe that none of these changes would matter.)

But the occasional visitor to American schools will note some changes that would cost much less, nothing at all, or even save money—and yet would improve at least the educational *environment* in American schools (once again, we ignore those skeptics who would insist that even a better educational environment cannot be guaranteed to improve educational achievement). In the spirit of evoking further cheap proposals, here is a

Reprinted by permission of *Daedalus* Journal, Journal of the American Academy of Arts and Sciences, "Values, Resources and Politics in America's Schools," Fall 1984, vol. 113, no. 4, 169–76.

small list of suggestions that, to my mind at least—and the mind I believe of any adult who visits American public schools—would mean a clear plus for American education:

1. *Disconnect all loudspeaker systems in American schools—or at least* 3 *reserve them, like the hotline between Moscow and Washington, for only the gravest emergencies.* The American classroom—and the American teacher and his or her charges—is continually interrupted by announcements from central headquarters over the loudspeaker system. These remind teachers to bring in some form or other; or students to bring in some form or other; or students engaged in some activity to remember to come to practice or rehearsal; or they announce a change of time for some activity. There is nothing so unnerving to a teacher engaged in trying to explain something, or a student engaged in trying to understand something, as the crackle of the loudspeaker prepared to issue an announcement, and the harsh and gravelly voice (the systems are not obviously of the highest grade) of the announcement itself.

Aside from questions of personal taste, why would this be a good idea? 4 As I have suggested, one reason is that the loudspeaker interrupts efforts to communicate complicated material that requires undivided attention. Second, it demeans the teacher as professional: every announcement tells her whatever she is doing is not very important and can be interrupted at any time. Third, it accentuates the notion of hierarchy in education—the principal and assistant principal are the important people, and command time and attention even in the midst of instruction. Perhaps I have been softened by too many years as a college teacher, but it would be unimaginable that a loud speaker, if one existed, would ever interrupt a college class except under conditions of the gravest and most immediate threat to life and limb. One way of showing students that education is important is not to interrupt it for band-rehearsal announcements.

2. *Disarm the school.* One of the most depressing aspects of the urban 5 school in the United States is the degree of security manifest within it, and that seems to me quite contradictory to what a school should be. Outer doors are locked. Security guards are present in the corridors. Internal doors are locked. Passes are necessary to enter the school or move within it, for outsiders and for students. Students are marched in groups from classroom to classroom, under the eye of the teachers. It is understandable that given the conditions in lower-class areas in our large cities—and not only lower-class areas—some degree of security-mindedness is necessary. There is valuable equipment—typewriters, computers, audio-visual equipment—that can be stolen; vandalism is a serious concern; marauders can enter the school in search for equipment, or teachers' pocketbooks, or to threaten directly personal safety in search of money or sex, and so on. School integration and busing, at least in their initial stages, have contributed to increased interracial tensions in schools and have in part severed the link

between community and school. The difference in ethnic and racial composition of faculty, other staff, administrators, and students contributes to
the same end.

Having acknowledged all this, I still believe the school should feel less   6
like a prison than it does. One should examine to what extent outside doors
must be closed; to what extent the security guard cannot be replaced by
local parents, volunteer or paid; the degree to which the endless bells
indicating "stop" and "go" are really necessary. I suspect that now that the
most difficult period of school integration has passed, now that teachers
and administrators and staff more closely parallel in race and ethnic background students and community owing to the increase in black and Hispanic teachers and administrators, we may be saddled with more security
than we need. Here we come to the sticky problem of *removing* security
measures whose need has decreased. What school board will open itself to
suit or to public criticism by deliberately providing *less* security? And yet
one must consider the atmosphere of the school and a school's primary
objective as a teaching agent: can this be reconciled with a condition of
maximum security? Perhaps there are lessons to be learned from colleges
and community colleges in older urban areas, which in my experience do
seem to manage with less security. One reason is that there are more adults
around in such institutions. Is that a hint as to how we could manage better
in public schools?

3. *Enlist the children in keeping the school clean.* Occasionally we see a   7
practice abroad that suggests possible transfer to the American scene. In
Japan, the children clean the school. There is a time of day when mops and
pails and brooms come out, and the children sweep up and wash up. This
does, I am sure, suggest to the children that this is *their* school, that it is not
simply a matter of being forced to go to a foreign institution that imposes
alien demands upon them. I can imagine some obstacles in the way of
instituting regular student clean-up in American schools—custodians'
unions, for example, might object. But they can be reassured that children
don't do that good of a job, and they will still be needed. Once again, as in
the case of the security problem, one wants to create in the school, if at all
possible, a common enterprise of teachers and students, without the latter
being bored and resistant, the former, in response, becoming equally indifferent. The school should be seen as everyone's workplace—and participation in cleaning the school will help.

4. *Save old schools.* Build fewer new ones. It has often surprised me that   8
while in schools such as Eton and Oxford—and indeed well-known private
schools and colleges in the United States—old buildings are prized, in so
many communities older public schools are torn down when to the naked
eye they have many virtues that would warrant their maintenance and use.
Only a few blocks from where I live, an excellent example of late
nineteenth-century fine brickwork and carved stonework that served as the

Cambridge Latin School came down for a remodeling. The carved elements are still displayed about the remodeled school, but why a building of such character should have deserved demolition escaped my understanding, particularly since one can take it almost as a given that a school building put up before the 1940s will be built of heavier and sturdier materials than one constructed today. Even the inconveniences of the old can possess a charm that makes them worthwhile. And indeed many of the reforms that seemed to require new buildings (for example, classrooms without walls, concentrated around activities centers in large open rooms) have turned out, on use, to be not so desirable. Our aim should be to give each school a history, a character, something that at least some students respond to. The pressures for new buildings are enormous, and sometimes perfectly legitimate (as when communities expand), but often illegitimate, as when builders and building-trades workers and contract-givers seek an opportunity or when state aid makes it appear as if a new building won't cost anything.

5. *Look on new hardware with a skeptical eye.* I think it likely that the passion for the new in the way of teaching-hardware not only does not contribute to higher educational achievement but may well serve as a temporary means to evade the real and hard tasks of teaching—which really require almost no hardware at all, besides textbooks, blackboard, and chalk. Admittedly, when one comes to high-school science, something more is called for. And yet our tendency is to always find cover behind new hardware. It's *fun* to get new audio-visual equipment, new rooms equipped with them in which all kinds of things can be done by flicking a switch or twisting a dial, or, as is now the case, to decide what kind of personal computers and software are necessary for a good educational program. Once again, foreign experience can be enlightening. When Japanese education was already well ahead of American, most Japanese schools were in prewar wooden buildings. (They are now as up-to-date as ours, but neither their age nor up-to-dateness has much to do with their good record of achievement.) Resisting the appeal of new hardware not only saves money, and provides less in the way of saleable goods to burglarize, but it also prevents distraction from the principal tasks of reading, writing, and calculating. When it turns out that computers and new software are shown to do a better job at these key tasks—I am skeptical as to whether this will ever be the case—there will be time enough to splurge on new equipment. The teacher, alone, up front, explaining, encouraging, guiding, is the heart of the matter—the rest is fun, and very helpful to corporate income, and gives an inflated headquarters staff something new to do. But students will have time enough to learn about computers when they get to college, and getting there will depend almost not at all on what they can do with computers, but how well they understand words and sentences, and how well they do at simple mathematics.

There is nothing wrong with old textbooks, too. Recently, reviewing   10
some recent high-school American history texts, I was astonished to discover they come out in new editions every two years or so, and not because
the main body of the text is improved, but because the textbook wants to be
able to claim it covers the very last presidential campaign, and the events of
the last few years. This is a waste of time and energy and money. There is
enough to teach in American history up to 1950 or 1960 not to worry about
whether the text includes Reagan's tax cuts. I suspect many new texts in
other areas also offer little advantage over the older ones. There is also a
virtue in a teacher becoming acquainted with a particular textbook. When I
read that a school is disadvantaged because its textbooks are old, I am
always mystified. Even the newest advances in physics and biology might
well be reserved for college.

6. *Expand the pool from which we draw good teachers.* This general   11
heading covers a number of simple and concrete things, such as: if a teacher
is considered qualified to teach at a good private school, that teacher should
be considered qualified to teach at a public school. It has always seemed to
me ridiculous that teachers accepted at the best private schools in New York
City or top preparatory schools in the country would not be allowed to
teach in the public school system of New York or Boston. Often, they are
willing—after all, the pay is better in public schools and there are greater
fringe benefits. They might, it is true, be driven out of those schools by the
challenge of lower- and working-class children. But when they are willing, it
seems unbelievable that the teacher qualified (or so Brearley thinks) for
Brearley will not be allowed to teach at P.S. 122. Greater use of part-time
teachers might also be able to draw upon people with qualities that we are
told the average teacher unfortunately doesn't possess—such as a higher
level of competence in writing and mathematics.

Our recurrent concern with foreign-language teaching should lead us   12
to recruit foreign-born teachers. There are problems in getting teaching jobs
today in Germany and France—yet teachers there are typically drawn from
pools of students with higher academic skills than is the case in this
country. Paradoxically, we make it easy for teachers of Spanish-language
background to get jobs owing to the expansion of bilingual programs—but
then their teaching is confined to children whose Spanish accent doesn't
need improvement. It would make more sense to expose children of foreign-
language background more to teachers with native English—and children
from English-speaking families to teachers who speak French, German,
Spanish, and, why not, Japanese, and Chinese natively. This would mean
that rules requiring that a teacher must be a citizen, or must speak English
without an accent, should be lifted for special teachers with special tasks.
Perhaps we could make the most of the oversupply of teachers in some
foreign countries by using them to teach mathematics—a subject where
accent doesn't count. The school system in Georgia is already recruiting

from Germany. Colleges often use teaching assistants whose English is not native and far from perfect, including Asians from Korea and China, to assist in science and mathematics courses. (There are many state laws which would not permit them to teach in elementary and secondary schools.)

All the suggestions above eschew any involvement with some great   13
issues of education—tradition or reform, the teaching of values, the role of religion in the schools—that have in the past dominated arguments over education and still do today. But I add one more proposal that is still, I am afraid, somewhat controversial:

7. *Let students, within reason, pick their schools, or let parents choose them*   14
for them. All those informed on school issues will sense the heaving depths of controversy under this apparently modest proposal. Does this mean they might choose parochial schools, without being required to pay tuition out of their own pockets? Or does this mean black children would be allowed to attend schools in black areas, and whites in white areas, or the reverse if each is so inclined? As we all know, the two great issues of religion and race stand in the way of any such simple and commonsensical arrangement. Students are regularly bused from one section of a city to another because of their race, and students cannot without financial penalty attend that substantial sector of schools—30 percent or so in most Northern and Midwestern cities—that are called "private." I ignore the question of whether, holding all factors constant, students do "better" in private or public schools, in racially well-mixed or hardly mixed schools. The evidence will always be uncertain. What is perhaps less arguable is that students will do better in a school that forms a community, in which teachers, parents, and students all agree that *that* is the school they want to teach in, to attend, to send their children to. I would guess that this is the kind of school most of the readers of this article have attended; it is the kind of school, alas, that our complex racial and religious history makes it harder and harder for those of minority race or of lower- and working-class status to attend.

I have eschewed the grand proposals—for curriculum change, for   15
improving the quality of entering teachers, for checking on the competence of teachers in service, for establishing national standards for achievement in different levels of education—all of which now form the agenda for many state commissions of educational reform and all of which seem reasonable to me. Rather, I have concentrated on a variety of other things that serve to remove distraction, to open the school to those of quality who would be willing to enter it to improve it, to concentrate on the essentials of teaching and learning as I (and many others) have experienced it. It would be possible to propose larger changes in the same direction: for example, reduce the size of the bureaucracies in urban school systems. Some of my modest proposals are insidiously intended to do this—if there were less

effort devoted to building new schools, buying new equipment, evaluating new textbooks, or busing children, there would be no need to maintain quite so many people at headquarters. Or so I would hope.

In the meantime, why not disconnect the loudspeakers?   16

Questions for Study and Discussion

1. In paragraph 11, Glazer proposes that there should be "greater use of part-time teachers." How does he intend the word "part-time"? Do you agree with his suggestion? Why or why not?

2. What does he mean when he ends his essay with the question: "In the meantime, why not disconnect the loudspeakers?"

3. According to Glazer, in what ways can a better learning environment lead to better educational achievements? Do you agree? Explain.

4. In paragraphs 5 and 6, Glazer proposes to "disarm the school." Why does he continue his argument by discussing busing and integration? Are they related to disarming the school? Does the disarming he refers to mean less security?

5. What types of school systems did Glazer have in mind while he was writing this essay? What parts of the country do these schools represent? Has Glazer overgeneralized, or does he portray public school as it is everywhere?

6. Glazer does not see the value of putting out new editions of textbooks (10). Is his argument effective? If not, how would you answer him? What, if any, is the benefit of teaching students about recent political campaigns?

7. In your opinion, would American schools be able to institute a student cleaning program? What kinds of problems would instituting such a program raise? How long would it last?

Writing Topics

1. Write an essay in which you give proposals to cut costs in a public school system. Name the programs, events, services, and parts of the curriculum that you think are not needed, and explain why. Can costs be cut without risking the loss of school spirit, educational potential, extracurricular activities, or a student's sense of belonging? How essential are each of these aspects of a public school education?

2. Busing students from cities into suburban areas has increased in the past twenty years. Write an essay in which you consider the pros and cons of busing to compensate for unequal educational opportunities.

ALLAN BLOOM

In 1987 Allan Bloom became an instant celebrity with the publication of his controversial best-seller *The Closing of the American Mind: How Higher Education Has Failed Democracy and Impoverished the Souls of Today's Students*, a thought-provoking critique of contemporary university education. A lifelong defender of the principles and purposes of America's great universities, Bloom was born in Indianapolis, Indiana, in 1930. Within the first few weeks of enrolling at the University of Chicago, Bloom recalls that "I somehow sensed that I had discovered my life." He eventually received his Ph.D from Chicago and joined the faculty there in 1955. After teaching at Yale, Cornell, and the University of Tel Aviv, in 1979 he returned to the University of Chicago, where he is currently the codirector of the John M. Olin Center for Inquiry into the Theory and Practice of Democracy. In academic circles, he is well known for his translations of works by Rousseau and Plato and his book *Shakespeare's Politics* (1964).

Starting in the late 1960s, Bloom has argued that "modern universities fail to give students the philosophical foundation necessary for addressing the fundamental questions of human life." His critical assessment of today's universities and their students culminated in *The Closing of the American Mind*. In the following selection from that book, Bloom criticizes our universities for not offering a "distinctive visage" to young, incoming students.

Today's University— Where Democracy Is Anarchy

What image does a first-rank college or university present today to a   1 teen-ager leaving home for the first time, off to the adventure of a liberal education? He has four years of freedom to discover himself—a space between the intellectual wasteland he has left behind and the inevitable dreary professional training that awaits him after the baccalaureate. In this short time he must learn that there is a great world beyond the little one he knows, experience the exhilaration of it and digest enough of it to sustain himself in the intellectual deserts he is destined to traverse. He must do this, that is, if he is to have any hope of a higher life. These are the charmed years when he can, if he so chooses, become anything he wishes and when he has the opportunity to survey his alternatives, not merely those current in his time or provided by careers, but those available to him as a human being. The importance of these years for an American cannot be overestimated. They are civilization's only chance to get to him.

In looking at him, we are forced to reflect on what he should learn if 2
he is to be called educated; we must speculate on what the human potential
to be fulfilled is. In the specialties we can avoid such speculation, and the
avoidance of them is one of specialization's charms. But here it is a simple
duty. What are we to teach this person? The answer may not be evident, but
to attempt to answer the question is already to philosophize and to begin to
educate. Such a concern in itself poses the question of the unity of man and
the unity of the sciences. It is childishness to say, as some do, that everyone
must be allowed to develop freely, that it is authoritarian to impose a point
of view on the student. In that case, why have a university? If the response is
to "provide an atmosphere for learning," we come back to our original
questions at the second remove. Which atmosphere? Choices and reflection
on the reasons for those choices are unavoidable. The university has to
stand for something. The practical effects of unwillingness to think
positively about the contents of a liberal education are, on the one hand, to
ensure that all the vulgarities of the world outside the university will
flourish within it, and, on the other, to impose a much harsher and more
illiberal necessity on the student—the one given by the imperial and imper-
ious demands of the specialized disciplines unfiltered by unifying thought.

The university now offers no distinctive visage to the young person. 3
He finds a democracy of the disciplines—which are there either because
they are autochthonous or because they wandered in recently to perform
some job that was demanded of the university. This democracy is really an
anarchy, because there are no recognized rules for citizenship and no
legitimate titles to rule. In short there is no vision, nor is there a set of
competing vision, of what an educated human being is. The question has
disappeared, for to pose it would be a threat to the peace. There is no
organization of the sciences, no tree of knowledge. Out of chaos emerges
dispiritedness, because it is impossible to make a reasonable choice. Better
to give up on liberal education and get on with a specialty in which there is
at least a prescribed curriculum and a prospective career. On the way the
student can pick up in elective courses a little of whatever is thought to
make one cultured. The student gets no intimation that great mysteries
might be revealed to him, that new and higher motives of action might be
discovered within him, that a different and more human way of life can be
harmoniously constructed by what he is going to learn.

Simply, the university is not distinctive. Equality for us seems to 4
culminate in the unwillingness and incapacity to make claims of superiority,
particularly in the domains in which such claims have always been made—
art, religion and philosophy. When Weber found that he could not choose
between certain high opposites—reason vs. revelation, Buddha vs. Jesus—
he did not conclude that all things are equally good, that the distinction
between high and low disappears. As a matter of fact, he intended to
revitalize the consideration of these great alternatives in showing the gravity

and danger involved in choosing among them; they were to be heightened in contrast to the trivial considerations of modern life that threatened to overgrow and render indistinguishable the profound problems the confrontation with which makes the bow of the soul taut. The serious intellectual life was for him the battleground of the great decisions, all of which are spiritual or "value" choices. One can no longer present this or that particular view of the educated or civilized man as authoritative; therefore one must say that education consists in knowing, really knowing, the small number of such views in their integrity. This distinction between profound and superficial—which takes the place of good and bad, true and false—provided a focus for serious study, but it hardly held out against the naturally relaxed democratic tendency to say, "Oh, what's the use? The first university disruptions at Berkeley were explicitly directed against the multiversity smorgasbord and, I must confess, momentarily and partially engaged my sympathies. It may have even been the case that there was some small element of longing for an education in the motivation of these students. But nothing was done to guide or inform their energy, and the result was merely to add multilife-styles to multidisciplines, the diversity of perversity to the diversity of specialization. . . .

Thus, when a student arrives at the university, he finds a bewildering 5 variety of departments and a bewildering variety of courses. And there is no official guidance, no university-wide agreement, about what he *should* study. Nor does he usually find readily available examples, either among students or professors, of a unified use of the university's resources. It is easiest simply to make a career choice and go about getting prepared for that career. The programs designed for those having made such a choice render their students immune to charms that might lead them out of the conventionally respectable. The sirens sing *sotto voce* these days, and the young already have enough wax in their ears to pass them by without danger. These specialties can provide enough courses to take up most of their time for four years in preparation for the inevitable graduate study. With the few remaining courses they can do what they please, taking a bit of this and a bit of that. No public career these days—not doctor nor lawyer nor politician nor journalist nor businessman nor entertainer—has much to do with humane learning. . . .

The real problem is those students who come hoping to find out what 6 career they want to have, or are simply looking for an adventure with themselves. There are plenty of things for them to do—courses and disciplines enough to spend many a lifetime on. Each department or great division of the university makes a pitch for itself, and each offers a course of study that will make the student an initiate. But how to choose among them? How do they relate to one another? The fact is they do not address one another. They are competing and contradictory, without being aware of it. The problem of the whole is urgently indicated by the very existence of the specialties, but it is never systematically posed. The net effect of the student's encounter with the college catalogue is bewilderment and very often demoralization. It is just a matter of chance whether he finds one or two professors who can give him an insight into one of the great visions of education that have been the distinguishing part of every civilized nation. Most professors are specialists, concerned only with their own fields, interested in the advancement of those fields in their own terms, or in their own personal advancement in a world where all the rewards are on the side of professional distinction. They have been entirely emancipated from the old structure of the university, which at least helped to indicate that they are incomplete, only parts of an unexamined and undiscovered whole. So the student must navigate among a collection of carnival barkers, each trying to lure him into a particular sideshow . . .

Questions for Study and Discussion

1. What is the purpose of the university system according to Bloom? Do you agree? Explain.

2. How would you characterize Bloom's attitude toward the professional life? How does this compare with the tone of the rest of the essay? Cite examples from the text to support your conclusion.

3. How does Bloom feel about the "smorgasbord of opportunities" at college? Is it realistic to provide such a wide variety of studies at a university? Explain.

4. Bloom thinks that the different courses of study contradict and do not address each other. Did you find his argument convincing? Why or why not?

5. Bloom's education and sophistication is evident in his vocabulary. Cite examples of the kinds of words that reveal this sophistication. Does his diction add or detract from the effectiveness of his essay?

6. In the first line of this essay Bloom asks a rhetorical question. In what sense is it rhetorical? What image does a college give to a teenager leaving home for the first time?

Writing Topics

1. Bloom does not address the fact that students are required to take general education courses as well as major studies, and that students have four or five semesters to "test the water" before declaring a major. In what ways do these policies defeat or defend Bloom's argument? Explain.

2. Some people feel that college is not only an educational opportunity but is also a stepping stone from the small world of family and friends to the bigger world outside. Write an essay explaining how college prepares a student, not just for a career, but for life.

THEODORE SIZER

Born in 1932 in Connecticut, Theodore Sizer received his A.B. from Yale in 1953 and his M.A.T. and Ph.D. from Harvard University. He later became dean of the Harvard Graduate School of Education. After serving as headmaster at Phillips Andover Academy, Sizer took two years off to visit secondary schools to talk with children, teachers, and administration in preparation for writing his book, *Horace's Compromise: The Dilemma of the American High School* (1984). Sizer's other publications include *Secondary Schools at the Turn of the Century* (1964), *The Age of Academies* (1964), *Religion and Public Education* (1967), *Moral Education: Five Lectures* (1970), and *Places for Learning, Places for Joy: Speculations on American School Reform* (1973).

In "Principals' Questions," taken from *Horace's Compromise*, Sizer offers an alternative to current high school curricula, which he claims are so cluttered that children are missing the essentials of a basic education.

Principals' Questions

As I traveled among schools, their principals pressed me with questions, many of which were practical, specific.   1

What's your curriculum . . . What subjects should be offered? they asked.   2

I replied: Let's not start with subjects; that usually leads us into the swamp called "coverage." What counts are positive answers to three questions: Can graduates of this high school teach themselves? Are they decent people? Can they effectively use the principal ways of looking at the world, ways represented by the major and traditional academic disciplines?   3

What do you mean, "teach themselves"?   4

Learning how to observe and analyze a situation or problem and being able to make sense of it, use it, criticize it, reject or accept it. This is more than simple "problem-solving," since many of the enriching things in life are not, in fact, problems. "Teaching oneself" is nothing more than knowing how to inform and enrich oneself. Ideally a school would like not only to equip a student with those skills, but also to inspire him or her to use them.   5

How is this done?   6

By directly giving students the task of teaching themselves and help-   7

287

ing them with it. It means providing fewer answers and insisting that
students find the right (or at least defensible) answers themselves. It means
that teachers must focus more on *how* kids think than on what they think.

This will take lots of time.   8

Yes, indeed. There will be far less opportunity for teachers to tell   9
things, and, as a result, less coverage, of fewer subject areas. Of course,
ultimately it means more coverage because the student is able to learn on
his or her own.

Which fewer areas? Be specific.   10

I will, but with the clear understanding that there is no One Best   11
Curriculum for all schools. While we all have to agree on some general
outcomes that give meaning to the high school diploma, the means to these
outcomes must be kept flexible. No two schools will or should have precisely the same characteristics; wise diversity is *essential* for quality. Furthermore, top-down edicts about "what" and "how" demonstrably do not work.
Each school must find its own way, and in so doing gain the energy that
such a search provides.

Let me give you the beginnings of one model. I would organize a high   12
school into four areas or large departments:

1. Inquiry and Expression
2. Mathematics and Science
3. Literature and the Arts
4. Philosophy and History

You will immediately note that "English," that pivotally important but
often misconstrued or even unconstrued "subject," would disappear. By
"expression," I mean all kinds of communication, but above all writing, the
litmus paper of thought. Some of "communication" is brute skill, such as
the use of a keyboard (that sine qua non for the modern citizen) and clear, if
rudimentary handwriting. Visual communication is included, as are gesture
and physical nuance and tone, those tools used so powerfully by such
masters as Winston Churchill and Ronald Reagan. A teacher cannot
ascertain a student's thought processes unless they are expressed.

Mathematics is the language of science, the language of certainties.   13
Science, of course, is full of uncertainty, as is much of higher mathematics,
but for beginners it is the certainties that dominate. Number systems work
in certain ways. Axioms hold. The pituitary gland secretes certain hormones; if it fails to do so, predictable consequences ensue. The world
around us has its share of certainties, and we should learn about them,
learn to be masters of them. Basic arithmetic, algebra, some geometry and
statistics, physics and biology, are the keys. I would merge the traditional
departments of mathematics and science, thus forcing coordination of the
real and abstract worlds of certainty. The fresh, modern necessity of study

in computer science can be the first bit of glue in this process of collaboration; that subject nicely straddles both areas.

Human expression cuts across written and spoken languages, theater, 14
song, and visual art. There is much common ground in these attempts of
man and woman to explain their predicament, yet English, music, and art
usually proceed in as much splendid isolation as do mathematics and
science. This is wasteful, as aesthetic expression and learning from others'
attempts to find meaning are of a piece. All need representation and benefit
from an alliance.

History, if it is responsibly taught, is perhaps the most difficult subject 15
for most high school students, because it involves the abstraction of time
past. One often can engage it well first through autobiography and then
through biography, proceeding finally to the "biographies" of communities,
which make up most conventional history. Things were as they were for
reasons, and from these incidents evolve concepts in geography, economics,
and sociology. For most students at this stage, these disciplines should
remain the handmaidens of history. The exception is philosophy, particularly moral and political philosophy. A political philosophy, essentially
that associated with American constitutionalism, is the bedrock of enlightened democratic citizenship, and adolescense, more than any other
stage of life, is filled with a search for values. The study of elementary ethics,
for example, not only provides excellent opportunities for learning intellectual skills, but also powerfully engages students' interest.

Why so few subjects? 16

There are several reasons. One is to lessen the splintered view of 17
knowledge that usually confronts high school students. Their world rarely
uses the fine distinctions between academic disciplines; insisting on them
confuses young scholars. A second serves teachers: strict specialization
hobbles much skill training. Good coaching cuts across academic specializa-
tions. The current organization is very wasteful. A third reason: a few areas,
taught in large time blocks, greatly reduce both the scheduling problems
and the frenetic quality of the school day. Finally, more broadly and
sensibly construed subject areas allow greater scope for teachers.

Won't students want electives? 18

Yes, in that they will want opportunities to study what interests them 19
and what helps them. However, this personalization can be well accommo-
dated *within* each broad area, rather than through a smorgasbord of unrelated courses.

This sounds deadly, very academic and removed from kids' lives. 20

It sounds deadly because it has often been taught in deadly ways. I am 21
regularly assaulted for being an "elitist" for proposing this program, yet no
critic will argue, when I press him, that any of the objectives I put forward is
inappropriate for every adolescent. A teacher must start where the students
are—and this may *not* be chapter one in the textbook. One works to engage

each student, to get him or her to experience some aspect of an area, and to feel that experience to be successful. It takes time, ingenuity, patience. Most difficult to reach will be the demoralized youngsters, the ones who see school as a hostile place. Many of these students come from low-income families. They will need special attention and classes that use extensive coaching—not only to help them gain the skills they often lack but also to promote some fresh self-assurance in them. Vast classes heavy with lecturing must be avoided.

You've left out physical education and vocational education.   22

Let's start with physical education. Much of what happens in schools   23
today under that rubric is neither education (or at best is disconnected applied biology) nor very physical (thirty minutes once a week playing volleyball does not mean much, except perhaps as a useful vent for built-up adolescent steam). Citizens should know about their bodies and be taught that the need for exercise is a good thing. These are worthy topics for a good science-mathematics area to present.

The same kind of argument can be made for vocational education.   24
Specific job training is a good thing, but not at the expense of a school's core. The best place to learn most jobs is on site. The common exception is business education, most prominently training for secretarial positions. The important points are ability to type and, beyond that, being well informed, literate, and able to handle numbers. If typing is a schoolwide requirement, and the other skills the inevitable consequence of the student's taking the core topics, the exception is moot.

Two more points about vocational education: tomorrow's economy   25
will be volatile and dependent on flexible workers with a high level of intellectual skills. Thus, the best vocational education will be one in general education in the use of one's mind. Second, we must remember that most of today's high school students are or wish to be in the labor market. As the age cohort shrinks, the demand for its labor in most communities will grow. Educators are not going to reverse this trend; it will be better if they seize it, and adapt schools in demanding, sensible ways to the reality of adolescent employment. Working per se can be good for adolescents.

All that may be true in the abstract. But the fact remains that you'll lose a   26
lot of kids if you cut out voc ed and athletics.

No, not necessarily. Remember that but a small minority of high   27
school students are significantly involved in vocational education and interscholastic athletics. Furthermore, to the extent that these activities form a bridge to the central subjects, I'm for them. Unfortunately, today in many schools they have a life of their own, at the expense of an education in mind and character.

What of foreign language?   28

The cry for its requirement in schooling is abroad in the land as a cure   29 for American isolation and chauvinism. For many adolescents, such study has merit; for others, little sense. If you cannot master your own language, it is inefficient to start another. If you have little immediate need to use a second language, the time spent in learning is largely wasted—unless that "foreign" language is English. An absolute requirement for study of a foreign tongue can divert from other topics time that is crucial for a particularly needy student. The issue of ethnocentrism is more important than language study and must be addressed through the history courses.

What of bilingual education?

30

Ideally, all Americans should enjoy it—but the real problem is that of non-English speaking students. They should be immersed in English intensively. Their nonlinguistic studies should continue—for no longer than necessary—in their mother tongues. Their self-confidence, often associated with their facility in language, should be reinforced. Empathy and patience are crucial here; rigid formulae passed down from central authorities *guarantee* inefficiency and frustration. The goal is confident youngsters, adept and effectively fluent in two languages.

31

I'm still skeptical about your overall plan. You can pull this off only if you had none but highly motivated students in your school. What of tracking and the turned-off student?

32

Just as now, some kids won't hook in; I know that. If they've shown themselves competent in the minima of literacy, numeracy, and civic understanding, let them leave high school—with the promise that they can come back in the future. The community college system in many regions makes this an easy alternative.

33

In addition, there are the troublemakers, the kids who don't want necessarily to leave school, but want just to stay there because it's fun, where their friends are. Of course, good teachers can work with them to try to change their attitudes. However, if they disrupt, they should be expelled, with the same opportunities to return later as all dropouts have. As long as they have met the state's requirements, no one should force them into school. Ideally, too, they should have a variety of programs from which to choose. Highly personalized alternative programs have frequently worked for this sort of student.

34

As to tracking: there would be none and there would be a great deal. Every student would be enrolled in each subject area all the time. There would therefore be none of the current tracks, usually called honors, college preparatory, general, technical, and so forth. But within each subject area, the students would progress at their own pace. This would create multiple tracks, ones that are flexible and that put no child in any dead end.

35

That will be very messy.

36

Yes, it will. Learning is messy. It can be handled if the units (separate high schools, or "houses" within high schools) are kept small enough to

37

allow a particular group of teachers to know particular students well and develop a track for each. Class patterns will vary by need, some larger for telling, some smaller for coaching and questioning. Students will be working much more on their own than they do now; there will be no strict age grading. One learns how to learn by experience, not by being told things.

Won't this add financial cost? 38

Some, perhaps. It need not, as long as schools retreat from the 39
objective of "comprehensiveness" and concentrate on classroom teaching. There are models of "zero-based budgets" which demonstrate that schools, if simply organized, can have well-paid faculty and fewer than eighty students per teacher, without increasing current per-pupil expenditure.

You haven't mentioned guidance counselors. 40

Counselors today act either as administrators, arranging schedules 41
and job and college interviews and the like, or as teachers, coaching and questioning young people about their personal concerns. Good teachers *are* good counselors, in that second sense; students turn to them for help, whether or not their titles identify them as "guidance" people. Most high school guidance departments are overloaded with obligations, many of which are contradictory—for example, serving both as a place where students can obtain confidential personal counsel and as a disciplinary arm of the school (perhaps running the "in school suspension" program for students who have repeatedly broken rules).

A decentralized school with small academic units has less need for 42
specialized counseling offices; improved faculty-student ratios make this possible. The administrative obligations now traditionally handled by such offices can be placed directly under the principal. Staff members who are well trained in counseling and testing skills can support the teachers in each small academic unit.

We are being asked often these days about "computer literacy" and the needs 43
of a "new technological society." How does your plan address these areas?

Computers, like calculators, books, and other familiar products of 44
technology, should be welcomed by schools. Well used, they might significantly extend teachers' coaching efforts as well as help students learn. While we should learn to employ the products of the new technologies, we should keep in mind two critical points: it is up to us to select the data to be put into them, and we must choose with care the uses we put them to.

Should public schools formally provide time for voluntary prayer? 45

No. There is ample time and opportunity outside school for religious 46
observances. Furthermore, the fact that public schools would not set time aside for prayer does not imply rejection of its importance. Schools should *not* claim to be comprehensive, arrogating to their routines every consequential aspect of an adolescent's life. High schools are limited to helping adolescents use their minds well—and this includes becoming thoughtful and decent people.

What of standards?   47

The existence of final "exhibitions" by students as a condition to   48
receiving their diplomas will give teachers a much greater control of standards than they currently have. These standards, combined with a variety
of external examinations, such as the Advanced Placement Examinations
of the College Board, Regents' Examinations in some states, and, it is
hoped, a growing list of other instruments that a school or an individual
student could adopt or take voluntarily, would give outside authorities,
like regional accrediting agencies, a good sense of the quality of work
being done.

A lot turns on those teachers. Are they good enough?   49

They've got to be.   50

Remedies like all these are neat, but abstractions, castles in the air.   51
Seeing adolescents in classrooms reminds one that, in substantial measure,
school is *their* castle, that they have to want to build it.

I arrived by car at the school at 7:15 A.M., thirty minutes before the   52
first bell. It was a cool day, and the first arrivals to the large high school I
was visiting were gathered in clots in the sun outside, around the low,
meandering structures that housed their classrooms. Parking lots and hard-
used lawns encircled the buildings. There were no side-walks in this neighborhood, even though it was quite built up; the school property was ringed
by small houses and business establishments. Everyone came to school by
bus or by private car.

I turned into one of the driveways leading toward what appeared to be   53
the school's central building and was immediately bounced out of the seat of
my rented Datsun by the first of a series of asphalt bumps in the road.
These barriers, it was painfully obvious, were there to slow down the dozens
of vehicles that used the driveway and were already lined up in the lots next
to the school, row on row of loyal steel beasts tethered by this pedagogical
water hole. I found a place and parked.

It was immediately clear from the stares I received from nearby stu-   54
dents that I picked a student lot, not one for staff or for visitors. Since it
seemed to me large enough to accommodate one more little car, I left the
Datsun where it was. It was ridiculously out of place, surrounded by pickup
trucks, high on their springs and mud spattered, and by jalopies, late sixties'
Chevrolets, old Ford Mustangs, Plymouth Satellites, each cumbrously settled upon great oversize rear tires. While all appeared poised, snouts down,
to roar purposefully off to God knows where, for the moment they simply
cowered here, submissive. Their masters and mistresses leaned against them
or sat on them, chatting. Many drank coffee out of paper cups. Some
smoked furtively as I drew near; though unfamiliar to them, I was wearing
the drab coat-tie-slacks uniform of the school administrator who might
admonish them.

My first instinct was to snicker at the parking lot scene. It was an 55
eighties' version of an *American Graffiti* strip, indeed an overdrawn one,
because the dusty trucks and drag-equipped cars were grotesquely numerous. My condescension disappeared, however, when I paid more attention to the students gathered around these vehicles, kids observing the
visitor who had taken a space on their turf. Their attitude was in no way
menacing, but it was freighted with an absence of interest. I was an object to
be observed and, if they were smoking, to be mildly reacted to. Beyond that,
I might have been a bird in the vast aviary of a boring zoo; I was a piece of
the scenery, glimpsed as part of hanging out before school. None of these
kids was playing principal's pet by coming and asking me whether I needed
help or directions to the office, but no one hassled me, either. The human
confrontation was neutral, nearly nonexistent.

These were older students, drivers. In their easy chatting among 56
themselves, in their self-absorption and nonchalance, they showed self-
assurance bordering on truculence. They had their own world.

My reaction was nervousness. I tried to smile a sorry-fellas-but- 57
I-didn't-know-where-the-visitors'-parking-lot-was message, but it did not
come off. I felt the awkward outsider, at distance from these composed
young people. Even as I knew that at the bell they would enter the buildings
and engage in the rituals of dutiful school-going and that they would get
more boisterous and engaging as the early morning mist over their spirits
parted, I also knew that these were considerable people, ones who would
play the game adult educators asked them to play only when and how they
wanted to. The fact that many of them, for a host of reasons, chose to go
along with the structures of the school did not lessen the force of the
observation: they possessed the autonomous power not to.

In this sense, kids run schools. Their apparent acquiescence to what 58
their elders want them to do is always provisional. Their ability to under-
mine even the illusions of certain adult authority and of an expectation of
deference was admirably if benignly displayed by the students on the
parking lot. A less benign challenge can be made by students in any
classroom when, for whatever reason, they collectively, quietly, but as-
suredly decide to say no. The fact that most go along with the system masks
the nascent power that students hold. Few adults outside the teaching
profession understand this.

The evening before, I had met the superintendent of this school 59
district. He was a man of great force and national reputation. His administration ran the district with efficiency and closely centralized authority. In
talking of his work, we had both used the ready metaphors of schoolkeep-
ing, most turning around an image of old folk (the teachers) passing
something of self-evident importance to young folk (the students). This
morning all of these metaphors seemed naïve. All assumed the young
student to be a passive receptacle or, at the least, a supplicant for knowl-

edge. The adolescents in that parking lot were neither passive nor suppliant. However much we adults may want them to be eagerly receptive and respectful of our agenda for their schooling, the choice to be that or something else—neutral, hostile, inattentive—was unequivocally theirs. If we want our well-intentioned plans to succeed, we'll have to *inspire* the adolescents to join in them—inspire even the sullen, uninterested kids one sees in parking lots at the start of a school day.

The vision of school as an uncomplicated place where teachers pass   60
along the torch of knowledge to eager students is sadly innocent.

Questions for Study and Discussion

1. How long would it take to implement the program that Sizer explains?

2. Do you think that Sizer's curriculum would be effective? What shortcomings do you see? What do you like about the program? Is it a real alternative to the problems he sees in the present system?

3. Do you believe that public school systems should include religion for students?

4. In paragraph 21 Sizer says, "Vast classes heavy with lecturing must be avoided." What alternatives, if any, does he offer? What would you suggest? Why?

5. Sizer's essay is divided into two parts. What kind of information is included in each part? Was this an effective way to organize his argument? Why of why not?

6. In paragraph 60, Sizer says it is "innocent" to envision schools as being uncomplicated. In your own words, in what ways is high school "complicated" both educationally and socially?

7. How would Sizer feel about individualized programs that allow students to progress at their own pace? In your opinion, what are the benefits and shortcomings of such programs?

Writing Topics

1. American schools rely heavily on grades to determine a student's achievement. In an essay, give your views on this means of ranking students' knowledge. How do you think grades help or hinder a student's progress in high school?

2. Sizer says that physical education, as it is currently offered in high school, is not worthwhile. In an essay argue for or against current physical education programs. If you agree with Sizer, offer suggestions to make athletics worthwhile.

RALPH WALDO EMERSON

One of the great philosophic writers of the American romantic period, Ralph Waldo Emerson (1803–1882) was born in Boston, but lived most of his life in Concord, Massachusetts. Emerson showed no literary potential during his adolescent years or while at Harvard where he graduated in 1821. An ordained minister, he was best known for his essay "Nature" and his addresses to the Phi Beta Kappa Society and to the Harvard Divinity School graduates. Emerson served as editor of *The Dial*, a transcendentalist magazine, from 1842 to 1844. His published works include *Essays* (1841), *Essays: Second Series* (1844), *Representative Men* (1849), and *Conduct of Life* (1860). The sixteen volumes of *The Journals and Miscellaneous Notebooks of Ralph Waldo Emerson* were reissued between 1960 and 1982.

"The American Scholar" was first presented as an address to the Phi Beta Kappa Society at Cambridge on August 31, 1837. In it Emerson explores the differences between scholars and thinkers and describes what he believes are the duties of the American scholar.

The American Scholar

Mr. President and Gentlemen:

I greet you on the recommencement of our literary year. Our anniversary is one of hope, and, perhaps, not enough of labor. We do not meet for games of strength or skill, for the recitation of histories, tragedies, and odes, like the ancient Greeks; for parliaments of love and poesy, like the Troubadours; nor for the advancement of science, like our contemporaries in the British and European capitals. Thus far, our holiday has been simply a friendly sign of the survival of the love of letters amongst a people too busy to give to letters any more. As such it is precious as the sign of an indestructible instinct. Perhaps the time is already come when it ought to be, and will be, something else; when the sluggard intellect of this continent will look from under its iron lids and fill the postponed expectation of the world with something better than the exertions of mechanical skill. Our day of dependence, our long apprenticeship to the learning of other lands, draws to a close. The millions that around us are rushing into life, cannot always be fed on the sere remains of foreign harvests. Events, actions arise, that must be sung, that will sing themselves. Who can doubt that poetry will revive and lead in a new age, as the star in the constellation Harp, which now flames in our zenith, astronomers announce, shall one day be the polestar for a thousand years?

In this hope I accept the topic which not only usage but the nature of our association seem to prescribe to this day—the AMERICAN SCHOLAR. Year by year we come up hither to read one more chapter of his biography. Let us inquire what light new days and events have thrown on his character and his hopes.

It is one of those fables which out of an unknown antiquity convey an unlooked-for wisdom, that the gods, in the beginning, divided Man into men, that he might be more helpful to himself; just as the hand was divided into fingers, the better to answer its end.

The old fable covers a doctrine ever new and sublime; that there is One Man—present to all particular men only partially, or through one faculty; and that you must take the whole society to find the whole man. Man is not a farmer, or a professor, or an engineer, but he is all. Man is priest, and scholar, and statesman, and producer, and soldier. In the *divided* or social state these functions are parcelled out to individuals, each of whom aims to do his stint of the joint work, whilst each other performs his. The fable implies that the individual, to possess himself, must sometimes return from his own labor to embrace all the other laborers. But, unfortunately, this original unit, this fountain of power, has been so distributed to multitudes, has been so minutely subdivided and peddled out, that it is spilled into drops, and cannot be gathered. The state of society is one in which the members have suffered amputation from the trunk, and strut about so many walking monsters—a good finger, a neck, a stomach, an elbow, but never a man.

Man is thus metamorphosed into a thing, into many things. The planter, who is Man sent out into the field to gather food, is seldom cheered by any idea of the true dignity of his ministry. He sees his bushel and his cart, and nothing beyond, and sinks into the farmer, instead of Man on the farm. The tradesman scarcely ever gives an ideal worth to his work, but is ridden by the routine of his craft, and the soul is subject to dollars. The priest becomes a form; the attorney a statute-book; the mechanic a machine; the sailor a rope of the ship.

In this distribution of functions the scholar is the delegated intellect. In the right state he is *Man Thinking.* In the degenerate state, when the victim of society, he tends to become a mere thinker, or still worse, the parrot of other men's thinking.

In this view of him, as Man Thinking, the theory of his office is contained. Him Nature solicits with all her placid, all her monitory pictures; him the past instructs; him the future invites. Is not indeed every man a student, and do not all things exist for the student's behoof? And finally, is not the true scholar the only true master? But the old oracle said, "All things have two handles: beware of the wrong one." In life, too often, the scholar errs with mankind and forfeits his privilege. Let us see him in his school, and consider him in reference to the main influences he receives.

I.   The first in time and the first in importance of the influences upon the mind is that of nature. Every day, the sun; and, after sunset, Night and her stars. Ever the winds blow; ever the grass grows. Every day, men and women, conversing—beholding and beholden. The scholar is he of all men whom this spectacle most engages. He must settle its value in his mind. What is nature to him? There is never a beginning, there is never an end, to the inexplicable continuity of this web of God, but always circular power returning into itself. Therein it resembles his own spirit, whose beginning, whose ending, he never can find—so entire, so boundless. Far too as her splendors shine, system on system shooting like rays, upward, downward, without centre, without circumference—in the mass and in the particle, Nature hastens to render account of herself to the mind. Classification begins. To the young mind every thing is individual, stands by itself. By and by, it finds how to join two things and see in them one nature; then three, then three thousand; and so, tyrannized over by its own unifying instinct, it goes on tying things together, diminishing anomalies, discovering roots running under ground whereby contrary and remote things cohere and flower out from one stem. It presently learns that since the dawn of history there has been a constant accumulation and classifying of facts. But what is classification but the perceiving that these objects are not chaotic, and are not foreign, but have a law which is also a law of the human mind? The astronomer discovers that geometry, a pure abstraction of the human mind, is the measure of planetary motion. The chemist finds proportions and intelligible method throughout matter; and science is nothing but the finding of analogy, identity, in the most remote parts. The ambitious soul sits down before each refractory fact; one after another reduces all strange constitutions, all new powers, to their class and their law, and goes on forever to animate the last fibre of organization, the outskirts of nature, by insight.

Thus to him, to this schoolboy under the bending dome of day, is 9 suggested that he and it proceed from one root; one is leaf and one is flower; relation, sympathy, stirring in every vein. And what is that root? Is not that the soul of his soul? A thought too bold, a dream too wild. Yet when this spiritual light shall have revealed the law of more earthly natures—when he has learned to worship the soul, and to see that the natural philosophy that now is, is only the first gropings of its gigantic hand, he shall look forward to an ever expanding knowledge as to a becoming creator. He shall see that nature is the opposite of the soul, answering to it part for part. One is seal and one is print. Its beauty is the beauty of his own mind. Its laws are the laws of his own mind. Nature then becomes to him the measure of his attainments. So much of nature as he is ignorant of, so much of his own mind does he not yet possess. And in fine, the ancient precept, "Know thyself," and the modern precept, "Study nature," become at last one maxim.

II. The next great influence into the spirit of the scholar is the mind 10 of the Past—in whatever form, whether of literature, of art, of institutions, that mind is inscribed. Books are the best type of the influence of the past, and perhaps we shall get at the truth—learn the amount of this influence more conveniently—by considering their value alone.

The theory of books is noble. The scholar of the first age received into him the world around; brooded thereon; gave it the new arrangement of his own mind, and uttered it again. It came into him life; it went out from him truth. It came to him shortlived actions; it went out from him immortal thoughts. It came to him business; it went from him poetry. It was dead fact; now, it is quick thought. It can stand, and it can go. It now endures, it now flies, it now inspires. Precisely in proportion to the depth of mind from which it issued, so high does it soar, so long does it sing.

Or, I might say, it depends on how far the process had gone, of transmuting life into truth. In proportion to the completeness of the distillation, so will the purity and imperishableness of the product be. But none is quite perfect. As no air-pump can by any means make a perfect vacuum, so neither can any artist entirely exclude the conventional, the local, the perishable from his book, or write a book of pure thought, that shall be as efficient, in all respects, to a remote posterity, as to contemporaries, or rather to the second age. Each age, it is found, must write its own books; or rather, each generation for the next succeeding. The books of an older period will not fit this.

Yet hence arises a grave mischief. The sacredness which attaches to the act of creation, the act of thought, is transferred to the record. The poet chanting was felt to be a divine man; henceforth the chant is divine also. The writer was a just and wise spirit; henceforward it is settled the book is perfect; as love of the hero corrupts into worship of his statue. Instantly the book becomes noxious; the guide is a tyrant. The sluggish and perverted mind of the multitude, slow to open to the incursions of Reason, having once so opened, having once received this book, stands upon it, and makes an outcry if it is disparaged. Colleges are built on it. Books are written on it by thinkers, not by Man Thinking; by men of talent, that is, who start wrong, who set out from accepted dogmas, not from their own sight of principles. Meek young men grow up in libraries, believing it their duty to accept the views which Cicero, which Locke, which Bacon have given; forgetful that Cicero, Locke, and Bacon were only young men in libraries when they wrote these books.

Hence, instead of Man Thinking, we have the bookworm. Hence the book-learned class, who value books, as such; not as related to nature and the human constitution, but as making a sort of Third Estate with the world and the soul. Hence the restorers of reading, the emendators, the bibliomaniacs of all degrees.

Books are the best of things, well used; abused, among the worst. What is the right use? What is the one end which all means go to effect? They are for nothing but to inspire. I had better never see a book than to be warped by its attraction clean out of my own orbit, and made a satellite instead of a system. The one thing in the world, of value, is the active soul.

This every man is entitled to; this every man contains within him, although in almost all men obstructed and as yet unborn. The soul active sees absolute truth and utters truth, or creates. In this action it is genius; not the privilege of here and there a favorite, but the sound estate of every man. In its essence it is progressive. The book, the college, the school of art, the institution of any kind, stop with some past utterance of genius. This is good, say they—let us hold by this. They pin me down. They look backward and not forward. But genius looks forward: the eyes of man are set in his forehead, not in his hindhead: man hopes: genius creates. Whatever talents may be, if the man create not, the efflux of the Deity is not his; cinders and smoke there may be, but not yet flame. There are creative manners, there are creative actions, and creative words; manners, actions, words, that is, indicative of no custom or authority, but springing spontaneous from the mind's own sense of good and fair.

On the other part, instead of being its own seer, let it receive from another mind its truth, though it were in torrents of light, without periods of solitude, inquest, and self-recovery, and a fatal disservice is done. Genius is always sufficiently the enemy of genius by over-influence. The literature of every nation bears me witness. The English dramatic poets have Shakspearized now for two hundred years. 16

Undoubtedly there is a right way of reading, so it be sternly subordinated. Man Thinking must not be subdued by his instruments. Books are for the scholar's idle times. When he can read God directly, the hour is too precious to be wasted in others men's transcripts of their readings. But when the intervals of darkness come, as come they must—when the sun is hid and the stars withdraw their shining—we repair to the lamps which were kindled by their ray, to guide our steps to the East again, where the dawn is. We hear, that we may speak. The Arabian proverb says, "A fig tree, looking on a fig tree, becometh fruitful." 17

It is remarkable, the character of the pleasure we derive from the best books. They impress us with the conviction that one nature wrote and the same reads. We read the verses of one of the great English poets, of Chaucer, of Marvell, of Dryden, with the most modern joy—with a pleasure, I mean, which is in great part caused by the abstraction of all *time* from their verses. There is some awe mixed with the joy of our surprise, when this poet, who lived in some past world, two or three hundred years ago, says that which lies close to my own soul, that which I also had well-nigh thought and said. But for the evidence thence afforded to the philosophical doctrine of the identity of all minds, we should suppose some preëstablished harmony, some foresight of souls that were to be, and some preparation of stores for their future wants, like the fact observed in insects, who lay up food before death for the young grub they shall never see. 18

I would not be hurried by any love of system, by any exaggeration of instincts, to underrate the Book. We all know, that as the human body can be nourished on any food, though it were boiled grass and the broth of 19 shoes, so the human mind can be fed by any knowledge. And great and heroic men have existed who had almost no other information than by the printed page. I only would say that it needs a strong head to bear that diet. One must be an inventor to read well. As the proverb says, "He that would bring home the wealth of the Indies, must carry out the wealth of the Indies." There is then creative reading as well as creative writing. When the mind is braced by labor and invention, the page of whatever book we read becomes luminous with manifold allusion. Every sentence is doubly significant, and the sense of our author is as broad as the world. We then see, what is always true, that as the seer's hour of vision is short and rare among heavy days and months, so is its record, perchance, the least part of his volume. The discerning will read, in his Plato or Shakspeare, only that least part—only the authentic utterances of the oracles; all the rest he rejects, were it never so many times Plato's and Shakspeare's.

Of course there is a portion of reading quite indispensable to a wise   20
man. History and exact science he must learn by laborious reading. Colleges, in like manner, have their indispensable office—to teach elements. But they can only highly serve us when they aim not to drill, but to create; when they gather from far every ray of various genius to their hospitable halls, and by the concentrated fires, set the hearts of their youth on flame. Thought and knowledge are natures in which apparatus and pretension avail nothing. Gowns and pecuniary foundations, though of towns of gold, can never countervail the least sentence or syllable of wit. Forget this, and our American colleges will recede in their public importance, whilst they grow richer every year.

III.   There goes in the world a notion that the scholar should be a   21
recluse, a valetudinarian—as unfit for any handiwork or public labor as a penknife for an axe. The so-called "practical men" sneer at speculative men, as if, because they speculate or *see*, they could do nothing. I have heard it said that the clergy—who are always, more universally than any other class, the scholars of their day—are addressed as women; that the rough, spontaneous conversation of men they do not hear, but only a mincing and diluted speech. They are often virtually disfranchised; and indeed there are advocates for their celibacy. As far as this is true of the studious classes, it is not just and wise. Action is with the scholar subordinate, but it is essential. Without it he is not yet man. Without it thought can never ripen into truth. Whilst the world hangs before the eye as a cloud of beauty, we cannot even see its beauty. Inaction is cowardice, but there can be no scholar without the heroic mind. The preamble of thought, the transition through which it passes from the unconscious to the conscious, is action. Only so much do I know, as I have lived. Instantly we know whose words are loaded with life, and whose not.

The world—this shadow of the soul, or *other me*—lies wide around. Its   22
attractions are the keys which unlock my thoughts and make me acquainted with myself. I run eagerly into this resounding tumult. I grasp the

hands of those next me, and take my place in the ring to suffer and to work, taught by an instinct that so shall the dumb abyss be vocal with speech. I pierce its order; I dissipate its fear; I dispose of it within the circuit of my expanding life. So much only of life as I know by experience, so much of the wilderness have I vanquished and planted, or so far have I extended my being, my dominion. I do not see how any man can afford, for the sake of his nerves and his nap, to spare any action in which he can partake. It is pearls and rubies to his discourse. Drudgery, calamity, exasperation, want, are instructors in eloquence and wisdom. The true scholar grudges every opportunity of action past by, as a loss of power. It is the raw material out of which the intellect moulds her splendid products. A strange process too, this by which experience is converted into thought, as a mulberry leaf is converted into satin. The manufacture goes forward at all hours.

The actions and events of our childhood and youth are now matters 23
of calmest observation. They lie like fair pictures in the air. Not so with our recent actions—with the business which we now have in hand. On this we are quite unable to speculate. Our affections as yet circulate through it. We no more feel or know it than we feel the feet, or the hand, or the brain of our body. The new deed is yet a part of life—remains for a time immersed in our unconscious life. In some contemplative hour it detaches itself from the life like a ripe fruit, to become a thought of the mind. Instantly it is raised, transfigured; the corruptible has put on incorruption. Henceforth it is an object of beauty, however base its origin and neighborhood. Observe too the impossibility of antedating this act. In its grub state, it cannot fly, it cannot shine, it is a dull grub. But suddenly, without observation, the selfsame thing unfurls beautiful wings, and is an angel of wisdom. So is there no fact, no event, in our private history, which shall not, sooner or later, lose its adhesive, inert form, and astonish us by soaring from our body into the empyrean. Cradle and infancy, school and playground, the fear of boys, and dogs, and ferrules, the love of little maids and berries, and many another fact that once filled the whole sky, are gone already; friend and relative, profession and party, town and country, nation and world, must also soar and sing.

Of course, he who has put forth his total strength in fit actions has the 24
richest return of wisdom. I will not shut myself out of this globe of action, and transplant an oak into a flowerpot, there to hunger and pine; nor trust the revenue of some single faculty, and exhaust one vein of thought, much like those Savoyards, who, getting their livelihood by carving shepherds, shepherdesses, and smoking Dutchmen, for all Europe, went out one day to the mountain to find stock, and discovered that they had whittled up the last of their pine trees. Authors we have, in numbers, who have written out their vein, and who, moved by a commendable prudence, sail for Greece or Palestine, follow the trapper into the prairie, or ramble round Algiers, to replenish their merchantable stock.

If it were only for a vocabulary, the scholar would be covetous of 25
action. Life is our dictionary. Years are well spent in country labors; in
town; in the insight into trades and manufactures; in frank intercourse with
many men and women; in science; in art; to the one end of mastering in all
their facts a language by which to illustrate and embody our preceptions. I
learn immediately from any speaker how much he has already lived,
through the poverty or the splendor of his speech. Life lies behind us as the
quarry from whence we get tiles and copestones for the masonry of to-day.
This is the way to learn grammar. Colleges and books only copy the
language which the field and the work-yard made.

But the final value of action, like that of books, and better than 26
books, is that it is a resource. That great principle of Undulation in nature,
that shows itself in the inspiring and expiring of the breath; in desire and
satiety; in the ebb and flow of the sea; in day and night; in heat and cold;
and, yet more deeply ingrained in every atom and every fluid, is known to
us under the name of Polarity—these "fits of easy transmission and reflection," as Newton called them, are the law of nature because they are the law
of spirit.

The mind now thinks, now acts, and each fit reproduces the other. 27
When the artist has exhausted his materials, when the fancy no longer
paints, when thoughts are no longer apprehended and books are a
weariness—he has always the resources to *live*. Character is higher than
intellect. Thinking is the function. Living is the functionary. The stream
retreats to its source. A great soul will be strong to live, as well as strong to
think. Does he lack organ or medium to impart his truths? He can still fall
back on this elemental force of living them. This is a total act. Thinking is a
partial act. Let the grandeur of justice shine in his affairs. Let the beauty of
affection cheer his lowly roof. Those "far from fame," who dwell and act
with him, will feel the force of his constitution in the doings and passages of
the day better than it can be measured by any public and designed display.
Time shall teach him that the scholar loses no hour which the man lives.
Herein he unfolds the sacred germ of his instinct, screened from influence.
What is lost in seemliness is gained in strength. Not out of those on whom
systems of education have exhaused their culture, comes the helpful giant to
destroy the old or to build the new, but out of unhandselled savage nature;
out of terrible Druids and Berserkers come at last Alfred and Shakspeare.

I hear therefore with joy whatever is beginning to be said of the 28
dignity and necessity of labor to every citizen. There is virtue yet in the hoe
and the spade, for learned as well as for unlearned hands. And labor is
everywhere welcome; always we are invited to work; only be this limitation
observed, that a man shall not for the sake of wider activity sacrifice any
opinion to the popular judgments and modes of action.

I have now spoken of the education of the scholar by nature, by 29
books, and by action. It remains to say somewhat of his duties.

They are such as become Man Thinking. They may all be comprised [30] in self-trust. The office of the scholar is to cheer, to raise, and to guide men by showing them facts amidst appearances. He plies the slow, unhonored, and unpaid task of observation. Flamsteed and Herschel, in their glazed observatories, may catalogue the stars with the praise of all men, and the results being splendid and useful, honor is sure. But he, in his private observatory, cataloguing obscure and nebulous stars of the human mind, which as yet no man has thought of as such—watching days and months sometimes for a few facts; correcting still his old records; must relinquish display and immediate fame. In the long period of his preparation he must betray often an ignorance and shiftlessness in popular arts, incurring the disdain of the able who shoulder him aside. Long he must stammer in his speech; often forego the living for the dead. Worse yet, he must accept—how often!—poverty and solitude. For the ease and pleasure of treading the old road, accepting the fashions, the education, the religion of society, he takes the cross of making his own, and, or course, the self-accusation, the faint heart, the frequent uncertainty and loss of time, which are the nettles and tangling vines in the way of the self-relying and self-directed; and the state of virtual hostility in which he seems to stand to society, and especially to educated society. For all this loss and scorn, what offset? He is to find consolation in exercising the highest functions of human nature. He is one who raises himself from private considerations and breathes and lives on public and illustrious thoughts. He is the world's eye. He is the world's heart. He is to resist the vulgar prosperity that retrogrades ever to barbarism, by preserving and communicating heroic sentiments, noble biographies, melodious verse, and the conclusion of history. Whatsoever oracles the human heart, in all emergencies, in all solemn hours, has uttered as its commentary on the world of actions—these he shall receive and impart. And whatsoever new verdict Reason from her inviolable seat pronounces on the passing men and events of to-day—this he shall hear and promulgate.

These being his functions, it becomes him to feel all confidence in [31] himself, and to defer never to the popular cry. He and he only knows the world. The world of any moment is the merest appearance. Some great decorum, some fetish of a government, some ephemeral trade, or war, or man, is cried up by half mankind and cried down by the other half, as if all depended on this particular up or down. The odds are that the whole question is not worth the poorest thought which the scholar has lost in listening to the controversy. Let him not quit his belief that a popgun is a popgun, though the ancient and honorable of the earth affirm it to be the crack of doom. In silence, in steadiness, in severe abstraction, let him hold by himself; add observation to observation, patient of neglect, patient of reproach, and bide his own time—happy enough if he can satisfy himself alone that this day he has seen something truly. Success treads on every right step. For the instinct is sure, that prompts him to tell his brother what he thinks. He then learns that in going down into the secrets of his own mind he has descended into the secrets of all minds. He learns that he who has mastered any law in his private thoughts, is master to that extent of all men whose language he speaks, and of all into whose language his own can be translated. The poet, in utter solitude remembering his spontaneous thoughts and recording them, is found to have recorded that which men in crowed cities find true for them also. The orator distrusts at first the fitness of his frank confessions, his want of knowledge of the persons he addresses, until he finds that he is the complement of his hearers; that they drink his words because he fulfills for them their own nature; the deeper he dives into his privatest, secretest presentiment, to his wonder he finds this is the most acceptable, most public, and universally true. The people delight in it; the better part of every man feels, This is my music; this is myself.

In self-trust all the virtues are comprehended. Free should the scholar be—free and brave. Free even to the definition of freedom, "without any hindrance that does not arise out of his own constitution." Brave; for fear is a thing which a scholar by his very function puts behind him. Fear always springs from ignorance. It is a shame to him if his tranquillity, amid dangerous times, arise from the presumption that like children and women his is a protected class; or if he seek a temporary peace by the diversion of his thoughts from politics or vexed questions, hiding his head like an ostrich in the flowering bushes, peeping into microscopes, and turning rhymes, as a boy whistles to keep his courage up. So is the danger a danger still; so is the fear worse. Manlike let him turn and face it. Let him look into its eye and search its nature, inspect its origin—see the whelping of this lion—which lies no great way back; he will then find in himself a perfect comprehension of its nature and extent; he will have made his hands meet on the other side, and can henceforth defy it and pass on superior. The world is his who can see through its pretension. What deafness, what stone-blind custom, what overgrown error you behold is there only by sufferance—by your sufferance. See it to be a lie, and you have already dealt it its mortal blow. 32

Yes, we are the cowed—we the trustless. It is a mischievous notion that we are come late into nature; that the world was finished a long time ago. As the world was plastic and fluid in the hands of God, so it is ever to so much of his attributes as we bring to it. To ignorance and sin, it is flint. They adapt themselves to it as they may; but in proportion as a man has any thing in him divine, the firmament flows before him and takes his signet and form. Not he is great who can alter matter, but he who can alter my state of mind. They are the kings of the world who give the color of their present thought to all nature and all art, and persuade men by the cheerful serenity of their carrying the matter, that this thing which they do is the apple which the ages have desired to pluck, now at last ripe, and inviting nations to the harvest. The great man makes the great thing. Wherever Macdonald sits, there is the head of the table. Linnaeus makes botany the 33 most alluring of studies, and wins it from the farmer and the herb-woman; Davy, chemistry; and Cuvier, fossils. The day is always his who works in it with serenity and great aims. The unstable estimates of men crowd to him whose mind is filled with a truth, as the heaped waves of the Atlantic follow the moon.

For this self-trust, the reason is deeper than can be fathomed—darker   34
than can be enlightened. I might not carry with me the feeling of my audience in stating my own belief. But I have already shown the ground of my hope, in adverting to the doctrine that man is one. I believe man has been wronged; he has wronged himself. He has almost lost the light that can lead him back to his prerogatives. Men are become of no account. Men in history, men in the world of to-day, are bugs, are spawn, and are called "the mass" and "the herd." In a century, in a millennium, one or two men; that is to say, one or two approximations to the right state of every man. All the rest behold in the hero or the poet their own green and crude being— ripened; yes, and are content to be less, so *that* may attain to its full stature. What a testimony, full of grandeur, full of pity, is borne to the demands of his own nature, by the poor clansman, the poor partisan, who rejoices in the glory of his chief. The poor and the low find some amends to their immense moral capacity, for their acquiescence in a political and social inferiority. They are content to be brushed like flies from the path of a great person, so that justice shall be done by him to that common nature which it is the dearest desire of all to see enlarged and glorified. They sun themselves in the great man's light, and feel it to be their own element. They cast the dignity of man from their downtrod selves upon the shoulders of a hero, and will perish to add one drop of blood to make that great heart beat, those giant sinews combat and conquer. He lives for us, and we live in him.

Men, such as they are, very naturally seek money or power; and power   35
because it is as good as money—the "spoils," so called, "of office." And why not? for they aspire to the highest, and this, in their sleep-walking, they dream is highest. Wake them and they shall quit the false good and leap to the true, and leave governments to clerks and desks. This revolution is to be wrought by the gradual domestication of the idea of Culture. The main enterprise of the world for splendor, for extent, is the upbuilding of a man. Here are the materials strewn along the ground. The private life of one man shall be a more illustrious monarchy, more formidable to its enemy, more sweet and serene in its influence to its friend, than any kingdom in history. For a man, rightly viewed, comprehendeth the particular natures of all men. Each philosopher, each bard, each actor has only done for me, as by a delegate, what one day I can do for myself. The books which once we valued more than the apple of the eye, we have quite exhausted. What is that but saying that we have come up with the point of view which the universal mind took through the eyes of one scribe; we have been that man, and have passed on. First, one, then another, we drain all cisterns, and

waxing greater by all these supplies, we crave a better and more abundant food. The man has never lived that can feed us ever. The human mind cannot be enshrined in a person who shall set a barrier on any one side to this unbounded, unboundable empire. It is one central fire, which, flaming now out of the lips of Etna, lightens the capes of Sicily, and now out of the throat of Vesuvius, illuminates the towers and vineyards of Naples. It is one light which beams out of a thousand stars. It is one soul which animates all men.

But I have dwelt perhaps tediously upon this abstraction of the 36 Scholar. I ought not to delay longer to add what I have to say of nearer reference to the time and to this country.

Historically, there is thought to be a difference in the ideas which 37 predominate over successive epochs, and there are data for marking the genius of the Classic, of the Romantic, and now of the Reflective or Philosophical age. With the views I have intimated of the oneness or the identity of the mind through all individuals, I do not much dwell on these differences. In fact, I believe each individual passes through all three. The boy is a Greek; the youth, romantic; the adult, reflective. I deny not, however, that a revolution in the leading idea may be distinctly enough traced.

Our age is bewailed as the age of Introversion. Must that needs be evil? 38 We, it seems, are critical; we are embarrassed with second thoughts; we cannot enjoy any thing for hankering to know whereof the pleasure consists; we are lined with eyes; we see with our feet; the time is infected with Hamlet's unhappiness—

"Sicklied o'er with the pale cast of thought."

It is so bad then? Sight is the last thing to be pitied. Would we be blind? Do we fear lest we should outsee nature and God, and drink truth dry? I look upon the discontent of the literary class as a mere announcement of the fact that they find themselves not in the state of mind of their fathers, and regret the coming state as untried; as a boy dreads the water before he has learned that he can swim. If there is any period one would desire to be born in, is it not the age of Revolution; when the old and the new stand side by side and admit of being compared; when the energies of all men are searched by fear and by hope; when the historic glories of the old can be compensated by the rich possibilities of the new era? This time, like all times, is a very good one, if we but know what to do with it.

I read with some joy of the auspicious signs of the coming days, as they 39 glimmer already through poetry and art, through philosophy and science, through church and state.

One of these signs is the fact that the same movement which effected 40 the elevation of what was called the lowest class in the state, assumed in literature a very marked and as benign an aspect. Instead of the sublime and beautiful, the near, the low, the common, was explored and poetized. That which had been negligently trodden under foot by those who were harnessing and provisioning themselves for long journeys into far countries, is suddenly found to be richer than all foreign parts. The literature of the poor, the feelings of the child, the philosophy of the street, the meaning of household life, are the topics of the time. It is a great stride. It is a sign—is it not?—of new vigor when the extremities are made active, when currents of warm life run into the hands and the feet. I ask not for the great, the remote, the romantic; what is doing in Italy or Arabia; what is Greek art, or Provencal minstrelsy. I embrace the common, I explore and sit at the feet of the familiar, the low. Give me insight into to-day, and you may have the antique and future worlds. What would we really know the meaning of? The meal in the firkin; the milk in the pan; the ballad in the street; the news of the boat; the glance of the eye; the form and the gait of the body; show me the ultimate reason of these matters; show me the sublime presence of the highest spiritual cause lurking, as always it does lurk, in these suburbs and extremities of nature; let me see every trifle bristling with the polarity that ranges it instantly on an eternal law; and the shop, the plough, and the ledger referred to the like cause by which light undulates and poets sing; and the world lies no longer a dull miscellany and lumber-room, but has form and order; there is no trifle, there is no puzzle, but one design unites and animates the farthest pinnacle and the lowest trench.

This idea has inspired the genius of Goldsmith, Burns, Cowper, and, in a newer time, of Goethe, Wordsworth, and Carlyle. This idea they have differently followed and with various success. In contrast with their writing, the style of Pope, of Johnson, of Gibbon, looks cold and pedantic. This writing is blood-warm. Man is surprised to find that things near are not less beautiful and wondrous than things remote. The near explains the far. The drop is a small ocean. A man is related to all nature. This perception of the worth of the vulgar is fruitful in discoveries. Goethe, in this very thing the most modern of the moderns, has shown us, as none ever did, the genius of the ancients. 41

There is one man of genius who has done much for this philosophy of life, whose literary value has never yet been rightly estimated; I mean Emanuel Swedenborg. The most imaginative of men, yet writing with the precision of a mathematician, he endeavored to engraft a purely philosophical Ethics on the popular Christianity of his time. Such an attempt of course must have difficulty which no genius could surmount. But he saw and showed the connection between nature and the affections of the soul. He pierced the emblematic or spiritual character of the visible, audible, tangible word. Especially did his shade-loving muse hover over and interpret the lower parts of nature; he showed the mysterious bond that allies moral evil to the foul material forms, and has given in epical parables a theory of insanity, of beasts, of unclean and fearful things. 42

Another sign of our times, also marked by an analogous political 43 movement, is the new importance given to the single person. Every thing that tends to insulate the individual—to surround him with barriers of natural respect, so that each man shall feel the world is his, and man shall treat with man as a sovereign state with a sovereign state—tends to true union as well as greatness. "I learned," said the melancholy Pestalozzi, "that no man in God's wide earth is either willing or able to help any other man." Help must come from the bosom alone. The scholar is that man who must take up into himself all the ability of the time, all the contributions of the past, all the hopes of the future. He must be an university of knowledges. If there be one lesson more than another which should pierce his ear, it is, The world is nothing, the man is all; in yourself is the law of all nature, and you know not yet how a globule of sap ascends; in yourself slumbers the whole of Reason; it is for you to know all; it is for you to dare all. Mr. President and Gentlemen, this confidence in the unsearched might of man belongs, by all motives, by all prophecy, by all preparation, to the American Scholar. We have listened too long to the courtly muses of Europe. The spirit of the American free-man is already suspected to be timid, imitative, tame. Public and private avarice make the air we breathe thick and fat. The scholar is decent, indolent, complaisant. See already the tragic consequence. The mind of this country, taught to aim at low objects, eats upon itself. There is no work for any but the decorous and the complaisant. Young men of the fairest promise, who begin life upon our shores, inflated by the mountain winds, shined upon by all the stars of God, find the earth below not in unison with these, but are hindered from action by the disgust which the principles on which business is managed inspire, and turn drudges, or die of disgust, some of them suicides. What is the remedy? They did not yet see, and thousands of young men as hopeful now crowding to the barriers for the career do not yet see, that if the single man plant himself indomitably on his instincts, and there abide, the huge world will come round to him. Patience—patience; with the shades of all the good and great for company; and for solace the perspective of your own infinite life; and for work the study and the communication of principles, the making those instincts prevalent, the conversion of the world. Is it not the chief disgrace in the world, not to be an unit; not to be reckoned one character; not to yield that peculiar fruit which each man was created to bear, but to be reckoned in the gross, in the hundred, or the thousand, of the party, the section, to which we belong; and our opinion predicted geographically, as the north, or the south? Not so, brothers and friends—please God, ours shall not be so. We will walk on our own feet; we will work with our own hands; we will speak our own minds. The study of letters shall be no longer a name for pity, for doubt, and for sensual indulgence. The dread of man and the love of man shall be a wall of defence and a wreath of joy around all. A nation of men will for the first time exist, because each believes himself inspired by the Divine Soul which also inspires all men.

Questions for Study and Discussion

1. How do the precepts "know thyself" and "study nature" relate to each other?

2. How does Emerson use symbols in this essay? Cite examples from the text to support your answer.

3. In paragraph 4, Emerson says men have "suffered amputation from the trunk, and strut about so many walking monsters—a good finger, a neck, a stomach, an elbow, but never a man." What does he mean by this? How is this fable related to the remainder of Emerson's essay?

4. Why should a student "join two things and see in them one nature?" What will a student gain from this?

5. What for Emerson are the three main influences on the young scholar's mind? How does he distinguish the different influences? How are they related?

6. Emerson argues against the "bookworm," for this is not truly "Man Thinking." What is the difference between the two? Why is this an important distinction for a scholar to grasp? Is his essay a useful tool for modern students? Explain.

Writing Topics

1. Emerson presents his ideas for education in the 1830s. How have the concepts, students, universities, and the attitudes about going to college changed since then? What are the duties of today's college graduate?

2. A battle has been raging in some public schools between "creationists" and "evolutionists." In an essay discuss the arguments each side brings to the issue. How do you imagine Emerson would react to the debate? How do you react to it after reading his essay?

Teaching and Testing

ALEXANDER CALANDRA

Tests in school and college are usually designed so that each question has only one correct answer, especially in such disciplines as the natural sciences. Yet many important discoveries have been made by individuals who have reached beyond the obvious and "known" answers—take Galileo, Columbus, and Einstein, for example. Alexander Calandra, a professor of physics at Washington University in St. Louis, once came across a college student who insisted on giving every answer but the expected one to a physics exam question. In this essay, originally published in *Saturday Review*, he tells what happened.

Angels on a Pin

Some time ago, I received a call from a colleague who asked if I would 1 be the referee on the grading of an examination question. He was about to give a student a zero for his answer to a physics question, while the student claimed he should receive a perfect score and would if the system were not set up against the student. The instructor and the student agreed to submit this to an impartial arbiter, and I was selected.

I went to my colleague's office and read the examination question: 2 "Show how it is possible to determine the height of a tall building with the aid of a barometer."

The student had answered: "Take the barometer to the top of the 3 building, attach a long rope to it, lower the barometer to the street, and then bring it up, measuring the length of the rope. The length of the rope is the height of the building."

I pointed out that the student really had a strong case for full credit, 4 since he had answered the question completely and correctly. On the other hand, if full credit were given, it could well contribute to a high grade for the student in his physics course. A high grade is supposed to certify competence in physics, but the answer did not confirm this. I suggested that the student have another try at answering the question. I was not surprised that my colleague agreed, but I was surprised that the student did.

I gave the student six minutes to answer the question, with the warning that his answer should show some knowledge of physics. At the end of five minutes, he had not written anything. I asked if he wished to give up, but he said no. He had many answers to this problem; he was just thinking of the best one. I excused myself for interrupting him, and asked him to please go on. In the next minute, he dashed off his answer, which read:

"Take the barometer to the top of the building and lean over the edge of the roof. Drop the barometer, timing its fall with a stopwatch. Then using the formula $S = \frac{1}{2} at^2$, calculate the height of the building."

At this point, I asked my colleague if *he* would give up. He conceded, and I gave the student almost full credit.

In leaving my colleague's office, I recalled that the student had said he had other answers to the problem, so I asked him what they were. "Oh, yes," said the student. "There are many ways of getting the height of a tall building with the aid of a barometer. For example, you could take the barometer out on a sunny day and measure the height of the barometer, the length of its shadow, and the length of the shadow of the building, and by the use of a simple proportion, determine the height of the building."

"Fine," I said. "And the others?"

"Yes," said the student. "There is a very basic measurement method that you will like. In this method, you take the barometer and begin to walk up the stairs. As you climb the stairs, you mark off the length of the barometer along the wall. You then count the number of marks, and this will give you the height of the building in barometer units. A very direct method.

"Of course, if you want a more sophisticated method, you can tie the barometer to the end of a string, swing it as a pendulum, and determine the value of 'g' at the street level and at the top of the building. From the difference between the two values of 'g', the height of the building can, in principle, be calculated."

Finally he concluded, there are many ways of solving the problem. "Probably the best," he said, "is to take the barometer to the basement and knock on the superintendent's door. When the superintendent answers, you speak to him as follows: 'Mr. Superintendent, here I have a fine barometer. If you will tell me the height of this building, I will give you this barometer.'"

At this point, I asked the student if he really did not know the conventional answer to this question. He admitted that he did, but said that he was fed up with high school and college instuctors trying to teach him how to think, to use the "scientific method," and to explore the deep inner logic of the subject in a pedantic way, as is often done in the new mathematics, rather than teaching him the structure of the subject. With this in mind, he decided to revive scholasticism as an academic lark to challenge the Sputnik-panicked classrooms of America.

Questions for Study and Discussion

1. What is the point of this essay? What makes the narrative more than a humorous story about a student and his physics exam?

2. What was the exam question supposed to test? Why did the question fail? How might the actual wording have caused this failure? How would you rewrite the question so that it would do what it was meant to do?

3. Why do you think the student gave the answer in paragraph 6 as the best one? Do you agree? What motivated him to avoid the conventional answer?

4. Why do you think the teacher accepted the answer in paragraph 6 but did not give the student full credit? Was he right to do so? Explain.

5. What relevant information does Calandra leave out of the essay? Why do you think he does this?

6. The scholastic philosophers of the Middle Ages used to debate theo-logical questions that seem pointless to us today, such as how many angels could dance on the head of a pin. In this context, what do you think is meant by the reference to scholasticism in the last sentence of the essay? What does the title contribute to the essay?

7. How would you characterize all of the student's answers? Granting their imaginativeness, what other quality do they all possess?

Writing Topics

1. History and everyday life are full of examples of what Edward de Bono calls "lateral thinking," going outside the conventional limits of a problem to find an unexpected but effective answer. The student in Calandra's essay is obviously an imaginative lateral thinker. What examples of lateral thinking can you find in your own experience, or from other sources? How can one set about thinking laterally? Write an essay in which you discuss the benefits of lateral thinking.

2. What are tests and exams normally used for? What should they be used for? How can you tell a good examination question from a bad one? Based on exams that you have taken, write an essay that examines the function of testing in the educational process.

ANDREW WARD

Photographer, former art teacher, and humorist, Andrew Ward was born in Chicago in 1946. He attended Oberlin College in Ohio and the Rhode Island School of Design and now makes his home in New Haven, Connecticut. His writing has appeared in a wide variety of publications including *Horizon*, *Inquiry*, *American Heritage*, and *Fantasy and Science Fiction Magazine*. He also published two collections of his essays: *Fits and Starts: The Premature Memoirs of Andrew Ward* (1978), and *Bits and Pieces* (1980). In 1980 he also published *Baby Bear and the Long Sleep*, a book for very young children.

"Pencils Down," taken from *Fits and Starts*, recounts with pity, pathos, nostalgia, and abrupt humor the many fearful testing situations Ward has faced throughout his school years.

Pencils Down

Everything will be going fine and then suddenly I will have that dream 1
again, the one in which I am walking across a campus and a classmate runs by me, waving his arms and shouting, "Come on! You're late!"

"Late?" I call after him. "Late for what?" 2

"Late for what?!" he exclaims. "Late for Bretko's final!" 3

In spite of myself, I begin to lope after him. "Bretko? Who's Bretko?" 4

"Jesus Christ!" he says as we dash toward the classroom building, 5
"where have you *been* all semester?"

It is just when we reach the classroom, where the final in a course I 6
have never heard of on a subject I know nothing about is already in progress, that I wake up in a tangle of bedding, my eyes bulging like eggs.

The first real test I remember taking was at a solemn little pedagogic 7
enterprise called the Lab School, to which the faculty of the University of Chicago sent its children and in which it tested out some of its educational theories. I spent four years guinea-pigging my way through the Lab School, but I don't remember very much about it. I do remember a wide, saintly kindergarten teacher who cured my stuttering ("Now, take your time, Andy," she would say as I stammered before her, "we have all the time in the world."). And I remember Miss Mums, a siren of a second-grade teacher with a flamboyant bust who used to hop up and down whenever one of us

answered her correctly. I still think the University was on to something when it hired Miss Mums; most of us did our best to keep her perpetually hopping before us.

In any case, sometime during the second grade a group of pale young men with attaché cases arrived at the school and established themselves in a little room which was usually devoted to hearing tests. We were called in one by one "to have a little fun," as Miss Mums put it, "with some nice big men." Some of us didn't want to have a little fun. One boy, whose mother made him wear some sort of prophylactic powder in his hair, fainted in the hallway when his turn came, and had to spend the rest of the day with the nurse.   8

When it came my turn, I walked down to the testing room and stood silently in the doorway, waiting to be noticed, which was my way of announcing myself in those days. I was finally beckoned in by a man with thick glasses that made his eyes look like fish suspended in ice.   9

"Now, Mark," he said brightly, "if you'll just take your seat right here, we can all start playing with blocks."   10

Much too polite to correct him about my name, I took my seat at a table around which four men with note pads loomed attentively. I was given six red plastic cubes and told, with many winks and nods, to do whatever I felt like doing with them. In truth, I didn't feel like doing anything with them. I was old enough to know that you couldn't build anything with six cubes. But the men looked so eager that I decided to do what I could, which was to line them all up into a row, then into two rows of three, then into three rows of two. The three rows of two seemed to go over very big. I could see out of the corner of my eye that they had begun to jot furiously, nodding to themselves as if entire life philosophies were being confirmed before their eyes.   11

I shoved the blocks around a while longer and finally leaned back. There was a pause, and then suddenly one of the men rose to his feet agitatedly and jabbed his pencil into the fish-eyed man's ribs.   12

"See?" he exclaimed. "See? What did I tell you?"   13

"You never told me *anything!*" the fish-eyed man hissed back, shoving the pencil aside. There was a scene, and in the confusion I got down off my chair and made my way back to Miss Mums' room. "Now," she asked me as I sat down at my desk, "wasn't that fun?"   14

"Yes," I said, and she gave a little hop.   15

My parents seemed to have had me down for college *in utero*. I remember working on a geography report about Bolivia when I was in the third grade and my mother standing over me with an anxious look and declaring, "They're going to count this for college."   16

As far as she was concerned, they were going to count everything for college. She used college in her disciplinary warnings the way some mothers used Santa Claus. This had the effect of simultaneously trivializing and   17

exalting my academic labors. On the one hand, I could not believe that my
knowledge that Bolivia was the only country in the world to lynch two
successive heads of state from the same lamp post was going to count for
anything in college. On the other hand, I could sometimes imagine a
tweedy admissions officer leaning back and asking, "By the way, Andrew,
what country was it that lynched two successive heads of state from the
same lamp post?"

"I believe that was Bolivia, sir." 18

"Excellent! Oh, excellent! Andrew, I believe you and Harvard are 19
going to get along very nicely."

I never did very well in school; in fact, the further along I got the 20
worse I did, until by senior year in high school I was just squeaking through.
I ascribe this to a difficulty I've always had with admitting to ignorance. It is
hard to learn anything when you are constantly trying to look as though
you know it already. I would rarely ask a question, for instance, unless it was
designed to demonstrate a precocious knowledge of the subject under
discussion. I would always start off my questions with, "Wouldn't you say
that . . . ," knowing full well that the teacher would, and congratulate me
for my insight. In math and science it got me nowhere.

My parents were perplexed by my performance in high school, to the 21
point of commissioning a university testing center in New York City to
determine what my problem was. Every Saturday for four weeks I made my
way into the Village to undergo batteries of five or six tests at a sitting. I
went in with my parents the first day, and we all sat around with a cheerful
man who kept asking me what I thought of myself. I told him I wanted to be
an artist, and had trouble studying. He smiled indulgently and said we
would see about that.

I guess I've blocked out a lot of the tests I took in the following weeks. 22
One of them was to check out my suitability for cost accounting. Another
consisted of a series of paintings depicting ambiguous scenes which I was to
interpret using multiple choice.

> The man and woman in the picture above have just: 23
> A. Had an argument.
> B. Made love.
> C. Poisoned themselves.
> D. Filed for joint return.

Another was a tricky test for artistic ability. There would be four 24
drawings of, say, a circle placed in a square. In one the circle would be
centered, in another it would be to one side, in another it would be to
another side, and so on. The idea was to select the one which was most
sound compositionally. I say this was tricky because at the time every
artistic convention was up for grabs, and I could have whipped up a
convincing aesthetic argument for any one of them. I decided, however,

that the centered circle was most likely to suit the testing center's artistic soul, and my high score bore this out.

One of the exams was an oral I.Q. test. The tester was an earnest man   25
in shirt sleeves who repeatedly told me to relax. "We're just going to kick around a few things," he said. "There's absolutely nothing to be afraid of."

He had me push blocks through holes, do something simple with   26
some checkers, and perform various other tasks, and then we came to a part of the test where I was to explain to him the derivation of different sayings. This proved a bumpier ride that he had expected, because I had never heard a lot of the sayings he read to me. "One swallow does not make a summer," for instance, troubled me deeply. I had never heard it, knew nothing about ornithology, and stammered along for several minutes, operating on the theory that he meant the act of swallowing. I think I said something about the wine of life and the flask of spring, and I could see from the way my tester fidgeted that he had not been provided with contingencies covering my interpretation.

I can't say I didn't get anything out of all this. I was given some   27
instruction on the ukelele by an old man in Washington Square during a testing break, and discovered a newsstand near the subway where I could buy *Gent* and *Nugget* without raising an eyebrow. When my parents and I were called back to hear the results, we were told that I was sharp as a tack, had trouble motivating myself to study, and should consider art as a profession. The cheerful man accepted my father's check for $125.00, and we all silently rode the train back to where I'd started.

I did pretty well on English and history College Boards, and miserably   28
in math and science, as was my pattern, My parents had me sign up for every testing date there was, and I swung at the ball in such varying locales as Danbury State Teachers' College, Tom's School of Business Success, and most of the high school auditoriums in southwestern Connecticut. One day, my mother saw an ad in the back of the *Times* for a College Board preparation class at a private school in the city, and in no time I was commuting again. It turned out that I was the only one in the class who did not come from midtown Manhattan, and the only male who didn't wear a yarmulke. The course turned out to be a fraud. The teacher, a shaky old fellow in gold framed bifocals, started off by informing us that there was no secret to doing well on College Boards, went on to talk a little about a sister of his who was about to undergo surgery, and then had us spend the rest of the time taking mock College Boards in exercise books we bought from the school for five dollars apiece.

Oberlin College was my first choice, naturally enough, because my   29
parents went there, and my brother, and all my aunts and uncles, because my grandfather was head of its art department, and my father was one of its trustees. Oberlin had strict admissions standards in those days, and there was considerable doubt on my parents' part that I would gain admittance.

When I had my admissions interview in a hotel suite in New York, I 30 had just received a D in chemistry, a course I had to pass in order to meet the science requirements, since I had flunked biology the year before. After several genial inquiries as to my family's health and whereabouts, the admissions officer proved remarkably encouraging. He hinted that I would be admitted under what he called Oberlin's "Tom Sawyer Program," which permitted students with "asymmetrical aptitudes," as he put it, to get in. He could not keep from wincing as his eyes descended row upon row of D's and C's in my high-school record, but he emphasized and reemphasized the positive side: high marks in art and English, soloist in the chorus, good attendance; and as the interview drew to a close, I got the impression that he was even more eager for me to go to Oberlin College than I was. As he waited with me for the elevator in the foyer outside his suite, he held my coat for me as I attempted, in vain, to get my second arm into its sleeve. We waltzed around in this way for some time, and as I finally stepped into the elevator, still lunging about for my elusive sleeve, he looked at me with the game, pained expression of a man at a dinner party who must smack his lips over something repugnant.

Oberlin didn't turn out to be quite what I had in mind, and vice 31 versa. As I went along, I had more and more trouble getting to class, until eventually I lost all track of where I was supposed to be, and when. Sometimes I would catch a glimpse of someone dimly familiar and follow him to his next class, in the hope that it would turn out to be one of my own. It never did turn out to be one of my own, but in this way I attended some fascinating lectures on subjects ranging from a historical review of the Albanian nation-state to the topical poetry of Po Chü-i.

I was well into my third, last-ditch semester at Oberlin College before 32 I finally managed to pinpoint my problem. I couldn't read. Not that I couldn't have stood up before a Wednesday Assembly and read aloud from my geology text in a clear, authoritative voice, making myself heard unto the last rows of Finney Chapel. It was just that to my own ears I wouldn't have made any sense.

As finals week approached, I tried to overcome this disability by locking 33 myself into my room in the dormitory, laying out my study materials in the lone beam of my Tensor desk lamp, and sitting there, hunched over my open textbook with a yellow felt-tip pen ready to underline important passages. I sat that way for hours at a time, waiting for the words over which my eyes passed to form phrases, sentences, ideas, and managing only an occasional flicker of recognition, enough to link perhaps twenty words together—"The exercise begins a rather extensive study to be continued in later sections of Chapter XXI"—never enough to gain me a foothold.

I was reduced to hoping that it was all penetrating my mind sub- 34 consciously, and I would tidily underline what I could only assume was important—headings, captions, opening and closing sentences, numbers, anything resembling a list, and sometimes a central sentence, a few of which, I figured, were probably important, too.

Underlining accomplished several purposes. It gave me something to do, demarcated the pages I had already gone through (I had no other way of knowing), and it hid from whoever might duck into my room the fact that I was, in effect, an illiterate, and had no business being in college in the first place.

My last final at Oberlin was in Geology I, a course I took because it was touted to have been designed for the scientifically inept. This touting did not, however, seem to have originated with the Geology Department. If there is more to know about rocks than was included in Geology I, I don't want to hear about it. By the time I took the final, I had missed all but seven of my classes, and had received an F on my research paper, a study of the Greenwich, Connecticut, reservoir system which I had based on a water company comic book starring a character made out of drain-pipe named Wally Water.

I took the exam with some fifty other geology cadets in a dark, gothic room overlooking Tappan Square. The proctor, a work-booted geology major, handed out the test sheet and bluebooks, and, stop-watch raised, signalled to us to begin.

The questions must have been mimeographed minutes before, because the ink still smelled sweet and dizzying. The first and second questions rang no bells at all, and as I read them my pen felt icy and useless in my fingers. In the third question I could barely make out the following: ". . . bituminous coal and discuss its suitability as a fuel. Use illustrations to explain your answer where necessary."

It was as if I had stumbled into someone else's identity. I didn't know anything about rocks. I didn't know anything about science. Why were they asking me these things? I stared up at the blackboard, where the proctor was already chalking up how much time we had left. He squinted back at me with suspicion, and I swerved my gaze ceilingward, as if searching for the appropriate phrasing with which to set down my brimming knowledge.

Coal. What did I know about coal? I thought of black lung, carbon paper, the heap of coal in my parents' basement in Chicago. Then, for a moment, a phrase sprang to my mind from an eighth-grade science text: "Coal results from the deterioration and mineralization of prehistoric tropical rainforests."

Quickly, before it sank back out of reach, I opened my bluebook and began to write. "Coal results from the deterioration and mineralization of prehistoric tropical rainforests. Coal deposits are apt to be found in those places where prehistoric tropical rainforests once stood. Thus, coal mines in present use are located in these places.

"Coal," I continued boldly, "contains some of the chemical elements of prehistoric tropical rainforests, but usually not all of them. Those that remain are those which have survived and, in a sense, resulted from, the deterioration and mineralization of prehistoric tropical rainforests."

That got me through three pages of large, loopy script. All around me, my classmates were filling one bluebook after another. One girl across the room wrote the ink out of one ballpoint, hurled it to the floor, and furiously scrawled on with another. All I could hear in the room was the steady scrape of pens and the rapid flutter of pages.   43

To drive home my point, I decided to deliver on a few illustrations. Carefully, but with a certain graphic flair, I drew: 44

1. a rainforest with arrows pointing to "trees," "scrub vegetation," "sun," and "topsoil,"
2. a rainforest deteriorating,
3. a deteriorated rainforest making its way underground,
4. a coal mine in full operation labelled "Thousands of years later," and,
5. a black lump labelled "resultant coal ore fragment."

These led to another drawing illustrating the chemical breakup of coal. I drew a circle and divided it into three parts, labelled "sulfur," "carbon," and "other." Coal was suitable as a fuel, I noted, because it burned.   45

As I underlined all my headings and captions I wondered about my alternatives. I could claim that I had overdosed on NoDoz, that I was reeling, hallucinating, unable to think. I could hand in a blank bluebook, copy out a C-level set of answers in another bluebook that evening, hand it in the next morning, and elegantly apologize for the mixup. I could feign a fainting spell or an epileptic fit or psychosomatic paralysis of my right hand. I could accuse the earnest, chalk-faced girl beside me of cheating and storm out the door, or punch out the proctor in a rebellious frenzy, becoming, overnight, a campus legend.   46

But it gradually became obvious to me that the college simply wanted me to answer these questions. Otherwise, I reasoned, they would not be asking them. And it was just as obvious that if I couldn't answer their questions, I had no business being there. Somehow, in the rustle of the testing room, this hit me like a revelation. I wanted to get up then, find the professor, and exclaim, "Say, sir I didn't *realize* any of this." He would understand. It must have happened before.   47

I looked at two of my friends a few rows away, both busily writing. At these times my friends seemed distant and unfamiliar. They were each into their third or fourth bluebook. What in God's name were they writing about?   48

The hinge of my jaw ached and trembled and as I yawned, the floor took on a soft, inviting look. I put down my pen and stretched out my legs and wondered if it would be all right if I just curled up for a little while on the scuffed, hardwood floor, closed my eyes, and slept.   49

"Pencils down," the proctor commanded, chopping at the air with his hand.   50

A resolute, perspiring girl in the front row raised her hand and asked if she could "just finish one last sentence."   51

The proctor nodded and a score of heads and hands ducked back down to finish sentences. I sat still for a moment, and then scribbled one last sentence, "Coal remains one of the most popular forms of fuel in use today."   52

"All right, that's it," the proctor declared, and everyone groaned and stretched and stacked their blue books. I signed mine with a bold hand, but glancing over my five pages I knew it was at last all over for me at Oberlin College. All that remained was one last explosion of red-inked exclamations expressing regrets, alarm, and grave concern for my future.   53

Questions for Study and Discussion

1. At what point in the essay were you first aware of Ward's humor? Examine several humorous passages and explain how the humor works in each case.

2. What point does Ward make about the examination or testing experience? How does humor help to make that point?

3. What role do Ward's parents play in his education? What does Ward mean when he says, "My parents seemed to have me down for college *in utero*"?

4. In paragraph 32 Ward says that he pinpointed his problem—he discovered he couldn't read. What does he mean when he says he "couldn't read," and how does the problem manifest itself?

5. Reread paragraphs 38–52. How would you characterize Ward's answer to the question of the Geology I final exam? What in particular about his answer is inadequate? Would he have fared better with this type of writing in a nonscientific course? Explain.

6. How has Ward organized his essay? How do paragraphs 1–6 fit into that organizational structure?

7. Discuss the extent to which examinations are specific to the academic environment. Are we ever tested elsewhere in life?

Writing Topics

1. Ward vividly remembers taking the College Boards and being enrolled in class to prepare for these examinations. Write an essay either for or against the use of College Board exams in the admissions process. You may want to interview your admissions director to determine how College Boards are used at your institution and how effective they are at predicting academic success.

2. It's well known that many students suffer from the anxiety of studying for and taking examinations. Write an essay in which you propose and describe

one or more alternatives to traditional academic testing. What problems would your proposal address? Can your proposal be readily or easily implemented? Explain.

3. Write an essay in which you analyze examination trauma and account for its major causes.

SAMUEL H. SCUDDER

Samuel H. Scudder (1837–1911) was a graduate of Williams College and Harvard University and was a university professor and leading scientist of his day. His special field of study was butterflies, grasshoppers, and crickets, and in 1888–1889 he published the result of his thirty years of research on butterflies in *The Butterflies of the Eastern United States and Canada with Special Reference to New England.*

Although the following article about the famous zoologist and geologist Louis Agassiz was first published in 1874, the approach Agassiz took with Scudder and the lesson he imparted to him are as valid for us today as when Scudder first met his great teacher.

Learning to See

It was more than fifteen years ago that I entered the laboratory of Professor Agassiz, and told him I had enrolled my name in the Scientific School as a student of natural history. He asked me a few questions about my object in coming, my antecedents generally, the mode in which I afterwards proposed to use the knowledge I might acquire, and, finally, whether I wished to study any special branch. To the latter I replied that, while I wished to be well grounded in all departments of zoology, I purposed to devote myself specially to insects.

"When do you wish to begin?" he asked.

"Now," I replied.

This seemed to please him, and with an energetic "Very well!" he reached from the shelf a huge jar of specimens in yellow alcohol.

"Take this fish," he said, "and look at it; we call it a haemulon; by and by I will ask what you have seen."

With that he left me, but in a moment returned with explicit instructions as to the care of the object entrusted to me.

"No man is fit to be a naturalist," said he, "who does not know how to take care of specimens."

I was to keep the fish before me in a tin tray, and occasionally moisten the surface with alcohol from the jar, always taking care to replace the stopper tightly. Those were not the days of ground-glass stoppers and elegantly shaped exhibition jars; all the old students will recall the huge neckless glass bottles with their leaky, wax-besmeared corks, half eaten by insects, and begrimed with cellar dust. Entomology was a cleaner science than ichthyology, but the example of the Professor, who had unhesitatingly plunged to the bottom of the jar to produce the fish, was infectious; and though this alcohol had a "very ancient and fishlike smell," I really dared

323

not show any aversion within these sacred precincts, and treated the alcohol as though it were pure water. Still I was conscious of a passing feeling of disappointment, for gazing at a fish did not commend itself to an ardent entomologist. My friends at home, too, were annoyed when they discovered that no amount of eau-de-Cologne would drown the perfume which haunted me like a shadow.

In ten minutes I had seen all that could be seen in that fish, and ⁹ started in search of the Professor—who had, however, left the Museum; and when I returned, after lingering over some of the odd animals stored in the upper apartment, my specimen was dry all over. I dashed the fluid over the fish as if to resuscitate the beast from a fainting-fit, and looked with anxiety for a return of the normal sloppy appearance. This little excitement over, nothing was to be done but to return to a steadfast gaze at my mute companion. Half an hour passed—an hour—another hour; the fish began to look loathsome. I turned it over and around; looked it in the face—ghastly; from behind, beneath, above, sideways, at a three-quarters' view—just as ghastly. I was in despair; at an early hour I concluded that lunch was necessary; so, with infinite relief, the fish was carefully placed in the jar, and for an hour I was free.

On my return, I learned that Professor Agassiz had been at the ¹⁰ Museum, but had gone, and would not return for several hours. My fellow-students were too busy to be disturbed by continued conversation. Slowly I drew forth that hideous fish, and with a feeling of desperation again looked at it. I might not use a magnifying-glass; instruments of all kinds were interdicted. My two hands, my two eyes, and the fish; it seemed a most limited field. I pushed my finger down its throat to feel how sharp the teeth were. I began to count the scales in the different rows, until I was convinced that that was nonsense. At last a happy thought struck me—I would draw the fish; and now with surprise I began to discover new features in the creature. Just then the Professor returned.

"That is right," said he, "a pencil is one of the best eyes. I am glad to ¹¹ notice, too, that you keep your specimen wet, and your bottle corked."

With these encouraging words, he added: ¹²

"Well, what is it like?" ¹³

He listened attentively to my brief rehearsal of the structure of parts ¹⁴ whose names were still unknown to me: the fringed gill-arches and movable operculum; the pores of the head, fleshy lips and lidless eyes; the lateral line, the spinous fins and forked tail; the compressed and arched body. When I had finished, he waited as if expecting more, and then, with an air of disappointment:

"You have not looked very carefully; why," he continued more ear- ¹⁵ nestly, "you haven't even seen one of the most conspicuous features of the animal, which is as plainly before your eyes as the fish itself; look again, look again!" and he left me to my misery.

I was piqued; I was mortified. Still more of that wretched fish! But now I set myself to my task with a will, and discovered one new thing after another, until I saw how just the Professor's criticism had been. The afternoon passed quickly; and when, toward its close, the Professor inquired:

"Do you see it yet?"

"No," I replied, "I am certain I do not, but I see how little I saw before."

"That is the next best," said he, earnestly, "but I won't hear you now; put away your fish and go home; perhaps you will be ready with a better answer in the morning. I will examine you before you look at the fish."

This was disconcerting. Not only must I think of my fish all night, studying, without the object before me, what this unknown but most visible feature might be; but also, without reviewing my discoveries, I must give an exact account of them the next day. I had a bad memory; so I walked home by Charles River in a distracted state, with my two perplexities.

The cordial greeting from the Professor the next morning was reassuring; here was a man who seemed to be quite as anxious as I that I should see for myself what he saw.

"Do you perhaps mean," I asked, "that the fish has symmetrical sides with paired organs?"

His thoroughly pleased "Of course! Of course!" repaid the wakeful hours of the previous night. After he had discoursed most happily and enthusiastically—as he always did—upon the importance of this point, I ventured to ask what I should do next.

"Oh, look at your fish!" he said, and left me again to my own devices. In a little more than an hour he returned, and heard my new catalogue.

"That is good, that is good!" he repeated; "but that is not all; go on"; and so for three long days he placed that fish before my eyes, forbidding me to look at anything else, or to use any artificial aid. "Look, look, look," was his repeated injunction.

This was the best entomological lesson I ever had—a lesson whose influence has extended to the details of every subsequent study; a legacy the Professor has left me, as he has left it to many others, of inestimable value, which we could not buy, with which we cannot part.

A year afterward, some of us were amusing ourselves with chalking outlandish beasts on the Museum blackboard. We drew prancing starfishes; frogs in mortal combat; hydra-headed worms; stately crawfishes, standing on their tails, bearing aloft umbrellas; and grotesque fishes with gaping mouths and staring eyes. The Professor came in shortly after, and was as amused as any at our experiments. He looked at the fishes.

"Haemulons, every one of them," he said; "Mr.——— drew them."

True; and to this day, if I attempt a fish, I can draw nothing but haemulons.

The fourth day, a second fish of the same group was placed beside the 30
first, and I was bidden to point out the resemblances and differences
between the two; another and another followed, until the entire family lay
before me, and a whole legion of jars covered the table and surrounding
shelves; the odor had become a pleasant perfume; and even now, the sight
of an old, six-inch, worm-eaten cork brings fragrant memories.

The whole group of haemulons was thus brought in review; and, 31
whether engaged upon the dissection of the internal organs, the preparation
and examination of the bony framework, or the description of the various
parts, Agassiz's training in the method of observing facts and their orderly
arrangement was ever accompanied by the urgent exhortation not to be
content with them.

"Facts are stupid things," he would say, "until brought into connec- 32
tion with some general law."

At the end of eight months, it was almost with reluctance that I left 33
these friends and turned to insects; but what I had gained by this outside
experience has been of greater value than years of later investigation in my
favorite groups.

Questions for Study and Discussion

1. What important lesson does Scudder learn from his experience with
Professor Agassiz? Where is the lesson referred to in the essay?

2. Briefly describe Professor Agassiz's teaching technique or method.
What about his style made it effective with Scudder? Would it be as effective
today? Explain.

3. How much time did Scudder spend studying haemulons? Was it necessary to spend this amount of time? Could the process have been speeded up
with the use of lectures or textbooks? Explain.

4. How did Scudder happen to draw the fish? How did his drawing the
fish help him better to understand or know the fish? What does Agassiz mean
when he says "a pencil is one of the best of eyes?"

5. What in Scudder's diction indicates his attitude toward the experience? What in Scudder's style and diction show that this essay was written in
the nineteenth century and not the twentieth?

6. What did Agassiz mean when he said, "Facts are stupid things until
brought into connection with some general law"?

Writing Topics

1. Using Scudder's essay as a model, write about a teacher who had a
significant impact or influence on you and your education. What was there in
the way this particular teacher approached learning that has stayed with you?

2. Professor Agassiz's comment "a pencil is one of the best of eyes" has been echoed by many writers over the years. For example, Anne Morrow Lindbergh has said, "I think best with a pencil in my hand." What for you is the relationship between writing, thinking, and learning? Does your understanding of a subject increase when you write about it? Do you see relationships or connections that you didn't see when reading and talking about a subject?

3. In education, how important do you think it is to find good answers to other people's questions, and how important to learn to ask good questions yourself? Where has the emphasis been in your education so far? Can good question-asking be taught and learned? If so, how? If not, why not?

LANGSTON HUGHES

Born in Joplin, Missouri, Langston Hughes (1902–1967) wrote poetry, fiction, and drama and regularly contributed a column to the *New York Post*. An important figure in the Harlem Renaissance, he is best known for *Weary Blues*, *The Negro Mother*, *Shakespeare in Harlem*, and *Ask Your Mama*, volumes of poetry which reflect his racial pride, his familiarity with the traditions of African-Americans, and his knowledge of jazz rhythms. The speaker of "Theme for English B" is a student at Columbia University, where Hughes had enrolled for a year in 1921. The poem, athough quite short, embodies the two great themes of Hughes's work and indeed of the Harlem Renaissance: the celebration of African-American culture and the demand for equal treatment and respect.

Theme for English B

The instructor said,

> *Go home and write*
> *a page tonight:*
> *And let that page come out of you—*
> *Then, it will be true.*   5

I wonder if it's that simple?
I am twenty-two, colored, born in Winston-Salem.
I went to school there, then Durham, then here
to this college on the hill above Harlem.[1]
I am the only colored student in my class.   10

The steps from the hill lead down into Harlem,
through a park, then I cross St. Nicholas,
Eighth Avenue, Seventh, and I come to the Y,
the Harlem Branch Y, where I take the elevator
up to my room, sit down, and write this page: 15

It's not easy to know what is true for you or me
at twenty-two, my age. But I guess I'm what

---

[1]Refers to Columbia University, which is located next to Harlem.

I feel and see and hear, Harlem, I hear you:
hear you, hear me—we two—you, me, talk on this page.
(I hear New York, too.) Me—who?   20

Well, I like to eat, sleep, drink, and be in love.
I like to work, read, learn, and understand life.
I like a pipe for a Christmas present,
or records—Bessie,[2] bop, or Bach.
I guess being colored doesn't make me *not* like   25
the same things other folks like who are other races.
So will my page be colored that I write?
Being me, it will not be white.
But it will be
a part of you, instructor.   30
You are white—
yet a part of me, as I am a part of you.
That's American.
Sometimes perhaps you don't want to be a part of me.
Nor do I often want to be a part of you.   35
But we are, that's true!
As I learn from you,
I guess you learn from me—
although you're older—and white—
and somewhat more free.   40

This is my page for English B.

Questions for Study and Discussion

1. What does the instructor mean when he tells the student that the writing should "come out of you"? Why would it then be "true"?

2. Is the student in the poem Hughes himself? What in the poem led you to your conclusion?

3. What is the significance of the student's speaking of Columbia as "on the hill above Harlem"?

4. The student says that he is a part of his instructor and that his instructor is a part of him. What does he mean? Are we all part of each other? If so, in what way? If not, why not?

5. The student ends by saying, "This is my page for English B." Is the "page" what the instructor asked for or wanted? Why, or why not?

----

[2]Bessie Smith (1898?–1937), American blues singer, considered by many critics to be the greatest jazz singer of her time.

Writing Topics

1. The poem says, "As I learn from you, / I guess you learn from me." What do you think teachers learn from their students, if anything? What should they learn? Write an essay in which you describe what for you is the ideal student-teacher relationship.

2. What constitutes a good writing assignment? Compose one or two essay assignments for your class, keeping in mind the purpose of the course and other students' backgrounds and interests.

TONI CADE BAMBARA

Toni Cade Bambara was born in New York City in 1939. After graduating from Queens College and City College, she taught at Livingston College of Rutgers University, Duke, Atlanta University, and Spellman College in Atlanta. In addition she has been employed by the New York State Department of Welfare and has studied mime and dance. Barbara has edited *The Black Woman* (1970) and *Tales and Stories of Black Folks* (1971). She is also the author of two collections of stories, *Gorilla, My Love* (1972) and *The Seabirds Are Still Alive* (1977), and the novel *The Salt Eaters* (1980).

In "The Lesson," included in *Gorilla, My Love*, Bambara presents a day in the life of Sylvia, a welfare child. Although on the surface the story seems to be no more than an anecdote, there is an important lesson to be learned.

The Lesson

Back in the days when everyone was old and stupid or young and 1
foolish and me and Sugar were the only ones just right, this lady moved on
our block with nappy hair and proper speech and no makeup. And quite
naturally we laughed at her, laughed the way we did at the junk man who
went about his business like he was some big-time president and his sorry-
ass horse his secretary. And we kinda hated her too, hated the way we did
the winos who cluttered up our parks and pissed on our handball walls and
stank up our hallways and stairs so you couldn't halfway play hide-and-seek
without a goddamn gas mask. Miss Moore was her name. The only woman
on the block with no first name. And she was black as hell, cept for her feet,
which were fish-white and spooky. And she was always planning these
boring-ass things for us to do, us being my cousin, mostly, who lived on the
block cause we all moved North the same time and to the same apartment
then spread out gradual to breathe. And our parents would yank our heads
into some kinda shape and crisp up our clothes so we'd be presentable for
travel with Miss Moore, who always looked like she was going to church,
though she never did. Which is just one of things the grownups talked about
when they talked behind her back like a dog. But when she came calling
with some sachet she'd sewed up or some gingerbread she'd made or some
book, why then they'd all be too embarrassed to turn her down and we'd

get handed over all spruced up. She'd been to college and said it was only right that she should take responsibility for the young ones' education, and she not even related by marriage or blood. So they'd go for it. Specially Aunt Gretchen. She was the main gofer in the family. You got some ole dumb shit foolishness you want somebody to go for, you send for Aunt Gretchen. She been screwed into the go-along for so long, it's a blood-deep natural thing with her. Which is how she got saddled with me and Sugar and Junior in the first place while our mothers were in a la-de-da apartment up the block having a good ole time.

So this one day Miss Moore rounds us all up at the mailbox and it's puredee hot and she's knocking herself out about arithmetic. And school suppose to let up in summer I heard, but she don't never let up. And the starch in my pinafore scratching the shit outta me and I'm really hating this nappy-head bitch and her goddamn college degree. I'd much rather go to the pool or to the show where it's cool. So me and Sugar leaning on the mailbox being surly, which is a Miss Moore word. And Flyboy checking out what everybody brought for lunch. And Fat Butt already wasting his peanut-butter-and-jelly sandwich like the pig he is. And Junebug punchin on Q.T.'s arm for potato chips. And Rosie Giraffe shifting from one hip to the other waiting for somebody to step on her foot or ask her if she from Georgia so she can kick ass, preferably Mercedes'. And Miss Moore asking us do we know what money is, like we a bunch of retards. I mean real money, she say, like it's only poker chips or monopoly papers we lay on the grocer. So right away I'm tired of this and say so. And would much rather snatch Sugar and go to the Sunset and terrorize the West Indian kids and take their hair ribbons and their money too. And Miss Moore files that remark away for next week's lesson on brotherhood, I can tell. And finally I say we oughta get to the subway cause it's cooler and besides we might meet some cute boys. Sugar done swiped her mama's lipstick, so we ready.

So we heading down the street and she's boring us silly about what things cost and what our parents make and how much goes for rent and how money ain't divided up right in this country. And then she gets to the part about we all poor and live in the slums, which I don't feature. And I'm ready to speak on that, but she steps out in the street and hails two cabs just like that. Then she hustles half the crew in with her and hands me a five-dollar bill and tells me to calculate 10 percent tip for the driver. And we're off. Me and Sugar and Junebug and Flyboy hanging out the window and hollering to everybody, putting lipstick on each other cause Flyboy a faggot anyway, and making farts with our sweaty armpits. But I'm mostly trying to figure how to spend this money. But they all fascinated with the meter ticking and Junebug starts laying bets as to how much it'll read when Flyboy can't hold his breath no more. Then Sugar lay bets as to how much it'll be when we get there. So I'm stuck. Don't nobody want to go for my plan, which is to jump out at the next light and run off to the first bar-b-que we can find. Then the driver tells us to get the hell out cause we there already. And the meter reads eight-five cents. And I'm stalling to figure out the tip and Sugar say give him a dime. And I decide he don't need it bad as I do, so later for him. But then he tries to take off with Junebug's foot still in the door so we talk about his mama something ferocious. Then we check out that we on Fifth Avenue and everybody dressed up in stockings. One lady in a fur coat, hot as it is. White folks crazy.

"This is the place," Miss Moore say, presenting it to us in the voice she 4 uses at the museum. "Let's look in the windows before we go in."

"Can we steal?" Sugar asks very serious like she's getting the ground 5 rules squared away before she plays. "I beg your pardon," say Miss Moore, and we fall out. So she leads us around the windows of the toy store and me and Sugar screamin, "This is mine, that's mine, I gotta have that, that was made for me, I was born for that," till Big Butt drowns us out.

"Hey, I'm going to buy that there." 6

"That there? You don't even know what it is, stupid." 7

"I do so," he say punchin on Rosie Giraffe. "It's a microscope." 8

"Whatcha gonna do with a microscope, fool?" 9

"Look at things." 10

"Like what, Ronald?" ask Miss Moore. And Big Butt ain't got the first 11 notion. So here go Miss Moore gabbing about the thousands of bacteria in a drop of water and the somethinorother in a speck of blood and the million and one living things in the air around us is invisible to the naked eye. And what she say that for? Junebug go to town on that "naked" and we rolling. Then Miss Moore ask what it cost. So we all jam into the window smudgin it up and the price tag say $300. So then she ask how long'd take for Big Butt and Junebug to save up their allowances. "Too long," I say. "Yeh," adds Sugar, "outgrown it by that time." And Miss Moore say no, you never outgrow learning instruments. "Why, even medical students and interns and," blah, blah, blah. And we ready to choke Big Butt for bringing it up in the first damn place.

"This here costs four hundred eighty dollars," say Rosie Giraffe. So we 12 pile up all over her to see what she pointin out. My eyes tell me it's a chunk of glass cracked with something heavy, and different-color inks dripped into the splits. then the whole thing put into a oven or something. But for $480 it don't make sense.

"That's a paperweight made of semi-precious stones fused together 13 under tremendous pressure," she explains slowly, with her hands doing the mining and all the factory work.

"So what's a paperweight?" asks Rosie Giraffe. 14

"To weigh paper with, dumbbell," say Flyboy, the wise man from the 15 East.

"Not exactly," say Miss Moore, which is what she say when you warm 16 or way off too. "It's to weigh paper down so it won't scatter and make your desk untidy." So right away me and Sugar curtsy to each other and then to Mercedes who is more the tidy type.

"We don't keep paper on top of the desk in my class," say Junebug, 17 figuring Miss Moore crazy or lyin one.

"At home, then," she say. "Don't you have a calendar and a pencil 18 case and a blotter and a letter-opener on your desk at home where you do your homework?" And she know damn well what our homes look like cause she nosys around in them every chance she gets.

"I don't even have a desk," say Junebug. "Do we?" 19

"No. And I don't get no homework neither," says Big Butt. 20

"And I don't even have a home," say Flyboy like he do at school to 21 keep the white folks off his back and sorry for him. Send this poor kid to camp posters, is his specialty.

"I do," says Mercedes. "I have a box of stationery on my desk and a 22 picture of my cat. My godmother bought the stationery and the desk. There's a big rose on each sheet and the envelopes smell like roses."

"Who wants to know about your smelly-ass stationery," say Rosie 23 Giraffe fore I can get my two cents in.

"It's important to have a work area all your own so that. . . ." 24

"Will you look at this sailboat, please," say Flyboy, cuttin her off and 25 pointin to the thing like it was his. So once again we tumble all over each other to gaze at this magnificent thing in the toy store which is just big enough to maybe sail two kittens across the pond if you strap them to the posts tight. We all start reciting the price tag like we in assembly. "Hand-crafted sailboat of fiberglass at one thousand one hundred ninety-five dollars."

"Unbelievable," I hear myself say and am really stunned. I read it 26 again for myself just in case the group recitation put me in a trance. Same thing. For some reason this pisses me off. We look at Miss Moore and she lookin at us, waiting for I dunno what.

"Who'd pay all that when you can buy a sailboat set for a quarter at 27 Pop's, a tube of glue for a dime, and a ball of string for eight cents? It must have a motor and a whole lot else besides," I say. "My sailboat cost me about fifty cents."

"But will it take water?" say Mercedes with her smart ass. 28

"Took mine to Alley Pond Park once," say Flyboy. "String broke. Lost 29 it. Pity."

"Sailed mine in Central Park and it keeled over and sank. Had to ask 30 my father for another dollar."

"And you got the strap," laugh Big Butt. "The jerk didn't even have a 31 string on it. My old man wailed on his behind."

Little Q.T. was staring hard at the sailboat and you could see he 32 wanted it bad. But he too little and somebody'd just take it from him. So what the hell. "This boat for kids, Miss Moore?"

"Parents silly to buy something like that just to get all broke up," say 33
Rosie Giraffe.

"That much money it should last forever," I figure. 34

"My father'd buy it for me if I wanted it." 35

"Your father, my ass," say Rosie Giraffe getting a chance to finally 36
push Mercedes.

"Must be rich people shop here," say Q.T. 37

"You are a very bright boy," say Flyboy. "What was your first clue?" 38
and he rap him on the head with the back of his knuckles, since Q.T. the
only one he could get away with. Though Q.T. liable to come up behind you
years later and get his licks in when you half expect it.

"What I want to know is," I says to Miss Moore though I never talk to 39
her, I wouldn't give the bitch that satisfaction, "is how much a real boat
costs? I figure a thousand'd get you a yacht any day."

"Why don't you check that out," she says, "and report back to the 40
group?" Which really pains my ass. If you gonna mess up a perfectly good
swim day least you could do is have some answers. "Let's go in," she say like
she got something up her sleeve. Only she don't lead the way. So me and
Sugar turn the corner to where the entrance is, but when we get there I
kinda hang back. Not that I'm scared, what's there to be afraid of, just a toy
store. But I feel funny, shame. But what I got to be shamed about? Got as
much right to go in as anybody. But somehow I can't seem to get hold of the
door, so I step away for Sugar to lead. But she hangs back too. And I look at
her and she looks at me and this is ridiculous. I mean, damn, I have never
ever been shy about doing nothing or going nowhere. But then Mercedes
steps up and then Rosie Giraffe and Big Butt crowd in behind and shove,
and next thing we all stuffed into the doorway with only Mercedes squeezing past us, smoothing out her jumper and walking right down the aisle.
Then the rest of us tumble in like a glued-together jigsaw done all wrong.
And people looking at us. And it's like the time me and Sugar crashed into
the Catholic church on a dare. But once we got in there and everything so
hushed and holy and the candles and the bowin and the handkerchiefs on
all the drooping heads, I just couldn't go through with the plan. Which was
for me to run up to the altar and do a tap dance while Sugar played the nose
flute and messed around in the holy water. And Sugar kept givin me the
elbow. Then later teased me so bad I tied her up in the shower and turned it
on and locked her in. And she'd be there till this day if Aunt Gretchen
hadn't finally figured I was lyin about the boarder takin a shower.

Same thing in the store. We all walkin on tiptoe and hardly touchin 41
the games and puzzles and things. And I watched Miss Moore who is steady
watchin us like she waiting for a sign. Like Mama Drewery watches the sky
and sniffs the air and takes note of just how much slant is in the bird
formation. Then me and Sugar bump smack into each other, so busy gazing
at the toys, 'specially the sailboat. But we don't laugh and go into our

fat-lady bump-stomach routine. We just stare at the price tag. Then Sugar ran a finger over the whole boat. And I'm jealous and want to hit her. Maybe not her, but I sure want to punch somebody in the mouth.

"Whatcha bring us here for, Miss Moore?"   42

"You sound angry, Sylvia. Are you mad about something?" Givin me   43
one of them grins like she tellin a grown-up joke that never turns out to be funny. And she's lookin very closely at me like maybe she plannin to do my portrait from memory. I'm mad, but I won't give her that satisfaction. So I slouch around the store bein very bored and say, "Let's go."

Me an Sugar at the back of the train watchin the tracks whizzin by   44
large then small then gettin gobbled up in the dark. I'm thinking about this tricky toy I saw in the store. A clown that somersaults on a bar then does chin-ups just cause you yank lightly at his leg. Cost $35. I could see me askin my mother for a $35 birthday clown. "You wanna who that costs what?" she'd say, cocking her head to the side to get a better view of the hole in my head. Thirty-five dollars and the whole household could go visit Granddaddy Nelson in the country. Thirty-five dollars would pay for the rent and the piano bill too. Who are these people that spend that much for performing clowns and $1000 for toy sailboats? What kinda work they do and how they live and how come we ain't in on it? Where we are is who we are, Miss Moore always pointin out. But it don't necessarily have to be that way, she always adds then waits for somebody to say that poor people have to wake up and demand their share of the pie and don't none of us know what kind of pie she talkin about in the first damn place. But she ain't so smart cause I still got her four dollars from the taxi and she sure ain't getting it. Messin up my day with this shit. Sugar nudges me in my pocket and winks.

Miss Moore lines us up in front of the mailbox where we started from,   45
seem like years ago, and I got a headache for thinkin so hard. And we lean all over each other so we can hold up under the draggy-ass lecture she always finishes us off with at the end before we thank her for borin us to tears. But she just looks at us like she readin tea leaves. Finally she say, "Well, what did you think of F.A.O. Schwartz?"

Rosie Giraffe mumbles, "White folks crazy."   46

"I'd like to go there again when I get my birthday money," says   47
Mercedes, and we shove her out the pack so she has to lean on the mailbox by herself.

"I'd like a shower. Tiring day," says Flyboy.   48

Then Sugar surprises me by sayin, "You know, Miss Moore, I don't   49
think all of us here put together eat in a year what that sailboat costs." And Miss Moore lights up like somebody goosed her. "And?" she say, urging Sugar on. Only I'm standin on her foot so she don't continue.

"Imagine for a minute what kind of society it is in which some people   50
can spend on a toy what it would cost to feed a family of six or seven. What do you think?"

"I think," say Sugar pushing me off her feet like she never done before, cause I whip her ass in a minute, "that this is not much of a democracy if you ask me. Equal chance to pursue happiness means an equal crack at the dough, don't it?" Miss Moore is besides herself and I am disgusted with Sugar's treachery. So I stand on her foot one more time to see if she'll shove me. She shuts up, and Miss Moore looks at me, sorrowfully I'm thinkin. And somethin weird is goin on. I can feel it in my chest. 51

"Anybody else learn anything today?" lookin dead at me. I walk away and Sugar has to run to catch up and don't even seem to notice when I shrug her arm off my shoulder. 52

"Well, we got four dollars anyway," she says. 53

"Uh hunh." 54

"We could go to Hascombs and get half a chocolate layer and then to the Sunset and still have plenty money for potato chips and ice cream sodas." 55

"Uh hunh." 56

"Race you to Hascombs," she say. 57

We start down the block and she gets ahead which is O.K. by me cause I'm going to the West End and then over to the Drive to think this day through. She can run if she want to and even run faster. But ain't nobody gonna beat me at nuthin. 58

Questions for Study and Discussion

1. In paragraph 1, Bambara says, "and quite naturally we laughed" at Miss Moore. Why do you think they laughed? Why does she state it as if she were saying, "Of course we laughed"?

2. While the other children admire the sailboat and discuss the price, Sylvia mutters that she is "pissed off." What makes her so mad?

3. Using examples of Bambara's diction to support your answer, choose a single word to describe her attitude toward Miss Moore.

4. What is the significance of Bambara's title? Would another title have been better? Why or why not?

5. What is the significance of the last paragraph? Why do you think the author chose this way to conclude her story?

Writing Topics

1. In an essay, describe something important you learned during an ordinary day or from the words of a friend.

2. Write a narrative essay that best presents you and your life-style. Although a moral should be implied, it need not be stated. Be sure to use characteristic diction and activities.

Campus Issues
of the 1990s

BRUCE WEBER

Born in 1953, Bruce Weber is an editor of *The New York Times Magazine* and is the author of many magazine and newspaper articles on writers, sports personalities, and contemporary social life. In 1986 he edited *Look Who's Talking: An Anthology of Modern American Short Stories*.

In "The Unromantic Generation," which appeared in the April 5, 1987, issue of *The New York Times Magazine*, Weber discusses the ways in which logic has triumphed over passion in modern times.

The Unromantic Generation

Here is a contemporary love story. 1

Twenty-four-year-old Clark Wolfsberger, a native of St. Louis, and 2 Kim Wright, twenty-five, who is from Chicago, live in Dallas. They've been going together since they met as students at Southern Methodist University three years ago. They are an attractive pair, trim and athletic, she dark and lissome, he broad-shouldered and square-jawed. They have jobs they took immediately after graduating—Clark works at Talent Sports International, a sports marketing and management company; Kim is an assistant account executive at Tracy-Locke, a large advertising agency— and they are in love.

"We're very compatible," she says. 3

"We don't need much time together to confirm our relationship," he 4 says.

When they speak about the future, they hit the two-career family 5 notes that are conventional now in the generations ahead of them. "At thirty, I'll probably be married and planning a family," says Kim. "I'll stay in advertising. I'll be a late parent."

"By thirty, I'll definitely be married; either that or water-skiing naked 6
in Monaco," Clark says and laughs. "No. I'll be married. Well-established in my line of work. Have the home, have the dog. Maybe not a kid yet, but eventually. I'm definitely in favor of kids."

In the month I spent last winter visiting several cities around the 7
country, interviewing recent college graduates about marriage, relationships, modern romance I heard a lot of this, life equations already written, doubt banished. I undertook the trip because of the impression so many of us have; that in one wavelike rush to business school and Wall Street, young Americans have succumbed to a culture of immediate gratification and gone deep-down elitist on us. I set out to test the image with an informal survey meant to take the emotional temperature of a generation, not far behind my own, that *seems* so cynical, so full of such "material" girls and boys.

The sixty or so people I interviewed, between the ages of twenty-two 8
and twenty-six, were a diverse group. They spoke in distinct voices, testifying to a range of political and social views. Graduate students, lawyers, teachers, entertainers, business people, they are pursuing a variety of interests. What they have in common is that they graduated from college, are living in or around an urban center, and are heterosexual, mirrors of myself when I graduated from college in 1975. And yet as I moved from place to place, beginning with acquaintances of my friends and then randomly pursuing an expanding network of names and phone numbers, another quality emerged to the degree that I'd call it characteristic: they are planners. It was the one thing that surprised me, this looking ahead with certainty. They have priorities. I'd ask about love, they'd give me a graph.

This isn't how I remember it. Twelve years ago, who knew? I was three 9
years away from my first full-time paycheck, six from anything resembling the job I have now. It was all sort of desultory and hopeful, a time of dabbling and waiting around for some event that would sprout a future. Frankly, I had it in mind that meeting a woman would do it.

My cultural prototype was Benjamin Braddock, the character played 10
by Dustin Hoffman in Mike Nichol's 1967 film *The Graduate*, who, returning home after his college triumphs, finds the prospect of life after campus daunting in the extreme, and so plunges into inertia. His refrain "I'm just a little worried about my future," served me nicely as a sort of wryly understated mantra.

What hauls Benjamin from his torpor is love. Wisely or not, he 11
responds to a force beyond logic and turns the world upside down for Elaine Robinson. And though in the end their future together is undetermined, the message of the movie is that love is meant to triumph, that its passion

and promise, however naïve, are its strength, and that if we are lucky it will seize us and transform our lives.

Today I'm still single and, chastened by that, I suppose, a little more rational about what to expect from love. Setting out on my trip, I felt as if I'd be plumbing a little of my past. But the people I spoke with reminded me more of the way I am now than the way I was then. I returned thinking that young people are older than they used to be, *The Graduate* is out of date, and for young people just out of college today, the belief that love is all you need no longer obtains.   12

"Kim's a great girl; I love her," Clark Wolfsberger says. "But she's very career-oriented. I am, too, and with our schedules the way they are, we haven't put any restrictions on each other. I think that's healthy."   13

"He might want to go back to St. Louis," Kim Wright says. "I want to go back to Chicago. If it works out, great. If not, that's fine, too. I can handle it either way."   14

They are not heartless, soulless, cold, or unimaginative. They *are* self-preoccupied, but that's a quality, it seems to me, for which youthful generations have always been known. What distinguishes this generation from mine, I think, is that they're aware of it. News-conscious, media-smart, they are sophisticated in a way I was not.   15

They have come of age, of course, at a time when American social traditions barely survive. Since 1975, there have been more than a million divorces annually, and it is well publicized that nearly half of all marriages now end in divorce. Yet the era of condoned casual promiscuity and sexual experimentation—itself once an undermining of the nation's social fabric—now seems to be drawing to a close with the ever-spreading plague of sexually transmitted disease.   16

The achievements of feminist activism—particularly the infusion of women into the work force—have altered the expectations that the sexes have for each other and themselves.   17

And finally, the new college graduates have been weaned on scarifying forecasts of economic gloom. They feel housing problems already; according to *American Demographics* magazine, the proportion of young people living at home with their parents was higher in 1985 than in the last three censuses. They're aware, too, of predictions that however affluent they are themselves, they're probably better off than their children will be.   18

With all this in mind, today's graduates seem keenly aware that the future is bereft of conventional expectations, that what's ahead is more chaotic than mysterious. I've come to think it ironic that in a youth-minded culture such as ours, one that ostensibly grants greater freedom of choice to young people than it ever has before, those I spoke with seem largely restrained. Concerned with, if not consumed by, narrowing the options   19 down, getting on track, they are aiming already at a distant comfort and security. I spoke, on my travels, with several college counselors and administrators, and they concur that the immediate concerns of today's graduates are more practical than those of their predecessors. "I talk to them about sex," says Gail Short Hanson, dean of students at George Washington University in Washington. "I talk about careers. And marriage, with women, because of the balancing act they have to perform these days. But love? I can't remember the last conversation I had about love."

Career-minded, fiercely self-reliant, they responded to me, a single   20
man with a good job, with an odd combination of comradeliness and respect. When the interviews were over, I fielded a lot of questions about what it's like to work at *The New York Times.* How did I get my job? Occasionally, someone would ask about my love life. Considering the subject of our discussions, I was surprised it happened so rarely. When it did, I told them I'd come reasonably close to marriage once, but it didn't work out. Nobody asked me why. Nobody asked if I was lonely.

Micah Materre, twenty-five, recently completed an internship at CBS   21
News in Chicago and is looking for a job in broadcast journalism. Like many of the young people I talked to, she is farsighted in her romantic outlook: "I went out with a guy last fall. He had a good job as a stockbroker. He was nice to me. But then he started telling me about his family. And there were problems. I thought, 'What happens if I fall in love and we get married? What then?' "

It may be a memory lapse, but I don't recall thinking about marriage   22
much at all until I fell in love. I was twenty-nine; late, that's agreed. But the point is that for me (and for my generation as a whole, I believe, though you hate to make a statement like that), marriage loomed only as an outgrowth of happenstance; you met a person. Todays graduates, however, seem uneasy with that kind of serendipity. All of the married couples I spoke with are delighted to be married, but they do say their friends questioned their judgment. "I heard a lot of reasons why I shouldn't do it," one recent bride told me. "Finally, I just said to myself, 'I feel happier than I've ever felt. Why should I give this up just because I'm young?' "

Most of them too young to remember the assassination of *either*   23
Kennedy, they are old enough to have romantic pasts, to have experienced the trauma of failure in love. What surprised me was how easily so many of them accepted it; it seems a little early to be resigned to the idea that things fall apart. In each interview, I asked about past involvements. Were you ever serious about anyone? Any marital close calls? And virtually everyone had a story. But I heard very little about heartbreak or lingering grief. Instead, with an almost uniform equanimity, they spoke of maturity gained, lessons learned. It isn't disillusionment exactly, and they *are* too young to be weary; rather, it sounds like determination.

Twenty-five-year-old Peter Mundy of San Francisco, for example, says   24
that until six months ago he'd had a series of steady girlfriends. "I'm down
on romance," he says. "There's too much pain, too much pressure. There
are so many variables, and you can't tell until you're in the middle of it
whether it'll be positive. It's only in retrospect that you can see how things
went wrong. In the meantime, you end up neglecting other things."

The prevalent notion is that chemistry is untrustworthy; partners   25
need to be up to snuff according to pretty rigorous standards. Ellen Lubin,
twenty-six, of Los Angeles, for example, has just gotten engaged to the man
she has been living with for two years. When she met him, she says: "I
wasn't that attracted to him right away. But there were things about him
that made me say, 'This is what I want in a man.' He's bright. He's a go-
getter. He was making tons of money at the age of twenty-five. He's well-
connected. He was like my mentor in coming to deal with life in the city."

At the end of *The Graduate*, Benjamin Braddock kidnaps his lady love   26
at the altar, an instant after she has sealed her vows to someone else, and
they manage to make their escape because Benjamin bolts the church door
from the outside with a cross. That was the 1960s, vehement times. When I
graduated, we were less obstreperous. Sacraments you could take or leave.
And marriage wasn't much of an issue. If we put it off, it wasn't for the sake
of symbolism so much as that it didn't seem necessary. In the last few years,
I have been to a number of weddings among my contemporaries, people in
their thirties, and that impression of us is still with me. What we did was
drift toward marriage, arriving at it eventually, and with some surprise.
Some of us are still drifting.

Today's graduates have forged a new attitude entirely. In spite of the   27
high divorce rate, many of those I spoke with have marriage in mind.
Overwhelmingly, they see it as not only desirable, but inevitable. Because of
the odds, they approach it with wariness and pragmatism. More cautious
than their parents (for American men in 1985, the median age at the time
of their first marriage was 25.5, the highest since the turn of the century; it
was 23.3 for women, a record), they are methodical in comparison with me.

Perhaps that explains why I find the way they speak about marriage so   28
unromantic. Men and women tend to couch their views in different terms,
but they seem to share the perception that marriage is necessarily restrict-
ing. Nonetheless they trust in its rewards, whatever they are. Overall, it
doesn't represent the kind of commitment that seems viable without adequate preparation.

"I've been dating someone for a year and a half," says Tom Grossman,   29
a twenty-four-year-old graduate of the University of Texas. "We don't talk
about marriage, and frankly I don't think it'll occur." Currently area sales
manager in San Antonio for the John H. Harland Company, a check-
printing concern, Grossman says he has professional success in mind first.
"I want to be really well-off financially, and I don't want that struggle to

interfere with the marriage. There are too many other stress factors involved. I want to be able to enjoy myself right away. And I never want to look back and think that if I hadn't gotten married, I could have accomplished more."

Many young women say they responded with some alarm to last year's   30
Newsweek report on the controversial demographic study conducted at Harvard, which concluded that once past thirty, a woman faces rapidly dwindling chances of marrying. At a time when women graduates often feel it incumbent on them to pursue careers, they worry that the possibility of "having it all" is, in fact, remote.

Janie Russell, twenty-five, graduated from the University of North   31
Carolina in 1983, left a serious boyfriend behind, and moved to Los Angeles to pursue a career in the film industry. Working now as a director of production services of New Visions Inc., like many other young women she believes the independence fostered by a career is necessary, not only for her own self-esteem but as a foundation for a future partnership. "I look forward to marriage," she says. "But this is a very selfish time for me. I have to have my career. I have to say to myself, 'I did this on my own.' It makes me feel more interesting than I would otherwise. Of course, what may happen is that I'll look up one day and say, 'O.K., husband, where are you?' and he won't be there."

About halfway through my trip I stopped interviewing married cou-   32
ples because they tended to say similar things. They consider themselves the lucky ones. As twenty-four-year-old Adam Cooper put it, at dinner with his wife, Melanee, also twenty-four, in their Chicago apartment: "The grass is not greener on the other side."

I came away thinking it is as true as ever: all happy families are the   33
same. But the couples I spoke with seemed to me part of a generation other than their own, older even than mine. Calling the Coopers to arrange an interview, I was invited for "a good, home-cooked meal."

The next day, I met Micah Materre, who expressed the prevailing   34
contemporary stance as well as anyone. Outgoing and self-possessed, she gave me a long list of qualities she's looking for in a man: good looks, sense of humor, old-fashioned values, but also professional success, financial promise, and a solid family background. "Why not?" she said. "I deserve the best." But as I was folding up my notebook, she added a plaintive note: "I'll get married, won't I? It's the American way, right?"

Very early on in my sexual experience I was flattered by a woman who   35
told me she ordinarily wouldn't go to bed with men who were under twenty-six. "Until then," she said, "all they're doing when they're with you is congratulating themselves." For whatever reason, she never returned my calls after that night. Not an untypical encounter, all in all. Congratulations to both of us.

We were a lusty, if callow, bunch, not least because we thought we   36
could afford to be. Encouraged by the expansive social mores spawned by
the sexual revolution, fortified by the advent of a widespread availability of
birth control and fundamentally unaware of germs, we interpreted sex, for
our convenience, as pure pleasure shared by "consenting parties." If it feels
good, do it. Remember that?

It is an attitude that the current generation inherited and put into   37
practice at an early age. Asked about her circle of friends in Los Angeles,
Lesley Bracker, twenty-three, puts it nonchalantly: "Oh, yeah, we were all
sexually active as teen-agers. When we were younger, it was considered O.K.
to sleep around."

Now, however, they are reconsidering. In general, on this topic, I   38
found them shy. They hesitate to speak openly about their sex lives, are
prone to euphemism ("I'm not exactly out there, you know, mingling"), and
say they worry about promiscuity only because they have friends who still
practice it. According to Laura Kavesh and Cheryl Lavin, who write a
column about single life, "Tales from the Front," for the *Chicago Tribune*
that is syndicated in some sixty other papers around the country, a letter
from a reader about the virtues of virginity generated more supportive mail
than anything that has appeared in the column in its two years of existence.
I'm not about to say there's a new celibacy among the young, but my
impression is that even if they're having twice as much sex as they say
they're having, it's not as much as you would think.

The AIDS scare, of course, is of primary relevance. "I talk about AIDS   39
on first dates," says Jill Rotenberg, twenty-five, publishing manager of a
rare-book company in San Francisco. "I talk about it all the time. I've
spoken with the guy I'm dating about taking an AIDS test. Neither one of
us is thrilled about condoms. But we use them. The first time we had sex, I
was the one who had one in my wallet."

Not everyone is so vehement. But seriously or jokingly, in earnest tête-à-   40
tête or idly at dinner parties, they all talk about it. To some, the new concern
is merely a source of disappointment. Several of the young people I spoke with
express the sense of having been robbed. It's tough to find sex when you want
it, tougher than it used to be, is the lament of many, mostly men. As it was put
to me at one point, "I wish I'd been born ten years earlier."

Jill Rotenberg says she feels betrayed: "I've had one long relationship   41
in my life. He was my first lover, and for a long time my only one. So I feel
I've had an untainted past. Now I feel I'm being punished anyway, even
though I've been a good girl."

"I feel like I'm over the hurdle," says Douglas Ertman, twenty-two, of   42
San Francisco, who got engaged last summer. "I'm really lucky to know that
I'll have one sexual partner forever."

Most agree that the solution is monogamy, at least on a temporary   43
basis. "It's a coupled-up society," says Alan Forman, twenty-six, a law

student of George Washington University who, for the last several months, has been in a monogamous relationship. "Now more than ever. A lot of people I know are feeling the pressure to get hooked up with somebody."

I ask Forman and his girlfriend, twenty-four-year-old Debra Golden, 44 about their future together. They say they don't know ("I'm too insecure to make a decision like that," she says), and I get the sense they never talk about it. Then she turns to him, genuinely curious. "Say you break up with me and go to New York next year," she says.

"I don't know," he says. "If I met someone and I like her, what do I 45 have to do, ask her to take a blood test?"

A decade ago, one of the privileges that my contemporaries and I 46 inferred from our sexual freedom was more or less to deny that there might be, in the sexual act, any innately implied emotional exchange. It's no longer feasible, however, to explain away sex as frivolity, inconsequential gratification. And that has complicated things for all of us, of course, whatever age, single or not.

But for young people, it's an issue, like marriage, that has been raised 47 early: what does sex mean, if it doesn't mean nothing?

It's clearly a struggle for them. In one of my first interviews, twenty- 48 five-year-old Karl Wright of Chicago told me: "Maybe there's a silver lining in all this. Maybe AIDS will bring back romance." The more I think about that, the more chilling it gets.

Beverly Caro, a twenty-five-year-old associate in the Dallas law firm of 49 Gardere & Wynne, graduated from Drake University, in Des Moines, in 1983, and attended law school there as well. Her office high above the street looks out on the city's jungle of futuristic skyscrapers. She had offers from firms in Denver and her hometown of Kansas City, Mo., she says, but chose to come to Dallas because, "I see upward mobility here; that's what I was looking for."

Ms. Caro has an attractive, thoughtful manner and a soft voice, but 50 like many of her contemporaries, given the chance to discuss her personal goals, she speaks with a certitude that borders on defiance. Currently, she sees two men "somewhat regularly," she says. "I'd like to have a companion. A friend, I guess. But finding a man is not a top priority. I want to travel. I want to establish myself in the community. I don't see any drastic changes in my life by the time I turn thirty. Except that I'll be a property owner."

During my interviews, the theme of getting on track and staying there 51 surfaced again and again. I came to think of it as the currency of self-definition. As a generation, they are not a particularly well-polled group, but certain figures bear out my impression.

According to annual surveys of 300,000 college freshmen conducted 52 by the Higher Education Research Institute at the Graduate School of Education of the University of California at Los Angeles, young people today, by the time they *enter* college, are more inclined to express concrete life objectives than they've been for many years. Of those surveyed last fall, 73.2 percent cited being "very well off financially" as an essential or very important objective. That's up from 63.3 percent in 1980, 49.5 percent in 1975. Other objectives that the survey shows have risen in importance include "obtain recognition from colleagues for contributions to my special field"; "have administrative responsibility for the work of others"; "be successful in my own business"; and "raise a family." At the same time, the percentage of freshmen who consider it important to "develop a meaningful philosophy of life" has declined from 64.2 percent in 1975 to 40.6 percent last year.

Many of the people I spoke to feel the pressure of peer scrutiny. A 53 status thing has evolved, to which many seem to have regretfully succumbed. Several expressed a weariness with meeting someone new and having to present themselves by their credentials. Yet, overwhelmingly, asked what they're looking for in a romantic partner, they responded first with phrases such as "an educated professional" and "someone with direction." They've conceded, more or less consciously, that unenlightened and exclusionary as it is, it's very uncool not to know what you want and not to be already chasing it.

"Seems like everyone in our generation has to be out there achieving," 54 says Scott Birnbaum, twenty-five, who is the chief accountant for TIC United Corp., a holding company in Dallas.

Birnbaum graduated from the University of Texas in 1984, where, he 55 says, "For me, the whole career-oriented thing kicked in." A native Texan with a broad drawl, he lives in the Greenville section of the city, an area populated largely by young singles. His apartment is comfortably roomy, not terribly well appointed. He shakes his head amiably as he points to the television set propped on a beer cooler. "What do I need furniture for?" he says. "Most of my time is taken up going to work."

Confident in himself professionally, Birnbaum was one of very few 56 interviewees who spoke frankly about the personal cost of career success. Many speculated that they'll be worried if, in their thirties, they haven't begun to settle their love lives; this was more true of women than men. But Birnbaum confesses a desire to marry now. "It's kind of lonely being single," he says. "I'd hate to find myself successful at thirty without a family. Maybe once I'm married and have children, that might make being successful career-wise less important."

The problem, he goes on, is the collective outlook he's part and parcel 57 of. "Here's how we think," he says. "Get to this point, move on. Get to that point, move on. Acquire, acquire. Career, career. We're all afraid to slow down for fear of missing out on something. That extends to your social life as well. You go out on a date and you're thinking, 'Hell, is there someone better for me?' I know how terrible that sounds but it seems to be my problem. Most of my peers are in the same position. Men and women. I tell you, it's tough out there right now."

When I returned to New York, I called Alex de Gramont, whom I'd   58
been saving to interview last. I've known Alex for a long time, since he was a gawky and curious high school student and I was his teacher. Handsome now, gentle-looking, he's a literary sort, prone to attractive gloom and a certain lack of perspective. He once told me that his paradigm of a romantic, his role model, was Heathcliff, the mad, doomed passion-monger from Emily Brontë's *Wuthering Heights*.[1]

A year out of Wesleyan University in Middletown, Conn., Alex has   59
reasons to be hopeful. His book-length senior thesis about Albert Camus[2] has been accepted for publication, and on the strength of it, he has applied to four graduate programs in comparative literature. But he's unenthusiastic, and he has applied to law schools, too. In the meantime, he is living with his parents in New Jersey.

He tells me that last summer he went to West Germany in pursuit of a   60
woman he'd met when he was in college. He expected to live there with her, but he was back in this country in a couple of weeks. "Camus has a line," Alex says, "'Love can burn or love can last. It can't do both.'" Like Benjamin Braddock, Alex is a little worried about his future.

Dustin Hoffman is forty-nine. I'm thirty-three. Both of us are doing   61
pretty well. Alex, at twenty-three, confesses to considerable unease. "Every minute I'm not accomplishing something, I feel is wasted," he says, sort of miserably. "I feel a lot of pressure to decide what to do with my life. I'm a romantic, but these are very unromantic times."

Questions for Study and Discussion

1. Why did Weber conduct his survey? What did he expect to find? What did he find that surprised him?
2. How would you characterize Weber's attitude toward contemporary young adults? Is it neutral, angry, supportive, or something else? Cite examples of his diction and phrasing to support your answer.
3. What kinds of people comprised Weber's survey group? How were they different? What did they have in common? Do you think they were representative enough? Why or why not?

---

[1]Emily Brontë (1818–1848) wrote *Wuthering Heights*, one of the most famous English novels, in 1847.

[2]French philosopher, dramatist, and novelist (1913–1960), who won the Nobel Prize for literature in 1957.

4. What qualities do modern young people look for in a relationship? What qualities inherent in old-fashioned romance make it unattractive to the modern generation? Where are these objections best stated?

5. What are some of the reasons Weber offers for the shift in romantic priorities? Can you think of any others?

6. In paragraphs 9–11, Weber explains the nature of romance in his day. Does he ever conclude that his way might have been better than the modern way? What are the advantages and disadvantages of the new way and the old way?

7. Weber waits until paragraph 28 to mention romance. How does he define it? Why do you think he waits so long to use the word?

8. In paragraph 48, Weber responds to the idea that the fear of AIDS may "bring back romance," by saying, "The more I think about that, the more chilling it gets." What does he mean by this remark? Do you agree or disagree?

Writing Topics

1. According to Weber, young people have become less romantic as material goals have taken precedence in their lives. Yet Weber quotes a source who predicts that the AIDS epidemic will bring back romance. Among your contemporaries, which factors in Weber's article seem to have the most influence on romantic style? How has the fear of AIDS and other sexually transmitted diseases affected relationships? What role does ambition play in modern romance? Do you and your friends "plan" your future to the extent that Weber suggests? What factors, other than the ones Weber discusses, do you see working to make relationships either more or less romantic?

2. The notion of "romantic love" is relatively new in western culture. Do some research to find out when it first became the standard. How were love and marriage viewed before that time? What kinds of relationships can you envision for the future? Can you imagine a relationship unlike either the "romantic" love Weber remembers or the "planned" relationship he finds in the present?

ELLEN SWEET

Born in 1942, Ellen Sweet was an editorial consultant for the book *I Never Call It Rape* (1988). While a senior editor at *Ms.* magazine, Sweet directed the *Ms.* magazine Campus Project on Sexual Assault. She is currently the managing editor of *New Choices* magazine.

In the following essay, first printed in *Ms.* in October 1985, Sweet proposes ways to prevent rape while making the reader aware that date or acquaintance rape is a much greater problem than society thinks it is.

Date Rape: The Story of an Epidemic and Those Who Deny It

It was the beginning of spring break when I was a junior. I was in good spirits and had been out to dinner with an old friend. We returned to his college [dorm]. There were some seniors on the ground floor, drinking beer, playing bridge. I'm an avid player, so we joined them, joked around a lot. One of them, John, wasn't playing, but he was interested in the game. I found him attractive. We talked, and it turned out we had a mutual friend, shared experiences. It was getting late, and my friend had gone up to bed, so John offered to see me safely home. We took our time, sat outside talking for a while. Then he said we could get inside one of the most beautiful campus buildings, which was usually locked at night. I went with him. Once we were inside, he kissed me. I didn't resist. I was excited. He kissed me again. But when he tried for more, I said no. He just grew completely silent. I couldn't get him to talk to me any more. He pinned me down and ripped off my pants. *I couldn't believe it was happening to me . . .*

Let's call this Yale graduate Judy. Her experience and her disbelief, as she describes them, are not unique. Gretchen, another student victim of date rape (or acquaintance rape, as it is also called), had known for five years the man who invited her to an isolated vacation cabin and then raped her. "I considered him my best friend," she says on a Stanford University videotape used in discussions of the problem. "I couldn't believe it. *I couldn't believe it was actually happening to me.*"

Such denial, the inability to believe that someone they know could have raped them, is a common reaction of victims of date rape, say psychologists and counselors who have researched the topic and treated these women. In fact, so much silence surrounds this kind of crime that many women are not even aware that they have been raped. In one study, Mary P. Koss, a psychology professor at Kent State University, Ohio, asked female students if they had had sexual intercourse against their will through use of or threat of force (the minimal legal definition of rape). Of those who answered yes, only 57 percent went on to identify their experience as rape. Koss also identified the other group (43 percent) as those who hadn't even acknowledged the rape to themselves.

"I can't believe it's happening on our campus," is usually the initial response to reports such as Koss's. She also found that one in eight women students had been raped, and another one in four were victims of attempted rape. Since only 4 percent of all those reported the attack, Koss concluded that "at least ten times more rapes occur among college students than are reflected in official crime statistics." (Rape is recognized to be the most underreported of all crimes, and date rape is among the least reported, least believed, and most difficult to prosecute, second only to spouse rape.) 3

Working independently of Koss, researchers at Auburn University, Alabama, and more recently, University of South Dakota and St. Cloud State University, Minnesota, all have found that one in five women students were raped by men they knew. 4

Koss also found a core group of highly sexually aggressive men (4.3 percent) who use physical force to compel women to have intercourse but who are unlikely to see their act as rape. These "hidden rapists" have "oversubscribed" to traditional male roles, she says. They believe that aggression is normal and that women don't really mean it when they say no to sexual advances. Such men answer "True" to statements like "most women are sly and manipulating when they want to attract a man," "a woman will only respect a man who will lay down the law to her," and "a man's got to show the woman who's boss right from the start or he'll end up henpecked." 5

In Koss's current study, one respondent who answered yes to a question about obtaining intercourse through physical force, wrote in the comment, "I didn't rape the chick, she was enjoying it and responding," and later, "I feel that sex is a very pleasant way to relieve stress. Especially when there are no strings attached." 6

"He acted like he had a right, like he *didn't believe me*," says a coed from Auburn University on a videotaped dramatization of date rape experiences. And several weeks later, when she confronts him, saying he forced her, he says no, she wanted it. "You raped me," she finally tells him. And the picture freezes on his look of incredulity. 7

Barry Burkhart, a professor of psychology at Auburn, who has also studied sexual aggression among college men, found that 10 percent had used physical force to have intercourse with a woman against her will, and a large majority admitted to various other kinds of aggression. "These are 8 ordinary males operating in an ordinary social context," he says. "So what we conclude is that there's something wrong with that social context."

The something wrong is that our culture fosters a "rape supportive belief system," according to social psychologist Martha Burt. She thinks that "there's a large category of 'real' rapes, and a much smaller category of what our culture is willing to call a 'real' rape. The question is, how does the culture manage to write off all those other rapes?" The way it's done, says Burt, currently director of the Social Services Research Center at the Urban Institute in Washington, D.C., is by believing in a series of myths about rape, including:

- *It didn't really happen (the woman was lying);*
- *Women like rape (so there's no such thing as rape);*
- *Yes, it happened, but no harm was done (she wasn't a virgin; she wasn't white);*
- *Women provoke it (men can't control themselves);*
- *Women deserve it anyway.*

It's easy to write off date rapes with such myths, coupled with what Burt calls our culture's "adversarial sexual beliefs": the gamesmanship theory that everybody is out for what they can get, and that all sexual relationships are basically exploitive and predatory. In fact, most victims of date rape initially blame themselves for what happened, and almost none report it to campus authorities. And most academic institutions prefer to keep it that way, judging from the lack of surveys on date rape—all of which makes one wonder if they don't actually blame the victim, too.

As long as such attacks continue to be a "hidden" campus phenomenon, unreported and unacknowledged by many college administrators, law enforcement personnel, and students, the problem will persist. Of course, the term has become much better known in the three years since *Ms.* reported on the prevalence of experiences such as Judy's and Gretchen's. (See "Date Rape: A Campus Epidemic?" September 1982.) It has been the subject of talk shows such as "The Donahue Show" and TV dramas ("Cagney and Lacey"). But for most people it remains a contradiction in terms. "Everybody has a stake in denying that it's happening so often," says Martha Burt. "For women, it's self-protective . . . if only bad girls get raped, then I'm personally safe. For men, it's the denial that 'nice' people like them do it."

The fault has not entirely been that of the institutions. "Ten years ago, we were telling women to look over your shoulder when you go out at night and lock your doors," says Py Bateman, director of a nationally known rape education program in Seattle, Alternatives to Fear. The prevailing myth was that most rapes were committed by strangers in dark alleys.

"If you have to think that sixty to eighty percent of rape is by people you know—that's hard to deal with," says Sylvia Callaway, who directed the Austin, Texas, Rape Crisis Center for more than eight years before leaving last July. "No rape center in a university community would be surprised that the university is not willing to deal with the problem." 13

Statistics alone will not solve the problem of date rape, but they could help bring it out into the open. Which is why *Ms.* undertook the first nationwide survey on college campuses. The *Ms.* Magazine Campus Project on Sexual Assault, directed by Mary P. Koss at Kent State and funded by the National Center for the Prevention and Control of Rape, reached more than seven thousand students at a nationally representative sample of thirty-five schools, to find out how often, under what circumstances, and with what aftereffects a wide range of sexual assaults, including date rape, took place. 14

Preliminary results are now ready, and the information is no surprise. Participating schools were promised anonymity, but each will receive the results applying to its student body. Our hope is that the reaction of "we can't believe it's happening on our campus" will be followed by "what can we do about it—now." 15

Just how entrenched is denial of this problem today? One gauge might be the difficulty our own researchers had in persuading schools to let us on campus. For every college that approved our study, two others rejected it. Their reasons (in writing and in telephone conversations) were themselves instructive: "we don't want to get involved," "limited foreseeable benefit," "too volatile a topic," "have not had any problems in this area," "worried about publicity," "can't allow surveys in classroom," "just can't invest the time now," "would be overintrusive," "don't want to be left holding the bag if something goes wrong." 16

Several schools rejected the study on the basis that filling out the questionnaire might upset some students, and that we were not providing adequate follow-up counseling. (Researchers stayed on campus for at least a day after the distribution of the questionnaire, gave students listings of counselors or rape crisis centers to consult if anything upset them, and offered to meet with school personnel to brief them.) But isn't it less upsetting for a student to recognize and admit that she has been the victim of an acquaintance rape than to have buried the trauma of that rape deep inside herself? 17

"It's a Catch-22 situation. You want a survey to publicize a problem that has tremendous psychological implications. And the school says, 'Don't do it, because it will get people psychologically upset,'" admits John Jung, who heads the human subjects review committee at California State University/Long Beach (a school that declined our study). 18

One wonders just who are the "people" who will get most psychologically upset: the students, or their parents who pay for their educations, or 19 the administrators who are concerned about the school's image. "There may have been an episode here," said John Hose, executive assistant to the president of Brandeis University, "but there is no cause célèbre surrounding the issue. In such cases, the reaction of Student Affairs is to encourage the student to be in touch with her parents and to take legal action."

"Student Affairs" at Brandeis is headed by Rodger Crafts, who moved   20
to this post about a year ago from the University of Rhode Island. "I don't think we have a significant problem here because we have a sophisticated and intelligent group of students," said Dean Crafts. As for the University of Rhode Island, more students there are "first generation college attenders," as he put it, and therefore have "less respect" for other people. Vandalism and physical harm are more likely to occur with "lower educational levels." Respect for other people goes along with "intelligence level."

Back at the University of Rhode Island, the counseling center is   21
sponsoring a twelve-week support and therapy group this fall for male students who are coercive and abusive in their relationships with women. Even though Nancy Carlson, director of Counseling and Career Services, is enthusiastic about such programs and workshops she notes, "the awareness about date rape has been a long time coming."

Another school where administrators were the last to confront the   22
challenge to their school's self-image is Yale. Last year, two student publications reported instances of date rape on campus that surprised students, faculty, and administration. "There are no full statistics available on rape between students at Yale anywhere. . . . There is no mention of rape in the 1983–1984 Undergraduate Regulations. There is no procedure for a victim to file a formal complaint of rape with the university. But there is rape between students at Yale," wrote Sarah Oates in the *Yale Daily News*. Partly in response to such charges, current Yale undergraduate regulations now list "sexual harassment" under "offenses that are subject to disciplinary action"—but still no mention of rape.

Yale students brave enough to bring a charge of sexual harassment   23
may go before the Yale College Executive Committee, a specially convened group of faculty, administrators, and students that can impose a series of penalties, graduated in severity, culminating in expulsion. All its hearings and decisions are kept secret (but can in theory be subpoenaed in a court of law). But Michael McBride, current chair of the committee, told me that cases of date rape have come up during the past year, leading in one instance to a student being asked to "resign" from the university, and in another, the conclusion that there was not "sufficient evidence." (In Judy's case, described at the beginning of this article, the senior she charged was penalized by being denied the privilege of graduating with his class. But she claims that after he demanded that the case be reconsidered, he was fully exonerated.) Said McBride, "What surprised me the most was how complicated these cases are. It's only one person's word against another's. It's amazing how different their perceptions can be."

Judy chose to take her case before the Executive Committee rather 24
than report it to the local police, because she felt she would have complete
confidentiality and quick action. Actually, there were many delays. And
then, because the man she accused hired a lawyer, she was forced to hire
one too. As a result, the meeting felt very much like a jury trial to her,
complete with cross-examinations that challenged her truthfulness and
raised excruciatingly embarrassing questions.

Judy's lawyer felt that such painful questions were necessary. But it 25
seems as if the lesson feminists in the sixties and seventies worked so hard
and successfully to make understood—not to blame the victim for stranger
rape—is one that will have to be learned all over again in the case of
acquaintance rape. Only this time, the woman who reports the rape suffers
a triple victimization. Not only is she attacked and then not believed, but
she carries the added burden of losing faith in her own judgment and trust
in other people.

In a recently published study of jurors in rape trials, University of 26
Illinois sociologist Barbara Reskin found that jurors were less likely to
convict a man if the victim knew him. "Consent is the preferred rape
defense and gets the highest acquittal rates," Reskin observes. "In a date
rape situation, I would think the jury would assume that the woman had
already accepted his invitation in a romantic sense. It would be a matter of
how *much* did she consent to."

Personal characteristics also influence jurors, Reskin says. Those she 27
studied couldn't imagine that certain men would commit a rape: if they
were attractive, had access to sexual partners such as a girlfriend or a wife.
More often than not, they'd say, "But he doesn't look like a rapist." Reskin
imagines that this pattern would be "magnified in date rape, because these
are men who could get a date, they're not complete losers."

It may turn out that solutions to the problem will turn up at places 28
with a less genteel image to protect. Jan Strout, director of Montana State
Women's Resource Center, wonders if schools such as hers, which recognize
that they are dealing with a more conservative student body and a "macho
cowboy image," aren't more willing to take the first step toward acknowledging the problem. A group called Students Against Sexual Assault was
formed there two-and-a-half years ago after several students who were raped
or resisted an attempted rape "went public." With men and women sharing
leadership, this group is cosponsored by the Women's Resource Center and
the student government.

Admitting to the problem isn't easy even when data is available, as 29
doctoral student Genny Sandberg found at University of South Dakota.
Last spring, she announced the results of a dating survey she coauthored
with psychologists Tom Jackson and Patricia Petretic-Jackson. The most
shocking statistic: 20 percent of the students (most from rural backgrounds
and living in a rural campus setting) has been raped in a dating situation.
The state board of regents couldn't believe it. "I just think that that's

absolutely ridiculous," former regent Michael Rost said, according to the Brookings *Daily Register*, "I can't believe we would allow that to occur. If it is true, it's a very serious problem." Regent William Srstka agreed, "If this is true it's absolutely intolerable."

Following testimony by one of the researchers, the board changed its 30 tune. Members are now discussing how to begin a statewide education and prevention program.

An inspiring example of how an administration can be led to new 31 levels of consciousness took place at the University of Michigan earlier this year. Spurred by an article in *Metropolitan Detroit* magazine, a group of students staged a sit-in at the office of a university vice-president who had been quoted as saying that "Rape is a red flag word. . . . [The university] wants to present an image that is receptive and palatable to the potential student cohort," and also that "Rape is an issue like Alzheimer's disease or mental retardation [which] impacts on a small but sizable part of the population. . . . Perhaps it has to become a crisis that is commonly shared in order to get things done."

The students who spent the entire day in Vice-President Henry 32 Johnson's office claimed that rape had already become a crisis on their campus. They presented a list of twelve demands, ranging from a rape crisis center on campus to better lighting and installation of outdoor emergency phones. By the end of the day, Johnson had started to change his mind. Although he insisted that he had been misquoted and quoted out of context in the press, he told me that "I did not realize [before that] acquaintance rape was so much a problem, that it was the most prevalent type of rape. There is a heightened awareness now on this campus. Whether we as a faculty and administration are as sensitive as we should be is another issue—and that will take some time."

In the meantime, members of the Michigan Student Assembly Wo- 33 men's Issues Committee (one of the groups active in organizing the protest) took their demands before the school's board of regents. The result: a $75,000 program for rape prevention and education on campus, directly reporting to Johnson's office. "We'll now be in a position to document the problem and to be proactive," says Johnson. Jennifer Faigel, an organizer of the protest, acknowledges a change in the administration's awareness but says the students themselves, disappointed in the amount of funding promised for the program, have already formed a group (Students Organized Against Rape) to develop programs in the dorms.

In just the three years since *Ms.* first reported on date rape [in 1982], 34 several new campus organizations have sprung up and other ongoing programs have surfaced.

But the real measure of a school's commitment to dealing with this 35 problem is the range of services it provides, says Mary Harvey, who did a nationwide study of exemplary rape programs for the National Center for the Prevention and Control of Rape. "It should have preventive services, crisis intervention, possibilities for long-term treatment, advocacy, and women's studies programs that educate about violence. The quality of a university's services to rape victims can be measured by the degree to which these other things are in place."

Minimally, rape counselors and educators feel, students need to be exposed to information about date rape as soon as they enter college. Studies show that the group most vulnerable to acquaintance rape are college freshmen, followed by high school seniors. In Koss's original survey, for example, the average age of the victim was eighteen.   36

"I'd like a program where no first-year students could finish their starting week at college without being informed about the problem of acquaintance rape," says Andrea Parrot, a lecturer in human service studies at Cornell University, who is developing a program to train students and dorm resident advisers as date rape awareness counselors. Parrot and others admit that this would be a bare minimum. Handing out a brochure to read, even conducting a workshop on the subject during the busy orientation week and counting on students voluntarily attending, needs to be followed up with sessions in dormitories or other living units. These are the most common settings for date rapes, according to a study by Parrot and Robin Lynk.   37

So how do we go about changing attitudes? And how do we do it without "setting student against student?" asks Gretchen Mieszkowski, chair of the Sexual Assault Prevention Committee at the University of Houston/Clear Lake. Chiefly a commuter campus, with a majority of married women students, Clear Lake nevertheless had seventeen acquaintance rapes reported to the local crisis hot line last year. "We had always focused on traditional solutions like lighting and escort services at night," Mieszkowski says. "But changing lighting in the parking lot is easy; it's only money."   38

Many who have studied the problem of rape education believe it has to begin with college-age women and men talking to each other more frankly about their beliefs and expectations about sex. Py Bateman of Alternatives to Fear thinks it has to start earlier, among teenagers, by developing rudimentary dating skills at the lower end of the sexual activity scale. "We need to learn more about holding hands than about sexual intercourse."   39

Bateman continues: "We've got to work on both sides. Boys don't know what they want any more than girls do. The way our sexual interaction is set up is that boys are supposed to push. Their peers tell them that scoring is what counts. They're as divorced from intimacy as girls."   40

Gail Abarbanel of the Rape Treatment Center at Santa Monica Hospital agrees. Her center conducts educational programs for schools in Los Angeles County. In a recent survey of more than five thousand teenagers, she found a high degree of misconception and lack of information about rape: "Most boys say yes to the question, 'If a girl goes back to a   41 guy's house when she knows no one is home, is she consenting to sex?' And most boys believe that girls don't mean no when they say it."

Women clearly need to get more convincing, and men clearly need to   42
believe them more. But until that ideal time, Montana State's Jan Strout warns, "Because men have been socialized to hear yes when women say no, we have to scream it."

Questions for Study and Discussion

1. In paragraph 16 Sweet says that some of the colleges she contacted would not allow *Ms.* magazine to conduct a survey of rape on campus. Those which did "were promised anonymity" (15). What reasons does she give for this reluctance? Do the reasons sound valid, or do you think there are other, unmentioned reasons? Explain.

2. Rodger Crafts of Brandeis University feels that the school does not have a problem with rape because of the intelligence of the students. Is this a valid argument? What factors, if any, is he overlooking?

3. In paragraph 24 Sweet explains that Judy was subjected to embarrassing questions during her jury trial. What kinds of questions do you think she was asked? Are these questions relevant to the crime?

4. Sweet says that "women clearly need to get more convincing." Do you agree? Why or why not?

5. Reread the accounts of the victims. What do these stories have in common? What other kinds of evidence does the author use to make her argument? Which did you find the most convincing?

6. In paragraph 27 Barbara Reskin says that people find it hard to imagine certain men committing a rape. She offers as examples men who have "access to sexual partners such as a girl friend or a wife." Does this example stand up against the notion that rape is not a sexual crime, but a crime of aggression? Is this distinction important?

7. Sweet says, "Rape is recognized to be the most underreported of all crimes, and date rape is among the least reported. . . ." What reasons, if any, does she offer for this phenomenon? What reasons can you offer?

Writing Topics

1. Often the subject of date rape is discussed as a college campus phenomenon. Do you think the problem occurs more frequently on college campuses? If so, what is it about the college campus that lends itself to this particular crime?

2. In an essay discuss the eventual effects of skirting a campus issue such as rape, venereal disease, or cheating. For example, most colleges denied *Ms.* the opportunity to conduct a survey on the topic of rape. What implications could this have later? Do colleges benefit from not allowing the topic to be brought up?

CAROLINE BIRD

Caroline Bird was born in New York City, attended Vassar College for three years, and received her B.A. from the University of Toledo and her M.A. from the University of Wisconsin. A feminist writer throughout most of her career, Bird has focused her attention on women's roles in the business world. She has published such influential and well-reviewed books as *The Invisible Scar: The Great Depression and What It Did to American Life, from Then Until Now* (1966) with Sarah Welles Briller, *Born Female: The High Cost of Keeping Women Down* (1968), *Everything a Woman Needs to Know to Get Paid What She's Worth* (1973), *Enterprising Women: Their Contribution to the American Economy, 1776–1976* (1976), *What Women Want* (1978), and *The Two-Paycheck Marriage: How Women at Work Are Changing Life in America* (1982).

In the following selection Bird turns her attention away from feminist issues and asks whether or not a college education is a worthwhile financial investment. What would be the result, for example, if you were to take the money that you will spend on your college education and invest it and become gainfully employed instead of attending school?

College Is a Waste of Time and Money

A great majority of our nine million college students are not in school 1 because they want to be or because they want to learn. They are there because it has become the thing to do or because college is a pleasant place to be; because it's the only way they can get parents or taxpayers to support them without working at a job they don't like; because Mother wanted them to go, or some other reason entirely irrelevant to the course of studies for which college is supposedly organized.

As I crisscross the United States lecturing on college campuses, I am 2 dismayed to find that professors and administrators, when pressed for a candid opinion, estimate that no more than 25 percent of their students are turned on by classwork. For the rest, college is at best a social center or aging vat, and at worst a young folks' home or even a prison that keeps them out of the mainstream of economic life for a few more years.

The premise—which I no longer accept—that college is the best place 3 for all high-school graduates grew out of a noble American ideal. Just as the United States was the first nation to aspire to teach every small child to read and write, so, during the 1950s, we became the first and only great nation to aspire to higher education for all. During the '60s, we damned the expense and built great state university systems as fast as we could. And adults—parents, employers, high-school counselors—began to push, shove, and cajole youngsters to "get an education."

It became a mammoth industry, with taxpayers footing more than half   4
the bill. By 1970, colleges and universities were spending more than 30 billion dollars annually. But still only half of our high-school graduates were going on. According to estimates made by the economist Fritz Machlup, if we had been educating every young person until age 22 in that year of 1970, the bill for higher education would have reached 47.5 billion dollars, 12.5 billion more than the total corporate profits for the year.

Figures such as these have begun to make higher education for all look   5
financially prohibitive, particularly now when colleges are squeezed by the pressures of inflation and a drop-off in the growth of their traditional market.

Predictable demography has caught up with the university empire   6
builders. Now that the record crop of postwar babies has graduated from college, the rate of growth of the student population has begun to decline. To keep their mammoth plants financially solvent, many institutions have begun to use hard-sell, Madison-Avenue techniques to attract students. They sell college like soap, promoting features they think students want: innovative programs, an environment conducive to meaningful personal relationships, and a curriculum so free that it doesn't sound like college at all.

Pleasing the customers is something new for college administrators.   7
Colleges have always known that most students don't like to study, and that at least part of the time they are ambivalent about college, but before the student riots of the 1960s educators never thought it either right or necessary to pay any attention to student feelings. But when students rebelling against the Vietnam war and the draft discovered they could disrupt a campus completely, administrators had to act on some student complaints. Few understood that the protests tapped the basic discontent with college itself, a discontent that did not go away when the riots subsided.

Today students protest individually rather than in concert. They turn   8
inward and withdraw from active participation. They drop out to travel to India or to feed themselves on subsistence farms. Some refuse to go to college at all. Most, of course, have neither the funds nor the self-confidence for constructive articulation of their discontent. They simply hang around college unhappily and reluctantly.

All across the country, I have been overwhelmed by the prevailing   9
sadness on American campuses. Too many young people speak little, and then only in drowned voices. Sometimes the mood surfaces as diffidence, weariness, or coolness, but whatever its form, it looks like a defense

mechanism, and that rings a bell. This is the way it used to be with women, and just as society had systematically damaged women by insisting that their proper place was in the home, so we may be systematically damaging 18-year-olds by insisting that their proper place is in college.

Campus watchers everywhere know what I mean when I say students are sad, but they don't agree on the reason for it. During the Vietnam war some ascribed the sadness to the draft; now others blame affluence or say it has something to do with permissive upbringing.

Not satisfied with any of these explanations, I looked for some an-swers with the journalistic tools of my trade—scholarly studies, economic analyses, the historical record, the opinions of the especially knowledgeable, conversations with parents, professors, college administrators, and em-ployers, all of whom spoke as alumni, too. Mostly I learned from my interviews with hundreds of young people on and off campuses all over the country.

My unnerving conclusion is that students are sad because they are not needed. Somewhere between the nursery and the employment office, they become unwanted adults. No one has anything in particular against them. But no one knows what to do with them either. We already have too many people in the world of the 1970s, and there is no room for so many newly minted 18-year-olds. So we temporarily get them out of the way by sending them to college where in fact only a few belong.

To make it more palatable, we fool ourselves into believing that we are sending them there for their own best interests, and that it's good for them, like spinach. Some, of course, learn to like it, but most wind up preferring green peas.

Educators admit as much. Nevitt Sanford, distinguished student of higher education, says students feel they are "capitulating to a kind of voluntary servitude." Some of them talk about their time in college as if it were a sentence to be served. I listened to a 1970 Mount Holyoke graduate: "For two years I was really interested in science, but in my junior and senior years I just kept saying, 'I've done two years; I'm going to finish.' When I got out I made up my mind that I wasn't going to school anymore because so many of my courses had been bullshit."

But bad as it is, college is often preferable to a far worse fate. It is better than the drudgery of an uninspiring nine-to-five job, and better than doing nothing when no jobs are available. For some young people, it is a graceful way to get away from home and become independent without losing the financial support of their parents. And sometimes it is the only alternative to an intolerable home situation.

It is difficult to assess how many students are in college reluctantly. The conservative Carnegie Commission estimates from 5 to 30 percent. Sol Linowitz, who was once chairman of a special committee on campus tension of the American Council on Education, found that "a significant number were not happy with their college experience because they felt they were there only in order to get the 'ticket to the big show' rather than to spend the years as productively as they otherwise could."

Older alumni will identify with Richard Baloga, a policeman's son, who stayed in school even though he "hated it" because he thought it would do him some good. But fewer students each year feel this way. Daniel Yankelovich has surveyed undergraduate attitudes for a number of years, and reported in 1971 that 74 percent thought education was "very important." But just two years earlier, 80 percent thought so.

The doubters don't mind speaking up. Leon Lefkowitz, chairman of the department of social studies at Central High School in Valley Stream, New York, interviewed 300 college students at random, and reports that 200 of them didn't think that the education they were getting was worth the effort. "In two years I'll pick up a diploma," said one student, "and I can honestly say it was a waste of my father's bread."

Nowadays, says one sociologist, you don't have to have a reason for going to college; it's an institution. His definition of an institution is an arrangement everyone accepts without question; the burden of proof is not on why you go, but why anyone thinks there might be a reason for not going. The implication is that an 18-year-old is too young and confused to know what he wants to do, and that he should listen to those who know best and go to college.

I don't agree. I believe that college has to be judged not on what other people think is good for students, but on how good it feels to the students themselves.

I believe that people have an inside view of what's good for them. If a child doesn't want to go to school some morning, better let him stay at home, at least until you find out why. Maybe he knows something you don't. It's the same with college. If high-school graduates don't want to go, or if they don't want to go right away, they may perceive more clearly than their elders that college is not for them. It is no longer obvious that adolescents are best off studying a core curriculum that was constructed when all educated men could agree on what made them educated, or that professors, advisors, or parents can be of any particular help to young people in choosing a major or a career. High-school graduates see college graduates driving cabs and decide it's not worth going. College students find no intellectual stimulation in their studies and drop out.

If students believe that college isn't necessarily good for them, you can't expect them to stay on for the general good of mankind. They don't go to school to beat the Russians to Jupiter, improve the national defense, increase the GNP, or create a new market for the arts—to mention some of the benefits taxpayers are supposed to get for supporting higher education.

Nor should we expect to bring about social equality by putting all young people through four years of academic rigor. At best, it's a roundabout and expensive way to narrow the gap between the highest and lowest in our society anyway. At worst, it is unconsciously elitist. Equalizing opportunity through universal higher education subjects the whole population to the intellectual mode natural only to a few. It violates the fundamental egalitarian principle of respect for the differences between people.

Of course, most parents aren't thinking of the "higher" good at all. 24 They send their children to college because they are convinced young people benefit financially from those four years of higher education. But if money is the only goal, college is the dumbest investment you can make. I say this because a young banker in Poughkeepsie, New York, Stephen G. Necel, used a computer to compare college as an investment with other investments available in 1974, and college did not come out on top.

For the sake of argument, the two of us invented a young man whose 25 rich uncle gave him, in cold cash, the cost of a four-year education at any college he chose, but the young man didn't have to spend the money on college. After bales of computer paper, we had our mythical student write to his uncle: "Since you said I could spend the money foolishly if I wished, I am going to blow it all on Princeton."

The much respected financial columnist Sylvia Porter echoed the 26 common assumption when she said last year, "A college education is among the very best investments you can make in your entire life." But the truth is not quite so rosy, even if we assume that the Census Bureau is correct when it says that as of 1972, a man who completed four years of college would expect to earn $199,000 more between the ages of 22 and 64 than a man who had only a high-school diploma.

If a 1972 Princeton-bound high-school graduate had put the $34,181 27 that his four years of college would have cost him into a savings bank at 7.5 percent interest compounded daily, he would have had at age 64 a total of $1,129,200, or $528,200 more than the earnings of a male college graduate, and more than five times as much as the $199,000 extra the more educated man could expect to earn between 22 and 64.

The big advantage of getting your college money in cash now is that 28 you can invest it in something that has a higher return than a diploma. For instance, a Princeton-bound high-school graduate of 1972 who liked fooling around with cars could have banked his $34,181, and gone to work at the local garage at close to $1,000 more per year than the average high-school graduate. Meanwhile, as he was learning to be an expert auto mechanic, his money would be ticking away in the bank. When he became 28, he would have earned $7,199 less on his job from age 22 to 28 than his college-educated friend, but he would have had $73,113 in his passbook—enough to buy out his boss, go into the used-car business, or acquire his own new car dealership. If successful in business, he could expect to make more than the average college graduate. And if he had the brains to get into Princeton, he would be just as likely to make money without the four years spent on campus. Unfortunately, few college-bound high-school graduates get the opportunity to bank such a large sum of money and then wait for it to make them rich. And few parents are sophisticated enough to understand that in financial returns alone, their children would be better off with the money than with the education.

Rates of return and dollar signs on education are fascinating brain   29
teasers, but obviously there is a certain unreality to the game. Quite aside from the noneconomic benefits of college, and these should loom larger once the dollars are cleared away, there are grave difficulties in assigning a dollar value to college at all.

In fact there is no real evidence that the higher income of college   30
graduates is due to college. College may simply attract people who are slated to earn more money anyway; those with higher IQs, better family back-grounds, a more enterprising temperament. No one who has wrestled with the problem is prepared to attribute all of the higher income to the impact of college itself.

Christopher Jencks, author of *Inequality*, a book that assesses the   31
effect of family and schooling in America, believes that education in general accounts for less than half of the difference in income in the American population. "The biggest single source of income differences," writes Jencks, "seems to be the fact that men from high-status families have higher incomes than men from low-status families even when they enter the same occupations, have the same amount of education, and have the same test scores."

Jacob Mincer of the National Bureau of Economic Research and   32
Columbia University states flatly that of "20 to 30 percent of students at any level, the additional schooling has been a waste, at least in terms of earnings." College fails to work its income-raising magic for almost a third of those who go. More than half of those people in 1972 who earned $15,000 or more reached that comfortable bracket without the benefit of a college diploma. Jencks says that financial success in the U.S. depends a good deal on luck, and the most sophisticated regression analyses have yet to demonstrate otherwise.

But most of today's students don't go to college to earn more money   33
anyway. In 1968, when jobs were easy to get, Daniel Yankelovich made his first nationwide survey of students. Sixty-five percent of them said they "would welcome less emphasis on money." By 1973, when jobs were scarce, that figure jumped to 80 percent.

The young are not alone. Americans today are all looking less to the   34
pay of a job than to the work itself. They want "interesting" work that permits them "to make a contribution," "express themselves" and "use their special abilities," and they think college will help them find it.

Jerry Darring of Indianapolis knows what it is to make a dollar. He   35
worked with his father in the family plumbing business, on the line at

Chevrolet, and in the Chrysler foundry. He quit these jobs to enter Wright State University in Dayton, Ohio, because "in a job like that a person only has time to work, and after that he's so tired that he can't do anything else but come home and go to sleep."

Jerry came to college to find work "helping people." And he is   36
perfectly willing to spend the dollars he earns at dull, well-paid work to prepare for lower-paid work that offers the reward of service to others.

Jerry's case is not unusual. No one works for money alone. In order to   37
deal with the nonmonetary rewards of work, economists have coined the concept of "psychic income," which according to one economic dictionary means "income that is reckoned in terms of pleasure, satisfaction or general feelings of euphoria."

Psychic income is primarily what college students mean when they   38
talk about getting a good job. During the most affluent years of the late 1960s and early 1970s college students told their placement officers that they wanted to be researchers, college professors, artists, city planners, social workers, poets, book publishers, archaeologists, ballet dancers, or authors.

The psychic income of these and other occupations popular with   39
students is so high that these jobs can be filled without offering high salaries. According to one study, 93 percent of urban university professors would choose the same vocation again if they had the chance, compared with only 16 percent of unskilled auto workers. Even though the monetary gap between college professor and auto worker is now surprisingly small, the difference in psychic income is enormous.

But colleges fail to warn students that jobs of these kinds are hard to   40
come by, even for qualified applicants, and they rarely accept the responsibility of helping students choose a career that will lead to a job. When a young person says he is interested in helping people, his counselor tells him to become a psychologist. But jobs in psychology are scarce. The Department of Labor, for instance, estimates there will be 4,300 new jobs for psychologists in 1975 while colleges are expected to turn out 58,430 B.A.s in psychology that year.

Of thirty psych majors who reported back to Vassar what they were   41
doing a year after graduation in 1973, only five had jobs in which they could possibly use their courses in psychology, and two of these were working for Vassar.

The outlook isn't much better for students majoring in other psychic-   42
pay disciplines: sociology, English, journalism, anthropology, forestry, education. Whatever college graduates want to do, most of them are going to wind up doing what there is to do.

John Shingleton, director of placement at Michigan State University,   43
accuses the academic community of outright hypocrisy. "Educators have never said, 'Go to college and get a good job,' but this has been implied,

and now students expect it. . . . If we care what happens to students after college, then let's get involved with what should be one of the basic purposes of education: career preparation."

In the 1970s, some of the more practical professors began to see that jobs for graduates meant jobs for professors too. Meanwhile, students themselves reacted to the shrinking job market, and a "new vocationalism" exploded on campus. The press welcomed the change as a return to the ethic of achievement and service. Students were still idealistic, the reporters wrote, but they now saw that they could best make the world better by healing the sick as physicians or righting individual wrongs as lawyers.   44

But there are no guarantees in these professions either. The American Enterprise Institute estimated in 1971 that there would be more than the target ratio of 100 doctors for every 100,000 people in the population by 1980. And the odds are little better for would-be lawyers. Law schools are already graduating twice as many new lawyers every year as the Department of Labor thinks will be needed, and the oversupply is growing every year.   45

And it's not at all apparent that what is actually learned in a "professional" education is necessary for success. Teachers, engineers, and others I talked to said they find that on the job they rarely use what they learned in school. In order to see how well college prepared engineers and scientists for actual paid work in their fields, The Carnegie Commission queried all the employees with degrees in these fields in two large firms. Only one in five said the work they were doing bore a "very close relationship" to their college studies, while almost a third saw "very little relationship at all." An overwhelming majority could think of many people who were doing their same work, but had majored in different fields.   46

Majors in nontechnical fields report even less relationship between their studies and their jobs. Charles Lawrence, a communications major in college and now the producer of "Kennedy & Co.," the Chicago morning television show, says, "You have to learn all that stuff and you never use it again. I learned my job doing it." Others employed as architects, nurses, teachers, and other members of the so-called learned professions report the same thing.   47

Most college administrators admit that they don't prepare their graduates for the job market. "I just wish I had the guts to tell parents that when you get out of this place you aren't prepared to do anything," the academic head of a famous liberal-arts college told us. Fortunately, for him, most people believe that you don't have to defend a liberal-arts education on those grounds. A liberal-arts education is supposed to provide you with a value system, a standard, a set of ideas, not a job. "Like Christianity, the liberal arts are seldom practiced and would probably be hated by the majority of the populace if they were," said one defender.   48

The analogy is apt. The fact is, of course, that the liberal arts are a religion in every sense of that term. When people talk about them, their   49 language becomes elevated, metaphorical, extravagant, theoretical and reverent. And faith in personal salvation by the liberal arts is professed in a creed intoned on ceremonial occasions such as commencements.

If the liberal arts are a religious faith, the professors are its priests. But disseminating ideas in a four-year college curriculum is slow and most expensive. If you want to learn about Milton, Camus, or even Margaret Mead you can find them in paperback books, the public library, and even on television. 50

And when most people talk about the value of a college education, they are not talking about great books. When at Harvard commencement, the president welcomes the new graduates into "the fellowship of educated men and women," what he could be saying is, "Here is a piece of paper that is a passport to jobs, power, and instant prestige." As Glenn Bassett, a personnel specialist at G.E., says, "In some parts of G.E., a college degree appears completely irrelevant to selection to, say, a manger's job. In most, however, it is a ticket of admission." 51

But now that we have doubled the number of young people attending college, a diploma cannot guarantee even that. The most charitable conclusion we can reach is that college probably has very little, if any, effect on people and things at all. Today, the false premises are easy to see: 52

First, college doesn't make people intelligent, ambitious, happy, or liberal. It's the other way around. Intelligent, ambitious, happy, liberal people are attracted to higher education in the first place. 53

Second, college can't claim much credit for the learning experiences that really change students while they are there. Jobs, friends, history, and most of all the sheer passage of time, have as big an impact as anything even indirectly related to the campus. 54

Third, colleges have changed so radically that a freshman entering in the fall of 1974 can't be sure to gain even the limited value research studies assigned to colleges in the '60s. the sheer size of undergraduate campuses of the 1970s makes college even less stimulating now than it was 10 years ago. Today even motivated students are disappointed with their college courses and professors. 55

Finally, a college diploma no longer opens as many vocational doors. Employers are beginning to realize that when they pay extra for someone with a diploma, they are paying only for an empty credential. The fact is that most of the work for which employers now expect college training is now or has been capably done in the past by people without higher educations. 56

College, then, may be a good place for those few young people who are really drawn to academic work, who would rather read than eat, but it has become too expensive, in money, time, and intellectual effort, to serve as a holding pen for large numbers of our young. We ought to make it possible for those reluctant, unhappy students to find alternative ways of growing up and more realistic preparation for the years ahead. 57

Questions for Study and Discussion

1. What reasons does Bird give for believing that college is a waste of time and money? Which reasons, if any, do you find most compelling? Explain why.

2. Why, according to Bird, do people go to college? Do you agree with her assessment? Why or why not?

3. In the 1960s and early 1970s students protested en masse on campuses across the country. How, according to Bird, do students protest today? Is this true of students on your campus? Explain.

4. In traveling to college campuses across the country Bird was struck by the "prevailing sadness." Why does she believe students are sad? Do you think she's right? Why or why not?

5. Why, after going through the exercises of showing the economic advantages of investing money instead of spending it on a college education, does Bird admit that "there is a certain unreality to the game"? Do you agree with her when she says, "few parents are sophisticated enough to understand that in financial returns alone, their children would be better off with the money than with the education"?

6. What, according to Bird, is psychic income? How can a person estimate the value of psychic income? How important is such income to you and your peers?

7. What is the "new vocationalism" of the 1970s that Bird refers to? Is this still a campus reality in the early 1990s? Explain.

8. What types of sources does Bird use to substantiate her argument? In what ways do these sources help her to avoid the charges of being opinionated, cynical, or sensational?

9. How are paragraphs 52–57 related to what comes before? Does this block of paragraphs function as an appropriate conclusion? Explain.

Writing Topics

1. Bird says that college is "at best a social center or aging vat, and at worst a young folks' home or even a prison that keeps them out of the mainstream of economic life for a few more years." She concludes her essay by saying "We ought to make it possible for those reluctant, unhappy students to find alternative ways of growing up and more realistic preparation for the years ahead." Write an essay in which you explore new learning experiences and opportunities for personal growth designed to prepare our youth for the years ahead.

2. The selections by David P. Gardner (pp. 267–75) and Caroline Bird address educational issues at the college level and approach the subject from different vantage points. Gardner's report sounds an alarm because the nation's post-secondary schools are not striving for excellence, and Bird claims that college is a waste of time and money. One is concerned with the nation's welfare and future, the other with students' potential financial gains. Compare and contrast the arguments made by each author. Are the issues raised really two

different ones or are they actually different sides of the same problem? If the nation's colleges were able to achieve the excellence Gardner's commission calls for, do you think Caroline Bird would still believe that college is a waste of time and money?

3. College is, or at least should be, something more than a place to get the credentials necessary to earn more money in your chosen career. Write an essay in which you explain what you hope to gain intellectually, morally, and socially from your college education.

GEORGE F. WILL

Born in 1941 in Champaign, Illinois, George F. Will graduated from Trinity College in Hartford, Connecticut, in 1962 and attended Oxford University from 1962 to 1964 before teaching political science at Michigan State University and the University of Toronto. Will is best known for his syndicated biweekly column in *Newsweek*. He has collected his columns in three books: *The Pursuit of Happiness and Other Sobering Thoughts* (1979), *The Pursuit of Virtue and Other Tory Notions* (1982), *The Morning After; American Successes and Excesses, 1981–1986* (1986), and *Men at Work* (1990). He has also written another book on politics, *Statecraft as Soulcraft: What Government Does* (1983).

In "Our Schools for Scandal," published in a September 1986 issue of *Newsweek*, Will gets away from politics to the horrors of the football recruiting system. He argues that players are often the losers when universities scramble to build winning teams.

Our Schools for Scandal

During a royal visit in 1957 Queen Elizabeth, at a Maryland–North Carolina football game, asked Maryland's governor, "Where do you get all those enormous players?" He replied: "Your Majesty, that's a very embarrassing question." Big-time college football is grinding into gear yet again, and permanent embarrassment may account for the tradition of nervous joking. A wit once defined college coaches as "a class of selfless sufferers who go on building character year after year, no matter how many states they have to import it from." A Cincinnati University coach once said that 90 percent of all colleges abide by the rules and the other 10 percent go to bowl games. When hired at Nebraska a coach joked, "I don't expect to win enough games to be put on NCAA probation. I just want to win enough to warrant an investigation." An Oklahoma University president joked, "We're trying to build a university our football team can be proud of." Ho, ho.

Not funny. Big-time college sports are a continuing scandal, corrupting and exploiting. A proximate cause of this is coaches' insecurity, but that insecurity is produced by the stakes: bushels of money and rabid legions of alumni. Insecurity? Lou Holtz, Notre Dame's new coach, once joked, "I have a lifetime contract. That means I can't be fired during the third quarter if we're ahead and moving the ball." A Michigan State coach once got this telegram from alumni: "Coach, we're all behind you—win or tie."

Out the back door: The worst scandal does not involve cash or convert- 3 ibles. It involves slipping academically unqualified young men in the back doors of academic institutions, insulating them from academic expectations, wringing them dry of their athletic-commercial usefulness, then slinging them out the back door even less suited to society than they were when they entered. They are less suited because they have spent four years acquiring the idea that they are exempt from normal standards. A Texas A&M basketball coach once joked to an athlete who received four F's and a D, "Son, looks to me like you're spending too much time on one subject." The sports system that generates such jokes has an ugly racial dimension.

Many football and basketball programs prosper by exploiting the 4 heartbreaking belief of ghetto boys that sports are a broad paved road to riches. This year the NCAA is implementing requirements for freshmen athletes—minimum grade-point average in a core high-school curriculum and a very minimal score on a standard aptitude test. At least 8 of the 47 football players on Parade magazine's 1985 high-school All-America team are ineligible to play this year. The Dallas Times Herald reports that in the 105 Division I football programs, 206 (9 percent) of 2,227 entering freshmen are ineligible. All but 31 of the 206 are black. High schools deserve a large dollop of blame for not having "no pass, no play" rules. But colleges are especially guilty of exploitation because they are the end of the road for most "student athletes."

A survey of 1,359 black athletes who entered colleges in 1977 revealed 5 that only 14 percent graduated in four years and only 31 percent in six years. Among 4,067 white athletes the figure was deplorable but better: 53 percent graduated in six years. But many "graduates" glided through on cushy courses. Remember Kevin Ross, who played basketball for Creighton University in Omaha and then enrolled in a seventh-grade class to learn to read and write.

Preposterous enterprise: Many athletes live in an atmosphere of perma- 6 nent exemption—exemption from all the rules and rigors of academic life. Not surprisingly, some young people come to think they are exempt also from physiological limits. "Cocaine? Can't hurt me." An attorney for some University of Georgia officials said: "We may not make a university student out of [an athlete], but if we can teach him to read and write, maybe he can work at the post office rather than as a garbage man when he gets through with his athletic career." However, even if the athletic departments had such kindness in mind, it is a preposterous enterprise for an institution of higher—higher than what?—education. Anyway, what is really involved is higher math. This season the 105 Division I football programs will raise and spend nearly $1 billion while entertaining 25 million spectators and zillions of TV viewers. Ticket and concession sales often top $500,000 for a single game. Winning teams go to bowl games and swim in gravy. Penn State's share from last year's Orange Bowl was $2.2 million.

In addition to money, a sprawling multiversity can get from a success-   7
ful team a unifying focus. As Alabama's Bear Bryant once noted, "It's kind of hard to rally round a math class." And sports can give useful glamour to an institution. A Boston college official gives much credit to the 1984 football team of quarterback Doug Flutie for the increase from 12,500 to 16,200 in freshman applications from 1984 to 1985. Also, it is not fair to say, as a wit did, that football bears the same relation to education that bullfighting does to agriculture. Sport is a realm of discipline, skill and excellence, and hence has a legitimate role on campuses. Furthermore, many institutions such as Penn State, Notre Dame, Georgetown and Duke are proving that athletic excellence is compatible with academic respon-sibility.

Many small reforms could make a big difference in big-time sports.   8
Freshmen should not be allowed to compete on varsity teams. Joe Paterno, Penn State's football coach, says something is out of whack when a kid plays football games before attending his first class. There should be none of those special dormitories where athletes eat and sleep and do not study together in splendid isolation from real students. Schools should not be allowed to give the full quota of athletic scholarships unless the graduation rate among athletes is as high as the rate for the entire student body. Eligibility and graduation should not be faked using ludicrous "courses" such as the one some University of Nevada at Las Vegas basketball players "took" during a 16-day playing tour of the South Pacific. Sports Illustrated reports that they were required to spend several hours a day on "field trips," read two books and write a term paper. Some players received six credits. The average full-term credit load at UNLV is 15. The course is called Contemporary Issues in Social Welfare, and should itself be an issue. Sports Illustrated suggested the title Palm Trees 101.

Questions for Study and Discussion

1. According to Will, what is the chief danger in allowing academically unqualified young men to play ball?
2. What is the chief contributing factor to the scandal Will describes? What are some other causes?
3. What is the meaning of Will's title? How does it relate to his thesis?
4. Prepare a scratch outline of Will's article. How has he organized his argument? Could he have organized it differently?
5. In paragraph 7, Will offers some of the legitimate reasons for including sports in the university setting. Why do you think he does this? Does including them strengthen or weaken his argument?

6. Who is Will writing for, and what is his purpose in writing this article?

7. Reread Will's essay, paying special attention to the quotes he uses. What do they have in common? How do they contribute to his argument?

8. What are the racial implications inherent in the football recruiting system according to Will? What are the racial implications of the solutions he offers?

Writing Topics

1. Campuses suffer problems other than scandalous sports recruitment practices. Campus rape, the increasing incidence of sexually transmitted diseases, and theft are just a few of them. Choose a problem that plagues your campus. What do you perceive as the factors contributing to that problem? What solutions can you offer? Pay attention to whether or not the solutions will create other problems.

2. Will suggests several reforms to the college sports system. Are these reforms practical? What would schools and universities have to do to make these changes possible? How likely is it that they would agree to the changes he suggests? Can you offer any suggestions that might be useful?

CHRIS MILLER

Chris Miller is a 1963 graduate of Dartmouth and a 1964 graduate of its Amos Tuck School of Business. While working for a major Madison Avenue advertising agency, he wrote the "I'm cuckoo for Coca Puffs" commercials. Miller is best known as the co-author of the screen play for the popular movie comedy *Animal House*, an insider's look at fraternity life in the early 1960s.

The following article was written for the *Dartmouth Alumni Magazine* in 1989, at the editor's request. It is written in response to a campaign by the administration to dissolve the Greek system.

Son of Animal House

In January of 1961, as a pledge in a Dartmouth fraternity, I underwent 1 a little number known as the "Night of the Seven Fires." My pledge partner and I, handed a smudged, mimeographed map, had to locate and climb a steep, snowy, wooded hillside in sub-zero temperatures. We then had to stop at each of seven bonfires and perform demented acts demanded of us by the brothers. Among many other things, most of them unsuitable for airing in an all-family magazine, we had to drop our pants and sit in the snow, drink impossible quantities of beer and wine, and vomit repeatedly, sometimes on each other.

It was one of the greatest nights of my life. 2

This is difficult for people to understand. Fraternity hijinks are a very 3 particular and specialized sort of behavior, and are regarded with neither sympathy nor affection by much of the world, especially mothers, police officers, campus administrators, and other societal voices of moderation and control. It's hard to explain to those who have missed the fraternity experience how richly satisfying booting, or mooning, or eating your underwear can be. People just don't get it.

Which is why, about ten years after graduation, I decided to write a 4 novel portraying fraternity life as it is. I wanted to put it all out there—the reverse value system, the fascination with the repugnant, the joyous flouting of authority. The book, alas, did not find a publisher, but parts of it, converted to short stories, appeared in National Lampoon, where their popularity inspired editor Doug Kenney to suggest that he, Harold Ramis, and I write a movie based on them. The movie, of course, was "Animal House."

This probably did not endear me to Parkhurst Hall, whose occupants have been laboring mightily to rid the College of its "Animal House image." Well, sorry folks—nothing personal. It just seemed like fraternities were endlessly getting a bum rap, and it was time someone spoke up for good old irresponsible, sophomoric, hedonistic, over-the-top fun.

The movie evidently tapped into something—it quickly became the highest-grossing comedy of its time. People who liked it didn't just see it once, they went ten or 20 times. Its release coincided with, and perhaps contributed to, the rebound of fraternities around the country from their Vietnam-era doldrums. Toga parties and food fights made comebacks. Beer sales rose sharply. Sheer, mindless fun-for-fun's-sake was in fashion once again.

The fraternities revived in Hanover, too, only to discover their popularity among other sectors of the College was at a low ebb. To be sure, Dartmouth has *usually* eyed its fraternities with something less than full-bore enthusiasm—the first time the College considered getting rid of them was in 1846—but this was different. *This* time, it looked like the administration, faculty, Trustees, and police were *serious*.

The opening gun was fired in 1978. An English professor, James A. Epherson, circulated a petition among the faculty to have fraternities abolished for "interfering with College life and the health and well-being of students." The real stunner came when the faculty voted 67–16 in favor of the proposal. Obviously, there was some serious resentment harbored against the fraternities at Dartmouth. And though the proposal ultimately did not fly, it marked the beginning of a crackdown that resulted in many houses being put on probation, and given shape-up-or-ship-out ultimata. Next came a reformist "plan of improvement," and then, in '83, the instituting of "Minimum Standards." Since this program called for expensive renovations to the deteriorating houses, it was widely perceived as an attempt to do away with fraternities by breaking them financially.

Then, in '87, the Board of Trustees released a "Residential Life Statement" calling for a reduction in the fraternity system's dominance of social life on campus, and, shortly after that, the Hanover Police, without notifying the administration, conducted their notorious undercover sting operation, recruiting an 18-year-old girl and sending her, with an out-of-town policeman posing as her boyfriend, on a round of fraternities during Green Key weekend. Naturally, she was served beer at some of them, and eight fraternities and two sororities were charged with serving alcohol to a minor. The houses were actually put on notice that they could face criminal indictments, though the College ultimately got them off the hook. This had a chilling effect on the admission of nonmember guests to parties. Finally, in 1988, the administration announced that starting with the class of '93, rush would be delayed until sophomore year. Since this would decrease fraternity membership—and their already pinched treasuries—there was bitter resistance to the measure, all the more so because it was a dictate from on high that ignored heavy student opposition.

Were these necessary reforms, or the overzealous programs of Dean Wormer-like administrators during a fundamentalist, neo-prohibitionist decade? What it sometimes *looked* like, to those of us on the outside, was that the College had declared *war* on its fraternities. Being in a house *these* days didn't look like much fun at all. So when the Alumni Magazine invited me up to research a piece on the state of fraternities at Dartmouth today, I thought twice. I mean, I wasn't sure I wanted to *know*. 10

I enter the AD house after all these years with trepidation. Here it is, the mythic fountainhead of the Animal House legend—what will it be like today? Reduced to a skeleton crew of intimidated weenies, sipping Oolong and discussing Proust? 11

But no. The first thing I notice is the smell. It's the *same smell*; it hasn't changed in 25 years! Mainly beer, with certain miscellaneous nuances. And the place *looks* pretty much the same, too. A bit more wrecked-up, maybe, but it's the same tube room, the same tap system, and, running the perimeter of the basement, the same beloved AD gutter (today known as the "gorf"). In the erstwhile basement bathroom—converted to a broom closet a few years ago after a brother tore out the toilet to mix punch in it—I can still make out the carved names of brothers from my era: Y. Bags, Lapes, Snot, Mag F. Pie, Hydrant, Dumptruck. . . . 12

Having recently concluded a very successful rush, the house has nearly a hundred members, and it looks like most of them are here tonight. They seem a little cool; I wonder if I'm welcome. Or maybe it's a generational style—they don't make a big deal about things. There's so *many* of them, though, over *twice* the number we had! The living room is like a subway car! And, God, how'd they get to be so *young*? 13

I have brought with me, on video-cassette, an assemblage of eight-millimeter movies taken by one of our better social chairmen, Bob Scott '61, back in the early sixties. As I show the old flicks—glimpses of snow statues, of the brothers cavorting at Hums, of parties and our great perennial R&B band, Lonnie Youngblood and the Redcoats (the original Otis Day and the Knights)—pledges are periodically sent to "run a rack." They return with lengths of plank covered with brimming beer cups so that the brothers may indulge their taste for malt beverage. The crowd especially appreciates the sequence in which several old ADs eat the shirt of Bert Rowley '62 off his back. When the show concludes, they give it a round of snaps and sing a friendly (albeit obscene) song to me. Then one of them hands me a full 16-ounce cup of beer, and I see all these faces looking at me with expectation. 14

Good God, I think, can I still chug one of these things? Well, it *takes* a little longer than it used to, but, yes, I can! All right—still got my chops! The 15

ADs cheer, the ice is broken. We repair to the basement, where fine music is played, multifarious brews are demolished, and whoops of laughter fill the room. Sometimes, it occurs to me, despite the passage of time, the essence of things remains the same.

The Coed Fraternity Sorority System, as it is currently called, is made 16 up of nine sororities, five coed houses, and 17 "mainstream" fraternities. That's 31 organizations in all, in 27 houses. (Pi Lambda Phi went defunct in '67, and its former house no longer holds a fraternity. The DKE house was razed in '72.) Two fraternities and two sororities are predominantly black. They tend to have smaller memberships, and are "achievement oriented," in contrast to the mainstream houses, which are seen as primarily social outlets.

Well, right. The main function of most Dartmouth fraternities, as it 17 was in your day and mine, is social. Let's face it—Hanover is still a long way from anything. Without the houses, there's nothing to do. Sure, you can take in a string quartet at the Hop, or a movie, but after a while this gets old. You're 19, you want to *party*. The College has tried to provide "social alternatives"—dances at Collis Center, parties at the cluster housing—but they're just not the same. For one thing, College-sponsored events cannot serve alcohol to anyone under 21, and most students at Dartmouth are under 21. For another, you can't *trash* Collis Center or a dormitory; they're public places and don't belong to you. What it boils down to—there's nothing like getting down with your own friends on your own turf. Social alternatives are diet sodas—healthier for you, probably, but nowhere near as satisfying.

Let us state the obvious. College is the first time most young people 18 get away from home. It's a short, four-year window of opportunity, between the oppressiveness of living under the control of your parents and the oppressiveness of adult responsibilities, to raise some serious hell, to get a life-time's's worth of rude, rebellious and disreputable behavior out of your system. And I would submit that, by and large, this is a normal and healthy process.

In America, the expression of youthful exuberance is typically done in 19 tribes. Laughter and raucous celebration come easier when you have company; that's why sit-coms have laugh tracks. When the youths in question are from the inner city, the tribes are called gangs. In the sixties, they were communes, and the hell-raising was often political. In colleges, we know them as fraternities and sororities. Whatever they're called, the tribes are a sort of halfway house between childhood and maturity.

And probably a rejection of both. I have long theorized that Dart- 20 mouth students' singular passion for booting (that's recreational vomiting, for the clueless among you) is a metaphorical regurgitation of their polite, proper upbringings. Similarly, the unwashed clothing (I knew a Skidmore sophomore who called underwear worn longer than a week "oldies but goodies"), amiably destroyed fraternity interiors, malodorous basements and public urinations constitute a living-out of a "natural" (as in "unrefined") lifestyle that will soon be utterly forbidden to them for the rest of their lives. A contemporary addition is the use of dip, or smokeless tobacco. I'm told a pinch of this stuff, tucked behind your lower lip, can give you a nice buzz, "make your head feel numb" as one AD brother put it. What may be more important is that it forces you to spit. Repeatedly. So fraternity guys now have a new disgusting thing to do, and the mung on fraternity floors has gained a component—saliva. How gross! How wonderful!

Any good tribe has its badges, symbols, and lingo. House members 21 have a variety of sweatshirts, t-shirts, baseball caps and club jackets bearing their Greek letters. As for lingo, part of the fun of Dartmouth has always been its lively alternative vocabulary. You still hear "tails," "rally," "chug," and many other terms from my day. Of course, many more have come along since. Dorky people are known as "lunch meats." Drinking is "hooking." "Sweet!" is an expression of approval. ("Hey, we just went on tap." "Sweet!") To "ding" someone is to reject them. I'll leave it to you to find out what "piling" is.

At the heart of the fraternity experience is this powerful drive to *do* 22 stuff—legendary feats of endurance and consumption, acts of absurd, non-linear behavior. Fraternity guys, in their collegiate way, are playing Ken Kesey and the Merry Pranksters' game—living in a state of mystical, spiritual brotherhood, pressing the envelope of human experience, trying to take things *further*. This is the drive that prompted three AD brothers to take off late one night for Truth or Consequences, New Mexico, for no other reason than that it had a funny name. And another fellow to drive his car hundreds of times around the town square of Lebanon, until he ran out of gas. And another guy to plant himself nude in the hose closet of the basement, where he waited patiently for three hours until enough of us were drinking down there for him to pop the door open and amaze us. It's what made one of my brothers swear he could live on beer alone for one week (he didn't make it), and another bet he could survive inside the refrigerator of the tap system for an hour (he succeeded, drank one congratulatory beer, and retired from the scene early, swathed in blankets). It's what prompts stair diving, mooning someone's grandmother, trick-or-treating wearing nothing but a jack-o-lantern, supplying its nose with a portion of your anatomy. There's no reason for this stuff—you just *do* it. It's existential, dadaist performance art.

Then there's hazing. In my day, there were pledge papers ("My 23 Sensations at Birth" was the mildest one), crew races, and a painful interview with a "Grand Inquisitor." Today, of course, there *is* no hazing at Dartmouth, so the following stories must be from somewhere else. One house drops its pledges a few miles out of town, naked with an axe. The point is to get back to campus. Ever try hitchhiking naked with an axe? Pledges of another fraternity are threatened with a punishment for pledging infractions known as the Rack of Gnarl—up to a dozen cups containing a mixture of catsup, soy sauce, dog food, mouthwash, and whatever other unappetizing liquid or semi-liquid substances happen to be on hand. You're supposed to drink every cup, and, sorry, it's bad form to boot too soon.

Hazing gets a lot of criticism. In many cases, it *deserves* a lot of criticism. Done right, though—which is to say, in a spirit of friendship—it's basically fun, and serves some important functions. During your pledge period, you find you can do things you didn't think you could do, face scary stuff and come through fine. You learn you can trust your brother, that, ultimately, he's not going to let anything too terrible happen to you. Surviving the shared ordeal bonds you to your pledge brothers, and, for that matter, to everyone who's ever been a member of your house. Why this should seem important, I don't know, but it does seem so. Maybe it's just that it's damned pleasant to be bonded with other people—the world's a lonely place.

There *are* questionable sides to fraternities. There's sexism, and elitism, and conformity, and anti-intellectual hedonism, just as the critics say. This is not surprising. Young men, in fraternities or out, have always had a problem viewing young women as persons rather than pastries. Which is in no way a justification of that posture—the objectification of women is a bad thing. It just shouldn't come as a shock that 21-year-old guys behave that way.

Their penchant for elitism—the "We're number one" syndrome—and the conformity seem more a function of age than of house membership. And as for anti-intellectual hedonism . . . *yeah!* I mean, the animal in us needs care and feeding, too, just as badly as the scholar, the visionary, and the spiritual seeker. Yes, fraternities have defects. But so do sewing circles, scout troops, and Congresses. Fraternities are no more perfectable than any of humanity's other inventions.

Which does not mean there's no room for improvement. In fact, a more balanced approach to the fun and madness seems to be evolving these days. Just about everyone I talked to, including some independents, said so. There's a heightened awareness about alcohol, for one thing; during parties, sober brothers guard the exits, and take your keys away if you're too ripped to drive. Nor, at least in some houses, is there the pressure to drink there once was. AD pledges, for instance, are told by their pledgemaster straight out—if you don't want to, you don't have to.

The houses are in better physical shape, too, due largely to the implementation of Minimum Standards. And numerous Dartmouth women told me the guys are even making progress with sexism, that things are much better than they were a few years ago. So, as it turns out, much of the reform demanded by the College during the eighties has actually improved things, without diminishing the partying in the least.

Perhaps you, too, had gotten the impression from the relentless media reports of controversy and divisiveness at Dartmouth that somehow the fun

24

25

26

27

28

29

was getting lost up there. Put aside your fears. I spent time at more than a dozen houses—fraternities, sororities, and coed—and I'm happy to report that the men and women of today's Dartmouth are having as much fun as we ever did, if not more. You'd be proud of 'em.

Saturday of Green Key, my last day; tomorrow it's back to the   30
freeways and smog and mortgages and diaper-changings of real life. Turns out the AD house has its major annual party this afternoon on the front lawn. They've got this terrific funk band on the front porch, and the dudes are wailing. The yard is as packed with people as it was Green Key Weekend 28 years ago, the Sunday afternoon Chuck Berry was supposed to play. But I'm not dancing—I'm feeling grumpy about having to go home tomorrow, and, hell, a little burned out generally from trying to keep up with these 20-year-olds the whole week.

Thanks to last night's killer rain, much of the yard is a mud puddle.   31
After a while, predictably enough, the brothers decide to do a little mud diving. In fact, half the guys in the house quickly join in, as do many of the dates and friends and onlookers, and it looks like "Return of the Mud Monsters" out there. And, then, uh-oh—I spot seven or eight beslimed brothers headed straight for me with crazed, demented smiles.

Well, I don't feel like going in any mud, that's for sure. Later for that,   32
Jack. "Come on, you guys, let's just forget it, okay?" They blithely ignore me; I barely have time to toss my wallet and shades to my amused wife (who's been egging them on), and then I am being carried across the yard by all these guys—Donk and Oddjob and Mulch and Scurvey and Snot II and Toast and Remus and Spock—and they find a particularly juicy mud hole. . . . and put me in it!

And, whadda ya know, it's great! Suddenly, I'm not tired and I'm not   33
grumpy—it's as if I've been shot up with adrenaline. And, man, I'm dancing my brains out, exchanging high fives and whooping like a maniac, and it all comes back, that total party feeling, where time suspends and you're in an eternal, fun-filled *now*. This is it—the thing people join fraternities for—one of those peak Bacchanalian moments that know no equal. I feel closer to these dancing mud maniacs—guys I'd never met until a week ago, and who are young enough to be my kids—than I do to most of the people I see in my everyday life. They're my brothers! This bonding thing really works, even all these long, weary years later, and I couldn't be happier.

Ah, fraternities.   34

Sweet!   35

Questions for Study and Discussion

1. Cite several examples of "frat talk" Miller uses in this essay. What does such language add to his discussion of fraternities and the Greek system? What, if anything, would be lost if he did not use it? Explain.

2. What does Miller feel has contributed to the recent resurgence of fraternity enrollment?

3. In paragraph 5 Miller says of *Animal House* "it was time someone spoke up for good old irresponsible, sophomoric, hedonistic, over-the-top fun." Does Miller accomplish this in his essay?

4. What reason does Miller give for college students "booting," foregoing their laundering, and urinating in public? Do you agree with his reasoning?

5. Which individuals or groups have been opposed to the Greek system? On what do they base their opposition?

Writing Topics

1. In paragraph 17 Miller defends his position that "without the (fraternity) houses there's nothing to do," because "college-sponsored events cannot serve alcohol to anyone under 21" and "you can't trash . . . a dormitory." Is Miller saying that the only way to have fun is to drink and trash a room? Is this the only way to have fun? In an essay, answer these questions and defend or attack college-sponsored events on your campus.

2. In an essay, argue to eliminate or maintain college fraternities. What contributions does it make to campus life both socially and financially? In what ways is it detrimental? Are the advantages it offers worth the disadvantages? Use Miller's article as a guide or your own personal experience to support your argument.

A society as adept as ours has become at propaganda—whether political or commercial—should know that "persuasion," which means the art of launching myths and artificially inducing inhibitions, is every bit as effective as force of law.
BRIGID BROPHY

A thing is not necessarily true because badly uttered, nor false because spoken magnificently.
ST. AUGUSTINE

It isn't language that is sexist, it is society.
VICTORIA FROMKIN AND ROBERT RODMAN

Media and Advertising

JIB FOWLES

An expert in the analysis of industrial culture, Jib Fowles was born in Hartford, Connecticut, in 1940, and graduated from Wesleyan University. After completing his graduate studies at Columbia University and New York University, he accepted a teaching post at the University of Houston, where he is currently professor of studies of the future. Fowles has written *Mass Advertising as Social Forecast* (1976) and is the editor of the *Handbook of Futures Research* (1978).

In the following article, published in *ETC: A Review of General Semantics*, Fowles discusses the basic emotions that advertisers appeal to. Not coincidentally, the appeals parallel a "hierarchy of needs" described by leading psychologists.

Advertising's Fifteen Basic Appeals

Emotional Appeals

The nature of effective advertisements was recognized full well by the late media philosopher Marshall McLuhan. In his *Understanding Media*, the first sentence of the section on advertising reads, "The continuous pressure is to create ads more and more in the image of audience motives and desires." 1

By giving form to people's deep-lying desires, and picturing states of being that individuals privately yearn for, advertisers have the best chance of arresting attention and affecting communication. And that is the immediate goal of advertising: to tug at our psychological shirt sleeves and slow us down long enough for a word or two about whatever is being sold. We glance at a picture of a solitary rancher at work, and "Marlboro" slips into our minds. 2

Reprinted from *Et Cetera*, Volume 39, Number 3, Fall 1982. By permission of International Society for General Semantics, San Francisco.

Advertisers (I'm using the term as a shorthand for both the products'   3
manufacturers, who bring the ambition and money to the process, and the
advertising agencies, who supply the know-how) are ever more compelled to
invoke consumers' drives and longings; this is the "continuous pressure"
McLuhan refers to. Over the past century, the American marketplace has
grown increasingly congested as more and more products have entered into
the frenzied competition after the public's dollars. The economics of other
nations are quieter than ours since the volume of goods being hawked does
not so greatly exceed demand. In some economies, consumer wares are
scarce enough that no advertising at all is necessary. But in the United
States, we go to the other extreme. In order to stay in business, an
advertiser must strive to cut through the considerable commercial hub-bub
by any means available—including the emotional appeals that some observers have held to be abhorrent and underhanded.

The use of subconscious appeals is a comment not only on conditions   4
among sellers. As time has gone by, buyers have become stoutly resistant to
advertisements. We live in a blizzard of these messages and have learned to
turn up our collars and ward off most of them. A study done a few years ago
at Harvard University's Graduate School of Business Administration ventured that the average American is exposed to some 500 ads daily from
television, newspapers, magazines, radio, billboards, direct mail, and so on.
If for no other reason than to preserve one's sanity, a filter must be
developed in every mind to lower the number of ads a person is actually
aware of—a number this particular study estimated at about seventy-five
ads per day. (Of these, only twelve typically produce a reaction—nine
positive and three negative, on the average.) To be among the few messages
that do manage to gain access to minds, advertisers must be strategic,
perhaps even a little underhanded at times.

There are assumptions about personality underlying advertisers'   5
efforts to communicate via emotional appeals, and while these assumptions
have stood the test of time, they still deserve to be aired. Human beings, it is
presumed, walk around with a variety of unfulfilled urges and motives
swirling in the bottom half of their minds. Lusts, ambitions, tenderness,
vulnerabilities—they are constantly bubbling up, seeking resolution. These
mental forces energize people, but they are too crude and irregular to be
given excessive play in the real world. They must be capped with the
competent, sensible behavior that permits individuals to get along well in
society. However, this upper layer of mental activity, shot through with
caution and rationality, is not receptive to advertising's pitches. Advertisers
want to circumvent this shell of consciousness if they can, and latch on to
one of the lurching, subconscious drives.

In effect, advertisers over the years have blindly felt their way around   6
the underside of the American psyche, and by trial and error have discovered the softest points of entree, the places where their messages have

the greatest likelihood of getting by consumers' defenses. As McLuhan says elsewhere, "Gouging away at the surface of public sales resistance, the ad men are constantly breaking through into the *Alice in Wonderland* territory behind the looking glass, which is the world of subrational impulses and appetites."

An advertisement communicates by making use of a specially selected   7
image (of a supine female, say, or a curly-headed child, or a celebrity) which is designed to stimulate "subrational impulses and desires" even when they are at ebb, even if they are unacknowledged by their possessor. Some few ads have their emotional appeal in the text, but for the greater number by far the appeal is contained in the artwork. This makes sense, since visual communication better suits more primal levels of the brain. If the viewer of an advertisement actually has the importuned motive, and if the appeal is sufficiently well-fashioned to call it up, then the person can be hooked. The product in the ad may then appear to take on the semblance of gratification for the summoned motive. Many ads seem to be saying, "If you have this need, then this product will help satisfy it." It is a primitive equation, but not an ineffective one for selling.

Thus, most advertisements appearing in national media can be under-   8
stood as having two orders of content. The first is the appeal to deep-running drives in the minds of consumers. The second is information regarding the good or service being sold: its name, its manufacturer, its picture, its packaging, its objective attributes, its functions. For example, the reader of a brassiere advertisement sees a partially undraped but blandly unperturbed woman standing in an otherwise commonplace public setting, and may experience certain sensations; the reader also sees the name "Maidenform," a particular brassiere style, and, in tiny print, words about the material, colors, price. Or, the viewer of a television commercial sees a demonstration with four small boxes labelled 650, 650, 650, and 800; something in the viewer's mind catches hold of this, as trivial as thoughtful consideration might reveal it to be. The viewer is also exposed to the name "Anacin," its bottle, and its purpose.

Sometimes there is an apparently logical link between an ad's emo-   9
tional appeal and its product information. It does not violate common sense that Cadillac automobiles be photographed at country clubs, or that Japan Air Lines be associated with Orientalia. But there is no real need for the linkage to have a bit of reason behind it. Is there anything inherent to the connection between Salem cigarettes and mountains, Coke and a smile, Miller Beer and comradeship? The link being forged in minds between product and appeal is a pre-logical one.

People involved in the advertising industry do not necessarily talk in   10
the terms being used here. They are stationed at the sending end of this communications channel, and may think they are up to any number of things—Unique Selling Propositions, explosive copywriting, the optimal use

of demographics or psychographics, ideal media buys, high recall ratings, or whatever. But when attention shifts to the receiving end of the channel, and focuses on the instant of reception, then commentary becomes much more elemental: an advertising message contains something primary and primitive, an emotional appeal, that in effect is the thin end of the wedge, trying to find its way into a mind. Should this occur, the product information comes along behind.

When enough advertisements are examined in this light, it becomes clear that the emotional appeals fall into several distinguishable categories, and that every ad is a variation on one of a limited number of basic appeals. While there may be several ways of classifying these appeals, one particular list of fifteen has proven to be especially valuable.

Advertisements can appeal to:

1. The need for sex
2. The need for affiliation
3. The need to nurture
4. The need for guidance
5. The need to aggress
6. The need to achieve
7. The need to dominate
8. The need for prominence
9. The need for attention
10. The need for autonomy
11. The need to escape
12. The need to feel safe
13. The need for aesthetic sensations
14. The need to satisfy curiosity
15. Physiological needs: food, drink, sleep, etc.

Murray's List

Where does this list of advertising's fifteen basic appeals come from? Several years ago, I was involved in a research project which was to have as one segment an objective analysis of the changing appeals made in post–World War II American advertising. A sample of magazine ads would have their appeals coded into the categories of psychological needs they seemed aimed at. For this content analysis to happen, a complete roster of human motives would have to be found.

The first thing that came to mind was Abraham Maslow's famous four-part hierarchy of needs. But the briefest look at the range of appeals made in advertising was enough to reveal that they are more varied, and more profane, than Maslow had cared to account for. The search led on to the work of psychologist Henry A. Murray, who together with his colleagues at the Harvard Psychological Clinic had constructed a full taxonomy of needs. As described in *Explorations in Personality*, Murray's team had conducted a lengthy series of depth interviews with a number of subjects in order to derive from scratch what they felt to be the essential variables of personality. Forty-four variables were distinguished by the Harvard group, of which twenty were motives. The need for achievement ("to overcome obstacles and obtain a high standard") was one, for instance; the need to defer was another; the need to aggress was a third; and so forth.

Murray's list had served as the groundwork for a number of subsequent projects. Perhaps the best-known of these was David C. McClelland's extensive study of the need for achievement, reported in his *The Achieving Society*. In the process of demonstrating that a people's high need for achievement is predictive of later economic growth, McClelland coded achievement imagery and references out of a nation's folklore, songs, legends, and children's tales.

Following McClelland, I too wanted to cull the motivational appeals from a culture's imaginative product—in this case, advertising. To develop categories expressly for this purpose, I took Murray's twenty motives and added to them others he had mentioned in passing in *Explorations in Personality* but not included on the final list. The extended list was tried out on a sample of advertisements, and motives which never seemed to be invoked were dropped. I ended up with eighteen of Murray's motives, into which 770 print ads were coded. The resulting distribution is included in the 1976 book *Mass Advertising as Social Forecast*.

Since that time, the list of appeals has undergone refinements as a result of using it to analyze television commercials. A few more adjustments have stemmed from the efforts of students in my advertising classes to decode appeals; tens of term papers surveying thousands of advertisements have caused some inconsistencies in the list to be hammered out. Fundamentally, though, the list remains the creation of Henry Murray. In developing a comprehensive, parsimonious inventory of human motives, he pinpointed the subsurface mental forces that are the least quiescent and the most susceptible to advertisings entreaties.

Fifteen Appeals

1. *Need for sex.* Let's start with sex, because this is the appeal which seems to pop up first whenever the topic of advertising is raised. Whole books have been written about this one alone, to find a large audience of mildly titillated readers. Lately, due to campaigns to sell blue jeans, concern with sex in ads has redoubled.

The fascinating thing is not how much sex there is in advertising, but how little. Contrary to impressions, unambiguous sex is rare in these messages. Some of this surprising observation may be a matter of definition: the Jordache ads with the lithe, blouse-less female astride a similarly clad male is clearly an appeal to the audience's sexual drives, but the same cannot be said about Brooke Shields in the Calvin Klein commercials. Directed at young women and their credit-card-carrying mothers, the image of Miss Shields instead invokes the need to be looked at. Buy Calvins and you'll be the center of much attention, just as Brooke is, the ads imply; they do not primarily inveigle their target audience's need for sexual intercourse.

In the content analysis reported in *Mass Advertising as Social Forecast*, only two percent of ads were found to pander to this motive. Even *Playboy* ads shy away from sexual appeals: a recent issue contained eighty-three full-page ads, and just four of them (or less than five percent) could be said to have sex on their minds. 20

The reason this appeal is so little used is that it is too blaring and tends to obliterate the product information. Nudity in advertising has the effect of reducing brand recall. The people who do remember the product may do so because they have been made indignant by the ad; this is not the response most advertisers seek. 21

To the extent that sexual imagery is used, it conventionally works better on men than women; typically a female figure is offered up to the male reader. A Black Velvet liquor advertisement displays an attractive woman wearing a tight black outfit, recumbent under the legend, "Feel the Velvet." The figure does not have to be horizontal, however, for the appeal to be present, as National Airlines revealed in its "Fly me" campaign. Indeed, there does not even have to be a female in the ad: "Flick my Bic" was sufficient to convey the idea to many. 22

As a rule, though, advertisers have found sex to be a tricky appeal, to be used sparingly. Less controversial and equally fetching are the appeals to our need for affectionate human contact. 23

2. *Need for affiliation.* American mythology upholds autonomous individuals, and social statistics suggest that people are ever more going it alone in their lives, yet the high frequency of affiliative appeals in ads belies this. Or maybe it does not: maybe all the images of companionship are compensation for what Americans privately lack. In any case, the need to associate with others is widely invoked in advertising and is probably the most prevalent appeal. All sorts of goods and services are sold by linking them to our unfulfilled desires to be in good company. 24

According to Henry Murray, the need for affiliation consists of desires "to draw near and enjoyably cooperate or reciprocate with another; to please and win affection of another; to adhere and remain loyal to a friend." The manifestations of this motive can be segmented into several different types of affiliation, beginning with romance. 25

Courtship may be swifter nowadays, but the desire for pair-bonding is far from satiated. Ads reaching for this need commonly depict a youngish 26 male and female engrossed in each other. The head of the male is usually higher than the female's, even at this late date; she may be sitting or leaning while he is standing. They are not touching in the Smirnoff vodka ads, but obviously there is an intimacy, sometimes frolicsome, between them. The couple does touch for Martell Cognac when "The moment was Martell." For Wind Song perfume they have touched, and "Your Wind Song stays on his mind."

Depending on the audience, the pair does not absolutely have to be 27 young—just together. He gives her a DeBeers diamond, and there is a tear in her laugh lines. She takes Geritol and preserves herself for him. And numbers of consumers, wanting affection too, follow suit.

Warm family feelings are fanned in ads when another generation is 28 added to the pair. Hallmark Cards brings grandparents into the picture, and Johnson and Johnson Baby Powder has Dad, Mom, and baby, all fresh from the bath, encircled in arms and emblazoned with "Share the Feeling." A talc has been fused to familial love.

Friendship is yet another form of affiliation pursued by advertisers. 29 Two women confide and drink Maxwell House coffee together; two men walk through the woods smoking Salem cigarettes. Miller Beer promises that afternoon "Miller Time" will be staffed with three or four good buddies. Drink Dr. Pepper, as Mickey Rooney is coaxed to do, and join in with all the other Peppers. Coca-Cola does not even need to portray the friendliness; it has reduced this appeal to "a Coke and a smile."

The warmth can be toned down and disguised, but it is the same 30 affiliative need that is being fished for. The blonde has a direct gaze and her friends are firm businessmen in appearance, but with a glass of Old Bushmill you can sit down and fit right in. Or, for something more upbeat, sing along with the Pontiac choirboys.

As well as presenting positive images, advertisers can play to the need 31 for affiliation in negative ways, by invoking the fear of rejection. If we don't use Scope, we'll have the "Ugh! Morning Breath" that causes the male and female models to avert their faces. Unless we apply Ultra-Brite or Close-Up to our teeth, it's goodbye romance. Our family will be cursed with "House-a-tosis" if we don't take care. Without Dr. Scholl's anti-perspirant foot spray, the bowling team will keel over.. There go all the guests when the supply of Dorito's nacho cheese chips is exhausted. Still more rejection if our shirts have ring-around-the-collar, if our car needs to be Midasized. But make a few purchases, and we are back in the bosom of human contact.

As self-directed as Americans pretend to be, in the last analysis we 32 remain social animals, hungering for the positive, endorsing feelings that only those around us can supply. Advertisers respond, urging us to "Reach out and touch someone," in the hopes our monthly bills will rise.

3. *Need to nurture.* Akin to affiliative needs is the need to take care of 33 small, defenseless creatures—children and pets, largely. Reciprocity is of less

consequence here, though; it is the giving that counts. Murray uses synonyms like "to feed, help, support, console, protect, comfort, nurse, heal." A strong need it is, woven deep into our genetic fabric, for if it did not exist we could not successfully raise up our replacements. When advertisers put forth the image of something diminutive and furry, something that elicits the word "cute" or "precious," then they are trying to trigger this motive. We listen to the childish voice singing the Oscar Mayer wiener song, and our next hot-dog purchase is prescribed. Aren't those darling kittens something, and how did this Meow Mix get into our shopping cart?

This pitch is often directed at women, as Mother Nature's chief   34
nurturers. "Make me some Kraft macaroni and cheese, please," says the elfin preschooler just in from the snowstorm, and mothers' hearts go out, and Kraft's sales go up. "We're cold, wet, and hungry," whine the husband and kids, and the little women gets the Manwiches ready. A facsimile of this need can be hit without children or pets; the husband is ill and sleepless in the television commercial, and the wife grudgingly fetches the NyQuil.

But it is not women alone who can be touched by this appeal. The   35
father nurses his son Eddie through adolescence while the John Deere lawn tractor survives the years. Another father counts pennies with his young son as the subject of New York Life Insurance comes up. And all over America are businessmen who don't know why they dial Qantas Airlines when they have to take a trans-Pacific trip; the koala bear knows.

4. Need for guidance. The opposite of the need to nurture is the need to   36
be nurtured: to be protected, shielded, guided. We may be loath to admit it, but the child lingers on inside every adult—and a good thing it does, or we would not be instructable in our advancing years. Who wants a nation of nothing but flinty personalities?

Parent-like figures can successfully call up this need. Robert Young   37
recommends Sanka coffee, and since we have experienced him for twenty-five years as television father and doctor, we take his word for it. Florence Henderson as the expert mom knows a lot about the advantages of Wesson oil.

The parent-ness of the spokesperson need not be so salient; sometimes   38
pure authoritativeness is better. When Orson Wells scowls and intones, "Paul Masson will sell no wine before its time," we may not know exactly what he means, but we still take direction from him. There is little maternal about Brenda Vaccaro when she speaks up for Tampax, but there is a certainty to her that many accept.

A celebrity is not a necessity in making a pitch to the need for   39
guidance, since a fantasy figure can serve just as well. People accede to the Green Giant, or Betty Crocker, or Mr. Goodwrench. Some advertisers can get by with no figure at all: "When E. F. Hutton talks, people listen."

Often it is tradition or custom that advertisers point to and consumers   40
take guidance from. Bits and pieces of American history are used to sell

whiskeys like Old Crow, Southern Comfort, Jack Daniels. We conform to traditional male/female roles and age-old social norms when we purchase Barclay cigarettes, which informs us "The pleasure is back."

The product itself, if it has been around for a long time, can constitute   41
a tradition. All those old labels in the ad for Morton salt convince us that we should continue to buy it. Kool-Aid says, "You loved it as a kid. You trust it as a mother," hoping to get yet more consumers to go along.

Even when the product has no history at all, our need to conform to   42
tradition and to be guided are strong enough that they can be invoked through bogus nostalgia and older actors. Country-Time lemonade sells because consumers want to believe it has a past they can defer to.

So far the needs and the ways they can be invoked which have been   43
looked at are largely warm and affiliative; they stand in contrast to the next set of needs, which are much more egoistic and assertive.

5. *Need to aggress.* The pressures of the real world create strong   44
retaliatory feelings in every functioning human being. Since these impulses can come forth as bursts of anger and violence, their display is normally tabooed. Existing as harbored energy, aggressive drives present a large, tempting target for advertisers. It is not a target to be aimed at thoughtlessly, though, for few manufacturers want their products associated with destructive motives. There is always the danger that, as in the case of sex, if the appeal is too blatant, public opinion will turn against what is being sold.

Jack-in-the-Box sought to abruptly alter its marketing by going after   45
older customers and forgetting the younger ones. Their television commercials had a seventy-ish lady command, "Waste him," and the Jack-in-the-Box clown exploded before our eyes. So did public reaction, until the commercials were toned down. Print ads for Club cocktails carried the faces of octogenarians under the headline, "Hit me with a Club"; response was contrary enough to bring the campaign to a stop.

Better disguised aggressive appeals are less likely to backfire: Triumph   46
cigarettes has models making a lewd gesture with their uplifted cigarettes, but the individuals are often laughing and usually in the close company of others. When Exxon said, "There's a Tiger in your tank," the implausibility of it concealed the invocation of aggressive feelings.

Depicted arguments are a common way for advertisers to tap the   47
audience's needs to aggress. Don Rickles and Linda Carter trade gibes, and consumers take sides as the name of Seven-Up is stitched on minds. The Parkay tub has a difference of opinion with the user; who can forget it, or who (or what) got the last word in?

6. *Need to achieve.* This is the drive that energizes people, causing them   48
to strive in their lives and careers. According to Murray, the need for achievement is signalled by the desires "to accomplish something difficult. To overcome obstacles and attain a high standard. To excel one's self. To

rival and surpass others." A prominent American trait, it is one that advertisers like to hook on to because it identifies their product with winning and success.

The Cutty Sark ad does not disclose that Ted Turner failed at his 49 latest attempt at yachting's America Cup; here he is represented as a champion on the water as well as off in his television enterprises. If we drink this whiskey, we will be victorious alongside Turner. We can also succeed with O. J. Simpson by renting Hertz cars, or with Reggie Jackson by bringing home some Panasonic equipment. Cathy Rigby and Stayfree Maxipads will put people out front.

Sports heroes are the most convenient means to snare consumers' 50 needs to achieve, but they are not the only one. Role models can be established, ones which invite emulation, as with the profiles put forth by Dewar's scotch. Successful, tweedy individuals relate they have "graduated to the flavor of Myer's rum." Or the advertiser can establish a prize: two neighbors play one-on-one basketball for a Michelob beer in a television commercial, while in a print ad a bottle of Johnnie Walker Black Label has been gilded like a trophy.

Any product that advertises itself in superlatives—the best, the first, 51 the finest—is trying to make contact with our needs to succeed. For many consumers, sales and bargains belong in this category of appeals, too; the person who manages to buy something at fifty percent off is seizing an opportunity and coming out ahead of others.

7. *Need to dominate.* This fundamental need is the craving to be 52 powerful—perhaps omnipotent, as in the Xerox ad where Brother Dominic exhibits heavenly powers and creates miraculous copies. Most of us will settle for being just a regular potentate, though. We drink Budweiser because it is the King of Beers, and here come the powerful Clydesdales to prove it. A taste of Wolfschmidt vodka and "The spirit of the Czar lives on."

The need to dominate and control one's environment is often thought 53 of as being masculine, but as close students of human nature advertisers know, it is not so circumscribed. Women's aspirations for control are suggested in the campaign theme, "I like my men in English Leather, or nothing at all." The females in the Chanel No. 19 ads are "outspoken" and wrestle their men around.

Male and female, what we long for is clout; what we get in its place is 54 Mastercard.

8. *Need for prominence.* Here comes the need to be admired and 55 respected, to enjoy prestige and high social status. These times, it appears, are not so egalitarian after all. Many ads picture the trappings of high position; the Oldsmobile stands before a manorial doorway, the Volvo is parked beside a steeplechase. A book-lined study is the setting for Dewar's 12, and Lenox China is displayed in a dining room chock full of antiques.

Beefeater gin represents itself as "The Crown Jewel of England" and 56 uses no illustrations of jewels or things British, for the words are sufficient indicators of distinction. Buy that gin and you will rise up the prestige hierarchy, or achieve the same effect on yourself with Seagram's 7 Crown, which unambiguously describes itself as "classy."

Being respected does not have to entail the usual accoutrements of wealth: "Do you know who I am?" the commercials ask, and we learn that the prominent person is not so prominent without his American Express card.   57

9. *Need for attention.* The previous need involved being *looked up to,* while this is the need to be *looked at.* The desire to exhibit ourselves in such a way as to make others look at us is a primitive, insuppressible instinct. The clothing and cosmetic industries exist just to serve this need, and this is the way they pitch their wares. Some of this effort is aimed at males, as the ads for Hathaway shirts and Jockey underclothes. But the greater bulk of such appeals is targeted singlemindedly at women.   58

To come back to Brooke Shields: this is where she fits into American marketing. If I buy Calvin Klein jeans, consumers infer, I'll be the object of fascination. The desire for exhibition has been most strikingly played to in a print campaign of many years duration, that of Maidenform lingerie. The woman exposes herself, and sales surge. "Gentlemen prefer Hanes" the ads dissemble, and women who want eyes upon them know what they should do. Peggy Fleming flutters her legs for L'eggs, encouraging females who want to be the star in their own lives to purchase this product.   59

The same appeal works for cosmetics and lotions. For years, the little girl with the exposed backside sold gobs of Coppertone, but now the company has picked up the pace a little: as a female, you are supposed to "Flash 'em a Coppertone tan." Food can be sold the same way, especially to the diet-conscious; Angie Dickinson poses for California avocadoes and says, "Would this body lie to you?" Our eyes are too fixed on her for us to think to ask if she got that way by eating mounds of guacamole.   60

10. *Need for autonomy.* There are several ways to sell credit card services, as has been noted: Mastercard appeals to the need to dominate, and American Express to the need for prominence. When Visa claims, "You can have it the way you want it," yet another primary motive is being beckoned forward—the need to endorse the self. The focus here is upon the independence and integrity of the individual; this need is the antithesis of the need for guidance and is unlike any of the social needs. "If running with the herd isn't your style, try ours," says Rotan-Mosle, and many Americans feel they have finally found the right brokerage firm.   61

The photo is of a red-coated Mountie on his horse, posed on a snow-covered ledge; the copy reads, "Windsor—one Canadian stands alone." This epitome of the solitary and proud individual may work best with male customers, as may Winston's man in the red cap. But one-figure advertisements also strike the strong need for autonomy among American women. As Shelly Hack strides for Charlie perfume, females respond to her obvious pride and flair; she is her own person. The Virginia Slims' tale is of people   62 who have come a long way from subservience to independence. Cachet perfume feels it does not need a solo figure to work this appeal, and uses three different faces in its ads; it insists, though, "It's different on every women who wears it."

Like many psychological needs, this one can also be appealed to in a   63
negative fashion, by invoking the loss of independence or self-regard. Guilt and regrets can be stimulated: "Gee, I could have had a V-8." Next time, get one and be good to yourself.

11. *Need to escape.* An appeal to the need for autonomy often co-   64
occurs with one for the need to escape, since the desire to duck out of our social obligations, to seek rest or adventure, frequently takes the form of one-person flight. The dashing image of a pilot, in fact, is a standard way of quickening this need to get away from it all.

Freedom is the pitch here, the freedom that every individual yearns   65
for whenever life becomes too oppressive. Many advertisers like appealing to the need for escape because the sensation of pleasure often accompanies escape, and what nicer emotional nimbus could there be for a product? "You deserve a break today," says McDonalds, and Stouffer's frozen foods chime in, "Set yourself free."

For decades men have imaginatively bonded themselves to the Marl-   66
boro cowboy who dwells untarnished and unencumbered in Marlboro Country some distance from modern life; smokers' aching needs for auton-omy and escape are personified by that cowpoke. Many women can identify with the lady ambling through the woods behind the words, "Benson and Hedges and mornings and me."

But escape does not have to be solitary. Other Benson and Hedges   67
ads, part of the same campaign, contain two strolling figures. In Salem cigarette advertisments, it can be several people who escape together into the mountaintops. A commercial for Levi's pictured a cloudbank above a city through which ran a whole chain of young people.

There are varieties of escape, some wistful like the Boeing "Someday"   68
campaign of dream vacations, some kinetic like the play and parties in soft drink ads. But in every instance, the consumer exposed to the advertise-ment is invited to momentarily depart his everyday life for a more carefree experience, preferably with the product in hand.

12. *Need to feel safe.* Nobody in their right mind wants to be intimi-   69
dated, menaced, battered, poisoned. We naturally want to do whatever it takes to stave off threats to our well-being, and to our families'. It is the instinct for self-preservation that makes us responsive to the ad of the St. Bernard with the keg of Chivas Regal. We pay attention to the stern talk of Karl Malden and the plight of the vacationing couples who have lost all their funds in the American Express travelers cheques commercials. We want the omnipresent stag from Hartford Insurance to watch over us too.

In the interest of keeping failure and calamity from our lives, we like to   70
see the durability of products demonstrated. Can we ever forget that Timex

takes a licking and keeps on ticking? When the American Tourister suitcase bounces all over the highway and the egg inside doesn't break, the need to feel safe has been adroitly plucked.

We take precautions to diminish future threats. We buy Volkswagen 71 Rabbits for the extraordinary mileage, and MONY insurance policies to avoid the tragedies depicted in their black-and-white ads of widows and orphans.

We are careful about our health. We consume Mazola margarine 72 because it has "corn goodness" backed by the natural food traditions of the American Indians. In the medicine cabinet is Alka-Seltzer, the "home remedy"; having it, we are snug in our little cottage.

We want to be safe and secure; buy these products, advertisers are 73 saying, and you'll be safer than you are without them.

13. *Need for aesthetic sensations.* There is an undeniable aesthetic 74 component to virtually every ad run in the national media: the photography or filming or drawing is near-perfect, the type style is well chosen, the layout could scarcely be improved upon. Advertisers know there is little chance of good communication occurring if an ad is not visually pleasing. Consumers may not be aware of the extent of their own sensitivity to artwork, but it is undeniably large.

Sometimes the aesthetic element is expanded and made into an ad's 75 primary appeal. Charles Jordan shoes may or may not appear in the accompanying avant-garde photographs; Kohler plumbing fixtures catch attention through the high style of their desert settings. Beneath the slightly out of focus photograph, languid and sensuous in tone, General Electric feels called upon to explain, "This is an ad for the hair dryer."

This appeal is not limited to female consumers: J and B scotch says "It 76 whispers" and shows a bucolic scene of lake and castle.

14. *Need to satisfy curiosity.* It may seem odd to list a need for 77 information among basic motives, but this need can be as primal and compelling as any of the others. Human beings are curious by nature, interested in the world around them, and intrigued by tidbits of knowledge and new developments. Trivia, percentages, observations counter to conventional wisdom—these items all help sell products. Any advertisement in a question-and-answer format is strumming this need.

A dog groomer has a question about long distance rates, and Bell 78 Telephone has a chart with all the figures. An ad for Porsch 911 is replete with diagrams and schematics, numbers and arrows. Lo and behold, Anacin pills have 150 more milligrams than its competitors; should we wonder if this is better or worse for us?

15. *Physiological needs.* To the extent that sex is solely a biological need, 79 we are now coming around full circle, back towards the start of the list. In this final category are clustered appeals to sleeping, eating, drinking. The art of photographing food and drink is so advanced, sometimes these temptations are wonderously caught in the camera's lens: the crab meat in

the Red Lobster restaurant ads can start us salivating, the Quarterpounder can almost be smelled, the liquor in the glass glows invitingly. Imbibe, these ads scream.

Styles

Some common ingredients of advertisements were not singled out for separate mention in the list of fifteen because they are not appeals in and of themselves. They are stylistic features, influencing the way a basic appeal is presented. The use of humor is one, and the use of celebrities is another. A third is time imagery, past and future, which goes to several purposes. [80]

For all of its employment in advertising, humor can be treacherous, because it can get out of hand and smother the product information. Supposedly, this is what Alka-Seltzer discovered with its comic commercials of the late sixties; "I can't believe I ate the whole thing," the sad-faced husband lamented, and the audience cackled so much it forgot the antacid. Or, did not take it seriously. [81]

But used carefully, humor can punctuate some of the softer appeals and soften some of the harsher ones. When Emma says to the Fruit-of-the-Loom fruits, "Hi, cuties. Whatcha doing in my laundry basket?" we smile as our curiosity is assuaged along with hers. Bill Cosby gets consumers tickled about the children in his Jell-O commercials, and strokes the need to nurture. [82]

An insurance company wants to invoke the need to feel safe, but does not want to leave readers with an unpleasant aftertaste; cartoonist Rowland Wilson creates an avalanche about to crush a gentleman who is saying to another, "My insurance company? New England Life, of course. Why?" The same tactic of humor undercutting threat is used in the cartoon commercials for Safeco when the Pink Panther wanders from one disaster to another. Often humor masks aggression: comedian Bob Hope in the outfit of a boxer promises to knock out the knock-knocks with Texaco; Rodney Dangerfield, who "can't get no respect," invites aggression as the comic relief in Miller Lite commercials. [83]

Roughly fifteen percent of all advertisements incorporate a celebrity, almost always from the fields of entertainment or sports. This approach can also prove troublesome for advertisers, for celebrities are human beings too, and fully capable of the most remarkable behavior; if anything distasteful about them emerges, it is likely to reflect on the product. The advertisers making use of Anita Bryant and Billy Jean King suffered several anxious moments. An untimely death can also reflect poorly on a product. But advertisers are willing to take these risks because celebrities can be such a good link between producers and consumers, performing the social role of introducer. [84]

There are several psychological needs these middlemen can play upon. Let's take the product class of cameras and see how different celebrities can [85] hit different needs. The need for guidance can be invoked by Michael Landon, who plays such a wonderful dad on "Little House on the Prairie"; when he says to buy Kodak equipment, many people listen. James Garner for Polaroid cameras is put in a similar authoritative role, so defined by a mocking spouse. The need to achieve is summoned up by Tracy Austin and other tennis stars for Canon AE-1; the advertiser first makes sure we see these athletes playing to win. When Cheryl Tiegs speaks up for Olympus cameras, it is the need for attention that is being targeted.

The past and future, being outside our grasp, are exploited by adver- 86 tisers as locales for the projection of needs. History can offer up heroes (and call up the need to achieve) or traditions (need for guidance) as well as art objects (need for aesthetic sensations). Nostalgia is a kindly version of personal history and is deployed by advertisers to rouse needs for affiliation and for guidance; the need to escape can come in here, too. The same need to escape is sometimes the point of futuristic appeals, but picturing the avant-garde can also be a way to get at the need to achieve.

Analyzing Advertisements

When analyzing ads yourself for their emotional appeals, it takes a bit 87 of practice to learn to ignore the product information (as well as one's own experience and feelings about the product). But that skill comes soon enough, as does the ability to quickly sort out from all the non-product aspects of an ad the chief element which is the most striking, the most likely to snag attention first and penetrate brains furthest. The key to the appeal, this element usually presents itself centrally and forwardly to the reader or viewer.

Another clue: the viewing angle which the audience has on the ad's 88 subjects is informative. If the subjects are photographed or filmed from below and thus are looking down at you much as the Green Giant does, then the need to be guided is a good candidate for the ad's emotional appeal. If, on the other hand, the subjects are shot from above and appear deferential, as is often the case with children or female models, then other needs are being appealed to.

To figure out an ad's emotional appeal, it is wise to know (or have a 89 good hunch about) who the targeted consumers are; this can often be inferred from the magazine or television show it appears in. This piece of information is a great help in determining the appeal and in deciding between two different interpretations. For example, if an ad features a partially undressed female, this would typically signal one appeal for readers of *Penthouse* (need for sex) and another for readers of *Cosmopolitan* (need for attention).

It would be convenient if every ad made just one appeal, were aimed at 90 just one need. Unfortunately, things are often not that simple. A cigarette ad with a couple at the edge of a polo field is trying to hit both the need for affiliation and the need for prominence; depending on the attitude of the male, dominance could also be an ingredient in this. An ad for Chimere perfume incorporates two photos: in the top one the lady is being commanding at a business luncheon (need to dominate), but in the lower one she is being bussed (need for affiliation). Better ads, however, seem to avoid being too diffused; in the study of post–World War II advertising described earlier, appeals grew more focused as the decades passed. As a rule of thumb, about sixty percent of ads make one paramount appeal; roughly twenty percent have two conspicuous appeals; the last twenty percent have three or more. Rather than looking for the greatest number of appeals, decoding ads is most productive when the loudest one or two appeals are discerned, since those are the appeals with the best chance of grabbing people's attention.

Finally, analyzing ads does not have to be a solo activity and probably   91
should not be. The greater number of people there are involved, the better chance there is of transcending individual biases and discovering the essential emotional lure built into an advertisement.

Do They or Don't They?

Do the emotional appeals made in advertisements add up to the   92
sinister manipulation of consumers?

It is clear that these ads work. Attention is caught, communication   93
occurs between producers and consumers, and sales result. It turns out to be difficult to detail the exact relationship between a specific ad and a specific purchase, or even between a campaign and subsequent sales figures, because advertising is only one of a host of influences upon consumption. Yet no one is fooled by this lack of perfect proof; everyone knows that advertising sells. If this were not the case, then tight-fisted American businesses would not spend a total of fifty billion dollars annually on these messages.

But before anyone despairs that advertisers have our number to the   94
extent that they can marshall us at will and march us like automatons to the check-out counters, we should recall the resiliency and obduracy of the American consumer. Advertisers may have uncovered the softest spots in minds, but that does not mean they have found truly gaping apertures. There is no evidence that advertising can get people to do things contrary to their self-interests. Despite all the finesse of advertisements, and all the subtle emotional tugs, the public resists the vast majority of the petitions. According to the marketing division of the A. C. Nielsen Company, a whopping seventy-five percent of all new products die within a year in the marketplace, the victims of consumer disinterest which no amount of advertising could overcome. The appeals in advertising may be the most

captivating there are to be had, but they are not enough to entrap the wiley consumer.

The key to understanding the discrepancy between, on the one hand, 95 the fact that advertising truly works, and, on the other, the fact that it hardly works, is to take into account the enormous numbers of people exposed to an ad. Modern-day comunications permit an ad to be displayed to millions upon millions of individuals; if the smallest fraction of that audience can be moved to buy the product, then the ad has been successful. When one percent of the people exposed to a television advertising campaign reach for their wallets, that could be one million sales, which may be enough to keep the product in production and the advertisements coming.

In arriving at an evenhanded judgment about advertisements and 96 their emotional appeals, it is good to keep in mind that many of the purchases which might be credited to these ads are experienced as genuinely gratifying to the consumer. We sincerely like the good or service we have bought, and we may even like some of the emotional drapery that an ad suggests comes with it. It has sometimes been noted that the most avid students of advertisements are the people who have just bought the product; they want to steep themselves in the associated imagery. This may be the reason that Americans, when polled, are not negative about advertising and do not disclose any sense of being misused. The volume of advertising may be an irritant, but the product information as well as the imaginative material in ads are partial compensation.

A productive understanding is that advertising messages involve costs 97 and benefits at both ends of the communications channel. For those few ads which do make contact, the consumer surrenders a moment of time, has the lower brain curried, and receives notice of a product; the advertiser has given up money and has increased the chance of sales. In this sort of communications activity, neither party can be said to be the loser.

Questions for Study and Discussion

1. In paragraph 4 Fowles states that buyers have become resistant to advertisements and we turn up our collars at most of them. Do you agree with this statement?

2. How would you define Fowles's tone? Use examples of diction to support your answer.

3. Fowles theorizes that in addition to using unsubstantiated or misleading text, TV advertisers appeal to viewers' emotions. What kind of evidence does he offer to support his argument? Is he convincing?

4. Where does Fowles feel the emotional appeal is contained in an ad?

5. How does Florence Henderson help sell Wesson Oil according to Fowles? What does his explanation reveal about his attitude toward consumers? What is your reaction to his attitude? Explain.

6. Fowles implies that viewer response brought a halt to Club Cocktails ad campaigns. Is his explanation realistic? What type of action do you think it would take to halt an ad campaign?

Writing Topics

1. One topic Fowles did not discuss in relation to advertising and psychology is subliminal advertising. This tactic works by hiding a message in a commercial, for example, inserting one frame of "Buy Krunchy Kookie Cereal" in an ad for this product. The eye never acknowledges it, but the mind picks up the message. In an essay, discuss your feelings regarding the use of psychology and subliminal advertising.

2. *Adweek*, an advertising trade journal, annually accepts nominations for the year's worst advertisements. Contributors to the "BADvertising" feature selected ads that they dislike for one reason or another. Nominate five ads that irritate you and another five that you consider ineffective. In an essay explain how each qualifies for an award in its category.

RON ROSENBAUM

Ron Rosenbaum was born in New York in 1946 and graduated from Yale University in 1968. He began his career as a writer by joining the staff of New York's weekly *Village Voice* and has contributed articles to magazines such as *Esquire* and *Harper's*. Some of these pieces have been collected in *Rebirth of a Salesman: Tales of the Song and Dance Seventies* (1978); he has also written a novel, *Murder at Elaine's* (1979). His latest book is *Manhattan Passions: True Tales of Power, Wealth, and Excess* (1987).

Rosenbaum concludes that advertising tells us more about ourselves and our times than does *Masterpiece Theatre* or "a week's worth of sit-coms." He noticed that television advertising began to change with the onset of the 1980s, and in this essay, published in *Mother Jones* in 1981, he points out what is new—and why.

The Hard Sell

Too many viewers, I'm afraid, miss out on the most exciting intellectual challenge offered by television: the commercials. That's right. I said the intellectual challenge of TV commercials and I don't mean just the task of choosing between Stove Top stuffing and potatoes. I mean the pleasure to be found in pitting your intellect against some of the cleverest minds in the country, the Masterminds of Madison Avenue, and trying to figure out how they've figured *you* out. 1

Too many TV watchers still leave the room during TV commercials for some trivial reason. As a result, they miss some of the best-produced, most skillfully scripted and edited dramas on TV: more thought, more research into human nature and, in some cases, more dollars go into creating those 30- and 60-second ads than into the development of most 30- and 60-minute prime-time programs. 2

I never leave the room during the commercials. I sit spellbound watching them. I take notes. The highpoint of an evening before the set for me can be discovering a new wrinkle in Mr. Whipple's war on secretive Charmin squeezers, or catching the debut of one of the grand, soaring production numbers the airline or beer people put on to get us in the mood for getting high. I find more intrigue in trying to figure out the mysterious appeal of Mrs. Olsen and Robert Young, those continuing characters in coffee commercials, than in the predictable puzzles of *Masterpiece Theatre*. 3

And I'm convinced that future archeologists will find more concentrated and reliable clues to the patterns of our culture in one Clorox ad than they could ever find in a week's worth of sit-coms.

Take a look at some of the key trends in TV ads of the 1980s, the changes in tone and technique, and you can see what they tell us about ourselves and consciousness of the new decade.

No More Nice Guys

The early '80s have witnessed the return of the Hard Sell, or what might be called the "no more Mr. Nice Guy" school of commercial strategy. If you had been watching closely you could have picked up an advance warning, a seismic tremor of the shift to come, in the Buick slogan change. In the fall of 1979 Buick abruptly yanked its confident slogan, the one that told us "Make it Buick. After all, life is to enjoy." Then, after that, everything changed.

The Buick ads of the '80s no longer take a firm position on the meaning of life. Instead they give us hard numbers and initials: EPA est. MPG.[1] Which leaves us to wonder; if life is no longer "to enjoy," what is life to? In the world of the new no-nonsense ads, life is to *struggle*, life is to fight for survival in a nasty brutish world. "Life got tougher," the makers of Excedrin tell us, so "we got stronger." And the airways are filled with new, tougher, hard-edged combative spirit. Little old ladies are seen savagely socking gas pumps in the midsections. Vicious tempers flare into public displays of anger in Sanka commercials. For years, tough guy Robert Conrad postured pugnaciously and challenged the unsuspecting viewer: "I dare you to call this an ordinary battery," threatening by implication to step right out of the tube and commit some assault and battery right there in our living rooms.

This aggressive stance is echoed by the take-it-or-leave-it approach of the Italian food canner who declares, "Make it Progresso, or make it yourself," and was heralded by the Japanese car maker who told us, "If you can find a better-built car than Toyota, buy it." This dismissive imperative tone of voice is the new keynote of ads in the 1980s.

You could see the philosophy of the new no-nonsense school being formulated by the deep-thinkers of Madison Avenue in the first year of the new decade. The pages of *Advertising Age* were filled with speculations by ad people about what to name the period. "The Aching '80s" was one suggestion. "The Decade of Difficult Decisions," "The Era of Uncertainty," "The Return to Reality" were others. Each sage of the new era wanted to distinguish the '80s from the previous decade, from what one advertising

[1]Environmental Protection Agency–estimated miles per gallon.

agency commentator called "the self-centered, the self-indulgent, self-gratifying of the Me Decade."

The battle between the old and the new is not confined to the pages of 9
Ad Age. If you want a quick tour of the combat zone, the best place to start is with the big-money brokerage battle. You can usually catch the clash on the Sunday interview shows (*Meet the Press* and the others). Here you can see four brokerage houses go after their potential client targets with two totally different advertising strategies. While Paine Webber and Dean Witter try to win hearts and minds with the Late-'70s-Wish-Fulfillment approach, Merrill Lynch and Smith Barney assault the viewer with the blasted landscape of Early '80s Angst.

To shift back and forth between the two worlds invites severe disorien- 10
tation. Start with Dean Witter's world, where ecstatic customers are always getting calls and letters from their broker that cause them to burst with joyful financial fulfillment as a heavenly-sounding choir croons:

"You look like you just heard from Dean Witter." 11

Contrast that with the lead character from another brokerage ad. He's 12
alone. He's lost. There is pain in his big sad eyes; he's cutting his hooves on icy rocks and crusts of snow as he slowly picks his way in search of shelter. This harsh winter scene is "today's investment climate," a voice-over tells us, a time to "protect your assets." We watch the bull finally find a dank cave in which to shelter his assets (a parable about tax shelters,[2] it seems) just as a terrifying crack of thunder bursts over the frozen wasteland outside. There hasn't been a storm more fraught with the sheer terror of existence since the third act of *King Lear*. This is no mere investment climate; this is all the cold and terror and loneliness of modern life.

In his most recent appearances, we see the solitary bull wandering a 13
barren desert wasteland beset by the tormenting trickery of a mirage; in another we see him stepping into a bewildering hedge maze, which conjures up the horror of the hedge maze chase in Stanley Kubrick's *The Shining* as much as it does the subtle securities offered by hedge funds[3] on the financial scene. Finally—it was inevitable—the poor beast becomes the proverbial "bull in the china shop," making his way through a maze of crystal and making us feel the frightening fragility of the most cloistered of civilized interiors.

A Bull Apart

That lonely bull. He's lonelier than ever now, farther off than ever 14
from any hope of reunion with his herd. Faithful bull-watchers realize that

---

[2]Investments that permit one to "shelter" income from taxes.

[3]Investments that protect, or "hedge" against losses.

the '80s have introduced the third major phase in the bull's relation to the herd. In the original Merrill Lynch ads of the early '70s, when Merrill Lynch was still unabashedly "bullish on America," he was joyfully romping with the whole happy herd. In fact, we didn't even single out any particular bull, such was the togetherness of the big beasts. A late '70s series of Merrill Lynch ads would open on a lone bull majestically patrolling scenic outposts on his own but rejoining the herd in the final shot because, in the modified slogan, Merrill Lynch was "still bullish on America."

Then at the very beginning of the new decade the herd disappeared   15
from the ads completely. (What has become of the other bulls? PBB poisoning? Cattle mutilations?) Gone too is any attempt to further refurbish the "bullish on America" slogan. (What could they say—"We're *really, truly,* still bullish on America"?)

The new slogan, "Merrill Lynch—a breed apart," tells us there's no   16
time to worry about the herd; you have to look after your own assets in today's cold and nasty economic climate, in which the market falls more every day.

But wait—ten minutes later, on a break in *Issues and Answers,* for instance, we're suddenly in a whole other America, the kind of place where everything goes right. We're back not just in civilization but at the summit of civilized achievements, where we hear the rattle of fine china teacups and the clink of crystal champagne glasses set to delicate waltz music. We're in the world of Paine Webber. Grateful clients are acquiring Renoirs, eating pâté or otherwise comforting themselves with the satisfied obliviousness of the courtiers of Louis XVI.[4] The ad includes a sort of disclaimer to the effect that while Paine Webber cannot guarantee you wealth, if you bring your money to them, maybe someday "you might say, 'Thank you, Paine Webber' too."

Ah, yes . . . *maybe someday* . . . It's that old wish-fulfillment witchcraft   18
working.

Another quick flick of the remote control button and the spell of such   19
summery sophistries shatters under the frosty glare with which John Houseman fixes us in the Smith Barney ads. It is a shock, the shift from the plush carpeted Paine Webber world to the trashy, torn-ticker-tape litter on the floor of the stock exchange, from the soaring choirs of Dean Witter to the bare ruined choirs of the Big Board.[5]

Houseman puts on a great performance. Smith Barney has invested   20
wisely in him. "The New York Stock Exchange. The day's trading is over,"

---

[4]The shimmering impressionist paintings of Pierre Auguste Renoir (1841–1919) are occasionally auctioned at very high prices. King Louis XVI of France (1754–1793) ruled in splendor—until he was deposed in the French Revolution and later executed.

[5]A quotation board for securities listed on the New York Stock Exchange.

he intones ominously in his classic debut spot. "Some tally their profits," he says with a wintry, dismissive smile that implies: "Fat chance that's you, fella." "Some," he concludes, impaling us with a veritable icicle of a glance, "lick their wounds."

Wounds. Suffering. Pain. Insecurity. The tragic view of life. Houseman's debut for Smith Barney was the perfect harbinger of the New Hard Sell. Unlike the old hard sell, with a fast-and-loud-talking salesperson pitching a product, the new sell portrays the world as cold, brutally tough. The product isn't pushed so much as the audience is impelled to reach—reach *hard*—for the hope of security the product offers. The *hope* of security—that is what the '80s hard sell offers to those of us frozen out by this brutal era.

The Tough Life

A recent editorial in *Ad Age* denounced the new Excedrin "Life got tougher" ads for "overkill," for giving the impression that "life is now akin to a forced march to the Gulag Archipelago[6] . . . a kind of doomsday feeling."

Even if life is not getting *that* tough, *tough* is definitely the key word in the world of today's TV commercials. Dodge trucks are "ram tough," and the Dodge ads feature hormone-crazed rams smashing horns against each other. Ford trucks are "built tough," and their promo featured a grueling tug of war with Toyota.

Then, too, the old-fashioned work ethic has returned to prominence. "They make money the old-fashioned way. They earn it," John Houseman says in a Smith Barney ad. Back to basics. Don't express yourself, protect yourself. Life is no longer to enjoy. Life is to avoid. The essence of this new technique is to arouse anxiety and offer relief. It means something, I think, that dollar for dollar Tylenol is the single most frequently purchased drugstore item in the United States today.

Certainly the older-type commercials, the softer, happier advertising pitches, continue to be the most popular with TV viewers. A look at two years of polls by Video Storyboards Test Inc. (a market research outfit that asks a cross-section of people what they think is the most outstanding TV commercial they have seen recently) consistently registers the popularity of the spiritual, emotional, celebratory ad campaigns. The warmth and emotion of the "Mean Joe Green and the Kid" Coke commercial made it the most popular in recent years. The stirring musical Americana of the soft drink spirituals, the lyrical beauty and hearty camaraderie of the beer ads

---

[6]The system of Soviet prison camps where Stalin's political enemies were confined in the 1940s.

and the blood-curdling cuteness of cat food commercials consistently push these upbeat celebrations of humanity, warmth and friendship into the Top 10 of such ad polls.

Whether or not they will continue to be popular with ad people as   26
selling tools is another question. There have been some interesting changes in the spiritual genre in the new season's ads.

Consider first the very popularity of the word. After a brief ap-   27
pearance and quick death in 1976, the word *spirit* has arisen again. We have the "catch that Pepsi spirit" campaign; we have the cloud-level soaring "spirit of Hyatt" and the plucky American Motors gas-saving model, Spirit.

But, hovering over the grand, "Main Street parade" Pepsi spirit spot is   28
an aura of anxiety. We watch the little drum majorette drop her baton in practice at home. Now it's the Fourth of July parade, and we are treated to the anxious glances of the parents and friends as they wait to see if their child will suffer public humiliation. Of course, she catches it; but anxiety and suspense giving way to relief, and people gulping Pepsi to soothe throats dry from tension are not the unambiguous hallmarks of joy that once reigned in soft drink ads. Even they now bode harder times. . . .

Something More than Feelings

Another technique of the late '70s school is the emphasis on feeling.   29
While this has been a good year for product feelings ("Feelin' 7-Up," "Oh, what a feeling . . . Toyota"), it has not been a particularly good season for feelings of love.

Why is love slighted? Why did AT&T cancel its love song theme,   30
"Feelings," and switch to the California hot-tub gestalt "Reach Out and Touch Someone" theme? What was the flaw for the ad people in "Feelings"?

Many to be sure would call it a criminally sentimental piece of trash,   31
but that never stopped other songs from making it. No, it is the fact that the Morris Albert classic is specifically a song about feelings of love. And with love there are always mixed feelings, touchy feelings, fiery feelings, not the comfortable nonthreatening warmth of reach-out-and-touch feelings. California closeness is a safer-selling feeling than those volatile feelings of love.

Increasingly, this year we find the notion of love ridiculed and   32
scorned. In one of those male-bonding, beer-bar get-togethers, a starry-eyed man bursts in to announce "I've found *the* woman."

"*Again*," some wise guy cracks scornfully to the roar of ridicule from a   33
crowd clearly disillusioned with the Western Romantic tradition.

While some wine commercials celebrate passion and *amore* between   34
men and women, the most conspicuous instance of love at first sight on screen these days is between man and car (Mazda's "Just one look . . . " theme), and the most conspicuous instance of erotic love is between a

woman and herself (the Rive Gauche[7] hard-driving, dawn-watching woman who "goes it alone," whose "auto-eroticism," as Jeff Greenfield called it before I got a chance to, is only thinly veiled—we even see the earth move as she watches the sun also rise).

In fact, the one new ad that treated love uncynically celebrated what   35
is actually pubescent puppy love—the two shy kids in the 1980 "Love's Baby Soft" teenybopper fragrance ad. It's a brilliant and beguiling piece of work, but nowhere do you find the equivalent for post-teenagers.

The only innovative use of love in the past few years is in the less-than   36
romantic name of a cleansing product—"Love My Carpet." (The most interesting new-product name on the market in recent years has got to be "Gee, Your Hair Smells Terrific!" Look for more of these exclamatory-sentence brand names in future TV commercials.)

Realm of Nightmare

In fact, there have been some vicious anti-Romance ads running   37
recently. The most insidious of the genre was the Longines spot that aired last Christmastime. A cozy marital scene; the man has just given his wife a watch he worked his heart out to afford. He's gazing at her, brimming over with loving generosity as she announces, "I love it."

She pauses. Only a microsecond, but one of the most deadly micro-   38
seconds ever aired. "But?" he asks. "No, really," she replies with just a fleeting smile.

The guy's heart is breaking. She's not even faking enthusiasm.   39
"C'mon, tell me," he pleads weakly.

"I guess I was hoping for a Longines," she says wistfully.   40

This is not Romance but a nasty little murder of it committed right   41
before our eyes.

Here, we have entered the realm of nightmare. Here, other kinds of   42
feelings reign. We are working not with human potential but with human paranoia. Anxiety. Loss. Fear of loss. Remember that nightmarish classic, the American Express Lost Traveler's Cheques series. Who can forget the smug sneer of the French concierge when the frantic young American couple confess that the traveler's checks they have lost were not American Express? "Ah," he says, as if gazing down from the frosty remoteness of Mont Blanc at a particularly distasteful specimen of grape blight. "Most people carry American Express."

What's shocking here is not the Gallic scorn but the supine response   43
of the American couple. Instead of grabbing the concierge by his starched, stuffed shirt and reminding him that his mother hadn't asked the

---

[7]Left Bank; refers to the bohemian district of Paris on the left bank of the Seine River.

Americans who liberated Paris what kind of bank checks they brought, the couple turns away in humiliation and self-abasement. We *are* such worms, we Americans, only good for our virtually worthless dollars, and here we are too stupid even to do what Most People do and at least avoid inconveniencing the concierge with our petty failures.

Certainly this abasement before foreigners must reflect more than the   44
lingering cringe of the colonials before continental civilization. It suggests a kind of sickening national self-image that masochistically relishes affronts to our representatives abroad.

Consider the slogan for the ad: "American Express Traveler's   45
Cheques—don't leave home without them." Isn't the net effect of that slogan—which follows portrait after panicked portrait of Americans robbed, humiliated, traumatized, everything but taken hostage, generally in foreign lands—isn't the net effect to feed the voice inside our national psyche, that fearful voice that simply says, "Don't leave home"?

The Humiliation Sell

Humiliation, embarrassment and slovenliness seem to be at the core   46
of not just Miller but Schlitz and other "lite" beer commercials. Ads for full-bodied beers are still some of the most beautiful, most lyrical, glowingly lit tributes to the romance of working people, the dignity of the work ethic and the nobility of adventure and athletic endeavor. But the Lite ads give us symbols of humiliation, such as comedians Rodney Dangerfield and malaprop-man Norm Crosby.

And there's Marv Throneberry, who has built a career out of two   47
humiliating seasons as last-place first baseman for the worst team in baseball. It's marvelous that Miller beer has made him a national celebrity—anybody's better than Bruce Jenner—but what does his popular following suggest about our new notion of the heroic figure? Rodney Dangerfield, of course, is famous for "I don't get no respect," but the "lite" beer ethos seems to play upon our feelings that we don't *deserve* respect.

There are also the repeated small moments of defeat for the non-   48
celebrity: the natural cereal eater who is constantly crestfallen at how many bowls of this brand it would take to equal the vitamins in Total; the shamefaced jerks ridiculed by their friends for forgetting the Prestone, failing to keep their guard up and stranding them all in the cold; the overachieving, overtime-working eager beavers who are constantly being whispered about because they "need a deodorant that works overtime"; the guy in the Yellow Pages ad who rips the bottom of his pants so embarrassingly that he has to wait in a telephone booth for a tailor to make him fit to appear in public again.

The Humiliation Sell goes hand in hand with what's happening in the   49
"real people" genre of TV commercials. The real people being selected to
appear in recent ads are, to put it bluntly, a much stupider, uglier breed
than those of the late '70s. This is not the cute, stupid and ugly urban look
of the late '60s "New York School" of filmic ad realists (the Alka-Seltzer "No
Matter What Shape Your Stomach's In" campaign, for instance). No, this is
a new kind of subhuman suburban subspecies. It is as if the ad people were
saying to the public and the FTC: "You want honesty? You want truth and
reality in ads? O.K. We'll rub your nose in realism! We'll show you 'real.'"

Someday, bits of this verité[8] material will be recognized as some of the   50
most accurate journalism of our time. Nothing captures the bleak reality of
the suburban teenager better than the picture of the "real kid" in a laundry
detergent ad, staring vacantly with what looks like angel-dust-blasted eyes
at two piles of white linen and grunting, "I'm not into wash, but like, that
one's cleaner."

Not only do these real people look vacant, they seem totally cut off   51
from the people closest to them; they exhibit not merely mistaken product
identification responses but an almost pathological failure to know the
world around them.

After all these years, how is it possible for a real person in a super-   52
market aisle, approached by a man with a microphone, not to know that he
or she ought to pick Stove Top stuffing instead of potatoes? And how could
all those mothers in the Procter & Gamble ads fail to know their sons and
husbands prefer clean clothes to dingy? Are ad people trying to rub the
noses of real people in their nitty-gritty griminess?

And talk about rubbing it in: have you seen the latest Charmin toilet   53
paper ad with Mr. Whipple? It's a remarkable example of ad people boasting
shamelessly about their manipulative trickery to the very people they have
successfully hoodwinked.

This crown jewel of the epic Charmin campaign (first begun a decade   54
ago, it transformed Charmin from a minor regional brand into the No. 1
product of its kind) takes place outside Whipple's supermarket. He has
taken down his old Don't Squeeze the Charmin signs and is ushering in a
new era, during which there will be no more silly prohibitions on squeezing.
As he does so, he reflects on the whole "Don't Squeeze" theme of the
campaign and confides at last the true motive behind the gimmick.
"Squeezing the Charmin wasn't so bad after all," Whipple confesses. His
"Don't Squeeze" prissiness was just a trick to provoke and then co-opt your
rebelliousness. Hence, the brand-new Charmin slogan: "The squeezing gets
you. The softness keeps you."

---

[8]Or *cinéma verité*, movies that present realistic slices of life.

In other words, Whipple is virtually coming out and saying, "We   55
tricked you into buying it." You can almost hear the triumphant crowing of
the ad people—you laughed at us for putting on such a ridiculous campaign,
but, Mr. and Mrs. America, the joke's on you: you bought it anyway.

Perhaps the final, most insulting touch to top off this trend was the   56
reappearance of ventriloquists' dummies in place of real people in some
campaigns. We have had one ventriloquist's dummy mouthing "ring around
the collar" in a Wisk ad and another saying "butter" in the Parkay margarine spots. Real people are so malleable, so willing to say whatever the ad
people want them to, they might as well be ventriloquists' dummies as far as
the ad people are concerned. This explains, perhaps, the birth of the
dummy trend and the displacement of their flesh-and-blood counterparts.

One gets the feeling that these commercials are expressing a certain   57
impatience with the consumer on the part of ad people, perhaps even a
subconscious hostility. Industry has become tired of trying to persuade us,
seduce us, flatter us, indulge our fantasies. The Me Decade is over on
Madison Avenue, and from now on it's no more Mr. Nice Guy. Tough times
are here, even for advertising.

Advertising is going through a period during which precipitous   58
agency-client shifts have raised cries of disloyalty and betrayal in some
quarters. Product "positioning" wars and head-to-head comparison ad conflicts grow more fierce, even vicious.[9] "ANOTHER ROUND IN COLA WARS"; "GF
SENDS 'MASTER BLEND' INTO BATTLE"—the images in the trade paper headlines
are grimly warlike. Even in the sweet little candy world, big battles are
erupting: "LIFE-SAVERS, CHICLE READY FOR CANDY ROLL MARKET CLASS" pro-
claimed one front page battle dispatch in *Ad Age.*

There are signs of even tougher times to come, both on the screen and   59
in the offices of Madison Avenue. The trade papers are reporting with
increasing frequency the problems agencies are having with slowpaying
buyers. Credit problems are cropping up and forcing the creation of a new
get-tough policy toward debtors.

It was around the turn of the decade that I first spotted a notice in *Ad*   60
Age for an outfit that said it specialized in "advertising debt-collection
problems." Their slogan: "We're gentlemen."

Were they hinting with that line that there are nongentlemen working   61
the suites of Madison Avenue, tough guys who specialize in more forceful,
no-nonsense ways of dealing with advertising debt collection? One cannot
help but imagine a *Rocky* type in a gray flannel suit visiting a Creative
Director and delivering the ultimatum, "Pay up or we'll mangle the syntax

---

[9]In advertising, "positioning" means tailoring a product and its advertising to appeal to a
specific group of consumers in a particular way.

of your slogan." Perhaps the only satisfaction we can get from all this is that if ads are getting tougher on life, life is certainly getting tougher on advertising.

Questions for Study and Discussion

1. Rosenbaum describes the "Hard Sell," the "Tough Life," the "Humiliation Sell," and "love" in advertising. Briefly, how does he distinguish among these categories? Are his distinctions useful? Explain.

2. What is the advantage to Rosenbaum of using the second-person plural, "we" and "us," as opposed to speaking in either the first or the third person?

3. Adwriters for Excedrin explain that "Life got tough, so we got stronger." Why do you think advertisers exploit the idea that life is tough? Is life as tough as advertisements would lead us to believe?

4. What kinds of words does Rosenbaum use for ads he likes? for ads he disapproves of? What would you say is his overall attitude toward ads?

5. Reread the essay, paying particular attention to Rosenbaum's vocabulary. Diction should be suited for the author's audience. Whom do you think Rosenbaum intended his audience to be? Compare Rosenbaum's vocabulary to Fowles's (pp. 385–401). What differences and similarities do you see?

Writing Topics

1. Society likes to name decades. What are the social tendencies that will characterize the 1990s? In an essay discuss the ways you think advertising might present these priorities.

2. Watch television for a week, paying close attention to the commercials. How many of the selling tactics Rosenbaum describes are used in one evening? In an essay describe the commercials and classify them according to their selling tactic.

Neil Postman, writer and professor of media ecology at New York University, was a voice for radical educational reform in the late sixties and early seventies. With coauthor Charles Weingartner, Postman argued in *The Soft Revolution* that students were being indentured to "years of servitude in a totalitarian environment." Later in his career, Postman said he had "changed his mind" and published *Teaching as a Conservative Activity* (1979). Postman explained the turnabout in his philosophy by arguing that while schools must change in times of social stagnation, in times of rapid social changes, they must be havens for stability.

Postman has written for several magazines including *Nation* and *Atlantic*. Among his many published works are: *The Uses of Language* (1965); *Exploring Your Language* (1966); two books with Charles Weingartner, *Linguistics: A Revolution in Teaching* (1966) and *The Soft Revolution: A Student Handbook for Turning the Schools Around* (1971); and *Crazy Talk, Stupid Talk: How We Defeat Ourselves by the Way We Talk and What to Do about It* (1976).

In the following essay from *Amusing Ourselves to Death* (1985), Postman examines the ways that the format for broadcast journalism has trivialized the news. Postman warns that the effort to keep the news hour entertaining not only keeps the public ignorant, ultimately it puts the entire culture at risk of extinction.

"Now . . . This"

The American humorist H. Allen Smith once suggested that of all the worrisome words in the English language, the scariest is "uh oh," as when a physician looks at your X-rays, and with knitted brow says, "Uh oh." I should like to suggest that the words which are the title of this chapter are as ominous as any, all the more so because they are spoken without knitted brow—indeed, with a kind of idiot's delight. The phrase, if that's what it may be called, adds to our grammar a new part of speech, a conjunction that does not connect anything to anything but does the opposite: separates everything from everything. As such, it serves as a compact metaphor for the discontinuities in so much that passes for public discourse in present-day America

"Now . . . this" is commonly used on radio and television newscasts to indicate that what one has just heard or seen has no relevance to what one

414

is about to hear or see, or possibly to anything one is ever likely to hear or see. The phrase is a means of acknowledging the fact that the world as mapped by the speeded-up electronic media has no order or meaning and is not to be taken seriously. There is no murder so brutal, no earthquake so devastating, no political blunder so costly—for that matter, no ball score so tantalizing or weather report so threatening—that it cannot be erased from our minds by a newscaster saying, "Now . . . this." The newscaster means that you have thought long enough on the previous matter (approximately forty-five seconds), that you must not be morbidly preoccupied with it (let us say, for ninety seconds), and that you must now give your attention to another fragment of news or a commercial.

Television did not invent the "Now . . . this" world view. As I have 3 tried to show, it is the offspring of the intercourse between telegraphy and photography. But it is through television that it has been nurtured and brought to a perverse maturity. For on television, nearly every half hour is a discrete event, separated in content, context, and emotional texture from what precedes and follows it. In part because television sells its time in seconds and minutes, in part because television must use images rather than words, in part because its audience can move freely to and from the television set, programs are structured so that almost each eight-minute segment may stand as a complete event in itself. Viewers are rarely required to carry over any thought or feeling from one parcel of time to another.

Of course, in television's presentation of the "news of the day," we 4 may see the "Now . . . this" mode of discourse in its boldest and most embarrassing form. For there, we are presented not only with fragmented news but with news without context, without consequences, without value, and therefore without essential seriousness; that is to say, news as pure entertainment.

Consider, for example, how you would proceed if you were given the 5 opportunity to produce a television news show for any station concerned to attract the largest possible audience. You would, first, choose a cast of players, each of whom has a face that is both "likable" and "credible." Those who apply would, in fact, submit to you their eight-by-ten-glossies, from which you would eliminate those whose countenances are not suitable for nightly display. This means that you will exclude woman who are not beautiful or who are over the age of fifty, men who are bald, all people who are overweight or whose noses are too long or whose eyes are too close together. You will try, in other words, to assemble a cast of talking hair-do's. At the very least, you will want those whose faces would not be unwelcome on a magazine cover.

Christine Craft has just such a face, and so she applied for a co- 6 anchor position on KMBC-TV in Kansas City. According to a lawyer who represented her in a sexism suit she later brought against the station, the management of KMBC-TV "loved Christine's look." She was accordingly hired in January 1981. She was fired in August 1981 because research indicated that her appearance "hampered viewer acceptance." What exactly does "hampered viewer acceptance" mean? And what does it have to do with the news? Hampered viewer acceptance means the same thing for television news as it does for any television show: Viewers do not like looking at the performer. It also means that viewers do not believe the performer, that she lacks credibility. In the case of a theatrical performance, we have a sense of what that implies: The actor does not persuade the audience that he or she is the character being portrayed. But what does lack of credibility imply in the case of a news show? What character is a co-anchor playing? And how do we decide that the performance lacks verisimilitude? Does the audience believe that the newscaster is lying, that what is reported did not in fact happen, that something important is being concealed?

It is frightening to think that this may be so, that the perception of the truth of a report rests heavily on the acceptability of the newscaster. In the ancient world, there was a tradition of banishing or killing the bearer of bad tidings. Does the television news show restore, in a curious form, this tradition? Do we banish those who tell us the news when we do not care for the face of the teller? Does television countermand the warnings we once received about the fallacy of the ad hominem argument?   7

If the answer to any of these questions is even a qualified "Yes," then here is an issue worthy of the attention or epistemologists. Stated in its simplest form, it is that television provides a new (or, possibly, restores an old) definition of truth: The credibility of the teller is the ultimate test of the truth of a proposition. "Credibility" here does not refer to the past record of the teller for making statements that have survived the rigors of reality-testing. It refers only to the impression of sincerity, authenticity, vulnerability or attractiveness (choose one or more) conveyed by the actor/reporter.   8

This is a matter of considerable importance, for it goes beyond the question of how truth is perceived on television news shows. If on television, credibility replaces reality as the decisive test of truth-telling, political leaders need not trouble themselves very much with reality provided that their performances consistently generate a sense of verisimilitude. I suspect, for example, that the dishonor that now shrouds Richard Nixon results not from the fact that he lied but that on television he looked like a liar. Which, if true, should bring no comfort to anyone, not even veteran Nixon-haters. For the alternative possibilities are that one may look like a liar but be telling the truth; or even worse, look like a truth-teller but in fact be lying.   9

As a producer of a television news show, you would be well aware of these matters and would be careful to choose your cast on the basis of criteria used by David Merrick and other successful impresarios. Like them, you would then turn your attention to staging the show on principles that   10 maximize entertainment value. You would, for example, select a musical theme for the show. All television news programs begin, end, and are somewhere in between punctuated with music. I have found very few Americans who regard this custom as peculiar, which fact I have taken as evidence for the dissolution of lines of demarcation between serious public discourse and entertainment. What has music to do with the news? Why is it there? It is there, I assume, for the same reason music is used in the theater and films—to create a mood and provide a leitmotif for the entertainment. If there were no music—as is the case when any television program is interrupted for a news flash—viewers would expect something truly alarming, possibly life-altering. But as long as the music is there as a frame for the program, the viewer is comforted to believe that there is nothing to be greatly alarmed about; that, in fact, the events that are reported have as much relation to reality as do scenes in a play.

This perception of a news show as a stylized dramatic performance   11
whose content has been staged largely to entertain is reinforced by several other features, including the fact that the average length of any story is forty-five seconds. While brevity does not always suggest triviality, in this case it clearly does. It is simply not possible to convey a sense of seriousness about any event if its implications are exhausted in less than one minute's time. In fact, it is quite obvious that TV news has no intention of suggesting that any story *has* any implications, for that would require viewers to continue to think about it when it is done and therefore obstruct their attending to the next story that waits panting in the wings. In any case, viewers are not provided with much opportunity to be distracted from the next story since in all likelihood it will consist of some film footage. Pictures have little difficulty in overwhelming words, and short-circuiting introspection. As a television producer, you would be certain to give both prominence and precedence to any event for which there is some sort of visual documentation. A suspected killer being brought into a police station, the angry face of a cheated consumer, a barrel going over Niagara Falls (with a person alleged to be in it), the President disembarking from a helicopter on the White House lawn—these are always fascinating or amusing, and easily satisfy the requirements of an entertaining show. It is, of course, not necessary that the visuals actually document the point of the story. Neither is it necessary to explain why such images are intruding themselves on public consciousness. Film footage justifies itself, as every television producer well knows.

It is also of considerable help in maintaining a high level of unreality   12
that the newscasters do not pause to grimace or shiver when they speak their prefaces or epilogs to the film clips. Indeed, many newscasters do not appear to grasp the meaning of what they are saying, and some hold a fixed and ingratiating enthusiasm as they report on earthquakes, mass killings and other disasters. Viewers would be quite disconcerted by any show of

concern or terror on the part of newscasters. Viewers, after all, are partners with the newscasters in the "Now . . . this" culture, and they expect the newscaster to play out his or her role as a character who is marginally serious but who stays well clear of authentic understanding. The viewers, for their part, will not be caught contaminating their responses with a sense of reality, any more than an audience at a play would go scurrying to call home because a character on stage has said that a murderer is loose in the neighborhood.

The viewers also know that no matter how grave any fragment of news may appear (for example, on the day I write a Marine Corps general has declared that nuclear war between the United States and Russia is inevitable), it will shortly be followed by a series of commercials that will, in an instant defuse the import of the news, in fact render it largely banal. This is a key element in the structure of a news program and all by itself refutes any claim that television news is designed as a serious form of public discourse. Imagine what you would think of me, and this book, if I were to pause here, tell you that I will return to my discussion in a moment, and then proceed to write a few words in behalf of United Airlines or the Chase Manhattan Bank. You would rightly think that I had no respect for you and, certainly, no respect for the subject. And if I did this not once but several times in each chapter, you would think the whole enterprise unworthy of your attention. Why, then, do we not think a news show similarly unworthy? The reason, I believe, is that whereas we expect books and even other media (such as film) to maintain a consistency of tone and a continuity of content, we have no such expectation of television, and especially television news. We have become so accustomed to its discontinuities that we are no longer struck dumb, as any sane person would be, by a newscaster who having just reported that a nuclear war is inevitable goes on to say that he will be right back after this word from Burger King; who says, in other words, "Now . . . this." One can hardly overestimate the damage that such juxtapositions do to our sense of the world as a serious place. The damage is especially massive to youthful viewers who depend so much on television for their clues as to how to respond to the world. In watching television news, they, more than any other segment of the audience, are drawn into an epistemology based on the assumption that all reports of cruelty and death are greatly exaggerated and, in any case, not to be taken seriously or responded to sanely.

I should go so far as to say that embedded in the surrealistic frame of a television news show is a theory of anticommunication, featuring a type of discourse that abandons logic, reason, sequence and rules of contradiction. In aesthetics, I believe the name given to this theory is Dadaism; in philosophy, nihilism; in psychiatry, schizophrenia. In the parlance of the theater, it is known as vaudeville.

For those who think I am here guilty of hyperbole, I offer the following description of television news by Robert MacNeil, executive editor and co-anchor of the "MacNeil-Lehrer Newshour." The idea, he writes, "is to keep everything brief, not to strain the attention of anyone but instead to provide constant stimulation through variety, novelty, action, and movement. You are required . . . to pay attention to no concept, no character, and no problem for more than a few seconds at a time." He goes on to say that the assumptions controlling a news show are "that bite-sized is best, that complexity must be avoided, that nuances are dispensable, that qualifications impede the simple message, that visual stimulation is a substitute for thought, and that verbal precision is an anachronism."

Robert MacNeil has more reason than most to give testimony about 16 the television news show as vaudeville act. The "MacNeil-Lehrer Newshour" is an unusual and gracious attempt to bring to television some of the elements of typographic discourse. The program abjures visual stimulation, consists largely of extended explanations of events and in-depth interviews (which even there means only five to ten minutes), limits the number of stories covered, and emphasizes background and coherence. But television has exacted its price for MacNeil's rejection of a show business format. By television's standards, the audience is minuscule, the program is confined to public-television stations, and it is a good guess that the combined salary of MacNeil and Lehrer is one-fifth of Dan Rather's or Tom Brokaw's.

If you were a producer of a television news show for a commercial 17 station, you would not have the option of defying television's requirements. It would be demanded of you that you strive for the largest possible audience, and, as a consequence and in spite of your best intentions, you would arrive at a production very nearly resembling MacNeil's description. Moreover, you would include some things MacNeil does not mention. You would try to make celebrities of your newscasters. You would advertise the show, both in the press and on television itself. You would do "news briefs," to serve as an inducement to viewers. You would have a weatherman as comic relief, and a sportscaster whose language is a touch uncouth (as a way of his relating to the beer-drinking common man). You would, in short, package the whole event as any producer might who is in the entertainment business.

The result of all this is that Americans are the best entertained and 18 quite likely the least well-informed people in the Western world. I say this in the face of the popular conceit that television, as a window to the world, has made Americans exceedingly well informed. Much depends here, of course, on what is meant by being informed. I will pass over the now tiresome polls that tell us that, at any given moment, 70 percent of our citizens do not know who is the Secretary of State or the Chief Justice of the Supreme Court. Let us consider, instead, the case of Iran during the drama that was called the "Iranian Hostage Crisis." I don't suppose there has been a story in years that received more continuous attention from television. We may assume, then, that Americans know most of what there is to know about this unhappy event. And now, I put these questions to you: Would it be an exaggeration to say that not one American in a hundred knows what language the Iranians speak? Or what the word "Ayatollah" means or implies? Or knows any details of the tenets of Iranian religious beliefs? Or the main outlines of their political history? Or knows who the Shah was, and where he came from?

Nonetheless, everyone had an opinion about this event, for in America everyone is entitled to an opinion, and it is certainly useful to have a few when a pollster shows up. But these are opinions of a quite different order from eighteenth- or nineteenth-century opinions. It is probably more accurate to call them emotions rather than opinions, which would account for the fact that they change from week to week, as the pollsters tell us. What is happening here is that television is altering the meaning of "being informed" by creating a species of information that might properly be called *disinformation*. I am using this word almost in the precise sense in which it is used by spies in the CIA or KGB. Disinformation does not mean false information. It means misleading information—misplaced, irrelevant, fragmented or superficial information—information that creates the illusion of knowing something but which in fact leads one away from knowing. In saying this, I do not mean to imply that television news deliberately aims to deprive Americans of a coherent, contextual understanding of their world. I mean to say that when news is packaged as entertainment, that is the inevitable result. And in saying that the television news show entertains but does not inform, I am saying something far more serious than that we are being deprived of authentic information. I am saying we are losing our sense of what it means to be well informed. Ignorance is always correctable. But what shall we do if we take ignorance to be knowledge?

Here is a startling example of how this process bedevils us. A *New York Times* article is headlined on February 15, 1983:

REAGAN MISSTATEMENTS GETTING LESS ATTENTION

The article begins in the following way:

> President Reagan's aides used to become visibly alarmed at suggestions that he had given mangled and perhaps misleading accounts of his policies or of current events in general. That doesn't seem to happen much anymore.
>
> Indeed, the President continues to make debatable assertions of fact but news accounts do not deal with them as extensively as they once did. In the view of White House officials, the declining news coverage mirrors a *decline in interest by the general public.* (my italics)

This report is not so much a news story as a story about the news, and our recent history suggests that it is not about Ronald Reagan's charm. It is about how news is defined, and I believe the story would be quite astonishing to both civil libertarians and tyrants of an earlier time. Walter

Lippmann, for example, wrote in 1920: "There can be no liberty for a community which lacks the means by which to detect lies." For all of his pessimism about the possibilities of restoring an eighteenth- and nineteenth-century level of public discourse, Lippmann assumed, as did Thomas Jefferson before him, that with a well-trained press functioning as a lie-detector, the public's interest in a President's mangling of the truth would be piqued, in both senses of that word. Given the means to detect lies, he believed, the public could not be indifferent to their consequences.

But this case refutes his assumption. The reporters who cover the   23
White House are ready and able to expose lies, and thus create the grounds for informed and indignant opinion. But apparently the public declines to take an interest. To press reports of White House dissembling, the public has replied with Queen Victoria's famous line: "We are not amused." However, here the words mean something the Queen did not have in mind. They mean that what is not amusing does not compel their attention. Perhaps if the President's lies could be demonstrated by pictures and accompanied by music the public would raise a curious eyebrow. If a movie, like *All the President's Men*, could be made from his misleading accounts of government policy, if there were a break-in of some sort or sinister characters laundering money, attention would quite likely be paid. We do well to remember that President Nixon did not begin to come undone until his lies were given a theatrical setting at the Watergate hearings. But we do not have anything like that here. Apparently, all President Reagan does is *say* things that are not entirely true. And there is nothing entertaining in that.

But there is a subtler point to be made here. Many of the President's   24
"misstatements" fall in the category of contradiction—mutually exclusive assertions that cannot possibly both, in the same context, be true. "In the same context" is the key phrase here, for it is context that defines contradiction. There is no problem in someone's remarking that he prefers oranges to apples, and also remarking that he prefers apples to oranges—not if one statement is made in the context of choosing a wallpaper design and the other in the context of selecting fruit for dessert. In such a case, we have statements that are opposites, but not contradictory. But if the statements are made in a single, continuous, and coherent context, then they are contradictions, and cannot both be true. Contradiction, in short, requires that statements and events be perceived as interrelated aspects of a continuous and coherent context. Disappear the context, or fragment it, and contradiction disappears. This point is nowhere made more clear to me than in conferences with my younger students about their writing. "Look here," I say. "In this paragraph you have said one thing. And in that you have said the opposite. Which is it to be?" They are polite and wish to please, but they are as baffled by the question as I am by the response. "I know," they will say, "but that is *there* and this is *here*." The difference between us is that I assume "there" and "here," "now" and "then," one

paragraph and the next to be connected, to be continuous, to be part of the same coherent world of thought. That is the way of typographic discourse, and typography is the universe I'm "coming from," as they say. But they are coming from a different universe of discourse altogether: the "Now . . . this" world of television. The fundamental assumption of that world is not coherence but discontinuity. And in a world of discontinuities, contradiction is useless as a test of truth or merit, because contradiction does not exist.

My point is that we are by now so thoroughly adjusted to the   25
"Now . . . this" world of news—a world of fragments, where events stand alone, stripped of any connection to the past, or to the future, or to other events—that all assumptions of coherence have vanished. And so, perforce, has contradiction. In the context of *no context*, so to speak, it simply disappears. And in its absence, what possible interest could there be in a list of what the President says *now* and what he said *then?* It is merely a rehash of old news, and there is nothing interesting or entertaining in that. The only thing to be amused about is the bafflement of reporters at the public's indifference. There is an irony in the fact that the very group that has taken the world apart should, on trying to piece it together again, be surprised that no one notices much, or cares.

For all his perspicacity, George Orwell would have been stymied by   26
this situation; there is nothing "Orwellian" about it. The President does not have the press under his thumb. *The New York Times* and the *Washington Post* are not *Pravda;* the Associated Press is not Tass. And there is no Newspeak here. Lies have not been defined as truth nor truth as lies. All that has happened is that the public has adjusted to incoherence and been amused into indifference. Which is why Aldous Huxley would not in the least be surprised by the story. Indeed, he prophesied its coming. He believed that it is far more likely that the Western democracies will dance and dream themselves into oblivion than march into it, single file and manacled. Huxley grasped, as Orwell did not, that it is not necessary to conceal anything from a public insensible to contradiction and narcoticized by technological diversions. Although Huxley did not specify that television would be our main line to the drug, he would have no difficulty accepting Robert MacNeil's observation that "Television is the *soma* of Aldous Huxley's *Brave New World.*" Big Brother turns out to be Howdy Doody.

I do not mean that the trivialization of public information is all   27
accomplished *on* television. I mean that television is the paradigm for our conception of public information. As the printing press did in an earlier time, television has achieved the power to define the form in which news must come, and it has also defined how we shall respond to it. In presenting news to us packaged as vaudeville, television induces other media to do the same, so that the total information environment begins to mirror television.

For example, America's newest and highly successful national news- 28 paper, *USA Today*, is modeled precisely on the format of television. It is sold on the street in receptacles that look like television sets. Its stories are uncommonly short, its design leans heavily on pictures, charts and other graphics, some of them printed in various colors. Its weather maps are a visual delight; its sports section includes enough pointless statistics to distract a computer. As a consequence, *USA Today*, which began publication in September 1982, has become the third largest daily in the United States (as of July 1984, according to the Audit Bureau of Circulations), moving quickly to overtake the *Daily News* and the *Wall Street Journal*. Journalists of a more traditional bent have criticized it for its superficiality and theatrics, but the paper's editors remain steadfast in their disregard of typographic standards. The paper's Editor-in-Chief, John Quinn, has said: "We are not up to undertaking projects of the dimensions needed to win prizes. They don't give awards for the best investigative paragraph." Here is an astonishing tribute to the resonance of television's epistemology: In the age of television, the paragraph is becoming the basic unit of news in print media. Moreover, Mr. Quinn need not fret too long about being deprived of awards. As other newspapers join in the transformation, the time cannot be far off when awards will be given for the best investigative sentence.

It needs also to be noted here that new and successful magazines such 29 as *People* and *Us* are not only examples of television-oriented print media but have had an extraordinary "ricochet" effect on television itself. Whereas television taught the magazines that news is nothing but entertainment, the magazines have taught television that nothing but entertainment is news. Television programs, such as "Entertainment Tonight," turn information about entertainers and celebrities into "serious" cultural content, so that the circle begins to close: Both the form and content of news become entertainment.

Radio, of course, is the least likely medium to join in the descent into 30 a Huxleyan world of technological narcotics. It is, after all, particularly well suited to the transmission of rational, complex language. Nonetheless, and even if we disregard radio's captivation by the music industry, we appear to be left with the chilling fact that such language as radio allows us to hear is increasingly primitive, fragmented, and largely aimed at invoking visceral response; which is to say, it is the linguistic analogue to the ubiquitous rock music that is radio's principal source of income. As I write, the trend in call-in shows is for the "host" to insult callers whose language does not, in itself, go much beyond humanoid grunting. Such programs have little content, as this word used to be defined, and are merely of archeological interest in that they give us a sense of what a dialogue among Neanderthals might have been like. More to the point, the language of radio newscasts has become, under the influence of television, increasingly decontextualized and discontinuous, so that the possibility of anyone's knowing about the world, as against merely knowing *of* it, is effectively blocked. In New York City, radio station WINS entreats it listeners to "Give us twenty-two minutes and we'll give you the world." This is said without irony, and its audience, we may assume, does not regard the slogan as the conception of a disordered mind.

And so, we move rapidly into an information environment which 31 may rightly be called trivial pursuit. As the game of that name uses facts as a source of amusement, so do our sources of news. It has been demonstrated many times that a culture can survive misinformation and false opinion. It has not yet been demonstrated whether a culture can survive if it takes the measure of the world in twenty-two minutes. Or if the value of its news is determined by the number of laughs it provides.

Questions for Study and Discussion

1. Postman assigns great importance to the words "now . . . this," not for themselves alone, but for what they represent. What does Postman find so frightening about the world view implied in the use of these words? How does the division of time on television nurture this view?

2. What is "hampered viewer acceptance"? How does Postman relate it to a theatrical performance?

3. How does Postman distinguish between the two kinds of truth he mentions in paragraph 8?

4. Postman asks several questions in his essay. Identify a few of the questions he asks and explain the different ways he uses them to engage the reader.

5. What are some of the features of a news show that contribute to its dramatic performance?

6. In paragraph 13 Postman illustrates his point that commercial breaks "defuse the import of the news." Did you find this illustration convincing? Why or why not?

7. What do you think is Postman's attitude toward television news and the public who tolerates it? Choose examples of his diction to support your answer.

8. In paragraph 31, Postman makes a subtle prediction. What is it, and how well do you think it works as a conclusion?

Writing Topics

1. Postman says "Americans are the best entertained and quite likely the least well-informed people in the Western world" (paragraph 18). What evidence does he give to support his statement? In a brief essay, use examples of your own observations of the nature of television news to argue for or against Postman's position.

2. Postman expresses his dread over the growing popularity of call-in shows. What is his fear? Listen to some of these shows in your area. Do you think his fear is valid? Why or why not? In a brief essay discuss your conclusions.

3. In paragraph 18 Postman discusses our lack of knowledge about Iran and Islam even though no other "story in years . . . received more attention from television" than the Iran hostage crisis. What are some of the facts we never got from watching that news story on television? Select several other significant news events of recent times, perhaps the Iraqi invasion of Kuwait or the savings and loan scandal, and in an essay discuss some of the information that the television news never mentioned in reporting them. Would you have been interested in knowing more?

CONSUMER REPORTS

Desiring greater credibility and wishing to avoid the high cost of advertising, some American businesses and their public relations agencies now provide "canned news" stories to television stations and newspapers throughout the country. The following essay first appeared in *Consumer Reports*, a consumer advocacy publication of the Consumers Union, in March 1986. The Consumers Union, a nonprofit organization, provides "consumers with information and counsel on consumer goods and services." Here the editors of *Consumer Reports* discuss the sophisticated techniques that businesses use to "insert product plugs in the media under the guise of news."

Advertising in Disguise: How the Hidden Hand of a Corporate Ghostwriter Can Turn a News Report into a Commercial

Last year, Procter & Gamble Co. launched a special promotion for 1
Spic and Span. Cubic zirconia—fake diamonds—were inserted in more than two million boxes of the powdered cleaner. But 500 boxes contained real diamonds worth about $600 each. You could tell which type of stone was in your package by taking it to a participating jeweler for a free evaluation.

The promotion got plenty of exposure on television. That might not 2
seem surprising, since Procter & Gamble is the nation's largest television advertiser, spending more than half a billion dollars a year on network and local television.

But in this case, the air time didn't cost the company a cent. Hill & 3
Knowlton, the large public-relations firm that represents Procter & Gamble, sent a package of materials to some 200 TV stations. It featured a 90-second videotape designed to be inserted into local news broadcasts. There was also supporting footage, prominently featuring the Spic and Span assembly line.

The story line ostensibly was that cubic zirconia are difficult to 4
distinguish from diamonds without special test equipment and that sales of

the low-priced diamond mimics were growing fast. But blended in were plenty of snippets about the Procter & Gamble promotion.

Hill & Knowlton says that its materials were used by stations in at least 27 cities nationwide, including San Francisco (KPIX), Dallas (WFAA), Boston (WBZ) and New York City (WCBS).   5

For Hill & Knowlton, the Spic and Span campaign proved a resounding success. But consumers have no reason to rejoice over such campaigns. By blurring the distinction between news and advertising, such activities imperil an important function of the media: providing consumers with accurate, unbiased information about the marketplace.   6

Passing out corporate handouts as news is nothing new. It's gone on for as long as there have been public-relations firms—and lazy journalists. In recent years, though, the techniques used to insert product plugs in the media under the guise of news have become more sophisticated.   7

For corporations, insinuating product plugs into news articles or news broadcasts can produce more impact than advertising can buy. "People like to think they're very savvy and hip to ads," says Hill & Knowlton broadcast specialist Colleen Growe. But, she says, "When it comes in the form of a news story, it has a lot more truth to the average viewer."   8

In the Can

The public-relations crowd has lately enjoyed a good deal of success placing product plugs on television. Many stations have introduced expanded newscasts; with more time to fill, they jump at the opportunity for free material.   9

PR people have honed their technique for preparing canned video news stories. Hill & Knowlton, for example, offers local TV stations a choice. They can run the report just as it's received or they can use narration by their own reporter over additional silent footage, called "B-Roll," that the public-relations firm supplies. For Spic and Span, Hill & Knowlton even suggested the following lead-in script that the local anchorperson could read.   10

"Diamonds are a personal gift. Very personal. Now a low-cost version is making its debut—in a soap box. (Blank) has the story."   11

Nor is the possible local angle overlooked. In the Spic and Span promotion, the public-relations firm supplied names of local participating supermarkets and jewelers in case the TV stations wanted to do its own interviews.   12

To make the fare look fresh instead of canned, PR firms use a trick that you might call "the vanishing interviewer." A PR person will interview an expert on some subject. When the footage is given to the TV stations, it's formatted so that a station can dub in the face or voice of its own   13 newspeople asking the prepackaged questions. In effect, the reporter serves as an actor in a commercial.

The canned news is packaged neatly. A TV station can take the material in familiar videocassette form. Or it can have the footage beamed in by satellite.

14

On the Page

On the newspaper side, such "canned news" is most often seen in special sections, such as those devoted to real estate, automobile, travel and food. The company that wants to promote its products will frequently hire a distribution service that devotes itself entirely to canned news. One such firm, Chicago-based Associated Release Service Inc., each month distributes between 40 and 100 articles to more than 3000 newspapers. "We send out original-quality proofs that are already typeset," says Ted Hathorn, Associated's president. "If they like the material, they can put it right into their page layout."

15

Hathorn finds that canned editorials—an oil company, for instance, might prepare an editorial advocating offshore drilling—don't have a very large market. What the newspapers mainly want, he says, "is anything that deals with the consumer. We send out a lot of food releases, a lot of consumer tips. For instance, All-State might have insurance ideas to help the consumer."

16

A skilled PR person will bury the commercial plug so that the reader won't easily guess the source of the story. As one example, Associated recently distributed a nine-paragraph article headlined "Heartburn—A Peril in the Night." Not until the story's eighth paragraph does the name of Associated's client pop up: "Another option is an over-the-counter antacid that works even when the nighttime heartburn sufferer is lying down. Gaviscon, a unique foaming antacid, is physician recommended and has been proven effective in relieving nighttime heartburn for many years."

17

In some cases, the "consumer information" can be extraordinarily self-serving. In a newspaper column called "Winter Driving Tips," we learn that "according to the experts, one cold start produces the equivalent of 2,000 miles of over-the-road engine wear. . . . This means that the family vehicle could rack up over 200,000 miles in engine wear in just one average 20-week cold season, with one cold start per day." But a worried reader quickly finds out that help is available. "A practical and economical solution to the problem of cold engine starts," the article continues, "is offered by Temro, a major Canadian manufacturer of automotive heating and starting aids." (CU's auto experts say that, while cold starts are indeed hard on your car, the mileage equivalency figures are "absurd.")

18

Who's Using It?

Who uses this sort of stuff? When Sun Color Service, another dis- 19
tribution agency, polled newspapers on the subject, only 25 percent said
they didn't want to receive its releases. Dorothy Rabb, a Sun Color
executive, says that "the large papers, with 200,000 circulation and up, for
the most part do their own articles. Most of our material is accepted by
papers with less than 80,000 circulation."

Still, big papers are not immune. In January, the *New York Times* ran a 20
special supplement on health, in the format known as an "advertorial." In
size and general appearance, it resembled the *New York Times Magazine*.
Conventional advertisements for health products alternated with other
material that looked like editorial matter. In fact, the entire supplement was
advertising. But while the supplement was labeled as advertising in small,
light print, the *New York Times* logo appeared on the cover, and the reader
would have had to read carefully to discern that the *New York Times* news
staff played no role in preparing it.

The number of papers willing to run advertisements in news stories' 21
clothing rises when the sponsor is a big advertiser. "If we do something for
Kraft's, we know it's going to go well," says Rabb. "For Kraft's, we'd expect
to have from 150 to 180 newspapers, totaling anywhere from four to six
million circulation."

One such Kraft-sponsored page or recipes, sent out by Sun Color last 22
summer, featured salads to take to picnics. Not surprisingly, all the recipes
included Miracle Whip or other Kraft dressings.

Ground That Eagle

On days with lots of news space to fill because of heavy ad volume, a 23
newspaper can brim with canned news. Last Thanksgiving, for example,
the *Wyoming Tribune-Eagle*, the newspaper of Cheyenne, the state capital,
carried 15 canned news articles—13 of them mentioning specific brand
names and two plugging generic products. The paper advised its readers to
use Blistex, a lip ointment, "on the mistletoe circuit," to fill their Christmas
stockings with Hazel Bishop Moisture Gloss Stick, and to install "the
watchful eye" of the Sony WatchCam security system, which "helps to make
certain it's just Santa stirring in the house and out."

"Isn't it deceptive to use this canned copy alongside legitimate news 24
articles? I've asked a number of times to label the copy advertising," says
Tribune-Eagle editor Don Hurlburt, who notes that the Wyoming paper's
canned articles are selected by the advertising department. "My voice has
fallen on deaf ears. I don't like it; I don't like the way they do it, but it's not
my decision to make."

A *Tribune-Eagle* advertising executive, who asked not to be identified,   25
insists that the canned news is justified. "Products that are usable by the
public are news," he contends. "It's the economics of the retail business that
keeps all of us going."

Plugs for Drugs

When the product plugged by a disguised advertisement is a drug, the   26
issues involved are more serious than usual. Under the law, a company can't
advertise a prescription drug without including a full and accurate account
of potential hazards and side effects. But drug companies can accomplish
the same end if they hook the press into serving as middleman.

"The area of press releases and videos gets a bit messy," says Ken   27
Feather, an official in the Drug Advertising Regulation Branch of the U.S.
Food and Drug Administration. "If they produce a pseudo-news kind of
blurb which they pass out for the press to use, we would object if it were inconsistent with the labeling. However, we have little opportunity to find out
about these things."

To see how a canned video news report on a drug works, consider the   28
case of Augmentin, manufactured by Beecham Laboratories. It combines a
penicillin derivative with a compound that breaks down bacterial resistance
to penicillin. In some instances Augmentin can be prescribed when penicillin alone wouldn't be effective.

In late 1984, Beecham received FDA approval to market Augmentin,   29
and turned to Hill & Knowlton to prepare a video news report. The public-
relations firm prepared the usual arsenal: a press kit, a videotape news
report, and additional footage that stations could use with their own
narration. Hill & Knowlton also sent the stations telexes with suggestions
for interviews with local doctors who had participated in testing Augmentin.

In some cases, local television stations prepared their own news re-   30
ports on Augmentin, and when they used Beecham-supplied material, they
noted that fact on the screen. But the station-prepared material and the
Beecham film clip sometimes seemed like fraternal twins.

The narrator of the Beecham video release said: "Infectious bacteria,   31
doubling their numbers every 20 minutes. And these are some of the
victims: children." The screen showed bacteria growing, followed by a scene
of children playing. Viewers of WNEW-TV in New York City saw those same
two scenes, only superimposed on the screen was "Dr. Max Gomez, The 10
O'Clock News, Ch. 5." The voice was that of scientist-reporter Gomez
saying, "Unchecked they can double their number in 20 minutes. And
these are some of the victims: young children."

We asked Gomez, who holds a Ph.D. in neurosciences and is now   32
health-and-science editor of KYW-TV in Philadelphia, about taking his narra-

tion from a script by publicity agents. "I can't say I'm not guilty of that," he notes, "but it would be unusual of me to do that."

In the Augmentin video news release, Dr. Richard Wallace, associate professor of research and clinical medicine at the University of Texas Health Center at Tyler, spoke about the drug. "We studied between 20 and 25 patients who were infected with these organisms," he said, "and all these patients were treated successfully with this agent Augmentin."   33

But the news clip didn't mention that 25 patients is a small-scale study, or that the study lacked a control group.   34

Dr. Wallace says that Hill & Knowlton paid him $1,000 to participate in the video clip, but that his comments were his own and not from a script. He says he put the money into a research fund as "my way of getting around any sense of obligation."   35

Is it proper for a doctor to be paid to appear in a film that will later appear on TV newscasts? Looking back on it, Dr. Wallace has some serious doubts. "I'm a scientist and am supposed to be separate from the company," he says. "They're selling a product; they want to package this so it sells to newspapers, radio and television. I probably would not do it again."   36

For Kenneth Rabin, who heads Hill & Knowlton's health unit, the Augmentin video clip was a total success. "It would not be an exaggeration to estimate that 50 to 100 TV stations used that clip in one part or another," he said. Rabin adds that "any time someone reads something in a magazine as news content or sees it on a TV news show, it carries a certain weight it doesn't in an ad."   37

The Oraflex Case

On May 19, 1982, Eli Lilly & Co. released news of its anti-arthritic drug Oraflex. Press kits went to news organizations all over the country, and a video news clip was prepared for use by television networks.   38

The Lilly material had omitted a key fact: On May 8, the *British Medical Journal* had published several articles about severe adverse reactions to Oraflex. According to the FDA, news of these articles had become widely known in the medical community by May 16.   39

The FDA found, however, that many TV and radio stations apparently took their reports on Oraflex directly from the Lilly material. According to an FDA internal memorandum dated July 10, 1982, "These broadcasts were of a uniform character: i.e., they all described Oraflex as being a potential remittive agent and as having a minimal potential for side effects. In fact, several broadcasts over different networks used nearly identical wording to these descriptions."   40

Oraflex, which had been approved by the FDA in April 1982, was pulled from the market that August. During that time, Federal investigators maintain it was a factor in the deaths of at least 26 Americans. Last   41 summer, Lilly pleaded guilty to criminal charges for not having informed Federal officials that Oraflex had been linked to deaths and illnesses in foreign countries.

The FDA's internal memorandum takes particular note of a report on   42
ABC-TV network news on May 19. The report, the memorandum says, "included a statement that physicians regard side effects related to Oraflex as being minor when compared to aspirin."

ABC science editor Jules Bergman, who prepared the Oraflex news   43
report, says he now consults a panel of doctors before doing any similar report.

The Way Out

Much of what businesses do is news. Certainly, we'd be the last to   44
discourage reports that name brands and companies, so long as the reporting is done with vigor and objectivity. But thinly disguised product plugs are not news, and shouldn't be passed off as such.

Companies and their public-relations agencies certainly aren't going   45
to stop playing the disguised ad game. For them, the appeal of canned news is understandable. It commands far more credibility than advertising—and it does it at a much lower cost. Sun Color Service, for instance, says that it can reach as many people by spending $1 on canned news as it can by spending $23 on advertising. Given that motivation, public relations people will keep trying to get the media to serve as shills.

It's up to the news media to avoid parroting plugs. When some news   46
reports are really ads in disguise, it casts doubt on everything presented as news.

Questions for Study and Discussion

1. What is the advantage to a corporation of plugging its product in a news story? In what way does this practice imperil the function of the media?

2. In paragraphs 10–14, *Consumer Reports* lists the ways that corporations have "honed their technique" for preparing canned video news stories. Briefly describe those techniques.

3. The selection includes two long examples of PR campaigns that were turned into news stories. Was it necessary to include such extensive evidence? Could the same point have been made in fewer words? Explain.

4. Who buys canned news and why? In what sections of the paper do newspapers usually use canned news? How do PR firms play down the fact that it's really an ad?

5. The PR firms who prepare the canned news are remarkably candid about their work. How did this strike you as you read the article?

6. The *Consumer Reports* article moves quickly and is easy to read. Who is its audience? Give examples of diction and organization to support your conclusion.

7. Why did *Consumer Reports* prepare this report? Is the purpose of this report stated or implied?

Writing Topics

1. *Consumer Reports* says, "We'd be the last to discourage reports that name brands and companies, so long as the reporting is done with vigor and objectivity." Watch television for a week and pay close attention to the way some reporting permits advertising of products while others are real news stories. What distinctions can you make between the two? Write an essay showing you understand the meaning of "vigor" and "objectivity" as used in the article.

2. Rewrite the opening story as straight news.

3. Reread the two cases of ads-as-news. Then describe in an essay what you believe is the harm, if any, of advertising disguised as news.

Prejudice and Sexism

GORDON ALLPORT

When Gordon Allport was writing *The Nature of Prejudice*, the influential book
from which the following essay is taken, much of the United States was still racially
segregated and Senator Joseph McCarthy was at the height of his sensational career,
chasing suspected communists and subversives from the national government.
Allport's book appeared in 1954, the year in which things began to change.
McCarthy's influence was finally ended by Senate censure. That same year the
Supreme Court ruled against racial segregation in public schools, and in 1955
Martin Luther King, Jr., led the boycott against Montgomery's segregated bus
system that began the modern civil rights movement.

Allport himself was not one to join the picket lines. He was born in 1897 in
Montezuma, Indiana, attended Harvard University, and ultimately returned there
as a professor of psychology; he retired in 1962 and died five years later. His articles
and books on personality established him as a leading authority in his field. *The
Nature of Prejudice* remains his most widely read book, however, as readable and
relevant today as it was when first published. In this selection, Allport identifies and
discusses some of the ways in which language itself, often very subtly, can express
prejudice and even cause it.

The Language of Prejudice

Without words we should scarcely be able to form categories at all. A   1
dog perhaps forms rudimentary generalizations, such as small-boys-are-to-
be-avoided—but this concept runs its course on the conditioned reflex level,
and does not become the object of thought as such. In order to hold a
generalization in mind for reflection and recall, for identification and for

action, we need to fix it in words. Without words our world would be, as William James said, an "empirical sand-heap."

Nouns That Cut Slices

In the empirical world of human beings there are some [four] billion   2
grains of sand corresponding to our category "the human race." We cannot possibly deal with so many separate entities in our thought, nor can we individualize even among the hundreds whom we encounter in our daily round. We must group them, form clusters. We welcome, therefore, the names that help us to perform the clustering.

The most important property of a noun is that it brings many grains   3
of sand into a single pail, disregarding the fact that the same grains might have fitted just as appropriately into another pail. To state the matter technically, a noun *abstracts* from a concrete reality some one feature and assembles different concrete realities only with respect to this one feature. The very act of classifying forces us to overlook all other features, many of which might offer a sounder basis than the rubric we select. Irving Lee gives the following example:

> I knew a man who lost the use of both eyes. He was called a "blind man." He could also be called an expert typist, a conscientious worker, a good student, a careful listener, a man who wanted a job. But he couldn't get a job in the department store order room where employees sat and typed orders which came over the telephone. The personnel man was impatient to get the interview over. "But you're a blind man," he kept saying, and one could almost feel his silent assumption that somehow the incapacity in one aspect made the man incapable in every other. So blinded by the label was the interviewer that he could not be persuaded to look beyond it.

Some labels, such as "blind man," are exceedingly salient and power-   4
ful. They tend to prevent alternative classification, or even cross-classification. Ethnic labels are often of this type, particularly if they refer to some highly visible feature, e.g., Negro, Oriental. They resemble the labels that point to some outstanding incapacity—*feeble-minded, cripple, blind man.* Let us call such symbols "labels of primary potency." These symbols act like shrieking sirens, deafening us to all finer discriminations that we might otherwise perceive. Even though the blindness of one man and the darkness of pigmentation of another may be defining attributes for some purposes, they are irrelevant and "noisy" for others.

Most people are unaware of this basic law of language—that every   5
label applied to a given person refers properly only to one aspect of his nature. You may correctly say that a certain man is *human, a philanthropist,*

a Chinese, a physician, an athlete. A given person may be all of these; but the chances are that *Chinese* stands out in your mind as the symbol of primary potency. Yet neither this nor any other classificatory label can refer to the whole of a man's nature. (Only his proper name can do so.)

Thus each label we use, especially those of primary potency, distracts our attention from concrete reality. The living, breathing, complex individual—the ultimate unit of human nature—is lost to sight. As in Figure 1 the label magnifies one attribute out of all proportion to its true significance, and masks other important attributes of the individual. . . .   6

A category, once formed with the aid of a symbol of primary potency, tends to attract more attributes that it should. The category labeled *Chinese* comes to signify not only ethnic membership but also reticence, impassivity, poverty, treachery. To be sure . . . there may be genuine ethnic-linked traits, making for a certain *probability* that the member of an ethnic stock may have these attributes. But our cognitive process is not cautious. The labeled category, as we have seen, includes indiscriminately the defining attribute, probable attributes, and wholly fanciful, nonexistent attributes.   7

Even proper names—which ought to invite us to look at the individual person—may act like symbols of primary potency, especially if they arouse ethnic associations. Mr. Greenberg is a person, but since his name is Jewish, it activates in the hearer his entire category of Jews-as-a-whole. An ingenious experiment performed by Razran shows this point clearly, and at the same time demonstrates how a proper name, acting like an ethnic symbol, may bring with it an avalanche of stereotypes.   8

> Thirty photographs of college girls were shown on a screen to 150 students. The subjects rated the girls on a scale from one to five for *beauty, intelligence, character, ambition, general likability*. Two months later the same subjects were asked to rate the same photographs (and fifteen additional ones introduced to complicate the memory factor). This time five of the original photographs were given Jewish surnames (Cohen, Kantor, etc.), five Italian (Valenti, etc.), five Irish (O'Brien, etc.); and the remaining girls were given names chosen from the signers of the Declaration of Independence and from the Social Register (Davis, Adams, Clark, etc.).
>
> When Jewish names were attached to photographs there occurred the following changes in ratings:
>
> decrease in liking
>
> decrease in character

decrease in beauty
increase in intelligence
increase in ambition

For those photographs given Italian names there occurred:

decrease in liking
decrease in character
decrease in beauty
decrease in intelligence

Thus a mere proper name leads to prejudgments of personal attributes. The individual is fitted to the prejudice ethnic category, and not judged in his own right.

While the Irish names also brought about depreciated judgment, the depreciation was not as great as in the case of the Jews and Italians. The falling of likability of the "Jewish girls" was twice as great as for "Italians" and five times as great as for "Irish." We note, however, that the "Jewish" photographs caused higher ratings in *intelligence* and in *ambition*. Not all stereotypes of out-groups are unfavorable.

The anthropologist, Margaret Mead, has suggested that labels of 9
primary potency lose some of their force when they are changed from nouns into adjectives. To speak of a Negro soldier, a Catholic teacher, or a Jewish artist calls attention to the fact that some other group classifications are just as legitimate as the racial or religious. If George Johnson is spoken of not only as a Negro but also as a *soldier*, we have at least two attributes to know him by, and two are more accurate than one. To depict him truly as an individual, of course, we should have to name many more attributes. It is a useful suggestion that we designate ethnic and religious membership where possible with *adjectives* rather than with *nouns*.

Emotionally Toned Labels

Many categories have two kinds of labels—one less emotional and one 10
more emotional. Ask yourself how you feel, and what thoughts you have, when you read the words *school teacher*, and then *school marm*. Certainly the second phrase calls up something more strict, more ridiculous, more disagreeable than the former. Here are four innocent letters: m-a-r-m. But they make us shudder a bit, laugh a bit, and scorn a bit. They call up an image of a spare, humorless, irritable old maid. They do not tell us that she is an individual human being with sorrows and troubles of her own. They force her instantly into a rejective category.

In the ethnic sphere even plain labels such as Negro, Italian, Jew, 11
Catholic, Irish-American, French-Canadian may have emotional tone for a

reason that we shall soon explain. But they all have their higher key equivalents: nigger, wop, kike, papist, harp, canuck. When these labels are employed we can be almost certain that the speaker *intends* not only to characterize the person's membership, but also to disparage and reject him.

Quite apart from the insulting intent that lies behind the use of certain labels, there is also an inherent ("physiognomic") handicap in many terms designating ethnic membership. For example, the proper names characteristic of certain ethnic memberships strike us as absurd. (We compare them, of course, with what is familiar and therefore "right.") Chinese names are short and silly; Polish names intrinsically difficult and outlandish. Unfamiliar dialects strike us as ludicrous. Foreign dress (which, of course, is a visual ethnic symbol) seems unnecessarily queer.

But of all these "physiognomic" handicaps the reference to color, clearly implied in certain symbols, is the greatest. The word Negro comes from the Latin *niger* meaning black. In point of fact, no Negro has a black complexion, but by comparison with other blonder stocks, he has come to be known as a "black man." Unfortunately *black* in the English language is a word having a preponderance of sinister connotations: the outlook is black, blackball, blackguard, blackhearted, black death, blacklist, blackmail, Black Hand. In his novel *Moby Dick*, Herman Melville considers at length the remarkably morbid connotations of black and the remarkably virtuous connotations of white.

Nor is the ominous flavor of black confined to the English language. A cross-cultural study reveals that the semantic significance of black is more or less universally the same. Among certain Siberian tribes, members of a privileged clan call themselves "white bones," and refer to all others as "black bones." Even among Uganda Negroes there is some evidence for a white god at the apex of the theocratic hierarchy; certain it is that a white cloth, signifying purity, is used to ward off evil spirits and disease.

There is thus an implied value-judgment in the very concept of *white race* and *black race*. One might also study the numerous unpleasant connotations of *yellow*, and their possible bearing on our conception of the people of the Orient.

Such reasoning should not be carried too far, since there are undoubtedly, in various contexts, pleasant associations with both black and yellow. Black velvet is agreeable; so too are chocolate and coffee. Yellow tulips are well liked; the sun and moon are radiantly yellow. Yet it is true that "color" words are used with chauvinistic overtones more than most people realize. There is certainly condescension indicated in many familiar phrases: dark as a nigger's pocket, darktown strutters, white hope (a term originated when a white contender was sought against the Negro heavyweight champion, Jack Johnson), the white man's burden, the yellow peril, black boy. Scores of everyday phrases are stamped with the flavor of prejudice, whether the user knows it or not.

We spoke of the fact that even the most proper and sedate labels for   17
minority groups sometimes seem to exude a negative flavor. In many
contexts and situations the very terms *French-Canadian, Mexican,* or *Jew,*
correct and nonmalicious though they are, sound a bit opprobrious. The
reason is that they are labels of social deviants. Especially in a culture where
uniformity is prized, the name of *any* deviant carries with it *ipso facto* a
negative value-judgment. Words like *insane, alcoholic, pervert* are presumably
neutral designations of a human condition, but they are more: they are
finger-pointings at deviance. Minority groups are deviants, and for this
reason, from the very outset, the most innocent labels in many situations
imply a shading of disrepute. When we wish to highlight the deviance and
denigrate it still further we use words of a higher emotional key: crackpot,
soak, pansy, greaser, Okie, nigger, harp, kike.

Members of minority groups are often understandably sensitive to   18
names given them. Not only do they object to deliberately insulting epithets, but sometimes see evil intent where none exists. Often the word
Negro is spelled with a small *n*, occasionally as a studied insult, more often
from ignorance. (The term is not cognate with white, which is not cap-
italized, but rather with Caucasian, which is.) Terms like "mulatto" or
"octoroon" cause hard feeling because of the condescension with which
they have often been used in the past. Sex differentiations are objectionable, since they seem doubly to emphasize ethnic difference: why speak of
Jewess and not of Protestantess, or of Negress and not of whitess? Similar
overemphasis is implied in the terms like Chinaman or Scotchman; why
not American man? Grounds for misunderstanding lie in the fact that
minority group members are sensitive to such shadings, while majority
members may employ them unthinkingly.

The Communist Label

Until we label an out-group it does not clearly exist in our minds. Take   19
the curiously vague situation that we often meet when a person wishes to
locate responsibility on the shoulders of some out-group whose nature he
cannot specify. In such a case he usually employs the pronoun "they"
without an antecedent. "Why don't they make these sidewalks wider?" "I
hear they are going to build a factory in this town and hire a lot of
foreigners." "I won't pay this tax bill; they can just whistle for their money."
If asked "who?" the speaker is likely to grow confused and embarrassed. The
common use of the orphaned pronoun *they* teaches us that people often
want and need to designate out-groups (usually for the purpose of venting
hostility) even when they have no clear conception of the out-group in
question. And so long as the target of wrath remains vague and ill-defined
specific prejudice cannot crystallize around it. To have enemies we need
labels.

Until relatively recently—strange as it may seem—there was no   20
agreed-upon symbol for *communist*. The word, of course, existed but it had
no special emotional connotation, and did not designate a public enemy.
Even when, after World War I, there was a growing feeling of economic and
social menace in this country, there was no agreement as to the actual
source of the menace.

A content analysis of the *Boston Herald* for the year 1920 turned up   21
the following list of labels. Each was used in a context implying some threat.
Hysteria had overspread the country, as it did after World War II. Someone
must be responsible for the postwar malaise, rising prices, uncertainty.
There must be a villain. But in 1920 the villain was impartially designated
by reporters and editorial writers with the following symbols:

> alien, agitator, anarchist, apostle of bomb and torch, Bolshevik, communist,
> communist laborite, conspirator, emissary of false promise, extremist, for-
> eigner, hyphenated-American, incendiary, IWW, parlor anarchist, parlor
> pink, parlor socialist, plotter, radical, red, revolutionary, Russian agitator,
> socialist, Soviet, syndicalist, traitor, undesirable.[1]

From this excited array we note that the *need* for an enemy (someone   22
to serve as a focus for discontent and jitters) was considerably more apparent than the precise *identity* of the enemy. At any rate, there was no clearly
agreed upon label. Perhaps partly for this reason the hysteria abated. Since
no clear category of "communism" existed there was no true focus for the
hostility.

But following World War II this collection of vaguely interchangeable   23
labels became fewer in number and more commonly agreed upon. The out-
group menace came to be designated almost always as *communist* or *red*. In
1920 the threat, lacking a clear label, was vague; after 1945 both symbol and
thing became more definite. Not that people knew precisely what they
meant when they said "communist," but with the aid of the term they were
at least able to point consistently to *something* that inspired fear. The term
developed the power of signifying menace and led to various repressive
measures against anyone to whom the label was rightly or wrongly attached.

Logically, the label should apply to specifiable defining attributes,   24
such as members of the Communist Party, or people whose allegiance is
with the Russian system, or followers, historically, of Karl Marx. But the
label came in for far more extensive use.

What seems to have happened is approximately as follows. Having   25
suffered through a period of war and being acutely aware of devastating
revolutions abroad, it is natural that most people should be upset, dreading

---

[1]The IWW, or Industrial Workers of the World, was a radical labor organization that
advocated violence. Syndicalism advocated that labor unions take over the government
and industry.

to lose their possessions, annoyed by high taxes, seeing customary moral and religious values threatened, and dreading worse disasters to come. Seeking an explanation for this unrest, a single identifiable enemy is wanted. It is not enough to designate "Russia" or some other distant land. Nor is it satisfactory to fix blame on "changing social conditions." What is needed is a human agent near at hand: someone in Washington, someone in our schools, in our factories, in our neighborhood. If we *feel* an immediate threat, we reason, there must be a near-lying danger. It is, we conclude, communism, not only in Russia but also in America, at our doorstep, in our government, in our churches, in our colleges, in our neighborhood.

Are we saying that hostility toward communism is prejudice? Not   26
necessarily. There are certainly phases of the dispute wherein realistic social conflict is involved. American values (e.g., respect for the person) and totalitarian values as represented in Soviet practice are intrinsically at odds. A realistic opposition in some form will occur. Prejudice enters only when the defining attributes of "communist" grow imprecise, when anyone who favors any form of social change is called a communist. People who fear social change are the ones most likely to affix the label to any persons or practices that seem to them threatening.

For them the category is undifferentiated. It includes books, movies,   27
preachers, teachers who utter what for them are uncongenial thoughts. If evil befalls—perhaps forest fires or a factory explosion—it is due to communist saboteurs. The category becomes monopolistic, covering almost anything that is uncongenial. On the floor of the House of Representatives in 1946, Representative Rankin called James Roosevelt a communist. Congressman Outland replied with psychological acumen, "Apparently everyone who disagrees with Mr. Rankin is a communist."

When differentiated thinking is at a low ebb—as it is in times of social   28
crises—there is a magnification of two-valued logic. Things are perceived as either inside or outside a moral order. What is outside is likely to be called "communist." Correspondingly—and here is where damage is done—whatever is called communist (however erroneously) is immediately cast outside the moral order.

This associative mechanism places enormous power in the hands of a   29
demagogue. For several years Senator McCarthy managed to discredit many citizens who thought differently from himself by the simple device of calling them a communist. Few people were able to see through this trick and many reputations were ruined. But the famous senator has no monopoly on the device. As reported in the *Boston Herald* on November 1, 1946, Representative Joseph Martin, Republican leader in the House, ended his election campaign against his Democratic opponent by saying, "The people will vote tomorrow between chaos, confusion, bankruptcy, state socialism or communism, and the preservation of our American life, with all its freedom and its opportunities." Such an array of emotional labels placed his opponent outside the accepted moral order. Martin was re-elected. . . .

Not everyone, of course, is taken in. Demagogy, when it goes too far, 30
meets with ridicule. Elizabeth Dilling's book, *The Red Network*, was so
exaggerated in its two-valued logic that it was shrugged off by many people
with a smile. One reader remarked, "Apparently if you step off the sidewalk
with your left foot you're a communist." But it is not easy in times of social
strain and hysteria to keep one's balance, and to resist the tendency of a
verbal symbol to manufacture large and fanciful categories of prejudiced
thinking.

Verbal Realism and Symbol Phobia

Most individuals rebel at being labeled, especially if the label is 31
uncomplimentary. Very few are willing to be called *fascistic*, *socialistic*, or
anti-Semitic. Unsavory labels may apply to others, but not to us.

An illustration of the craving that people have to attach favorable 32
symbols to themselves is seen in the community where white people banded
together to force out a Negro family that had moved in. They called
themselves "Neighborly Endeavor" and chose as their motto the Golden
Rule.[2] One of the first acts of this symbol-sanctified band was to sue the
man who sold property to Negroes. They then flooded the house which
another Negro couple planned to occupy. Such were the acts performed
under the banner of the Golden Rule.

Studies made by Stagner and Hartmann show that a person's political 33
attitudes may in fact entitle him to be called a fascist or a socialist, and yet
he will emphatically repudiate the unsavory label, and fail to endorse any
movement or candidate that overtly accepts them. In short, there is a *symbol
phobia* that corresponds to *verbal realism*. We are more inclined to the
former when we ourselves are concerned, though we are much less critical
when epithets of "fascist," "communist," "blind man," "school marm" are
applied to others.

When symbols provoke strong emotions they are sometimes regarded 34
no longer as symbols, but as actual things. The expressions "son of a bitch"
and "liar" are in our culture frequently regarded as "fighting words." Softer
and more subtle expressions of contempt may be accepted. But in these
particular cases, the epithet itself must be "taken back." We certainly do not
change our opponent's attitude by making him take back a word, but it
seems somehow important that the word itself be eradicated.

Such verbal realism may reach extreme length. 35

The City Council of Cambridge, Massachusetts, unanimously passed a resolution (December, 1939) making it illegal "to possess, harbor, sequester,
introduce or transport, within the city limits, any book, map, magazine,

---

[2]"Do onto others as you would have others do unto you."

newspaper, pamphlet, handbill or circular containing the words Lenin or Leningrad."

Such naiveté in confusing language with reality is hard to comprehend unless we recall that word-magic plays an appreciable part in human thinking. The following examples, like the one preceding, are taken from Hayakawa.[3]

> The Malagasy soldier must eschew kidneys, because in the Malagasy language the word for kidney is the same as that for "shot"; so shot he would certainly be if he ate a kidney.

> In May, 1937, a state senator of New York bitterly opposed a bill for the control of syphilis because "the innocence of children might be corrupted by a widespread use of the term. . . . This particular word creates a shudder in every decent woman and decent man."

This tendency to reify words underscores the close cohesion that exists between category and symbol. Just the mention of "communist," "Negro," "Jew," "England," "Democrats," will send some people into a panic of fear or a frenzy of anger. Who can say whether it is the word or the thing that annoys them? The label is an intrinsic part of any monopolistic category. Hence to liberate a person from ethnic or political prejudice it is necessary at the same time to liberate him from *word fetishism*. This fact is well known to students of general semantics who tell us that prejudice is due in large part to verbal realism and to symbol phobia. Therefore any program for the reduction of prejudice must include a large measure of semantic therapy. 36

Questions for Study and Discussion

1. Where does Allport state his main point? How does he support and develop that point in this essay?
2. Names and nouns are essential if we are to make sense of the world, as Allport suggests in his opening paragraph, yet he goes on to say that nouns are inherently unfair. Why is this so?
3. Why are "labels of primary potency" so important? Should we always avoid the use of such labels? Does Allport suggest any ways in which the force of these labels can be diminished. If so, what are they?
4. In paragraphs 10–18, Allport observes that different words with approximately the same literal meaning often express different attitudes. What about this passage had the greatest impact on you? Did any of it seem no longer

---

[3]S. I. Hayakawa, author of *Language in Thought and Action*.

valid? Why? What does the passage, and your response to it, suggest about the relation between language and prejudice?

5. Paragraphs 19–30 deal with an attitude that was widespread in the early 1950s but is much rarer now. Is Allport's point nonetheless still relevant? Why? If so, what present-day examples would you give to make its relevance plain?

6. What does Allport mean by "symbol phobia" and "verbal realism"? Give your own examples of each.

Writing Topics

1. Everyone can be placed in various categories according to sex, race, religion, cultural background, and even appearance. How would you categorize yourself? What is your own image of the categories to which you belong? How do outsiders view these categories? In what ways has language been used to stigmatize you or the categories to which you belong? How do you feel about it?

2. In recent years, members of various groups have sought to have new labels applied to themselves, labels that express their own views rather than those of outsiders. Two prominent examples are women and African-Americans. Choose a group and trace how it has named itself and how this has influenced the labels others use. What conclusions can you draw from that history?

MICHAEL NOVAK

Michael Novak was born in 1933 to immigrant parents in Johnstown, Pennsylvania. A prolific writer on social, religious, and political issues, Novak had a rich and varied education. At the age of fourteen he became a junior seminarian in the Congregation of the Holy Cross; he received his B.A. in 1956 from Stonehill, a Catholic college near Boston, and his B.Th. from Gregorian University in Rome in 1958, but left before his ordination. He holds a master's from Harvard University and has taught philosophy, humanities, and religion at Stanford University, the State University of New York, and Syracuse University.

Novak began his career as a democratic socialist but has steadily moved to the right and since 1978 has been a resident scholar at the American Enterprise Institute for Public Policy Research, a conservative think tank in Washington, D.C. Novak has written many books, including *The Spirit of Democratic Capitalism* (1982), *Confessions of a Catholic* (1983), *Moral Clarity in a Nuclear Age* (1983), and *Will It Liberate? Questions about Liberation Theology* (1986).

In the following selection, taken from his book *The Rise of the Unmeltable Ethnics* (1971), Novak explains the ways in which ethnic behavior is the result and not the cause of negative attitudes from WASPs.

Neither WASP nor Jew nor Black

Growing up in America has been an assault upon my sense of worthiness. It has also been a kind of liberation and delight. 1

There must be countless women in America who have known for years that something is peculiarly unfair, yet who only recently have found it possible, because of Women's Liberation, to give tongue to their pain. In recent months I have experienced a similar inner thaw, a gradual relaxation, a willingness to think about feelings heretofore shepherded out of sight. 2

I am born of PIGS—those Poles, Italians, Greeks, and Slavs, those non-English-speaking immigrants numbered so heavily among the working-men of this nation. Not particularly liberal or radical; born into a history not white Anglo-Saxon and not Jewish; born outside what, in America, is considered the intellectual mainstream—and thus privy to neither power nor status nor intellectual voice. 3

Those Poles of Buffalo and Milwaukee—so notoriously taciturn, sul- 4
len, nearly speechless. Who has ever understood them? It is not that Poles
do not feel emotion—what is their history if not dark passion, romanticism,
betrayal, courage, blood? But where in America is there anywhere a language for voicing what a Christian Pole in this nation feels? He has no
Polish culture left him, no Polish tongue.[1] Yet Polish feelings do not go easily
into the idiom of happy America, the America of the Anglo-Saxons and
yes, in the arts, the Jews. (The Jews have long been a culture of the word,
accustomed to exile, skilled in scholarship and in reflection. The Christian
Poles are largely of peasant origin, free men for hardly more than a hundred
years.) Of what shall the young man of Lackawanna think on his way to
work in the mills, departing his relatively dreary home and street? What
roots does he have? What language of the heart is available to him?[2]

The PIGS are not silent willingly. The silence burns like hidden coals 5
in the chest.

All four of my grandparents, unknown to one another, arrived in 6
America from the same county in Slovakia. My grandfather had a small
farm in Pennsylvania; his wife died in a wagon accident. Meanwhile,
Johanna, fifteen, arrived on Ellis Island, dizzy from witnessing births and
deaths and illnesses aboard the crowded ship. She had a sign around her
neck lettered PASSAIC. There an aunt told her of a man who had lost his wife
in Pennsylvania. She went. They were married. She inherited his three
children.

Each year for five years Grandma had a child of her own. She was 7
among the lucky; only one died. When she was twenty-two and the mother
of seven (my father was the last), her husband died. "Grandma Novak," as I
came to know her many years later, resumed the work she had begun in
Slovakia at the town home of a man known to my father only as "the
Professor"; she housecleaned and she laundered.

I heard this story only weeks ago. Strange that I had not asked 8
insistently before. Odd that I should have such shallow knowledge of my
roots. Amazing to me that I do not know what my family suffered, endured,
learned, and hoped these last six or seven generations. It is as if there were
no project in which we all have been involved, as if history in some way
began with my father and with me.

---

[1]See Andrew R. Sisson's chapter "Our Kooky English Language" in his *Applehood and
Mother Pie* (Peterborough, N.H.: Orchard Press, 1971), pp. 1–16, for a discussion of the
ways in which Continental languages differ from English according to their respective
cultural divergencies.

[2]Royko wrote in his *Chicago Daily News* column: "I imagine that the ethnic in Buffalo is
thinking the same thing that the white Southerner in Birmingham is thinking, or the
Okie oil workers in Tulsa: Another day, another dollar. In fact, that's probably what the
guy in Warsaw is thinking on his way to work." There is at least one point Royko
overlooks—the bottled-up anger of workers in America.

The estrangement I have come to feel derives not only from lack of   9
family history. Early in life, I was made to feel a slight uneasiness when I said
my name.[3]

Later "Kim" helped. So did Robert. And "Mister Novak" on TV. The   10
name must be one of the most Anglo-Saxon of the Slavic names. Nevertheless, when I was very young, the "American" kids still made something out
of names unlike their own, and their earnest, ambitious mothers thought
long thoughts when I introduced myself.

Under challenge in grammar school concerning my nationality, I had   11
been instructed by my father to announce proudly: "American." When my
family moved from the Slovak ghetto of Johnstown to the WASP suburb on
the hill, my mother impressed upon us how well we must be dressed, and
show good manners, and behave—people think of us as "different" and we
mustn't give them any cause. "Whatever you do, marry a Slovak girl," was
the other advice to a similar end: "They cook. They clean. They take good
care of you. For your own good." I was taught to be proud of being Slovak,
but to recognize that others wouldn't know what it meant, or care.

When I had at last pierced the deception—that most movie stars and   12
many other professionals had abandoned their European names in order to
feed American fantasies—I felt only a little sadness. One of my uncles, for
business reasons and rather late in life, changed his name, too, to a simple
German variant—not long, either, after World War II.

Nowhere in my schooling do I recall any attempt to put me in touch   13
with my own history. The strategy was clearly to make an American of me.
English literature, American literature, and even the history books, as I
recall them, were peopled mainly by Anglo-Saxons from Boston (where
most historians seemed to live). Not even my native Pennsylvania, let alone
my Slovak forebears, counted for very many paragraphs. (We did have
something called "Pennsylvania History" somewhere; I seem to remember
its puffs for industry. It could have been written by a Mellon.) I don't
remember feeling envy or regret: a feeling, perhaps, of unimportance, of
remoteness, of not having heft enough to count.

The fact that I was born a Catholic also complicated life. What is a   14
Catholic but what everybody else is in reaction against? Protestants re-
formed "the whore of Babylon." Others were "enlightened" from it, and
Jews had reason to help Catholicism and the social structure it was rooted
in fall apart. The history books and the whole of education hummed in
upon that point (for during crucial years I attended a public school): to
be modern is decidedly not to be medieval; to be reasonable is not to be
dogmatic; to be free is clearly not to live under ecclesiastical authority; to be

---

[3]See Victor R. Greene's "Sons of Hunkies: Men with a Past?" *Slovakia*, vol. XVI, No. 39,
1966, pp. 85–86.

scientific is not to attend ancient rituals, cherish irrational symbols, indulge in mythic practices. It is hard to grow up Catholic in America without becoming defensive, perhaps a little paranoid, feeling forced to divide the world between "us" and "them."

English Catholics have little of the sense of inferiority in which many   15
other Catholic groups tend to share—Irish Catholics, Polish Catholics, Lithuanians, Germans, Italians, Lebanese, and others. Daniel Callahan (*The Mind of the Catholic Layman, Generation of the Third Eye*) and Garry Wills ("Memories of a Catholic Boyhood," in *Esquire*) both identify, in part, with the more secure Catholicism of an Anglo-Catholic parent. The French around New Orleans have a social ease different from the French Catholics of Massachusetts. Still, as Catholics, especially vis-à-vis the national liberal culture, nearly all have felt a certain involuntary defensiveness. Granted our diverse ethnic circumstances, we share a certain communion of memories.

We had a special language all our own, our own pronunciation for   16
words we shared in common with others (Augústine, contémplative), sights and sounds and smells in which few others participated (incense at benediction of the Most Blessed Sacrament, Forty Hours, wakes, and altar bells at the silent consecration of the Host); and we had our own politics and slant on world affairs. Since earliest childhood, I have known about a "power elite" that runs America: the boys from the Ivy League in the State Department as opposed to the Catholic boys in Hoover's FBI who (as Daniel Moynihan once put it) keep watch on them. And on a whole host of issues, my people have been, though largely Democratic, conservative: on censorship, on communism, on abortion, on religious schools, etc. "Harvard" and "Yale" long meant "them" to us.

The language of Spiro Agnew, the language of George Wallace, except-   17
ing its idiom, awakens childhood memories in me: of men arguing in the barbershop, of my uncle drinking so much beer he threatened to lay his dick upon the porch rail and wash the whole damn street with steaming piss—while cursing the niggers in the mill below, and the Yankees in the mill above—millstones he felt pressing him. Other relatives were duly shocked, but everybody loved Uncle George; he said what he thought.

We did not feel this country belonged to us. We felt fierce pride in it,   18
more loyalty than anyone could know. But we felt blocked at every turn. There were not many intellectuals among us, not even very many professional men. Laborers mostly. Small businessmen, agents for corporations perhaps. Content with a little, yes, modest in expectation, and content. But somehow feeling cheated. For a thousand years the Slovaks survived Hungarian hegemony and our strategy here remained the same: endurance and steady work. Slowly, one day, we would overcome.

A special word is required about a complicated symbol: sex. To this   19
day my mother finds it hard to spell the work intact, preferring to write

"s--." Not that much was made of sex in our environment. And that's the point: silence. Demonstrative affection, emotive dances, and exuberance Anglo-Saxons seldom seem to share; but on the realities of sex, discretion. Reverence, perhaps; seriousness, surely. On intimacies, it was as though our tongues had been stolen, as though in peasant life for a thousand years—as in the novels of Tolstoi, Sholokhov, and even Kosinski—the context had been otherwise. Passion, certainly; romance, yes; family and children, certainly; but sex rather a minor if explosive part of life.

Imagine, then, the conflict in the generation of my brothers, sister, and myself. (The reviewer for the *New York Times* reviews on the same day two new novels of fantasy—one a pornographic fantasy to end all such fantasies [he writes], the other in some comic way representing the redemption wrought by Jesus Christ. In language and verve, the books are rated evenly. In theme, the reviewer notes his embarrassment in even reporting a religious fantasy, but no embarrassment at all about preposterous pornography.) Suddenly, what for a thousand years was minor becomes an all-absorbing investigation. Some view it as a drama of "liberation" when the ruling classes (subscribers to the *New Yorker*, I suppose) move progressively, generation by generation since Sigmund Freud, toward concentration upon genital stimulation, and latterly toward consciousness-raising sessions in Clit. Lib. But it is rather a different drama when we stumble suddenly upon mores staggering any expectation our grandparents ever cherished. Fear of becoming "sexual objects" is an ancient fear that appears in many shapes. The emotional reaction of Maria Wyeth in Joan Didion's *Play It as It Lays* is exactly what the ancient morality would have predicted.

Yet more significant in the ethnic experience in America is the intellectual world one meets: the definition of values, ideas, and purposes emanating from universities, books, magazines, radio, and television. One hears one's own voice echoed back neither by spokesmen of "middle America" (so complacent, smug, nativist, and Protestant), nor by the "intellectuals." Almost unavoidably, perhaps, education in America leads the student who entrusts his soul to it in a direction which, lacking a better word, we might call liberal: respect for individual conscience, a sense of social responsibility, trust in the free exchange of ideas and procedures of dissent, a certain confidence in the ability of men to "reason together" and adjudicate their differences, a frank recognition of the vitality of the unconscious, a willingness to protect workers and the poor against the vast economic power of industrial corporations, and the like.

On the other hand, the liberal imagination has appeared to be astonishingly universalist and relentlessly missionary. Perhaps the metaphor "enlightenment" offers a key. One is *initiated into light*. Liberal education tends to separate children from their parents, from their roots, from their history, in the cause of a universal and superior religion. One is taught regarding the unenlightened (even if they be one's uncles George and Peter, one's parents, one's brothers, perhaps) what can only be called a modern equivalent of *odium theologicum*. Richard Hofstadter described anti-intellectualism in America (more accurately, in nativist America rather than in ethnic America), but I have yet to encounter a comparable treatment of anti-unenlightenment among our educated classes.

In particular, I have regretted and keenly felt the absence of that sympathy for PIGS which simple human feeling might have prodded intelligence to muster, that same sympathy which the educated find so easy to conjure up for black culture, Chicano culture, Indian culture, and other cultures of the poor. In such cases one finds the universalist pretensions of liberal culture suspended; some groups, at least, are entitled to be both different and respected. Why do the educated classes find it so difficult to want to understand the man who drives a beer truck, or the fellow with a helmet working on a site across the street with plumbers and electricians, while their sensitivities race easily to Mississippi or even Bedford-Stuyvesant?   23

There are deep secrets here, no doubt, unvoiced fantasies and scarcely admitted historical resentments. Few persons in describing "middle Americans" "the silent majority," or Scammon and Wattenberg's typical American voter" distinguish clearly enough between the nativist American and the ethnic American. The first is likely to be Protestant, the second Catholic. Both may be, in various ways, conservative, loyalist, and unenlightened. Each has his own agonies, fears, betrayed expectations. Neither is ready, quite, to become an ally of the other. Neither has the same history behind him here. Neither has the same hopes. Neither lives out the same psychic voyage, shares the same symbols, has the same sense of reality. The rhetoric and metaphors proper to each differ from those of the other.   24

There is overlap, of course. But country music is not a polka; a successful politician in a Chicago ward needs a very different "common touch" from the one needed by the county clerk in Normal. The urban experience of immigration lacks that mellifluous, optimistic, biblical vision of the good America which springs naturally to the lips of politicians from the Bible Belt. The nativist tends to believe with Richard Nixon that he "knows America, and the American heart is good." The ethnic tends to believe that every American who preceded him has an angle, and that he, by God, will some day find one, too. (Often, ethnics complain that by working hard, obeying the law, trusting their political leaders, and relying on the American dream, they now have only their own naiveté to blame for rising no higher than they have.)   25

It goes without saying that the intellectuals do not love "Middle America," and that for all the good, warm discovery of America that preoccupied them during the 1950s no strong tide of respect accumulated in their hearts for the Yahoos, Babbitts, Agnews, and Nixons of the land. Willie Morris in *North Toward Home* writes poignantly of the chill, parochial   26 outreach of the liberal sensibility, its failure to engage the humanity of the modest, ordinary little man west of the Hudson. The Intellectual's Map of the United States is succinct: "Two coasts connected by United Airlines."

Unfortunately, it seems, the ethnics erred in attempting to American- 27 ize themselves before clearing the project with the educated classes. They learned to wave the flag and to send their sons to war. They learned to support their President—an easy task, after all, for those accustomed to obeying authority. And where would they have been if Franklin Roosevelt had not sided with them against established interests? They knew a little about communism—the radicals among them in one way, and by far the larger number of conservatives in another. To this day not a few exchange letters with cousins and uncles who did not leave for America when they might have, whose lot is demonstrably harder than their own and less than free.

Finally, the ethnics do not like, or trust, or even understand the 28 intellectuals. It is not easy to feel uncomplicated affection for those who call you "pig," "fascist," "racist." One had not yet grown accustomed to not hearing "hunkie," "Polack," "spic," "Mick," "dago," and the rest. A worker in Chicago told reporter Lois Wille in a vividly home-centered outburst:

> The liberals always have despised us. We've got these mostly little jobs, and we drink beer and, my God, we bowl and watch television and we don't read. It's goddamn vicious snobbery. We're sick of all these phoney integrated TV commercials with these upper-class Negroes. We know they're phoney.
>
> The only time a Pole is mentioned it's to make fun of him. He's Ignatz Dumbrowski, 274 pounds and 5-foot-4, and he got his education by writing in to a firm on a matchbook cover. But what will we do about it? Nothing because we're the new invisible man, the new whipping boy, and we still think the measure of a man's what he does and how he takes care of his children and what he's doing in his own home, not what he thinks about Vietnam.[4]

At no little sacrifice, one had apologized for foods that smelled too 29 strong for Anglo-Saxon noses; moderated the wide swings of Slavic and Italian emotion; learned decorum; given oneself to education, American style; tried to learn tolerance and assimilation. Each generation criticized the earlier for its authoritarian and European and old-fashioned ways. "Up-to-date" was a moral lever. And now when the process nears completion, when a generation appears that speaks without accent and goes to college, still you are considered "pigs," "fascists," and "racists."

---

[4]Lois Wille, "Fear Rises in the Suburbs," a reprint from the *Chicago Daily News*, in *The Anxious Majority* (New York: Institute on Human Relations, 1970), p. 8.

Racists? Our ancestors owned no slaves. Most of us ceased being serfs   30
only in the last two hundred years—the Russians in 1861. Italians, Lithuanians, Slovaks, Poles are not, in principle, against "community control," or
even against ghettoes of our own.

Whereas the Anglo-Saxon model appears to be a system of atomic in-   31
dividuals and high mobility, our model has tended to stress communities of
our own, attachment to family and relatives, stability, and roots. Ethnics
tend to have a fierce sense of attachment to their homes, having been
homeowners for less than three generations: a home is almost fulfillment
enough of one man's life. Some groups save arduously in a passion to *own*;
others rent. We have most ambivalent feelings about suburban assimilation
and mobility. The melting pot is a kind of homogenized soup, and its mores
only partly appeal to ethnics: to some, yes, and to others, no.

It must be said that ethnics think they are better people than the   32
blacks. Smarter, tougher, harder working, stronger in their families. But
maybe many are not sure. Maybe many are uneasy. Emotions here are
delicate; one can understand the immensely more difficult circumstances
under which the blacks have suffered; and one is not unaware of peculiar
forms of fear, envy, and suspicion across color lines. How much of this we
learned in America by being made conscious of our olive skin, brawny
backs, accents, names, and cultural quirks is not plain to us. Racism is not
our invention; we did not bring it with us; we had prejudices enough and
would gladly have been spared new ones. Especially regarding people who
suffer more than we.

When television commentators and professors say "humanism" or   33
"progress," it seems to ethnics like moral pressure to abandon their own
traditions, their faith, their associations, in order to reap higher rewards in
the culture of the national corporations. Ethnic neighborhoods usually do
not like interviewers, consultants, government agents, organizers, sociologists. Usually they resent the media. Almost all spokesmen they meet from
the world of intellect have disdain for them. It shows. Do museums, along
with "Black art" and "Indian art," have "Italo-American" exhibitions or
"Lithuanian-American" days? Dvořák wrote the *New World Symphony* in a
tiny community of Bohemian craftsmen in Iowa. All over the nation in
print studios and metal foundries, when the craftsmen immigrants from
Europe die, their crafts will die with them. Who here supports such skills?

Questions for Study and Discussion

1. In his opening sentence, Novak says that "Growing up in America has
been an assault upon my sense of worthiness. It has also been a kind of
liberation and delight." Clearly he describes the negative aspects of growing up
in America. Does he ever describe the "delight"?

2. Novak is known for his conservative thinking. What elements of a conservative point of view do you find in his article? Is his philosophy expressed mainly through examples, diction, or something else? Select examples of his writing to support your answer.

3. Novak distinguishes subgroups in American culture that either share similar concerns or become the enemies of ethnic Americans. Name the subgroups he identifies. What characteristics do they share?

4. What is Novak's thesis? Where is it best stated?

5. Novak has organized his article into several "explanations" for the character of ethnic Americans. In each case, who is to blame for the subjugation of ethnic Americans? How does this organization contribute to the overall tone of Novak's article? Do you agree with Novak in every case? Why or why not?

6. In paragraph 30, Novak offers an explanation for the racist attitudes of ethnic groups toward blacks. Why do you think he included this explanation? What is the effect of this paragraph on the reader?

7. How would you define the word "ethnic" as used by Novak? Does it have positive or negative connotations? How is the word "ethnic" defined in your dictionary? What are the differences and similarities between its denotative and connotative meanings?

8. Who is Novak's audience? Cite examples from the selection that led you to your conclusion.

Writing Topics

1. Michael Novak is obviously an educated, articulate American, possessing many of the qualities he says are the exclusive domain of WASPs. By necessity and historically it falls to the educated and articulate members of an oppressed group to speak out against their oppressors. But what effect does this seeming contradiction have on the reader? Does it work to strengthen or weaken the argument of an advocate? What are some of the ways an oppressed people make themselves visible other than through educated speech? Which do you find most effective?

2. Construct a causal argument in which you explain the behavior of a group to which you belong, such as a racial minority, a woman's group, or a fraternal organization. Decide who your readers are and then determine the kinds of evidence you will need to convince them of your point of view. How important is it to assume some responsibility for your behavior in your argument? Does assuming that responsibility weaken or strengthen your position?

CASEY MILLER AND KATE SWIFT

Casey Miller was born in Toledo, Ohio, in 1919 and graduated from Smith College in 1940. She has worked in various editorial positions at the Seabury Press and elsewhere before becoming a free-lance writer and editor in 1964. Kate Swift, born in Yonkers, New York, in 1923, attended Connecticut College and graduated from the University of North Carolina in 1944. She started work as a newsroom copy runner with NBC and later became an editorial assistant at *Time* magazine. Since 1948 she has served as a public relations writer for the Girl Scouts of the U.S.A., as a science writer for the American Museum of Natural History, and most recently as the director of the news bureau of the Yale University School of Medicine. In 1970 she formed a free-lance editorial partnership with Casey Miller. Together they have written numerous articles for such popular magazines as *New York*, *Ms.*, and *The New York Times Magazine* and several books, including *Words and Women* (1976) and *The Handbook of Nonsexist Writing (second edition, 1988)*

Since the early 1970s, Miller and Swift have been pioneers in the study of sexism and language. "It was out of our work as free-lance editors that we became interested in the effect of language on women," they stated in a recent interview. "We document many changes occurring in English today as a result of women's changing perception of themselves." "One Small Step for Genkind," first published in 1972 in *The New York Times Magazine*, was one of the first articles to bring widespread attention to the ways in which language discriminates against women. Here they discuss traditional gender words, prefixes, suffixes, and pronouns that reveal deep-seated biases against women in our male-dominated English language. Their analysis raises important questions about the possibility of establishing equal rights for women in this country.

One Small Step for Genkind

A riddle is making the rounds that goes like this: A man and his young son were in an automobile accident. The father was killed and the son, who was critically injured, was rushed to a hospital. As attendants wheeled the unconscious boy into the emergency room, the doctor on duty looked down at him and said, "My God, it's my son!" What was the relationship of the doctor to the injured boy?

If the answer doesn't jump to your mind, another riddle that has been around a lot longer might help: The blind beggar had a brother. The blind beggar's brother died. The brother who died had no brother. What relation was the blind beggar to the blind beggar's brother?

As with all riddles, the answers are obvious once you see them: The doctor was the boy's mother and the beggar was her brother's sister. Then why doesn't everyone solve them immediately? Mainly because our language, like the culture it reflects, is male oriented. To say that a woman in medicine is an exception is simply to confirm that statement. Thousands of doctors are women, but in order to be seen in the mind's eye, they must be called women doctors.

Except for words that refer to females by definition (mother, actress, Congresswoman), and words for occupations traditionally held by females (nurse, secretary, prostitute), the English language defines everyone as male. The hypothetical person ("If a man can walk 10 miles in two hours . . ."), the average person ("the man in the street") and the active person ("the man on the move") are male. The assumption is that unless otherwise identified, people in general—including doctors and beggars—are men. It is a semantic mechanism that operates to keep women invisible: *man* and *mankind* represent everyone; *he* in generalized use refers to either sex; the "land where our fathers died" is also the land of our mothers—although they go unsung. As the beetle-browed and mustachioed man in a Steig cartoon says to his two male drinking companions, "When I speak of mankind, one thing I *don't* mean is womankind."

Semantically speaking, woman is not one with the species of man, but a distinct subspecies. "Man," says the 1971 edition of Britannica Junior Encyclopedia, "is the highest form of life on earth. His superior intelligence, combined with certain physical characteristics, have enabled man to achieve things that are impossible for other animals." (The prose style has something in common with the report of a research team describing its studies on "the development of the uterus in rats, guinea pigs and men.") As though quoting the Steig character, still speaking to his friends in McSorley's, the Junior Encyclopedia continues: "Man must invent most of his behavior, because he lacks the instincts of lower animals. . . . Most of the things he learns have been handed down from his ancestors by language and symbols rather than by biological inheritance."

Considering that for the last 5,000 years society has been patriarchal, that statement explains a lot. It explains why Eve was made from Adam's rib instead of the other way around, and who invented all those Adam-rib words like *female* and *woman* in the first place. It also explains why, when it is necessary to mention woman, the language makes her a lower caste, a class separate from the rest of man; why it works to "keep her in her place."

This inheritance through language and other symbols begins in the home (also called a man's castle) where man and wife (not husband and wife, or man and woman) live for a while with their children. It is reinforced by religious training, the educational system, the press, government, commerce and the law. As Andrew Greeley wrote not long ago in his magazine, "man is a symbol-creating animal. He orders and interprets his reality by his symbols, and he uses the symbols to reconstruct that reality."

Consider some of the reconstructed realities of American history. 8 When school children learn from their textbooks that the early colonists gained valuable experience in governing themselves, they aren't told that the early colonists who were women were denied the privilege of self-government; when they learn that in the 18th century the average man had to manufacture many of the things he and his family needed, they are not told that this "average man" was often a woman who manufactured much of what she and her family needed. Young people learn that intrepid pioneers crossed the country in covered wagons with their wives, children and cattle; they do not learn that women themselves were intrepid pioneers rather than part of the baggage.

In a paper published this year in Los Angeles as a guide for authors 9 and editors of social-studies textbooks, Elizabeth Burr, Susan Dunn and Norma Farquhar document unintentional skewings of this kind that occur either because women are not specifically mentioned as affecting or being affected by historical events, or because they are discussed in terms of outdated assumptions. "One never sees a picture of women captioned simply 'farmers' or 'pioneers,'" they point out. The subspecies nomenclature that requires a caption to read "women farmers" or "women pioneers" is extended to impose certain jobs on women by definition. The textbook guide gives as an example the word *housewife*, which it says not only "suggests that domestic chores are the exclusive burden of females," but gives "female students the idea that they were born to keep house and teaches male students that they are automatically entitled to laundry, cooking and housecleaning services from the women in their families."

Sexist language is any language that expresses such stereotyped atti- 10 tudes and expectations, or that assumes the inherent superiority of one sex over the other. When a woman says of her husband, who has drawn up plans for a new bedroom wing and left out closets, "Just like a man," her language is as sexist as the man's who says, after his wife has changed her mind about needing the new wing after all, "Just like a woman."

Male and female are not sexist words, but masculine and feminine 11 almost always are. Male and female can be applied objectively to individual people and animals and, by extension, to things. When electricians and plumbers talk about male and female couplings, everyone knows or can figure out what they mean. The terms are graphic and culture free.

Masculine and feminine, however, are as sexist as any words can be, 12 since it is almost impossible to use them without invoking cultural stereotypes. When people construct lists of "masculine" and "feminine" traits they almost always end up making assumptions that have nothing to do with innate differences between the sexes. We have a friend who happens to be going through the process of pinning down this very phenomenon. He is 7 years old and his question concerns why his coats and shirts button left over right while his sisters button the other way. He assumes it must have something to do with the differences between boys and girls, but he can't see how.

What our friend has yet to grasp is that the way you button your coat, like most sex-differentiated customs, has nothing to do with real differences but much to do with what society wants you to feel about yourself as a male or female person. Society decrees that it is appropriate for girls to dress differently from boys, to act differently, and to think differently. Boys must be masculine, whatever that means, and girls must be feminine.   13

Unabridged dictionaries are a good source for finding out what society decrees to be appropriate, though less by definition than by their choice of associations and illustrations. Words associated with males—*manly, virile* and *masculine*, for example—are defined through a broad range of positive attributes like strength, courage, directness and independence, and they are illustrated through such examples of contemporary usage as "a manly determination to face what comes," "a virile literary style," "a masculine love of sports." Corresponding words associated with females are defined with fewer attributes (though weakness is often one of them) and the examples given are generally negative if not clearly pejorative: "feminine wiles," "womanish tears," "a womanlike lack of promptness," "convinced that drawing was a waste of time, if not downright womanly."   14

Male-associated words are frequently applied to females to describe something that is either incongruous ("a mannish voice") or presumably commendable ("a masculine mind," "she took it like a man"), but female-associated words are unreservedly derogatory when applied to males, and are sometimes abusive to females as well. The opposite of "masculine" is "effeminate," although the opposite of "feminine" is simply "unfeminine."   15

One dictionary, after defining the word *womanish* as "suitable to or resembling a woman," further defines it as "unsuitable to a man or to a strong character of either sex." Words derived from "sister" and "brother" provide another apt example, for whereas "sissy," applied either to a male or female, conveys the message that sisters are expected to be timid and cowardly, "buddy" makes clear that brothers are friends.   16

The subtle disparagement of females and corresponding approbation of males wrapped up in many English words is painfully illustrated by "tomboy." Here is an instance where a girl who likes sports and the out-of-doors, who is curious about how things work, who is adventurous and bold instead of passive, is defined in terms of something she is not—a boy. By denying that she can be the person she is and still be a girl, the word surreptitiously undermines her sense of identity: it says she is unnatural. A "tomboy," as defined by one dictionary, is a "girl, especially a young girl, who behaves like a spirited boy." But who makes the judgment that she is   17 acting like a spirited boy, not a spirited girl? Can it be a coincidence that in the case of the dictionary just quoted the editor, executive editor, managing editor, general manager, all six members of the Board of Linguists, the usage editor, science editor, all six general editors of definitions, and 94 out of the 104 distinguished experts consulted on usage—are men?

It isn't enough to say that any invidious comparisons and stereotypes   18
lexicographers perpetuate are already present in the culture. There are ways to define words like womanly and tomboy that don't put women down, though the tradition has been otherwise. Samuel Johnson, the lexicographer, was the same Dr. Johnson who said, "A woman preaching is like a dog's walking on his hind legs. It is not done well; but you are surprised to find it done at all."

Possibly because of the negative images associated with womanish and   19
womanlike, and with expressions like "woman driver" and "woman of the street," the word woman dropped out of fashion for at time. The women at the office and the women on the assembly line and the women one first knew in school all became ladies or girls or gals. Now a countermovement, supported by the very term women's liberation, is putting back into words like woman and sister and sisterhood the meaning they were losing by default. It is as though, in the nick of time, women had seen that the language itself could destroy them.

Some long-standing conventions of the news media add insult to   20
injury. When a woman or girl makes news, her sex is identified at the beginning of a story, if possible in the headline or its equivalent. The assumption, apparently, is that whatever event or action is being reported, a woman's involvement is less common and therefore more newsworthy than a man's. If the story is about achievement, the implication is: "pretty good for a woman." And because people are assumed to be male unless otherwise identified, the media have developed a special and extensive vocabulary to avoid the constant repetition of "woman." The results, "Grandmother Wins Nobel Prize," "Blonde Hijacks Airliner," "Housewife to Run for Congress," convey the kind of information that would be ludicrous in comparable headlines if the subjects were men. Why, if "Unsalaried Husband to Run for Congress" is unacceptable to editors, do women have to keep explaining that to describe them through external or superficial concerns reflects a sexist view of women as decorative objects, breeding machines and extensions of men, not real people?

Members of the Chicago Chapter of the National Organization for   21
Women recently studied the newspapers in their area and drew up a set of guidelines for the press. These include cutting out descriptions of the "clothes, physical features, dating life and marital status of women where such references would be considered inappropriate if about men"; using language in such a way as to include women in copy that refers to home-owners, scientists and business people where "newspaper descriptions often

convey the idea that all such persons are male"; and displaying the same discretion in printing generalizations about women as would be shown toward racial, religious and ethnic groups. "Our concern with what we are called may seem trivial to some people," the women said, "but we regard the old usages as symbolic of women's position within this society."

The assumption that an adult woman is flattered by being called a girl   22
is matched by the notion that a woman in a menial or poorly paid job finds compensation in being called a lady. Ethel Strainchamps has pointed out that since lady is used as an adjective with nouns designating both high and low occupations (lady wrestler, lady barber, lady doctor, lady judge), some writers assume they can use the noun form without betraying value judgments. Not so, Strainchamps says, rolling the issue into a spitball: "You may write, 'He addressed the Republican ladies,' or 'The Democratic ladies convened' . . . but I have never seen 'the Communist ladies' or 'the Black Panther ladies' in print."

Thoughtful writers and editors have begun to repudiate some of the   23
old usages. "Divorcée, "grandmother" and "blonde," along with "vivacious," "pert," "dimpled" and "cute," were dumped by the Washington Post in the spring of 1970 by the executive editor, Benjamin Bradlee. In a memo to his staff, Bradlee wrote, "The meaningful equality and dignity of women is properly under scrutiny today . . . because this equality has been less than meaningful and the dignity not always free of stereotype and condescension."

What women have been called in the press—or at least the part that   24
operates above ground—is only a fraction of the infinite variety of alternatives to "women" used in the subcultures of the English-speaking world. Beyond "chicks," "dolls," "dames," "babes," "skirts" and "broads" are the words and phrases in which women are reduced to their sexuality and nothing more. It would be hard to think of another area of language in which the human mind has been so fertile in devising and borrowing abusive terms. In "The Female Eunuch," Germaine Greer devotes four pages to anatomical terms and words for animals, vegetables, fruits, baked goods, implements and receptacles, all of which are used to dehumanize the female person. Jean Faust, in an article aptly called "Words That Oppress," suggests that the effort to diminish women through language is rooted in a male fear of sexual inadequacy. "Woman is made to feel guilty for and akin to natural disasters," she writes; "hurricanes and typhoons are named after her. Any negative or threatening force is given a feminine name. If a man runs into bad luck climbing up the ladder of success (a male-invented game), he refers to the 'bitch goddess' success."

The sexual overtones in the ancient and no doubt honorable custom   25
of calling ships "she" have become more explicit and less honorable in an age of air travel: "I'm Karen. Fly me." Attitudes of ridicule, contempt and disgust toward female sexuality have spawned a rich glossary of insults and epithets not found in dictionaries. And the usage in which four-letter words

meaning copulate are interchangeable with cheat, attack and destroy can scarcely be unrelated to the savagery of rape.

In her updating of Ibsen's "A Doll's House," Clare Booth Luce has   26
Nora tell her husband she is pregnant—"In the way only men are supposed to get pregnant." "Men, pregnant?" he says, and she nods; "With ideas. Pregnancies there [*she taps his head*] are masculine. And a very superior form of labor. Pregnancies here [*taps her tummy*] are feminine—a very inferior form of labor."

Public outcry followed a revised translation of the New Testament   27
describing Mary as "pregnant" instead of "great with child." The objections were made in part on esthetic grounds: there is no attractive adjective in modern English for a woman who is about to give birth. A less obvious reason was that replacing the euphemism with a biological term undermined religious teaching. The initiative and generative power in the conception of Jesus are understood to be God's; Mary, the mother, was a vessel only.

Whether influenced by this teaching or not, the language of human   28
reproduction lags several centuries behind scientific understanding. The male's contribution to procreation is still described as though it were the entire seed from which a new life grows: the initiative and generative power involved in the process are thought of as masculine, receptivity and nurturance as feminine. "Seminal" remains a synonym for "highly original," and there is no comparable word to describe the female's equivalent contribution.

An entire mythology has grown from this biological misunderstand-   29
ing and its semantic legacy; its embodiment in laws that for centuries made women nonpersons was a key target of the 19th-century feminist movement. Today, more than 50 years after women finally won the basic democratic right to vote, the word "liberation" itself, when applied to women, means something less than when used of other groups of people. An advertisement for the N.B.C. news department listed Women's Liberation along with crime in the streets and the Vietnam war as "bad news." Asked for his views on Women's Liberation, a highly placed politician was quoted as saying, "Let me make one thing perfectly clear. I wouldn't want to wake up next to a lady pipe-fitter."

One of the most surprising challenges to our male-dominated culture   30
is coming from within organized religion, where the issues are being stated, in part, by confronting the implications of traditional language. What a growing number of theologians and scholars are saying is that the myths of the Judeo-Christian tradition, being the products of patriarchy, must be reexamined, and that the concept of an exclusively male ministry and the image of a male god have become idolatrous.

Women are naturally in the forefront of this movement, both in their   31
efforts to gain ordination and full equality and through their contributions to theological reform, although both these efforts are often subtly

diminished. When the Rev. Barbara Anderson was ordained by the American Lutheran Church, one newspaper printed her picture over a caption headed "Happy Girl." *Newsweek's* report of a protest staged last December by women divinity students at Harvard was jocular ("another tilt at the windmill") and sarcastic: "Every time anyone in the room lapsed into what [the students] regarded as male chauvinism—such as using the word 'mankind' to describe the human race in general—the outraged women . . . drowned out the offender with earpiercing blasts from party-favor kazoos. . . . What annoyed the women most was the universal custom of referring to God as 'He.' "

The tone of the report was not merely unfunny; it missed the connection between increasingly outmoded theological language and the accelerating number of women (and men) who are dropping out of organized religion, both Jewish and Christian. For language, including pronouns, can be used to construct a reality that simply mirrors society's assumptions. To women who are committed to the reality of religious faith, the effect is doubly painful. Professor Harvey Cox, in whose classroom the protest took place, stated the issue directly: The women, he said, were raising the "basic theological question of whether God is more adequately thought of in personal or suprapersonal terms." 32

Toward the end of Don McLean's remarkable ballad "American Pie," a song filled with the imagery of abandonment and disillusion, there is a stanza that must strike many women to the quick. The church bells are broken, the music has died; then: 33

And the three men I admire most,
The Father, Son and the Holy Ghost,
They caught the last train for the Coast—
The day the music died.

Three men I admired most. There they go, briefcases in hand and topcoats buttoned left over right, walking down the long cold platform under the city, past the baggage wagons and the hissing steam onto the Pullman. Bye, bye God—all three of you—made in the image of male supremacy. Maybe out there in L.A. where the weather is warmer, someone can believe in you again. 34

The Roman Catholic theologian Elizabeth Farians says "the bad theology of an overmasculinized church continues to be one of the root causes of women's oppression." The definition of oppression is "to crush or burden by abuse of power or authority; burden spiritually or mentally as if by pressure." 35

When language oppresses, it does so by any means that disparage and belittle. Until well into the 20th century, one of the ways English was manipulated to disparage women was through the addition of feminine endings to nonsexual words. Thus a women who aspired to be a poet was 36 excluded from the company of real poets by the label poetess, and a woman who piloted an airplane was denied full status as an aviator by being called an aviatrix. At about the time poetess, aviatrix, and similar Adam-ribbisms were dropping out of use, H. W. Fowler was urging that they be revived. "With the coming expansion of women's vocations," he wrote in the first edition (1926) of "Modern English Usage," "feminines for vocation-words are a special need of the future." There can be no doubt he subconsciously recognized the relative status implied in the *-ess* designations. His criticism of a woman who wished to be known as an author rather than an authoress was that she had no need "to raise herself to the level of the male author by asserting her right to his name."

Who has the prior right to a name? The question has an interesting bearing on words that were once applied to men alone, or to both men and women, but now, having acquired abusive associations, are assigned to women exclusively. Spinster is a gentle case in point. Prostitute and many of its synonyms illustrate the phenomenon better. If Fowler had chosen to record the changing usage of harlot from hired man (in Chaucer's time) through rascal and entertainer to its present definition, would he have maintained that the female harlot is trying to raise herself to the level of the male harlot by asserting her right to his name? Or would he have plugged for harlotress? 37

The demise of most *-ess* endings came about before the start of the new feminist movement. In the second edition of "Modern English Usage," published in 1965, Sir Ernest Gowers frankly admitted what his predecessors had been up to. "Feminine designations," he wrote, "seem now to be falling into disuse. Perhaps the explanation of this paradox is that it symbolizes the victory of women in their struggle for equal rights; it reflects the abandonment by men of those ideas about women in the professions that moved Dr. Johnson to his rude remark about women preachers." 38

If Sir Ernest's optimism can be justified, why is there a movement back to feminine endings in such words as chairwoman, councilwoman and congresswoman? Betty Hudson, of Madison, Conn., is campaigning for the adoption of "selectwomen" as the legal title for a female member of that town's executive body. To have to address a woman as "Selectman," she maintains, "is not only bad grammar and bad biology, but it implies that politics is still, or should be, a man's business." A valid argument, and one that was, predictably, countered by ridicule, the surefire weapon for undercutting achievement. When the head of the Federal Maritime Commission, Helen D. Bentley, was named "Man of the Year" by an association of shipping interests, she wisely refused to be drawn into light-hearted debate with interviewers who wanted to make the award's name a humorous issue. Some women, of course, have yet to learn they are invisible. An 8-year-old who visited the American Museum of Natural History with her Brownie scout troop went through the impressive exhibit on pollution and over- 39 population called "Can Man Survive?" Asked afterward, "Well, can he?" she answered, "I don't know about him, but we're working on it in Brownies."

Nowhere are women rendered more invisible by language than in   40
politics. The United States Constitution, in describing the qualifications for Representative, Senator and President, refers to each as *he*. No wonder Shirley Chisholm, the first woman since 1888 to make a try for the Presidential nomination of a major party, has found it difficult to be taken seriously.

The observation by Andrew Greeley already quoted—that "man"   41
uses "his symbols" to reconstruct "his reality"—was not made in reference to the symbols of language but to the symbolic impact the "nomination of a black man for Vice-Presidency" would have on race relations in the United States. Did the author assume the generic term "man" would of course be construed to include "woman"? Or did he deliberately use a semantic device to exclude Shirley Chisholm without having to be explicit?

Either way, his words construct a reality in which women are ignored.   42
As much as any other factor in our language, the ambiguous meaning of *man* serves to deny women recognition as people. In a recent magazine article, we discussed the similar effect on women of the generic pronoun *he*, which we proposed to replace by a new common gender pronoun *tey*. We were immediately told, by a number of authorities, that we were dabbing in the serious business of linguistics, and the message that reached us from these scholars was loud and clear: It-is-absolutely-impossible-for-anyone-to-introduce-a-new-word-into-the-language-just-because-there-is-a-need-for-it, so-stop-wasting-your-time.

When words are suggested like "herstory" (for history), "sportsone-   43
ship" (for sportsmanship) and "mistresspiece" (for the work of a Virginia Woolf) one suspects a not-too-subtle attempt to make the whole language problem look silly. But unless Alexander Pope, when he wrote "The proper study of mankind is man," meant that women should be relegated to the footnotes (or, as George Orwell might have put it, "All men are equal, but men are more equal than women"), viable new words will surely someday supersede the old.

Without apologies to Freud, the great majority of women do not wish   44
in their hearts that they were men. If having grown up with a language that tells them they are at the same time men and not men raises psychic doubts for women, the doubts are not of their sexual identity but of their human identity. Perhaps the recent unrest surfacing in the Women's Movement is part of the evolutionary change in our particular form of life—the one form of all in the animal and plant kingdoms that orders and interprets its reality by symbols. The achievements of the species called man have brought us to the brink of self-destruction. If the species survives into the next century with the expectation of going on, it may only be because we have become

part of what Harlow Shapley calls the psychozoic kingdom, where brain overshadows brawn and rationality has replaced superstition.

Searching the roots of Western civilization for a word to call this new   45
species of man and woman, someone might come up with *gen*, as in genesis and generic. With such a word, *man* could be used exclusively for males as *woman* is used for females, for gen would include both sexes. Like the words deer and bison, gen would be both plural and singular. Like progenitor, progeny, and generation, it would convey continuity. Gen would express the warmth and generalized sexuality of generous, gentle, and genuine; the specific sexuality of genital and genetic. In the new family of gen girls and boys would grow to genhood, and to speak of genkind would be to include all the people of the earth.

Questions for Study and Discussion

1. What is the authors' thesis, and where is it stated?
2. How, according to Miller and Swift, does the English language operate to "keep women invisible"?
3. Miller and Swift believe that language works to keep women in their place. They argue that this is "reinforced by religious training, the educational system, the press, government, commerce, and the law." What evidence do they present to document this assertion? What examples can you add from your own experience or observations?
4. What, according to the authors, is sexist language? What do they mean when they say, "Male and female are not sexist words, but masculine and feminine are"?
5. In paragraph 17 Miller and Swift present a long example of the word "tomboy." What point about language is this example meant to illustrate?
6. According to Miller and Swift, how important is it to eliminate the automatic use of *he* and *his* and *him* when the person referred to could just as easily be female? How important an issue is it for you? Explain.
7. Why do you suppose Miller and Swift use so many examples and quotations? What effect did they have on you as you read the essay?
8. What is the tone of this essay? How do Miller and Swift maintain this tone? Is their tone appropriate for their subject and audience? Explain.
9. Explain the meaning of the essay's title. To what, if anything, are the authors alluding, and how is the allusion related to their thesis?

Writing Topics

1. Write an essay in which you discuss the power of language to shape society's attitudes toward women or another minority.
2. Miller and Swift provide us with an extensive catalog of words that reveal a disparaging attitude toward women. They argue that changes must be

made in our language if we are going to eliminate sexist language. Write an essay in which you discuss the possible things that you as a user of language, lexicographers as makers of dictionaries, and women and men as leaders of the equal-rights movement can do to bring about change and improve the lot of women in this country.

3. Miller and Swift believe that "the usage in which four-letter words meaning copulate are interchangeable with cheat, attack and destroy can scarcely be unrelated to the savagery of rape." What exactly do they mean here? Do you commonly use sexual obscenities and feel justified in doing so? Or do such words offend you when you hear them? How would you describe your feelings about such words? Write an essay in which you defend your feelings to someone who does not share them.

4. Miller and Swift wrote this essay for *The New York Times Magazine* in the spring of 1972. Certainly, the world has changed greatly in the intervening years. But much has remained unchanged. Write an essay describing the progress that has been made to eliminate sexist language from English. What areas have remained problems and still need attention? Do you have reason to be optimistic or pessimistic about the future? Why?

ALLEEN PACE NILSEN

Alleen Pace Nilsen is a teacher and writer who specializes in children's literature and the study of sexist language. Born in 1936 in Phoenix, Arizona, she is a graduate of Brigham Young University and the University of Iowa. Currently she is a professor and administrator at Arizona State University. Her books on language study include *Pronunciation Contrasts in English* (1971), *Language Play: An Introduction to Linguistics* (1983), and *The Language of Humor / The Humor of Language* (1983).

The following selection has been taken from *Sexism and Language*, a collection of essays published by the National Council of Teachers of English in 1971. Here she analyzes the ways that sexist language reveals the antifemale bias in our culture. According to Nilsen, the "chicken metaphor" tells the whole story: A young girl is a *chick*, then she marries and begins feeling *cooped up*, so she goes to *hen parties* where she *cackles* with her friends. Then she has her *brood*. And when they *leave the nest*, she begins to *henpeck* her husband, finally turning into an *old biddy*.

Sexism and Language

Over the last hundred years, American anthropologists have travelled to the corners of the earth to study primitive cultures. They either became linguists themselves or they took linguists with them to help in learning and analyzing languages. Even if the culture was one that no longer existed, they were interested in learning its language because besides being tools of communication, the vocabulary and structure of a language tell much about the values held by its speakers.

However, the culture need not be primitive, nor do the people making observations need to be anthropologists and linguists. Anyone living in the United States who listens with a keen ear or reads with a perceptive eye can come up with startling new insights about the way American English reflects our values.

Animal Terms for People—Mirrors of the Double Standard

If we look at just one semantic area of English, that of animal terms in relation to people, we can uncover some interesting insights into how our culture views males and females. References to identical animals can have negative connotations when related to a female, but positive or neutral connotations when related to a male. For example, a *shrew* has come to mean "a scolding, nagging, evil-tempered woman," while *shrewd* means "keen-witted, clever, or sharp in practical affairs; astute . . . businessman, etc." (*Webster's New World Dictionary of the American Language*, 1964).

A *lucky dog* or a *gay dog* may be a very interesting fellow, but when a   4 woman is a *dog*, she is unattractive, and when she's a *bitch* she's the personification of whatever is undesirable in the mind of the speaker. When a man is self-confident, he may be described as *cocksure* or even *cocky*, but in a woman this same self-confidence is likely to result in her being called a *cocky bitch*, which is not only a mixed metaphor, but also probably the most insulting animal metaphor we have. *Bitch* has taken on such negative connotations—children are taught it is a swear word—that in everyday American English, speakers are hesitant to call a female dog a *bitch*. Most of us feel that we would be insulting the dog. When we want to insult a man by comparing him to a dog, we call him a *son of a bitch*, which quite literally is an insult to his mother rather than to him.

If the female is called a *vixen* (a female fox), the dictionary says this   5 means she is "an ill-tempered, shrewish, or malicious woman." The female seems both to attract and to hold on longer to animal metaphors with negative connotations. A *vampire* was originally a corpse that came alive to suck the blood of living persons. The word acquired the general meaning of an unscrupulous person such as a blackmailer, and then the specialized meaning of "a beautiful but unscrupulous woman who seduces men and leads them to their ruin." From this latter meaning we get the word *vamp*. The popularity of this term and of the name *vampire bat* may contribute to the idea that a female being is referred to in a phrase such as *the old bat*.

Other animal metaphors do not have definitely derogatory connota-   6 tions for the female, but they do seem to indicate frivolity or unimportance, as in *social butterfly* or *flapper*. Look at the differences between the connotations of participating in a *hen party* and in a *bull session*. Male metaphors, even when they are negative in connotation, still relate to strength and conquest. Metaphors related to aggressive sex roles, for example, *buck*, *stag*, *wolf*, and *stud*, will undoubtedly remain attached to males. Perhaps one of the reasons that in the late sixties it was so shocking to hear policemen called *pigs* was that the connotations of *pig* are very different from the other animal metaphors we usually apply to males.

When I was living in Afghanistan, I was surprised at the cruelty and   7 unfairness of a proverb that said, "When you see an old man, sit down and take a lesson; when you see an old woman, throw a stone." In looking at Afghan folk literature. I found that young girls were pictured as delightful and enticing, middle-aged women were sometimes interesting but more often just tolerable, while old women were always grotesque and villainous. Probably the reason for the negative connotation of old age in women is that women are valued for their bodies while men are valued for their accomplishments and their wisdom. Bodies deteriorate with age but wisdom and accomplishments grow greater.

When we returned home from Afghanistan, I was shocked to discover   8
that we have remnants of this same attitude in America. We see it in our animal metaphors. If both the animal and the woman are young, the connotation is positive, but if the animal and the woman are old, the connotation is negative. Hugh Hefner might never have made it to the big time if he had called his girls *rabbits* instead of *bunnies*. He probably chose *bunny* because he wanted something close to, but not quite so obvious as *kitten* or *cat*—the all-time winners for connotating female sexuality. Also *bunny*, as in the skiers' *snow bunny*, already had some of the connotations Hefner wanted. Compare the connotations of *filly* to *old nag*; *bird* to *old crow* or *old bat*; and *lamb* to *crone* (apparently related to the early modern Dutch *kronje*, *old ewe* but now *withered old woman*).

Probably the most striking examples of the contrast between young   9
and old women are animal metaphors relating to cats and chickens. A young girl is encouraged to be *kittenish*, but not *catty*. And though most of us wouldn't mind living next door to a *sex kitten*, we wouldn't want to live next door to a *cat house*. Parents might name their daughter *Kitty* but not *Puss* or *Pussy*, which used to be a fairly common nickname for girls. It has now developed such sexual connotations that it is used mostly for humor, as in the James Bond movie featuring Pussy Galore and her flying felines.

In the chicken metaphors, a young girl is a *chick*. When she gets old   10
enough she marries and soon begins feeling *cooped up*. To relieve the boredom she goes to *hen parties* and *cackles* with her friends. Eventually she has her *brood*, begins to *henpeck* her husband, and finally turns into an *old biddy*.

How English Glorifies Maleness

Throughout the ages physical strength has been very important, and   11
because men are physically stronger than women, they have been valued more. Only now in the machine age, when the difference in strength between males and females pales into insignificance in comparison to the strength of earth-moving machinery, airplanes, and guns, males no longer have such an inherent advantage. Today a man of intellect is more valued than a physical laborer, and since women can compete intellectually with men, their value is on the rise. But language lags far behind cultural changes, so the language still reflects this emphasis on the importance of

being male. For example, when we want to compliment a male, all we need to do is stress the fact that he is male by saying he is a *he-man*, or he is *manly*, or he is *virile*. Both *virile* and *virtuous* come from the Latin *vir*, meaning *man*.

The command or encouragement that males receive in sentences like   12
"Be a man!" implies that *to be a man* is to be honorable, strong, righteous, and whatever else the speaker thinks desirable. But in contrast to this, a girl is never told to be a *woman*. And when she is told to be a *lady*, she is simply being encouraged to "act feminine," which means sitting with her knees together, walking gracefully, and talking softly.

The armed forces, particularly the Marines, use the positive masculine   13
connotation as part of their recruitment psychology. They promote the idea that to join the Marines (or the Army, Navy, or Air Force) guarantees that you will become a man. But this brings up a problem, because much of the work that is necessary to keep a large organization running is what is traditionally thought of as *women's work*. Now, how can the Marines ask someone who has signed up for a *man-sized job* to do *women's work*? Since they can't, they euphemize and give the jobs titles that either are more prestigious or, at least, don't make people think of females. Waitresses are called *orderlies*, secretaries are called *clerk-typists*, nurses are called *medics*, assistants are called *adjutants*, and cleaning up an area is called *policing* the area. The same kind of word glorification is used in civilian life to bolster a man's ego when he is doing such tasks as cooking and sewing. For example, a *chef* has higher prestige than a *cook* and a *tailor* has higher prestige than a *seamstress*.

Little girls learn early in life that the boy's role is one to be envied and   14
emulated. Child psychologists have pointed out that experimenting with the role of the opposite sex is much more acceptable for little girls than it is for little boys. For example, girls are free to dress in boys' clothes, but certainly not the other way around. Most parents are amused if they have a daughter who is a *tomboy*, but they are genuinely distressed if they have a son who is a *sissy*. The names we give to young children reflect this same attitude. It is all right for girls to have boys' names, but pity the boy who has a girl's name! Because parents keep giving boys' names to girls, the number of acceptable boys' names keeps shrinking. Currently popular names for girls include *Jo, Kelly, Terri, Chris, Pat, Shawn, Toni,* and *Sam* (short for *Samantha*). *Evelyn, Carroll, Gayle, Hazel, Lynn, Beverly, Marion, Francis,* and *Shirley* once were acceptable names for males. But as they were given to females, they became less and less acceptable. Today, men who are stuck with them self-consciously go by their initials or by abbreviated forms such as *Haze, Shirl, Frank,* or *Ev*. And they seldom pass these names on to their sons.

Many common words have come into the language from people's   15
names. These lexical items again show the importance of maleness com-

pared to the triviality of the feminine activities being described. Words derived from the names of women include *Melba toast*, named for the Australian singer Dame Nellie Melba; *Sally Lunn cakes*, named after an eighteenth-century woman who first made them; *pompadour*, a hair style named after Madame Pompadour; and the word *maudlin*, as in *maudlin sentiment*, from Mary Magdalene, who was often portrayed by artists as displaying exaggerated sorrow.

There are trivial items named after men—*teddy bear* after Theodore 16 Roosevelt and *sideburns* after General Burnside—but most words that come from men's names relate to significant inventions or developments. These include *pasteurization* after Louis Pasteur, *sousaphone* after John Philip Sousa, *mason jar* after John L. Mason, *boysenberry* after Rudolph Boysen, *pullman car* after George M. Pullman, *braille* after Louis Braille, *franklin stove* after Benjamin Franklin, *diesel engine* after Rudolf Diesel, *ferris wheel* after George W. G. Ferris, and the verb *to lynch* after William Lynch, who was a vigilante captain in Virginia in 1780.

The latter is an example of a whole set of English words dealing with 17 violence. These words have strongly negative connotations. From research using free association and semantic differentials, with university students as subjects, James Ney concluded that English reflects both an anti-male and an anti-female bias because these biases exist in the culture (*Etc.: A Review of General Semantics*, March 1976, pp.67–76). The students consistently marked as masculine such words as *killer, murderer, robber, attacker, fighter, stabber, rapist, assassin, gang, hood, arsonist, criminal, hijacker, villain,* and *bully*, even though most of these words contain nothing to specify that they are masculine. An example of bias against males, Ney observed, is the absence in English of a pejorative term for women equivalent to *rapist*. Outcomes of his free association test indicated that if "English speakers want to call a man something bad, there seems to be a large vocabulary available to them but if they want to use a term which is good to describe a male, there is a small vocabulary available. The reverse is true for women."

Certainly we do not always think positively about males; witness such 18 words as *jerk, creep, crumb, slob, fink,* and *jackass*. But much of what determines our positive and negative feelings relates to the roles people play. We have very negative feelings toward someone who is hurting us or threatening us or in some way making our lives miserable. To be able to do this, the person has to have power over us and this power usually belongs to males.

On the other hand, when someone helps us or makes our life more 19 pleasant, we have positive feelings toward that person or that role. *Mother* is one of the positive female terms in English, and we see such extensions of it as *Mother Nature, Mother Earth, mother lode, mother superior,* etc. But even though a word like *mother* is positive it is still not a word of power. In the minds of English speakers being female and being powerless or passive are so closely related that we use the terms *feminine* and *lady* either to mean female or to describe a certain kind of quiet and unobtrusive behavior.

Words Labelling Women as Things

Because of our expectations of passivity, we like to compare females to items that people acquire for their pleasure. For example, in a recent commercial for the television show "Happy Days," one of the characters announced that in the coming season they were going to have not only "cars, motorcycles, and girls," but also a band. Another example of this kind of thinking is the comparison of females to food since food is something we all enjoy, even though it is extremely passive. We describe females as such delectable morsels as a *dish*, a *cookie*, a *tart*, *cheesecake*, *sugar and spice*, a *cute tomato*, *honey*, a *sharp cookie*, and *sweetie pie*. We say a particular girl has a *peaches and cream complexion* or "she looks good enough to eat." And parents give their daughters such names as *Candy* and *Cherry*. 20

Other pleasurable items that we compare females to are toys. Young girls are called *little dolls* or *China dolls*, while older girls—if they are attractive—are simply called *dolls*. We might say about a woman, "She's pretty as a picture," or "She's a fashion plate." And we might compare a girl to a plant by saying she is a *clinging vine*, a *shrinking violet*, or a *wallflower*. And we might name our daughters after plants such as *Rose*, *Lily*, *Ivy*, *Daisy*, *Iris*, and *Petunia*. Compare these names to boys' names such as *Martin* which means warlike, *Ernest* which means resolute fighter, *Nicholas* which means victory, *Val* which means strong or valiant, and *Leo* which means lion. We would be very hesitant to give a boy the name of something as passive as a flower although we might say about a man that he is a *late-bloomer*. This is making a comparison between a man and the most active thing a plant can do, which is to bloom. The only other familiar plant metaphor used for a man is the insulting *pansy*, implying that he is like a woman. 21

Questions for Study and Discussion

1. What is Nilsen's thesis? Is it stated directly or is it implied?
2. What are the different areas of language in which antifemale bias is shown, according to Nilsen? Why does she use so many examples in each category?
3. Nilsen often states her own opinion for the reasoning behind the use of antifemale-biased language. How do her opinions strike you? Do you agree with them or do they weaken her argument? What other kinds of evidence does she

use to support her argument? Which kinds of evidence do you find most convincing?

4. According to Nilsen, the language used to describe men and women differs in its implications. In general, what are the implications for each sex?

5. According to Nilsen, how has the machine age been a boon to women?

6. Sexist language is an emotional issue that has been at the center of the women's movement. Is Nilsen's tone emotionally charged or is it neutral? How appropriate is her tone for the purpose of this essay?

7. In paragraphs 17 and 18 Nilsen discusses antimale-biased language. What argument does she use to suggest that it is not as harmful as antifemale language? Do you agree or disagree with her reasoning? Explain.

Writing Topics

1. Listen to yourself and your friends for a week or two. What, if any, gender-biased language do you hear? Remember, sexist language can be anti-male as well as antifemale. What do you learn from your investigation? Are you surprised? Is the language you hear more or less biased than you expected? What attitudes about the opposite sex does it reveal? What attitudes do the members of your group hold about their own sex? Do you see any need for change?

2. Nilsen does not offer any solutions to the problem of sexism in language. What solutions can you think of? Often a problem will suggest its own solution. Is this the case with any of the kinds of gender-biased language that Nilsen discusses? Can our language or any language ever be rid entirely of gender-biased language? Why or why not?

RALPH ELLISON

Ralph Ellison, born in 1914 in Oklahoma City, Oklahoma, gained his literary reputation with one novel, *The Invisible Man* (1952). Drawing on the author's own experience, the story follows a nameless young African-American as he struggles to find a place for himself in a hostile world. In 1964 Ellison published *Shadow and Act*, a collection of essays discussing issues of society, race, and the artist. Since 1970, Ellison has been the Albert Schweitzer Professor in the Humanities at New York University.

In the short story "King of the Bingo Game," first published in *Tomorrow* in 1944, Ellison's protagonist challenges fate and the odds in a desperate attempt to win money to pay his beloved's doctor bills.

King of the Bingo Game

The woman in front of him was eating roasted peanuts that smelled so good that he could barely contain his hunger. He could not even sleep and wished they'd hurry and begin the bingo game. There, on his right, two fellows were drinking wine out of a bottle wrapped in a paper bag, and he could hear soft gurgling in the dark. His stomach gave a low, gnawing growl. "If this was down South," he thought, "all I'd have to do is lean over and say, 'Lady, gimme a few of those peanuts, please ma'am,' and she'd pass me the bag and never think nothing of it." Or he could ask the fellows for a drink in the same way. Folks down South stuck together that way; they didn't even have to know you. But up here it was different. Ask somebody for something, and they'd think you were crazy. Well, I ain't crazy. I'm just broke, 'cause I got no birth certificate to get a job, and Laura 'bout to die 'cause we got no money for a doctor. But I ain't crazy. And yet a pinpoint of doubt was focused in his mind as he glanced toward the screen and saw the hero stealthily entering a dark room and sending the beam of a flashlight along a wall of bookcases. This is where he finds the trapdoor, he remembered. The man would pass abruptly through the wall and find the girl tied to a bed, her legs and arms spread wide, and her clothing torn to rags. He laughed softly to himself. He had seen the picture three times, and this was one of the best scenes. 1

On his right the fellow whispered wide-eyed to his companion, "Man, look a-yonder!" 2

"Damn!"   3

"Wouldn't I like to have her tied up like that . . ."   4

"Hey! That fool's letting her loose!"   5

"Aw, man, he loves her."   6

"Love or no love!"   7

The man moved impatiently beside him, and he tried to involve   8
himself in the scene. But Laura was on his mind. Tiring quickly of watching
the picture he looked back to where the white beam filtered from the
projection room above the balcony. It started small and grew large, specks of
dust dancing in its whiteness as it reached the screen. It was strange how the
beam always landed right on the screen and didn't mess up and fall
somewhere else. But they had it all fixed. Everything was fixed. Now
suppose when they showed that girl with her dress torn the girl started
taking off the rest of her clothes, and when the guy came in he didn't untie
her but kept her there and went to taking off his own clothes? *That* would
be something to see. If a picture got out of hand like that those guys up
there would go nuts. Yeah, and there'd be so many folks in here you
couldn't find a seat for nine months! A strange sensation played over his
skin. He shuddered. Yesterday he'd seen a bedbug on a woman's neck as
they walked out into the bright street. But exploring his thigh through a
hole in his pocket he found only goose pimples and old scars.

The bottle gurgled again. He closed his eyes. Now a dreamy music was   9
accompanying the film and train whistles were sounding in the distance,
and he was a boy again walking along a railroad trestle down South, and
seeing the train coming, and running back as fast as he could go, and
hearing the whistle blowing, and getting off the trestle to solid ground just
in time, with the earth trembling beneath his feet, and feeling relieved as he
ran down the cinder-strewn embankment onto the highway, and looking
back and seeing with terror that the train had left the track and was
following him right down the middle of the street, and all the white people
laughing as he ran screaming . . .

"Wake up there, buddy! What the hell do you mean hollering like   10
that? Can't you see we trying to enjoy this here picture?"

He stared at the man with gratitude.   11

"I'm sorry, old man," he said. "I musta been dreaming."   12

"Well, here, have a drink. And don't be making no noise like that,   13
damn!"

His hands trembled as he tilted his head. It was not wine, but whiskey.   14
Cold rye whiskey. He took a deep swoller, decided it was better not to take
another, and handed the bottle back to its owner.

"Thanks, old man," he said.   15

Now he felt the cold whiskey breaking a warm path straight through   16
the middle of him, growing hotter and sharper as it moved. He had not
eaten all day, and it made him light-headed. The smell of the peanuts
stabbed him like a knife, and he got up and found a seat in the middle aisle.

But no sooner did he sit than he saw a row of intense-faced young girls, and got up again, thinking, "You chicks, musta been Lindy-hopping somewhere." He found a seat several rows ahead as the lights came on, and he saw the screen disappear behind a heavy red and gold curtain; then the curtain rising, and the man with the microphone and a uniformed attendant coming on the stage.

He felt for his bingo cards, smiling. The guy at the door wouldn't like   17
it if he knew about his having *five* cards. Well, not everyone played the bingo game; and even with five cards he didn't have much of a chance. For Laura, though, he had to have faith. He studied the cards, each with its different numerals, punching the free center hole in each and spreading them neatly across his lap; and when the lights faded he sat slouched in his seat so that he could look from his cards to the bingo wheel with but a quick shifting of his eyes.

Ahead, at the end of the darkness, the man with the microphone was   18
pressing a button attached to a long cord and spinning the bingo wheel and calling out the number each time the wheel came to rest. And each time the voice rang out his finger raced over the cards for the number. With five cards, he had to move fast. He became nervous; there were too many cards, and the man went too fast with his grating voice. Perhaps he should just select one and throw the others away. But he was afraid. He became warm. Wonder how much Laura's doctor would cost? Damn that, watch the cards! And with despair he heard the man call three in a row which he missed on all five cards. This way he'd never win . . .

When he saw the row of holes punched across the third card, he sat   19
paralyzed and heard the man call three more numbers before he stumbled forward, screaming.

"Bingo! Bingo!"   20

"Let that fool up there," someone called.   21

"Get up there, man!"   22

He stumbled down the aisle and up the steps to the stage into a light   23
so sharp and bright that for a moment it blinded him, and he felt that he had moved into the spell of some strange, mysterious power. Yet it was as familiar as the sun, and he knew it was the perfectly familiar bingo.

The man with the microphone was saying something to the audience   24
as he held out his card. A cold light flashed from the man's finger as the card left his hand. His knees trembled. The man stepped closer, checking the card against the numbers chalked on the board. Suppose he had made a mistake? The pomade on the man's hair made him feel faint, and he backed away. But the man was checking the card over the microphone now, and he had to stay. He stood tense, listening.

"Under the O, forty-four," the man chanted. "Under the I, seven.   25
Under the G, three. Under the B, ninety-six. Under the N, thirteen!"

His breath came easier as the man smiled at the audience   26

"Yessir, ladies and gentlemen, he's one of the chosen people!"   27

The audience rippled with laughter and applause.   28

"Step right up to the front of the stage."   29

He moved slowly forward, wishing that the light was not so bright.   30

"To win to-night's jackpot of $36.90 the wheel must stop between the   31
double zero, understand?"

He nodded, knowing the ritual from the many days and nights he had   32
watched the winners march across the stage to press the button that
controlled the spinning wheel and receive the prizes. And now he followed
the instructions as though he'd crossed the slippery stage a million prize-
winning times.

The man was making some kind of a joke, and he nodded vacantly. So   33
tense had he become that he felt a sudden desire to cry and shook it away.
He felt vaguely that his whole life was determined by the bingo wheel; not
only that which would happen now that he was at last before it, but all that
had gone before, since his birth, and his mother's birth and the birth of his
father. It had always been there, even though he had not been aware of it,
handing out the unlucky cards and numbers of his days. The feeling
persisted, and he started quickly away. I better get down from here before I
make a fool of myself, he thought.

"Here, boy," the man called, "You haven't started yet."   34

Someone laughed as he went hesitantly back.   35

"Are you all reet?"   36

He grinned at the man's jive talk, but no words would come, and he   37
knew it was not a convincing grin. For suddenly he knew that he stood on
the slippery brink of some terrible embarrassment.

"Where are you from, boy?" the man asked.   38

"Down South."   39

"He's from down South, ladies and gentlemen," the man said. "Where   40
from? Speak right into the mike."

"Rocky Mont," he said. "Rock' Mont, North Car'lina."   41

"So you decided to come down off that mountain to the U. S.," the   42
man laughed. He felt that the man was making a fool of him, but then
something cold was placed in his hand, and the lights were no longer
behind him.

Standing before the wheel he felt alone, but that was somehow right,   43
and he remembered his plan. He would give the wheel a short quick twirl.
Just a touch of the button. He had watched it many times, and always it
came close to double zero when it was short and quick. He steeled himself;
the fear had left, and he felt a profound sense of promise, as though he were
about to be repaid for all the things he'd suffered all his life. Trembling, he
pressed the button. There was a whirl of lights, and in a second he realized
with finality that though he wanted to, he could not stop. It was as though
he held a high-powered line in his naked hand. His nerves tightened. As the
wheel increased its speed it seemed to draw him more and more into its
power, as though it held his fate; and with it came a deep need to submit, to

whirl, to lose himself in its swirl of color. He could not stop it now. So let it be.

The button rested snugly in his palm where the man had placed it. 44
And now he became aware of the man beside him advising him through the microphone, while behind the shadowy audience hummed with noisy voices. He shifted his feet. There was still that feeling of helplessness within him, making part of him desire to turn back, even now that the jackpot was right in his hand. He squeezed the button until his fist ached. Then, like the sudden shriek of a subway whistle, a doubt tore through his head. Suppose he did not spin the wheel long enough? What could he do, and how could he tell? And then he knew, even as he wondered, that as long as he pressed the button, he could control the jackpot. He and only he could determine whether or not it was to be his. Not even the man with the microphone could do anything about it now. He felt drunk. Then, as though he had come down from a high hill into a valley of people, he heard the audience yelling.

"Come down from there, you jerk!" 45

"Let somebody else have a chance . . ." 46

"Ole Jack thinks he done found the end of the rainbow . . ." 47

The last voice was not unfriendly, and he turned and smiled dreamily 48
into the yelling mouths. Then he turned his back squarely on them.

"Don't take too long, boy," a voice said. 49

He nodded. They were yelling behind him. Those folks did not 50
understand what had happened to him. They had been playing the bingo game day in and night out for years, trying to win rent money or hamburger change. But not one of those wise guys had discovered this wonderful thing. He watched the wheel whirling past the numbers and experienced a burst of exaltation: This is God! This is the really truly God! He said it aloud, "This is God!"

He said it with such absolute conviction that he feared he would fall 51
fainting into the footlights. But the crowd yelled so loud that they could not hear. Those fools, he thought. I'm here trying to tell them the most wonderful secret in the world, and they're yelling like they gone crazy. A hand fell upon his shoulder.

"You'll have to make a choice now, boy. You've taken too long." 52

He brushed the hand violently away. 53

"Leave me alone, man. I know what I'm doing!" 54

The man looked surprised and held on to the microphone for support. 55
And because he did not wish to hurt the man's feelings he smiled, realizing with a sudden pang that there was no way of explaining to the man just why he had to stand there pressing the button forever.

"Come here," he called tiredly. 56

The man approached, rolling the heavy microphone across the stage. 57

"Anybody can play this bingo game, right?" he said. 58

"Sure, but . . ." 59

He smiled, feeling inclined to be patient with this slick looking white 60
man with his blue shirt and his sharp gabardine suit.

"That's what I thought," he said. "Anybody can win the jackpot as 61
long as they get the lucky number, right?"

"That's the rule, but after all . . ." 62

"That's what I thought," he said. "And the big prize goes to the man 63
who knows how to win it?"

The man nodded speechlessly. 64

"Well then, go on over there and watch me win like I want to. I ain't 65
going to hurt nobody," he said, "and I'll show you how to win. I mean to
show the whole world how it's got to be done."

And because he understood, he smiled again to let the man know that 66
he held nothing against him for being white and impatient. Then he refused
to see the man any longer and stood pressing the button, the voices of the
crowd reaching him like sounds in distant streets. Let them yell. All the
Negroes down there were just ashamed because he was black like them. He
smiled inwardly, knowing how it was. Most of the time he was ashamed of
what Negroes did himself. Well, let them be ashamed for something this
time. Like him. He was like a long thin black wire that was being stretched
and wound upon the bingo wheel; wound until he wanted to scream;
wound, but this time himself controlling the winding and the sadness and
the shame, and because he did, Laura would be all right. Suddenly the
lights flickered. He staggered backwards. Had something gone wrong? All
this noise. Didn't they know that although he controlled the wheel, it also
controlled him and unless he pressed the button forever and forever and
ever it would stop, leaving him high and dry, dry and high on this hard high
slippery hill and Laura dead? There was only one chance. He had to do
whatever the wheel demanded. And gripping the button in despair, he
discovered with surprise that it imparted a nervous energy. His spine
tingled. He felt a certain power.

Now he faced the raging crowd with defiance, its screams penetrating 67
his eardrums like trumpets shrieking from a juke-box. The vague faces
glowing in the bingo lights gave him a sense of himself that he had never
known before. He was running the show, by God! They had to react to him,
for he was their luck. This is *me*, he thought. Let the bastards yell. Then
someone was laughing inside him, and he realized that somehow he had
forgotten his own name. It was a sad, lost feeling to lose your name, and a
crazy thing to do. That name had been given him by the white man who
had owned his grandfather a long lost time ago down South. But maybe
those wise guys knew his name.

"Who am I?" he screamed. 68

"Hurry up and bingo, you jerk!" 69

They didn't know either, he thought sadly. They didn't even know 70
their own names, they were all poor nameless bastards. Well, he didn't need
that old name; he was reborn. For as long as he pressed the button he was

The-man-who-pressed-the-button-who-held-the-prize-who-was-the-King-of-Bingo. That was the way it was, and he'd have to press the button even if nobody understood, even though Laura did not understand.

"Live!" he shouted.   71

The audience quieted like the dying of a huge fan.   72

"Live, Laura, baby. I got holt of it now, sugar. Live!"   73

He screamed it, tears streaming down his face. "I got nobody but   74
YOU!"

The screams tore from his very guts. He felt as though the rush of   75
blood to his head would burst out in baseball seams of small red droplets, like a head beaten by police clubs. Bending over he saw a trickle of blood splashing the toe of his shoe. With his free hand he searched his head. It was his nose. God, suppose something has gone wrong? He felt that the whole audience had somehow entered him and was stamping its feet in his stomach and he was unable to throw them out. They wanted the prize, that was it. They wanted the secret for themselves. But they'd never get it; he would keep the bingo wheel whirling forever, and Laura would be safe in the wheel. But would she? It had to be, because if she were not safe the wheel would cease to turn; it could not go on. He had to get away, *vomit* all, and his mind formed an image of himself running with Laura in his arms down the tracks of the subway just ahead of an A train, running desperately *vomit* with people screaming for him to come out but knowing no way of leaving the tracks because to stop would bring the train crushing down upon him and to attempt to leave across the other tracks would mean to run into a hot third rail as high as his waist which threw blue sparks that blinded his eyes until he could hardly see.

He heard singing and the audience was clapping its hands.   76

Shoot the liquor to him, Jim, boy!
Clap-clap-clap
Well a-calla the cop
He's blowing his top!
Shoot the liquor to him, Jim, boy!

Bitter anger grew within him at the singing. They think I'm crazy. Well   77
let 'em laugh. I'll do what I got to do.

He was standing in an attitude of intense listening when he saw that   78
they were watching something on the stage behind him. He felt weak. But when he turned he saw no one. If only his thumb did not ache so. Now they were applauding. And for a moment he thought that the wheel had stopped. But that was impossible, his thumb still pressed the button. Then he saw them. Two men in uniform beckoned from the end of the stage. They were coming toward him, walking in step, slowly, like a tap-dance team returning for a third encore. But their shoulders shot forward, and he backed away, looking wildly about. There was nothing to fight them with. He had only the long black cord which led to a plug somewhere back stage,

and he couldn't use that because it operated the bingo wheel. He backed slowly, fixing the men with his eyes as his lips stretched over his teeth in a tight, fixed grin; moved toward the end of the stage and realizing that he couldn't go much further, for suddenly the cord became taut and he couldn't afford to break the cord. But he had to do something. The audience was howling. Suddenly he stopped dead, seeing the men halt, their legs lifted as in an interrupted step of a slow-motion dance. There was nothing to do but run in the other direction and he dashed forward, slipping and sliding. The men fell back, surprised. He struck out violently going past.

"Grab him!" 79

He ran, but all too quickly the cord tightened, resistingly, and he 80 turned and ran back again. This time he slipped them, and discovered by running in a circle before the wheel he could keep the cord from tightening. But this way he had to flail his arms to keep the men away. Why couldn't they leave a man along? He ran, circling.

"Ring down the curtain," someone yelled. But they couldn't do that. 81 If they did the wheel flashing from the projection room would be cut off. But they had him before he could tell them so, trying to pry open his fist, and he was wrestling and trying to bring his knees into the fight and holding on to the button, for it was his life. And now he was down, seeing a foot coming down, crushing his wrist cruelly, down, as he saw the wheel whirling serenely above.

"I can't give it up," he screamed. Then quietly, in a confidential tone, 82 "Boys, I really can't give it up."

It landed hard against his head. And in the blank moment they had it 83 away from him, completely now. He fought them trying to pull him up from the stage as he watched the wheel spin slowly to a stop. Without surprise he saw it rest at double-zero.

"You see," he pointed bitterly. 84

"Sure, boy, sure, it's O.K.," one of the men said smiling. 85

And seeing the man bow his head to someone he could not see, he felt 86 very, very happy; he would receive what all the winners received.

But as he warmed in the justice of the man's tight smile he did not see 87 the man's slow wink, nor see the bow-legged man behind him step clear of the swiftly descending curtain and set himself for a blow. He only felt the dull pain exploding in his skull, and he knew even as it slipped out of him that his luck had run out on the stage.

Questions for Study and Discussion

1. Ellison doesn't reveal the race of the protagonist until well into the story. What else do you know about him by then? Did you suspect he is an African-American before you read it? Explain?

2. How would you describe the state of mind of the protagonist? Is he really mad?

3. Ellison wants us to experience the man's feelings of alienation, not only from the white man on the stage, but also from the other blacks in the audience. What are some of the means Ellison uses to achieve this sense of separateness?

4. Are you surprised to learn the dollar amount of the big prize? When must this story take place? Cite other clues from the text to support your conclusion.

5. Our nameless protagonist comes to identify with the bingo wheel more and more as the story moves forward. In what way is the wheel an appropriate metaphor for his life, for the life of all African-Americans at that time in history? What other figures of speech does Ellison use in his story? How effective are they?

6. Why does the man refuse to let go of the wheel? What is he afraid of? What does he mean when he calls himself the "King of Bingo"?

7. What is the irony contained in the last paragraph of Ellison's story? In what way is it a fitting ending to his story?

Writing Topics

1. Using a metaphor to make your point, write a story in which you describe feelings of alienation experienced by you or someone you know well.

2. During the Depression, people like Ellison's protagonist participated in dance marathons (grueling and humiliating ordeals that spanned many days of no sleep and little food) in the hopes of winning money to pay the bills. Do some research to compare the bingo game of Ellison's story and the dance marathons of the thirties. How were they similar? Were they popular during the same period of history? Were they exclusively for one race or another? Who were the people most likely to participate? In what way can modern-day lotteries be compared to the bingo game?

Language and Propaganda

GEORGE ORWELL

In the totalitarian state of George Orwell's novel *1984* (1949), the government has imposed on its subjects a simplified language, Newspeak, which is continually revised to give them fewer and fewer words with which to express themselves. Words like *terrible, abhorrent*, and *evil*, for example, have all been replaced by the single expression, *double-plus-ungood*. The way people use language, Orwell maintained, is both a result of the way they think and an important influence on their thought as well. This is also the point of his classic essay, "Politics and the English Language." Though published in 1946, the essay is as accurate and relevant now as it was then. Indeed, during the war in Vietnam various American officials were still using euphemisms such as "pacification" and "transfer of population," as if Orwell hadn't long since exposed those phrases as doubletalk. But Orwell goes beyond exposé. He not only holds up to public view and ridicule some choice examples of political language at its worst, but also offers a few short, simple, and effective rules for writers who want to do better. (For biographical information about Orwell, see page 36.)

Politics and the English Language

Most people who bother with the matter at all would admit that the 1 English language is in a bad way, but it is generally assumed that we cannot by conscious action do anything about it. Our civilization is decadent and our language—so the argument runs—must inevitably share in the general collapse. It follows that any struggle against the abuse of language is a sentimental archaism, like preferring candles to electric light or hansom cabs to aeroplanes. Underneath this lies the half-conscious belief that language is a natural growth and not an instrument which we shape for our own purposes.

Now, it is clear that the decline of a language must ultimately have political and economic causes: it is not due simply to the bad influence of this or that individual writer. But an effect can become a cause, reinforcing the original cause and producing the same effect in an intensified form, and so on indefinitely. A man may take to drink because he feels himself to be a failure, and then fail all the more completely because he drinks. It is rather the same thing that is happening to the English language. It becomes ugly and inaccurate because our thoughts are foolish, but the slovenliness of our language makes it easier for us to have foolish thoughts. The point is that the process is reversible. Modern English, especially written English, is full of bad habits which spread by imitation and which can be avoided if one is willing to take the necessary trouble. If one gets rid of these habits one can think more clearly, and to think clearly is a necessary first step toward political regeneration: so that the fight against bad English is not frivolous and is not the exclusive concern of professional writers. I will come back to this presently, and I hope that by that time the meaning of what I have said here will have become clearer. Meanwhile, here are five specimens of the English language as it is now habitually written.

These five passages have not been picked out because they are especially bad—I could have quoted far worse if I had chosen—but because they illustrate various of the mental vices from which we now suffer. They are a little below the average, but are fairly representative samples. I number them so that I can refer back to them when necessary:

> (1) I am not, indeed, sure whether it is not true to say that the Milton who once seemed not unlike a seventeenth-century Shelley had not become, out of an experience even more bitter in each year, more alien [*sic*] to the founder of that Jesuit sect which nothing could induce him to tolerate.
>
> Professor Harold Laski (Essay in *Freedom of Expression*)

> (2) Above all, we cannot play ducks and drakes with[1] a native battery of idioms which prescribes such egregious collections of vocables as the Basic *put up with* for *tolerate* or *put at a loss* for *bewilder.*
>
> Professor Lancelot Hogben (*Interglossa*)

> (3) On the one side we have the free personality: by definition it is not neurotic, for it has neither conflict nor dream. Its desires, such as they are, are transparent, for they are just what institutional approval keeps in the forefront of consciousness; another institutional pattern would alter their number and intensity; there is little in them that is natural, irreducible, or culturally

---

[1]Squander.

dangerous. But *on the other side*, the social bond itself is nothing but the mutual reflection of these self-secure integrities. Recall the definition of love. Is not this the very picture of a small academic? Where is there a place in this hall of mirrors for either personality or fraternity?

Essay on psychology in Politics (New York)

(4) All the "best people" from the gentlemen's clubs, and all the frantic fascist captains, united in common hatred of Socialism and bestial horror of the rising tide of the mass revolutionary movement, have turned to acts of provocation, to foul incendiarism, to medieval legends of poisoned wells, to legalize their own destruction of proletarian organizations, and rouse the agitated petty-bourgeoisie to chauvinistic fervor on behalf of the fight against the revolutionary way out of the crisis.

Communist pamphlet

(5) If a new spirit *is* to be infused into this old country, there is one thorny and contentious reform which must be tackled, and that is the humanization and galvanization of the B.B.C.[2] Timidity here will bespeak canker and atrophy of the soul. The heart of Britain may be sound and of strong beat, for instance, but the British Lion's roar at present is like that of Bottom in Shakespeare's *Midsummer Night's Dream*—as gentle as any sucking dove. A virile new Britain cannot continue indefinitely to be traduced in the eyes or rather ears, of the world by the effete languors of Langham Place, brazenly masquerading as "standard English." When the Voice of Britain is heard at nine o'clock, better far and infinitely less ludicrous to hear aitches honestly dropped than the present priggish, inflated, inhibited, schoolma'amish arch braying of blameless bashful mewing maidens!

Letter in Tribune

Each of these passages has faults of its own, but, quite apart from avoidable ugliness, two qualities are common to all of them. The first is staleness of imagery; the other is lack of precision. The writer either has a meaning and cannot express it, or he inadvertently says something else, or he is almost indifferent as to whether his words mean anything or not. This mixture of vagueness and sheer incompetence is the most marked characteristic of modern English prose, and especially of any kind of political writing. As soon as certain topics are raised, the concrete melts into the abstract and no one seems able to think of turns of speech that are not hackneyed: prose consists less and less of *words* chosen for the sake of their meaning, and more and more of *phrases* tacked together like the sections of a prefabricated henhouse. I list below, with notes and examples, various of the tricks by means of which the work of prose-construction is habitually dodged:

---

[2]British Broadcasting Corporation, the government-run radio and television network. "B.B.C. English" is meant to reflect standard pronunciation in England.

Dying Metaphors

A newly invented metaphor assists thought by evoking a visual image, [5] while on the other hand a metaphor which is technically "dead" (e.g., *iron resolution*) has in effect reverted to being an ordinary word and can generally be used without loss of vividness. But in between these two classes there is a huge dump of worn-out metaphors which have lost all evocative power and are merely used because they save people the trouble of inventing phrases for themselves. Examples are: *Ring the changes on, take up the cudgels for, toe the line, ride roughshod over, stand shoulder to shoulder with, play into the hands of, no axe to grind, grist to the mill, fishing in troubled waters, on the order of the day, Achilles' heel, swan song, hotbed.* Many of these are used without knowledge of their meaning (what is a "rift," for instance?), and incompatible metaphors are frequently mixed, a sure sign that the writer is not interested in what he is saying. Some metaphors now current have been twisted out of their original meaning without those who use them even being aware of the fact. For example, *toe the line* is sometimes written *tow the line.* Another example is *the hammer and the anvil*, now always used with the implication that the anvil gets the worst of it. In real life it is always the anvil that breaks the hammer, never the other way about: a writer who stopped to think what he was saying would be aware of this, and would avoid perverting the original phrase.

Operators or Verbal False Limbs

These save the trouble of picking out appropriate verbs and nouns, [6] and at the same time pad each sentence with extra syllables which give it an appearance of symmetry. Characteristic phrases are *render inoperative, militate against, make contact with, be subjected to, give rise to, give grounds for, have the effect of, play a leading part (role) in, make itself felt, take effect, exhibit a tendency to, serve the purpose of*, etc., etc. The keynote is the elimination of simple verbs. Instead of being a single word, such as *break, stop, spoil, mend, kill*, a verb becomes a *phrase*, made up of a noun or adjective tacked on to some general-purpose verb such as *prove, serve, form, play, render.* In addition, the passive voice is wherever possible used in preference to the active, and noun constructions are used instead of gerunds (*by examination of* instead of *by examining*). The range of verbs is further cut down by means of the *-ize* and *de-* formations, and the banal statements are given an appearance of profundity by means of the *not un-* formation. Simple conjunctions and prepositions are replaced by such phrases as *with respect to, having regard to, the fact that, by dint of, in view of, in the interests of, on the hypothesis that*; and the ends of sentences are saved from anticlimax by such resounding commonplaces as *greatly to be desired, cannot be left out of account, a* *development to be expected in the near future, deserving of serious consideration, brought to a satisfactory conclusion*, and so on and so forth.

Pretentious Diction

Words like *phenomenon, element, individual* (as noun), *objective, categori-* 7 *cal, effective, virtual, basic, primary, promote, constitute, exhibit, exploit, utilize, eliminate, liquidate,* are used to dress up simple statements and give an air of scientific impartiality to biased judgments. Adjectives like *epoch-making, epic, historic, unforgettable, triumphant, age-old, inevitable, inexorable, veritable,* are used to dignify the sordid processes of international politics, while writing that aims at glorifying war usually takes on an archaic color, its characteristic words being: *realm, throne, chariot, mailed fist, trident, sword, shield, buckler, banner, jackboot, clarion.* Foreign words and expressions such as *cul de sac, ancien régime, deus ex machina, mutatis mutandis, status quo, gleichschaltung, weltanschauung,* are used to give an air of culture and elegance. Except for the useful abbreviations *i.e., e.g.,* and *etc.,* there is no real need for any of the hundreds of foreign phrases now current in English. Bad writers, and especially scientific, political, and sociological writers, are nearly always haunted by the notion that Latin or Greek words are grander than Saxon ones, and unnecessary words like *expedite, ameliorate, predict, extraneous, deracinated, clandestine, subaqueous,* and hundreds of others constantly gain ground from their Anglo-Saxon opposite numbers.[3] The jargon peculiar to Marxist writing (*hyena, hangman, cannibal, petty bourgeois, these gentry, lackey, flunkey, mad dog, White Guard,* etc.) consists largely of words and phrases translated from Russian, German, or French; but the normal way of coining a new word is to use a Latin or Greek root with the appropriate affix and, where necessary, the size formation. It is often easier to make up words of this kind (*deregionalize, impermissible, extramarital, nonfragmentary* and so forth) than to think up the English words that will cover one's meaning. The result, in general, is an increase in slovenliness and vagueness.

Meaningless Words

In certain kinds of writing, particularly in art criticism and literary 8 criticism, it is normal to come across long passages which are almost

---

[3]An interesting illustration of this is the way in which the English flower names which were in use till very recently are being ousted by Greek ones, *snapdragon* becoming *antirrhinum, forget-me-not* becoming *myosotis,* etc. It is hard to see any practical reason for this change of fashion: it is probably due to an instinctive turning away from the more homely word and a vague feeling that the Greek word is scientific. [Orwell's note]

completely lacking in meaning.[4] Words like *romantic, plastic, values, human, dead, sentimental, natural, vitality*, as used in art criticism, are strictly mean-ingless, in the sense that they not only do not point to any discoverable object, but are hardly ever expected to do so by the reader. When one critic writes, "The outstanding feature of Mr. X's work is its living quality," while another writes, "The immediately striking thing about Mr. X's work is its peculiar deadness," the reader accepts this as a simple difference of opinion. If words like *black* and *white* were involved, instead of the jargon words *dead* and *living*, he would see at once that language was being used in an improper way. Many political words are similarly abused. The word *Fascism* has now no meaning except in so far as it signifies "something not desir-able." The words *democracy, socialism, freedom, patriotic, realistic, justice*, have each of them several different meanings which cannot be reconciled with one another. In the case of a word like *democracy*, not only is there no agreed definition, but the attempt to make one is resisted from all sides. It is almost universally felt that when we call a country democratic we are praising it: consequently the defenders of every kind of régime claim that it is a democracy, and fear that they might have to stop using the word if it were tied down to any one meaning. Words of this kind are often used in a consciously dishonest way. That is, the person who uses them has his own private definition, but allows his hearer to think he means something quite different. Statements like *Marshal Pétain was a true patriot*,[5] *The Soviet press is the freest in the world, The Catholic Church is opposed to persecution*, are almost always made with intent to deceive. Other words used in variable meanings, in most cases more or less dishonestly, are: *class, totalitarian, science, progressive, reactionary, bourgeois, equality*.

Now that I have made this catalogue of swindles and perversions, let me give another example of the kind of writing that they lead to. This time it must of its nature be an imaginary one. I am going to translate a passage of good English into Modern English of the worst sort. Here is a well-known verse from *Ecclesiastes*:

> I returned and saw under the sun, that the race is not to the swift, nor the battle to the strong, neither yet bread to the wise, nor yet riches to men of understanding, nor yet favour to men of skill; but time and chance happeneth to them all.

---

[4]Example: "[Alex] Comfort's catholicity of perception and image, strangely Whitman-esque in range, almost the exact opposite in aesthetic compulsion, continues to evoke that trembling atmospheric accumulative hinting at a cruel, an inexorably serene timelessness. . . . Wrey Gardiner scores by aiming at simple bull's-eyes with precision. Only they are not so simple, and through this contented sadness runs more than the surface bittersweet of resignation." (*Poetry Quarterly*.) [Orwell's note]

[5]In fact, Pétain was the Nazi-supported ruler of much of France from 1940 to 1944, and was convicted of treason in 1945.

Here it is in modern English:

> Objective considerations of contemporary phenomena compels the conclusion that success or failure in competitive activities exhibits no tendency to be commensurate with innate capacity, but that a considerable element of the unpredictable must invariably be taken into account.

This is a parody, but not a very gross one. Exhibit (3), above, for   10
instance, contains several patches of the same kind of English. It will be seen that I have not made a full translation. The beginning and ending of the sentence follow the original meaning fairly closely, but in the middle the concrete illustrations—race, battle, bread—dissolve into the vague phrase "success or failure in competitive activities." This had to be so, because no modern writer of the kind I am discussing—no one capable of using phrases like "objective consideration of contemporary phenomena"—would ever tabulate his thoughts in that precise and detailed way. The whole tendency of modern prose is away from concreteness. Now analyze these two sentences a little more closely. The first contains forty-nine words but only sixty syllables, and all its words are those of everyday life. The second contains thirty-eight words of ninety syllables: eighteen of its words are from Latin roots, and one from Greek. The first sentence contains six vivid images, and only one phrase ("time and chance") that could be called vague. The second contains not a single fresh, arresting phrase, and in spite of its ninety syllables it gives only a shortened version of the meaning contained in the first. Yet without a doubt it is the second kind of sentence that is gaining ground in modern English. I do not want to exaggerate. This kind of writing is not yet universal, and outcrops of simplicity will occur here and there in the worst-written page. Still, if you or I were told to write a few lines on the uncertainty of human fortunes, we should probably come much nearer to my imaginary sentence than to the one from *Ecclesiastes*.

As I have tried to show, modern writing at its worst does not consist in   11
picking out words for the sake of their meaning and inventing images in order to make the meaning clearer. It consists in gumming together long strips of words which have already been set in order by someone else, and making the results presentable by sheer humbug. The attraction of this way of writing is that it is easy. It is easier—even quicker, once you have the habit—to say *In my opinion it is not an unjustifiable assumption that* than to say *I think.* If you use ready-made phrases, you not only don't have to hunt about for words; you also don't have to bother with the rhythms of your sentences, since these phrases are generally so arranged as to be more or less euphonious. When you are composing in a hurry—when you are dictating to a stenographer, for instance, or making a public speech—it is natural to fall into a pretentious, Latinized style. Tags like *a consideration which we should do well to bear in mind* or *a conclusion to which all of us would readily assent* will save many a sentence from coming down with a bump. By using

stale metaphors, similes, and idioms, you save much mental effort, at the cost of leaving your meaning vague, not only for your reader but for yourself. This is the significance of mixed metaphors. The sole aim of a metaphor is to call up a visual image. When these images clash—as in *The Fascist octopus has sung its swan song, the jackboot is thrown into the melting pot*—it can be taken as certain that the writer is not seeing a mental image of the objects he is naming; in other words he is not really thinking. Look again at the examples I gave at the beginning of this essay. Professor Laski (1) uses five negatives in fifty-three words. One of these is superfluous, making nonsense of the whole passage, and in addition there is the slip—*alien* for akin—making further nonsense, and several avoidable pieces of clumsiness which increase the general vagueness. Professor Hogben (2) plays ducks and drakes with a battery which is able to write prescriptions, and, while disapproving of the everyday phrase *put up with*, is unwilling to look *egregious* up in the dictionary and see what it means; (3), if one takes an uncharitable attitude towards it, is simply meaningless: probably one could work out its intended meaning by reading the whole of the article in which it occurs. In (4), the writer knows more or less what he wants to say, but an accumulation of stale phrases chokes him like tea leaves blocking a sink. In (5), words and meaning have almost parted company. People who write in this manner usually have a general emotional meaning—they dislike one thing and want to express solidarity with another—but they are not interested in the detail of what they are saying. A scrupulous writer, in every sentence that he writes, will ask himself at least four questions, thus: What am I trying to say? What words will express it? What image or idiom will make it clearer? Is this image fresh enough to have an effect? And he will probably ask himself two more: Could I put it more shortly? Have I said anything that is avoidably ugly? But you are not obliged to go to all this trouble. You can shirk it by simply throwing your mind open and letting the ready-made phrases come crowding in. They will construct your sentences for you—even think your thoughts for you, to a certain extent—and at need they will perform the important service of partially concealing your meaning even from yourself. It is at this poinit that the special connection between politics and the debasement of language becomes clear.

In our time it is broadly true that political writing is bad writing. 12 Where it is not true, it will generally be found that the writer is some kind of rebel, expressing his private opinions and not a "party line." Orthodoxy, of whatever color, seems to demand a lifeless, imitative style. The political dialects to be found in pamphlets, leading articles, manifestoes, White Papers and the speeches of undersecretaries do, of course, vary from party to party, but they are all alike in that one almost never finds in them a fresh, vivid, homemade turn of speech. When one watches some tired hack on the platform mechanically repeating the familiar phrases—*bestial atrocities, iron heel, bloodstained tyranny, free peoples of the world, stand shoulder to shoulder*—

one often has a curious feeling that one is not watching a live human being but some kind of dummy: a feeling which suddenly becomes stronger at moments when the light catches the speaker's spectacles and turns them into blank discs which seem to have no eyes behind them. And this is not altogether fanciful. A speaker who uses that kind of phraseology has gone some distance toward turning himself into a machine. The appropriate noises are coming out of his larynx, but his brain is not involved as it would be if he were choosing his words for himself. If the speech he is making is one that he is accustomed to make over and over again, he may be almost unconscious of what he is saying, as one is when one utters the responses in church. And this reduced state of consciousness, if not indispensable, is at any rate favorable to political conformity.

In our time, political speech and writing are largely the defense of the 13 indefensible. Things like the continuance of British rule in India, the Russian purges and deportations, the dropping of the atom bombs on Japan, can indeed be defended, but only by arguments which are too brutal for most people to face, and which do not square with the professed aims of political parties. Thus political language has to consist largely of euphemism, question-begging and sheer cloudy vagueness. Defenseless villages are bombarded from the air, the inhabitants driven out into the countryside, the cattle machine-gunned, the huts set on fire with incendiary bullets: this is called *pacification*. Millions of peasants are robbed of their farms and sent trudging along the roads with no more than they can carry: this is called *transfer of population* or *rectification of frontiers*. People are imprisoned for years without trial, or shot in the back of the neck or sent to die of scurvy in Arctic lumber camps: this is called *elimination of unreliable elements*. Such phraseology is needed if one wants to name things without calling up mental pictures of them. Consider for instance some comfortable English professor defending Russian totalitarianism. He cannot say outright, "I believe in killing your opponents when you get good results by doing so." Probably, therefore, he will say something like this:

"While freely conceding that the Soviet régime exhibits certain fea- 14 tures which the humanitarian may be inclined to deplore, we must, I think, agree that a certain curtailment of the right to political opposition is an unavoidable concomitant of transitional periods, and that the rigors which the Russian people have been called upon to undergo have been amply justified in the sphere of concrete achievement."

The inflated style is itself a kind of euphemism. A mass of Latin words 15 falls upon the facts like soft snow, blurring the outlines and covering up all the details. The great enemy of clear language is insincerity. When there is a gap between one's real and one's declared aims, one turns as it were instinctively to long words and exhausted idioms, like a cuttlefish squirting out ink. In our age there is no such thing as "keeping out of politics." All issues are political issues, and politics itself is a mass of lies, evasions, folly, hatred, and schizophrenia. When the general atmosphere is bad, language must suffer. I should expect to find—this is a guess which I have not sufficient knowledge to verify—that the German, Russian and Italian languages have all deteriorated in the last ten or fifteen years, as a result of dictatorship.

But if thought corrupts language, language can also corrupt thought.   16
A bad usage can spread by tradition and imitation, even among people who should and do know better. The debased language that I have been discussing is in some ways very convenient. Phrases like *a not unjustifiable assumption, leaves much to be desired, would serve no good purpose, a consideration which we should do well to bear in mind*, are a continuous temptation, a packet of aspirins always at one's elbow. Look back through this essay, and for certain you will find that I have again and again committed the very faults I am protesting against. By this morning's post I have received a pamphlet dealing with conditions in Germany. The author tells me that he "felt impelled" to write it. I open it at random, and here is almost the first sentence that I see: "[The Allies] have an opportunity not only of achieving a radical transformation of Germany's social and political structure in such a way as to avoid a nationalistic reaction in Germany itself, but at the same time of laying the foundations of a co-operative and unified Europe." You see, he "feels impelled" to write—feels, presumably, that he has something new to say—and yet his words, like cavalry horses answering the bugle, group themselves automatically into the familiar dreary pattern. This invasion of one's mind by ready-made phrases (*lay the foundations, achieve a radical transformation*) can only be prevented if one is constantly on guard against them, and every such phrase anaesthetizes a portion of one's brain.

I said earlier that the decadence of our language is probably curable.   17
Those who deny this would argue, if they produced an argument at all, that language merely reflects existing social conditions, and that we cannot influence its development by any direct tinkering with words and constructions. So far as the general tone or spirit of a language goes, this may be true, but it is not true in detail. Silly words and expressions have often disappeared, not through any evolutionary process but owing to the conscious action of a minority. Two recent examples were *explore every avenue* and *leave no stone unturned*, which were killed by the jeers of a few journalists. There is a long list of flyblown metaphors which could similarly be got rid of if enough people would interest themselves in the job; and it should also be possible to laugh the *not un-* formation out of existence,[6] to reduce the amount of Latin and Greek in the average sentence, to drive out foreign phrases and strayed scientific words, and, in general, to make pretentious-

---

[6]One can cure oneself of the *not un-* formation by memorizing this sentence: *A not unblack dog was chasing a not unsmall rabbit across a not ungreen field.*

ness unfashionable. But all these are minor points. The defense of the English language implies more than this, and perhaps it is best to start by saying what it does *not* imply.

To begin with it has nothing to do with archaism, with the salvaging of obsolete words and turns of speech, or with the setting up of a "standard English" which must never be departed from. On the contrary, it is especially concerned with the scrapping of every word or idiom which has outworn its usefulness. It has nothing to do with correct grammar and syntax, which are of no importance so long as one makes one's meaning clear, or with the avoidance of Americanisms, or with having what is called a "good prose style." On the other hand it is not concerned with fake simplicity and the attempt to make written English colloquial. Nor does it even imply in every case preferring the Saxon word to the Latin one, though it does imply using the fewest and shortest words that will cover one's meaning. What is above all needed is to let the meaning choose the word, and not the other way about. In prose, the worst thing one can do with words is to surrender to them. When you think of a concrete object, you think wordlessly, and then, if you want to describe the thing you have been visualizing you probably hunt about till you find the exact words that seem to fit it. When you think of something abstract you are more inclined to use words from the start, and unless you make a conscious effort to prevent it, the existing dialect will come rushing in and do the job for you, at the expense of blurring or even changing your meaning. Probably it is better to put off using words as long as possible and get one's meaning as clear as one can through pictures or sensations. Afterward one can choose—not simple *accept*—the phrases that will best cover the meaning, and then switch round and decide what impression one's words are likely to make on another person. This last effort of the mind cuts out all stale or mixed images, all prefabricated phrases, needless repetitions, and humbug and vagueness generally. But one can often be in doubt about the effect of a word or a phrase, and one needs rules that one can rely on when instinct fails. I think the following rules will cover most cases:

(i) Never use a metaphor, simile, or other figure of speech which you are used to seeing in print.

(ii) Never use a long word where a short one will do.

(iii) If it is possible to cut a word out, always cut it out.

(iv) Never use the passive where you can use the active.

(v) Never use a foreign phrase, a scientific word, or a jargon word if you can think of an everyday English equivalent.

(vi) Break any of these rules sooner than say anything outright barbarous.

These rules sound elementary, and so they are, but they demand a deep change of attitude in anyone who has grown used to writing in the style now fashionable. One could keep all of them and still write bad English, but one could not write the kind of stuff that I quoted in those five specimens at the beginning of this article.

I have not here been considering the literary use of language, but merely language as an instrument of expressing and not for concealing or preventing thought. Stuart Chase and others have come near to claiming that all abstract words are meaningless, and have used this as a pretext for advocating a kind of political quietism. Since you don't know what Fascism is, how can you struggle against Fascism? One need not swallow such absurdities as this, but one ought to recognize that the present political chaos is connected with the decay of language, and that one can probably bring about some improvement by starting at the verbal end. If you simplify your English, you are freed from the worst follies of orthodoxy. You cannot speak any of the necessary dialects, and when you make a stupid remark its stupidity will be obvious, even to yourself. Political language—and with variations this is true of all political parties, from Conservatives to Anarchists—is designed to make lies sound truthful and murder respectable, and to give an appearance of solidity to pure wind. One cannot change this all in a moment, but one can at least change one's own habits, and from time to time one can even, if one jeers loudly enough, send some worn-out and useless phrase—some *jackboot, Achilles' heel, hotbed, melting pot, acid test, veritable inferno*, or other lump of verbal refuse—into the dustbin where it belongs.

Questions for Study and Discussion

1. In your own words, explain the relationship Orwell sees between politics and the English language. Do you agree with him? Why or why not?
2. What terms and concepts does Orwell define in his essay? What is his purpose in defining them? How does he go about it?
3. Our world is becoming increasingly prefabricated. In what way does the concept of prefabrication relate to Orwell's observations about the prevalence of habitual and trite phrases?
4. Orwell uses the following comparisons in his essay. How does each of them reinforce or clarify his meaning?
   a. "But in between these two classes there is a huge dump of worn-out metaphors which have lost all evocative power. . . ." (paragraph 5)
   b. "The writer knows more or less what he wants to say, but an accumulation of stale phrases chokes him like tea leaves blocking a sink." (paragraph 11)
   c. "A mass of Latin words falls upon the facts like soft snow, blurring the outlines and covering up all the details." (paragraph 15)
   d. "When there is a gap between one's real and one's declared aims, one turns as it were instinctively to long words and exhausted idioms, like a cuttlefish squirting out ink." (paragraph 15)

e. "He 'feels impelled' to write—feels, presumably, that he has something new to say—and yet his words, like cavalry horses answering the bugle, group themselves automatically into the familiar dreary pattern." (paragraph 16)

5. Orwell confesses that he himself is guilty, in this essay, of some of the errors he is pointing out. Can you detect any of them? What is the effect on you of these "errors" and of Orwell's confession?

6. The last of Orwell's six rules for better English reads, "Break any of these rules sooner than say anything outright barbarous." What do you think he means by this?

Writing Topics

1. As some of Orwell's examples suggest, language is sometimes used not to express our meanings but to conceal them. Is this true only of politics? Can you think of any situations in which you, or others you know, have been under pressure to say something yet had nothing you were ready or willing to say? What happened? How can one handle such situations honestly?

2. Gather five examples of recent American political English that you consider, in Orwell's words, "ugly and inaccurate." Can you analyze them using Orwell's terms? If not, what new terms would you invent to classify them?

3. Read Orwell's discussion of Newspeak in *1984*. What is the relation between politics and language in Oceania? How does it connect with Orwell's views in "Politics and the English Language"?

DONNA WOOLFOLK CROSS

Most people are opposed to propaganda in principle, but few know exactly what it is and how it works. Donna Woolfolk Cross has looked closely at the subject, and her observations have been published in *Word Abuse: How the Words We Use, Use Us* (1979). She was born in New York City in 1947, and graduated from the University of Pennsylvania and UCLA. She now teaches at Onondaga Community College in New York State. For several years prior to teaching she worked in publishing and advertising, practicing as well as observing some of the techniques she writes about in her book *Mediaspeak* (1983).

Propaganda is a Latin term meaning "that which is to be made known" and is basically a means of persuasion. As such, it can be used "for good causes as well as bad." In the following essay, adapted by the author from *Speaking of Words* (1986), Cross discusses thirteen fallacies that propagandists can use to trick and mislead us and offers advice on how we can avoid being manipulated by the propaganda that is part of our everyday lives.

Propaganda: How Not to Be Bamboozled

Propaganda. If an opinion poll were taken tomorrow, we can be sure that nearly everyone would be against it because it *sounds* so bad. When we say, "Oh, that's just propaganda," it means, to most people, "That's a pack of lies." But really, propaganda is simply a means of persuasion and so it can be put to work for good causes as well as bad—to persuade people to give to charity, for example, or to love their neighbors, or to stop polluting the environment.

For good or evil, propaganda pervades our daily lives, helping to shape our attitudes on a thousand subjects. Propaganda probably determines the brand of toothpaste you use, the movies you see, the candidates you elect when you get to the polls. Propaganda works by tricking us, by momentarily distracting the eye while the rabbit pops out from beneath the cloth. Propaganda works best with an uncritical audience. Joseph Goebbels, Propaganda Minister in Nazi Germany, once defined his work as "the conquest of the masses." The masses would not have been conquered, however, if they had known how to challenge and to question, how to make distinctions between propaganda and reasonable argument.

People are bamboozled mainly because they don't recognize propaganda when they see it. They need to be informed about the various devices that can be used to mislead and deceive—about the propagandist's overflowing bag of tricks The following, then, are some common pitfalls for the unwary.

1. Name-Calling

As its title suggests, this device consists of labeling people or ideas   4
with words of bad connotation, literally, "calling them names." Here the propagandist tries to arouse our contempt so we will dismiss the "bad name" person or idea without examining its merits.

Bad names have played a tremendously important role in the history   5
of the world. They have ruined reputations and ended lives, sent people to prison and to war, and just generally made us mad at each other for centuries.

Name-calling can be used against policies, practices, beliefs and ideals,   6
as well as against individuals, groups, races, nations. Name-calling is at work when we hear a candidate for office described as a "foolish idealist" or a "two-faced liar" or when an incumbent's policies are denounced as "reckless," "reactionary," or just plain "stupid." Some of the most effective names a public figure can be called are ones that may not denote anything specific: "Congresswoman Jane Doe is a *bleeding heart!*" (Did she vote for funds to help paraplegics?) or "The Senator is a *tool of Washington!*" (Did he happen to agree with the President?) Senator Yakalot uses name-calling when he denounces his opponent's "radical policies" and calls them (and him) "socialist," "pinko," and part of a "heartless plot." He also uses it when he calls small cars "puddle-jumpers," "canopeners," and "motorized baby buggies."

The point here is that when the propagandist uses name-calling, he   7
doesn't want us to think—merely to react, blindly, unquestioningly. So the best defense against being taken in by name-calling is to stop and ask, "Forgetting the bad name attached to it, what are the merits of the idea itself? What does this name really mean, anyway?"

2. Glittering Generalities

Glittering generalities are really name-calling in reverse. Name-calling   8
uses words with bad connotations; glittering generalities are words with good connotations—"virtue words," as the Institute for Propaganda Analysis has called them. The Institute explains that while name-calling tries to get us to *reject* and *condemn* someone or something without examining the evidence, glittering generalities try to get us to *accept* and *agree* without examining the evidence.

We believe in, fight for, live by "virtue words" which we feel deeply   9
about: "justice," "motherhood," "the American way," "our Constitutional

rights," "our Christian heritage." These sound good, but when we examine them closely, they turn out to have no specific, definable meaning. They just make us feel good. Senator Yakalot uses glittering generalities when he says, "I stand for all that is good in America, for our American way and our American birthright." But what exactly *is* "good for America"? How can we define our "American birthright"? Just what parts of the American society and culture does "our American way" refer to?

We often make the mistake of assuming we are personally unaffected   10
by glittering generalities. The next time you find yourself assuming that, listen to a political candidate's speech on TV and see how often the use of glittering generalities elicits cheers and applause. That's the danger of propaganda; it *works*. Once again, our defense against it is to ask questions: Forgetting the virtue words attached to it, what are the merits of the idea itself? What does "Americanism" (or "freedom" or "truth") really *mean* here? . . .

Both name-calling and glittering generalities work by stirring our   11
emotions in the hope that this will cloud our thinking. Another approach that propaganda uses is to create a distraction, a "red herring," that will make people forget or ignore the real issues. There are several different kinds of "red herrings" that can be used to distract attention.

3. Plain Folks Appeal

"Plain folks" is the device by which a speaker tries to win our con-   12
fidence and support by appearing to be a person like ourselves—"just one of the plain folks." The plain-folks appeal is at work when candidates go around shaking hands with factory workers, kissing babies in supermarkets, and sampling pasta with Italians, fried chicken with Southerners, bagels and blintzes with Jews. "Now I'm a businessman like yourselves" is a plain-folks appeal, as is "I've been a farm boy all my life." Senator Yakalot tries the plain-folks appeal when he says, "I'm just a small-town boy like you fine people." The use of such expressions once prompted Lyndon Johnson to quip, "Whenever I hear someone say, 'I'm just an old country lawyer,' the first thing I reach for is my wallet to make sure it's still there."

The irrelevancy of the plain-folks appeal is obvious: even if the man *is*   13
"one of us" (which may not be true at all), that doesn't mean his ideas and programs are sound—or even that he honestly has our best interests at heart. As with glittering generalities, the danger here is that we may mistakenly assume we are immune to this appeal. But propagandists wouldn't use it unless it had been proved to work. You can protect yourself by asking, "Aside from his 'nice guy next door' image, what does this man stand for? Are his ideas and his past record really supportive of my best interests?"

4. *Argumentum ad Populum (Stroking)*

Argumentum ad populum means "argument to the people" or "telling   14
the people what they want to hear." The colloquial term from the Watergate
era is "stroking," which conjures up pictures of small animals or children
being stroked or soothed with compliments until they come to like the
person doing the complimenting—and, by extension, his or her ideas.

We all like to hear nice things about ourselves and the group we belong   15
to—we like to be liked—so it stands to reason that we will respond warmly
to a person who tells us we are "hard-working taxpayers" or "the most
generous, free-spirited nation in the world." Politicians tell farmers they are
the "backbone of the American economy" and college students that they
are the "leaders and policy makers of tomorrow." Commercial advertisers
use stroking more insidiously by asking a question which invites a flattering
answer: "What kind of a man reads *Playboy*?" (Does he really drive a
Porsche and own $10,000 worth of sound equipment?) Senator Yakalot is
stroking his audience when he calls them the "decent law-abiding citizens
that are the great pulsing heart and the life blood of this, our beloved
country," and when he repeatedly refers to them as "you fine people," "you
wonderful folks."

Obviously, the intent here is to sidetrack us from thinking critically   16
about the man and his ideas. Our own good qualities have nothing to do
with the issue at hand. Ask yourself, "Apart from the nice things he has to
say about me (and my church, my nation, my ethnic group, my neighbors),
what does the candidate stand for? Are his or her ideas in my best
interests?"

5. *Argumentum ad Hominem*

Argumentum ad hominem means "argument to the man," and that's   17
exactly what it is. When a propagandist uses *argumentum ad hominem*, he
wants to distract our attention from the issue under consideration with
personal attacks on the people involved. For example, when Lincoln issued
the Emancipation Proclamation, some people responded by calling him the
"baboon." But Lincoln's long arms and awkward carriage had nothing to
do with the merits of the Proclamation or the question of whether or not
slavery should be abolished.

Today *argumentum ad hominem* is still widely used and very effective.   18
You may or may not support the Equal Rights Amendment, but you should
be sure your judgment is based on the merits of the idea itself, and not the
result of someone's denunciation of the people who support the ERA as
"fanatics" or "lesbians" or "frustrated old maids." Senator Yakalot is using

argumentum ad hominem when he dismisses the idea of using smaller automobiles with a reference to the personal appearance of one of its supporters, Congresswoman Doris Schlepp. Refuse to be waylaid by *argumentum ad hominem* and ask, "Do the personal qualities of the person being discussed have anything to do with the issues at hand? Leaving him or her aside, how good is the idea itself?"

6. *Transfer (Guilt or Glory by Association)*

In *argumentum ad hominem*, an attempt is made to associate negative [19] aspects of a person's character or personal appearance with an issue or idea he supports. The transfer device uses this same process of association to make us accept or condemn a given person or idea.

A better name for the transfer device is guilt (or glory) by association. [20] In glory by association, the propagandist tries to transfer the positive feelings of something we love and respect to the group or idea he wants us to accept. "This bill for a new dam is in the best tradition of this country, the land of Lincoln, Jefferson, and Washington," is glory by association at work. Lincoln, Jefferson, and Washington were great leaders that most of us revere and respect, but they have no logical connection to the proposal under consideration—the bill to build a new dam. Senator Yakalot uses glory by association when he says full-sized cars "have always been as American as Mom's apple pie or a Sunday drive in the country."

The process works equally well in reverse, when guilt by association is [21] used to transfer our dislike or disapproval of one idea or group to some other idea or group that the propagandist wants us to reject and condemn. "John Doe says we need to make some changes in the way our government operates; well, that's exactly what the Ku Klux Klan has said, so there's a meeting of great minds!" That's guilt by association for you; there's no logical connection between John Doe and the Ku Klux Klan apart from the one the propagandist is trying to create in our minds. He wants to distract our attention from John Doe and get us thinking (and worrying) about the Ku Klux Klan and its politics of violence. (Of course, there are sometimes legitimate associations between the two things; if John Doe had been a *member* of the Ku Klux Klan, it would be reasonable and fair to draw a connection between the man and his group.) Senator Yakalot tries to trick his audience with guilt by association when he remarks that "the words 'Community' and 'Communism' look an awful lot alike!" He does it again when he mentions that Mr. Stu Pott "sports a Fidel Castro beard."

How can we learn to spot the transfer device and distinguish between [22] fair and unfair associations? We can teach ourselves to *suspend judgment* until we have answered these questions: "Is there any legitimate connection between the idea under discussion and the thing it is associated with?

Leaving the transfer device out of the picture, what are the merits of the idea by itself?"

7. Bandwagon

Ever hear of the small, ratlike animal called the lemming? Lemmings   23
are arctic rodents with a very odd habit: periodically, for reasons no one entirely knows, they mass together in a large herd and commit suicide by rushing into deep water and drowning themselves. They all run in together, blindly, and not one of them ever seems to stop and ask, "*Why* am I doing this? Is this really what I want to do?" and thus save itself from destruction. Obviously, lemmings are driven to perform their strange mass suicide rites by common instinct. People choose to "follow the herd" for more complex reasons, yet we are still all too often the unwitting victims of the bandwagon appeal.

Essentially, the bandwagon urges us to support an action or an   24
opinion because it is popular—because "everyone else is doing it." This call to "get on the bandwagon" appeals to the strong desire in most of us to be one of the crowd, not to be left out or alone. Advertising makes extensive use of the bandwagon appeal ("join the Pepsi people"), but so do politicians ("Let us join together in this great cause"). Senator Yakalot uses the bandwagon appeal when he says that "More and more citizens are rallying to my cause every day," and asks his audience to "join them—and me—in our fight for America."

One of the ways we can see the bandwagon appeal at work is in the   25
overwhelming success of various fashions and trends which capture the interest (and the money) of thousands of people for a short time, then disappear suddenly and completely. For a year or two in the fifties, every child in North America wanted a coonskin cap so they could be like Davy Crockett; no one wanted to be left out. After that there was the hulahoop craze that helped to dislocate the hips of thousands of Americans. More recently, what made millions of people rush out to buy their very own "pet rocks"?

The problem here is obvious: just because everyone's doing it doesn't   26
mean that *we* should too. Group approval does not prove that something is true or is worth doing. Large numbers of people have supported actions we now condemn. Just a generation ago, Hitler and Mussolini rose to absolute and catastrophically repressive rule in two of the most sophisticated and cultured countries of Europe. When they came into power they were welled up by massive popular support from millions of people who didn't want to be "left out" at a great historical moment.

Once the mass begins to move—on the bandwagon—it becomes   27
harder and harder to perceive the leader *riding* the bandwagon. So don't be a lemming, rushing blindly on to destruction because "everyone else is

doing it." Stop and ask, "Where is this bandwagon headed? Never mind about everybody else, is this what is best for *me?*" . . .

As we have seen, propaganda can appeal to us by arousing our   28
emotions or distracting our attention from the real issues at hand. But there's a third way that propaganda can be put to work against us—by the use of faulty logic. This approach is really more insidious than the other two because it gives the appearance of reasonable, fair argument. It is only when we look more closely that the holes in the logical fiber show up. The following are some of the devices that make use of faulty logic to distort and mislead.

8. Faulty Cause and Effect

As the name suggests, this devise sets up a cause-and-effect relation-   29
ship that may not be true. The Latin name for this logical fallacy is *post hoc ergo propter hoc*, which means "after this, therefore because of this." But just because one thing happened after another doesn't mean that one *caused* the other.

An example of false cause-and-effect reasoning is offered by the story   30
(probably invented) of the woman aboard the ship *Titanic*. She woke up from a nap and, feeling seasick, looked around for a call button to summon the steward to bring her some medication. She finally located a small button on one of the walls of her cabin and pushed it. A split second later, the *Titanic* grazed an iceberg in the terrible crash that was to send the entire ship to its destruction. The woman screamed and said, "Oh, God, what have I done? What have I done?" The humor of that anecdote comes from the absurdity of the woman's assumption that pushing the small red button resulted in the destruction of a ship weighing several hundred tons: "It happened after I pushed it, therefore it must be *because* I pushed it"—*post hoc ergo propter hoc* reasoning. There is, of course, no cause-and-effect relationship there.

The false cause-and-effect fallacy is used very often by political candi-   31
dates. "After I came to office, the rate of inflation dropped to 6 percent." But did the person do anything to cause the lower rate of inflation or was it the result of other conditions? Would the rate of inflation have dropped anyway, even if he hadn't come to office? Senator Yakalot uses false cause and effect when he says "our forefathers who made this country great never had free hot meal handouts! And look what they did for our country!" He does it again when he concludes that "driving full-sized cars means a better car safety record on our American roads today."

False cause-and-effect reasoning is terribly persuasive because it seems   32
so logical. Its appeal is apparently to experience. We swallowed X product— and the headache went away. We elected Y official and unemployment went down. Many people think, "There *must* be a connection." But causality is

an immensely complex phenomenon; you need a good deal of evidence to prove that an event that follows another in time was "therefore" caused by the first event.

Don't be taken in by false cause and effect; be sure to ask, "Is there   33 enough evidence to prove that this cause led to that effect? Could there have been any *other* causes?"

9. False Analogy

An analogy is a comparison between two ideas, events, or things. But   34 comparisons can be fairly made only when the things being compared are alike in significant ways. When they are not, false analogy is the result.

A famous example of this is the old proverb "Don't change horses in   35 the middle of a stream," often used as analogy to convince voters not to change administrations in the middle of a war or other crisis. But the analogy is misleading because there are so many differences between the things compared. In what ways is a war or a political crisis like a stream? Is the President or head of state really very much like a horse? And is a nation of millions of people comparable to a man trying to get across a stream? Analogy is false and unfair when it compares two things that have little in common and assumes that they are identical. Senator Yakalot tries to hoodwink his listeners with false analogy when he says, "Trying to take Americans out of the kind of cars they love is as undemocratic as trying to deprive them of the right to vote."

Of course, analogies can be drawn that are reasonable and fair. It   36 would be reasonable, for example, to compare the results of busing in one small Southern city with the possible results in another, *if* the towns have the same kind of history, population, and school policy. We can decide for ourselves whether an analogy is false or fair by asking, "Are the things being compared truly alike in significant ways? Do the differences between them affect the comparison?"

10. Begging the Question

Actually, the name of this device is rather misleading, because it does   37 not appear in the form of a question. Begging the question occurs when, in discussing a questionable or debatable point, a person assumes as already established the very point that he is trying to prove. For example, "No thinking citizen could approve such a completely unacceptable policy as this one." But isn't the question of whether or not the policy *is* acceptable the very point to be established? Senator Yakalot begs the question when he announces that his opponent's plan won't work "because it is unworkable."

We can protect ourselves against this kind of faulty logic by asking,   38
"What is assumed in this statement? Is the assumption reasonable, or does it need more proof?"

11. The Two Extremes Fallacy (False Dilemma)

Linguists have long noted that the English language tends to view   39
reality in sets of two extremes or polar opposites. In English, things are either black or white, tall or short, up or down, front or back, left or right, good or bad, guilty or not guilty. We can ask for a "straightforward yes-or-no answer" to a question, the understanding being that we will not accept or consider anything in between. In fact, reality cannot always be dissected along such strict lines. There may be (usually are) *more* than just two possibilities or extremes to consider. We are often told to "listen to both sides of the argument." But who's to say that every argument has only two sides? Can't there be a third—even a fourth or fifth—point of view?

The two-extremes fallacy is at work in this statement by Lenin, the   40
great Marxist leader: "You cannot eliminate *one* basic assumption, one substantial part of this philosophy of Marxism (it is as if it were a block of steel), without abandoning truth, without falling into the arms of bourgeois-reactionary falsehood." In other words, if we don't agree 100 percent with every premise of Marxism, we must be placed at the opposite end of the political-economic spectrum—for Lenin, "bourgeois-reactionary falsehood." If we are not entirely *with* him, we must be against him; those are the only two possibilities open to us. Of course, this is a logical fallacy; in real life there are any number of political positions one can maintain *between* the two extremes of Marxism and capitalism. Senator Yakalot uses the two-extremes fallacy in the same way as Lenin when he tells his audience that "in this world a man's either for private enterprise or he's for socialism."

One of the most famous examples of the two-extremes fallacy in recent   41
history is the slogan, "America, Love it or leave it," with its implicit suggestion that we either accept everything just as it is in America today without complaint—or get out. Again, it should be obvious that there is a whole range of action and belief between the two extremes.

Don't be duped; stop and ask, "Are those really the only two options I   42
can choose from? Are there other alternatives not mentioned that deserve consideration?"

12. Card Stacking

Some questions are so multifaceted and complex that no one can   43
make an intelligent decision about them without considering a wide variety

of evidence. One selection of facts could make us feel one way or another selection could make us feel just the opposite. Card stacking is a device of propaganda which selects only the facts that support the propagandist's point of view, and ignores all the others. For example, a candidate could be made to look like a legislative dynamo if you say, "Representative McNerd introduced more new bills than any other member of the Congress," and neglect to mention that most of them were so preposterous that they were laughed off the floor.

Senator Yakalot engages in card stacking when he talks about the 44 proposal to use smaller cars. He talks only about jobs without mentioning the cost to the taxpayers or the very real—though still denied—threat of depletion of resources. He says he wants to help his countrymen keep their jobs, but doesn't mention that the corporations that offer the jobs will also make large profits. He praises the "American chrome industry," overlooking the fact that most chrome is imported. And so on.

The best protection against card stacking is to take the "Yes, but . . ." 45 attitude. This device of propaganda is not untrue, but then again it is not the *whole* truth. So ask yourself, "Is this person leaving something out that I should know about? Is there some other information that should be brought to bear on this question?" . . .

So far, we have considered three approaches that the propagandist can 46 use to influence our thinking: appealing to our emotions, distracting our attention, and misleading us with logic that may appear to be reasonable but is in fact faulty and deceiving. But there is a fourth approach that is probably the most common propaganda trick of them all.

13. Testimonial

The testimonial device consists in having some loved or respected 47 person give a statement of support (testimonial) for a given product or idea. The problem is that the person being quoted may *not* be an expert in the field; in fact, he may know nothing at all about it. Using the name of a man who is skilled and famous in one field to give a testimonial for something in another field is unfair and unreasonable.

Senator Yakalot tries to mislead his audience with testimonial when 48 he tells them that "full-sized cars have been praised by great Americans like John Wayne and Jack Jones, as well as by leading experts on car safety and comfort."

Testimonial is used extensively in TV ads, where it often appears in 49 such bizarre forms as Joe Namath's endorsement of a pantyhose brand. Here, of course, the "authority" giving the testimonial not only is no expert about pantyhose, but obviously stands to gain something (money!) by making the testimonial.

When celebrities endorse a political candidate, they may not be 50
making money by doing so, but we should still question whether they are in
any better position to judge than we ourselves. Too often we are willing to
let others we like or respect make our decisions *for us*, while we follow along
acquiescently. And this is the purpose of testimonial—to get us to agree and
accept *without* stopping to think. Be sure to ask, "Is there any reason to
believe that this person (or organization or publication or whatever) has
any more knowledge or information than I do on this subject? What does
the idea amount to on its own merits, without the benefit of testimonial?"

The cornerstone of democratic society is reliance upon an informed 51
and educated electorate. To be fully effective citizens we need to be able to
challenge and to question wisely. A dangerous feeling of indifference toward
our political processes exists today. We often abandon our right, our duty, to
criticize and evaluate by dismissing *all* politicians as "crooked," *all* new bills
and proposals as "just more government bureaucracy." But there are important distinctions to be made, and this kind of apathy can be fatal to
democracy.

If we are to be led, let us not be led blindly, but critically, intelligently, 52
with our eyes open. If we are to continue to be a government "by the
people," let us become informed about the methods and purposes of
propaganda, so we can be the masters, not the slaves of our destiny.

Questions for Study and Discussion

1. What are the four general types of propaganda devices that Cross
discusses?

2. What, according to Cross, is the most common propaganda trick of
them all? Give some examples from your experience.

3. What organization does Cross use for each of her discussions of a
propaganda device? Do you see any purpose for the order in which she presents
the thirteen devices?

4. Who is Senator Yakalot? What is his significance in Cross's essay?

5. Cross uses an analogy in her discussion of bandwagon appeal. How
does this analogy work? Is it a true or a false analogy, according to Cross's own
definitions? Explain.

Writing Topics

1. As Cross says in the beginning of her essay, propaganda "can be put to
work for good causes as well as bad." Using materials from the Red Cross,
United Way, or some other public service organization, write an essay in which
you discuss the propaganda used by such organizations. How would you charac-

terize their appeals? Do you ever find such propaganda objectionable? Does the end always justify the means?

2. In an effort to better understand the thought processes involved in propaganda, try writing a piece yourself. Using the devices described by Cross, try to persuade your classmates to (a) join a particular campus organization, (b) support, either spiritually or financially, a controversial movement or issue on campus, or (c) vote for one candidate and not another in a campus election.

THE NEW YORK TIMES

In every presidential election year the *New York Times* puts together a "basic" campaign speech for each candidate by synthesizing the material and messages of a number of the candidate's past speeches. The following selection is a melding of the issues and ideas that speech writers developed for Ronald Reagan to repeat throughout his 1984 campaign for the presidency.

The Ronald Reagan Basic 1984 Campaign Speech

I think there's a new feeling of patriotism in our land, a recognition that by any standard America is a decent and generous place, a force for good in the world. And I don't know about you but I'm a little tired of hearing people run her down. 1

We've come through some tough times but we've come through them together, all of us from every race, every religion and every ethnic background. And we're going forward with values that have never failed us when we lived up to them: dignity of work, love for family and neighborhood, faith in God, belief in peace through strength, and a commitment to protect the freedom which is our legacy as Americans. 2

All that we've done, and all that we mean to do, is to make this country freer still. America's future rests in a thousand dreams inside your hearts. And helping you make those dreams come true is what this job of mine is all about. 3

We hear shrill words from some who were in charge four years ago. But may I suggest that those who gave us double-digit inflation, record interest rates, tax increases, credit controls, farm embargoes, long lines at the gas stations, no growth at home, weakness abroad, and told us that it was our fault that we suffered from a malaise, they're not exactly experts on the future of growth and fairness in America. 4

I will say, however, their policies were fair. They didn't discriminate— they made everybody miserable. But I didn't come to dwell on their failures. I came to talk about how, together, we're going to make this great nation even greater. 5

Economic Expansion

With your help, we've knocked down inflation from 12.4 to 4.1   6
percent. And today, from the Jersey shore to San Francisco Bay, economic
expansion is carrying America forward. I'd like to ask you some questions, if
I could. I know there are some young people present—some questions about
a certain country. Now, I won't give away the answer by naming the
country, but I will give you a little hint. It has three initials, and its first two
are U.S. Now, of all the great industrialized nations in the world, which has
shown by far the strongest, most sustained economic growth?

AUDIENCE: U.S.A.

THE PRESIDENT: All right, what country can say its investment is   7
up, its productivity is up, its take-home pay is up, and its consumer
spending is up?

A.: U.S.A.

THE PRESIDENT: And what country during the past 20 months   8
created six million new jobs?

A.: U.S.A.

THE PRESIDENT: And what country created, on an average, more   9
new jobs each month during the past 12—than all the countries of Western
Europe created over the past 19 years, all put together?

A.: U.S.A.

THE PRESIDENT: Now, you get one hundred. You got it right. And   10
my friends, you ain't' seen nothing yet.

Today, more of your earnings are staying with your families in your   11
neighborhoods, in your state, where they belong. And we have the rare
opportunity to give our children the gift of peace and prosperity without
inflation. America has worked too hard for this progress to let anybody
destroy it with a massive tax and spending scheme. That would be the
equivalent of about $1,800 more in taxes per household, and it would ruin
the growth and your opportunities for the future.

Blueprint for Bondage

For them to introduce that blueprint for bondage in Philadelphia, the   12
very birthplace of our liberty, was a betrayal of the American people. Now,
they could have introduced their tax increase in Atlantic City. But, then,
that would have been unfair. The people who go to Atlantic City gamble
with their own money, not yours.

But we won't let them put that ball and chain around America's neck.   13
I don't think that you believe your families were put on this Earth just to
help them make Government bigger. They want to enact a massive tax

increase to put in their new so-called trust fund. We don't want their new Government trust fund; we want a Government that trusts you.

You know, I have to tell you, I'm afraid that the age issue may be a   14
factor in this election after all. My opponent's ideas are just too old.

We're talking about two different worlds. They see America wringing   15
her hands. We see America raising her hands. They see America divided by envy, each of us challenging our neighbor's success. We see America in-spired by opportunity, all of us challenging the best in ourselves. We believe in knowing when opportunity knocks. They go out of the way to knock opportunity. They see an America where every day is April 15th, tax day. We see an America where every day is the Fourth of July.

Aren't you saying, we want to think big and aim high? And aren't you   16
saying, don't hold us back, give us a chance and see how high we fly? Well, that's what we want to help you do. So I have some bad news for our opponents: Our economy will still be healthy come the November election. But I have some worse news for them: Our economy will still be that way in November of 1988.

Future Is Waiting

Our work isn't done. The future is waiting to be seized, great frontiers   17
in science, in technology, in space waiting to be discovered and pushed back. And we can do it.

We can do it because, as we saw with our great Olympic athletes,   18
when America goes for the gold, nothing is going to hold her back. And I think one challenge we're ready to meet as a nation, because it's so crucial to our future, is to make America's educational system a great center of leadership for excellence.

And we've begun already. The average Scholastic Aptitude Test score,   19
that thing we call "SAT," the college entrance exams, has gone up a full four points. And that's after nearly 20 years of steady decline of more than a hundred points. And this is the second increase in three years. And it's the biggest increase—it doesn't sound like much, four points; but it's the biggest increase in 21 years. But it's not enough. We've got to do better.

It's time for America to lift her sights. Time for us to resolve that,   20
before this decade is out, we'll raise Scholastic Aptitude Test scores nation-wide. We'll make up half of all the ground that was lost over the last 20 years and reduce the dropout rate from 27 percent to 10 percent or less. And this will require a great national commitment by students, teachers, administra-tors and, most certainly, by America's parents.

The challenge isn't easy but my friends we can meet it. Just as we can   21
continue to champion strong economic growth with greater individual

opportunity. We can simplify our tax system, make it more fair, easier to understand so that we can bring yours and everybody's income tax rates further down, not up.

Lower Tax Rates

You know when I say make it easier to understand, did you know that   22
Albert Einstein once said that he found the 1040 income tax form too difficult for him to understand?

We can pass an enterprise zones bill that would encourage people   23
through lower tax rates to start up businesses and to train and hire workers in distressed areas. The House Democratic leadership has bottled up that bill for two years in committee.

And we could add to enterprise zones a youth unemployment oppor-   24
tunity wage for teenagers so that employers would be encouraged to hire those who are disadvantaged and members of minority groups and young people who are just starting out with no job experience to get their first job.

We have, as I said, created six million jobs in the last 20 months.   25
That's a good record, better than any other nation, but it's not good enough. I pledge to you I won't rest until every American who wants a job can find a job. Now I propose also that we lift our sights toward a second challenge. By this time next year we must have found ways to simplify that tax system, passed the enterprise zones, passed a youth opportunity wage, and all of us must make this expansion so strong that millions of jobs will be created in distressed areas where our fellow citizens need help the most. This America can and must do.

Our goal is an American opportunity society giving everyone not only   26
an equal chance but a greater chance to pursue that American dream. And we can build that future together if you elect people to the Congress who will not vote for tax increases but vote for growth and economic progress.

To all those Democrats, and I hope there are many here, who have   27
been loyal to the party of F.D.R. and Harry Truman and J.F.K., people who believe in protecting the interests of working people, who are not ashamed or afraid of America's standing for freedom in the world—we say to you: Join us. Come walk with us down that new path of hope and opportunity.

I was a Democrat most of my adult life. I didn't leave my party and   28
we're not suggesting you leave yours. I am telling you that what I felt was that the leadership of the Democratic Party had left me and millions of patriotic Democrats in this country who believed in freedom.

Walk with us down that path of hope and opportunity, and together   29
we can and we will lift America up to meet our greatest days.

Questions for Study and Discussion

1. Patriotism is defined in the first paragraph. Do you agree with this definition? Why or why not?

2. In paragraph 3 Reagan promises to make this country "freer still." Is it clear to you what he means by this? Explain.

3. Who is the "they" Reagan mentions in paragraph 5? Why doesn't he name them?

4. Reagan cites several improvements made in the first four years of his presidency. Are his numbers convincing? Can a president reasonably take credit for the improvements Reagan mentions?

5. Reagan claims that he never left the Democratic Party. What do you suppose is his strategy in this statement?

6. Reagan is known for his ability to inspire emotions of fierce patriotism. One way he does this is to put everyone on horseback, with the good guys in white hats and the bad guys in black. However, in this generic speech the bad guys are not Russians but Democrats. Give examples of the words and phrases he uses to characterize the "we" and the "they" that makes the other side appear unpatriotic.

7. Reagan is known as the "Great Communicator" as much for his delivery as for the content of his speeches. Read this speech out loud. What do you notice? What identifies this as oral rather than written English? Consider diction, phrasing, and organization of material.

Writing Topics

1. In paragraph 18 Reagan uses Olympic athletes as a standard for the American public. In your own words, how does this one example typify his rhetoric? Before answering you will have to read and analyze some of his other speeches, noting the examples and references he most often makes and what image of the country he most often tries to evoke.

2. In his essay (pp. 483–94) George Orwell charges that political rhetoric is filled with "meaningless words," such as patriotism, democracy, and freedom. Selecting two of the words Orwell mentions or two of your own, review the works of Jefferson (pp. 671–74), Stanton (pp. 693–97), and Seattle (pp. 699–701) with these words in mind. Does each person define the words in the same way? In an essay discuss any differences you find in the use of these terms and what you think each of them hopes to gain in using the words in this way.

HENRY REED

Poet, dramatist, and translator Henry Reed is probably best known for his book of verse, *A Map of Verona* (1946), from which the following poem, "Naming of Parts," was taken. The poem has been included in many anthologies and was inspired by Reed's experiences in the Army during World War II. Born in 1914, Reed is also known for his radio dramas of the fifties, which have been published in two collections: *The Streets of Pompeii* (1971) and *Hilda Tablet and Others* (1971), four comedies of contemporary life based on the central character of composer Hilda Tablet.

In his poem, Reed juxtaposes the metallic parts of a gun with the soft warmth of a summer garden to heighten our awareness of the brittle, chill nature of war.

Naming of Parts

To-day we have naming of parts. Yesterday,
We had daily cleaning. And to-morrow morning,
We shall have what to do after firing. But to-day,
To-day we have naming of parts. Japonica
Glistens like coral in all of the neighboring gardens,   5
     And to-day we have naming of parts.

This is the lower sling swivel. And this
Is the upper sling swivel, whose use you will see,
When you are given your slings. And this is the piling swivel,
Which in your case you have not got. The branches   10
Hold in the gardens their silent, eloquent gestures,
     Which in our case we have not got.

This is the safety-catch, which is always released
With an easy flick of the thumb. And please do not let me
See anyone using his finger. You can do it quite easy   15
If you have any strength in your thumb. The blossoms
Are fragile and motionless, never letting anyone see
     Any of them using their finger.

And this you can see is the bolt. The purpose of this
Is to open the breech, as you see. We can slide it   20

Rapidly backwards and forwards: we call this
Easing the spring. And rapidly backwards and forwards
The early bees are assaulting and fumbling the flowers:
    They call it easing the Spring.

They call it easing the Spring: it is perfectly easy   25
If you have any strength in your thumb: like the bolt,
And the breech, and the cocking-piece, and the point of balance,
Which in our case we have not got; and the almond-blossom
Silent in all of the gardens and the bees going backwards and forwards,
    For to-day we have naming of parts.   30

Questions for Study and Discussion

    1. In Reed's poem, who is speaking and to whom is he speaking?
    2. Why has the author placed the action of the poem in a garden? What is the effect on the reader?
    3. How does the rhythm of the poem change from mention of the garden to mention of the gun parts?
    4. What is it that "you" and "we" have not got?
    5. How does Reed use repetition in his poem?
    6. What statement is the author making about war?

Writing Topics

    1. Write an essay in which you describe the various meanings of the phrases "easing the Spring" and "point of balance" as they are used in Reed's poem.
    2. Reed was born during World War I and reached young manhood during World War II. For much of his youth, the world and his country were involved in full-scale war. For today's young adults contemplating the effects of war, the situation is very different. The last full-scale U.S. involvement in war ended when most of today's young adults were still babies, when the U.S. withdrew from Vietnam in 1973. At the same time, television brings us face to face with the effects of war on other people's families and other nations' lives. Is this enough? Do we need the proximity of war to contemplate its effects on lives? Or can we contemplate it from the distance of our own country and our own generation? Write an essay in which you consider these points. How would you describe the effects of war on the lives of the people it touches?

KURT VONNEGUT, JR.

Our Declaration of Independence states as a "self-evident truth" that all men are created equal. But what does it mean to be "equal"? In the following story, Kurt Vonnegut, Jr., shows what it does *not* mean. Vonnegut was born in 1922 in Indianapolis, Indiana. While he was a student at Cornell University, he joined the Army to serve in World War II and was sent to Europe. Taken prisoner by the German Army, he witnessed the Allied firebombing of Dresden in 1945, a bloody and pointless incident that inspired his novel *Slaughterhouse-Five* (1969). After the war he completed his education at the University of Chicago, then from 1947 to 1950 worked in the public relations department of General Electric; since then, he has worked full time as a writer. Probably his best known novels besides *Slaughterhouse-Five* are *Player Piano* (1952) and *Cat's Cradle* (1963), and some of his short stories have been collected in *Welcome to the Monkey House* (1968). More recently he's written *Deadeye Dick* (1985), *Galapagos* (1986), and *Bluebeard* (1987). "Harrison Bergeron," from *Welcome to the Monkey House*, is set in 2081, but like much science fiction it offers a critique of the present as much as a prediction of the future.

Harrison Bergeron

The year was 2081, and everybody was finally equal. They weren't only equal before God and the law. They were equal every which way. Nobody was smarter than anybody else. Nobody was better looking than anybody else. Nobody was stronger or quicker than anybody else. All this equality was due to the 211th, 212th, and 213th Amendments to the Constitution, and to the unceasing vigilance of agents of the United States Handicapper General.   1

Some things about living still weren't quite right, though. April, for instance, still drove people crazy by not being springtime. And it was in that clammy month that the H-G men took George and Hazel Bergeron's fourteen-year-old son, Harrison, away.   2

It was tragic, all right, but George and Hazel couldn't think about it very hard. Hazel had a perfectly average intelligence, which meant she couldn't think about anything except in short bursts. And George, while   3 his intelligence was way above normal, had a little mental handicap radio in his ear. He was required by law to wear it at all times. It was tuned to a government transmitter. Every twenty seconds or so, the transmitter would send out some sharp noise to keep people like George from taking unfair advantage of their brains.

George and Hazel were watching television. There were tears on Hazel's cheeks, but she'd forgotten for the moment what they were about.   4

On the television screen were ballerinas.   5

A buzzer sounded in George's head. His thoughts fled in panic, like bandits from a burglar alarm.   6

"That was a real pretty dance, that dance they just did," said Hazel.   7

"Huh?" said George.   8

"That dance—it was nice," said Hazel.   9

"Yup," said George. He tried to think a little about the ballerinas.   10
They weren't really very good—no better than anybody else would have been, anyway. They were burdened with sashweights and bags of birdshot, and their faces were masked, so that no one, seeing a free and graceful gesture or a pretty face, would feel like something the cat drug in. George was toying with the vague notion that maybe dancers shouldn't be handicapped. But he didn't get very far with it before another noise in his ear radio scattered his thoughts.

George winced. So did two out of the eight ballerinas.   11

Hazel saw him wince. Having no mental handicap herself, she had to ask George what the latest sound had been.   12

"Sounded like somebody hitting a milk bottle with a ball peen hammer," said George.   13

"I'd think it would be real interesting, hearing all the different sounds," said Hazel, a little envious. "All the things they think up."   14

"Um," said George.   15

"Only, if I was Handicapper General, you know what I would do?" said Hazel. Hazel, as a matter of fact, bore a strong resemblance to the Handicapper General, a woman named Diana Moon Glampers. "If I was Diana Moon Glampers," said Hazel, "I'd have chimes on Sunday—just chimes. Kind of in honor of religion."   16

"I could think, if it was just chimes," said George.   17

"Well—maybe make 'em real loud," said Hazel. "I think I'd make a good Handicapper General."   18

"'Good as anybody else," said George.   19

"Who knows better'n I do what normal is?" said Hazel.   20

"Right," said George. He began to think glimmeringly about his abnormal son who was now in jail, about Harrison, but a twenty-one gun salute in his head stopped that.   21

"Boy!" said Hazel, "that was a doozy, wasn't it?"   22

It was such a doozy that George was white and trembling, and tears   21
stood on the rims of his red eyes. Two of the eight ballerinas had collapsed
to the studio floor, were holding their temples.

"All of a sudden you look so tired," said Hazel. "Why don't you   24
stretch out on the sofa, so's you can rest your handicap bag on the pillows,
honeybunch." She was referring to the forty-seven pounds of birdshot in a
canvas bag, which was padlocked around George's neck. "Go on and rest
the bag for a little while," she said. "I don't care if you're not equal to me for
a while."

George weighed the bag with his hands. "I don't mind it," he said. "I   25
don't notice it any more. It's just a part of me."

"You been so tired lately—kind of wore out," said Hazel. "If there was   26
just some way we could make a little hole in the bottom of the bag, and just
take out a few of them lead balls. Just a few."

"Two years in prison and two thousand dollars fine for every ball I   27
took out," said George. "I don't call that a bargain."

"If you could just take a few out when you came home from work,"   28
said Hazel. "I mean—you don't compete with anybody around here. You
just set around."

"If I tried to get away with it," said George, "then other people'd get   29
away with it—and pretty soon we'd be right back to the dark ages again,
with everybody competing against everybody else. You wouldn't like that,
would you?"

"I'd hate it," said Hazel.   30

"There you are," said George. "The minute people start cheating on   31
laws, what do you think happens to society?"

If Hazel hadn't been able to come up with an answer to this question,   32
George couldn't have supplied one. A siren was going off in his head.

"Reckon it'd fall all apart," said Hazel.   33

"What would?" said George blankly.   34

"Society," said Hazel uncertainly. "Wasn't that what you just said?"   35

"Who knows?" said George.   36

The television program was suddenly interrupted for a news bulletin.   37
It wasn't clear at first as to what the bulletin was about, since the announcer, like all announcers, had a serious speech impediment. For about
half a minute, and in a state of high excitement, the announcer tried to say,
"Ladies and gentlemen—"

He finally gave up, handed the bulletin to a ballerina to read.   38

"That's all right—" Hazel said to the announcer, "he tried. That's the   39
big thing. He tried to do the best he could with what God gave him. He
should get a nice raise for trying so hard."

"Ladies and gentlemen—" said the ballerina, reading the bulletin. She   40
must have been extraordinarily beautiful, because the mask she wore was

hideous. And it was easy to see that she was the strongest and most graceful of all the dancers, for her handicap bags were as big as those worn by two-hundred-pound men.

And she had to apologize at once for her voice, which was a very unfair voice for a woman to use. Her voice was a warm, luminous, timeless melody. "Excuse me—" she said, and she began again, making her voice absolutely uncompetitive.

"Harrison Bergeron, age fourteen," she said in a grackle squawk, "has just escaped from jail, where he was held on suspicion of plotting to overthrow the government. He is a genius and an athlete, is underhandicapped, and should be regarded as extremely dangerous."

A police photograph of Harrison Bergeron was flashed on the screen— upside down, then sideways, upside down again, then right side up. The picture showed the full length of Harrison against a background calibrated in feet and inches. He was exactly seven feet tall.

The rest of Harrison's appearance was Halloween and hardware. Nobody had ever born heavier handicaps. He had outgrown hindrances faster than the H-G men could think them up. Instead of a little ear radio for a mental handicap, he wore a tremendous pair of earphones, and spectacles with thick wavy lenses. The spectacles were intended to make him not only half blind, but to give him whanging headaches besides.

Scrap metal was hung all over him. Ordinarily, there was a certain symmetry, a military neatness to the handicaps issued to strong people, but Harrison looked like a walking junkyard. In the race of life, Harrison carried three hundred pounds.

And to offset his good looks, the H-G men required that he wear at all times a red rubber ball for a nose, keep his eyebrows shaved off, and cover his even white teeth with black caps at snaggle-tooth random.

"If you see this boy," said the ballerina, "do not—I repeat, do not—try to reason with him."

There was the shriek of a door being torn from its hinges.

Screams and barking cries of consternation came from the television set. The photograph of Harrison Bergeron on the screen jumped again and again, as though dancing to the tune of an earthquake.

George Bergeron correctly identified the earthquake, and well he might have—for many was the time his own home had danced to the same crashing tune. "My God—" said George, "that must be Harrison!"

The realization was blasted from his mind instantly by the sound of an automobile collision in his head.

When George could open his eyes again, the photograph of Harrison was gone. A living, breathing Harrison filled the screen.

Clanking, clownish, and huge, Harrison stood in the center of the studio. The knob of the uprooted studio door was still in his hand.

Ballerinas, technicians, musicians, and announcers cowered on their knees before him, expecting to die.

"I am the Emperor!" cried Harrison. "Do you hear? I am the Emperor! 54 Everybody must do what I say at once!" He stamped his foot and the studio shook.

"Even as I stand here—" he bellowed, "crippled, hobbled, sickened— I 55 am a greater ruler than any man who ever lived! Now watch me become what I *can* become!"

Harrison tore the straps of his handicap harness like wet tissue paper, 56 tore straps guaranteed to support five thousand pounds.

Harrison's scrap-iron handicaps crashed to the floor. 57

Harrison thrust his thumbs under the bar of the padlock that secured 58 his head harness. The bar snapped like celery. Harrison smashed his headphones and spectacles against the wall.

He flung away his rubber-ball nose, revealed a man that would have 59 awed Thor, the god of thunder.

"I shall now select my Empress!" he said, looking down on the 60 cowering people. "Let the first woman who dares rise to her feet claim her mate and her throne!"

A moment passed, and then a ballerina arose, swaying like a willow. 61

Harrison plucked the mental handicap from her ear, snapped off her 62 physical handicaps with marvelous delicacy. Last of all, he removed her mask.

She was blindingly beautiful. 63

"Now—" said Harrison, taking her hand, "shall we show the people 64 the meaning of the word dance? Music!" he commanded.

The musicians scrambled back into their chairs, and Harrison strip- 65 ped them of their handicaps, too. "Play your best," he told them, "and I'll make you barons and dukes and earls."

The music began. It was normal at first—cheap, silly, false, but Har- 66 rison snatched two musicians from their chairs, waved them like batons as he sang the music as he wanted it played. He slammed them back into their chairs.

The music began again and was much improved. 67

Harrison and his Empress merely listened to the music for a while— 68 listened gravely, as though synchronizing their heartbeats with it.

They shifted their weights to their toes. 69

Harrison placed his big hands on the girl's tiny waist, letting her sense 70 the weightlessness that would soon be hers.

And then, in an explosion of joy and grace, into the air they sprang! 71

Not only were the laws of the land abandoned, but the law of gravity 72 and the laws of motion as well.

They reeled, whirled, swiveled, flounced, capered, gamboled, and 73 spun.

They leaped like deer on the moon.   74

The studio ceiling was thirty feet high, but each leap brought the   75
dancers nearer to it.

It became their obvious intention to kiss the ceiling.   76

They kissed it.   77

And then, neutralizing gravity with love and pure will, they remained   78
suspended in air inches below the ceiling, and they kissed each other for a
long, long time.

It was then that Diana Moon Glampers, the Handicapper General,   79
came into the studio with a double-barreled ten-gauge shotgun. She fired
twice, and the Emperor and the Empress were dead before they hit the
floor.

Diana Moon Glampers loaded the gun again. She aimed it at the mu-   80
sicians and told them they had ten seconds to get their handicaps back on.

It was then that the Bergerons' television tube burned out.   81

Hazel turned to comment about the blackout to George. But George   82
had gone out into the kitchen for a can of beer.

George came back in with the beer, paused while a handicap signal   83
shook him up. And then he sat down again. "You've been crying?" he said
to Hazel.

"Yup," she said.   84

"What about?" he said.   85

"I forget," she said. "Something real sad on television."   86

"What was it?" he said.   87

"It's all kind of mixed up in my mind," said Hazel.   88

"Forget sad things," said George.   89

"I always do," said Hazel.   90

"That's my girl," said George. He winced. There was the sound of a   91
rivetting gun in his head.

"Gee—I could tell that one was a doozy," said Hazel.   92

"You can say that again," said George.   93

"Gee—" said Hazel, "I could tell that one was a doozy."   94

Questions for Study and Discussion

1. In what ways is Vonnegut's world of 2081 little changed from the
present? What is different? What can you infer from this about Vonnegut's
message in this story?

2. Why does George refer to the competitive past as the "dark ages"?
What solution does "handicapping" offer? In what ways does being underhandicapped make Harrison dangerous?

3. Consider the specific handicaps that above-average people have to
wear in the story. How do you respond to Vonnegut's descriptions? What do
those handicaps suggest about the collective mentality of 2081 society?

4. Why does Vonnegut make Harrison a fourteen-year-old child? What qualities of a teenager does Harrison display.

5. Vonnegut's story is plausible up to the point where Harrison and the ballerina "defy the law of gravity and the laws of motion. . . ." Why do you think Vonnegut shifts to fantasy at this point? Would the story have been better or worse if he had kept to the physically possible? Why do you think so?

6. What can you say about the Handicapper General, Diane Moon Glampers? What does the story tell you, or allow you to infer, about her position in 2081 society and her way of doing her job?

7. The words *equality* and *average* refer to similar but essentially different concepts. In what significant way do they differ? How does this difference relate to the theme of Vonnegut's story?

Writing Topics

1. Is there a typical American attitude toward people of exceptional talent or achievement? What is your attitude? Are there dangers in too much respect for such people—or too little? Write an essay in which you present your views on this important social issue. Use examples from your own experiences whenever appropriate.

2. Choose an area of contemporary society in which handicaps are imposed to achieve social ends, such as affirmative action in employment, open admissions in schools and colleges, or the progressive income tax. What social ends does the handicap serve? What are its benefits? What harm does it do? Write an essay in which you discuss the pros and/or cons of imposing handicaps to achieve equality in the area of contemporary society you have selected.

3. In an essay, compare and contrast "Harrison Bergeron" with W. H. Auden's "The Unknown Citizen" (pp. 718–19) as depictions of society.

Poetry fettered fetters the human race. Nations are destroyed, or flourish, in proportion as their poetry, painting, and music are destroyed or flourish!

WILLIAM BLAKE

People like to put the television down
But we are just good friends.

DAVID BYRNE

AARON COPLAND

Aaron Copland, American composer, was born in Brooklyn, New York, in 1900. Considered by many to be one of the most important twentieth-century composers, Copland has experimented with polyrhythms and jazz to arrive at the complicated style he has used in his many symphonies. In his ballets, such as *Billy the Kid* (1938) and *Rodeo* (1942), Copland astounded and delighted audiences with his bold use of American folk idiom. A musical genius, Copland once held the chair of the composition department of the Berkshire Music Center at Tanglewood, Lenox, Massachusetts, and he is known internationally for his career as a world-famous conductor. He has received numerous awards, including the Presidential Medal of Freedom.

Copland's books include *What to Listen for in Music* (1939), *Copland on Music* (1960), and *The New Music 1900—1960* (1968). *Billy the Kid* and *Appalachian Spring*, which he wrote for the Martha Graham dance company, are just two of his many famous ballets. Among his best known compositions are *Dance Symphony* and *Orchestral Variations*. In the following essay, Copland discusses the different "planes" on which music exists and suggests that we may tend to overinterpret music.

How We Listen

We all listen to music according to our separate capacities. But, for the   1
sake of analysis, the whole listening process may become clearer if we break
it up into its component parts, so to speak. In a certain sense we all listen to
music on three separate planes. For lack of a better terminology, one might
name these: (1) the sensuous plane, (2) the expressive plane, (3) the sheerly
musical plane. The only advantage to be gained from mechanically splitting
up the listening process into these hypothetical planes is the clearer view to
be had of the way in which we listen.

The simplest way of listening to music is to listen for the sheer pleasure   2
of the musical sound itself. That is the sensuous plane. It is the plane on
which we hear music without thinking, without considering it in any way.
One turns on the radio while doing something else and absentmindedly
bathes in the sound. A kind of brainless but attractive state of mind is
engendered by the mere sound appeal of the music.

You may be sitting in a room reading this book. Imagine one note   3
struck on the piano. Immediately that one note is enough to change the
atmosphere of the room—proving that the sound element in music is a
powerful and mysterious agent, which it would be foolish to deride or
belittle.

The surprising thing is that many people who consider themselves   4
qualified music lovers abuse that plane in listening. They go to concerts in
order to lose themselves. They use music as a consolation or an escape.
They enter an ideal world where one doesn't have to think of the realities of
everyday life. Of course they aren't thinking about the music either. Music
allows them to leave it, and they go off to a place to dream, dreaming
because of and apropos of the music yet never quite listening to it.

Yes, the sound appeal of music is a potent and primitive force, but you   5
must not allow it to usurp a disproportionate share of your interest. The
sensuous plane is an important one in music, a very important one, but it
does not constitute the whole story.

There is no need to digress further on the sensuous plane. Its appeal to   6
every normal human being is self-evident. There is, however, such a thing as
becoming more sensitive to the different kinds of sound stuff as used by
various composers. For all composers do not use that sound stuff in the
same way. Don't get the idea that the value of music is commensurate with
its sensuous appeal or that the loveliest sounding music is made by the
greatest composer. If that were so, Ravel would be a greater creator than
Beethoven. The point is that the sound element varies with each composer, that his usage of sound forms an integral part of his style and must be
taken into account when listening. The reader can see, therefore, that a
more conscious approach is valuable even on this primary plane of music
listening.

The second plane on which music exists is what I have called the   7
expressive one. Here, immediately, we tread on controversial ground. Composers have a way of shying away from any discussion of music's expressive
side. Did not Stravinsky himself proclaim that this music was an "object," a
"thing," with a life of its own, and with no other meaning than its own
purely musical existence? This intransigent attitude of Stravinsky's may be
due to the fact that so many people have tried to read different meanings
into so many pieces. Heaven knows it is difficult enough to say precisely
what it is that a piece of music means, to say it definitely, to say it finally so
that everyone is satisfied with your explanation. But that should not lead
one to the other extreme of denying to music the right to be "expressive."

My own belief is that all music has an expressive power, some more   8
and some less, but that all music has a certain meaning behind the notes
and that that meaning behind the note constitutes, after all, what the piece
is saying, what the piece is about. This whole problem can be stated quite

simply by asking, "Is there a meaning to music?" My answer to that would be, "Yes." And "Can you state in so many words what the meaning is?" My answer to that would be, "No." Therein lies the difficulty.

Simple-minded souls will never be satisfied with the answer to the second of these questions. They always want music to have a meaning, and the more concrete it is the better they like it. The more the music reminds them of a train, a storm, a funeral, or any other familiar conception the more expressive it appears to be to them. This popular idea of music's meaning—stimulated and abetted by the usual run of musical commentator—should be discouraged wherever and whenever it is met. One timid lady once confessed to me that she suspected something seriously lacking in her appreciation of music because of her inability to connect it with anything definite. That is getting the whole thing backward, of course.

Still, the question remains, How close should the intelligent music lover wish to come to pinning a definite meaning to any particular work? No closer than a general concept, I should say. Music expresses, at different moments, serenity or exuberance, regret or triumph, fury or delight. It expresses each of these moods, and many others, in a numberless variety of subtle shadings and differences. It may even express a state of meaning for which there exists no adequate word in any language. In that case, musicians often like to say that it has only a purely musical meaning. They sometimes go farther and say that *all* music has only a purely musical meaning. What they really mean is that no appropriate word can be found to express the music's meaning and that, even if it could, they do not feel the need of finding it.

But whatever the professional musician may hold, most musical novices still search for specific words with which to pin down their musical reactions. That is why they always find Tchaikovsky easier to "understand" than Beethoven. In the first place, it is easier to pin a meaning-word on a Tchaikovsky piece than on a Beethoven one. Much easier. Moreover, with the Russian composer, every time you come back to a piece of his it almost always says the same thing to you, whereas with Beethoven it is often quite difficult to put your finger right on what he is saying. And any musician will tell you that that is why Beethoven is the greater composer. Because music which always says the same thing to you will necessarily soon become dull music, but music whose meaning is slightly different with each hearing has a greater chance of remaining alive.

Listen, if you can, to the forty-eight fugue themes of Bach's *Well Tempered Clavichord*. Listen to each theme, one after another. You will soon realize that each theme mirrors a different world of feeling. You will also soon realize that the more beautiful a theme seems to you the harder it is to find any word that will describe it to your complete satisfaction. Yes, you will certainly know whether it is a gay theme or a sad one. You will be able, in other words, in your own mind, to draw a frame of emotional feeling around your theme. Now study the sad one a little closer. Try to pin down the exact quality of its sadness. Is it pessimistically sad or resignedly sad; is it fatefully sad or smiling sad?

Let us suppose that you are fortunate and can describe to your own 13 satisfaction in so many words the exact meaning of your chosen theme. There is still no guarantee that anyone else will be satisfied. Nor need they be. The important thing is that each one feel for himself the specific expressive quality of a theme or, similarly, an entire piece of music. And if it is a great work of art, don't expect it to mean exactly the same thing to you each time you return to it.

Themes or pieces need not express only one emotion, of course. Take 14 such a theme as the first main one of the *Ninth Symphony*, for example. It is clearly made up of different elements. It does not say only one thing. Yet anyone hearing it immediately gets a feeling of strength, a feeling of power. It isn't a power that comes simply because the theme is played loudly. It is a power inherent in the theme itself. The extraordinary strength and vigor of the theme results in the listener's receiving an impression that a forceful statement has been made. But one should never try to boil it down to "the fateful hammer of life," etc. That is where the trouble begins. The musician, in his exasperation, says it means nothing but the notes themselves, whereas the nonprofessional is only too anxious to hang on to any explanation that gives him the illusion of getting closer to the music's meaning.

Now, perhaps, the reader will know better what I mean when I say 15 that music does have an expressive meaning but that we cannot say in so many words what that meaning is.

The third plane on which music exists is the sheerly musical plane. 16 Besides the pleasurable sound of music and the expressive feeling that it gives off, music does exist in terms of the notes themselves and of their manipulation. Most listeners are not sufficiently conscious of this third plane. . . .

Professional musicians, on the other hand, are, if anything, too con- 17 scious of the mere notes themselves. They often fall into the error of becoming so engrossed with their arpeggios and staccatos that they forget the deeper aspects of the music they are performing. But from the layman's standpoint, it is not so much a matter of getting over bad habits on the sheerly musical plane as of increasing one's awareness of what is going on, in so far as the notes are concerned.

When the man in the street listens to the "notes themselves" with any 18 degree of concentration, he is most likely to make some mention of the melody. Either he hears a pretty melody or he does not, and he generally lets it go at that. Rhythm is likely to gain his attention next, particularly if it seems exciting. But harmony and tone color are generally taken for granted, if they are thought of consciously at all. As for music's having a definite form of some kind, that idea seems never to have occurred to him.

It is very important for all of us to become more alive to music on its   19
sheerly musical plane. After all, an actual musical material is being used.
The intelligent listener must be prepared to increase his awareness of the
musical material and what happens to it. He must hear the melodies, the
rhythms, the harmonies, the tone colors in a more conscious fashion. But
above all he must, in order to follow the line of the composer's thought,
know something of the principles of musical form. Listening to all of these
elements is listening on the sheerly musical plane.

Let me repeat that I have split up mechanically the three separate   20
planes on which we listen merely for the sake of greater clarity. Actually, we
never listen on one or the other of these planes. What we do is to correlate
them—listening in all three ways at the same time. It takes no mental effort,
for we do it instinctively.

Perhaps an analogy with what happens to us when we visit the theater   21
will make this instinctive correlation clearer. In the theater, you are aware of
the actors and actresses, costumes and sets, sounds and movements. All
these give one the sense that the theater is a pleasant place to be in. They
constitute the sensuous plane in our theatrical reactions.

The expressive plane in the theater would be derived from the feeling   22
that you get from what is happening on the stage. You are moved to pity,
excitement, or gayety. It is this general feeling, generated aside from the
particular words being spoken, a certain emotional something which exists
on the stage, that is analogous to the expressive quality in music.

The plot and plot development are equivalent to our sheerly musical   23
plane. The playwright creates and develops a character in just the same way
that a composer creates and develops a theme. According to the degree of
your awareness of the way in which the artist in either field handles his
material will you become a more intelligent listener.

It is easy enough to see that the theatergoer never is conscious of any   24
of these elements separately. He is aware of them all at the same time. The
same is true of music listening. We simultaneously and without thinking
listen on all three planes.

In a sense, the ideal listener is both inside and outside the music at the   25
same moment, judging it and enjoying it, wishing it would go one way and
watching it go another—almost like the composer at the moment he com-
poses it; because in order to write his music, the composer must also be
inside and outside his music, carried away by it and yet coldly critical of it.
A subjective and objective attitude is implied in both creating and listening
to music.

What the reader should strive for, then, is a more *active* kind of   26
listening. Whether you listen to Mozart or Duke Ellington, you can deepen
your understanding of music only by being a more conscious and aware
listener—not someone who is just listening, but someone who is listening *for*
something.

Questions for Study and Discussion

1. Why does Copland feel Beethoven is a greater composer than Tchaikovsky? Do nonmusicians agree?

2. How does Copland distinguish among the three planes on which he says music exists? Do you find these distinctions helpful? Why or why not?

3. In paragraphs 21–23 Copland presents an analogy. What is the analogy? How does it work in the context of his argument?

4. Does music have one meaning for all listeners? Is music composed so that it will have universal meaning?

5. What does Copland mean by the "tone color" of music?

6. Copland disspells certain beliefs about the meaning of music. What are some of these beliefs? Were you surprised by what he had to say? Explain.

7. Is Copland writing for musicians or a general readership? Choose examples of his diction that lead you to this conclusion.

Writing Topics

1. Using the audio resource section of your library, check out either a composition that Copland mentions or another that you like. After listening to the piece of music several times, evaluate the music based on Copland's three "planes."

2. Like some pieces of classical music, Shakespeare's works are considered by some to be difficult to read and interpret, and at times, boring. In an essay, discuss a Shakespearean play that you have read or seen on stage. Did you find it inaccessible or boring? How can Copland's essay be applied to classical literature and drama?

JOAN DIDION

Joan Didion was born in 1934 in Sacramento, California, and received her degree at the University of California at Berkeley in 1955. Her essays and fiction have won her a distinguished reputation as a writer and such awards as *Vogue's* Prix de Paris (1956) and the Bread Loaf Fellowship (1963). Didion has served as associate editor of *Vogue* and has taught creative writing at Berkeley. Her novels include *Run River* (1963), *Play It As It Lays* (1970), and *A Book of Common Prayer* (1975). She has written two screenplays and three collections of essays, *Slouching Towards Bethlehem* (1968), *The White Album* (1979), and *Salvador* (1983).

Following an innocent assumption on the nature of art expressed by her daughter, Didion analyzes whether or not a work of art is a true interpretation of the artist's emotions. "Georgia O'Keeffe" is taken from Didion's *The White Album*.

Georgia O'Keeffe

"Where I was born and where and how I have lived is unimportant," 1 Georgia O'Keeffe told us in the book of paintings and words published in her ninetieth year on earth. She seemed to be advising us to forget the beautiful face in the Stieglitz photographs. She appeared to be dismissing the rather condescending romance that had attached to her by then, the romance of extreme good looks and advanced age and deliberate isolation. "It is what I have done with where I have been that should be of interest." I recall an August afternoon in Chicago in 1973 when I took my daughter, then seven, to see what Georgia O'Keeffe had done with where she had been. One of the vast O'Keeffe "Sky Above Clouds" canvases floated over the back stairs in the Chicago Art Institute that day, dominating what seemed to be several stories of empty light, and my daughter looked at it once, ran to the landing, and kept on looking. "Who drew it," she whispered after a while. I told her. "I need to talk to her," she said finally.

My daughter was making, that day in Chicago, an entirely uncon- 2 scious but quite basic assumption about people and the work they do. She was assuming that the glory she saw in the work reflected a glory in its maker, that the painting was the painter as the poem is the poet, that every choice one made alone—every word chosen or rejected, every brush stroke laid or not laid down—betrayed one's character. *Style is character.* It seemed to me that afternoon that I had rarely seen so instinctive an application of this familiar principle, and I recall being pleased not only that my daughter responded to style as character but that it was Georgia O'Keeffe's particular style to which she responded: this was a hard woman who had imposed her 192 square feet of clouds on Chicago.

"Hardness" has not been in our century a quality much admired in women, nor in the past twenty years has it even been in official favor for men. When hardness surfaces in the very old we tend to transform it into "crustiness" or eccentricity, some tonic pepperiness to be indulged at a distance. On the evidence of her work and what she has said about it, Georgia O'Keeffe is neither "crusty" nor eccentric. She is simply hard, a straight shooter, a woman clean of received wisdom and open to what she sees. This is a woman who could early on dismiss most of her contemporaries as "dreamy," and would later single out one she liked as "a very poor painter." (And then add, apparently by way of softening the judgment: "I guess he wasn't a painter at all. He had no courage and I believe that to create one's own world in any of the arts take courage.") This is a woman who in 1939 could advise her admirers that they were missing her point, that their appreciation of her famous flowers was merely sentimental. "When I paint a red hill," she observed coolly in the catalogue for an exhibition that year, "you say it is too bad that I don't always paint flowers. A flower touches almost everyone's heart. A red hill doesn't touch everyone's heart." This is a woman who could describe the genesis of one of her most well-known paintings—the "Cow's Skull: Red, White and Blue" owned by the Metropolitan—as an act of quite deliberate and derisive orneriness. "I thought of the city men I had been seeing in the East," she wrote. "They talked so often of writing the Great American Novel—the Great American Play—the Great American Poetry. . . . So as I was painting my cow's head on blue I thought to myself, 'I'll make it an American painting. They will not think it great with the red stripes down the sides—Red, White and Blue—but they will notice it.'"

The city men. The men. They. The words crop up again and again as 4 this astonishingly aggressive woman tells us what was on her mind when she was making her astonishingly aggressive paintings. It was those city men who stood accused of sentimentalizing her flowers: "I made you take time to look at what I saw and when you took time to really notice my flower you hung all your associations with flowers on my flower and you write about my flower as if I think and see what you think and see—and I don't." *And I don't.* Imagine those words spoken, and the sound you hear is *don't tread on me.* "The men" believed it impossible to paint New York, so Georgia O'Keeffe painted New York. "The men" didn't think much of her bright color, so she made it brighter. The men yearned toward Europe so she went to Texas, and then New Mexico. The men talked about Cézanne, "long involved remarks about the 'plastic quality' of his form and color," and took

3

one another's long involved remarks, in the view of this angelic rattlesnake in their midst, altogether too seriously. "I can paint one of those dismal-colored paintings like the men," the woman who regarded herself always as an outsider remembers thinking one day in 1922, and she did: a painting of a shed "all low-toned and dreary with the tree beside the door." She called this act of rancor "The Shanty" and hung it in her next show. "The men seemed to approve of it," she reported fifty-four years later, her contempt undimmed. "They seemed to think that maybe I was beginning to paint. That was my only low-toned dismal-colored painting."

Some women fight and others do not. Like so many successful guer- 5 rillas in the war between the sexes, Georgia O'Keeffe seems to have been equipped early with an immutable sense of who she was and a fairly clear understanding that she would be required to prove it. On the surface her upbringing was conventional. She was a child on the Wisconsin prairie who played with china dolls and painted watercolors with cloudy skies because sunlight was too hard to paint and, with her brother and sisters, listened every night to her mother read stories of the Wild West, of Texas, of Kit Carson and Billy the Kid. She told adults that she wanted to be an artist and was embarrassed when they asked what kind of artist she wanted to be: she had no idea "what kind." She had no idea what artists did. She had never seen a picture that interested her, other than a pen-and-ink Maid of Athens in one of her mother's books, some Mother Goose illustrations printed on cloth, a tablet cover that showed a little girl with pink roses, and the painting of Arabs on horseback that hung in her grandmother's parlor. At thirteen, in a Dominican convent, she was mortified when the sister corrected her drawing. At Chatham Episcopal Institute in Virginia she painted lilacs and sneaked time alone to walk out to where she could see the line of the Blue Ridge Mountains on the horizon. At the Art Institute in Chicago she was shocked by the presence of live models and wanted to abandon anatomy lessons. At the Art Students League in New York one of her fellow students advised her that, since he would be a great painter and she would end up teaching painting in a girl's school, any work of hers was less important than modeling for him. Another painted over her work to show her how the Impressionists did trees. She had not before heard how the Impressionists did trees and she did not much care.

At twenty-four she left all those opinions behind and went for the first 6 time to live in Texas, where there were no trees to paint and no one to tell her how not to paint them. In Texas there was only the horizon she craved. In Texas she had her sister Claudia with her for a while, and in the late afternoons they would walk away from town and toward the horizon and watch the evening star come out." That evening star fascinated me," she wrote. "It was in some way very exciting to me. My sister had a gun, and as we walked she would throw bottles into the air and shoot as many as she could before they hit the ground. I had nothing but to walk into nowhere and the wide sunset space with the star. Ten watercolors were made from that star." In a way one's interest is compelled as much by the sister Claudia with the gun as by the painter Georgia with the star, but only the painter left us this shining record. Ten watercolors were made from that star.

Questions for Study and Discussion

1. In her essay Didion says that her daughter assumes "the painting was the painter as the poem is the poet." What does she mean by this?

2. In your opinion, what importance would O'Keeffe put on an art degree comprised heavily of art appreciation and history of art classes?

3. In paragraph 5, Didion lists several examples of the attitudes prevalent in the art world when O'Keeffe was studying art. How would you describe these attitudes? What kind of thinking united them? What in O'Keeffe's character helped her to overcome these attitudes?

4. How would you describe Didion's attitude toward O'Keeffe? Is it admiring, neutral, disdaining, or something else? Cite examples from the essay to support your answer.

5. Does Didion agree or disagree that "style is character"?

Writing Topics

1. O'Keeffe was known for her individuality of style. How important is this for an artist? How important is this quality in a writer? What other qualities might writers and artists share?

2. Using Didion's writing style, write a biography of someone significant to you. Make sure your impression of the person comes through in your choice of anecdotes, tone, and diction.

KATHERINE KUH

Historians seek to discover and explain major movements and trends in human events of the past; art historians attempt to do the same for their subject. In her book *Break-up: The Core of Modern Art* (1965), from which the following selection is taken, Katherine Kuh offers her interpretation of what has been happening in painting and sculpture over the past hundred years. Kuh was born in 1904 in St. Louis and educated at Vassar College and the University of Chicago. She has been curator of modern painting and sculpture at the Chicago Art Institute, and in 1959 she became art editor for the *Saturday Review*. Her books include *Art Has Many Faces* (1951), *The Artist's Voice* (1962), and *The Open Eye* (1971). Her thesis in *Break-up*, and in this essay from that book, is that modern art is an art of fragmentation, and that the tendency to fragmentation has increased as time has passed.

Modern Art

The art of our century has been characterized by shattered surfaces, broken color, segmented compositions, dissolving forms and shredded images. Curiously insistent is this consistent emphasis on break-up. However, dissolution today does not necessarily mean lack of discipline. It can also mean a new kind of discipline, for disintegration is often followed by reconstruction, the artist deliberately smashing his material only to reassemble it in new and unexpected relationships. Moreover, the process of breaking up is quite different from the process of breaking down. And during the last hundred years, every aspect of art has been broken up— color, light, pigment, form, line, content, space, surface and design. 1

In the nineteenth century, easels were moved out-of-doors and color 2 was broken into relatively minute areas in order to approximate the reality of sunlight and to preserve on canvas nature's own fleeting atmospheric effects. Known as Impressionism, this movement was the first step in a long sequence of experiments that finally banished the Renaissance emphasis on humanism, on three-dimensional form and on a traditional center of interest. Here was the beginning of a gradual but steady tendency toward diffusion in art. A few years later, Vincent Van Gogh transformed broken color into broken pigment. Less interested in realistic light than in his own highly charged emotions, he allowed smashing rhythmic brushstrokes to

From *Break-up: The Core of Modern Art* by Katherine Kuh. Copyright © 1965 by Cory, Adams, McKay, Ltd., London, England. By permission of Little, Brown and Company, in conjunction with the New York Graphic Society.

mirror his personal turbulence. In doing so he foretold twentiety-century Expressionism, that aptly named movement which relied on pitted surfaces, broken outlines, unpredictable color and scarred textures to intensify emotional expression. As the Impressionists were bent on freeing nature from sham, so the Expressionists hoped to liberate their own feelings from all trace of artificiality.

Perhaps the most revolutionary break-up in modern art took place a little more than fifty years ago with the advent of Cubism. It was the Cubists, Picasso, Braque, Duchamp, Picabia, Léger, Delaunay and Juan Gris, who responded to the inordinate multiplicity of present-day life by breaking up and arbitrarily rearranging transparent planes and surfaces so that all sides of an object could be seen at once. As the Cubists broke through the boundaries of conventional form to show multiple aspects simultaneously, their Italian colleagues, the Futurists, hoped to encompass the uninterrupted motion of an object at one time. This they tried to do by a series of overlapping transparent forms illustrating the path of an object as it moved through space.

With Surrealism came still another kind of break-up, the break-up of chronology. Frankly influenced by Freudian discoveries, this movement splintered time sequence with an abandon borrowed from the world of fragmented dreams. Content was purposely unhinged in denial of all rational expression, allowing disconnected episodes to recreate the disturbing life of our unconscious. At the same time, perspective and distance often became severely dislocated. Denying the orderly naturalism of the Renaissance, painters today project space and distance from innumerable eye levels, intentionally segmenting their compositions into conflicting perspectives. We look from above, from below, from diverse angles, from near, from far—all at one and the same time (not an unfamiliar experience for eyes accustomed to air travel). Here again is the Cubist idea of simultaneity, the twentieth-century urge to approach a scene from many different directions in a single condensed encounter.

Finally we come to the total break-up of Abstract Expressionism, a technique that celebrates the specific act of painting (sometimes appropriately called Action Painting). Now everything is shattered—line, light, color, form, pigment, surface and design. These canvases defy all the old rules as they reveal the immediate spontaneous feelings of the artist in the process of painting. There is no one central idea, no beginning, no end—only an incessant flow and flux where lightning brushstrokes report the artist's impulsive and compulsive reactions. The pigment actually develops a life of its own, almost strong enough to hypnotize the painter. Here break-up turns into both content and form, with the impetuous paint itself telling the full story. No naturalistic image is needed to describe these artists' volatile feelings.

As one looks back over the last hundred years, the history of break-up   6
becomes a key to the history of art. Why painters and sculptors of this
period have been so involved with problems of dissolution is a question
only partly answered by the obvious impact of modern scientific methods of
destruction. One cannot deny that the last two devastating wars and the
possibility of a still more devasting one to come do affect our daily thinking.
Since the discovery of the atom bomb, science has become almost synonymous with destruction. The influence of contemporary warfare with its
colossal explosions and upheavals has unquestionably had much to do with
the tendency toward fragmentation in art, but there have been other and
earlier causes.

From the beginning, it was science in one form or another that   7
affected modern painting and sculpture. In nineteenth-century Europe the
interest in atmospheric phenomena was not an isolated expression limited
to the Impressionists. At that time, numerous scientists were experimenting
with all manner of optical color laws, writing widely on the subject as they
investigated the relationship of color to the human eye. Artists like Monet
and Seurat were familiar with these findings and not unnaturally applied
them to their paintings. It would be a grave mistake to underestimate the
influence of contemporary scientific research on the development of Impressionism. The wonders of natural light became a focus for nineteenth-
century artists exactly as the magic of artificial light stimulated painters of
the precentury. If the earlier men were interested in rural landscapes seen
out-of-doors in the sunlight, the later artists quite reasonably concentrated
on city scenes, preferably at night when man-made luminosity tends to
puncture both form and space.

Other scientific investigations also exerted considerable influence on   8
present-day painters and sculptors. Inventions like the microscope and
telescope, with their capacity to enlarge, isolate and probe, offer the artist
provocative new worlds to explore. These instruments, which break up
structures only to examine them more fully, demonstrate how details can be
magnified and separated from the whole and operate as new experiences.
Repeatedly artists in recent years have exploited this idea, allowing one
isolated symbol to represent an entire complex organism. Miró often needs
merely part of a woman's body to describe all women, or Léger, one
magnified letter of the alphabet to conjure up the numberless printed words
that daily bombard us.

As scientists smash the atom, so likewise artists smash traditional   9
forms. For how, indeed, can anyone remain immune to the new mushroom
shape that haunts us day and night? The American painter, Morris Graves,
put it well recently, "You simply can't keep the world out any longer. Like
everyone else, I've been caught in our scientific culture." This is not to say
that painters are interested in reproducing realistic scenes of atomic explo-

sions, but rather that they are concerned with the reactions accompanying these disasters. It is just possible that, with their extra-sensitized intuition, artists may have unconsciously predicted the discovery of atomic energy long before "the bomb" became a familiar household word, for the history of break-up in art antedates the history of nuclear break-up.

Even the invention of the X-ray machine has brought us closer to   10
penetrating form. We no longer think of outer coverings as solid or final; we know they can be visually pierced merely by rendering them transparent. We have also learned from science that space penetrates everything.

The sculptor Gabo claims, "Space is a reality in all of our experiences   11
and it is present in every object. . . . That's what I've tried to show in certain of my stone carvings. When they turn, observe how their curved forms seem interpenetrated by space." For the artist today, nothing is static or permanent. The new popular dances are no more potently kinetic than the new staccato art forms that everywhere confront us.

With the dramatic development of speedier transportation and swifter   12
communication comes a visual overlapping responsible for much of contemporary art. In modern life one is simultaneously subjected to countless experiences that become fragmented, superimposed, and finally rebuilt into new experiences. Speed is a cogent part of our daily life.

How natural, then, that artists reflect this pressure by showing all   13
sides of an object, its entire motion, its total psychological content in one concerted impact. It is almost as if the pressures of time had necessitated a visual speed-up not unlike the industrial one associated with the assembly line and mass production. Speed with its multiple overlays transforms our surroundings into jagged, interrupted images.

Modern technology and science have produced a wealth of new   14
materials and new ways of using old materials. For the artist this means wider opportunities. There is no doubt that the limitations of materials and nature of tools both restrict and shape a man's work. Observe how the development of plastics and light metals along with new methods of welding and brazing have changed the direction of sculpture. Transparent plastic materials allow one to look through an object, to see its various sides superimposed on each other (as in Cubism or in an X ray). Today, welding is as prevalent as casting was in the past. This new method encourages open designs, often of great linear agility, where surrounding and intervening space becomes as important as form itself. In fact, it becomes a kind of negative form. While bronze casting and stone carving are techniques more readily adapted to solid volumes, welding permits perforated metal designs of extreme versatility that free sculpture from the static restrictions which for centuries have moored it to the floor.

More ambiguous than other scientific inventions familiar to modern   15
artists, but no less influential, are the psychoanalytic studies of Freud and his followers, discoveries that have infiltrated recent art, especially Surreal-

ism. The Surrealists, in their struggle to escape the monotony and frustrations of everyday life, claimed that dreams were the only hope. Turning to the irrational world of their unconscious, they banished all time barriers and moral judgments to combine disconnected dream experiences from the past, present and intervening psychological states. The Surrealists were concerned with overlapping emotions more than with overlapping forms. Their paintings often become segmented capsules of associative experiences. For them, obsessive and often unrelated images replaced the direct emotional messages of Expressionism. They did not need to smash pigment and texture; they went beyond this to smash the whole continuity of logical thought.

There is little doubt that contemporary art has taken much from 16 contemporary life. In a period when science has made revolutionary strides, artists in their studios have not been unaware of scientists in their laboratories. But this has rarely been a one-way street. Painters and sculptors, though admittedly influenced by modern science, have also molded and changed our world. If break-up has been a vital part of their expression, it has not always been a symbol of destruction. Quite the contrary: it has been used to examine more fully, to penetrate more deeply, to analyze more thoroughly, to enlarge, isolate and make more familiar certain aspects of life that earlier we were apt to neglect. In addition, it sometimes provides rich multiple experiences so organized as not merely to reflect our world, but in fact to interpret it.

Questions for Study and Discussion

1. What does Kuh mean by "break-up"?
2. How does Kuh feel science has influenced art? What does Kuh say have been other influences over art? Do you agree? Can you think of any others?
3. How does Kuh distinguish among the five different areas of art presentation? Are these distinctions both clear and useful? Explain.
4. How has Kuh organized her essay? Is the essay easy to read? Why or why not?
5. What is Kuh's thesis? Is her main idea directly stated or implied?

Writing Topics

1. Choose an art form that you enjoy, such as dance, poetry, music, sculpture, or photography. How has this art form progressed in our century? Do you prefer the contemporary or classical version of this art form?
2. Do artists have an obligation to please their audience or present their interpretations to please themselves? In an essay discuss what should and

should not govern an artist's work. Incorporate a discussion about research projects in which you contrast a class in which you are handed a topic and a class in which you may develop your own. How does this relate to artists? What are the differences, if any, when you are told what to produce rather than producing from the heart?

EDWARD HOAGLAND

Though he has written many short stories and three novels, Edward Hoagland is probably best known as an essayist. He is particularly interested in the North American wilderness and in the animals that live there; his books of essays include *The Courage of Turtles* (1970), *Walking the Dead Diamond River* (1973), *Red Wolves and Black Bears* (1976), *Seven Rivers West* (1986), and *Heart's Desire: The Best of Edward Hoagland* (1988). And yet he is a confirmed city dweller, born in 1932 in New York City and still a resident there. He graduated from Harvard College in 1954 (in the same class as John Updike) and then served in the Army for two years, meanwhile publishing *Cat Man* (1956), a novel of circus life. Since then he has taught writing occasionally at various colleges in the New York area and at the University of Iowa's famous creative writing program. A selection of his works is available as *The Edward Hoagland Reader* (1979). "On Essays" was first published in 1976 and is included in *The Tugman's Passage* (1982). In it Hoagland explores his own attitude toward the personal essay, offering at the same time an example of this form and an explanation of what it is.

On Essays

We sometimes hear that essays are an old-fashioned form, that so-and-so is the "last essayist," but the facts of the marketplace argue quite otherwise. Essays of nearly any kind are so much easier than short stories for a writer to sell, so many more see print, it's strange that though two fine anthologies remain that publish the year's best stories, no comparable collection exists for essays. Such changes in the reading public's taste aren't always to the good, needless to say. The art of telling stories predated even cave painting, surely; and if we ever find ourselves living in caves again, it (with painting and drumming) will be the only art left, after movies, novels, photography, essays, biography, and all the rest have gone down the drain—the art to build from.

One has the sense with the short story as a form that while everything may have been done, nothing has been overdone; it has a permanence. Essays, if a comparison is to be made, although they go back four hundred years to Montaigne,[1] seem a mercurial, newfangled, sometimes hokey affair

[1] Michel de Montaigne, the French essayist.

that has lent itself to many of the excesses of the age, from spurious autobiography to spurious hallucination, as well as to the shabby careerism of traditional journalism. It's a greased pig. Essays are associated with the way young writers fashion a name—on plain, crowded newsprint in hybrid vehicles like the *Village Voice, Rolling Stone,* the *New York Review of Books,* instead of the thick paper stock and thin readership of *Partisan Review.*

Essays, however, hang somewhere on a line between two sturdy poles: 3
this is what I think, and this is what I am. Autobiographies which aren't novels are generally extended essays, indeed. A personal essay is like the human voice talking, its order the mind's natural flow, instead of a systematized outline of ideas. Though more wayward or informal than an article or treatise, somewhere it contains a point which is its real center, even if the point couldn't be uttered in fewer words than the essayist has used. Essays don't usually boil down to a summary, as articles do, and the style of the writer has a "nap" to it, a combination of personality and originality and energetic loose ends that stand up like the nap on a piece of wool and can't be brushed flat. Essays belong to the animal kingdom, with a surface that generates sparks, like a coat of fur, compared with the flat, conventional cotton of the magazine article writer, who works in the vegetable kingdom, instead. But, essays, on the other hand, may have fewer "levels" than fiction, because we are not supposed to argue much about their meaning. In the old distinction between teaching and storytelling, the essayist, however cleverly he camouflages his intentions, is a bit of a teacher or reformer, and an essay is intended to convey the same point to each of us.

This emphasis upon mind speaking to mind is what makes essays less   4
universal in their appeal than stories. They are addressed to an educated, perhaps a middle-class, reader, with certain presuppositions, a frame of reference, even a commitment to civility that is shared—not the grand and golden empathy inherent in every man or woman that a storyteller has a chance to tap.

Nevertheless, the artful "I" of an essay can be as chameleon as any   5
narrator in fiction; and essays do tell a story quite as often as a short story stakes a claim to a particular viewpoint. Mark Twain's piece called "Cornpone Opinions," for example, which is about public opinion, begins with a vignette as vivid as any in *Huckleberry Finn.* Twain says that when he was a boy of fifteen, he used to hang out a back window and listen to the sermons preached by a neighbor's slave standing on top of a woodpile: "He imitated the pulpit style of the several clergyman of the village, and did it well and with fine passion and energy. To me he was a wonder. I believed he was the greatest orator in the United States and would some day be heard from. But it did not happen; in the distribution of rewards he was overlooked. . . . He interrupted his preaching now and then to saw a stick of wood, but the sawing was a pretense—he did it with his mouth, exactly imitating the

sound the bucksaw makes in shrieking its way through the wood. But it served its purpose, it kept his master from coming out to see how the work was getting along."

A novel would go on and tell us what happened next in the life of the slave—and we miss that. But the extraordinary flexibility of essays is what has enabled them to ride out rough weather and hybridize into forms that suit the times. And just as one of the first things a fiction writer learns is that he needn't actually be writing fiction to write a short story—that he can tell his own history or anybody else's as exactly as he remembers it and it will be "fiction" if it remains primarily a story—an essayist soon discovers that he doesn't have to tell the whole truth and nothing but the truth; he can shape or shave his memories, as long as the purpose is served of elucidating a truthful point. A personal essay frequently is not auto-biographical at all, but what it does keep in common with autobiography is that, through its tone and tumbling progression, it conveys the quality of the author's mind. Nothing gets in the way. Because essays are directly concerned with the mind and the mind's idiosyncrasy, the very freedom the mind possesses is bestowed on this branch of literature that does honor to it, and the fascination of the mind is the fascination of the essay.

Questions for Study and Discussion

1. What does Hoagland say is the root of art? In what way do you feel this is true?

2. What does Hoagland mean by "this is what I think, and this is what I am?"

3. Paragraph 3 contains a simile. What is it? How well does it work in the context of his argument?

4. Do essays need to tell the truth?

5. What kinds of evidence does Hoagland use to defend his arguments? How well does his system of organization help to move his argument along? Explain.

6. What distinctions does Hoagland make between a novel and an essay? Are the differences clear to you?

Writing Topics

1. Hoagland says, "through its tone and tumbling progression, [an essay] conveys the quality of the author's mind." Choose an essay from one of the early nineteenth-century writers, Henry David Thoreau, Edgar Allan Poe, Ralph Waldo Emerson, or one that you prefer. Write an essay in which you explain what the essay tells you about the author?

2. Hoagland defines an essay based on his own experience as a writer and a reader. How would you define "essay"? How should an essay differ from a novel, magazine article, or short story? In your opinion, what makes an essay good or bad? Write an essay in which you present your own definition of an essay.

RICHARD ROSEN

Born in 1949, in Chicago, Richard Rosen has lived in Cambridge, Massachusetts, since graduating from Harvard in 1972. Rosen began his writing career as an assistant editor of *Playboy Magazine* and later became senior editor of the *Boston Phoenix*, Boston's alternative newspaper. He left a full-time career as a writer to teach and is currently a professor of expository writing at Harvard, maintaining a tie to the magazine world with a column called "Dining Out" for *Boston Magazine*. Rosen's books include *Me and My Friends* (1971), *Psycho Babble* (1977), *Strike Three You're Dead* (1984), for which he won the Edgar Allan Poe Award, *Fadeaway* (1986), and *Saturday Night Dead* (1988).

 In the following essay, published in *New York Magazine*, Rosen bemoans the fact that instead of reading books whole, people nowadays consider themselves well read if they have digested just the review of a current book.

Bullcrit

 In the well-educated, gossip-rich world of the media, in the circles that 1
process and recycle and enhance with rumor all manner of literary and
crypto-literary data—how to put this delicately?—nobody who can help it
reads books anymore.

 This, naturally, doesn't stop anyone from talking about books. In a 2
culturally acquisitive milieu, there is nothing worse than—no egg so yolky
on one's face—not knowing what the writers people are talking about are
writing about in the books we are not reading. So we refer more than ever
to the universe of secondary and tertiary information about books—reviews
of books, movies based on books, gossip about authors, gossip about
publication parties—as if they were the books themselves.

 At a recent weekend house party where five of the six assembled were 3
media professionals, the dinner conversation turned to a new nonfiction
book, Charles Kaiser's *1968 in America.*

 "I saw the review," said the editor of a popular national magazine, 4
expertly summarizing the contents of *The New York Times Book Review*
coverage.

 "I was at a book party for him," a writer for one of the newsweeklies 5
said, offering a brief anecdote.

"Someone I know," I volunteered, "thinks that all this nostalgia for   6
the late sixties is"—and I vaguely paraphrased a theory that I had heard
secondhand and that itself had been hastily concocted by its originator.

At this juncture, the only person present for whom books are in no   7
sense a business said, "You know, I read the book—"

And he stopped, startled by the dark silence that suddenly descended   8
over the dinner table.

"You read the book?" I said, breaking the awkward pause. "Well, then,   9
I don't think you're qualified to pass judgment on it."

"You have an obvious emotional investment in it," added the editor.   10
"Your prejudice is unmistakable."

"Anything you say," the network television producer told him,   11
"would merely be your opinion."

Any phenomenon so pervasive that it is already being satirized by   12
some of its prepetrators desperately needs an identity. So, to the increasingly popular mode of discourse that combines all the virtues of literary
expertise with none of the inconveniences of reading book-length material
we may finally give a name: Bullcrit.

Bullcrit is judgmentalism without judgment, familiarity without knowl-   13
edge, received wisdom without emotional response, informedness without
information. In a world clogged with cultural artifacts, this species of specious
profundity has come to dominate and define certain civilized discussions. It is
the spicy patter of media people who have the time only to know *about* things.
It is not insight but outsight. In our widely spaced moments of intellectual
reckoning, what we dimly know ourselves to be is Bullcrit artists.

"My extremely well defended, morally correct, absolutely committed,   14
and frequently expressed opinion of Bret Easton Ellis's work," says Daniel
Okrent, a former New York book editor and now editor of *New England
Monthly*, "is based on the fact that I haven't read him."

"I was talking to my editor on a magazine piece I was doing," one New   15
York writer confessed to me, "and the subject of Mona Simpson's novel
Anywhere but Here came up. I mentioned that I thought she was really good
and had a big imagination, etc., and I hate to admit it, but it was only when
my editor remarked that she had actually read the novel that it occurred to
me that I hadn't."

Over dinner at a French restaurant in Manhattan—there were four of   16
us—the subject of Ayn Rand came up, and the air was soon full of
thoughtful remarks about "enlightened self-interest" and "the way Fascism
and libertarianism meet each other halfway in her books." Under subsequent mutual interrogation, we all confessed that Rand was among the
authors we had always meant to read. One guilty diner tried to win the
court's sympathy by saying, "Well, my best friend in high school read
everything Ayn Rand wrote."

"Hey," says an editor of a national monthly magazine, "that's why   17
we're all in journalism, isn't it? It's a Bullcrit profession. We've made an
adult strategy out of normal adolescent bulls––– behavior."

Yet it would be a mistake to think of Bullcrit as mere intellectual   18
window dressing. "I had a conversation the other morning with a writer
about Susan Sontag's book on AIDS," a successful free-lance writer told me
over lunch. "That afternoon, I happened to be talking with another writer
about the book, and I got a chance to sharpen my ideas. I began to feel
passionate about it. The point is, I got what it was all about. But"—she
smiled faintly and shrugged—"who knows what's in the book? Does it even
matter? I may not have been debating anything Sontag actually wrote, but I
was feeling it all very deeply."

In the mediacracy, which thrives on the bulk consumption and recita-   19
tion of premium tidbits, an investment on the scale of reading an entire
book—how undergraduate!—could not possibly pay a conversational and
informational dividend high enough to make it worthwhile. Indeed, intimate knowledge of a book's contents can severely limit the reader's range of
cocktail-party commentary on it.

"Look," Okrent says, "if I invest four to six hours in reading a book, I   20
feel I have to like it and defend it from attack. When you're familiar enough
with a book to say in conversation, 'He makes a very interesting point in
the penultimate chapter,' when you're in that deep, you can't say it's wrong
or bad. But if you spend only ten minutes reading a review of the same
book, then you can say anything you like."

"If you read a book," Ruth Adams Bronz, owner and chef of Manhat-   21
tan's Miss Ruby's Café, says with admirable logic, "in all conscience, you're
obliged to defend it from dumb reviews. If you don't read it, for all you know
all the juicy negative stuff in the reviews just might be true."

What is important now is not book reading but book sightings: to   23
spot mentions of a book in print and conversation and report these
sightings in still other conversations, thereby helping create a book's
"buzz." In this atmosphere, nothing could be more lethal to a book's reputation than its being read.

Granted, lying about what you've read has always been one of those   24
natural social instincts, like padding your income or lowering the age at
which your children began sleeping through the night. The truly alarming
development is that among members of the mediacracy, all pretense has
been dropped. The rules have changed. *There is no longer any need to pretend
that one has read a book, because it is a social and intellectual disadvantage to
have done so.* In the time it takes to read a book, you could be consuming
enough magazines, newspapers, and television shows to arm yourself for
months of cocktail-party battle. No, the act of reading a book today
requires an almost archaic gentility, a nineteenth-century obliviousness to

the lava of product belching out of this nation's publishers, film studios, and television networks.

Bullcrit is the quick efficient way of coping with media overload, a   25 problem exacerbated in media circles by the preference for creating culture over appreciating it. As Gore Vidal put it fifteen years ago, "It has always been true that in the United States the people who ought to read books write them." In certain loosely defined New York circles, you can reach a point while still in your thirties where you do not even have the time to *skim* all the new books written by friends and acquaintances, let alone attempt that old cover-to-cover thing. As a matter of sheer etiquette, it becomes second nature to affect a familiarity with unopened books. Bullcrit allows us to squeeze still more into what Daniel Boorstin 30 years ago called our "overpopulated consciousness."

On a deeper level, Bullcrit "resolves" the contradiction between peo-   26 ple's need to feel a community of literary interests and the forbidding facts that there are too many books and too little time to achieve any unity. Once you get beyond a few bestsellers—a *Bonfire of the Vanities* or a *Presumed Innocent*—it's a hopelessly atomized situation. New York's media elite often turn out to have little in common except their privileged role as cogs in the well-oiled wheels of cultural commerce. Sadly, the pleasures that books give to readers in the hinterlands are rarely enjoyed at headquarters. Pathetic as it may be, Bullcrit is our noble attempt to preserve for book reading, that most private cultural experience, an acceptable public dimension.

That public dimension is increasingly absent even from the publishing   27 industry itself. A book editor I know served not long ago as a fiction judge for the National Book Award and was sent almost every serious novel of that particular year. "For once, I was extremely well read," he says. "I'd have lunch with literary agents and be able to say, 'Oh, you represent so-and-so; I loved his book.' I'd really read it! And the agents would say to me, 'I can't tell you how nice it is to meet someone in publishing who's really read the book.' And I couldn't admit that I'd read it because I had to."

Book reviews are the bedrock of Bullcrit. By providing instant sec-   28 ondhand opinions handsomely designed for cocktail parties and intellectual self-aggrandizement, book reviews render an invaluable service. (Even when reviewers themselves are Bullcriting. According to a National Book Critics Circle survey reported in January 1988, 36 percent of book reviewers said it was sometimes ethical to review a book without having finished it. How many more, one wonders, think it's unethical but do it anyway?) In the reading of any book review, there is a critical point we might call the Release—that glorious, cathartic moment at which you realize you've now absorbed enough information about the book to feel released from the obligation to read it.

To paraphrase Emily Dickinson, there is no frigate like a book review,   29 to take us lands away.

The Bullcrit artist's bible is *The New York Times Book Review*, the chief   30
maker, keeper, and destroyer of literary reputation. To be able to quote,
paraphrase, or, failing that, fake the gist of a book review in that publication
has become a leading mark of erudition. To tell an author at a Manhattan
get-together that you "saw the review" is considered tantamount to having
read—and liked—the book itself.

"At a party to celebrate the publication of my last novel," says a New   31
York author, "an editor I've known for years sidled up to me and said, 'Well,
I can see that you're really coming up in the world. Your first novel wasn't
reviewed at all in the *Times*, your second was given an "In Short" review,
and this one was reviewed in the daily *Times*.' The fact that he had
diligently tracked my review history in the New York *Times* was intended as
the very highest praise. Mind you, I've never had the slightest shred of
evidence that he's read a single word of any of my books. Generally, when
people say to me, 'I saw the review'—and you'd be amazed how many people
say that and nothing else—I always want to reply, 'Thank you, but I didn't
write that, I wrote the book.' But I usually hold my tongue, because I know
that books are meant to be seen and not read."

The rise of Bullcrit has been smoothed by a couple of other factors,   32
the dominant one being the influence of the cultural standards set by
television and the movies. The communal experience denied adult readers is
readily available to moviegoers and television watchers. A line from a
screenplay can within weeks enjoy a national familiarity only a few lines of
Shakespeare have achieved in centuries. Kevin Costner's egregious line from
Bull Durham—"I believe in long, slow, deep, soft, wet kisses that last for
three days"—was recently canonized by *People* magazine for its 23 million
readers as "the most repeated movie quote of the year." The disparity
between the impact made by even the worst movie and all but a very few
books has created a growing pressure on books to behave, if they want to be
noticed, like creatures of the movie world. In a recent ad for a new book,
The DeMilles: An American Family, by Anne Edwards, the publisher chose
as the ad's headline a quotation from the *Publishers Weekly* review: "A great
story . . . the kind [Cecil B.] would have optioned for the movies." The
breathless question most often asked by those to whom I have just been
introduced as someone who writes novels is "Are they going to be made into
movies?" Often, this is not only the first question asked but the only one. In
the questioner's voice I can hear the hidden panic: "Novels? For God's sake,
man, are they going to get it into a form my system can tolerate?"

Bullcrit has important roots in the movie industry. Hollywood has   33
always reviled writers, no matter how indispensable they may be, and long
ago institutionalized a kind of smiling contempt for them. As Neal Gabler
reminds us in his excellent recent book, *An Empire of Their Own: How the
Jews Invented Hollywood* (all right, I saw the review), the Warner brothers
and their fellow moguls, despite their high cultural claims for movies, were

not readers. After getting a wire from director Mervyn LeRoy telling him to read Hervey Allen's long-winded 1933 best-seller, *Anthony Adverse*, Jack Warner cabled back, "Read it? I can't even lift it." Today's equivalent of this story? When the producer of a hit television show tells you several months after he receives your five-page treatment for an episode that it is "too long to read" and asks if it can be condensed to a single paragraph.

"You know," says Dongan Lowndes, the half-broken-down writer in   34
Robert Stone's 1985 novel *Children of Light*, "a lot of times when Hollywood people tell you they like a book it turns out they're referring to the studio synopsis." Gore Vidal, who once boasted that "I am that rarest of reviewers who actually reads every word, and rather slowly," wrote in 1973 that "there is evidence that a recent best-seller by a well-known writer was never read by its publisher or by the book club that took it or by the film company that optioned it."

There is something chilling about a culture in which the purpose of a   35
book is no longer presumed by many to be tied up with the reading of it. More than ever, books are status symbols, fashion accessories, interior-decorating touches, matching gewgaws; they accent the coffee tables of our consciousness. A foot or so of color-coded Vintage Contemporary paperbacks on your shelf is the macramé wall hanging of the late eighties. When Kirk Douglas was on the *Tonight Show* recently, guest host Jay Leno thanked him for an inscribed copy of Douglas's autobiography, *The Ragman's Son*, not by saying, "I look forward to reading it" but by saying, "It'll go right up there on my bookshelf."

"You hear it all the time," says critic Stephen Schiff. "Somebody says,   36
'That's a great book. I saw it on the *Today Show*.' "

The advertising for the comedy film *The Naked Gun* reads: "You've   37
read the ad. Now see the movie." It's a gag that inadvertently underlines the degree to which advertising copy is this country's preferred reading material.

In a recent article about Italian novelist Umberto Eco and the publica-   38
tion of his new book, *Foucault's Pendulum*, Eco "estimated that *The Name of the Rose*"—his previous novel—"had a potential audience of 16 million. 'Let's be completely pessimistic and say that only 10 percent actually read it,' he said. 'That's 1.6 million people. All right, that's not bad for a writer, having 1.6 million friends.' " But it's still one out of ten.

"Why do authors bother?" *New Republic* editor Michael Kinsley   39
lamented only half-facetiously in 1985. "As a magazine editor, I often beg journalists who contemplate spending a year or two writing a book on some worthwhile or even important subject to save themselves the agony, cut out the middleman, and just write the review."

Or, better yet, write the blurb. The rise of the blurb culture is the   40
second major factor underlying Bullcrit. As *Spy* magazine has been documenting regularly, we live in a you-scratch-my-book-jacket-and-I'll-scratch-

yours world. (Example: Robert Coover on Angela Carter's *Saints and Strangers*: "One of the greatest prose masters of our time." Carter on Coover's *Gerald's Party*: "A master.") A culture in which book-jacket blurbs are prized by the publishing industry even though they are widely understood to be little more than a system of favors extended and debts discharged is a culture that has already begun to falsify the whole idea of literary appraisal. In the blurbocracy, all blurbs are created equally meaningless. As the mystery writer Robert B. Parker, quoting John Kenneth Galbraith, likes to say to novelists petitioning him for a line of praise, "I'll blurb your book or I'll read it, but not both."

Bullcrit is the conversational form of blurb, used to assign some   41
largely random value to books and other cultural artifacts as they cruise silently across our radar screens. In an era shamelessly defined by celebrity journalism and the trivial pursuit of informed gossip, the object of book writing is now to provide a pretext for the meta-experience by which the book is known.

Under the circumstances, Bullcrit is almost impossible to resist. Wher-   42
ever the knowing meet, one is liable to feel the symptoms—tightness in the chest, brain coughing up some idle judgment, lips twitching in reluctant anticipation of uttering it to hold one's own in the Bullcrit session. To this peer pressure Andrew Heyward, executive producer of CBS's *48 Hours*, has given the name "gangst." "It's that horrible feeling," Heyward says, "almost matched by that agonizing second just after you've given in and made your comment, during which you're wondering, 'Did I get away with it again?'"

Of course you got away with it. In a world of shattered attention   43
spans, Bullcrit has taken its place as a new aesthetic of knowledge. It attests—like State Department spokesmen and answering machines—to the sacredness of the secondhand.

Questions for Study and Discussion

1. In your own words, what is "bullcrit"? What does Rosen imply about humankind in his discussion about "bullcrit"?

2. What motivates writers to publish books that they know will sit on a coffee table or go directly to the bookshelf?

3. Does Rosen agree or disagree with the notion that in order to write well, a person must read "well"? How does "bullcrit" relate to this notion?

4. Why do people lie about their age, weight, salary, and their children's development? In your opinion, do people achieve the desired results from these lies?

5. Rosen presents two ideas in this essay. Those who have not read a book are not qualified to comment on it, and those who have read it have an emotional stake in it and thus are also not qualified to comment on it. Does he resolve this dilemma? How would you resolve it?

6. Rosen says people panic when asked if they've read a novel. They need "a form [their] system can tolerate." Why do they need form? What type of form do they want?

Writing Topics

1. Explain a time, perhaps after giving an oral report you were not prepared for, when you wondered, "Did I get away with it?" Why weren't you sure that you had gotten away with it? What does it mean to "get away with it"? When did you find out you had or had not gotten away with it? What were the results? Have you done it since?

2. When novels are made into movies, parts of the book are often changed or deleted and scenes that did not appear in the book are added. In an essay discuss the differences between such a movie and novel that you are familiar with. If the title has been changed, discuss the ways the new title reflects the "new" story.

Born in 1944, Leo Cawley fought in Vietnam during the early years of the war. After completing his own education, he taught political economy at Columbia, Vassar, and Georgetown. Cawley now hosts "Fearful Symmetry," a radio talk show on New York's WBAI. Cawley's writing appears regularly in such magazines as *The Nation* and *Monthly Review*.

In the following essay, first published in *The Village Voice*, Cawley points out that more than a decade after America's involvement in Vietnam ended Hollywood has finally started to make films about our part in that war. Cawley questions the accuracy of these films, exposing the "truths" of the war that America is still unwilling to believe.

Refighting the War: Why the Movies Are in Vietnam

Twelve years after the fall of Saigon, it's hard to get a hotel room in Bangkok, because American crews on location for Vietnam War movies have taken all the space. Oliver Stone's *Platoon* and Stanley Kubrick's *Full Metal Jacket* are filling the theaters back home. John Irvin's *Hamburger Hill* is hoping to do the same; *Apocalypse Now* and *Go Tell the Spartans* are being re-released; and a Vietnam TV series will open this fall on CBS,[1] opposite *The Cosby Show*. Something is clearly going on. They are at last making movies about the war "we put behind us"—indeed, we've gone from suppression to saturation in a handful of months.

Is this a moment of turning toward the truth, where the American people will gain some insight into the Vietnam War? Or will it be hammering of the history of that war into the boilerplate of myth? Is it time for the mastication of that period's pain and conflict into domestic familiarity, the Hogan's Heroization of the war America lost?

A census of the whole Vietnam film library to date, from right to left or from militarist to antimilitarist, would show a lopsided count with the right-wing, militarist end badly overcrowded. It is not even clear that any recent example of a 100 percent antimilitary, anti-imperialist film exists. *Cutter's Way*, Ivan Passer's film about an embittered veteran and a corrupt,

[1]The show was "Tour of Duty."

murderous business executive (symbol of corporate power and militarism), comes close. So unusual was the film's perspective that many critics misunderstood even the basic plot elements. More common is the mixed message of *The Deer Hunter* and *Go Tell the Spartans*, that misguided policy led to an unworthy or overly cruel war. Promilitary films rely on the inherent drama of war-is-hell, until, at the farthest right and most populous end of the spectrum, with Rambo and Chuck Norris, war becomes exciting and fun. But locating Vietnam movies according to their position on a political spectrum of attitudes toward the war or militarism is oddly uninformative. Much more is going on.

The only romance shared by all America is the one we got at the movies. Into film go all the love and longing for what America is missing and can't find in the mass cultural cornucopia of the twentieth century. And this passion has not gone unrequited. Hollywood has been our constant lover. Even if all the old smoothy wanted was to score, Hollywood has responded to every prompting and every need, it has always found a language to speak to the longings in that unhappy heart.   4

What Americans seem to crave most is assurance of their goodness, their essential morality. While the French might insist on their intelligence and the English their status, Americans will confess to, even boast of, their undistinguished status or intelligence but demand that their essential goodness be conceded. Nowhere is this craving more consistently served than in film. But the Vietnam War challenged American innocence, and so film found it impossible to embrace its issues.   5

One of the deepest facts revealed about us by the Vietnam movies is how trapped we are in the perceptions of World War II. We liked that war too much and are reluctant to surrender the sense of unity and righteousness it brought. We liked the way we felt about ourselves during it. Nearly all the Vietnam films, left or right, share with World War II films premises like the following: 6

- *A moral impulse is behind every American war. Wars are undertaken by Americans, even if the cause is mistaken, as crusades.*

- *Individuals prove themselves by participating in combat, which teaches truths impossible to learn elsewhere.*

- *The foreignness of the enemy is a sign for evil—the only good foreigners are those who have acquired the cultural traits of Americans (like chewing gum or using slang) or at least admire those traits.*

- *Americans themselves are better, friendlier than other nationalities and want nothing selfish in relations with foreigners.*

- *But if there is conflict, Americans are inherently better at violence and will win.*

The issue most elaborately evaded by Vietnam films is the domestic 7
conflict over the war itself. Some of the bitterest dramas of the war years are
absent from the movies, the struggles in schools, churches, unions, homes,
the accusations of "murderer" and "communist" at family gatherings.
There is still no serious film about the antiwar movement of the more than
fifty thousand draft-age men who went to Canada or prison. The closest
Hollywood got may have been *Coming Home*, in which Jon Voight's para-
plegic vet stages a one-man antiwar protest at a time when this was
conspicuously a group activity. One result of this silence is that in the latest
Vietnam films, the rebellion against the war is present in the most deformed
ways: Bill Graham's braying, Nehru-jacketed peacenik in *Gardens of Stone*,
or *Hamburger Hill*'s uncritical retailing of the paranoid GI fantasy of dog-
shit-throwing hippies greeting him on his return.

Because of its marked unwillingness to face the question of the war's 8
justification, the Vietnam film differs sharply from World War II movies in
that it shows the rise of "lesser" loyalties, which supplant older causes like
anticommunism or democratic principle. The war left such issues hopelessly
tainted in any case, along with the whole idea of American goodness;
Vietnam films, whatever their place on the left-right spectrum, tend to
reflect a view of government as a dishonest, self-serving bureaucracy unworthy of loyalty. The M*A*S*H film and television show, which were really a
crypto discussion of Vietnam, started a trend that can be labeled "the
devolution of personal loyalties." What to fight for became as much a
question for the filmmaker as it was for the grunt in the rifle company. In
movie after movie, characters "soldier on" out of a host of other loyalties,
including self, family, friends, ethnic group, and in Francis Ford Coppola's
loopy *Gardens of Stone*, the U.S. Army itself. No one has asked what it is
that these new old values are replacing. And any new old values will do.
What matters is that the line holds, that nobody cuts and runs even if
American democracy and anticommunism don't turn people on anymore.
The sergeant hero of *Hamburger Hill* states for his men the personal morality of senescent imperialism: "You don't have to like it, you just have to
show up."

In *Rambo*, it is proletarian rage that seeps away other allegiances. He 9
is the soldier without a cause, although the militarist stupidity of the films
obscures the startling antipatriotism of the character. Stallone's hero has
been betrayed by his government, the army, even the Special Forces. The
only claim the inarticulate and inaccessible Rambo still recognizes is that of
his fellow veterans and MIAs. He still hates the Vietnamese but he also
hates his nation, his government et al. because, having started the war and
expended "American lives," they quit.

In this flight from politics, the Vietnam film emphasizes the personal 10
anguish of individual involvement. Accordingly, it continues the World

War II film tradition of portraying war as an arena for the display of a man's fundamental traits, such as ferocity, courage, capacity for sacrifice, etc. It is easy to underestimate the effort of imagination and will needed to keep coming up with plots that allow military men to undertake these solitary missions in total opposition to the doctrine and practice of the U.S. military. Not only do Rambo and Chuck Norris go in to fight alone; so, too, do Martin Sheen in *Apocalypse Now* and Robert De Niro in *The Deer Hunter*. But no human activity is as intensely social as modern warfare. The breakthrough realism of *Platoon*, *Full Metal Jacket*, and *Hamburger Hill* results partly from their focus on the interaction within the unit. By highlighting the personal encounter with violence, most Vietnam films have lost any connection with this reality.

The Vietnam film accepts the convention of U.S. political culture 11 that foreign conflicts are easy to sort out, with adorable underdog villains. Americans do not see themselves, and Hollywood does not show them, as B-52 pilots or as military aides in the caudillo's palace. Our mass culture presents Americans as underdogs or as the allies of underdogs. Rambo, although an American, becomes the guerrilla fighter, the Vietcong in the jungle armed with will and primitive weapons who successfully battles helicopters and superior fire-power. In Vietnam movies across the political spectrum, the American martial spirit is embodied either in the grunt or in the Special Forces soldier fighting with the partisans.

But this moral egotism has developed a sullen flip side. The World War 12 II movie showed Germans and Japanese with ferocious or sadistic traits, but it did not insist, as some recent films do, that viciousness confers real military advantage. This new wrinkle, which meshes with the right-wing theory of the defeat in Vietnam, should be called "the doctrine of restrained ferocity." Most explicit in *Rambo*, it holds that the U.S. fights according to rules while its opponents don't. Rambo explains, in one of his rare utterances, that he was made to lose in Vietnam by having to fight fair. Clint Eastwood has said, "I disagree with the [John] Wayne concept. . . . I play bigger-than-life characters, but I'll shoot a guy in the back. I go by the expediency of the moment."

The Iranian hostage crisis brought out the national tendency to think 13 of the Third World as a kind of right-wing theme park, where mindless military rambunctiousness can be indulged at no cost to oneself. There was a warlike mood in Washington in those fading days of Carter "wimpishness," and my students at Georgetown University were far from immune to it. A class in the economics of developing countries voted 60–3 in favor of war with Iran. But when I asked them how many favored the return of the draft, the vote ran 59–4 against, with an Iranian student switching sides. Security from the sobering threat of the draft is an insufficiently recognized ingredient in the revival of Reagan-Rambo toughness. Here we were a few short years after the fall of Saigon, and the nation's young, the Future Veterans of Foreign Wars, or FVFW, as I like to think of them, were raring to go again.

And no wonder. Film has presented a rich menu of pleasures to be   14
had from war. The array of heady intoxicants includes service to ideals of transcendent value, the destruction of empires of infinite evil, the discharge of aggression, the fellowship of heroes, illusions of invulnerability, the gratitude of the defended, etc. Vietnam films are no exception. They persist in fetishizing the skills of the warrior, treating survival and success in war as the result of skill and mastery, and devoting substantial dialogue to explaining how formidable a combatant the central character is. From *Rambo* to *Platoon*, the convention is rarely violated. This is an important part of the make-believe, that it isn't all just dumb luck. It is true that bad luck seems to follow incompetents around, but the John Wayne supertrooper stereotype is an object of contempt by troops in combat for good reason.

Everyone learns very soon in combat that modern war kills tough guys   15
in much the same way that it kills everybody else. Mortar rounds in the sky, fired by people miles away, do not know and do not care how fast your reflexes are or how good your marksmanship is or whether you are brave. Grunts may come to this awareness reluctantly; after all, most of them were brought up on the red-blooded American cowboy, tough guy ethic. But combat usually wises up the ones it doesn't kill. None of this is visible in any of the Vietnam films.

The use of middle-aged stars as combat infantrymen is a distortion too   16
widespread to be accidental. In *The Deer Hunter*, Michael Cimino had the gall to show a thirtyish Robert De Niro leave a good job in a steel mill to go fight in Vietnam. *Platoon* is the first film not to make the mistake of featuring men the age of De Niro, Sylvester Stallone, or Chuck Norris, who are far too old to withstand the rigors of jungle war. But this use of overage stars depicts war as the business of real men, mature men, rather than the luckless adolescents who actually fight it. Like all wars, Vietnam was fought by teenage males, disproportionately the high school dropouts, the poor, the black, and Hispanic. On this Reagan and Gorbachev and the Ayatollah all agree: the Future Veterans of Foreign Wars are economically and socially expendable. The films show gratifying fantasies of power and rage to the least powerful; they present combat infantrymen as valued and indispensable members of an exclusive society to people who are seen as neither by society at large.

The complaints that Vietnam films inspire in veterans, the obsession   17
with hardware and tactics that never worked, the middle-age combat heroes, the fire-power that could be avoided by an enemy who maintained close contact, the improbable heroics, are the product of film-making that is far from laissez-faire. The Pentagon has had an active hand in film production at least since Frank Capra's World War II *Why We Fight* series. The War

Department established basic combat film conventions, like the racial focus for the depiction of Japanese. It rejected several of Capra's scripts because they blamed the emperor and the Japanese ruling elite and were therefore likely to elicit "too much sympathy for Jap people." Finally the offending scriptwriter, Joris Ivens, was fired, and a script was written that blamed the culture, history, and people of Japan for the war. The convention is still observed that Asian enemies are evil for ethnic reasons, while Europeans merely have evil governments, like the Third Reich.

More recently, former congressman Benjamin Rosenthal estimated   18
the cost to the Pentagon for assistance in the making of *The Green Berets* to be over a million dollars. John Wayne was billed $18,623.64 for help, which included eighty-five hours of helicopter flying time and thirty-eight hundred man days of borrowed military personnel. Army cooperation was "extensive" in the making of *Gardens of Stone*. The price was a series of script changes to depict army personnel more favorably. The result of this gold thumb on the scales has been a whole clatch of propagandistic films that would otherwise have been strangled in the cradle by the magic of the marketplace.

It is hard to tell if *Platoon* and *Full Metal Jacket* will set standards or be   19
exceptions in the flood of films descending on us. But if film is going to tear itself away from the contemplation of American mythic obsessions and tell what happened in Vietnam, here are some of the incidents it will see when it opens its eyes. This list is conceived with the FVFW in mind. In this war the air strikes are as dangerous to us as to the people who are shooting at the infantrymen. The helicopters don't come promptly when there are wounded. You hear on the sound track guys who have been tough in the earlier reels screaming, especially the ones who have lost limbs. They've been shot up with morphine and the corpsmen have begged them to shut up because they are giving away their position. But the morphine won't work for twenty minutes and they don't care who hears them. Their legs are gone at the knees and they're howling and thrashing around, crying for their mothers, yelling "Mommy! Mommy!" over and over again at the top of their lungs. No shame. They don't care anymore. The others wouldn't mind if they'd die, if only they'd shut up. It's not so much that they're giving the position away. It's the howling, the bottomless woe. Those wounded are only ten or twenty meters away in the dark, but they're signaling how horrible it can be, how anybody can sound if their luck runs out. This would be a whole different order of screaming from the kind you'd need later in the hospital ward scenes. (There is a striking absence of hospital scenes in the Vietnam genre film.) The screaming in the hospital wards on the day the corpsmen clean the stumps would present new challenges to the audio engineers.

Platoon exposed the illusion that the war was "brought into the living room," the myth that Vietnam was on television every night in all its violence and gore. Of the forty-one hundred network news reports on the war, about 10 percent actually had "bang, bang" in them. The bulk of the stories were the body counts, the pacification programs, Westmoreland inspecting the ARVN. In the part of *Platoon* some critics called the My Lai scene, the audience sees all the familiar images, the peasant huts, the water buffaloes, the conical hats. You can almost feel the audience's sense of being at home with the images, of thinking, "I know, I know"—until the Americans start to kill villagers. At this point there is a palpable wincing and turning away, as if to say, "No! This isn't how it goes. It goes some other way." But that was how it went too often, more often than any of us will ever know.

But it is not easy to go against a culture of not wanting to know. Or even to identify where in the circle of not knowing we need to break in. The columnist Anthony Lewis, who wrote a good deal about Vietnam, said *Platoon* told him things he hadn't known about the war. How did he not know these things? And the great American mass has its own convictions about "offensive incidents." At the end of the war, Richard Nixon used the need to prevent a bloodbath as the only excuse for continuing the fighting and cited the "Hue massacre" as proof that this would happen should the North gain control.

At that time I was active in Vietnam Veterans Against the War. A CBS file clerk sent us an outline of a documentary project that had been killed. The proposed project had located a number of credible, i.e., non-Vietnamese, sources who said that what the marine corps claimed were massacre victims were in fact killed by the marine corps bombing raids during the retaking of Hue. As the Vietnamese forces held out against the marines for weeks after Tet, the corpses became a health hazard, and the city's residents pushed the dead into mass graves. It was these mass graves that the marine corps used in its massacre claims and still stands by. Even Kubrick's antiwar *Full Metal Jacket* shows the uncovering of these graves and naïvely offers the marine corp's version of how they came to be.

Armed with the internal documents concerning the proposed documentary, VVAW staged a sit-in at CBS, where it became clear the network would give no ground and would soon call the police. We gave in. But the episode exposed me to CBS thinking. I was told the network "had taken so much heat over My Lai" that it was just impossible to go with another story like the one we were then proposing. As Barry Richardson, then VP for public relations, told me, "One of those is enough." So one of those was all America was allowed to have.

In the Vietnam films I would like to see, not all of these evaded realities have to be horrific. Some could be subtle. There could be a depiction of the quiet vomiting of members of an infantry squad before they leave the perimeter for a night patrol. Previous movies have missed the small ways that fear affects you. The way it grinds you down, and diminishes and degrades you. And they've missed fear's aftereffects, like the screaming nightmares of GIs in the field hospitals who rave about "gooks," GIs who have been wounded and who now would like to kill all of "them," even the Vietnamese who sweep up the ward.

And, of course, there are the Vietnamese. It would seem lopsided if   25
the films kept focusing exclusively on our story. Will we keep thinking the tragedy is that of the invader, of his painful self-knowledge, his loss of innocence, his recognition of limits? This suits the national character so depressingly well. It would be interesting to take other lives into account. There should be scenes about the legions of whores and barbers and laundresses and spies who were all the Vietnam American troops ever knew. In Da Nang, the command had the whorehouses working two shifts, one daytime for the enlisted men, one at night for the officers. We used to joke that it was because of the damage to morale and leadership if the officers saw the enlisted men going to the bordellos.

And what about our "allies," the ones we went there to defend? Who   26
were those people whose daughters wore white *ao dais* and rode bicycles to the Lycée Blaise Pascal on Doc Lap Street? Who were the families with the Citroëns? One day in the spring of '66, some local Buddhists were going into Da Nang, dressed in their best clothes, to protest something or other. Some ARVN soldiers fired an antitank weapon at their bus. A horrible mess, all those bright clothes covered with blood. We were ordered to fire on the ones who fired the antitank weapon if they fired again. It was a national controversy. We could learn about it in a film that might be made one day when, after growing curious about what we were like and learning about ourselves, we acquired an interest in other lives, including those of the Vietnamese. There could be a film about their experience. Our memorial wall in Washington has fifty-eight thousand or so dead on it. The Vietnamese suffered more than two million dead. Allowing for the greater number of dead and the fact that there are fewer—one-fifth as many— Vietnamese than Americans, their memorial wall of names, if they had one, would be two hundred times larger than ours.

Questions for Study and Discussion

1. In paragraph 2 Cawley asks two questions. Does he answer those questions?

2. What does Cawley say are "some of the bitterest dramas of the war years"? How does he explain those dramas?

3. Cawley feels that Americans "crave" the "assurance of their goodness." How do the movies of the Vietnam War fulfill this need?

4. In paragraph 7, Cawley presents a "GI fantasy of dog-shit-throwing hippies greeting him on his return." Did this happen? Who was the GI fighting for in Vietnam?

5. What is Cawley's attitude toward the modern films about Vietnam? Cite examples of his diction that show how you arrived at your conclusion.

6. In paragraph 16, Cawley says that Reagan, Gorbachev, and the Ayatollah all feel that the "luckless adolescents," the "Future Veterans of Foreign Wars," are expendable. What is your reaction to this assertion?

Writing Topics

1. According to Cawley, the motion picture industry has misrepresented the reality of war, for example by portraying most soldiers as adults when they are really just kids. Do you think these misrepresentations are intentional? What image of America do these depictions maintain? How have more recent movies changed the way the war is depicted?

2. Individuals and organizations withhold information to protect their own and society's interests. In an essay discuss the circumstances under which you think it might be beneficial to shade the truth. If it is never an ethical choice for you, explain your position. Use examples from your own experience or from current events, such as the NASA "O-ring" disclosure or the Iran-Contra affair.

STEPHEN KING

Stephen King, the reigning king of horror in the United States, was born in 1947, in Portland, Maine. He graduated in 1970 with a B.S in English from the University of Maine at Orono. Early in his writing career King was a janitor and a laundry worker. He was living in a trailer and teaching high-school English when he made it big with his first best-seller *Carrie* (1974). The rest is history to horror fans.

King's list of best-sellers grows longer by a book or two every year. King's many works include the following novels: *Salem's Lot* (1975), *The Shining* (1977), *The Dead Zone* (1979), *Firestarter* (1980), *Christine* (1983), *Pet Sematary* (1983), *Tommyknockers* (1988), and *The Dark Half* (1989). A short story from the collection *Night Shift* (1978) was made into a critically acclaimed film *Stand by Me*.

The widespread popularity of horror books and films attest to the fact that many people share King's fascination with the macabre. In the following selection, which appeared in *Playboy* in 1982, King analyzes the reasons we all flock to good horror movies.

Why We Crave Horror Movies

I think that we're all mentally ill; those of us outside the asylums only   1
hide it a little better—and maybe not all that much better, after all. We've all known people who talk to themselves, people who sometimes squinch their faces into horrible grimaces when they believe no one is watching, people who have some hysterical fear—of snakes, the dark, the tight place, the long drop . . . and, of course, those final worms and grubs that are waiting so patiently underground.

When we pay our four or five bucks and seat ourselves at tenth-row   2
center in a theater showing a horror movie, we are daring the nightmare.

Why? Some of the reasons are simple and obvious. To show that we   3
can, that we are not afraid, that we can ride this roller coaster. Which is not to say that a really good horror movie may not surprise a scream out of us at some point, the way we may scream when the roller coaster twists through a complete 360 or plows through a lake at the bottom of the drop. And horror movies, like roller coasters, have always been the special province of the young; by the time one turns 40 or 50, one's appetite for double twists or 360-degree loops may be considerably depleted.

We also go to re-establish our feelings of essential normality; the   4
horror movie is innately conservative, even reactionary. Freda Jackson as
the horrible melting woman in *Die, Monster, Die!* confirms for us that no
matter how far we may be removed from the beauty of a Robert Redford or
a Diana Ross, we are still light-years from true ugliness.

And we go to have fun.   5

Ah, but this is where the ground starts to slope away, isn't it? Because   6
this is a very peculiar sort of fun indeed. The fun comes from seeing others
menaced—sometimes killed. One critic has suggested that if pro football has
become the voyeur's version of combat, then the horror film has become the
modern version of the public lynching.

It is true that the mythic, "fairytale" horror film intends to take away   7
the shades of gray. . . . It urges us to put away our more civilized and adult
penchant for analysis and to become children again, seeing things in pure
blacks and whites. It may be that horror movies provide psychic relief on
this level because this invitation to lapse into simplicity, irrationality and
even outright madness is extended so rarely. We are told we may allow our
emotions a free rein . . . or no rein at all.

If we are all insane, then sanity becomes a matter of degree. If your   8
insanity leads you to carve up women like Jack the Ripper or the Cleveland
Torso Murderer, we clap you away in the funny farm (but neither of those
two amateur-night surgeons was ever caught, heh-heh-heh); if, on the other
hand your insanity leads you only to talk to yourself when you're under
stress or to pick your nose on your morning bus, then you are left alone to
go about your business . . . though it is doubtful that you will ever be
invited to the best parties.

The potential lyncher is in almost all of us (excluding saints, past and   9
present; but then, most saints have been crazy in their own ways), and every
now and then, he has to be let loose to scream and roll around in the grass.
Our emotions and our fears form their own body, and we recognize that it
demands its own exercise to maintain proper muscle tone. Certain of these
emotional muscles are accepted—even exalted—in civilized society; they
are, of course, the emotions that tend to maintain the status quo of
civilization itself. Love, friendship, loyalty, kindness—these are all the emotions that we applaud, emotions that have been immortalized in the cou-
plets of Hallmark cards and in the verses (I don't dare call it poetry) of
Leonard Nimoy.

When we exhibit these emotions, society showers us with positive   10
reinforcement; we learn this even before we get out of diapers. When, as
children, we hug our rotten little puke of a sister and give her a kiss, all the
aunts and uncles smile and twit and cry, "Isn't he the sweetest little thing?"
Such coveted treats as chocolate-covered graham crackers often follow. But
if we deliberately slam the rotten little puke of a sister's fingers in the door,

sanctions follow—angry remonstrance from parents, aunts and uncles; instead of a chocolate-covered graham cracker, a spanking.

But anticivilization emotions don't go away, and they demand   11
periodic exercise. We have such "sick" jokes as, "What's the difference between a truckload of bowling balls and a truckload of dead babies? (You can't unload a truckload of bowling balls with a pitchfork . . . a joke, by the way, that I heard originally from a ten-year-old.) Such a joke may surprise a laugh or a grin out of us even as we recoil, a possibility that confirms the thesis: If we share a brotherhood of man, then we also share an insanity of man. None of which is intended as a defense of either the sick joke or insanity but merely as an explanation of why the best horror films, like the best fairy tales, manage to be reactionary, anarchistic, and revolutionary all at the same time.

The mythic horror movie, like the sick joke, has a dirty job to do. It   12
deliberately appeals to all that is worst in us. It is morbidity unchained, our most base instincts let free, our nastiest fantasies realized . . . and it all happens, fittingly enough, in the dark. For those reasons, good liberals often shy away from horror films. For myself, I like to see the most aggressive of them—*Dawn of the Dead*, for instance—as lifting a trap door in the civilized forebrain and throwing a basket of raw meat to the hungry alligators swimming around in that subterranean river beneath.

Why bother? Because it keeps them from getting out, man. It keeps   13
them down there and me up here. It was Lennon and McCartney who said that all you need is love, and I would agree with that.

As long as you keep the gators fed.   14

Questions for Study and Discussion

1. According to King, what are several of the reasons people go to horror movies? What other reasons can you add to King's list?

2. Identify the analogy King uses in paragraph 3, and explain how it works.

3. What does King mean when he says in paragraph 4 "the horror movie is innately conservative, even reactionary"?

4. What emotions does society applaud? Why? Which ones does King label "anticivilization" emotions?

5. In what ways is a horror movie like a sick joke? What is the "dirty job" that the two have in common (12)?

6. King starts his essay with the attention-grabbing sentence "I think that we're all mentally ill." How does he develop this idea of insanity in his essay? What does King mean when he says "the potential lyncher is in almost all of us" (9)? How does King's last line relate to the theme of mental illness?

7. What is King's tone in the essay? Point to particular words or sentences that led you to this conclusion.

Writing Topics

1. Many recent television dramas suggest a vigilante action as the ordinary citizen's solution to the threat of violent crime. What attitudes and emotions must the writers of such dramas perceive in the average person? How do these attitudes and emotions relate to the emotions King dicusses in his essay? Write an essay in which you explore the "personality" of a culture that is receptive to such a solution.

2. Write an essay in which you analyze, in light of King's remarks, a horror movie you've seen. In what ways do you think King is right about our craving for such movies? How did you feel before going to the theater? How did you feel when leaving?

ALLAN BLOOM

Rock music has always had its detractors, people who thought that it was immoral and corrupting the nation's youth. In recent years their numbers seem to be growing and their voices seem to be getting louder. Irate parents and religious leaders are outraged by the explicit lyrics of today's songs. They want compact discs, cassettes, and record albums to be given ratings, similar to those given to movies. It's difficult to disagree with people like Allan Bloom who say, "Nothing is more singular about this generation than its addiction to music." If young people are indeed addicted to rock music, perhaps we are justified in wondering what effect this addiction will have on them.

In the following selection from Bloom's controversial best-seller *The Closing of the American Mind* (1987), portions of which first appeared in an essay in the *National Review* in 1982, Bloom speculates about the negative influence that rock music is having on the education of American students. (Biographical information about Allan Bloom is on page 283).

Music

Though students do not have books, they most emphatically do have music. Nothing is more singular about this generation than its addiction to music. This is the age of music and the states of soul that accompany it. To find a rival to this enthusiasm, one would have to go back at least a century to Germany and the passion for Wagner's[1] operas. They had the religious sense that Wagner was creating the meaning of life and that they were not merely listening to his works but experiencing that meaning. Today, a very large proportion of young people between the ages of ten and twenty live for music. It is their passion; nothing else excites them as it does; they cannot take seriously anything alien to music. When they are in school and with their families, they are longing to plug themselves back into their music. Nothing surrounding them—school, family, church—has anything to do with their musical world. At best that ordinary life is neutral, but mostly it is an impediment, drained of vital content, even a thing to be rebelled against. Of course, the enthusiasm for Wagner was limited to a small class, could be indulged only rarely and only in a few places, and had to wait on

[1]Richard Wagner (1813–1883), famous German composer, primarily noted for grand opera.

the composer's slow output. The music of the new votaries, on the other hand, knows neither class nor nation. It is available twenty-four hours a day, everywhere. There is the stereo in the home, in the car; there are concerts; there are music videos, with special channels exclusively devoted to them, on the air nonstop; there are the Walkmans so that no place—not public transportation, not the library—prevents students from communing with the Muse, even while studying. And, above all, the musical soil has become tropically rich. No need to wait for unpredictable genius. Now there are many geniuses, producing all the time, two new ones rising to take the place of every fallen hero. There is no dearth of the new and the startling.

The power of music in the soul—described to Jessica marvelously by   2
Lorenzo in the *Merchant of Venice*—has been recovered after a long period of desuetude. And it is rock music alone that has effected this restoration. Classical music is dead among the young. This assertion will, I know, be hotly disputed by many who, unwilling to admit tidal changes, can point to the proliferation on campuses of classes in classical music appreciation and practice, as well as performance groups of all kinds. Their presence is undeniable, but they involve not more than 5 to 10 percent of the students. Classical music is now a special taste, like Greek language or pre-Columbian archeology, not a common culture of reciprocal communication and psychological shorthand. Thirty years ago, most middle-class families made some of the old European music a part of the home, partly because they liked it, partly because they thought it was good for the kids. University students usually had some early emotive association with Beethoven, Chopin, and Brahms, which was a permanent part of their makeup and to which they were likely to respond throughout their lives. This was probably the only regularly recognizable class distinction between educated and uneducated in America. Many, or even most, of the young people of that generation also swung with Benny Goodman,[2] but with an element of self-consciousness—to be hip, to prove they weren't snobs, to show solidarity with the democratic ideal of a pop culture out of which would grow a new high culture. So there remained a class distinction between high and low, although private taste was beginning to create doubts about whether one really liked the high very much. But all that has changed. Rock music is as unquestioned and unproblematic as the air the students breathe, and very few have any acquaintance at all with classical music. This is a constant surprise to me. And one of the strange aspects of my relations with good students I come to know well is that I frequently introduce them to Mozart. This is a pleasure to me, inasmuch as it is always pleasant to give people gifts that please them. It is interesting to see whether and in what ways their studies are complemented by such music. But this is something utterly new

---

[2]American jazz clarinetist and band leader (1909–1986).

to me as a teacher; formerly my students usually knew much more classical music than I did.

Music was not all that important for the generation of students   3 preceding the current one. The romanticism that had dominated serious music since Beethoven appealed to refinements—perhaps overrefinements—of sentiments that are hardly to be found in the contemporary world. The lives people lead or wish to lead and their prevailing passions are of a different sort than those of the highly educated German and French bourgeoisie, who were avidly reading Rousseau and Baudelaire, Goethe and Heine,[3] for their spiritual satisfaction. The music that had been designed to produce, as well as to please, such exquisite sensibilities had a very tenuous relation to American lives of any kind. So romantic musical culture in America had had for a long time the character of a veneer, as easily susceptible to ridicule as were Margaret Dumont's displays of coquettish chasteness, so aptly exploited by Groucho Marx in *A Night at the Opera.* I noticed this when I first started teaching and lived in a house for gifted students. The "good" ones studied their physics and then listened to classical music. The students who did not fit so easily into the groove, some of them just vulgar and restive under the cultural tyranny, but some of them also serious, were looking for things that really responded to their needs. Almost always they responded to the beat of the newly emerging rock music. They were a bit ashamed of their taste, for it was not respectable. But I instinctively sided with the second group, with real, if coarse, feelings as opposed to artificial and dead ones. Then their musical sans-culotteism won the revolution and reigns unabashed today. No classical music has been produced that can speak of this generation.

Symptomatic of this change is how seriously students now take the   4 famous passages on musical education in Plato's *Republic.* In the past, students, good liberals that they always are, were indignant at the censorship of poetry, as a threat to free inquiry. But they were really thinking of science and politics. They hardly paid attention to the discussion of music itself and, to the extent that they even thought about it, were really puzzled by Plato's devoting time to rhythm and melody in a serious treatise on political philosophy. Their experience of music was as an entertainment, a matter of indifference to political and moral life. Students today, on the contrary, know exactly why Plato takes music so seriously. They know it affects life very profoundly and are indignant because Plato seems to want to rob them of their most intimate pleasure. They are drawn into argument with Plato about the experience of music, and the dispute centers on how to

---

[3]Prominent French and German literary figures of the eighteenth and nineteenth centuries; the French philosopher Jean-Jacques Rousseau, the French poet Charles Baudelaire, the German man of letters Johann Wolfgang von Goethe, and the German lyric poet Heinrich Heine.

evaluate it and deal with it. This encounter not only helps to illuminate the phenomenon of contemporary music, but also provides a model of how contemporary students can profitably engage with a classic text. The very fact of their fury shows how much Plato threatens what is dear and intimate to them. They are little able to defend their experience, which has seemed unquestionable until questioned, and it is most resistant to cool analysis. Yet if a student can—and this is most difficult and unusual—draw back, get a critical distance on what he clings to, come to doubt the ultimate value of what he loves, he has taken the first and most difficult step toward the philosophic conversion. Indignation is the soul's defense against the wound of doubt about its own; it reorders the cosmos to support the justice of its cause. It justifies putting Socrates to death. Recognizing indignation for what it is constitutes knowledge of the soul, and is thus an experience more philosophic than the study of mathematics. It is Plato's teaching that music, by its nature, encompasses all that is today most resistant to philosophy. So it may well be that through the thicket of our greatest corruption runs the path to awareness of the oldest truths.

Plato's teaching about music is, put simply, that rhythm and melody,   5 accompanied by dance, are the barbarous expression of the soul. Barbarous, not animal. Music is the medium of the *human* soul in its most ecstatic condition of wonder and terror. Nietzsche,[4] who in large measure agrees with Plato's analysis, says in *The Birth of Tragedy* (not to be forgotten is the rest of the title, *Out of the Spirit of Music*) that a mixture of cruelty and coarse sensuality characterized this state, which of course was religious, in the service of gods. Music is the soul's primitive and primary speech and it is *alogon*, without articulate speech or reason. It is not only not reasonable, it is hostile to reason. Even when articulate speech is added, it is utterly subordinate to and determined by the music and the passions it expresses.

Civilization or, to say the same thing, education is the taming or   6 domestication of the soul's raw passions—not suppressing or excising them, which would deprive the soul of its energy—but forming and informing them as art. The goal of harmonizing the enthusiastic part of the soul with what develops later, the rational part, is perhaps impossible to attain. But without it, man can never be whole. Music, or poetry, which is what music becomes as reason emerges, always involves a delicate balance between passion and reason, and, even in its highest and most developed forms— religious, warlike, and erotic—that balance is always tipped, if ever so slightly, toward the passionate. Music, as everyone experiences, provides an unquestionable justification and a fulfilling pleasure for the activities it accompanies: the soldier who hears the marching band is enthralled and reassured; the religious man is exalted in his prayer by the sound of the

---

[4]Friedrich Nietzche (1844–1900), German philosopher.

organ in the church; and the lover is carried away and his conscience stilled by the romantic guitar. Armed with music, man can damn rational doubt. Out of the music emerge the gods that suit it, and they educate men by their example and their commandments.

Plato's Socrates disciplines the ecstasies and thereby provides little consolation or hope to men. According to the Socratic formula, the lyrics— speech and, hence, reason—must determine the music—harmony and rhythm. Pure music can never endure this constraint. Students are not in a position to know the pleasures of reason; they can only see it as a disciplinary and repressive parent. But they do see, in the case of Plato, that that parent has figured out what they are up to. Plato teaches that, in order to take the spirtual temperature of an individual or a society, one must "mark the music." To Plato and Nietzsche, the history of music is a series of attempts to give form and beauty to the dark, chaotic, premonitory forces in the soul—to make them serve a higher purpose, an ideal, to give man's duties a fullness. Bach's religious intentions and Beethoven's revolutionary and humane ones are clear enough examples. Such cultivation of the soul uses the passions and satisfies them while sublimating them and giving them an artistic unity. A man whose noblest activities are accompanied by a music that expresses them while providing a pleasure extending from the lowest bodily to the highest spiritual, is whole, and there is no tension in him between the pleasant and the good. By contrast a man whose business life is prosaic and unmusical and whose leisure is made up of coarse, intense entertainments, is divided, and each side of his existence is undermined by the other.

Hence, for those who are interested in psychological health, music is at the center of education, both for giving the passions their due and for preparing the soul for the unhampered use of reason. The centrality of such education was recognized by all the ancient educators. It is hardly noticed today that in Aristotle's *Politics* the most important passages about the best regime concern musical education, or that the *Poetics* is an appendix to the *Politics*. Classical philosophy did not censor the singers. It persuaded them. And it gave them a goal, one that was understood by them, until only yesterday. But those who do not notice the role of music in Aristotle and despise Plato went to school with Hobbes, Locke, and Smith,[5] where such considerations have become unnecessary. The triumphant Enlightenment rationalism thought that it had discovered other ways to deal with the irrational part of the soul, and that reason needed less support from it. Only in those great critics of Enlightenment and rationalism, Rousseau and Nietzsche, does music return, and they were the most musical of philoso-

---

[5]Major British political and moral philosophers of the seventeenth and eighteenth centuries: Thomas Hobbes, John Locke, and Adam Smith.

phers. Both thought that the passions—and along with them their minis-
terial arts—had become thin under the rule of reason and that, therefore,
man *himself* and what he sees in the world have become correspondingly
thin. They wanted to cultivate the enthusiastic states of the soul and to re-
experience the Corybantic[6] possession deemed a pathology by Plato.
Nietzsche, particularly, sought to tap again the irrational sources of vitality,
to replenish our dried-up stream from barbaric sources, and thus encouraged the Dionysian[7] and the music derivative from it.

This is the significance of rock music. I do not suggest that it has any   9
high intellectual sources. But it has risen to its current heights in the
education of the young on the ashes of classical music, and in an atmosphere in which there is no intellectual resistance to attempts to tap the
rawest passions. Modern-day rationalists, such as economists, are indifferent to it and what it represents. The irrationalists are all for it. There is
no need to fear that "the blond beasts" are going to come forth from the
bland souls of our adolescents. But rock music has one appeal only, a
barbaric appeal, to sexual desire—not love, not *eros*, but sexual desire
undeveloped and untutored. It acknowledges the first emanations of children's emerging sensuality and addresses them seriously, eliciting them and
legitimating them, not as little sprouts that must be carefully tended in
order to grow into gorgeous flowers, but as the real thing. Rock gives
children, on a silver platter, with all the public authority of the entertainment industry, everything their parents always used to tell them they had to
wait for until they grew up and would understand later.

Young people know that rock has the beat of sexual intercourse. That   10
is why Ravel's[8] *Bolero* is the one piece of classical music that is commonly
known and liked by them. In alliance with some real art and a lot of pseudo-
art, an enormous industry cultivates the taste for the orgiastic state of
feeling connected with sex, providing a constant flood of fresh material for
voracious appetites. Never was there an art form directed so exclusively to
children.

Ministering to and according with the arousing and cathartic music,   11
the lyrics celebrate puppy love as well as polymorphous attractions, and
fortify them against traditional ridicule and shame. The words implicitly
and explicitly describe bodily acts that satisfy sexual desire and treat them
as its only natural and routine culmination for children who do not yet
have the slightest imagination of love, marriage, or family. This has a much
more powerful effect than does pornography on youngsters, who have no

---

[6]From Greek mythology, referring to a spirit of wild music and dance.

[7]From Greek mythology, relating to Dionysus, the god of wine. The word refers to
frenzied, uninhibited behavior.

[8]Maurice Ravel (1875–1937), French composer.

need to watch others do grossly what they can so easily do themselves. Voyeurism is for old perverts; active sexual relations are for the young. All they need is encouragement.

The inevitable corollary of such sexual interest is rebellion against the parental authority that represses it. Selfishness thus becomes indignation and then transforms itself into morality. The sexual revolution must overthrow all the forces of domination, the enemies of nature and happiness. From love comes hate, masquerading as social reform. A worldview is balanced on the sexual fulcrum. What were once unconscious or half-conscious childish resentments become the new Scripture. And then comes the longing for the classless, prejudice-free, conflictless, universal society that necessarily results from liberated consciousness—"We Are the World," a pubescent version of *Alle Menschen werden Brüder*,[9] the fulfillment of which has been inhibited by the political equivalents of Mom and Dad. These are the three great lyrical themes: sex, hate, and a smarmy, hypocritical version of brotherly love. Such polluted sources issue in a muddy stream where only monsters can swim. A glance at the videos that project images on the wall of Plato's cave since MTV took it over suffices to prove this. Hitler's image recurs frequently enough in exciting contexts to give one pause. Nothing noble, sublime, profound, delicate, tasteful, or even decent can find a place in such tableaux. There is room only for the intense, changing, crude, and immediate, which Tocqueville[10] warned us would be the character of democratic art, combined with a pervasiveness, importance, and content beyond Tocqueville's wildest imagination. 12

Picture a thirteen-year-old boy sitting in the living room of his family home doing his math assignment while wearing his Walkman headphones or watching MTV. He enjoys the liberties hard won over centuries by the alliance of philosophic genius and political heroism, consecrated by the blood of martyrs; he is provided with comfort and leisure by the most productive economy ever known to mankind; science has penetrated the secrets of nature in order to provide him with the marvelous, lifelike electronic sound and image reproduction he is enjoying. And in what does progress culminate? A pubescent child whose body throbs with orgasmic rhythms; whose feelings are made articulate in hymns to the joys of onanism or the killing of parents; whose ambition is to win fame and wealth in imitating the drag-queen who makes the music. In short, life is made into a nonstop, commercially prepackaged masturbational fantasy. 13

This description may seem exaggerated, but only because some would prefer to regard it as such. The continuing exposure to rock music is a 14

---

[9]German song: "All Men Will Be Brothers."

[10]Alexis de Tocqueville (1805–1859). French statesman and author of an influential foreign assessment of American life, *Democracy in America*.

reality, not one confined to a particular class or type of child. One need only ask first-year university students what music they listen to, how much of it, and what it means to them, in order to discover that the phenomenon is universal in America, that it begins in adolescence or a bit before and continues through the college years. It is *the* youth culture and, as I have so often insisted, there is now no other countervailing nourishment for the spirit. Some of this culture's power comes from the fact that it is so loud. It makes conversation impossible, so that much of friendship must be without the shared speech that Aristotle asserts is the essence of friendship and the only true common ground. With rock, illusions of shared feelings, bodily contact and grunted formulas, which are supposed to contain so much meaning beyond speech, are the basis of association. None of this contradicts going about the business of life, attending classes, and doing the assignments for them. But the meaningful inner life is with the music.

This phenomenon is both astounding and indigestible, and is hardly   15
noticed, routine and habitual. But it is of historic proportions that a society's best young and their best energies should be so occupied. People of future civilizations will wonder at this and find it as incomprehensible as we do the caste system, witch-burning, harems, cannibalism, and gladiatorial combats. It may well be that a society's greatest madness seems normal to itself. The child described has parents who have sacrificed to provide him with a good life and who have a great stake in his future happiness. They cannot believe that the musical vocation will contribute very much to that happiness. But there is nothing they can do about it. The family spiritual void has left the field open to rock music, and they cannot possibly forbid their children to listen to it. It is everywhere; all children listen to it; forbidding it would simply cause them to lose their children's affection and obedience. When they turn on the television, they will see President Reagan warmly grasping the daintily proffered gloved hand of Michael Jackson and praising him enthusiastically. Better to set the faculty of denial in motion—avoid noticing what the words say, assume the kid will get over it. If he has early sex, that won't get in the way of his having stable relationships later. His drug use will certainly stop at pot. School is providing real values. And popular historicism provides the final salvation; there are new lifestyles for new situations, and the older generation is there not to impose its values but to help the younger one to find its own. TV, which compared to music plays a comparatively small role in the formation of young people's character and taste, is a consensus monster—the Right monitors its content for sex, the Left for violence, and many other interested sects for many other things. But the music has hardly been touched, and what efforts have been made are both ineffectual and misguided about the nature and extent of the problem.

The result is nothing less than parents' loss of control over their   16
children's moral education at a time when no one else is seriously concerned

with it. This has been achieved by an alliance between the strange young males who have the gift of divining the mob's emergent wishes—our versions of Thrasymachus, Socrates' rhetorical adversary—and the record-company executives, the new robber barons, who mine gold out of rock. They discovered a few years back that children are one of the few groups in the country with considerable disposable income, in the form of allowances. Their parents spend all they have providing for the kids. Appealing to them over their parents' heads, creating a world of delight for them, constitutes one of the richest markets in the postwar world. The rock business is perfect capitalism, supplying to demand and helping to create it. It has all the moral dignity of drug trafficking, but it was so totally new and unexpected that nobody thought to control it, and now it is too late. Progress may be made against cigarette smoking because our absence of standards or our relativism does not extend to matters of bodily health. In all other things the market determines the value. (Yoko Ono is among America's small group of billionaires, along with oil and computer magnates, her late husband having produced and sold a commodity of worth comparable to theirs.) Rock is a very big business, bigger than the movies, bigger than professional sports, bigger than television, and this accounts for much of the respectability of the music business. It is difficult to adjust our vision to the changes in the economy and to see what is really important. McDonald's now has more employees than U.S. Steel, and likewise the purveyors of junk food for the soul have supplanted what still seem to be more basic callings.

This change has been happening for some time. In the late fifties, De Gaulle gave Brigitte Bardot[11] one of France's highest honors. I could not understand this, but it turned out that she, along with Peugot, was France's biggest export item. As Western nations became more prosperous, leisure, which had been put off for several centuries in favor of the pursuit of property, the means to leisure, finally began to be of primary concern. But, in the meantime, any notion of the serious life of leisure, as well as men's taste and capacity to live it, had disappeared. Leisure became entertainment. The end for which they had labored for so long has turned out to be amusement, a justified conclusion if the means justify the ends. The music business is peculiar only in that it caters almost exclusively to children, treating legally and naturally imperfect human beings as though they were ready to enjoy the final or complete satisfaction. It perhaps thus reveals the nature of all our entertainment and our loss of a clear view of what adulthood or maturity is, and our incapacity to conceive ends. The emptiness of *values* results in the acceptance of the natural *facts* as the ends. In

17

---

[11]Popular French movie actress of the 1950s and 60s, known mainly for sexually provocative roles.

this case infantile sexuality is the end, and I suspect that, in absence of other ends, many adults have to agree that it is.

It is interesting to note that the Left, which prides itself on its critical approach to "late capitalism" and is unrelenting and unsparing in its analysis of our other cultural phenomena, has in general given rock music a free ride. Abstracting from the capitalist element in which it flourishes, they regard it as a people's art, coming from beneath the bourgeoisie's layers of cultural repression. Its antinomianism and its longing for a world without constraint might seem to be the clarion of the proletarian revolution, and Marxists certainly do see that rock music dissolves the beliefs and morals necessary for liberal society and would approve of it for that alone. But the harmony betwen the young intellectual Left and rock is probably profounder than that. Herbert Marcuse[12] appealed to university students in the sixties with a combination of Marx and Freud. In *Eros and Civilization* and *One Dimensional Man* he promised that the overcoming of capitalism and its false consciousness will result in a society where the greatest satisfactions are sexual, of a sort that the bourgeois moralist Freud called polymorphous and infantile. Rock music touches the same chord in the young. Free sexual expression, anarchism, mining of the irrational unconscious and giving it free rein are what they have in common. The high intellectual life . . . and the low rock world are partners in the same entertainment enterprise. They must both be interpreted as parts of the cultural fabric of late capitalism. Their success comes from the bourgeois's need to feel that he is not bourgeois, to have undangerous experiments with the unlimited. He is willing to pay dearly for them. The Left is better interpreted by Nietzsche than by Marx. The critical theory of late capitalism is at once late capitalism's subtlest and crudest expression. Antibourgeois ire is the opiate of the Last Man.

This strong stimulant, which Nietzsche called Nihiline, was for a very long time, almost fifteen years, epitomized in a single figure, Mick Jagger. A shrewd, middle-class boy, he played the possessed lower-class demon and teen-aged satyr up until he was forty, with one eye on the mobs of children of both sexes whom he stimulated to a sensual frenzy and the other eye winking at the unerotic, commercially motivated adults who handled the money. In his act he was male and female, heterosexual and homosexual; unencumbered by modesty, he could enter everyone's dreams, promising to do everything with everyone; and, above all, he legitimated drugs, which were the real thrill that parents and policemen conspired to deny his youthful audience. He was beyond the law, moral and political, and thumbed his nose at it. Along with all this, there were nasty little appeals to the suppressed inclinations toward sexism, racism, and violence, indulgence

18

19

---

[12]German philosopher who taught in American universities (1898–1979).

in which is not now publicly respectable. Nevertheless, he managed not to appear to contradict the rock ideal of a universal classless society founded on love, with the distinction between brotherly and bodily blurred. He was the hero and the model for countless young persons in universities, as well as elsewhere. I discovered that students who boasted of having no heroes secretly had a passion to be like Mick Jagger, to live his life, have his fame. They were ashamed to admit this in a university, although I am not certain that the reason has anything to do with a higher standard of taste. It is probably that they are not supposed to have heroes. Rock music itself and talking about it with infinite seriousness are perfectly respectable. It has proved to be the ultimate leveler of intellectual snobbism. But it is not respectable to think of it as providing weak and ordinary persons with a fashionable behavior, the imitation of which will make others esteem them and boost their own self-esteem. Unaware and unwillingly, however, Mick Jagger played the role in their lives that Napoleon played in the lives of ordinary young Frenchmen throughout the nineteenth century. Everyone else was so boring and unable to charm youthful passions. Jagger caught on.

In the last couple of years, Jagger has begun to fade. Whether Michael Jackson, Prince, or Boy George can take his place is uncertain. They are even weirder than he is, and one wonders what new strata of taste they have discovered. Although each differs from the others, the essential character of musical entertainment is not changing. There is only a constant search for variations on the theme. And this gutter phenomenon is apparently the fulfillment of the promise made by so much psychology and literature that our weak and exhausted Western civilization would find refreshment in the true source, the unconscious, which appeared to the late romantic imagination to be identical to Africa, the dark and unexplored continent. Now all has been explored; light has been cast everywhere; the unconscious has been made conscious, the repressed expressed. And what have we found? Not creative devils, but show business glitz. Mick Jagger tarting it up on the stage is all we brought back from the voyage to the underworld. 20

My concern here is not with the moral effects of this music—whether it leads to sex, violence, or drugs. The issue here is its effect on education, and I believe it ruins the imagination of young people and makes it very difficult for them to have a passionate relationship to the art and thought that are the substance of liberal education. The first sensuous experiences are decisive in determining the taste for the whole of life, and they are the link between the animal and spiritual in us. The period of nascent sensuality has always been used for sublimation, in the sense of making sublime, for attaching youthful inclinations and longings to music, pictures, and stories that provide the transition to the fulfillment of the human duties and the enjoyment of the human pleasures. Lessing, speaking of Greek sculpture, said "beautiful men made beautiful statues, and the city 21 had beautiful statues in part to thank for beautiful citizens." This formula encapsulates the fundamental principle of the esthetic education of man. Young men and women were attracted by the beauty of heroes whose very bodies expressed their nobility. The deeper understanding of the meaning of nobility comes later, but is prepared for by the sensuous experience and is actually contained in it. What the senses long for as well as what reason later sees as good are thereby not at tension with one another. Education is not sermonizing to children against their instincts and pleasures, but providing a natural continuity between what they feel and what they can and should be. But this is a lost art. Now we have come to exactly the opposite point. Rock music encourages passions and provides models that have no relation to any life the young people who go to universities can possibly lead, or to the kinds of admiration encouraged by liberal studies. Without the cooperation of the sentiments, anything other than technical education is a dead letter.

Rock music provides premature ecstasy and, in this respect, is like the drugs with which it is allied. It artificially induces the exaltation naturally attached to the completion of the greatest endeavors—victory in a just war, consummated love, artistic creation, religious devotion, and discovery of the truth. Without effort, without talent, without virtue, without exercise of the faculties, anyone and everyone is accorded the equal right to the enjoyment of their fruits. In my experience, students who have had a serious fling with drugs—and gotten over it—find it difficult to have enthusiasms or great expectations. It is as though the color has been drained out of their lives and they see everything in black and white. The pleasure they experienced in the beginning was so intense that they no longer look for it at the end, or as the end. They may function perfectly well, but dryly, routinely. Their energy has been sapped, and they do not expect their life's activity to produce anything but a living, whereas liberal education is supposed to encourage the belief that the good life is the pleasant life and that the best life is the most pleasant life. I suspect that the rock addiction, particularly in the absence of strong counterattractions, has an effect similar to that of drugs. The students will get over this music, or at least the exclusive passion for it. But they will do so in the same way Freud says that men accept the reality principle—as something harsh, grim, and essentially unattractive, a mere necessity. These students will assiduously study economics or the professions and the Michael Jackson costume will slip off to reveal a Brooks Brothers suit beneath. They will want to get ahead and live comfortably. But this life is as empty and false as the one they left behind. The choice is not between quick fixes and dull calculation. This is what liberal education is meant to show them. But as long as they have the Walkman on, they cannot hear what the great tradition has to say. And, after its prolonged use, when they take it off, they find they are deaf.

22

Questions for Study and Discussion

1. In paragraph 2, Bloom says, "this was probably the only regularly recognizable class distinction between educated and uneducated in America." What is the "this" Bloom refers to? Do you agree with Bloom? How well does he support this idea throughout his essay? What kinds of evidence does he use?

2. In paragraph 4, Bloom speaks repeatedly of indignation. How does he intend his use of the word? How does this word set the tone of the essay?

3. How useful is Bloom's reference to Plato? What assumptions about his reader is Bloom making?

4. Who are "the Lefts" and "the Rights?" How can they influence the music industry?

5. Bloom says that, compared to rock music, television "plays a comparatively small role in the formation of young people's character." Why does he believe this to be true? Do you agree? Why or why not?

6. What does Bloom say is responsible for "respectability" in the music industry? In what ways, if any, does this contradict what he says in the rest of the essay? Explain.

Writing Topics

1. Some parent groups are working to convince record manufacturers to label music albums to reflect their content. Critics inside and outside the music industry say any such labeling is a form of censorship. In an essay, offer your point of view. Is labeling a form of censorship? Why or why not? What would be the effect of such labeling on musicians and the consumer? Would it have the results concerned parents hope for?

2. MTV and other video channels gained in popularity during the late 1980s. Discuss the effect of these channels on the music industry. In what ways if any has commercial music changed? How has it stayed the same? In your opinion have the changes been for the better or for the worse?

PAT AUFDERHEIDE

Not too long ago, the popular music world was dominated by records and cassettes. Today we have CDs and music videos. "Music videos are more than a fad, or fodder for spare hours and dollars of young consumers," says media expert Pat Aufderheide. "They are pioneers in video expression."

Born in 1948, Pat Aufderheide is an associate professor of communications at American University in Washington, D.C. She is also a senior editor at *In These Times*, a weekly alternative newspaper.

In "The Look of the Sound," Aufderheide examines the influence of music videos on "a populist industrial society." A bold new experiment, music videos, according to Aufderheide, amplify a mood of instability that characterizes American youth.

The Look of the Sound

Music videos are more than a fad, or fodder for spare hours and dollars of young consumers. They are pioneers in video expression, and the results of their reshaping of the form extend far beyond the TV set.

Music videos have broken through TV's most hallowed boundaries. As commercials in themselves, they have erased the very distinction between the commercial and the program. As nonstop sequences of discontinuous episodes, they have erased the boundaries between programs.

Music videos have also set themselves free from the television set, inserting themselves into movie theaters, popping up in shopping malls and department store windows, becoming actors in both live performances and the club scene. As omnivorous as they are pervasive, they draw on and influence the traditional image-shaping fields of fashion and advertising. Even political campaigning is borrowing from these new bite-sized packages of desire.

With nary a reference to cash or commodities, music videos cross the consumer's gaze as a series of mood states. They trigger moods such as nostalgia, regret, anxiety, confusion, dread, envy, admiration, pity, titillation—attitudes at one remove from primal expression such as passion, ecstasy, and rage. The moods often express a lack, an incompletion, an instability, a searching for location. In music videos, those feelings are carried on flights of whimsy, extended journeys into the arbitrary.

In appealing to and playing on these sensations, music videos have animated and set to music a tension basic to American youth culture. It is that feeling of instability that fuels the search to buy-and-belong, to possess a tangible anchor in a mutable universe while preserving the essence of that universe—its mutability. It allows the viewer to become a piece of the action in a continuous performance.

Music videos did not discover the commercial application of anxiety, of course. The manufacturer of Listerine was selling mouthwash on anxiety sixty years ago. Nor did music videos succeed in making themselves widely appealing by somehow duping passive audiences into an addiction to commercial dreams. Music videos are authentic expressions of a populist industrial society. For young people struggling to find a place in communities dotted with shopping malls but with few community centers, in an economy whose major product is information, music videos play to the adolescent's search for identity and an improvised community.

The success of MTV has been based on understanding that the channel offers not videos but environment, a context that creates mood. The goal of MTV executive Bob Pittman, the man who designed the channel, is simple: His job, he says, is to "amplify the mood and include MTV in the mood." Young Americans, he argues, are "television babies," particularly attracted to appeals to heart rather than head. "If you can get their emotions going," he says, "forget their logic, you've got 'em." Other executives describe MTV as "pure environment," in which not performers but music is the star of the perpetual show.

MTV's "pure environment" is expertly crafted. The pace is relentless, set by the music videos, which offer, in the words of one producer, "short bursts of sensual energy." But the image of the program service is casual and carefree. The channel's VJs are chosen for their fresh, offhand delivery and look. They are "themselves," celebrities whose only claim to fame is their projection of a friendly image to youthful viewers. The sets are designed to look like a basement hideaway a fifteen-year-old might dream of, with rock memorabilia and videocassettes adorning walls and shelves. Lighting is intentionally "shitty," instead of the classic no-shadow bright lighting of most TV productions. MTV intends to offer viewers not just a room of their own, but a room that is an alternate world.

MTV promotes itself as the populist, even democratic expression of its viewers. Rock stars in promo spots call on viewers to say, "I want my Em Tee Vee!", as if someone were threatening to take it away from them. "Their" MTV, as its own ads portray it, is the insouciant,[1] irreverent rejection of a tedious other world—not the real-life one of work and family, but the world as network news reports it. One commercial spoofs network news promos.

---

[1] *insouciant*: carefree, indifferent, unbothered.

Flashing the familiar "Coming at 11" slogan, the ad promises, "MTV provides *reason to live*, despite news of *botched world!*" On a miniature TV set, a logo reads, "Botched World." MTV superimposes its own version of reality on television's historic moments as well. Space flights—which made history not least for television's live coverage of them—are a favorite subject for MTV's own commercials. One shows astronauts planting an MTV flag on the moon. Another asks, "What if time had never been invented!," showing a space launch countdown without numbers. MTV's promise to remove the viewer from history is succinctly put into the slogan "24 hours every day . . . so you'll be able to live forever!"

Wherever they appear, music videos are distinctive because they   10
imitate dreams rather than the plot or event structure of bounded pro-grams. Even the usually thin narrative threads in song lyrics rarely provide the basis for a video's look and action. ("If you can hear them, the words help a bit," says video producer Zelda Barron wryly; her videos for Culture Club feature the bizarre, supernatural, and exotic, and use hectic montage[2] rather than narrative logic. Her explanation for her style—that the budgets aren't big enough to produce a coherent story—fails to explain why the features have the heady dream elements they do.) In *Film Quarterly*, Marsha Kinder has noted strong parallels between dreams and music videos. She cites five elements: unlimited access (MTV's continuous format and peo-ple's ability to both sleep and daydream); structural discontinuity (for instance, abrupt scene shifts); decentering (a loosely connected flow of action around a theme); structural reliance on memory retrieval (both videos and dreams trigger blocks of associations with pungent images); and the omnipresence of the spectator. In *Fabula*, Margaret Morse notes many of the same features, particularly the absence of reliance on narrative; she focuses on the magical quality of the word, as lip-synched by the performer who can appear anywhere in the video without being linked with the images or events, as if a dreamer who could create a world.

Many videos in fact begin with someone dreaming or daydreaming.   11
For instance, Kool and the Gang's "Misled" begins with a band member in his bedroom, launching into a dream-adventure in which he is both himself and a small Third World boy, threatened by a glamorous white female ghost and engaged in an adventure that imitates *Raiders of the Lost Ark*[3]— significantly, another commercial fantasy. The dream never really ends, since after his band members wake him up, they all turn into ghosts. Thelma Houston's "Heat Medley" shows the performer daydreaming to escape an unpleasant morning conflict with her husband. She daydreams a

---

[2]*montage*: a composite picture; a rapid sequence of images in motion pictures in TV.

[3]*Raiders of the Lost Ark*: a popular action/adventure movie by American director Steven Spielberg.

central role for herself on a *Love Boat*–like episode that turns into a nightmare of disastrous romance.

While the fantasies of music videos are open-ended, they do play on classic story lines, such as boy-meets-loses-wins-girl and child-is-menaced-by-monster-and-conquers-it. Some weave fairy tale themes—in which the protagonist is either a preschooler or is infantilized—into the dream. But performers easily switch identities, magical transportations occur, and sets are expressionistically large or small. In Midnight Star's "Operator," giant telephones dwarf performers, and a telephone booth magically pops up and disappears on highways. In Billy Joel's "Keeping the Faith," a judge's bench becomes a giant jukebox on a set featuring commercial talismans of the 1950s. In ABC's "The Look of Love," Central Park becomes a cartoon set (commercial kiddie culture), and Nolan Thomas' "Yo' Little Brother" looks like a Saturday morning cartoon version of *The Cabinet of Dr. Caligari*.[4]   12

Kinder believes that manufactured fantasy may have a much more far-reaching effect on people's subconscious attitudes and expectations than we now imagine, perhaps conditioning not only our expectations today but our dreams tomorrow. Her fears are far-reaching—and unprovable—but her careful analysis of parallels between dream structure and music video structure have fascinating implications for the form. Music videos offer a ready-made alternative to social life. With no beginnings or endings—no history—there may be nightmarish instability, even horror, but not tragedy. Tragedy is rooted in the tension between an individual and society. Likewise, there is no comedy, which provokes laughter with sharp, unexpected shifts of context, making solemnity slip on a banana peel. Dreams by contrast create gestalts,[5] in which sensations build and dissolve. And so they nicely match the promise and threat of consumer-constructed identity, endlessly flexible, depending on your income and taste. Obsolescence[6] is built in. Like fashion, identity can change with a switch of scene, with a change in the beat. The good news is: You can be anything, anywhere. That is also the bad news—which whets the appetite for more "news," more dreams.   13

Music video's lack of a clear subject carries into its constant play with the outward trappings of sex roles. Male images include sailors, thugs, gang members, and gangsters. Female images include prostitutes, nightclub performers, goddesses, temptresses, and servants. Most often, these images are drawn not from life or even myth, but from old movies, ads, and other pop culture clichés.   14

---

[4]*The Cabinet of Dr. Caligari*: Fritz Lang's 1919 silent film, noted for its bizarre lighting and distorted sets.

[5]*gestalts*: in Gestalt psychology, the integrated patterns that make up experience; forms or patterns.

[6]*obsolescence*: the process of becoming obsolete, out of date, or outmoded.

Social critics, especially feminists, have denounced sadomasochistic   15
trappings and stereotypes of exotic women (especially East Asians) in
videos. This may indeed be evidence of entrenched prejudice in the culture.
For instance, women are often portrayed in videos as outsiders and agents
of trouble, which reflects in part the macho traditions of rock. The fetishistic[7] female costumery of many videos probably reflects the role of artifice in
shaping feminine sex roles in the culture; there is a fuller cultural grab bag
for feminine than for masculine sexual objects.

Male or female, grotesquerie is the norm. Combine grotesquerie with   16
shifting identities and you get androgyny,[8] as with Culture Club's flamboyant Boy George. Androgyny may be the most daring statement that an
entire range of sex roles is fair game for projecting one's own statement of
the moment. Gender is no longer fixed; male and female are fractured into a
kaleidoscope of images.

Fashion's unstable icons also exist in a spooky universe. The land-   17
scape on which transient images take shape participates in the self-
dramatizing style of the performer-icons. Ordinary sunlight is uncommon;
night colors—especially blue and silver—are typical; and neon light, light
that designs itself and comes in brilliantly artificial colors, is everywhere.
Natural settings are extreme—desert sands, deep tropical forests, oceans.
Weather often becomes an actor, buffeting performers and evoking moods.
The settings are hermetic and global at the same time, locked into color
schemes in which colors complement each other but no longer refer to a
natural universe.

It can be a lonely world, but even the loneliness is hypnotically   18
engrossing. One music video visual cliché that provides continuity in the
absence of plot is the shot of the performer simply gazing, often at himself
or herself in the previous shot. In Roxy Music's "The Main Thing," Bryan
Ferry gazes from an armchair at his own just projected image. In Chicago's
"You're the Inspiration," members of the group pretend to practice in a
nostalgically lit loft. Intercut are scenes of couples in wistful moods and
shots of performers brooding individually. It is images like these that
provoke Marsha Kinder to call videos solipsistic.[9]

Their world, however, is also one of cosmic threat and magical power.   19
The self-transforming figures are menaced by conglomerate figures of authority, which often trigger all-powerful fantasy acts of destruction and
salvation. Parents, school principals, teachers, police, and judges provide a
cultural iconography of repression. In Heaven's "Rock School," a principal

---

[7]*fetishistic:* relating to any object that commands unusual or unreasonable admiration or
devotion.

[8]*androgyny:* the state of being both male and female or of having attributes of both sexes.

[9]*solipsistic:* concerned with the self in an exaggerated or extreme way.

wears a stocking mask, and a school guard menaces students with a Doberman. Bon Jovi's "Runaway" features a girl in miniskirted rebellion against her parents (harking back nostalgically to an era when miniskirts could express rebellion). In retaliation against restrictions, she incinerates them with powers reminiscent of those used in the films *Carrie* and *Firestarter*; we're seeing word magic, the power of dream-song, at work. Sammy Hagar, in "I Can't Drive 55," exercises his "right" to drive as fast as he wants to (desire being asserted as a right); he ends up before a judge whose name is Julius Hangman, from whom he escapes by waking up. Videos often play on the overlapping sexual and political iconography of power in Naziesque sadomasochistic fetishes, with symbols connoting total power without moral or social context. In Billy Idol's "Flesh for Fantasy," as he sings "Face to face and back to back / You see and feel my sex attack," the video shows Idol strutting, preening, performing Nazi-like salutes. Cutting into this one-man parade is a sequence of body parts and geometric forms, some of them drawn from the starkly abstract set. Idol's "sex attack" is not directed; while he sometimes looks directly at the camera, the video's "story" is the construction of a movie-picture portrait of Idol in his stormtrooper/S&M outfit.

The National Coalition on Television Violence, among other groups, 20 has criticized the violence, "especially senseless violence and violence between men and women," in music videos. The criticisms are grounded in a history of objections to violence in TV programs. These violent actions are seen by NCTV analysts (and the middle-class consumers who support the pressure group) as virtual prescriptions to violence in life. But it is hard to assign a prescriptive meaning to random violence that is used not as action but as atmosphere and aestheticizer. Even Central American conflict has been retailed in videos by Don Henley and Mick Jagger, as a backdrop for the dislocated performers making a stand amid rubble and military action in which no side stands for anything. George Gerbner, dean of the Annenberg School of Communications at the University of Pennsylvania, has reassessed the implications of violence in music video, saying, "Many videos express a sense of defiance and basic insensitivity, an unemotional excitement." The sensations evoked by video imagery are disconnected from the realm of social responsibility altogether.

. . . But music video's fulcrum position may best be revealed in the 21 way it has traveled beyond television, especially in its use by fashion designers. There, the construction of identity through fashion is at the center of the business. Since 1977, when Pierre Cardin began making video recordings of his fashion shows, designers have been incorporating video into their presentations. Videos now run continuously in retail store windows and on floor displays. For many designers, what sells records already sells fashion, and some foresee a fashion channel. The Cooperative Video

Network, a television news service, already offers a half-hour program, *Video Fashion News*, with three-minute segments on current designer models. Some designers regard video as a primary mode of expression. Norma Kamali now shows her work only on video, both in stores and on programs. One of her best-known works is a video called "The Shoulder Pad Song." Another designer, Lloyd Allen, makes videos that sensually evoke his own fashion career. Designer Bill Tice demands that his contracts for personal appearances include showings of his fashion videos. Kamali, saying that her tapes allow her to approach customers "without interpretation," also thinks that video adds a dimension to her work, because it "extends my fantasy," which of course is the reality of her business.

The marketing crossover is becoming global, a kind of perpetual feedback system. Michael Jackson has begun to sell fashion licenses for his look, and Christie Brinkley, a supermodel who starred in Billy Joel's "Uptown Girl," recently started her own fashion line. The videos undertaken at Perkins Productions are seen as prospective vehicles for extensive cross-promotion, in which a performer may use a prominently featured soap and a designer fragrance. The video may then circulate freely—in hotel lobbies, stores, and on airplane flights as well as on television programs. Video thrills are moving into all aspects of daily life. McDonald's has installed TV monitors at many cash registers, offering tempting images of food and giving shoppers the sense that fast food is part of a high-tech media world, a piece of the fashion action. "Video wallpaper" is being produced for bars and discos, with commercial products deliberately inserted into the montages in a style called by one producer "bordering on subliminal advertising."[10] In general, the boundary between commercial and noncommercial images is eroding. One Manhattan boutique asked General Electric for a copy of a music videoesque commercial to use in its floor display, "for atmosphere," not for any message but simply for its style.

As media image-making comes to dominate electoral politics, music video has invaded that domain too. Consultants to both the Democratic and Republican parties have used music video to explore the mind-set of younger generations. "You can see the tensions among kids rising in their music," said pollster Patrick Caddell, "as they struggle to figure out what they will become." Or, he might have added, what they are. Republican strategist Lee Atwater decided, "We've got a bunch of very confused kids out there." That hasn't stopped politicians from using music videos as ads; videos were also enlisted (without marked results) in voter registration campaigns in 1984. The collision of music video with traditional political mobilizing brings one world—that of the consumer, concerned with individ-

22

23

---

[10]*subliminal advertising*: advertising that appeals directly to the unconscious through the suggestiveness of hidden or deliberately obscured words and images.

ual choice—smack up against another—that of the citizen, charged with responsibility for public decisions. It is this collision that led fashion analyst Gerri Hirshey, noting the passionate investment of the young in their "look," to write: "If one's strongest commitment is to a pair of red stiletto heel pumps, style has a higher price tag than we'd imagine." In one sense, politics is fully ready for music video, if the success of Ronald Reagan—whose popularity rests on a pleasant media image to which "nothing sticks" while critics search in vain for a corresponding reality—is any guide.

The enormous popularity and rapid evolution of music videos give the lie to conspiracy theorists who think commodity culture is force-fed into the gullets of unwilling spectators being fattened for the cultural kill. But it should also chasten free-market apologists who trust that whatever sells is willy-nilly an instrument of democracy. Music videos are powerful, if playful, postmodern art. Their raw materials are aspects of commercial popular culture; their structures those of dreams; their premise the constant permutation of identity in a world without social relationships. These are fascinating and disturbing elements of a form that becomes not only a way of seeing and of hearing but of being. Music videos invent the world they represent. And people whose "natural" universe is that of shopping malls are eager to participate in the process. Watching music videos may be diverting, but the process that music videos embody, echo, and encourage—the constant re-creation of an unstable self—is a full-time job.

Questions for Study and Discussion

1. What is Aufderheide's thesis? Where is it best stated?
2. In what way are music videos "pioneers"?
3. Why are music videos successful? What "mood" do they reflect? What are the several ways in which they achieve that mood?
4. How has Aufderheide organize her essay?
5. What elements of the dream state distinguish the music video? According to one expert, what are the dangers of manufactured fantasy?
6. What kinds of details does Aufderheide use to support her argument? Are some more convincing than others? Explain.
7. In what way is "androgyny" a suitable image for the music video?
8. In paragraph 22, Aufderheide says "In general, the boundary between commercial and noncommercial images is eroding." How does she support this claim? What conclusions, if any, does she draw from it?

Writing Topics

1. The National Coalition on Television Violence has criticized the violence (especially against women) that is portrayed in music videos. The group

fears that these portrayals become prescriptions for violence in real life. Feminists also are concerned that sadomasochistic trappings in some videos are dangerous and reflect an ongoing macho tradition in rock. Are you equally concerned? How do you and your friends interpret the images in music videos?

2. Respond to the following quote from a fashion expert in Aufderheide's essay, "If one's strongest commitment is to a pair of red stiletto heel pumps, style has a higher price tag than we'd imagine."

3. For a week or two pay attention to the ways fashion and other consumer goods are advertised on television and in the malls. How well does Aufderheide's analysis bear out? To what extent has the music video traveled beyond MTV? How is the "mood" Aufderheide describes in her essay reflected in ads?

DONNA WOOLFOLK CROSS

Donna Woolfolk Cross is a linguist and writer who was born in New York in 1947. She received a B.A. from the University of Pennsylvania and an M.A. from UCLA. Once an advertising copywriter, Cross now teaches at Onondaga Community College in New York. She has written extensively on the ways language affects our perception of reality both for the good and for the bad. Her books include *Word Abuse* (1979), *Mediaspeak: How Television Makes Up Your Mind* (1983), *Daddy's Little Girl* (1983) (with her father, novelist William Woolfolk), and *Speaking of Words* (1986), a college text (with James McKillop).

"Sin, Suffer, and Repent" is the opening chapter of *Mediaspeak*. In it Cross uses humor to discuss the detrimental effects of the way reality is portrayed on television soap operas.

Sin, Suffer, and Repent

Soap operas reverse Tolstoy's famous assertion in Anna Karenina *that "Happy families are all alike; every unhappy family is unhappy in its own way." On soaps, every family is unhappy, and each is unhappy in more or less the same way.*
MARJORIE PERLOFF

It is the hope of every advertiser to habituate the housewife to an engrossing narrative whose optimum length is forever and at the same time to saturate all levels of her consciousness with the miracle of a given product, so she will be aware of it all the days of her life and mutter its name in her sleep.
JAMES THURBER

In July 1969, when the entire nation was glued to television sets watching the first man walk on the moon, an irate woman called a Wausau, Wisconsin, TV station to complain that her favorite soap opera was not being shown that day and why was that. The station manager replied, "This is probably the most important news story of the century, something you may never again see the equal of." Unimpressed, the lady replied, "Well, I hope they crash."

One can hardly blame her. For weeks, she had been worrying that Audrey might be going blind, that Alice would marry that scoundrel

Michael, and that Dr. Hardy might not discover his patient Peter to be his long-lost natural son before the boy died of a brain tumor. Suddenly, in the heat of all these crises, she was cut off from all information about these people and forced to watch the comings and goings of men in rubber suits whom she had never met. It was enough to unhinge anybody.

Dedicated watchers of soap operas often confuse fact with fiction.[1] 3 Sometimes this can be endearing, sometimes ludicrous. During the Senate Watergate hearings (which were broadcast on daytime television), viewers whose favorite soap operas were preempted simply adopted the hearings as substitute soaps. Daniel Shorr reports that the listeners began "telephoning the networks to criticize slow-moving sequences, suggesting script changes and asking for the return of favorite witnesses, like 'that nice John Dean.'"

Stars of soap operas tell hair-raising stories of their encounters with 4 fans suffering from this affliction. Susan Lucci, who plays the promiscuous Erica Kane on "All My Children," tells of a time she was riding in a parade: "We were in a crowd of about 250,000, traveling in an antique open car moving ver-r-ry slowly. At that time in the series I was involved with a character named Nick. Some man broke through, came right up to the car and said to me, 'Why don't you give *me* a little bit of what you've been giving Nick?'" The man hung onto the car, menacingly, until she was rescued by the police. Another time, when she was in church, the reverent silence was broken by a woman's astonished remark, "Oh my god, Erica prays!" Margaret Mason, who plays the villainous Lisa Anderson in "Days of Our Lives," was accosted by a woman who poured a carton of milk all over her in the supermarket. And once a woman actually tried to force her car off the Ventura Freeway.

Just as viewers come to confuse the actors with their roles, so too they 5 see the soap image of life in America as real. The National Institute of Mental Health reported that a majority of Americans actually adopt what they see in soap operas to handle their own life problems. The images are not only "true to life"; they are a guide for living.

What, then, is the image of life on soap operas? For one thing, 6 marriage is touted as the *ne plus ultra* of a woman's existence. Living together is not a respectable condition and is tolerated only as long as one of the partners (usually the woman) is bucking for eventual marriage. Casual sex is out; only the most despicable villains engage in it: "Diane has no respect for marriage or any of the values we were brought up with. She's a vicious, immoral woman." Occasionally, a woman will speak out against marriage,

---

[1]Contrary to popular belief, soap operas are not the harmless pastime of lonely house-wives only. Recent surveys show that many high school and college students, as well as many working and professional people, are addicted to soaps. A sizable chunk of the audience is men. Such well-known people as Sammy Davis, Jr., Van Cliburn, John Connally, and Supreme Court Justice Thurgood Marshall admit to being fans of one or more soap operas.

but it's clear that in her heart of hearts she really wants it. Women who are genuinely not interested in marriage do not appear on soap operas except as occasional caricatures, misguided and immature in their thinking. Reporter Martha McGee appeared on "Ryan's Hope" just long enough to titillate the leading man with remarks like, "I don't know if you're my heart's desire, but you're sexy as hell." Punished for this kind of heretical remark, she was last seen sobbing brokenly in a telephone booth.

No, love and marriage still go together like a horse and carriage in soap operas, though many marriages don't last long enough for the couple to put away all the wedding gifts. As Cornell professor Rose Goldsen says, this is a world of "fly-apart marriages, throwaway husbands, throwaway wives." There is rarely any clear logic behind the dissolution of these relationships; indeed, the TV formula seems to be: the happier the marriage, the more perilous the couple's future. A blissful marriage is the kiss of death: "I just can't believe it about Alice and Steve. I mean they were the *perfect* couple, the absolute *perfect* couple!"

Most marriages are not pulled apart by internal flaws but by external tampering—often by a jealous rival: "C'mon, Peter. Stay for just one more drink. Jan won't mind. And anyway, the night's still young. Isn't it nice to be together all nice and cozy like this?"

Often the wife has willfully brought this state of affairs on herself by committing that most heinous of all offenses: neglecting her man. "NHM" almost always occurs when the woman becomes too wrapped up in her career. Every time Rachel Corey went to New York City for a weekend to further her career as a sculptress, her marriage tottered. At this writing, Ellen Dalton's marriage to Mark appears to be headed for big trouble as a result of her business trip to Chicago:

ERICA: I warned you, Ellen, not to let your job interfere with your marriage.
ELLEN: I have tried to do my best for my marriage *and* my job . . . Mark had no right to stomp out of here just now.
ERICA: Don't you understand? He just couldn't take anymore.
ELLEN: What do you mean?
ERICA: It's not just the trip to Chicago that Mark resents. It's your putting your job before having a family.
ELLEN: I demand the right to be treated as an equal. I don't have to apologize because I don't agree to have a child the minute my husband snaps his fingers. I'm going to Chicago like a big girl and I'm going to do the job I was hired to do. (stalks out the door)
ERICA: (musing to herself) Well, I may be old-fashioned, but that's no way to hold onto your man.

Career women do appear frequently on soap operas, but the ones who are romantically successful treat their careers as a kind of sideline. Female cardiologists devote fifteen years of their lives to advanced medical training, then spend most of their time in the hospital coffee shop. One man remarked to a career woman who was about to leave her job, "Oh, Kate, you'll miss working. Those long lunches, those intimate cocktail hours!" Women residents apparently schedule all their medical emergencies before dinnertime, because if they should have to stay late at the hospital, it's the beginning of the end for their marriages. It's interesting to speculate how they might work this out:

> NURSE: Oh my God, Dr. Peterson, the patient's hemorrhaging!
> DR. PETERSON: Sorry, nurse, it'll have to wait. If I don't get my meat loaf in by a quarter to six, it'll never be ready before my husband gets home.

Husbands, weak-minded souls, cannot be expected to hold out against the advances of any attractive woman, even one for whom they have contempt, if their wives aren't around. Meatloafless, they are very easily seduced. The clear suggestion is that they could hardly have been expected to do otherwise:

> Well, after all, Karen, you weren't around very much during that time. It's not surprising that Michael turned to Pat for a little comfort and understanding.

If, in the brief span of time allotted to them, a couple manage to have intercourse, the woman is certain to become pregnant. Contraception on soap operas is such a sometime thing that even the Pope could scarcely object to it. The birth rate on soaps is eight times as high as the United States birthrate; indeed it's higher than the birthrate of any under-developed nation in the world. This rabbitlike reproduction is fraught with peril. One recent study revealed that out of nineteen soap opera pregnancies, eight resulted in miscarriages and three in death for the mother. Rose Goldsen has estimated that the odds are 7 to 10 against any fetus making it to full term, worse if you include getting through the birth canal. Women on soap operas miscarry at the drop of a pin. And of course, miscarriages are rarely caused by any defect with mother or baby: again, external forces are to blame. Often, miscarriage is brought on by an unappreciative or unfaithful mate. For example, on "Another World," Alice, the heroine, suffered a miscarriage when her husband visited his ex-wife Rachel. One woman lost her baby because her husband came home drunk. This plot twist is no doubt particularly appealing to women viewers because of the instant revenge visited upon the transgressing mate. They can fantasize about similar punishment for husbandly malfeasance in their own lives—and about his inevitable guilt and repentance:

> HUSBAND: (stonily) Jennifer, these potatoes are too gluey. I can't eat this!
> WIFE: (clutches her belly) Oh no!
> HUSBAND: What? What is it?
> WIFE: It's the baby! Something's wrong—call the doctor!
> HUSBAND: Oh my God, what have I done?
> *Later, at the hospital:*

DOCTOR: I'm sorry, Mr. Henson, but your wife has lost the baby.

HUSBAND: (brokenly) I didn't know, I didn't know. How could I have attacked her potatoes so viciously with her in such a delicate condition!

DOCTOR: Now, now. You mustn't blame yourself. We still don't know exactly what causes miscarriages except that they happen for a complicated set of physical and emotional reasons.

HUSBAND: Oh, thank you, Doctor.

DOCTOR: Of course, carping about the potatoes couldn't have *helped*.

Miscarriage is effective as a punishment because it is one of the very 13 worst things that can happen to a woman on a soap opera. In the world of soaps, the one thing every good and worthwhile woman wants is a baby. Soap operas never depict childless women as admirable. These "real people" do not include women like Katharine Hepburn, who once announced that she never wanted to have children because "the first time the kid said no to me, I'd kill it!" Childless women are either to be pitied, if there are physical reasons that prevent them from getting pregnant, or condemned, if they are childless by choice.

Second only to neglecting her man in her hierarchy of female crime is 14 having an abortion. No admirable character *ever* gets an abortion on a soap opera. Occasionally, however, a virtuous woman will consider it, usually for one of two reasons: she doesn't want the man she loves to feel "trapped" into marrying her; or she has been "violated" by her husband's best friend, a member of the underworld, or her delivery boy, who may also be her long-lost half brother. But she always "comes around" in the end, her love for "the new life growing inside me" conquering her misgivings. If the baby should happen to survive the perilous journey through the birth canal (illegitimate babies get miscarried at a far higher rate than legitimate ones), she never has any regrets. Why should she? Babies on soap operas never drool, spit up, or throw scrambled eggs in their mothers' faces. Babyhood (and its inevitable counterpart, motherhood) is "sold" to American women as slickly as soap. Kimberly, of "Ryan's Hope," is so distressed when she finds out she is pregnant that she runs away from home. She has the baby, prematurely, while alone and unattended on a deserted houseboat. It is a difficult and dangerous birth. But once the baby is born, Kimberly is all maternal affection. "Where is she?" she shouts. "Why won't they let me see my little girl?" By the end of the day, she announces, "If anything happens to this baby, I don't know what I'll do!"

Mothers are never tired, sleepless, or discouraged. Radiant, they boast 15 about the baby's virtues:

Well, he's just the smartest, best little baby in the whole wide world!

He looks just like his daddy—those big blue eyes, that enchanting smile!

Look at her little hands and feet. Have you ever seen anything more adorable! And she's good as gold—really, no trouble at all. She's Mommy's precious little princess, aren't you, darling?

One producer of a (now defunct) soap opera actually wanted, as a   16
promotion gimmick for one of the plotlines, to give away one baby a week as a prize! The idea was abandoned only because of the lack of cooperation from adoption agencies.

After the age of about ten months, children are of no interest in soap   17
operas unless they are hit by a car or contract a fever of unknown origin, in which case they occasion a lot of hand-wringing and pious sentiments from all the adults. If the producers cannot arrange any such misfortune, the rule is that children are not to be seen or heard. Having a young child around would interrupt the endless raveling of the sleeve of romance. It won't do to have little Bobby need to go on the potty or have his nose blown in the middle of the adults' complicated lives, which have, as one critic says, "all the immediacy of a toothache and the urgency of a telegram."

You may hear a good deal of pious talk about a young child's need for   18
stability and love, but usually only when a couple's marriage is on the rocks. Children on soap operas still go to sleep at night having no idea whether one or both of their parents will be around in the morning—a situation which brings to mind Lady Bracknell's remark in *The Importance of Being Earnest*: "Losing one parent might be regarded as a misfortune; losing two seems like carelessness."

Children on soap operas are secondary. Because they serve largely as   19
foils for the adult characters, their development does not follow the slow, steady pattern of the rest of the action.[2] Their growth is marked by a series of sudden and unsettling metamorphoses as new and older juvenile actors assume the role. On Tuesday, little Terence is cooing in his cradle. On Monday next, he is the terror of the Little League. By Thursday, his voice begins to change. Friday night is his first date. He wakes up on Monday a drug-crazed teenager, ready to be put to use creating heartbreak and grief for his devoted mother and her new husband. He stays fifteen years old for

---

[2]The pace of many soap operas has picked up considerably in the last few years, as audience surveys have revealed a strong viewer interest in action-and-adventure stories. Before 1980, however, plot movement on the soaps was glacierlike, and on the earliest soaps, almost imperceptible. James Thurber claimed that it took one male character in a soap three days to get an answer to the simple question. "Where have you been?" He wrote, "If . . . you missed an automobile accident that occurred on a Monday broadcast, you could pick it up the following Thursday and find the leading woman character still unconscious and her husband still moaning over her beside the wrecked car. In one program . . . [a character] said, 'It doesn't seem possible to me that Ralph Wilde arrived here only yesterday.' It should not have seemed possible to anyone else, either, since Ralph Wilde had arrived, as mortal time goes, thirteen days before."

about two to five years (more if he managed to get into lots of scrapes), and then one day he again emerges from the off-camera cocoon transformed into a full-fledged adult, with all the rights, privileges, pain, and perfidy of that elite corps. And so the cycle continues.

Under the surface of romantic complications, soap operas sell a vision 20
of morality and American family life, of a society where marriage is the highest good, sex the greatest evil, where babies are worshiped and abortion condemned, where motherhood is exalted and children ignored. It is a vision of a world devoid of social conflict. There are hardly any short-order cooks, bus drivers, mechanics, construction workers, or farmers on soap operas. Blue-collar problems do not enter these immaculate homes. No one suffers from flat feet or derrière spread from long hours spent at an un-rewarding or frustrating job. The upwardly mobile professionals who populate soap operas love their work, probably because they are hardly ever at it—one lawyer clocked in at his office exactly once in three months. Their problems are those of people with time on their hands to covet the neigh-bor's wife, track down villains, betray friends, and enjoy what one observer has called "the perils of Country Club Place."

Questions for Study and Discussion

1. Cross begins her essay with an anecdote. Why do you think she chose this beginning? How effective is it?

2. In what ways do soap fans confuse reality and the soaps? What are the potentially harmful effects of this confusion?

3. What information is included in the footnotes to this article? Why has Cross presented this information separately?

4. How is the ideal woman depicted on soap operas?

5. What figure of speech does Cross use in paragraph 19? Why has she presented this information this way? Does it detract from or enhance her argument? Explain.

6. What are some of the contradictions in the vision of American family life depicted on soaps? In what ways is it a world "devoid of social conflict"?

7. What would you say is Cross's attitude toward the soap operas she warns us against? Cite examples from the text to support your answer.

Writing Topics

1. If you are a soap fan, you will be in a good position to decide whether or not Cross has made an accurate assessment of the soaps. Do you agree with her analyses? What new directions have the soaps taken since this article was published in 1983?

2. Are soaps the only villains, or does much of television news and drama misrepresent reality? Write an essay in which you discuss the ways other television programming misrepresents "real life." Before you begin writing you may want to reread Pat Aufderheide's article (pp. 579–86) and Neil Postman's article (pp. 414–424).

Human history becomes more and more a race between education and catastrophe.

H. G. WELLS

While it is unlikely that we could ever extinguish life in an absolute manner, we are eliminating species at a rate never before known in historic time and in a manner never known in biologic time.

THOMAS BERRY

More than any other time in history, mankind faces a crossroads. One path leads to despair and utter hopelessness. The other, to total extinction. Let us pray we have the wisdom to choose correctly.

WOODY ALLEN

The Abundance
of Nature

ANNIE DILLARD

Annie Dillard was born in Pittsburgh, Pennsylvania, in 1945 and earned both her B.A. and M.A. from Hollins College. Dillard now teaches at Wesleyan University in Middletown, Connecticut. It is her years living in the Roanoke Valley of Virginia, though, that inspired her Pulitzer Prize–winning *Pilgrim at Tinker Creek* (1974). Among her other works are *Tickets for a Prayer Wheel* (1974), *Holy the Firm* (1978), *Teaching a Stone to Talk* (1982), *Living by Fiction* (1982), *Encounters with Chinese Writers* (1984), and *Writing Life* (1989).

In the following essay, from *Teaching a Stone to Talk*, Dillard recounts her experience in a village on the Napo River. Dillard's charm as a writer is her ability to enable the reader to see what she sees and share her sense of wonder.

In the Jungle

Like any out-of-the-way place, the Napo River in the Ecuadorian jungle seems real enough when you are there, even central. Out of the way of *what*? I was sitting on a stump at the edge of a bankside palm-thatch village, in the middle of the night, on the headwaters of the Amazon. Out of the way of human life, tenderness, or the glance of heaven? 1

A nightjar in a deep-leaved shadow called three long notes, and hushed. The men with me talked softly in clumps: three North Americans, four Ecuadorians who were showing us the jungle. We were holding cool drinks and idly watching a hand-sized tarantula seize moths that came to the lone bulb on the generator shed beside us. 2

It was February, the middle of summer. Green fireflies spattered lights across the air and illumined for seconds, now here, now there, the pale 3 trunks of enormous, solitary trees. Beneath us the brown Napo River was rising, in all silence; it coiled up the sandy bank and tangled its foam in vines that trailed from the forest and roots that looped the shore.

Each breath of night smelled sweet, more moistened and sweet than any kitchen, or garden, or cradle. Each star in Orion seemed to tremble and stir with my breath. All at once, in the thatch house across the clearing behind us, one of the village's Jesuit priests began playing an alto recorder, playing a wordless song, lyric, in a minor key, that twined over the village clearing, that caught in the big trees' canopies, muted our talk on the bankside, and wandered over the river, dissolving downstream. 4

This will do, I thought. This will do, for a weekend, or a season, or a home. 5

Later that night I loosed my hair from its braids and combed it smooth—not for myself, but so the village girls could play with it in the morning. 6

We had disembarked at the village that afternoon, and I had slumped on some shaded steps, wishing I knew some Spanish or some Quechua so I could speak with the ring of little girls who were alternately staring at me and smiling at their toes. I spoke anyway, and fooled with my hair, which they were obviously dying to get their hands on, and laughed, and soon they were all braiding my hair, all five of them, all fifty fingers, all my hair, even my bangs. And then they took it apart and did it again, laughing, and teaching me Spanish nouns, and meeting my eyes and each other's with open delight, while their small brothers in blue jeans climbed down from the trees and began kicking a volleyball around with one of the North American men. 7

Now, as I combed my hair in the little tent, another of the men, a free-lance writer from Manhattan, was talking quietly. He was telling us the tale of his life, describing his work in Hollywood, his apartment in Manhattan, his house in Paris. . . . "It makes me wonder," he said, "what I'm doing in a tent under a tree in the village of Pompeya, on the Napo River, in the jungle of Ecuador." After a pause he added, "It makes me wonder why I'm going *back*." 8

The point of going somewhere like the Napo River in Ecuador is not to see the most spectacular anything. It is simply to see what is there. We are here on the planet only once, and might as well get a feel for the place. We might as well get a feel for the fringes and hollows in which life is lived, for the Amazon basin, which covers half a continent, and for the life that—there, like anywhere else—is always and necessarily lived in detail: on the tributaries, in the riverside villages, sucking this particular white-fleshed guava in this particular pattern of shade. 9

What is there is interesting. The Napo River itself is wide (I mean   10
wider than the Mississippi at Davenport) and brown, opaque, and smeared
with floating foam and logs and branches from the jungle. White egrets
hunch on shoreline deadfalls and parrots in flocks dart in and out of the
light. Under the water in the river, unseen, are anacondas—which are
reputed to take a few village toddlers every year—and water boas, stingrays,
crocodiles, manatees, and sweet-meated fish.

Low water bares gray strips of sandbar on which the natives build tiny   11
palm-thatch shelters, arched, the size of pup tents, for overnight fishing
trips. You see these extraordinarily clean people (who bathe twice a day in
the river, and whose straight black hair is always freshly washed) paddling
down the river in dugout canoes, hugging the banks.

Some of the Indians of this region, earlier in the century, used to sleep   12
naked in hammocks. The nights are cold. Gordon MacCreach, an American explorer in these Amazon tributaries, reported that he was startled to
hear the Indians get up at three in the morning. He was even more startled,
night after night, to hear them walk down to the river slowly, half asleep,
and bathe in the water. Only later did he learn what they were doing: they
were getting warm. The cold woke them; they warmed their skins in the
river, which was always ninety degrees; then they returned to their hammocks and slept through the rest of the night.

The riverbanks are low, and from the river you see an unbroken wall   13
of dark forest in every direction, from the Andes to the Atlantic. You get a
taste for looking at trees: trees hung with the swinging nests of yellow
troupials, trees from which ant nests the size of grain sacks hang like black
goiters, trees from which seven-colored tanagers flutter, coral trees, teak,
balsa and breadfruit, enormous emergent silk-cotton trees, and the pale-
barked *samona* palms.

When you are inside the jungle, away from the river, the trees vault   14
out of sight. It is hard to remember to look up the long trunks and see the
fans, strips, fronds, and sprays of glossy leaves. Inside the jungle you are
more likely to notice the snarl of climbers and creepers round the trees'
boles, the flowering bromeliads and epiphytes in every bough's crook, and
the fantastic silk-cotton tree trunks thirty or forty feet across, trunks
buttressed in flanges of wood whose curves can make three high walls of a
room—a shady, loamy-aired room where you would gladly live, or die.
Butterflies, iridescent blue, striped, or clear-winged, thread the jungle paths
at eye level. And at your feet is a swath of ants bearing triangular bits of
green leaf. The ants with their leaves look like a wide fleet of sailing
dinghies—but they don't quit. In either direction they wobble over the
jungle floor as far as the eye can see. I followed them off the path as far as I
dared, and never saw an end to ants or to those luffing chips of green they
bore.

Unseen in the jungle, but present, are tapirs, jaguars, many species of   15
snake and lizard, ocelots, armadillos, marmosets, howler monkeys, toucans
and macaws and a hundred other birds, deer, bats, peccaries, capybaras,
agoutis, and sloths. Also present in this jungle, but variously distant, are
Texaco derricks and pipelines, and some of the wildest Indians in the world,
blowgun-using Indians, who killed missionaries in 1956 and ate them.

Long lakes shine in the jungle. We traveled one of these in dugout   16
canoes, canoes with two inches of freeboard, canoes paddled with machete-
hewn oars chopped from buttresses of silk-cotton trees, or poled in the
shallows with peeled cane or bamboo. Our part-Indian guide had cleared
the path to the lake the day before; when we walked the path we saw where
he had impaled the lopped head of a boa, open-mouthed, on a pointed stick
by the canoes, for decoration.

The lake was wonderful. Herons, egrets, and ibises plodded the   17
sawgrass shores, kingfishers and cuckoos clattered from sunlight to shade,
great turkeylike birds fussed in dead branches, and hawks lolled overhead.
There was all the time in the world. A turtle slid into the water. The boy in
the bow of my canoe slapped stones at birds with a simple sling, a rubber
thong and leather pad. He aimed brilliantly at moving targets, always, and
always missed; the birds were out of range. He stuffed his sling back in his
shirt. I looked around.

The lake and river waters are as opaque as rain-forest leaves; they are   18
veils, blinds, painted screens. You see things only by their effects. I saw the
shoreline water roil and the sawgrass heave above a thrashing *paichi*, an
enormous black fish of these waters; one had been caught the previous week
weighing 430 pounds. Piranha fish live in the lakes, and electric eels. I
dangled my fingers in the water, figuring it would be worth it.

We would eat chicken that night in the village, and rice, yucca,   19
onions, beets, and heaps of fruit. The sun would ring down, pulling
darkness after it like a curtain. Twilight is short, and the unseen birds of
twilight wistful, uncanny, catching the heart. The two nuns in their dazzling
white habits—the beautiful-boned young nun and the warm-faced old—
would glide to the open cane-and-thatch schoolroom in darkness, and start
the children singing. The children would sing in piping Spanish, high-
pitched and pure; they would sing "Nearer My God to Thee" in Quechua,
very fast. (To reciprocate, we sang for them "Old MacDonald Had a Farm";
I thought they might recognize the animal sounds. Of course they thought
we were out of our minds.) As the children became excited by their own
singing, they left their log benches and swarmed around the nuns, hopping,
smiling at us, everyone smiling, the nuns' faces bursting in their cowls, and
the clear-voiced children still singing, and the palm-leafed roofing stirred.

The Napo River: it is not out of the way. It is *in* the way, catching   20
sunlight the way a cup catches poured water; it is a bowl of sweet air, a basin
of greenness, and of grace, and, it would seem, of peace.

Questions for Study and Discussion

1. Dillard makes repeated references to trees in her works. What, for her, is their significance?

2. What is the purpose of Dillard's exposing the "Manhattan writer's" thoughts?

3. Why is Dillard's essay more than just a travel brochure? Does the Napo River sound like somewhere you would want to go to spend time? Explain.

4. Dillard presents both ends of a spectrum—from nature's untouched beauty to the ravages of human materialism. How does her tone change in writing of each of these extremes? Cite examples of Dillard's diction to support your answer.

5. Dillard uses a metaphor in the last paragraph. Explain how the metaphor works. In what way is it a fitting conclusion to her essay?

Writing Topics

1. In an essay, use descriptive techniques, similar to Dillard's, to describe the aspects of a place you find beautiful despite its downfalls.

2. In what ways has nature suffered the effects of human materialism? Is there any way in which it can be said that the losses have been "worth it"?

ROBERT FINCH

Born in 1943, Robert Finch, a resident of West Brewster, Massachusetts, combines poetic prose with a scientific eye in sharing the mysteries of seaside nature with his readers. In *Common Ground: A Naturalist's Cape Cod* (1981) and *Primal Place* (1983), collections of essays, Finch reveals the natural world of Cape Cod with wit, wisdom, and keen observation. "Snowy," like Finch's other works, first appeared in "Soundings," his weekly nature column that runs in four Cape Cod newspapers. In addition to his writing, Finch is the director of publications for the Cape Cod Museum of Natural History.

In "Snowy," Finch records a longed-for but unlikely encounter with a snowy owl on the icy, wind-swept Nauset Beach just north of Orleans, Massachusetts.

Snowy

She sat and watched me across the barren sandy plain with silent 1 indifferent eyes, as though I were a piece of driftwood. A flock of winter dunlins swept and crisscrossed the marsh behind her, emphasizing her immobility. She was a large bird, more gray than white at a distance, and highly marked—the signs of a female. Her breast was flecked with lateral black markings like those of a great horned owl, and the wing and back feathers were also tipped in black. The head markings started in a widow's peak, then carried back around and down like sideburns over the ear openings. The male, by contrast, is usually smaller and much less marked, often nearly pure white.

This was the first time I had ever seen a snowy owl in the wild and all 2 these details and comparisons did not surface in my mind until much later. At the time I was only aware of watching, and being watched by, one of the most beautiful creatures I had ever seen.

Seeing a snowy on Cape Cod is largely a matter of being in the right 3 place at the right time. These occasional arctic visitors to the Cape's winter beaches are not that uncommon, but their appearances vary greatly from year to year. During so-called 'flight years,' up to fifty or more of these great white birds, largest of all our North American owls, have been reported here.

Ornithologists still debate over the precise causes of these en masse 4 southern migrations, which seem to occur roughly every five years. Still, they appear to be definitely linked with the cyclical abundance of the owls' arctic prey, mainly lemmings and northern hares. An exceptionally snowy winter on their home grounds might also make the rodent food supply less available and thus drive some of the population south. I don't believe that this winter was a flight year, at least not here, but even in off years one or two of these birds can be expected along our outer shores.

Over Christmas week a snowy had been reported on Nauset Beach a couple of miles north of the Orleans parking lot. One morning after New Year's I drove down to have a look. It was a semi-raw day, overcast, with the wind north-northeast and cold when you headed into it. The ocean had a magnificent, bruised look about it, and pawed at the upper beach with dark, polished claws.

I took the landward route north, walking inside the wall of low dunes up toward the inlet. I saw where a recent northeaster had washed over their crest and spilled considerable beach sand down their backsides, burying the beach grass and then crusting over in the cold, so that the sand continually broke through as I walked over it, as salt ice will on a frozen marsh.

There was not much to be seen on the way out, and I knew that my expectations were based a great deal on faith. With its keen hearing and daytime vision, the owl might easily spot me and slip away long before I saw it. There was also no guarantee it would be on the Orleans spit in the first place. It might have flown across the inlet to Coast Guard Beach, or out to New Island, created a few winters ago when the ocean made a new inlet into Nauset Harbor and sheared off the southern end of the Eastham spit. It might even be gone completely, or have been shot—though it is now a protected species.

I remembered reading that during the great flight year of 1926–27 over 2300 snowy owls were shot and kept as trophies in the United States alone. One of the greatest difficulties for modern conservationists, I think, is to rightly conceive how much we have lost. We trudge so far today to see so little, that the result is often a strangely pathetic elation.

When I came to where the dunes tapered down and ended, the beach spread out into a large, wide, bare plain separating ocean and marsh. Here in summer is a large least tern colony, the area posted and protected from human interference. One owl could wreak unbelievable damage on such a colony, but snowys almost always leave for the north again by March. On this same plain in other winters I have sometimes surprised a flock of a thousand gulls, standing in solemn congregation, and have run among them like a banshee, turning the air into a gray and white screaming turbulence. But today there was nothing, only an empty vastness and a darkening sky.

I stood atop the last dune, where I had an unobstructed view of the sands as far north as the inlet, and looked through my glasses for several minutes. Nothing. My ears began to grow cold and my hopes flagged. I was about to leave and scanned the barren plain one last time. By chance I noticed near a slight rise a little gray post the top of which suddenly cocked over. It was the owl, slouched against a lump of sand with a tuft of grass growing on its top, about two hundred yards off on the inlet side. I walked obliquely but openly northeast across the plain toward the ocean side until I was slightly north of the bird, some hundred yards away, forcing it to look into the wind at me. Then I sat down and looked at the owl carefully through field glasses for the first time.

11   The owl indolently turned her head from side to side and then deliberatly rested her gaze on me. She stared down the barrels of my binoculars with heavily-lidded yellow eyes. The masked face resembled that of a hockey goalie, a ritual mask of hidden strength and violence.

12   The snowy owl's peculiarly lidded eyes—"bedroom eyes," my father calls them—give it a sleepy, dreamy aspect, causing most people who see one for the first time to assume that it is sick or exhausted. It also has a peculiar stance. Unlike most owls, a snowy tends not to perch upright, but leans or slouches over against the ground, almost touching its breast. It will sometimes fish along a stream, lying at full length on its side beside the bank, utterly motionless until a fish swims by and a hidden talon darts out with lightning speed. When at rest everything about the snowy owl suggests sloth and unawareness; it is a beautiful ruse.

13   On their breeding grounds in the far north these snowy owls are said to possess a formidable and somewhat eerie repertoire of hoots, grunts and barks. But like wise men in strange lands they keep silent during their erratic southern migrations.

14   In their normal range these birds are not exclusively coastal residents, but it was suddenly clear to me why, when they visit the Cape, they prefer our outer beaches to our woodlands. Here everything conspired to remind her of her northern home. The small sand hummock, in the lee of which she now rested, was a sandy reproduction of the frost-heaved rises, called *pingaluks*, which dot her native tundra. On these pingaluks the owls nest and scan the moss- and lichen-covered terrain for prey. New Island, out in the inlet, was said to have a healthy population of voles, a highly acceptable substitute for arctic lemmings in her diet.

15   Geese and ducks fed in the water of the marshes beyond her, as they do in the summer-thawed lakes and swamps of the arctic. Earlier that week a friend of mine had watched the owl rip apart the carcass of a Canada goose with her powerful talons and beak on the banks of the island. She had probably found the goose dead, although these four-pound predators have been known to kill, and even fly off with, full-grown geese twice their own weight.

16   Under her unyielding gaze the plain was transformed into a frozen northern tundra, the sand into windswept snow. The parking lot twenty

minutes to the south withdrew a thousand miles away, and I, not the owl, became the intruder and temporary visitor.

Keeping my binoculars trained on her, I began to inch slowly toward 17 her on my seat, hoping that this unconventional or low-profile approach might distract her. If this sounds like a stupid ploy, it probably was; but I had seen it work with other birds. At any rate, the owl let me play my game for only about thirty feet and then lifted into the air on great, white creamy wings, drifting swiftly and effortlessly south for a hundred yards, where she came to rest on an old beached timber.

This time I crawled toward her on my stomach, hoping to keep below 18 her line of sight. But she soon rose and again sailed south, this time slipping down behind the low dune from which I had first spotted her.

Obviously she was not interested in escaping me, which she could 19 have done easily by flying across the inlet. It seemed I was merely disturbing some comfortable psychological distance within which she would not tolerate me—about two hundred and fifty feet, it seemed. I wondered if this distance might bear some relationship to the effective and hereditary range of an Eskimo arrow.

This time, however, the dune that hid us from each other was high 20 enough so that I might approach her unseen. I headed swiftly toward it, wondering if her keen ears would pick up my footsteps on the hardened sand; but no owl rose. Finally I reached the dune, crawled carefully up its side, peered through the grass on its ridge and saw—nothing. The owl was gone. It was as though the dune were a magician's cloak that had been spread momentarily over a beautiful women, and then had been withdrawn to reveal her vanished!

I was certain I had been outfoxed—or outowled; that the bird had 21 slipped away between the dunes, skimming low and unseen out over the sands and down the beach as marsh hawks will do. And then I realized that I was watching a remarkable piece of avian camouflage.

Behind the dune and parallel to the beach was a row of upended 22 wooden pallets placed in the sand as windbreaks for many rows of nearly buried but still visible beach grass plantings. On the top of one of these pallets, perched so that her darker, gray-streaked sides lined up with two of the vertical, wind-bleached boards, sat the owl. At first glance she had looked exactly like an extension of the pallet.

Had the ploy been intentional? I was ready to believe it. But I did not 23 have time to ponder the question. As soon as I realized what it was I was looking at and established eye contact with the owl, she once again lifted into the air with no visible effort. This time she passed deliberately and directly over me, heading with slow, deep wingbeats into the wind. As she passed not thirty feet above my head, I had a glimpse of sheer, cool competence sailing by on pure milk-white wings nearly five feet across. The yellow eyes peered down at me as though I might be a mouse or a lemming, and I was very glad I wasn't.

The owl continued north nearly two hundred yards, then stooped   24
and went into a long low sweet glide that gradually slowed to a halt. Stretching out her talons before her, she came to rest in the precise spot by the low hummock where I had first spotted her a half-hour before. Again she turned her head casually and looked at me with faintly contemptuous indifference, as much as to say, "Well, we can play this game all day, if *you* care to."

But I had taken up enough of her time. Somehow I had the feeling   25
that I had not seen a snowy owl so much as been seen by one. Certain encounters always turn out that way, whatever the intention. It seems a matter of character. I turned and headed south, back to the car, leaving her to her undisturbed and unchallenged isolation.

Questions for Study and Discussion

1. What was Finch's first impression of the snowy owl? Why didn't he begin his essay with those impressions instead of the details and comparisons that occurred to him later?

2. What is a "flight year"? What was remarkable about the flight year of 1926–27?

3. In paragraph 8, Finch mentions the "strangely pathetic elation" experienced by the modern conservationist. In your own words, what does he mean by this?

4. Finch devotes several paragraphs to descriptions other than the owl. Why do you think he includes this information? Could he have done without them?

5. Finch uses several figures of speech in "Snowy." Identify a few of them and describe how they are used to enhance his essay.

6. In what ways does the Cape compare to the owl's arctic home?

7. What qualities of the owl does Finch include? What attitude toward the owl is revealed in Finch's presentation of her qualities?

8. What does Finch mean by his use of the word "character" in the final paragraph?

Writing Topics

1. Write about a sighting of your own in the wild. How do you plan to organize your essay? Along with the technical information on the creature you describe, include a description of the landscape and the environment you encounter.

2. Finch says that one of the greatest difficulties for modern conservationists is to conceive of "how much we have lost." In the face of this loss, what unique pleasures are possible for modern conservationists? What are the special pleasures, if any, that you derive from your encounters with animals in the wild?

WILLIAM LONGGOOD

Born in 1917, Longgood began his extensive career writing for radio, then became a reporter for the *Newark News* and the *New York World Telegram and Sun*. In the mid-sixties he free-lanced, writing stories mostly about nature and the environment. Since 1968 he has been *The New York Times* Cape Cod correspondent and a teacher of feature writing at the New School for Social Research in New York City.

Longgood has said that his "greatest writing satisfaction" came from his book *The Queen Must Die and Other Affairs of Bees and Men* (1985), from which the following essay was taken. "The real and enduring reward is when readers write or say it has given them a new perspective on another form of life." Among Longgood's many other works are *The Poisons in Your Food* (1960) and *The Darkening Land* (1972). Longgood also contributes to numerous magazines.

In "The Analogous Bee," Longgood provides a detailed description of activity in the hive and describes the similarities and differences between bees and people.

The Analogous Bee

The bees are flying today and that is not according to the book. Bees usually don't fly unless the air temperature reaches fifty-five degrees Fahrenheit. This is a winter day, in late December, and the temperature is under fifty. The sun must have been shining directly on the hives and driven the temperature up inside, deceiving the bees. It must be a bit of a shock to them to venture outside, expecting benign warmth, and getting a blast of chilling air. It may be that the bees were not deceived but are merely being perverse. Bees almost never follow the rules laid down for them by their tenders. Beekeepers are forever grumbling about "those damned bees." But we have only ourselves to fault because we wrote the book, not the bees. We created our own false expectations.

Apparently, once outside and on the wing, the bees decide to complete the business that made them leave the hives. The snow is soiled with their droppings. It is startling how many brown spots there are; they dapple the snow and white hives as if someone had flicked a wet paintbrush.

Every couple of weeks the bees need a "cleansing flight" in the winter to rid themselves of accumulated wastes or they may come down with a severe bowel disease that, left untreated, can cause a colony to weaken or lead to heavy loss of life. Worker bees are so incredibly clean that they will risk death by flying in cold weather rather than befoul their home. Only the boorish males are guilty of soiling the hive, and there are not likely to be any of them in the winter colony.

When there is a long spell of cold and the bees can't get out to relieve 4 themselves, on the first warm day they fairly explode from the hive; it is not unusual to see the snow splashed almost solid brown for several hundred feet in all directions. Generally bees do not go far from the hive on cleansing flights. This is sensible on their part. If they went any distance and the temperature suddenly dropped, they probably wouldn't make it back.

Bees, unlike humans, have a sound sense of their life mission. They 5 work hard in the spring, summer, and fall, and in the winter they loaf, or take it fairly easy, like retirees at leisure. But that is not an altogether accurate statement. The bees that work so diligently from April through September are probably not the same ones that more or less knock off during the cold months. In the summer the field bees work so hard that their average life is only four to six weeks. Their wings beat about two hundred times a minute, which musicians say is the key of C sharp below middle C. The fragile wings become ragged and torn, and finally wear out altogether so that they no longer will support flight. An experienced beekeeper can usually tell a bee's approximate age by the condition of her wings.

Hive values are such that when a bee no longer can fly and be an asset 6 to the colony, she will remove herself from the hive rather than be a burden. If she lacks the grace to commit suicide, or to depart of her own will, she will be kicked out of the hive or killed outright by those she served so faithfully while she could. Human societies have no monopoly on ingratitude and treachery.

There is little sentiment in a hive. The motto, indelibly and invisibly 7 etched in bee genes, is "work or die." Every female bee, except the queen, is expected to give full measure in hard labor for her keep, and the queen has her own biological obligations. This is a completely socialistic society, the direct opposite of the competitiveness and spirit of individual advantage that governs most human societies. No goods are owned privately. The collective wealth is the pooled honey in the combs and dedication to a common goal. The individual bee owns nothing, and owes full allegiance to the colony. In exchange she is provided a place to live and work while she is a productive member of the community.

Many human communes could have used bees as their models, but 8 such experiments seldom come off. Humans rarely are capable of the self-sacrifice and dedication of bees. On the other hand, bees are not wracked and diverted by sexual desire as humans are, and such wholehearted fidelity to ceaseless work may be a questionable virtue: is this drive motivated by pleasure or compulsion? Is it socially useful or only for personal gain?

In a beehive every effort is directed toward the common good. Every individual, except the queen, is expendable, but under certain circumstances even she is eliminated in a dark bee plot euphemisitcally known as "supersedure," which usually involves the queen's murder by her own daughters, but more about that later. The most ordinary colony is better organized than the most efficient man-made factory. And yet, even these models of nature's organizational efficiency and industry are sometimes less than perfect, beset by such human failings as sloppy workmanship, useless endeavor, and what appears to be poor management or faulty judgment. Bee colonies, like human societies, vary in the standards they set for themselves and in the life-styles they adopt. Some prosper while others barely manage to struggle along, existing on the bee equivalent of welfare provided by their keeper, and some fail altogether, often victims of their own shortcomings.

Worker bees make up almost the entire population of the hive. These are females that lack the ability to produce a fertilized egg necessary to generate a female worker bee like themselves. There is only one queen to a hive, although there have been cases in which a second or even a third have been tolerated, but this is so rare that it suggests some kind of perversion of nature's intentions.

The queen's only function is to lay eggs, as many as two thousand a day. Indeed, she is known as an "egg-laying machine." Completing the makeup of the hive are those comic-tragic, but vital, lusting clowns, the drones. There are relatively few of them in each hive and the number may represent less a necessity than a bee equivalent of conspicuous consumption. Drones are males conceived from unfertilized eggs laid by the queen. Their sole function is to mate with virgin queens, and most live and die without ever fulfilling this mission. The drone lives a life of bullying, nonproductive ease, like the worst free-loading relative, unless summoned to duty, in which case he may sacrifice his life, probably to his own surprise and dismay. For their intemperate ways, the surviving males eventually get their comeuppance in a bloody fall rite known as the "massacre of the drones," a drama that will unfold here in its place.

A worker bee's existence is regulated by a biological timetable, which is one of the profound mysteries that govern a hive. During her brief life, she performs many diverse chores: scavenger, nurse, producer of wax, molder of honeycomb, housekeeper, forager, fanner, water carrier, undertaker, guard, warrior, and finally, martyr. She passes from one of these roles to another, depending on age and experience. A bee is like a worker in industry who is rewarded for her experience and length of service with successive raises and promotions, until the employee is considered more liability than asset and the employer seeks to unload her and bring in a successor who is young, inexperienced, and inexpensive; success often bears a price tag of diminishing returns.

For the bee, indignity rarely accompanies old age. As noted pre- 13 viously, she either resolves the problem by working herself to death or is dispatched by her younger sisters. The climax role for a worker is that of forager, or field bee, gathering pollen and the nectar that will be converted into honey; but at the same time she is expected to perform other, often menial, hive duties. Efficiency and hive demands and not personal status or job assignment determine her roles throughout life and into death. We know of no prima donnas or egotists in the hive. The function of a bee is always contingent on community need.

Scientists believe that bees, next to humans, have the most elaborate 14 social structure and specialization of labor in the animal kingdom, one far more complex and sophisticated than formerly thought. Only ants and termites approach bees in the intricacy of their societies.

For the multiple, specialized tasks a worker bee performs, she has no 15 training or prior knowledge that we are aware of, but takes to each succeeding role naturally. How does this extraordinary progression come about? Is it genetic transference? Some unidentified dietary substance or secretion that is responsible? Is it due to an abiding animus that dwells secretly in the hive, invisible and indecipherable, and provides this ability, this profound intelligence, that we observe without comprehending?

The mystery is compounded because each phase of a bee's develop- 16 ment occurs on a fairly predictable timetable. One thing we know, as observers, is that from the moment of a bee's "birth" she is destined to work until she no longer can do so, but no one has the least notion what dictates this pattern of behavior. The queen and drones are equally condemned by the same invisible forces, although their roles differ. We watch the miracle that unfolds from their various labors with wonder but with little or no understanding of the origins or imperatives.

The colony, as noted, is ruled by one fixed law: those who do not or 17 cannot work cannot remain in the hive and be a drain on its resources. There is no charity, no exception, no compassion. If a bee is born deformed, too weak, or not willing to work, it is ruthlessly killed or thrown out of the hive. The same fate awaits those who become too old or infirm to work. It also applies to victims of mishaps and heroines maimed in combat while guarding the hive against invaders.

There is, for the worker bee, no honorable retirement, no pension, no 18 welfare program or reward for service to the community, no compromising of hive values. The individual bee means nothing. Only the continuing life of the colony counts. This is the first commandment of the hive—a manifestation of that mysterious and dispassionate force that guides all bee life.

It is called, with little understanding of what it means, "the spirit of the hive."

The primary rule is inflexible: work or die.   19

Questions for Study and Discussion

1. According to Longgood, in what ways are bees and humans similar? In what ways do they differ? Can you add to his lists?

2. What is a "cleansing flight"?

3. Several times in his essay Longgood makes the point that bees must "work or die." Why do you think he makes this point so often? Is it necessary or does it weaken his essay?

4. Longgood has written this essay to compare humans and bees, yet he does not mention humans until paragraph 5. Why has he waited so long to mention them? What is the effect on the reader?

5. How does Longgood make the transition from one paragraph to another in his essay? Is his method effective? Explain.

Writing Topics

1. In paragraph 8, Longgood asks "wholehearted fidelity to ceaseless work may be a questionable virtue: is this drive motivated by pleasure or compulsion? Is it socially useful or only for personal gain?" In an essay address the issue of "workaholicism" with Longgood's questions in mind.

2. Longgood suggests that bees conduct their business in a "completely socialistic society." Is his definition of socialism complete? What aspects, if any, of a socialistic system are lacking in the hive? What rules of the hive would not be included in the ideal socialistic society?

JANE VAN LAWICK–GOODALL

Born in 1934 in London, Jane van Lawick–Goodall has spent most of her life living a dream she says she has had since she was a child of eight. Since 1968, van Lawick–Goodall has studied the behavior of chimpanzees in the Gombe Stream Game Preserve in East Africa. Her observations, which have made her the foremost authority on chimpanzees and other primates, have appeared in books for both the scientific community and general readers.

Interestingly, van Lawick–Goodall had no formal training for her career, but began with on-the-job training with renowned anthropologist Dr. Louis S. B. Leakey. "He wanted someone with a mind uncluttered and unbiased by theory who would make the study for no other reason than a real desire for knowledge: and, in addition, someone with a sympathetic understanding of animals," van Lawick–Goodall once explained. Among her many published works are *Primate Behavior* (1965); *My Friends, the Wild Chimpanzees* (1967); *The Bush Baby*, a story of the author's son (1972); and *In the Shadow of Man* (1971), from which the following selection is taken.

In "*First Observations*," the author includes insights into the behavior of the chimpanzee culture. However, she also includes reflections on the behavior of the observer.

First Observations

For about a month I spent most of each day either on the Peak or overlooking Mlinda Valley where the chimps, before or after stuffing themselves with figs, ate large quantities of small purple fruits that tasted, like so many of their foods, as bitter and astringent as sloes or crab apples. Piece by piece, I began to form my first somewhat crude picture of chimpanzee life.

The impression that I had gained when I watched the chimps at the msulula tree of temporary, constantly changing associations of individuals within the community was substantiated. Most often I saw small groups of four to eight moving about together. Sometimes I saw one or two chimpanzees leave such a group and wander off on their own or join up with a different association. On other occasions I watched two or three small groups joining to form a larger one.

Often, as one group crossed the grassy ridge separating the Kasekela 3
Valley from the fig trees in the home valley, the male chimpanzee, or
chimpanzees, of the party would break into a run, sometimes moving in an
upright position, sometimes dragging a fallen branch, sometimes stamping
or slapping the hard earth. These charging displays were always accompanied by loud pant-hoots and afterward the chimpanzee frequently would
swing up into a tree overlooking the valley he was about to enter and sit
quietly, peering down and obviously listening for a response from below. If
there were chimps feeding in the fig trees they nearly always hooted back, as
though in answer. Then the new arrivals would hurry down the steep slope
and, with more calling and screaming, the two groups would meet in the fig
trees. When groups of females and youngsters with no males present joined
other feeding chimpanzees, usually there was none of this excitement; the
newcomers merely climbed up into the trees, greeted some of those already
there, and began to stuff themselves with figs.

While many details of their social behavior were hidden from me by 4
the foliage, I did get occasional fascinating glimpses. I saw one female, newly
arrived in a group, hurry up to a big male and hold her hand toward him.
Almost regally he reached out, clasped her hand in his, drew it toward him,
and kissed it with his lips. I saw two adult males embrace each other in
greeting. I saw youngsters having wild games through the treetops, chasing
around after each other or jumping again and again, one after the other,
from a branch to a springy bough below. I watched small infants dangling
happily by themselves for minutes on end, patting at their toes with one
hand, rotating gently from side to side. Once two tiny infants pulled on
opposite ends of a twig in a gentle tug-of-war. Often, during the heat of
midday or after a long spell of feeding, I saw two or more adults grooming
each other, carefully looking through the hair of their companions.

At that time of year the chimps usually went to bed late, making their 5
nests when it was too dark to see properly through binoculars, but sometimes they nested earlier and I could watch them from the Peak. I found that
every individual, except for infants who slept with their mothers, made his
own nest each night. Generally this took about three minutes: the chimp
chose a firm foundation such as an upright fork or crotch, or two horizontal
branches. Then he reached out and bent over smaller branches onto this
foundation, keeping each one in place with his feet. Finally he tucked in the
small leafy twigs growing around the rim of his nest and lay down. Quite
often a chimp sat up after a few minutes and picked a handful of leafy twigs,
which he put under his head or some other part of his body before settling
down again for the night. One young female I watched went on and on
bending down branches until she had constructed a huge mound of green-
ery on which she finally curled up.

I climbed up into some of the nests after the chimpanzees had left 6
them. Most of them were built in trees that for me were almost impossible to

climb. I found that there was quite complicated interweaving of the branches in some of them. I found, too, that the nests were never fouled with dung; and later, when I was able to get closer to the chimps, I saw how they were always careful to defecate and urinate over the edge of their nests, even in the middle of the night.

During that month I really came to know the country well, for I often went on expeditions from the Peak, sometimes to examine nests, more frequently to collect specimens of the chimpanzees' food plants, which Bernard Verdcourt had kindly offered to identify for me. Soon I could find my way around the sheer ravines and up and down the steep slopes of three valleys—the home valley, the Pocket, and Mlinda Valley—as well as a taxi driver finds his way about the main streets and byways of London. It is a period I remember vividly, not only because I was beginning to accomplish something at last, but also because of the delight I felt in being completely by myself. For those who love to be alone with nature I need add nothing further; for those who do not, no words of mine could ever convey, even in part, the almost mystical awareness of beauty and eternity that accompanies certain treasured moments. And, though the beauty was always there, those moments came upon me unaware: when I was watching the pale flush preceding dawn; or looking up through the rustling leaves of some giant forest tree into the greens and browns and black shadows that occasionally ensnared a bright fleck of the blue sky; or when I stood, as darkness fell, with one hand on the still-warm trunk of a tree and looked at the sparkling of an early moon on the never still, sighing water of the lake. 7

One day, when I was sitting by the trickle of water in Buffalo Wood, pausing for a moment in the coolness before returning from a scramble in Mlinda Valley, I saw a female bushbuck moving slowly along the nearly dry streambed. Occasionally she paused to pick off some plant and crunch it. I kept absolutely still, and she was not aware of my presence until she was little more than ten yards away. Suddenly she tensed and stood staring at me, one small forefoot raised. Because I did not move, she did not know what I was—only that my outline was somehow strange. I saw her velvet nostrils dilate as she sniffed the air, but I was downwind and her nose gave her no answer. Slowly she came closer, and closer—one step at a time, her neck craned forward—always poised for instant flight. I can still scarcely believe that her nose actually touched my knee; yet if I close my eyes I can feel again, in imagination, the warmth of her breath and the silken impact of her skin. Unexpectedly I blinked and she was gone in a flash, bounding away with loud barks of alarm until the vegetation hid her completely from my view. 8

It was rather different when, as I was sitting on the Peak, I saw a leopard coming toward me, his tail held up straight. He was at a slightly lower level than I, and obviously had no idea I was there. Ever since arrival in Africa I had had an ingrained, illogical fear of leopards. Already, while 9 working at the Gombe, I had several times nearly turned back when, crawling through some thick undergrowth, I had suddenly smelled the rank smell of cat. I had forced myself on, telling myself that my fear was foolish, that only wounded leopards charged humans with savage ferocity.

On this occasion, though, the leopard went out of sight as it started to 10 climb up the hill—the hill on the peak of which I sat. I quickly hastened to climb a tree, but halfway there I realized that leopards can climb trees. So I uttered a sort of halfhearted squawk. The leopard, my logical mind told me, would be just as frightened of me if he knew I was there. Sure enough, there was a thudding of startled feet and then silence. I returned to the Peak, but the feeling of unseen eyes watching me was too much. I decided to watch for the chimps in Mlinda Valley. And, when I returned to the Peak several hours later, there, on the very rock which had been my seat, was a neat pile of leopard dung. He must have watched me go and then, very carefully, examined the place where such a frightening creature had been and tried to exterminate my alien scent with his own.

As the weeks went by the chimpanzees became less and less afraid. 11 Quite often when I was on one of my food-collecting expeditions I came across chimpanzees unexpectedly, and after a time I found that some of them would tolerate my presence provided they were in fairly thick forest and I sat still and did not try to move closer than sixty to eighty yards. And so, during my second month of watching from the Peak, when I saw a group settle down to feed I sometimes moved closer and was thus able to make more detailed observations.

It was at this time that I began to recognize a number of different 12 individuals. As soon as I was sure of knowing a chimpanzee if I saw it again, I named it. Some scientists feel that animals should be labeled by numbers—that to name them is anthropomorphic—but I have always been interested in the *differences* between individuals, and a name is not only more individual than a number but also far easier to remember. Most names were simply those which, for some reason or other, seemed to suit the individuals to whom I attached them. A few chimps were named because some facial expression or mannerism reminded me of human acquaintances.

The easiest individual to recognize was old Mr. McGregor. The crown 13 of his head, his neck, and his shoulders were almost entirely devoid of hair, but a slight frill remained around his head rather like a monk's tonsure. He was an old male—perhaps between thirty and forty years of age (the longevity record of a captive chimp is forty-seven years). During the early months of my acquaintance with him, Mr. McGregor was somewhat belligerent. If I accidentally came across him at close quarters he would threaten me with an upward and backward jerk of his head and a shaking of branches before climbing down and vanishing from sight. He reminded me, for some reason, of Beatrix Potter's old gardener in *The Tale of Peter Rabbit*.

Ancient Flo with her deformed, bulbous nose and ragged ears was   14
equally easy to recognize. Her younger offspring at that time were two-year-
old Fifi, who still rode everywhere on her mother's back, and her juvenile
son, Figan, who was always to be seen wandering around with his mother
and little sister. He was then about six years old; it was approximately a year
before he would attain puberty. Flo often traveled with another old mother,
Olly. Olly's long face was also distinctive; the fluff of hair on the back of her
head—though no other feature—reminded me of my aunt, Olwen. Olly, like
Flo, was accompanied by two children, a daughter younger than Fifi, and
an adolescent son about a year older than Figan.

Then there was William, who, I am certain, must have been Olly's   15
blood brother. I never saw any special signs of friendship between them, but
their faces were amazingly alike. They both had long upper lips that
wobbled when they suddenly turned their heads. William had the added
distinction of several thin, deeply etched scar marks running down his
upper lip from his nose.

Two of the other chimpanzees I knew well by sight at that time were   16
David Graybeard and Goliath. Like David and Goliath in the Bible, these
two individuals were closely associated in my mind because they were very
often together. Goliath, even in those days of his prime, was not a giant, but
he had a splendid physique and the springy movements of an athlete. He
probably weighed about one hundred pounds. David Graybeard was less
afraid of me from the start than were any of the other chimps. I was always
pleased when I picked out his handsome face and well-marked silvery beard
in a chimpanzee group, for with David to calm the others, I had a better
chance of approaching to observe them more closely.

Before the end of my trial period in the field I made two really exciting   17
discoveries—discoveries that made the previous months of frustration well
worth while. And for both of them I had David Graybeard to thank.

One day I arrived on the Peak and found a small group of chimps just   18
below me in the upper branches of a thick tree. As I watched I saw that one
of them was holding a pink-looking object from which he was from time to
time pulling pieces with his teeth. There was a female and a youngster and
they were both reaching out toward the male, their hands actually touching
his mouth. Presently the female picked up a piece of the pink thing and put
it to her mouth: it was at this moment that I realized the chimps were eating
meat.

After each bite of meat the male picked off some leaves with his lips   19
and chewed them with the flesh. Often, when he had chewed for several
minutes on this leafy wad, he spat out the remains into the waiting hands of
the female. Suddenly he dropped a small piece of meat, and like a flash the
youngster swung after it to the ground. Even as he reached to pick it up the
undergrowth exploded and an adult bushpig charged toward him. Screaming, the juvenile leaped back into the tree. The pig remained in the open,

snorting and moving backward and forward. Soon I made out the shapes of three small striped piglets. Obviously the chimps were eating a baby pig. The size was right and later, when I realized that the male was David Graybeard, I moved closer and saw that he was indeed eating piglet.

For three hours I watched the chimps feeding. David occasionally let   20
the female bite pieces from the carcass and once he actually detached a small piece of flesh and placed it in her outstretched hand. When he finally climbed down there was still meat left on the carcass; he carried it away in one hand, followed by the others.

Of course I was not sure, then, that David Graybeard had caught the   21
pig for himself, but even so, it was tremendously exciting to know that these chimpanzees actually ate meat. Previously scientists had believed that although these apes might occasionally supplement their diet with a few insects or small rodents and the like they were primarily vegetarians and fruit eaters. No one had suspected that they might hunt larger mammals.

It was within two weeks of this observation that I saw something that   22
excited me even more. By then it was October and the short rains had begun. The blackened slopes were softened by feathery new grass shoots and in some places the ground was carpeted by a variety of flowers. The Chimpanzees' Spring, I called it. I had had a frustrating morning, tramping up and down three valleys with never a sign or sound of a chimpanzee. Hauling myself up the steep slope of Mlinda Valley I headed for the Peak, not only weary but soaking wet from crawling through dense undergrowth. Suddenly I stopped, for I saw a slight movement in the long grass about sixty yards away. Quickly focusing my binoculars I saw that it was a single chimpanzee, and just then he turned in my direction. I recognized David Graybeard.

Cautiously I moved around so that I could see what he was doing. He   23
was squatting beside the red earth mound of a termite nest, and as I watched I saw him carefully push a long grass stem down into a hole in the mound. After a moment he withdrew it and picked something from the end with his mouth. I was too far away to make out what he was eating, but it was obvious that he was actually using a grass stem as a tool.

I knew that on two occasions casual observers in West Africa had seen   24
chimpanzees using objects as tools: one had broken open palm-nut kernels by using a rock as a hammer, and a group of chimps had been observed pushing sticks into an underground bees' nest and licking off the honey. Somehow I had never dreamed of seeing anything so exciting myself.

For an hour David feasted at the termite mound and then he wan-   25
dered slowly away. When I was sure he had gone I went over to examine the mound. I found a few crushed insects strewn about, and a swarm of worker termites sealing the entrances of the nest passages into which David had obviously been poking his stems. I picked up one of his discarded tools and carefully pushed it into a hole myself. Immediately I felt the pull of several

termites as they seized the grass, and when I pulled it out there were a number of worker termites and a few soldiers, with big red heads, clinging on with their mandibles. There they remained, sticking out at right angles to the stem with their legs waving in the air.

Before I left I trampled down some of the tall dry grass and constructed   26
a rough hide—just a few palm fronds leaned up against the low branch of a tree and tied together at the top. I planned to wait there the next day. But it was another week before I was able to watch a chimpanzee "fishing" for termites again. Twice chimps arrived, but each time they saw me and moved off immediately. Once a swarm of fertile winged termites—the princes and princesses, as they are called—flew off on their nuptial flight, their huge white wings fluttering frantically as they carried the insects higher and higher. Later I realized that it is at this time of year, during the short rains, when the worker termites extend the passages of the nest to the surface, preparing for these emigrations. Several such swarms emerge between October and January. It is principally during these months that the chimpanzees feed on termites.

On the eighth day of my watch David Graybeard arrived again,   27
together with Goliath, and the pair worked there for two hours. I could see much better: I observed how they scratched open the sealed-over passage entrances with a thumb or forefinger. I watched how they bit the ends off their tools when they became bent, or used the other end, or discarded them in favor of new ones. Goliath once moved at least fifteen yards from the heap to select a firm-looking piece of vine, and both males often picked three or four stems while they were collecting tools, and put the spares beside them on the ground until they wanted them.

Most exciting of all, on several occasions they picked small leafy twigs   28
and prepared them for use by stripping off the leaves. This was the first recorded example of a wild animal not merely *using* an object as a tool, but actually modifying an object and thus showing the crude beginnings of tool*making*.

Previously man had been regarded as the only toolmaking animal.   29
Indeed, one of the clauses commonly accepted in the definition of man was that he was a creature who "made tools to a regular and set pattern." The chimpanzees, obviously, had not made tools to any set pattern. Nevertheless, my early observations of their primitive toolmaking abilities convinced a number of scientists that it was necessary to redefine man in a more complex manner than before. Or else, as Louis Leakey put it, we should by definition have to accept the chimpanzee as Man.

Questions for Study and Discussion

1. In paragraph 7, van Lawick–Goodall is her most personal, describing her delight at being alone. Why do you suppose she has included this passage?

2. Throughout her essay, she refers to species and places unknown to the general reader. What is the effect of her use of this vocabulary on the reader? Should she have explained all her terms as she went along?

3. What is the point of van Lawick–Goodall's narrative about the leopard in paragraphs 9 and 10?

4. The author explains that some scientists prefer to refer to animals by number. They claim that naming animals under observation is anthropomorphic. How does van Lawick–Goodall argue against this point? Which argument is more convincing?

5. What are some of the characteristics of chimpanzees that van Lawick–Goodall names? Which do you find the most surprising? the least surprising? Explain.

6. What two new discoveries does van Lawick–Goodall make? Why are they exciting to her?

7. What is the problem with defining chimpanzees as toolmakers?

Writing Topics

1. Van Lawick–Goodall includes many of the elements of a good narrative, such as purpose, point of view, plot, figures of speech, and suspense, in her account of chimpanzee behavior. Observe a creature of your choice, either at home or in the wild. Then, using van Lawick–Goodall's essay as a guide, write an account of it in narrative form. Be sure to review the elements of good narration before you begin.

2. In the last paragraph of her essay, van Lawick–Goodall says that her discovery of the toolmaking tendencies of chimpanzees has convinced scientists that man (previously believed to be the only toolmaker) may have to be redefined "in a more complex way." Faced with the challenge, how would you define man in a way that would distinguish him from all other species? You may want to discuss your definition with teachers and classmates in the fields of anthropology and zoology.

3. Van Lawick–Goodall says, "My early observations of their primitive toolmaking abilities convinced a number of scientists that it was necessary to redefine man in a more complex manner than before. Or else, as Louis Leakey put it, we should by definition have to accept the chimpanzee as Man." What are your views on this issue? Is it legitimate to insist on the distinction between man and the other species? Or are such efforts based on chauvinistic attitudes that have no basis in real science?

JOHN McPHEE

As much as any wild creature, the grizzly evokes feelings of terror and awe. His keen sense of survival and crushing strength make him a formidable enemy for those foolish enough to underestimate him and a respected adversary for those who are not. John McPhee counts himself among the latter, especially after spending a few days in the grizzly's turf. Born in 1931 in Princeton, New Jersey, McPhee attended the university there, then moved to New York to work as a television writer before settling in as a staff writer for the *New Yorker*. Although McPhee is strictly a city man, he is comfortable in the woods and has written extensively on nature and the environment in such books as *The Pine Barrens* (1968) and *Coming into the Country* (1977).

In "The Grizzly," McPhee conveys a sense of the awesome power of the bear without ever attempting to romanticize the animal. Instead of pretending some kind of silent nobility or cunning on the part of the grizzly, McPhee makes it clear that the bear's trump card in the game of survival is his power to kill, swiftly and without hesitation.

The Grizzly

We passed first through stands of fireweed, and then over ground that   1
was wine-red with the leaves of bearberries. There were curlewberries, too, which put a deep-purple stain on the hand. We kicked at some wolf scat, old as winter. It was woolly and white and filled with the hair of a snowshoe hare. Nearby was a rich inventory of caribou pellets and, in increasing quantity as we moved downhill, blueberries—an outspreading acreage of blueberries. Fedeler stopped walking. He touched my arm. He had in an instant become even more alert than he usually was, and obviously apprehensive. His gaze followed straight on down our intended course. What he saw there I saw now. It appeared to me to be a hill of fur. "Big boar grizzly," Fedeler said in a near-whisper. The bear was about a hundred steps away, in the blueberries, grazing. The head was down, the hump high. The immensity of muscle seemed to vibrate slowly—to expand and contract, with the grazing. Not berries alone but whole bushes were going into the bear. He was big for a barren-ground grizzly. The brown bears of Arctic

Alaska (or grizzlies; they are no longer thought to be different) do not grow to the size they will reach on more ample diets elsewhere. The barren-ground grizzly will rarely grow larger than six hundred pounds.

"What if he got too close?" I said. 2

Fedeler said, "We'd be in real trouble." 3

"You can't outrun them," Hession said. 4

A grizzly, no slower than a racing horse, is about half again as fast as 5
the fastest human being. Watching the great mound of weight in the blueberries, with a fifty-five-inch waist and a neck more than thirty inches around, I had difficulty imagining that he could move with such speed, but I believed it, and was without impulse to test the proposition. Fortunately, a light southerly wind was coming up the Salmon valley. On its way to us, it passed the bear. The wind was relieving, coming into our faces, for had it been moving the other way the bear would not have been placidly grazing. There is an old adage that when a pine needle drops in the forest the eagle will see it fall; the deer will hear it when it hits the ground; the bear will smell it. If the boar grizzly were to catch our scent, he might stand on his hind legs, the better to try to see. Although he could hear well and had an extraordinary sense of smell, his eyesight was not much better than what was required to see a blueberry inches away. For this reason, a grizzly stands and squints, attempting to bring the middle distance into focus, and the gesture is often misunderstood as a sign of anger and forthcoming attach. If the bear were getting ready to attack, he would be on four feet, head low, ears cocked, the hair above his hump muscle standing on end. As if that message were not clear enough, he would also chop his jaws. His teeth would make a sound that would carry like the ringing of an axe.

One could predict, but not with certainty, what a grizzly would do. 6
Odds were very great that one touch of man scent would cause him to stop his activity, pause in a moment of absorbed and alert curiosity, and then move, at a not undignified pace, in a direction other than the one from which the scent was coming. That is what would happen almost every time, but there was, to be sure, no guarantee. The forest Eskimos fear and revere the grizzly. They know that certain individual bears not only will fail to avoid a person who comes into their country but will approach and even stalk the trespasser. It is potentially inaccurate to extrapolate the behavior of any one bear from the behavior of most, since they are both intelligent and independent and will do what they choose to do according to mood, experience, whim. A grizzly that has ever been wounded by a bullet will not forget it, and will probably know that it was a human being who sent the bullet. At sight of a human, such a bear will be likely to charge. Grizzlies hide food sometimes—a caribou calf, say, under a pile of scraped-up moss—and a person the bear might otherwise ignore might suddenly not be ingored if the person were inadvertently to step into the line between the food cache and the bear. A sow grizzly with cubs, of course, will charge

anything that suggests danger to the cubs, even if the cubs are nearly as big as she is. They stay with their mother two and a half years.

None of us had a gun. (None of the six of us had brought a gun on the trip.) Among nonhunters who go into the terrain of the grizzly, there are several schools of thought about guns. The preferred one is: Never go without a sufficient weapon—a high-powered rifle or a shotgun and plenty of slug-loaded shells. The option is not without its own inherent peril. A professional hunter, some years ago, spotted a grizzly from the air and—with a client, who happened to be an Anchorage barber—landed on a lake about a mile from the bear. The stalking that followed was evidently conducted not only by the hunters but by the animal as well. The professional hunter was found dead from a broken neck, and had apparently died instantly, unaware of danger, for the cause of death was a single bite, delivered from behind. The barber, noted as clumsy with a rifle, had emptied his magazine, missing the bear with every shot but one, which struck the grizzly in the foot. The damage the bear did to the barber was enough to kill him several times. After the corpses were found, the bear was tracked and killed. To shoot and merely wound is worse than not to shoot at all. A bear that might have turned and gone away will possibly attack if wounded.

Questions for Study and Discussion

1. In only a few pages, McPhee conveys a sense of the incredible strength of the grizzly. What kinds of details does he include to bring the reader face to face with the bear's power?
2. Why is it difficult to make generalizations about the grizzly's behavior?
3. What is the point of McPhee's narrative? Whom do you think he intends as his audience?
4. How would you characterize McPhee and his comrades? Are they hunters, scientists, or something else? After everything McPhee tells us about the grizzly, why do he and his friends venture into bear territory without weapons? Is their reasoning convincing?
5. McPhee says, "The forest Eskimos fear and revere the grizzly." Why? What do you suspect is McPhee's attitude toward the bear? Cite examples of his diction to support your answer.

Writing Topics

1. Would you venture into grizzly territory knowing what you now know? Why or why not? What kinds of dangerous adventures have you had? What forces impelled you? What kinds of emotions did you experience before, during, and after the adventure?

2. What do the animals see when they watch us? Keep a journal account of the behavior of a particular person you know. Reread the essays in this section as guides to the kind of information to include. What conclusions do you reach? What differences, if any, do you see between the studies of people and animals?

E. E. CUMMINGS

e. e. (Edward Estin) cummings (1894–1962) was born in Cambridge, Massachusetts, and graduated from Harvard in 1915. While cummings' poems and stories are exceptional for their unconventional visual appearance and whimsical style, they are also well-loved for their joyful celebration of love and nature. His fifteen volumes of poetry include *Tulips & Chimneys* (1923) and *95 Poems* (1958). *The Enormous Room* (1922), a prose chronicle of his internment in France during World War I, is acknowledged to be one of the finest books written about war.

cummings' interest in the visual appearance of his poems on the page can be traced to his artistic talents. His paintings and drawings have been exhibited widely in one-man shows both here and abroad. A two-volume edition of his poetic works, *Complete Poems, 1913–1962*, appeared in 1972.

In "O sweet spontaneous earth," cummings gives voice to nature's response to the self-conscious attempts of science, philosophy, and religion to explain its mysteries.

O sweet spontaneous earth

O sweet spontaneous
earth how often have
the
doting

     fingers of   5
prurient philosophers pinched
and
poked

thee
, has the naughty thumb   10
of science prodded
thy

---

beauty   . how
often have religions taken
thee upon their scraggy knees   15
squeezing and

buffeting thee that thou mightest conceive
gods
    (but
true   20

to the incomparable
couch of death thy
rhythmic
lover

    thou answerest   25

them only with

      spring)

Questions for Study and Discussion

1. What is the question the three disciplines ask of earth in cummings's poem? What is the meaning of earth's reply?

2. Does the use of alliteration have any special function in cummings's poem, or is it used merely to create a rhythm?

3. What familiar family situation does cummings evoke through the personification of philosophy, science, and religion? What role do they play? What is the role of earth? How appropriate is this image for the purpose of his poem?

4. What is "the incomparable couch of death" cummings refers to in his poem?

5. What is the dominant impression of cummings's poem? Is it morbid, playful, or something else? Choose examples of his diction to support your answer.

Writing Topics

1. In an essay discuss your views on the role of science, religion, and philosophy in unraveling the mysteries of the universe. Which, if any, is best suited to the task? How would cummings respond to your conclusions?

2. Choose a poem of your liking that also celebrates the glory of spring. How does the poet evoke a sense of wonder and renewal? Do his or her views coincide with cummings's or do they express a different world view?

The Attack on Nature

DAVID QUAMMEN

David Quammen was born in Cincinnati, Ohio, in 1948, and graduated from Yale University in 1970. After studying literature at Oxford University as a Rhodes Scholar, he nurtured his interests in the natural world by pursuing graduate studies in zoology at the University of Montana. Quamman has written two novels and his essays appear regularly in such diverse magazines as *Esquire*, *Audubon*, and *Rolling Stone*. Quammen currently writes a column for *Outside* magazine titled "Natural Acts," which also is the title for a collection of his essays on science.

    In the following essay from *Natural Acts*, Quammen uses a light touch as an improbable means of prophesizing the extinction of the human race.

The Big Goodbye

    There are extinctions, and then again there are Extinctions.	1

    Inevitably every once in a while a single species passes quietly into	2
oblivion. At other and much rarer times large groups of species—entire
genera and families of animals and plants, entire civilizations of interrelated
organisms—disappear suddenly in a great catastrophic wipeout. During the
Permian Extinction, for instance, roughly 225 million years ago, half of all
the families of marine creatures (which were then the predominant form of
life) died away in a brief few million years. No one knows why, and the
question is still debated, but most likely the cause was habitat loss, when the
rich oceanic shells were left high and dry by falling sea levels. The Cretaceous Extinction, 65 million years ago, was equally drastic and even more
puzzling: After more than 100 million years of unrivaled success, the
dinosaurs rather abruptly disappeared, as did the various flying and fishlike
reptiles, and many more groups of marine invertebrates. Again there is no
proven explanation but the suggested causes include global temperature

change, reversal of the polar magnetic field, and the impact of a hypothetical asteroid six miles across which raised such an atmospheric dust cloud that no sunlight could penetrate and no green plants could grow for ten years. Finally and most dramatically, the Late Quaternary Extinction, during which more than a million species of living things perished within just a century. This quickest of all mass extinctions occurred (according to the local time system) in the span 1914–2014 A.D. The main cause was once again habitat loss, and the agent of that loss was the killer–primate *Homo sapiens*, now itself extinct. *Sapiens* unaccountably violated the first rule of a successful parasite: modernization. *Sapiens* was suicidally rapacious.

That's the way it will look to some being on the planet Tralfamadore   3
with an idle interest in the paleontology of Earth. Life has existed on this mudball for about 3½ billion years, and we are just now in the midst of what looks to shape up as the third great mass extinction of species. This episode threatens to be larger in consequence than the Permian and the Cretaceous and the other major die-offs put together. One-fifth of all forms of earthly organism could be gone within thirty years.

After that, things would get ugly for the survivors. Global climatic   4
conditions would change, with accelerated buildup of carbon dioxide in the atmosphere, disruption of wind currents, cycles of vastly increasing erosion despite decreasing rainfall, breakdown of natural processes for the purification of fresh water, warmer average temperatures, the eventual failure of domestic food crops—and that would only be the beginning. We have all heard about snail darters and whooping cranes until our eyes glaze over, but what in fact is at issue here is the overall biological stability of a world. The Late Quaternary Extinction wants you.

In a broad sense the LQE began about 400 years ago, with the   5
European age of empires, when humankind reached a stage smart enough to sail all over the planet and still stupid enough to kill much of what we found when we got there. Dutch settlers arrived on the island of Mauritius in 1598 and the dodo was extinct by 1681. On Bering Island off Alaska, the last Steller's sea cow was killed by a party of Russian scalers in 1768. Icelandic hunters killed a lonely pair of great auk in June of 1844, and no great auk has been seen alive since. But these were just the preliminaries. In a stricter sense the start of the Late Quaternary Extinction can be set, with precision that is artificial but emblematic, as September 1, 1914. That day the last passenger pigeon, name of Martha, died in the Cincinnati Zoo.

Martha is significant because her species—despite incredibly intense   6
hunting pressure against them—succumbed chiefly to loss of habitat. The passenger pigeon, which had once been perhaps the most numerous bird on earth, needed huge, continuous areas of oak and beechnut forest for its gregarious patterns of feeding and nesting. With the great hardwood forests east of the Mississippi cut back to small pockets, the passenger pigeon had

no more chance of surviving than, literally, a fish out of water. And at this end of the century the same thing is happening, say eminent biologists like Thomas Lovejoy and Norman Myers, to hundreds of species—*poof:* gone forever—each year.

Eventual extinction is as natural for every species as eventual death is 7 for every individual creature. What matters for biological stability are (1) patterns of extinction, and (2) rate of extinction. As long as extinctions occur no more rapidly than new species arise, and are not so clustered in particular areas as to destroy the conditions from which new species *can* arise, then ecosystems remain stable and healthy. While the Cretaceous Extinction was in full swing, paleontologists estimate, the rate of disappearance was one species every thousand years. Between 1600 and 1900 A.D., with our improved capabilities for travel and hunting, mankind eliminated roughly seventy-five species of known mammals and birds. Since 1900 we have killed off another seventy-five species of conspicuous animal—just less than one per year. For a single new species of bird to diverge from another species probably takes at least 10,000 years.

A bad balance, but growing still worse: Norman Myers, having stud- 8 ied the problem for years from his base in Nairobi, figures we might say goodbye to *one million* further species by the year 2000. That amounts to about 100 species driven extinct every day.

Numbers, yes. Boggling, dulling numbers. Finally it doesn't sound 9 real. *What are all these vanishing species? Where are they? And what's killing them?*

But it is real. They are, for the most part, inconspicuous but ecolog- 10 ically crucial organisms: plants, insects, fungi, crustaceans, mites, nematode worms. They inhabit those ecological zones that are richest in living diversity but have been least investigated by man: estuaries, shallow oceanic shells, coral reefs, and in particular, tropical rainforests. They are being extinguished, like the passenger pigeon, by human activities that alter their habitats.

We are poisoning the estuaries with our industrial and municipal 11 wastes, we are drilling for oil and spilling it on the ocean shells, but most egregious and most critical is the destruction of tropical rainforests. Rainforests comprise only 6 percent of the Earth's land surface, yet may hold as many as half the Earth's total number of species, and two-thirds of all species of plant. The rainforests of Central America and the Amazon are today being mown down for pulpwood, and to graze cattle on the cleared land so that American hamburger chains can buy cheap beef. Rainforests of the Philippines, Indonesia and other parts of tropical Asia are being lumbered, to fill the demand for plywood and exotic hardwoods in more affluent countries. In West Africa the forests are falling chiefly to slash-and-burn agricultural methods by starving peasants who can't feed their growing families off small permanent fields, partly because world oil demand has priced them out of any chance for petroleum–based fertilizer. Altogether the planet may be losing 3,000 acres of rainforest—and four irreplaceable living species—every hour. We are gaining rosewood and mahogany trinkets, profligate use of personal autos, and the Big Mac.

There is complicity involved here, more than a share for us all. Norman Myers says that "the main problem for declining wildlife is not the person with conscious intent to exploit or kill: it is the citizen who, by virtue of his consumerist lifestyle, stimulates economic processes that lead to disruption of natural environments." 12

All of this is tenaciously intertangled—the guilt, the patterns of demand, the good selfish considerations that should dictate species preservation—as intertangled as the life cycles of the species themselves. 13

Plants, for instance. The educated guess is that each species of plant supports ten to thirty species of dependent animal. Eliminate just one species of insect and you may have destroyed the sole specific pollinator for a flowering plant; when that plant consequently vanishes, so may another twenty-nine species of insects that rely on it for food; each of those twenty-nine species might be an important parasite upon still another species of insect, a pest, which when left uncontrolled by parasitism will destroy further whole populations of trees, which themselves had been important because. . . . 14

And so on, into the endless reticulation, the endless fragile chain of interdependence that is a tropical ecosystem. Of course it is possible that the most dire projections will not become reality, that the trend will change, that mankind at the last minute will show unexpected forebearance—as economist Julian Simon and other bullish anthropocentrists are fond of predicting. Possible, yes. It is *possible*, for that matter, that with a hundred years of trying genetic engineers at the General Electric laboratories might find a way to re-invent the passenger pigeon. (If so, they would probably patent it.) Possible but not likely. Neither of those cheerful miracles can sensibly be counted on. 15

What seems all *too* likely is that the present trend will continue; that mankind will have cut down and bulldozed away most of the world's rainforests before the year 2000. If so, by direct action alone we will have thereby exterminated perhaps 150,000 species of plants—with indirect consequences, among other creatures and for the biosphere as a whole, that would be geometrically larger. Maybe 900,000 species of insect lost; and the 291 species of tropical bird already known to be threatened; and the fewer than fifty remaining Sumatran rhino; and the nine surviving representatives of the Mauritius kestrel. Enough numbers. 16

No, one final number: 300. Just that many years have passed since 1681. In this tricentennial year of the extinction of *Raphus cucullatus*, the giant flightless Mauritian pigeon, it is worth remembering that *Homo sapiens* too could become part of the Late Quaternary Extinction, engineer- 17 ing ourselves a place among the next group of species bidding this planet the Dodo's Farewell.

Questions for Study and Discussion

1. Quammen begins his essay on extinction with a touch of fantasy. How appropriate is it to the subject of his essay? Is it effective or should he have chosen a different beginning? Explain.

2. In what way is Quammen's dating of the Late Quaternary Extinction "artificial but emblematic"? How is the loss of Martha significant?

3. What two factors in the extinction process are relevant to stability? How is the Late Quaternary Extinction dramatic in those terms?

4. Quammen delivers his doomsday message in the eccentric, witty tone that has made his essays popular. Is his tone appropriate for this essay? Would a more serious tone have been more appropriate? Why or why not?

5. Quammen uses several devices to get the reader's attention, among them sentence fragments, statistics, and italicized words. Locate other attention grabbers in his essay and discuss the ways in which each of them is effective or ineffective.

6. What kinds of human activities does Quammen say are responsible for destroying animal and plant habitats?

7. Quammen suggest that there is no solution to the eventual extinction of the race. Then why do you suppose he has bothered to write this essay?

8. Quammen uses the word "Dodo" in paragraph 17. Look up the word in the dictionary. Are you surprised at the definition? In what ways could it be considered a perfect ending for Quammen's essay?

Writing Topics

1. Quammen delivers a doomsday message while offering nothing in the way of redemption. Talk to teachers in environmental studies. Do all of them agree with Quammen? What does the opposition have to say? What kinds of arguments are there for human beings being able to reverse their fate? What kinds of evidence do these other voices use?

2. Depending on how you look at it, modern science fiction is less apocalyptic than it was just a few years ago. Instead of an Armegeddon triggered by nuclear holocaust, the world of the future will be modeled after a giant corporation in which individuality is subservient to the good of the company. Which vision do you share or do you see a different future for humankind? What kinds of evidence can you provide to support your vision?

JACQUES-YVES COUSTEAU AND YVES PACCALET

Born in 1910, Jacques-Yves Cousteau, French naval officer and marine biologist, is best known for his underwater documentaries that emphasize not only the wonders of ocean life, but also highlight the need to protect it. Cousteau is also renowned for his invention (with Emil Gagnon) of the self-contained underwater breathing apparatus (SCUBA) or aqualung. In 1945 he founded the French Navy's undersea research group and in 1957 was appointed director of Monaco's oceanographic museum. Since 1951 he has undertaken yearly ocean research voyages that are chronicled in such books as *The Silent World* (1953), *The Living Sea* (1963), *The Shark* (1970), and *Cousteau's Amazon Journey* (1984). His films include *World without Sun* (1964), *Desert Whales* (1970), and *Tragedy of Red Salmon* (1970). Yves Paccalet has shared in the Cousteau team's adventures and undertakings for a number of years. An alumnus of the Ecole Supérieure and deeply involved in all nature-related issues, he met Cousteau while working on the 20-volume series, *The Ocean World of Jacques Cousteau*. Since then, they have enjoyed a special rapport rooted in a mutual passion for the sea. Paccalet is in charge of the two periodicals published by the Cousteau Foundation.

In the following introduction to their book *Whales* (1988), Cousteau and Paccalet argue for the preservation of the whales on the grounds that man, too, would suffer if the whales are hunted into oblivion.

The Assault on Whales

Let our imagination transport us high above our planet. Earth spins below us; only the vast oceans that gird the continents and islands seem to be alive. From our lofty vantage point, the living creatures that dwell on the dry surface of the globe are no longer visible; we can no longer make out rhinoceroses or elephants or crocodiles or huge snakes. But on the surface of the seas we can still see large herds of animals swiftly plying measureless expanses of water, cavorting with mountainous, storm-tossed waves. These creatures—which from our imaginary perch in space we might well think the only things on earth—are the cetaceans.
LACÉPÈDE (1804)

The whale is the most astonishing animal the earth has ever known. It does not merely inspire superlatives—it is a living superlative. Some whales are much larger than the gigantic dinosaurs of the Mesozoic. It would take

1

25 elephants, or 2,000 human beings, to equal the weight of a single blue whale; its tongue alone weighs as much as an elephant. The blue whale is as long as four buses placed end to end. Its skeleton weighs 18 tons, its blubber 30, its meat 44. When it blows at the ocean's surface, the spout looks for all the world like a new cloud in the sky.

When it swims, however, this mountain of muscle and fat is as fluid as the element it calls home. The whale can be a gregarious, intelligent, peaceable creature that coaxes and cajoles its young; comes to the defense of its fellow whales, converses with them in an enigmatic language, and sings with all its might in raging storms.

So: what has mankind made of these creatures? We've made them into oil for our lamps, stays for our corsets, meat for our pets. We have made them into lipstick for our makeup kits and lubricants to keep our engines of war running smoothly. While *Homo sapiens* probe outer space for life on other planets, certain members of our species are eradicating wondrous forms of life right here on earth!

As recently as thirty years ago, this slaughter did not strike everyone as unusual or illogical. "It is extraordinary how few people realize that a whale secretes a prodigious amount of oil, that greasy substance coveted by the entire world," wrote Georges Blond in 1953. "The modern demand for oil for machinery, war industries, and the armies they supply rises day by day. Modern chemistry extracts from whale oil not only lubricants but glycerine, margarine, soap, skin-foods, and cosmetics. . . . "

More than fifty million years of peace in the oceans came to an end when man started butchering whales by the thousands. The carnage went from bad to worse. More whales have been wiped out in the last fifty years than in the four centuries previous: between 1929 and 1979, more than 2 million were caught and flensed, for an annual average of 40,000. Every whaling season, whales collectively shed as much blood as the *Amoco Cadiz* lost oil during its disastrous spill. But this slick turns the seas red.

Today there is not a single whale product or by-produce that chemists cannot produce synthetically or extract from plant or mineral substances, and at competitive prices; yet we go right on taking whales. There is no longer any economic justification for keeping whaling fleets in operation. To be sure, it can still pay to whale: a harpooned whale can be worth between $15,000 and $25,000, depending on its size. But the profit margin is growing smaller and smaller; whale stocks are dwindling, while the cost of fuel and manpower is going up. The absurd result? Subsidies. Thus an activity that deprives the citizens of the world of a fabulous sight is supported at taxpayer expense? The titans of the animal kingdom are vanishing, and our planet is that much poorer for it. This massacre not only upsets the balance of the marine ecosystem, but also deprives our dreams and musings of creatures beyond belief—all to line the pockets of a handful of shipowners and fishing magnates.

Whaling advocates usually fall back on two arguments, and we might   7
just as well dispose of them right away. First, they say, suspending operations would be unfair to all the people on factory ships or shore stations,
who would be thrown out of work. Second, mankind is in dire need of every
possible source of protein.

We have all heard the unemployment argument before; it is the refuge   8
of those too lazy to come up with a better rationale. Out it pops at us like a
jack-in-the-box every time a commercial venture stands accused of de-
spoiling nature. Applied to whales, the argument is less convincing than
ever. The number of people whose livelihood depends on factory vessels,
shore stations, and whaling-related industries does not exceed a few thousand worldwide. In Japan and the Soviet Union—the only two countries
where this sector of the population is of any consequence—whalers account
for 2 to 3 percent of all fishery employees. The Soviet and Japanese fisheries
derive no more than 4 percent of their total income from whaling. In 1973,
whaling operations accounted for a scant 0.024 percent of Japan's gross
national product; by now, this figure is probably one-tenth of what it was—
hardly worth considering. We might point out that substituting plant or
mineral derivatives for whale products generates new jobs. Moreover, the
recovery of whale populations has opened up another important source of
revenue: tourism.

The animal protein argument is not worth a single yen or ruble more.   9
The Soviet Union feeds its whale meat to animals (primarily on fur farms)
or exports it to Japan. Whale meat is an important part of the diet of
Eskimos and a few other aboriginal hunters, but their dependence on it is
decreasing.

Only in Japan is whale meat eaten with any regularity; it accounts for   10
exactly 0.9 percent of total protein intake, 2.1 percent of all animal-derived
protein, and 4 percent of protein from seafood (according to a 1976 report
by the Food and Agricultural Organization's Advisory Committee on
Marine Resources Research). These minuscule proportions cannot possibly
justify a continuation of the butchery. As a leading economic power, Japan
wins no respect by marshaling its vast industrial and technological resources for an activity that is nothing more than plunder. No one denies
that whaling is a centuries-old tradition in Japan, but the past does not
excuse the present.

Can nations be persuaded to stop shedding the blood of whales?   11
Many countries have already done so, but a few are determined not to give
in. The ideology of state doctrine is not easily swayed. Soviet officials tell us
that whaling is consistent with the Marxist-Leninist concept of man's
relationship with nature. But the Soviet people are not unmoved by the
wonders of our planet, and the champions of the whale are gaining ground
in Moscow and Leningrad.

With regard to Japan (and the countries it has enlisted to carry on its 12 whaling operations by proxy—South Korea, Taiwan, Brazil, and Chile), the problem is different. Here we are dealing with a situation that is analogous to the illicit trade in fur or ivory: a handful of clever, greedy individuals versed in the ins-and-outs of manipulating officials and markets, and forming pressure groups. The whaling lobby is a fact of life; it puts up a good fight, and nowhere better than in the halls of the International Whaling Commission, where it battles a worldwide movement that asks that whales be left in peace.

Nevertheless, the picture is changing, because the laws of economics 13 are working in favor of the whales. The animals cannot breed fast enough for capitalist fleets to turn a profit. Whales have become a scarce commodity, and tracking them down across vast ocean expanses uses up equally vast amounts of costly fuel. In this respect, it may be said that OPEC has been more effective in safeguarding whales than have all the preservationist societies put together.

In addition, a growing number of citizens now understand that eco- 14 nomic arguments become unacceptable as soon as they threaten the survival of even a single species. We live in an age of sweeping change; things once reserved for a privileged few—manufactured consumer goods—are becoming commonplace, while commodities once plentiful and free—clean air and water, nature in all its exuberance—are growing scarce. If we gauge things this way, a single sperm whale could be reckoned more valuable than a whole fleet of whaling ships.

There is still hope, but time is of the essence. For some local stocks, 15 the drop in population is so severe that, even if all whaling were to cease overnight, there is no guarantee that the animals could ever recover.

Furthermore, whales (like all marine life) are reeling from the effects of 16 overdevelopment and pollution. They suffer from oil spills and the discharge of toxic waste from homes, farms, and factories; demolitions at sea, the building of seawalls, and the intrusion of overzealous tourists.

Compared with other endangered species, whales are at a special 17 disadvantage: because of their enormous size, they are presumed indestructible. After all, people reason, the whales roam vast expanses of water; surely they can manage to give harpoon gunners the slip. But anyone who believes this rationale is deluding himself: man is everywhere.

It is time we gave these animals a fighting chance. We owe it to 18 ourselves, to our children, and to generations yet unborn. If we do not, we shall have to use the past tense when we talk about the right whale and its bonnet of barnacles, the fabulously large blue whale, the swift, streamlined rorquals, the singing humpbacks, the gray whales that migrate through the waters off the California coast, and the brawny, once dreaded sperm whale.

This book is a labor of love—and of anger. It is an indignant outcry 19 against pointless slaughter and a solemn declaration of unswerving friendship for the nation of the whales. If we lose the whales, we lose something of incalculable value from our dreams, our myths, our finest poetry—from all the things that made us human before we defined ourselves in terms of heavy industry. In *Whales*, we endeavor to explain that mankind is annihilating species that may have countless wonderful secrets to share with us. Whales may yet guide us to the ocean depths or open our ears to the pulse of the seas.

This is our hope: that the children born today may still have, twenty   20
years hence, a bit of green grass under their bare feet, a breath of clean air to breathe, a patch of blue water to sail upon, and a whale on the horizon to set them dreaming.

Questions for Study and Discussion

1. The authors begin their essay with a claim about whales. What was your first reaction to this statement? After reading the essay did you feel the authors had supported their claim? Explain.

2. What two arguments do advocates of whaling use? What kinds of evidence do the authors use to counter these arguments? Is their evidence convincing? Why or why not?

3. What changes are at work to safeguard the whale? Which do you think will be the most effective in the long run? Why? What irony do the authors use in paragraph 13?

4. Why is it imperative that we save the whales? What is it that the authors say whales embody?

5. The authors describe their book as "a labor of love—and of anger." Cite examples of the authors' diction that support this claim. Does the authors' choice of language strengthen or weaken their argument? Explain.

6. The authors have organized their essay into several sections. Identify these sections and point out the kinds of information contained in each one. Would you have arranged the sections in the same order? Why or why not? What other sections, if any, might they have included?

7. The International Whaling Commission establishes nonbinding regulations for the taking of whales. After reading the essay, what areas of concern do you suspect the commission might have to address other than the direct killing of whales for profit?

Writing Topics

1. As Cousteau and Paccalet suggest, pollution plays a major role in the assault on whales. Using the authors' essay as a guide, write an essay in which you argue for the preservation of humankind as if it were another species threatened by pollution. What qualities of humankind are worth its preserva-

tion? What are the major threats to its existence? What is being done about it? Is there hope? Why is the situation urgent?

2. The 1980s might be remembered as the "Decade of Causes," for the proliferation of concerns related to ourselves, our neighbors, and the preservation of our planet. Bumper stickers, T-shirts, and lapel buttons broadcast the issues people care about, not only to advertise them but also to generate converts. But with so many perceived dangers and so little time, how does anyone decide which issues should receive time and energy? Which causes are you concerned about? How did you choose them? In what ways do you feel you can effect change?

DENNIS OVERBYE

The increasing danger to the environment resulting from our industrialized society has been one of the major issues of the late 1980s and will probably continue to dominate political and social discussion throughout the nineties. On one side of the issue are the doomsayers who say it is too lalte to make the needed changes to save our planet. At the other end of the spectrum are the optimists who say we broke it and we can fix it.

Dennis Overbye, a contributing essayist to *Time* magazine, is one of the latter. In the following essay, which appeared in an October 1989 issue of *Time*, Overbye suggest a paradox—that we are fortunate to have the technology to aid us in charting and repairing the environmental damage created by the unwise use of technology.

Fear in a Handful of Numbers

Everybody talks about the weather, goes the saying (often wrongly attributed to Mark Twain), *but nobody does anything about it.* The word from scientists is that whoever said this was wrong. All of us, as we go about the mundane business of existence, are helping change the weather and every other aspect of life on this fair planet: Los Angelenos whipping their sunny basin into a brown blur on the way to work every morning; South Americans burning and cutting their way through the rain forest in search of a better life; a billion Chinese, their smokestacks belching black coal smoke, marching toward the 21st century and a rendezvous with modernization. 1

On the flanks of Mauna Loa in Hawaii, an instrument that records the concentration of carbon dioxide dumped into the atmosphere as a result of all this activity traces a wobbly rising line that gets steeper and steeper with time. Sometime in the next 50 years, say climatologists, all that carbon dioxide, trapping the sun's heat like a greenhouse, could begin to smother the planet, raising temperatures, turning farmland to desert, swelling oceans anywhere from four feet to 20 feet. Goodbye Venice, goodbye Bangladesh. Goodbye to millions of species of animals, insects and plants that haven't already succumbed to acid rain, ultraviolet radiation leaking through the damaged ozone layer, spreading toxic wastes or bulldozers. 2

A species that can change its planet's chemistry just by day-to-day coming and going has, I suppose, achieved a kind of coming-of-age. We could celebrate or tremble. What do we do when it is not war that is killing us but progress? When it is not the actions of a deranged dictator threatening the world but the ordinary business of ordinary people? When there are no bombs dropping, nobody screaming, nothing to fear but a line on a graph or a handful of numbers on a computer printout? Dare we change the world on the basis of a wobbly line on a graph? We can change the world, and those numbers, slowly, painfully—we can ration, recycle, carpool, tax and use the World Bank to bend underdeveloped nations to our will. But the problem is neither the world nor those numbers. The problem is ourselves.

In our relations with nature, we've been playing a deadly game of cowboys and Indians. We all started as Indians. Many primitive cultures— and the indigenous peoples still clinging today to their pockets of underdevelopment—regarded the earth and all its creatures as alive. Nature was a whistling wind tunnel of spirits. With the rise of a scientific, clockwork cosmos and of missionary Christianity, with its message of man's dominion and relentless animus against paganism, nature was metaphorically transformed. It became dead meat.

The West was won, Los Angeles and the 20th century were built, by the cowboy mind. To the cowboy, nature was a vast wilderness waiting to be tamed. The land was a stage, a backdrop against which he could pursue his individual destiny. The story of the world was the story of a man, usually a white man, and its features took their meaning from their relationship to him. A mountain was a place to test one's manhood; an Asian jungle with its rich life and cultures was merely a setting for an ideological battle. The natives are there to be "liberated." By these standards even Communists are cowboys.

The cowboys won—everywhere nature is being tamed—but victory over nature is a kind of suicide. The rules change when there is only one political party allowed in a country or there is only one company selling oil or shoes. So too when a species becomes numerous and powerful enough to gain the illusion of mastery. What we have now is a sort of biological equivalent to a black hole, wherein a star becomes so massive and dense that it bends space and time totally around itself and then pays the ultimate price of domination by disappearing.

Modern science, a cowboy achievement, paradoxically favors the Indian view of life. Nature is alive. The barest Antarctic rock is crawling with microbes. Viruses float on the dust. Bacteria help digest our food for us. According to modern evolutionary biology, our very cells are cities of formerly independent organisms. On the molecular level, the distinction between self and nonself disappears in a blur of semipermeable membranes. Nature goes on within and without us. It wafts through us like a breeze through a screened porch. On the biological level, the world is a seamless continuum of energy and information passing back and forth, a vast complicated network of exchange. Speech, food, posture, infection, respiration, scent are but a few pathways of communication. Most of those circuits are still a mystery, a labyrinth we have barely begun to acknowledge or explore.

The great anthropologist and philosopher Gregory Bateson pointed out 20 years ago that this myriad of feedback circuits resemble the mathematical models of thinking being developed for the new science of artificial intelligence. A forest or a coral reef or a whole planet, then, with its checks and balances and feedback loops and delicate adjustments always striving for light and equilibrium, is like *a mind*. In this way of thinking, pollution is literal insanity (Bateson was also a psychologist). To dump toxic waste in a swamp, say, is like trying to repress a bad thought or like hitting your wife every night and assuming that because she doesn't fight back, you can abuse her with impunity—30 years later she sets your bed on fire. 8

Some of these circuits are long and slow, so that consequences may take years or generations to manifest themselves. That helps sustain the cowboy myth that nature is a neutral, unchanging backdrop. Moreover, evolution seems to have wired our brains to respond to rapid changes, the snap of a twig or a movement in the alley, and to ignore slow ones. When these consequences do start to show up, we don't notice them. Anyone who has ever been amazed by an old photograph of himself or herself can attest to the merciful ignorance of slow change, that is, aging—*Where did those clothes and that strange haircut come from? Was I really that skinny?* 9

We weren't born with the ability to taste carbon dioxide or see the ozone layer, but science and technology have evolved to fill the gap to help us measure what we cannot feel or taste or see. We have old numbers with which, like old photographs, we can gauge the ravages of time and our own folly. In that sense, the "technological fix" that is often wishfully fantasized—cold fusion, anyone?—has already appeared. The genius of technology has already saved us, as surely as the Ghost of Christmas Future saved Scrooge by rattling the miser's tight soul until it cracked. A satellite photograph is technology, and so are the differential equations spinning inside a Cray supercomputer. There is technology in the wobbly rising trace on a piece of graph paper. There is technology in a handful of numbers. 10

The trick is to become more like Indians without losing the best parts of cowboy culture—rationalism and the spirit of inquiry. We need more science now, not less. How can we stretch our nerves around those numbers and make them as real and as ominous as our cholesterol readings? Repeat them each night on the evening news? We need feedback, as if we were the audience in a giant public radio fund-raising drive hitting the phones and making pledges. Like expert pilots navigating through a foggy night, we need the faith to fly the planet collectively by our instruments and not by 11 the seat of our pants. In the West we need the faith and courage to admit the bitter truth, that our prosperity is based as much on cheap energy as on free markets. A long-postponed part of the payment for that energy and prosperity is coming due if we want to have any hope of dissuading the Chinese and the rest of the Third World from emulating us and swaddling the planet with fumes and wastes.

What if the spirit doesn't hit? We can't afford to wait if we want to survive. While we are waiting for this sea change of attitude, we could pretend—a notion that sounds more whimsical than it is. Scientists have found that certain actions have a feedback effect on the actor. Smilers actually feel happier; debaters become enamored of their own arguments; a good salesman sells himself first. You become what you pretend to be. We can pretend to be unselfish and connected to the earth. We can pretend that 30-ft.-long, black-tinted-glass, air-conditioned limos are unfashionable because we know that real men don't need air conditioning. We can pretend that we believe it is wrong to loot the earth for the benefit of a single generation of a single species. We can pretend to care about our children's world. 12

The air has been poisoned before, 3 billion years ago, when the blue-green algae began manufacturing oxygen. That was the first ecological crisis. Life survived then. Life will not vanish now, but this may be the last chance for humans to go along gracefully. 13

Questions for Study and Discussion

1. Irony is the use of words to suggest something other than their literal meaning. What is the irony in Overbye's use of the expression "Everybody talks about the weather, but nobody does anything about it"? How is the expression generally intended? What is its meaning in the context of Overbye's essay?

2. Overbye uses the analogy of cowboys and Indians to argue that progress is killing us. In what ways is this analogy particularly fitting for his argument? What does it reveal about whom he intends for his audience?

3. Throughout his essay, Overbye asks the reader several questions. How does he answer them? How would you respond?

4. In what ways is pollution a "kind of suicide"?

5. Overbye uses several metaphors in his essay. Identify a few of them and discuss how they work to help him make his point.

6. In your own words, what is the paradox of science that Overbye mentions in paragraph 7?

7. Overbye says, "We need more science now, not less." How do numbers figure in his solution? In light of his point that progress is killing us, his emphasis on the "technological fix" can be seen as a contradiction. How well does he resolve it for the reader?

8. What is the "long-postponed" payment Overbye refers to in paragraph 11?

9. Overbye wrote his essay in October 1989 when readers were already well aware of the dangers of the greenhouse effect. In what ways, if any, are the solutions he offers to the problem of pollution new and unexpected.

Writing Topics

1. Choose one of Overbye's solutions to the greenhouse effect and explain the ways in which it might be implemented. What would be the difficulties in implementing it? Whom would you approach first? What expectations for success would you have?

2. Compare "The Big Goodbye" by David Quammen (pp. 629–33) in this section with Overbye's essay. What differences do you find in the tone and approach of the two writers to the subject of pollution? How might you account for those differences? Which one more closely parallels your feelings on the subject? Explain.

DON MITCHELL

Don Mitchell (b. 1947) is a writer, farmer, and teacher who received his B.A. in philosophy from Swarthmore College in 1969. Mitchell has written two novels, *Thumb Tripping* (1970) and *Four-stroke* (1974), and a fable, *The Souls of Lambs* (1979). His essays have appeared in numerous magazines such as *Esquire*, the *Atlantic*, *Yankee*, and *Vermont Life*. For the last twelve years Mitchell has written the "R.F.D." column for *Boston Magazine*. Essays from the column have been compiled in two books, *Moving Upcountry* (1984) and *Living Upcountry* (1986). In addition to writing, Mitchell raises sheep in Vermont and lectures on creative writing at Middlebury College.

"Dancing with Nature" was written as part of Mitchell's contribution to a panel discussion on nature writing held at the annual Breadloaf Writers' Conference in Ripton, Vermont. The essay later appeared in a Breadloaf anthology.

Dancing with Nature

I think of myself as many things—farmer, carpenter, teacher, essayist— 1
but I never thought of myself as a *nature writer* until a friend accused me of being one. It was a brand new term to me, and I was immediately suspicious as to whether "nature writing" constituted a bona fide genre of literature. The more I thought about this issue, the more problematic it seemed.

An initial difficulty is that "nature writing" cuts across the categories 2
in which we ordinarily consider literary enterprise, e.g. fiction, nonfiction, and poetry. To throw out formal considerations and attempt to organize disparate texts according to their subject matter strikes me as somewhat convenient for critics, but mainly unhelpful for students and teachers of literary craft.

A second problem—or a second question I asked myself, was: what is 3
not "nature writing"? Because there's a sense in which nearly all writing is about "nature." Possible exceptions might be nonsense verse or science fiction about aliens in imaginary galaxies—but even these examples may not hold up. All literary texts are uniquely human artifacts, and humans are natural organisms existing within nature's rather unforgiving bounds.

But with further thought, I came to believe there *is* a distinction worth 4
making here; "nature writing" need not be a wrong-headed or vacuous

term. The key is that nature writers are chiefly concerned with something larger than *human* nature—which, let me suggest, has become the over-whelming preoccupation of most modern writing. Nature writers often do address the human situation, but only as part of a larger puzzle. In a psychological age—an age of widespread self-absorption, in which a great many writers have chosen to study their psycho-emotional navels in re-markable detail—both the breadth and the outward focus of a nature writer's gaze is apt to make him seem eccentric, even anachronistic. I confess I find these attractive traits.

The hallmark of "nature writing," I came to realize, is its primary   5
attention to the world *outside* the author and indeed sometimes outside human culture. Rocks, trees, birds, furry creatures, geologic time, hazards of climate, astronomic speculation—deep, abiding interest in subjects like these distinguish the nature writer and mark him or her as different from fellow literary craftsmen. For the nature writer, interest in *character*—the fundamental vehicle of most modern literature—is usually restricted to the question: where do humans fit into the general environmental soup? What is the appropriate relation that humans ought to seek with the rest of the cosmos?

And I suppose that, on this definition, much of my own work could   6
be classified as nature writing. My friend had not so much forced me into a pigeonhole as forced me to think analytically about my efforts. This task, while never easy, does have certain benefits.

Now that I recognized what species I belonged to, though, I felt a   7
curious aversion to being lumped together with "nature writers." Part of my annoyance, I'm sure, was caused by my personal version of the streak of cussed independence all writers cultivate; beyond that, however, I felt genuine embarrassment about certain mistakes and misconceptions com-monly offered to the reading public by my fellow toilers in this modest literary vineyard. If one is writing about, say, trees, one ought on the face of things to have an easier time speaking truthfully than the writer who sets up to do business on the vagaries of human personality. I regret it is not so. I've made plenty of mistakes myself, writing on perfectly ordinary subjects like raising sheep and building barns and managing a woodlot; but I have usually managed to find my compatriots' mistakes a great deal more alarm-ing. And—since this is my essay, not theirs—I'd like to explore certain pitfalls in "nature writing" by picking almost exclusively on others.

I take it as axiomatic that what anybody sees in life depends on where   8
he or she stands, and as human beings we always approach "nature" from the perspective of civilization, of human culture. This gives rise to a tremendous paradox, though: the fact is that humans created civilization because the conditions of life *in nature* were and are unacceptable. Unpre-dictable. Capricious. Often inhospitable, and sometimes downright in-humane—or at least unable to reliably nurture what we value in the human

spirit and the human potential. Civilization shaves the peak excesses of nature, much as a power company strives to even-out demand for electricity.

Yes, of course, we've gone too far—in Northern, Western culture—in the direction of civilization. Many people now live lives *bereft* of nature, of any sense of rootedness in or oneness with or connection to natural cycles. Such people, however well-off, are deeply impoverished and this is a tragedy. But I think it's also a tragedy when their condition leads to an idealization or romanticization of "nature," as though a "state of nature" were a state of grace, or innocence, or goodness, or purity, because it's just not so. If you want to find out, try experimenting with some modern analog to Walden Pond. But bear in mind that even Thoreau couldn't stand Walden for more than a couple of years.

I get bothered and worried when I hear about people who live in urban highrises, ride subways to and from their work in glass office towers, and then take up *birding* as a weekend hobby. They learn the names of all the different birds, they place rolled-up balls of suet on their concrete balconies, they take Audubon birdwalks on Sunday mornings and believe they're discovering important truths about something called "nature." This behavior is more like scratching an itch—and yes, I know such scratching feels good, and I'll accept that its probably healthy and therapeutic. But it's not a process apt to lend much insight, and it's not what I regard as a likely source for either compelling or *true* writing about nature.

I mention these urban birders—straw men, to be sure—because I think we should admit that most "nature writing" is appreciated *by readers* in exactly the manner of an Audubon hike. Or of joining the Sierra Club. Or sending a check to Defenders of Wildlife to help save the coyotes. (I get testy about coyotes these days, since I raise sheep and coyotes prey on my flock. I certainly don't want to make coyotes extinct, but a rough analog to having urban folks defend and romanticize the wily coyotes that kill my lambs would be for me, a farmer in Vermont, to defend and romanticize the rats that carouse in the cupboards of city dwellers.) Much or most of what passes for nature writing, in short, seems to me little more than shameless pandering to specific needs and longings caused by modern man's alienation from the natural world. And this audience's uninformed, uncritical *neediness* makes me feel extremely uncomfortable.

Again, in the manner of an Audubon birdwalk, writers engaged in explicitly *non-nature* writing usually feel the need to add obligatory paragraphs here and there referring to the natural setting in which a story or poem or novel is placed. These passages are typically long on taxonomy—naming some half-dozen species of trees, or specifying just *what kind* of clouds are in the sky—and short on knowledge. In fact, quite often these passages are startlingly misinformed. I point the finger at myself, here, too; what writer hasn't cooked up utterly perfunctory "nature" passages out of a

9

10

11

12

perceived need to add descriptive color or texture to a manuscript? Such work, though, amounts to little more than a verbal birdwalk. Let's not fool ourselves into thinking it is authentic.

So how does a person write truly about nature?   13

It seems to me that the first obligation of a serious writer is to decide   14
what, in life, he wants to understand—what he's interested in telling the truth about, or trying to. And then his project is to develop his life along lines that will allow him to explore his concerns. Our lives are *long*, and there's time enough for the writer to explore many things, and to try and maybe fail or maybe succeed at many different ventures. But if what he wants to explore is human personality—in the manner of Henry James, or Marcel Proust—he had better not become a hermit. And if what he wants to explore is his psyche—if self-explanation or self-understanding or self-analysis is his primary artistic project—then he may not want to become a social butterfly. Or have six kids and try to raise them.

I believe writers have a serious responsibility—*if* they're serious—not   15
to drift or bumble through their lives but to shape them, actively, in ways that are going to help them study and reflect and work on the issues or problems or questions that interest them; in this sense a writer's life *is* a work of art, and certainly ought to be treated as such. So, if you want to write about nature, you've got to shape your life in ways that will afford continual, abundant opportunities to *engage* nature and render yourself vulnerable to natural forces. To the extent that a writer does this, he's more and more apt to avoid the most common and dreadful mistakes in "nature writing"—those that arise from the author's not really knowing what he's talking about.

I want to distinguish three separate levels of engagement with nature: 16
first, what I'm going to call Mere Observation—although observation is never mere and learning to observe is a big part of our continual education as writers. I say Mere Observation, though, in the sense that we might notice, "There are some big round bales of hay in that meadow across the road." And we could describe the bales in various ways, maybe come up with some arresting imagery or some piquant, metaphoric language to nail down the way they look, or smell, or feel; and I want to distinguish this from a second level of engagement which I'm going to call Appreciation.

In moving from Mere Observation to Appreciation of nature, we   17
might say: "Gee, there seems to be a pattern here, something's going on here, somebody let the grasses in that field grow up to a certain point, then mowed them down and let them dry in the sun and baled them up with a baler so as to have winter fodder for livestock because animals can't graze pastures when there's two feet of snow on the ground, and winter is coming." Appreciation represents a higher order of understanding than Mere Observation; in Appreciation, we tend to start investing natural phenomena with symbolic meanings, tend to start developing metaphors

that go well beyond description—or at least this is when we *should* begin such work. Some of the worst mistakes we can make come from getting the cart before the horse, i.e. hurrying to start up the process of Appreciation—and of developing symbolic meanings—before we've observed enough.

I want to recommend a third level of engagement, which I'll call Involvement or Investment: this happens when one engages nature as an actor, which usually means as a manager of one kind or another. To flesh out the haymaking analogy, if it's *your* hay you're asking questions like: "Is it going to rain today? Is it going to rain tomorrow? Are these grasses at the right stage of maturity to maximize energy and protein? Is the ground dry enough to bear my tractor's weight? Has last winter's frost heaved new rocks out of the soil? Is my baler about to break for lack of grease in any one of fifty bearings?" You'd be wondering about things like that, asking those sorts of questions—and, not incidentally, you'd be equipping yourself masterfully to write about hay. I want to suggest that a good way to avoid mistakes in nature writing is for the writer to get his hands dirty—just as dirty as possible—so that he can write from the perspective of active Involvement with nature.

This Involvement, as I've suggested, usually takes some form of management. A host of human activities could fill the bill: forester, game warden, wildlife biologist, fisherman, firefighter, snowplow driver. It depends on what the writer wants to learn about. In my case, fifteen years ago, I was interested in these questions: Where does food come from, and how do you make it grow? How can a person eat meat joyfully? How do machines work? What holds buildings up, and what can cause them to fall down? I admit these are somewhat eccentric questions for a writer to get excited about, but at any rate they were my questions and I wanted firsthand answers. And a sensible solution—for me—was to become a farmer, which is a very interesting form of engagement with nature and also a source of income at least as dependable as writing has proved for me—although that's not saying too much. Over time, I've learned quite a few surprising things.

I want to offer a short list of discoveries I've made by Involvement with nature as a farmer—discoveries which I never would have made as a Mere Observer of my chosen landscape, or even as a thoughtful Appreciator of it. To learn these things I had to become an actor, a manager; but I think that non-farmers may find these discoveries surprising, too.

1. The persistence of meadows in a landscape like Vermont, where the climax vegetation is a hardwood forest—where nature really wants to grow trees, not grass—is no accident. These meadows require endless, persistent, dedicated care. By humans. Year after year. They're beautiful—New England meadows can be perfect jewels of landscape—they're not here thanks to nature. They're here by the assertion of human will against what natural forces would prefer to grow. People, not nature, put these meadows here. And people are

working hard to keep them here, in a continuing feat of human will and intention and deliberate caring.

2. Nature, in fact, is not much interested in producing foods of the quantity and types required to feed humanity. All farming consists, in Thoreau's phrase, of trying to get the earth to say *beans*, rather than burdocks or milkweek or something else that we can't eat. It takes enormous persuasion on the part of humans to get nature to put dinner on our tables.

3. Wild animals, left to do their own thing ad libidinem, are not an unmitigated blessing. In fact, at this point in history wild animal populations frequently need to be controlled for the benefit of the animals themselves, not to mention the benefit of human beings.

4. Acid rain is a net *benefit* to the forage-based agriculture of the Northeast. I happen to be an environmentalist, and I expect most thoughtful readers to be environmentalists, and we're all aware that acid rain has been implicated with serious environmental deterioration . . . but my hayfields and my neighbors' hayfields happen to be benefitting. Like most natural phenomena, acid rain is not entirely destructive.

5. Livestock-based agriculture, which allows meat-based human diets, can be and often is the most appropriate way to conserve soil & water resources, to "tread lightly" over the earth, to leave the planet in richer shape than we found it. In contrast, tillage-based farming—the basis for nearly all "vegetarian" diets—is extremely hard on the soil.

Now, we've all read nature writers who assert the opposite of these surprising things I've learned, so let's consider how they could have made such mistakes. How *do* mistakes get made, in writing about nature? I want to suggest three ways: first, fallacies simply caused by faulty observation. Second, fallacies caused by *overeagerness* to "appreciate" nature, to invest observation with symbolic meaning. And thirdly, fallacies caused by unfortunate, all-too-human combinations of the two.

I think I can explain all three of these roads to error simultaneously, by discussing one spectacular example of a "combo-fallacy" in writing about nature, a fallacy built on both faulty observation and over-eager appreciation. The example comes from a famous passage in Annie Dillard's book *Pilgrim at Tinker Creek*, published in 1974 and admired—on the whole, justly—ever since. In this passage, Dillard has discovered a female praying mantis in a field, and she pauses to watch her project of laying eggs. Dillard writes:

> The male was nowhere in sight. The female had probably eaten him. Fabre [the nineteenth-century French entomologist, quoted extensively by Dillard] says that, at least in captivity, the female will mate with and devour up to seven males, whether she has laid her egg cases or not. The mating rites of mantises are well known: a chemical produced in the head of the male insect says, in effect: "No, don't go near her, you fool, she'll eat you alive." At the same time a chemical in his abdomen says, "Yes, by all means, now and forever yes."

While the male is making up what passes for his mind, the female tips   29
the balance in her favor by eating his head. He mounts her.

And the passage goes on from there. I regard this as a gorgeous piece   30
of writing, but when I was teaching *Pilgrim at Tinker Creek* a couple of years
ago, one of my students—a biology major—came in with a brief article from
the magazine *Science 85*. This cross-fertilization is the beauty of working at a
liberal arts college; the magazine had published a wonderful photograph of
two praying mantises having fun together, and—lo and behold!—the male
had not lost his head. The caption read: Mating with a female praying
mantis is a lot easier on the male mantis than previously believed." And the
article went on to note: "The problem with previous studies [going back to
Fabre] . . . was privacy. Apparently . . . the mantises were distracted by the
well-lit scientists watching them." The writer went on to suggest that
previous researchers perhaps hadn't *fed* their mantises adequately, noting
that these insects have voracious appetites.

Well, now! In light of this new information, Dillard's passage—which   31
is *not* based on first-hand observation of mantises actually mating, but on a
"borrowed" observation from Fabre—amounts to sustaining a hundred-
year-old libel on praying mantises, and investing it with startling new
symbolic meanings. So startling as to make a libel-by-suggestion on human
beings, too. It's not hard to make several harsh inferences from the Dillard
passage, inferences that seem virtually inherent in her analysis. Such as:
sexual response in the male is a hydraulic, abdominal reflex better accomplished without benefit of cerebration. Or, indeed: the male brain may be
an absolute *impediment* to successful copulation. Or, again: females harbor
an unconscious instinct to devour their male sex partners.

Unlike Fabre, we live—and Annie Dillard writes—in an age of wide-   32
spread misogyny, misanthropy (in the narrow sense) and general mistrust
between the sexes. At the time I taught this passage from *Pilgrim At Tinker
Creek*, a hit record happened to be "Maneater" by Darryl Hall and John
Oates. The chorus went: "Whoa, here she comes / Watch out, boy, she'll
chew you up!" It's not surprising, in such an age, that a writer should invest
the recorded sex habits of praying mantises with the symbolic meanings
Dillard chooses—but what a tower of symbolic nonsense if the evidence
turns out to be false!

So, in light of what we *now* know about praying mantises, consider the   33
new symbolic meanings we could readily develop and attribute to the
evidence of "nature." For example, Never have sex before dinner, particularly if the woman is hungry. Or, Never have sex in front of scientific
researchers. Or, If you want to survive sex, young man, first get the lighting
right.

It's a wonderful example, at any rate, because it illustrates so much.   34
The best antidote to making such mistakes, though—I think—is by having
the writer get committed to a life of authentic involvement with nature, if

that's what he wants to write about. And then to be extremely patient about deciding what "Nature" means or Who She Is.

In my pre-rural, pre-agrarian life, I used to feel comfortable with the   35 trite, profound personification of nature as some cosmic Mother. Involvement with her, though, on a sheep farm in Vermont has gradually forced me to reject this image. Nature as my Mother? No—certainly not in the sense of a persistently reliable, nurturing, creating force. She has disappointed me far too many times. In farming, though, it's not hard to think of nature as a sort of silent "business partner"; as business partner, I've found nature to be somewhat careless and capricious about little things . . . though seldom about big ones. No business partner is perfect, of course. And business would be *awfully* hard without this partner's capital.

Both as farmer and as writer, it strikes me as crucial at this time in   36 history to tell humanity that we are not at war with nature, not in a battle against nature. Because that attitude, if we adopt it, will doom us. At the same time, though, we need to recognize that nature is not concerned with our human predicament. When Thoreau was dying, a relative asked him if he'd made peace with his Creator; Thoreau's answer was, "We've never quarrelled." That's always struck me as a wonderful sentiment, but I can't say it's true in my own case. I've quarrelled plenty, and farming often feels like an endless, low-grade disputation with someone one suspects is not even listening. So I think I would prefer to put it like this: I've come to look on Nature as a necessary dancing partner. An extremely *difficult* dancing partner, to be sure—but we've all just got to keep trying to learn the steps, always listening for the beat. Don't we?

Questions for Study and Discussion

1. Mitchell begins his essay by attempting to define the "nature writer," but ends by doing something else as well. What is it?

2. Mitchell uses several systems of organization to make his argument clear. Name these systems and discuss how each fits his purpose. What system of organization does he use for the overall essay? Why is it particularly appropriate?

3. According to Mitchell, what distinguishes the "true" nature writer from the "untrue" nature writer? In your opinion, is this distinction valid? Explain.

4. What "myth" of nature does Mitchell debunk? Do you agree? Why or why not?

5. Mitchell uses several italicized words in his essay. What do they have in common? Why do you think he uses them?

6. In his essay, Mitchell attacks the work of Annie Dillard, the respected and well-known "nature writer." How does she fail to fit his definition of a "true" nature writer? Does his attack on her weaken or strengthen his argument? Explain.

7. What is the meaning of Mitchell's title? When does its meaning become clear to you? Why do you suppose Mitchell waited so long to make this connection for the reader?

Writing Topics

1. Think of something about yourself you take for granted—for example, an interest in antique cars, dance, or hiking. In an essay develop a definition of an "authentic pursuer" of this hobby or passion. What are the vital characteristics of an antique car buff or a rock-and-roll fan? What distinguishes you from a casual hobbyist?

2. Reread the essay by Annie Dillard (pp. 599–602) in an earlier section. What occurs to you in comparing her work with the definition of a nature writer Mitchell describes in his essay? Is she a "true" nature writer or not? Explain.

NATHANIEL HAWTHORNE

As a master American novelist and short-story writer, Nathaniel Hawthorne (1804–1864) devoted much of his life to perfecting—and contemplating—his craft. He was born to a prominent Puritan family in Salem, Massachusetts. After graduating in 1825 from Bowdoin College in Maine, he returned to his mother's home in Salem, where he lived in seclusion for twelve years, working at his craft. Apart from one or two short stories he published in magazines and a novel that he himself published but immediately withdrew, he produced little that he was willing to have others read. Finally, in 1837, he published *Twice-Told Tales*, a collection of short stories that brought him success as well as some fame, and in the same year he "reentered" society. In 1850 the first of his great novels appeared, *The Scarlet Letter*, followed by *The House of the Seven Gables* (1851) and *The Blithedale Romance* (1852). Hawthorne's works all deal with moral and spiritual conflicts, and his characters are often lonely or frustrated or frail. In "The Birth-Mark," Hawthorne tells the story of how Aylmer, a scientist, attempts to remove a birthmark from his wife's cheek. In his obsession to make her "perfect," Aylmer fails to see that it is our imperfections that make us human and that nature can not be made to serve science.

The Birth-Mark

In the latter part of the last century, there lived a man of science—an 1
eminent proficient in every branch of natural philosophy—who, not long before our story opens, had made experience of a spiritual affinity, more attractive than any chemical one. He had left his laboratory to the care of an assistant, cleared his fine countenance from the furnace-smoke, washed the stain of acids from his fingers, and persuaded a beautiful woman to become his wife. In those days, when the comparatively recent discovery of electricity, and other kindred mysteries of nature, seemed to open paths into the region of miracle, it was not unusual for the love of science to rival the love of woman, in its depth and absorbing energy. The higher intellect, the imagination, the spirit, and even the heart, might all find their congenial aliment in pursuits which, as some of their ardent votaries believed, would ascend from one step of powerful intelligence to another, until the philosopher should lay his hand on the secret of creative force, and perhaps make new worlds for himself. We know not whether Aylmer possessed this degree of faith in man's ultimate control over nature. He had devoted himself, however, too unreservedly to scientific studies, ever to be weaned from them by any second passion. His love for his young wife might prove the stronger of the two; but it could only be by intertwining itself with his love of science, and uniting the strength of the latter to its own.

Such a union accordingly took place, and was attended with truly 2 remarkable consequences, and a deeply impressive moral. One day, very soon after their marriage, Aylmer sat gazing at his wife, with a trouble in his countenance that grew stronger, until he spoke.

"Georgiana," said he, "has it never occurred to you that the mark upon your cheek might be removed?"

"No, indeed," said she, smiling; but perceiving the seriousness of his manner, she blushed deeply. "To tell you the truth, it has been so often called a charm, that I was simple enough to imagine it might be so."

"Ah, upon another face, perhaps it might," replied her husband. "But never on yours! No, dearest Georgiana, you came so nearly perfect from the hand of Nature, that this slightest possible defect—which we hesitate whether to term a defect or a beauty—shocks me, as being the visible mark of earthly imperfection."

"Shocks you, my husband!" cried Georgiana, deeply hurt; at first reddening with momentary anger, but then bursting into tears. "Then why did you take me from my mother's side? You cannot love what shocks you!"

To explain this conversation, it must be mentioned, that, in the centre of Georgiana's left cheek, there was a singular mark, deeply interwoven, as it were, with the texture and substance of her face. In the usual state of her complexion—a healthy, though delicate bloom—the mark wore a tint of deeper crimson, which imperfectly defined its shape amid the surrounding rosiness. When she blushed, it gradually became more indistinct, and finally vanished amid the triumphant rush of blood, that bathed the whole cheek with its brilliant glow. But, if any shifting emotion caused her to turn pale, there was the mark again, a crimson stain upon the snow, in what Aylmer sometimes deemed an almost fearful distinctness. Its shape bore not a little similarity to the human hand, though of the smallest pigmy size. Georgiana's lovers were wont to say, that some fairy, at her birth-hour, had laid her tiny hand upon the infant's cheek, and left this impress there, in token of the magic endowments that were to give her such sway over all hearts. Many a desperate swain would have risked life for the privilege of pressing his lips to the mysterious hand. It must not be concealed, however, that the impression wrought by this fairy sign-manual varied exceedingly, according to the difference of temperament in the beholders. Some fastidious persons—but they were exclusively of her own sex—affirmed that the Bloody Hand, as they chose to call it, quite destroyed the effect of Georgiana's beauty, and rendered her countenance even hideous. But it would be as reasonable to say, that one of those small blue stains, which sometimes occur in the purest statuary marble, would convert the Eve of Powers[1] to a monster. Masculine observers, if the birth-mark did not heighten their

---

[1]"Eve before the Fall" (1839?), a statue by Hiram Powers (1805–1873), American sculptor famous for his idealized representations of feminine purity and innocence.

admiration, contented themselves with wishing it away, that the world might possess one living specimen of ideal loveliness, without the semblance of a flaw. After his marriage—for he thought little or nothing of the matter before—Aylmer discovered that this was the case with himself.

Had she been less beautiful—if Envy's self could have found aught else to sneer at—he might have felt his affection heightened by the prettiness of this mimic hand, now vaguely portrayed, now lost, now stealing forth again, and glimmering to-and-fro with every pulse of emotion that throbbed within her heart. But, seeing her otherwise so perfect, he found this one defect grow more and more intolerable, with every moment of their united lives. It was the fatal flaw of humanity, which Nature, in one shape or another, stamps ineffaceably on all her productions, either to imply that they are temporary and finite, or that their perfection must be wrought by toil and pain. The Crimson Hand expressed the ineludible gripe, in which mortality clutches the highest and purest of earthly mould, degrading them into kindred with the lowest, and even with the very brutes, like whom their visible frames return to dust. In this manner, selecting it as the symbol of his wife's liability to sin, sorrow, decay, and death, Alymer's sombre imagination was not long in rendering the birth-mark a frightful object, causing him more trouble and horror than ever Georgiana's beauty, whether of soul or sense, had given him delight. 8

At all the seasons which should have been their happiest, he invariably, and without intending it—nay, in spite of a purpose to the contrary—reverted to this one disastrous topic. Trifling as it at first appeared, it so connected itself with innumerable trains of thought, and modes of feeling, that it became the central point of all. With the morning twilight, Aylmer opened his eyes upon his wife's face, and recognized the symbol of imperfection; and when they sat together at the evening hearth, his eyes wandered stealthily to her cheek, and beheld, flickering with the blaze of the wood fire, the spectral Hand that wrote mortality, where he would fain have worshipped. Georgiana soon learned to shudder at his gaze. It needed but a glance, with the peculiar expression that his face often wore, to change the roses of her cheek into a deathlike paleness, amid which the Crimson Hand was brought strongly out, like a bas-relief of ruby on the whitest marble. 9

Late, one night, when the lights were growing dim, so as hardly to betray the stain on the poor wife's cheek, she herself, for the first time, voluntarily took up the subject. 10

"Do you remember, my dear Aylmer," said she, with a feeble attempt at a smile—"have you any recollection of a dream, last night, about this odious Hand?" 11

"None!—none whatever!" replied Aylmer, starting; but then he added in a dry, cold tone, affected for the sake of concealing the real depth of his emotion:—"I might well dream of it: for before I fell asleep, it had taken a pretty firm hold of my fancy." 12

"And you did dream of it," continued Georgiana, hastily; for she dreaded lest a gush of tears should interrupt what she had to say—"A terrible dream! I wonder that you can forget it. Is it possible to forget this one expression?—'It is in her heart now—we must have it out!'—Reflect, my husband; for by all means I would have you recall that dream." 13

The mind is in a sad note, when Sleep, the all-involving, cannot confine her spectres within the dim region of her sway, but suffers them to break forth, affrighting this actual life with secrets that perchance belong to a deeper one. Aylmer now remembered his dream. He had fancied himself, with his servant Aminadab, attempting an operation for the removal of the birth-mark. But the deeper went the knife, the deeper sank the Hand, until at length its tiny grasp appeared to have caught hold of Georgiana's heart; whence, however, her husband was inexorably resolved to cut or wrench it away. 14

When the dream had shaped itself perfectly in his memory, Aylmer sat in his wife's presence with a guilty feeling. Truth often finds its way to the mind close-muffled in robes of sleep, and then speaks with uncompromising directness of matters in regard to which we practise an unconscious self-deception, during our waking moments. Until now, he had not been aware of the tyrannizing influence acquired by one idea over his mind, and of the lengths which he might find in his heart to go, for the sake of giving himself peace. 15

"Aylmer," resumed Georgiana, solemnly, "I know not what may be the cost to both of us, to rid me of this fatal birth-mark. Perhaps its removal may cause cureless deformity. Or, it may be, the stain goes as deep as life itself. Again, do we know that there is a possibility, on any terms, of unclasping the firm gripe of this little Hand, which was laid upon me before I came into the world?" 16

"Dearest Georgiana, I have spent much thought upon the subject," hastily interrupted Aylmer—"I am convinced of the perfect practicability of its removal." 17

"If there be the remotest possibility of it," continued Georgiana, "let the attempt be made, at whatever risk. Danger is nothing to me; for life—which this hateful mark makes me the object of your horror and disgust—life is a burthen which I would fling down with joy. Either remove this dreadful Hand, or take my wretched life! You have deep science! All the world bears witness of it. You have achieved great wonders! Cannot you remove this little, little mark, which I cover with the tips of two small fingers? Is this beyond your power, for the sake of your own peace, and to save your poor wife from madness?" 18

"Noblest—dearest—tenderest wife!" cried Aylmer, rapturously. "Doubt not my power, I have already given this matter the deepest thought—thought which might almost have enlightened me to create a being less perfect than yourself. Georgiana, you have led me deeper than ever into the heart of science. I feel myself fully competent to render this 19 dear cheek as faultless as its fellow: and then, most beloved, what will be my triumph, when I shall have corrected what Nature left imperfect, in her fairest work! Even Pygmalion,[2] when his sculptured woman assumed life, felt not greater ecstasy than mine will be."

"It is resolved, then," said Georgiana, faintly smiling—"And, Aylmer, spare me not, though you should find the birth-mark take refuge in my heart at last."   20

Her husband tenderly kissed her cheek—her right cheek—not that which bore the impress of the Crimson Hand.   21

The next day, Aylmer apprized his wife of a plan that he had formed, whereby he might have opportunity for the intense thought and constant watchfulness, which the proposed operation would require; while Georgiana, likewise, would enjoy the perfect repose essential to its success. They were to seclude themselves in the extensive apartments occupied by Aylmer as a laboratory, and where, during his toilsome youth, he had made discoveries in the elemental powers of nature, that had roused the admiration of all the learned societies in Europe. Seated calmly in this laboratory, the pale philosopher had investigated the secrets of the highest cloud-region, and of the profoundest mines; he had satisfied himself of the causes that kindled and kept alive the fires of the volcano; and had explained the mystery of fountains, and how it is that they gush forth, some so bright and pure, and others with such rich medicinal virtues, from the dark bosom of the earth. Here, too, at an earlier period, he had studied the wonders of the human frame, and attempted to fathom the very process by which Nature assimilates all her precious influences from earth and air, and from the spiritual world, to create and foster Man, her masterpiece. The latter pursuit, however, Aylmer had long laid aside, in unwilling recognition of the truth, against which all seekers sooner or later stumble, that our great creative Mother, while she amuses us with apparently working in the broadest sunshine, is yet severely careful to keep her own secrets, and, in spite of her pretended openness, shows us nothing but results. She permits us indeed, to mar, but seldom to mend, and, like a jealous patentee, on no account to make. Now, however, Aylmer resumed these half-forgotten investigations; not, of course, with such hopes or wishes as first suggested them; but because they involved much physiological truth, and lay in the path of his proposed scheme for the treatment of Georgiana.   22

As he led her over the threshold of the laboratory, Georgiana was cold and tremulous. Aylmer looked cheerfully into her face, with intent to reassure her, but was so startled with the intense glow of the birth-mark upon the whiteness of her cheek, that he could not restrain a strong convulsive shudder. His wife fainted.   23

------

[2]King of Cyprus, in Greek mythology, who fell in love with a statue he had sculptured. In answer to his prayers Aphrodite, the goddess of love, brought the statue to life.

"Aminadab! Aminadab!" shouted Aylmer, stamping violently on the floor.   24

Forthwith, there issued from an inner apartment a man of low stature,   25
but bulky frame, with shaggy hair hanging about his visage, which was
grimed with the vapors of the furnace. This personage had been Aylmer's
under-worker during his whole scientific career, and was admirably fitted
for that office by his great mechanical readiness, and the skill with which,
while incapable of comprehending a single principle, he executed all the
practical details of his master's experiments. With his vast strength, his
shaggy hair, his smoky aspect, and the indescribable earthiness that in-
crusted him, he seemed to represent man's physical nature; while Aylmer's
slender figure, and pale, intellectual face, were no less apt a type of the
spiritual element.

"Throw open the door of the boudoir, Aminadab," said Aylmer, "and   26
burn a pastille."[3]

"Yes, master," answered Aminadab, looking intently at the lifeless   27
form of Georgiana; and then he muttered to himself:—"If she were my wife,
I'd never part with that birth-mark."

When Georgiana recovered consciousness, she found herself   28
breathing an atmosphere of penetrating fragrance, the gentle potency of
which had recalled her from her deathlike faintness. The scene around her
looked like enchantment. Aylmer had converted those smoky, dingy,
sombre rooms, where he had spent his brightest years in recondite pursuits,
into a series of beautiful apartments, not unfit to be the secluded abode of a
lovely woman. The walls were hung with gorgeous curtains, which imparted
the combination of grandeur and grace, that no other species of adornment
can achieve; and as they fell from the ceiling to the floor, their rich and
ponderous folds, concealing all angles and straight lines, appeared to shut in
the scene from infinite space. For aught Georgiana knew, it might be a
pavilion among the clouds. And Aylmer, excluding the sunshine, which
would have interfered with his chemical processes, had supplied its place
with perfumed lamps, emitting flames of various hue, but all uniting in a
soft, empurpled radiance. He now knelt by his wife's side, watching her
earnestly, but without alarm: for he was confident in his science, and felt
that he could draw a magic circle round her, within which no evil might
intrude.

"Where am I?—Ah, I remember!" said Georgiana, faintly; and she   29
placed her hand over her cheek, to hide the terrible mark from her
husband's eyes.

"Fear not, dearest!" exclaimed he. "Do not shrink from me! Believe   30
me, Georgiana, I even rejoice in this single imperfection, since it will be
such rapture to remove it."

---

[3]Incense.

"Oh, spare me!" sadly replied his wife—"Pray do not look at it again. I   31
never can forget that convulsive shudder."

In order to soothe Georgiana, and, as it were, to release her mind from   32
the burden of actual things, Aylmer now put in practice some of the light
and playful secrets, which science had taught him among its profounder
lore. Airy figures, absolutely bodiless ideas, and forms of unsubstantial
beauty, came and danced before her, imprinting their momentary footsteps
on beams of light. Though she had some indistinct idea of the method of
these optical phenomena, still the illusion was almost perfect enough to
warrant the belief, that her husband possessed sway over the spiritual
world. Then again, when she felt a wish to look forth from her seclusion,
immediately, as if her thoughts were answered, the procession of external
existence flitted across a screen. The scenery and the figures of actual life
were perfectly represented, but with that bewitching, yet indescribable
difference, which always makes a picture, an image, or a shadow, so much
more attractive than the original. When wearied of this, Aylmer bade her
cast her eyes upon a vessel, containing a quantity of earth. She did so, with
little interest at first, but was soon startled, to perceive the germ of a plant,
shooting upward from the soil. Then came the slender stalk—the leaves
gradually unfolded themselves—and amid them were a perfect and lovely
flower.

"It is magical!" cried Georgiana. "I dare not touch it."   33

"Nay, pluck it," answered Aylmer, "pluck it, and inhale its brief   34
perfume while you may. The flower will wither in a few moments, and leave
nothing save its brown seed-vessels—but thence may be perpetuated a race
as ephemeral as itself."

But Georgiana had no sooner touched the flower than the whole   35
plant suffered a blight, its leaves turning coal-black, as if by the agency of
fire.

"There was too powerful a stimulus," said Aylmer thoughtfully.   36

"To make up for this abortive experiment, he proposed to take her   37
portrait by a scientific process of his own invention. It was to be effected by
rays of light striking upon a polished plate of metal. Georgiana assented—
but, on looking at the result, was affrighted to find the features of the
portrait blurred and indefinable; while the minute figure of a hand appeared where the cheek should have been. Aylmer snatched the metallic
plate, and threw it into a jar of corrosive acid.

Soon, however, he forgot these mortifying failures. In the intervals of   38
study and chemical experiment, he came to her, flushed and exhausted, but
seemed invigorated by her presence, and spoke in glowing language of the
resources of his art. He gave a history of the long dynasty of the Alchemists,
who spent so many ages in quest of the universal solvent, by which the
Golden Principle might be elicited from all things vile and base. Aylmer
appeared to believe, that, by the plainest scientific logic, it was altogether

within the limits of possibility to discover this long-sought medium; but, he added, a philosopher who should go deep enough to acquire the power, would attain too lofty a wisdom to stoop to the exercise of it. Not less singular were his opinions in regard to the Elixir Vitae. He more than intimated, that it was his option to concoct a liquid that should prolong life for years—perhaps interminably—but that it would produce a discord in nature, which all the world, and chiefly the quaffer of the immortal nostrum, would find cause to curse.

"Aylmer, are you in earnest?" asked Georgiana, looking at him with amazement and fear; "it is terrible to possess such power, or even to dream of possessing it!" 39

"Oh, do not tremble, my love!" said her husband, "I would not wrong either you or myself by working such inharmonious effects upon our lives. But I would have you consider how trifling, in comparison, is the skill requisite to remove this little Hand." 40

At the mention of the birth-mark, Georgiana, as usual, shrank, as if a red-hot iron had touched her cheek. 41

Again, Aylmer applied himself to his labors. She could hear his voice in the distant furnace-room, giving directions to Aminadab, whose harsh, uncouth, misshapen tones were audible in response, more like the grunt or growl of a brute than human speech. After hours of absence, Aylmer reappeared, and proposed that she should now examine his cabinet of chemical products, and natural treasures of the earth. Among the former he showed her a small vial, in which, he remarked, was contained a gentle yet most powerful fragrance, capable of impregnating all the breezes that blow across a kingdom. They were of inestimable value, the contents of that little vial; and, as he said so, he threw some of the perfume into the air, and filled the room with piercing and invigorating delight. 42

"And what is this?" asked Georgiana, pointing to a small crystal globe, containing a gold-colored liquid. "It is so beautiful to the eye, that I could imagine it the Elixir of Life." 43

"In one sense it is," replied Aylmer, "or rather the Elixir of Immortality. It is the most precious poison that ever was concocted in this world. By its aid, I could apportion the lifetime of any mortal at whom you might point your finger. The strength of the dose would determine whether he were to linger out years, or drop dead in the midst of a breath. No king, on his guarded throne, could keep his life, if I, in my private station, should deem that the welfare of millions justified me in depriving him of it." 44

"Why do you keep such a terrible drug?" inquired Georgiana in horror. 45

"Do not mistrust me, dearest!" said her husband, smiling; "its virtuous potency is yet greater than its harmful one. But, see! here is a powerful cosmetic. With a few drops of this, in a vase of water, freckles may be 46 washed away as easily as the hands are cleansed. A stronger infusion would take the blood out of the cheek, and leave the rosiest beauty a pale ghost."

"Is it with this lotion that you intend to bathe my cheek?" asked   47
Georgiana anxiously.

"Oh, no!" hastily replied her husband—"this is merely superficial.   48
Your case demands a remedy that shall go deeper."

In his interviews with Georgiana, Aylmer generally made minute   49
inquiries as to her sensations, and whether the confinement of the rooms, and the temperature of the atmosphere, agreed with her. These questions had such a particular drift, that Georgiana began to conjecture that she was already subjected to certain physical influences, either breathed in with the fragrant air, or taken with her food. She fancied likewise—but it might be altogether fancy—that there was a stirring up of her system,—a strange indefinite sensation creeping through her veins, and tingling, half painfully, half pleasurably, at her heart. Still, whenever she dared to look into the mirror, there she beheld herself, pale as a white rose, and with the crimson birth-mark stamped upon her cheek. Not even Aylmer now hated it so much as she.

To dispel the tedium of the hours which her husband found it   50
necessary to devote to the processes of combination and analysis, Georgiana turned over the volumes of his scientific library. In many dark old tomes, she met with chapters full of romance and poetry. They were the works of the philosophers of the middle ages, such as Albertus Magnus, Cornelius Agrippa, Paracelsus, and the famous friar who created the prophetic Brazen Head. All these antique naturalists stood in advance of their centuries, yet were imbued with some of their credulity, and therefore were believed, and perhaps imagined themselves, to have acquired from the investigation of nature a power above nature, and from physics a sway over the spiritual world. Hardly less curious and imaginative were the early volumes of the Transactions of the Royal Society, in which the members, knowing little of the limits of natural possibility, were continually recording wonders, or proposing methods whereby wonders might be wrought.

But, to Georgiana, the most engrossing volume was a large folio from   51
her huband's own hand, in which he had recorded every experiment of his scientific career, with its original aim, the methods adopted for its development, and its final success or failure, with the circumstances to which either event was attributable. The book, in truth, was both the history and emblem of his ardent, ambitious, imaginative, yet practical and laborious, life. He handled physical details, as if there were nothing beyond them; yet spiritualized them all, and redeemed himself from materialism, by his strong and eager aspiration towards the infinite. In his grasp, the veriest clod of earth assumed a soul. Georgiana, as she read, reverenced Aylmer, and loved him more profoundly than ever, but with a less entire dependence on his judgment than heretofore. Much as he had accomplished, she could not but observe that his most splendid successes were almost invariable failures, if

compared with the ideal at which he aimed. His brightest diamonds were the merest pebbles, and felt to be so by himself, in comparison with the inestimable gems which lay hidden beyond his reach. The volume, rich with achievements that had won renown for its author, was yet as melancholy a record as ever mortal hand had penned. It was the sad confession, and continual exemplification, of the short-comings of the composite man—the spirit burthened with clay and working in matter—and of the despair that assails the higher nature, at finding itself so miserably thwarted by the earthly part. Perhaps every man of genius, in whatever sphere, might recognize the image of his own experience in Aylmer's journal.

So deeply did these reflections affect Georgiana, that she laid her face 52 upon the open volume, and burst into tears. In this situation she was found by her husband.

"It is dangerous to read in a sorcerer's books," said he, with a smile, 53 though his countenance was uneasy and displeased. "Georgiana, there are pages in that volume, which I can scarcely glance over and keep my senses. Take heed lest it prove as detrimental to you!"

"It has made me worship you more than ever," said she. 54

"Ah! wait for this one success," rejoined he, "then worship me if you 55 will. I shall deem myself hardly unworthy of it. But, come! I have sought you for the luxury of your voice. Sing to me, dearest!"

So she poured out the liquid music of her voice to quench the thirst of 56 his spirit. He then took his leave, with a boyish exuberance of gaiety, assuring her that her seclusion would endure but a little longer, and that the result was already certain. Scarcely had he departed, when Georgiana felt irresistibly impelled to follow him. She had forgotten to inform Aylmer of a symptom, which, for two or three hours past, had begun to excite her attention. It was a sensation in the fatal birth-mark, not painful, but which induced a restlessness throughout her system. Hastening after her husband, she intruded, for the first time, into the laboratory.

The first thing that struck her eye was the furnace, that hot and 57 feverish worker, with the intense glow of its fire, which, by the quantities of soot clustered above it, seemed to have been burning for ages. There was a distilling apparatus in full operation. Around the room were retorts, tubes, cylinders, crucibles, and other apparatus of chemical research. An electrical machine stood ready for immediate use. The atmosphere felt oppressively close, and was tainted with gaseous odors, which had been tormented forth by the processes of science. The severe and homely simplicity of the apartment, with its naked walls and brick pavement, looked strange, accustomed as Georgiana had become to the fantastic elegance of her boudoir. But what chiefly, indeed almost solely, drew her attention, was the aspect of Aylmer himself.

He was pale as death, anxious, and absorbed, and hung over the 58 furnace as if it depended upon his utmost watchfulness whether the liquid, which it was distilling, should be the draught of immortal happiness or misery. How different from the sanguine and joyous mien that he had assumed for Georgiana's encouragement!

"Carefully now, Aminadab! Carefully, thou human machine! Carefully, thou man of clay!" muttered Aylmer, more to himself than his assistant. "Now, if there be a thought too much or too little, it is all over!" 59

"Hoh! hoh!" mumbled Aminadab—"look, master, look!" 60

Aylmer raised his eyes hastily, and at first reddened, then grew paler than ever, on beholding Georgiana. He rushed towards her, and seized her arm with a gripe that left the print of his fingers upon it. 61

"Why do you come hither? Have you no trust in your husband?" cried he impetuously. "Would you throw the blight of that fatal birth-mark over my labors? It is not well done. Go, prying woman, go!" 62

"Nay, Alymer," said Georgiana, with the firmness of which she possessed no stinted endowment, "it is not you that have a right to complain. You mistrust your wife! You have concealed the anxiety with which you watch the development of this experiment. Think not so unworthily of me, my husband! Tell me all the risk we run; and fear not that I shall shrink, for my share in it is far less than your own!" 63

"No, no, Georgiana!" said Aylmer impatiently, "it must not be." 64

"I submit," replied she calmly. "And, Aylmer, I shall quaff whatever draught you bring me; but it will be on the same principle that would induce me to take a dose of poison, if offered by your hand." 65

"My noble wife," said Aylmer, deeple moved. "I knew not the height and depth of your nature, until now. Nothing shall be concealed. Know, then, that this Crimson Hand, superficial as it seems, has clutched its grasp into your being, with a strength of which I had no previous conception. I have already administered agents powerful enough to do aught except to change your entire physical system. Only one thing remains to be tried. If that fail us, we are ruined!" 66

"Why did you hesitate to tell me this?" asked she. 67

"Because, Georgiana," said Aylmer, in a low voice, "there is danger!" 68

"Danger? There is but one danger—that this horrible stigma shall be left upon my cheek!" cried Georgiana. "Remove it! remove it!—whatever be the cost—or we shall both go mad!" 69

"Heaven knows, your words are too true," said Aylmer, sadly. "And now, dearest, return to your boudoir. In a little while, all will be tested." 70

He conducted her back, and took leave of her with a solemn tenderness, which spoke far more than his words how much was now at stake. After his departure, Georgiana became wrapt in musings. She considered the character of Alymer, and did it completer justice than at any previous moment. Her heart exulted, while it trembled, at his honorable love, so pure and lofty that it would accept nothing less than perfection, nor miserably make itself contented with an earthlier nature than he had dreamed of. She felt how much more precious was such a sentiment, than 71 that meaner kind which would have borne with the imperfection for her sake, and have been guilty of treason to holy love, by degrading its perfect idea to the level of the actual. And, with her whole spirit, she prayed, that, for a single moment, she might satisfy his highest and deepest conception. Longer than one moment, she well knew, it could not be; for his spirit was ever on the march—ever ascending—and each instant required something that was beyond the scope of the instant before.

The sound of her husband's footsteps aroused her. He bore a crystal goblet, containing a liquor colorless as water, but bright enough to be the draught of immortality. Aylmer was pale; but it seemed rather the consequence of a highly wrought state of mind, and tension of spirit, than of fear or doubt.   72

"The concoction of the draught has been perfect," said he, in answer to Georgiana's look. "Unless all my science have deceived me, it cannot fail."   73

"Save on your account, my dearest Aylmer," observed his wife, "I might wish to put off this birth-mark of mortality by relinquishing mortality itself, in preference to any other mode. Life is but a sad possession to those who have attained precisely the degree of moral advancement at which I stand. Were I weaker and blinder, it might be happiness. Were I stronger, it might be endured hopefully. But, being what I find myself, methinks I am of all mortals the most fit to die."   74

"You are fit for heaven without tasting death!" replied her husband. "But why do we speak of dying? The draught cannot fail. Behold its effect upon this plant!"   75

On the window-seat there stood a geranium, diseased with yellow blotches, which had overspread all its leaves. Aylmer poured a small quantity of the liquid upon the soil in which it grew. In a little time, when the roots of the plant had taken up the moisture, the unsightly blotches began to be extinguished in a living verdure.   76

"There needed no proof," said Georgiana, quietly. "Give me the goblet. I joyfully stake all upon your word."   77

"Drink, then, thou lofty creature!" exclaimed Aylmer, with fervid admiration. "There is no taint of imperfection on thy spirit. Thy sensible frame, too, shall be all perfect!"   78

She quaffed the liquid, and returned the goblet to his hand.   79

"It is grateful," said she, with a placid smile. "Methinks it is like water from a heavenly fountain; for it contains I know not what of unobtrusive fragrance and deliciousness. It allays a feverish thirst, that had parched me for many days. Now, dearest, let me sleep. My earthly senses are closing over my spirit, like the leaves round the heart of a rose, at sunset."   80

She spoke the last words with a gentle reluctance, as if it required almost more energy than she could command to pronounce the faint and lingering syllables. Scarcely had they loitered through her lips, ere she was   81 lost in slumber. Aylmer sat by her side, watching her aspect with the emotions proper to a man, the whole value of whose existence was involved in the process now to be tested. Mingled with this mood, however, was the philosophic investigation, characteristic of the man of science. Not the minutest symptom escaped him. A heightened flush of the check—a slight irregularity of breath—a quiver of the eyelid—a hardly perceptible tremor through the frame—such were the details which, as the moments passed, he wrote down in his folio volume. Intense thought had set its stamp upon every previous page of that volume; but the thoughts of years were all concentrated upon the last.

While thus employed, he failed not to gaze often at the fatal Hand, 82 and not without a shudder. Yet once, by a strange and unaccountable impulse, he pressed it with his lips. His spirit recoiled, however, in the very act, and Georgiana, out of the midst of her deep sleep, moved uneasily and murmured as if in remonstrance. Again, Aylmer resumed his watch. Nor was it without avail. The Crimson Hand, which at first had been strongly visible upon the marble paleness of Georgiana's cheek, now grew more faintly outlined. She remained not less pale than ever; but the birth-mark, with every breath that came and went, lost somewhat of its former distinctness. Its presence had been awful; its departure was more awful still. Watch the stain of the rainbow fading out of the sky; and you will know how that mysterious symbol passed away.

"By Heaven, it is well nigh gone!" said Alymer to himself, in almost 83 irrepressible ecstacy. "I can scarcely trace it now. Success! Success! And now it is like the faintest rose-color. The slightest flush of blood across her cheek would overcome it. But she is so pale!"

He drew aside the window-curtain, and suffered the light of natural 84 day to fall into the room, and rest upon her cheek. At the same time, he heard a gross, hoarse chuckle, which he had long known as his servant Aminadab's expression of delight.

"Ah, clod! Ah, earthly mass!" cried Aylmer, laughing in a sort of 85 frenzy. "You have served me well! Matter and Spirit—Earth and Heaven— have both done their part in this! Laugh, thing of senses! You have earned the right to laugh."

These exclamations broke Georgiana's sleep. She slowly unclosed her 86 eyes, and gazed into the mirror, which her husband had arranged for that purpose. A faint smile flitted over her lips, when she recognized how barely perceptible was now that Crimson Hand, which had once blazed forth with such disastrous brilliancy as to scare away all their happiness. But then her eyes sought Aylmer's face, with a trouble and anxiety that he could by no means account for.

"My poor Aylmer!" murmured she. 87

"Poor? Nay, richest! Happiest! Most favored!" exclaimed he. "My 88 peerless bride, it is successful! You are perfect!"

"My poor Aylmer!" she repeated, with a more than human tenderness. "You have aimed loftily!—you have done nobly! Do not repent, that, with so high and pure a feeling, you have rejected the best that earth could offer. Aylmer—dearest Aylmer—I am dying!"

Alas, it was too true! The fatal Hand had grappled with the mystery of life, and was the bond by which an angelic spirit kept itself in union with a mortal frame. As the last crimson tint of the birth-mark—that sole token of human imperfection—faded from her cheek, the parting breath of the now perfect woman passed into the atmosphere, and her soul, lingering a moment near her husband, took its heavenward flight. Then a hoarse, chuckling laugh was heard again! Thus ever does the gross Fatality of Earth exult in its invariable triumph over the immortal essence, which, in this dim sphere of half-development, demands the completeness of a higher state. Yet, had Aylmer reached a profounder wisdom, he need not thus have flung away the happiness, which would have woven his mortal life of the self-same texture with the celestial. The momentary circumstance was strong for him; he failed to look beyond the shadowy scope of Time, and living once for all in Eternity, to find the perfect Future in the present.

Questions for Study and Discussion

1. Why do you think Hawthorne chose a birthmark for the wife's imperfection? Why did he choose the figure of a hand for that mark? What does it represent? In what way can the symbolism be extended beyond the immediate story?

2. Hawthorne's story is an example of "romanticism," which is characterized by its celebration of nature, imagination, emotion, introspection, the individual, and the transcendent. Choose elements from Hawthorne's story that exemplify these various aspects of romanticism and explain in what ways they do so.

3. In Hawthorne's story what is the role of the husband, the wife, the laboratory assistant? What differing view of mortality and perfection does each of them represent? Which one most closely resembles the author's point of view? How do you know?

4. The husband can be said to have been "marked" by his obsession with his work. How was the husband's "fatal flaw" revealed and developed in Hawthorne's story? In what way did his flaw compare to the author's treatment of the birthmark?

5. What is the dominant impression or mood of Hawthorne's story? What kinds of details does he use to create that mood? Were you surprised by the ending of Hawthorne's story?

6. What is the meaning of the wife's final words to her husband? What do these words reveal to you about Hawthorne's position on the nature of science and the transcendent?

Writing Topics

1. Hawthorne's protagonist is a scientist whose work was his obsession even at the expense of the wife he professed to love. His law was simple and inviolate: the work of the scientist can achieve transcendence and so by definition is above the laws which apply to other mortals. How do we regard the scientific community today? Should we impose limits on scientific experimentation? If not, why not? If so, how does a society impose limits and guidelines on intellectual growth?

2. In an essay, describe a person you know with the qualitites portrayed in the scientist's assistant in Hawthorne's story. What motivates someone like him? What does he value? How are you like him? how different?

The right to freedom also necessarily includes the means to execute that right. If I have no income and no resources whatever and am then offered a job at two dollars an hour, am I really free not to take it?

WILLIAM RYAN

Present day civilization is full of evils, but it is also full of good; and it has the capacity in it to rid itself of those evils.

JAWAHARLAL NEHRU

Some Classic
Statements

THOMAS JEFFERSON

In June 1776 the Continental Congress chose a committee of five to draft a justification for revolution. Benjamin Franklin, John Adams, and Thomas Jefferson were among its members. The committee in turn asked Jefferson to write a first draft. Born in 1743 in Albemarle County, Virginia, Jefferson was the youngest delegate to the Congress. He was, in time, to become a governor, secretary of state, and president before he died on July 4, 1826, but in 1776 he was known only as a talented lawyer out of William and Mary College with a gift for words. His draft was lightly revised by Adams and Franklin and amended during the Congress's debate, but it remains essentially the work not of a committee but of one man with the political insight, the vision, and the rhetorical skill to speak for his people.

The Declaration of Independence

When in the course of human events, it becomes necessary for one   1
people to dissolve the political bands which have connected them with another, and to assume among the Powers of the earth, the separate and equal station to which the Laws of Nature and of Nature's God entitle them, a decent respect to the opinions of mankind requires that they should declare the causes which impel them to the separation.

We hold these truths to be self-evident, that all men are created equal,   2
that they are endowed by their Creator with certain unalienable Rights, that among these are Life, Liberty and the pursuit of Happiness. That to secure these rights, Governments are instituted among Men deriving their just powers from the consent of the governed. That whenever any Form of Government becomes destructive of these ends, it is the Right of the People to alter or to abolish it, and to institute new Government, laying its foundation on such principles and organizing its powers in such form, as to them shall seem most likely to effect their Safety and Happiness. Prudence, indeed, will dictate that Governments long established should not be changed for light and transient causes; and accordingly all experience hath

671

shown, that mankind are more disposed to suffer, while evils are sufferable, than to right themselves by abolishing the forms to which they are accustomed. But when a long train of abuses and usurpations pursuing invariably the same Object evinces a design to reduce them under absolute Despotism, it is their right, it is their duty, to throw off such government, and to provide new Guards for their future security. Such has been the patient sufferance of these Colonies; and such is now the necessity which constrains them to alter their former Systems of Government. The history of the present King of Great Britain is a history of repeated injuries and usurpations, all having in direct object the establishment of an absolute Tyranny over these States. To prove this, let Facts be submitted to a candid world.

He has refused his Assent to laws, the most wholesome and necessary   3
for the public good.

He has forbidden his Governors to pass Laws of immediate and   4
pressing importance, unless suspended in their operation till his Assent should be obtained; and when so suspended, he has utterly neglected to attend to them.

He has refused to pass other Laws for the accommodation of large   5
districts of people, unless those people would relinquish the right of Representation in the Legislature, a right inestimable to them and formidable to tyrants only.

He has called together legislative bodies at places unusual, uncomfort-   6
able, and distant from the depository of their Public Records, for the sole purpose of fatiguing them into compliance with his measures.

He has dissolved Representative Houses repeatedly, for opposing with   7
manly firmness his invasions on the rights of the people.

He has refused for a long time, after such dissolutions, to cause others   8
to be elected; whereby the Legislative Powers, incapable of Annihilation, have returned to the People at large for their exercise; the State remaining in the mean time exposed to all the dangers of invasion from without, and convulsions within.

He has endeavoured to prevent the population of these States; for that   9
purpose obstructing the Laws of Naturalization of Foreigners; refusing to pass others to encourage their migration hither, and raising the conditions of new Appropriations of Lands.

He has obstructed the Administration of Justice, by refusing his   10
Assent to Laws for establishing Judiciary Powers.

He has made Judges dependent on his Will alone, for the tenure of   11
their offices, and the amount and payment of their salaries.

He has erected a multitude of New Offices, and sent hither swarms of   12
Officers to harass our People, and eat out their substance.

He has kept among us, in time of peace, Standing Armies without the   13
Consent of our Legislature.

He has affected to render the Military independent of and superior to 14
the Civil Power.

He has combined with others to subject us to jurisdictions foreign to 15
our constitution, and unacknowledged by our laws; giving his Assent to
their acts of pretended Legislation:

For quartering large bodies of armed troops among us: 16

For protecting them, by a mock Trial, from Punishment for any 17
Murders which they should commit on the Inhabitants of these States:

For cutting off our Trade with all parts of the world: 18

For imposing Taxes on us without our Consent: 19

For depriving us in many cases, of the benefits of Trial by Jury: 20

For transporting us beyond Seas to be tried for pretended offenses: 21

For abolishing the free System of English Laws in a Neighbouring 22
Province, establishing therein an Arbitrary government, and enlarging its
boundaries so as to render it at once an example and fit instrument for
introducing the same absolute rule into these Colonies:

For taking away our Charters, abolishing our most valuable Laws, and 23
altering fundamentally the Forms of our Governments:

For suspending our own Legislatures, and declaring themselves in- 24
vested with Power to legislate for us in all cases whatsoever.

He has abdicated Government here, by declaring us out of his Protec- 25
tion and waging War against us.

He has plundered our seas, ravaged our Coasts, burnt our towns and 26
destroyed the Lives of our people.

He is at this time transporting large Armies of foreign Mercenaries to 27
compleat works of death, desolation and tyranny, already begun with
circumstances of Cruelty & perfidy scarcely paralleled in the most barbarous ages, and totally unworthy the Head of a civilized nation.

He has constrained our fellow Citizens taken Captive on the high Seas 28
to bear Arms against their Country, to become the executioners of their
friends and Brethren, or to fall themselves by their Hands.

He has excited domestic insurrections amongst us, and has endeav- 29
oured to bring on the inhabitants of our frontiers, the merciless Indian
Savages, whose known rule of warfare, is an undistinguished destruction of
all ages, sexes and conditions.

In every stage of these Oppressions We Have Petitioned for Redress in 30
the most humble terms: Our repeated petitions have been answered only by
repeated injury. A Prince, whose character is thus marked by every act
which may define a Tyrant, is unfit to be the ruler of a free People.

Nor have We been wanting in attention to our British brethren. We 31
have warned them from time to time of attempts by their legislature to
extend an unwarrantable jurisdiction over us. We have reminded them of
the circumstances of our emigration and settlement here. We have appealed
to their native justice and magnanimity and we have conjured them by the

ties of our common kindred to disavow these usurpations, which would inevitably interrupt our connections and correspondence. They too have been deaf to the voice of justice and of consanguinity. We must, therefore, acquiesce in the necessity, which denounces our Separation, and hold them, as we hold the rest of mankind, Enemies in War, in Peace Friends.

We, therefore, the Representatives of the United States of America, in General Congress, Assembled, appealing to the Supreme Judge of the world for the rectitude of our intentions, do, in the Name, and by Authority of the good People of these Colonies, solemnly publish and declare, That these United Colonies are, and of Right ought to be Free and Independent States; that they are Absolved from all Allegiance to the British Crown, and that all political connection between them and the State of Great Britain, is and ought to be totally dissolved; and that as Free and Independent States, they have full power to levy War, conclude Peace, contract Alliances, establish Commerce, and to do all other Acts and Things which Independent States may of right do. And for the support of this Declaration, with a firm reliance on the protection of Divine Providence, we mutually pledge to each other our lives, our Fortunes and our sacred Honor. 32

Questions for Study and Discussion

1. According to the Declaration of Independence, what is the purpose of government? Are there other legitimate purposes that governments serve? If so, what are they?

2. What is the chief argument offered by the Declaration for "abolishing" English rule over the American colonies? How is that argument supported?

3. What argument does the Declaration make for overthrowing any unacceptable government? What assumptions underlie this argument? Where does sovereignty lie, according to the Declaration?

4. According to the Declaration, how did the colonists try to persuade the English king to rule more justly?

5. Is the language of the Declaration of Independence coolly reasonable or emotional, or does it change from one to the other? Give examples to support your answer.

Writing Topics

1. To some people the Declaration of Independence still accurately reflects America's political philosophy and way of life; to others it does not. What is your position? Discuss your analysis of the Declaration's contemporary relevance.

2. The adoption of the Declaration of Independence was, among other things, a matter of practical politics. Using library sources, research the deliberations of the Continental Congress and explain how and why the final version of the Declaration differs from Jefferson's first draft.

HENRY DAVID THOREAU

In 1845, at the age of twenty-eight, Henry David Thoreau built a cabin in the woods near Walden Pond and moved in. He wanted to live alone with nature and hoped to free his life from materialistic concerns. He stayed there for more than two years, an experience he later described in his greatest literary work, *Walden, or Life in the Woods* (1854).

Thoreau was born in 1817 in Concord, Massachusetts. After graduating from Harvard College, he worked as a schoolteacher, a house-painter, and a handyman—the latter for his mentor and friend, Ralph Waldo Emerson. Thoreau was always an activist, once going to jail rather than pay a poll tax to a government that made war with Mexico and supported slavery. This act of civil disobedience in protest of actions that he considered unjust is the subject of his essay "Civil Disobedience" (1849), which later inspired both Gandhi and Martin Luther King, Jr., in their nonviolent protests. Thoreau died in 1862.

Civil Disobedience

I heartily accept the motto, "That government is best which governs least;" and I should like to see it acted up to more rapidly and systematically. Carried out, it finally amounts to this, which also I believe—"That government is best which governs not at all;" and when men are prepared for it, that will be the kind of government which they will have. Government is at best but an expedient; but most governments are usually, and all governments are sometimes, inexpedient. The objections which have been brought against a standing army, and they are many and weighty, and deserve to prevail, may also at last be brought against a standing government. The standing army is only an arm of the standing government. The government itself, which is only the mode which the people have chosen to execute their will, is equally liable to be abused and perverted before the people can act through it. Witness the present Mexican war, the work of comparatively a few individuals using the standing government as their tool; for, in the outset, the people would not have consented to this measure.

This American government—what is it but a tradition, though a recent one, endeavoring to transmit itself unimpaired to posterity, but each instant losing some of its integrity? It has not the vitality and force of a single living man; for a single man can bend it to his will. It is a sort of wooden gun to the people themselves. But it is not the less necessary for this; for the people must have some complicated machinery or other, and hear its din, to satisfy that idea of government which they have. Governments show thus how successfully men can be imposed on, even impose on themselves, for their own advantage. It is excellent, we must all allow. Yet this government never of itself furthered any enterprise, but by the alacrity with which it got out of its way. *It* does not keep the country free. *It* does not settle the West. *It* does not educate. The character inherent in the American people has done all that has been accomplished; and it would have done somewhat more, if the government had not sometimes got in its way. For government is an expedient by which men would fain succeed in letting one another alone; and, as has been said, when it is most expedient, the governed are most let alone by it. Trade and commerce, if they were not made of india-rubber, would never manage to bounce over the obstacles which legislators are continually putting in their way; and, if one were to judge these men wholly by the effects of their actions and not partly by their intentions, they would deserve to be classed and punished with those mischievous persons who put obstructions on the railroads.

But, to speak practically and as a citizen, unlike those who call themselves no-government men, I ask for, not at once no government, but *at once* a better government. Let every man make known what kind of government would command his respect, and that will be one step toward obtaining it. 3

After all, the practical reason why, when the power is once in the hands of the people, a majority are permitted, and for a long period continue, to rule is not because they are most likely to be in the right, nor because this seems fairest to the minority, but because they are physically the strongest. But a government in which the majority rule in all cases cannot be based on justice, even as far as men understand it. Can there not be a government in which majorities do not virtually decide right and wrong, but conscience?—in which majorities decide only those questions to which the rule of expediency is applicable? Must the citizen ever for a moment, or in the last degree, resign his conscience to the legislator? Why has every man a conscience, then? I think that we should be men first, and subjects afterwards. It is not desirable to cultivate a respect for the law, so much as for the right. The only obligation which I have a right to assume is to do at any time what I think right. It is truly enough said that a corporation has no conscience; but a corporation of conscientious men is a corporation *with* a conscience. Law never made men a whit more just; and, by means of their respect for it, even the well-disposed are daily made the agents of injustice. A common and natural result of an undue respect for law is, that you may see a file of soldiers, colonel, captain, corporal, privates, powder-monkeys, and all, marching in admirable order over hill and dale to the wars, against their wills, ay, against their common sense and consciences, which makes it very steep marching indeed, and produces a palpitation of the heart. They have no doubt that it is a damnable business in which they are concerned; they are all peaceably inclined. Now, what are they? Men at all? or small movable forts and magazines, at the service of some unscrupulous man in power? Visit the Navy-Yard, and behold a 4 marine, such a man as an American government can make, or such as it can make a man with its black arts—a mere shadow and reminiscence of humanity, a man laid out alive and standing, and already, as one may say, buried under arms with funeral accompaniments, though it may be,—

Not a drum was heard, not a funeral note,
   As his corse to the rampart we hurried;
Not a soldier discharged his farewell shot
   O'er the grave where our hero was buried.[1]

     The mass of men serve the state thus, not as men mainly, but as 5 machines, with their bodies. They are the standing army, and the militia, jailers, constables, *posse comitatus*, etc. In most cases there is no free exercise whatever of the judgment or of the moral sense; but they put themselves on a level with wood and earth and stones; and wooden men can perhaps be manufactured that will serve the purpose as well. Such command no more respect than men of straw or a lump of dirt. They have the same sort of worth only as horses and dogs. Yet such as these even are commonly esteemed good citizens. Others—as most legislators, politicians, lawyers, ministers, and office-holders—serve the state chiefly with their heads; and, as they rarely make any moral distinctions, they are as likely to serve the devil, without *intending* it, as God. A very few—as heroes, patriots, martyrs, reformers in the great sense, and *men*—serve the state with their consciences also, and so necessarily resist it for the most part; and they are commonly treated as enemies by it. A wise man will only be useful as a man, and will not submit to be "clay," and "stop a hole to keep the wind away,"[2] but leave that office to his dust at least:—

I am too high-born to be propertied,
To be a secondary at control,
Or useful serving-man and instrument
To any sovereign state throughout the world.[3]

     He who gives himself entirely to his fellow-men appears to them 6 useless and selfish; but he who gives himself partially to them is pronounced a benefactor and philanthropist.

     How does it become a man to behave toward this American govern- 7 ment today? I answer, that he cannot without disgrace be associated with it. I cannot for an instant recognize that political organization as *my* government which is the *slave's* government also.

---

[1]Charles Wolfe, "Burial of Sir John Moore at Corunna" (1817).
[2]*Hamlet*, V, i, ll. 236–237.
[3]*King John*, V, ii, ll. 79–82.

All men recognize the right of revolution; that is, the right to refuse   8
allegiance to, and to resist, the government, when its tyranny or its inefficiency are great and unendurable. But almost all say that such is not the
case now. But such was the case, they think, in the Revolution of '75. If one
were to tell me that this was a bad government because it taxed certain
foreign commodities brought to its ports, it is most probable that I should
not make an ado about it, for I can do without them. All machines have
their friction; and possibly this does enough good to counterbalance the
evil. At any rate, it is a great evil to make a stir about it. But when the
friction comes to have its machine, and oppression and robbery are
organized, I say, let us not have such a machine any longer. In other words,
when a sixth of the population of a nation which has undertaken to be the
refuge of liberty are slaves, and a whole country is unjustly overrun and
conquered by a foreign army, and subjected to military law, I think that it is
not too soon for honest men to rebel and revolutionize. What makes this
duty the more urgent is the fact that the country so overrun is not our own,
but ours is the invading army.

Paley,[4] a common authority with many on moral questions, in his   9
chapter on the "Duty of Submission to Civil Government," resolves all civil
obligation into expediency; and he proceeds to say that "so long as the
interest of the whole society requires it, that is, so long as the established
government cannot be resisted or changed without public inconveniency, it
is the will of God . . . that the established government be obeyed—and no
longer. The principle being admitted, the justice of every particular case of
resistance is reduced to a computation of the quantity of the danger and
grievance on the one side, and of the probability and expense of redressing
it on the other." Of this, he says, every man shall judge for himself. But
Paley appears never to have contemplated those cases to which the rule of
expediency does not apply, in which a people, as well as an individual, must
do justice, cost what it may. If I have unjustly wrested a plank from a
drowning man, I must restore it to him though I drown myself.[5] This,
according to Paley, would be inconvenient. But he that would save his life,
in such a case, shall lose it.[6] This people must cease to hold slaves, and to
make war on Mexico, though it cost them their existence as a people.

In their practice, nations agree with Paley; but does any one think   10
that Massachusetts does exactly what is right at the present crisis?

A drab of state, a cloth-o'-silver slut,
To have her train borne up, and her soul trail in the dirt.

---

[4]Rev. William Paley, *Principles of Moral and Political Philosophy* (1785), a text Thoreau is
known to have studied at Harvard College.

[5]Cited by Cicero, *De Officiis*, III, a text Thoreau knew at college.

[6]Luke IX: 24; Matthew X: 39.

Practically speaking, the opponents to a reform in Massachusetts are not a hundred thousand politicians at the South, but a hundred thousand merchants and farmers here, who are more interested in commerce and agriculture than they are in humanity, and are not prepared to do justice to the slave and to Mexico, *cost what it may*. I quarrel not with far-off foes, but with those who, near at home, coöperate with, and do the bidding of, those far away, and without whom the latter would be harmless. We are accustomed to say, that the mass of men are unprepared; but improvement is slow, because the few are not materially wiser or better than the many. It is not so important that many should be as good as you, as that there be some absolute goodness somewhere; for that will leaven the whole lump.[7] There are thousands who are *in opinion* opposed to slavery and to the war, who yet in effect do nothing to put an end to them; who, esteeming themselves children of Washington and Franklin, sit down with their hands in their pockets, and say that they know not what to do, and do nothing; who even postpone the question of freedom to the question of free trade, and quietly read the prices-current along with the latest advices from Mexico, after dinner, and, it may be, fall asleep over them both. What is the price-current of an honest man and patriot today? They hestitate, and they regret, and sometimes they petition; but they do nothing in earnest and with effect. They will wait, well disposed, for others to remedy the evil, that they may no longer have it to regret. At most, they give only a cheap vote, and a feeble countenance and God-speed, to the right, as it goes by them. There are nine hundred and ninety-nine patrons of virtue to one virtuous man. But it is easier to deal with the real possessor of a thing than with the temporary guardian of it.

All voting is a sort of gaming, like checkers or backgammon, with a slight moral tinge to it, a playing with right and wrong, with moral questions; and betting naturally accompanies it. The character of the voters is not staked. I cast my vote, perchance, as I think right; but I am not vitally concerned that that right should prevail. I am willing to leave it to the majority. Its obligation, therefore, never exceeds that of expediency. Even voting *for the right* is *doing* nothing for it. It is only expressing to men feebly your desire that it should prevail. A wise man will not leave the right to the mercy of chance, nor wish it to prevail through the power of the majority. There is but little virtue in the action of masses of men. When the majority shall at length vote for the abolition of slavery, it will be because they are indifferent to slavery, or because there is but little slavery left to be abolished by their vote. *They* will then be the only slaves. Only *his* vote can hasten the abolition of slavery who asserts his own freedom by his vote.

I hear of a convention to be held at Baltimore, or elsewhere, for the

11

12

---

[7] I Corinthians V: 6.

selection of a candidate for the Presidency, made up chiefly of editors, and men who are politicians by profession; but I think, what is it to any independent, intelligent, and respectable man what decision they may come to? Shall we not have the advantage of his wisdom and honesty, nevertheless? Can we not count upon some independent votes? Are there not many individuals in the country who do not attend conventions? But no: I find that the respectable man, so called, has immediately drifted from his position, and despairs of his country, when his country has more reason to despair of him. He forthwith adopts one of the candidates thus selected as the only *available* one, thus proving that he is himself *available* for any purposes of the demagogue. His vote is of no more worth than that of any unprincipled foreigner or hireling native, who may have been bought. O for a man who is a *man*, and, as my neighbor says, has a bone in his back which you cannot pass your hand through! Our statistics are at fault: the population has been returned too large. How many *men* are there to a square thousand miles in this country? Hardly one. Does not America offer any inducement for men to settle here? The American has dwindled into an Odd Fellow—one who may be known by the development of his organ of gregariousness, and a manifest lack of intellect and cheerful self-reliance; whose first and chief concern, on coming into the world, is to see that the almshouses are in good repair; and, before yet he has lawfully donned the virile garb, to collect a fund for the support of the widows and orphans that may be; who, in short, ventures to live only by the aid of the Mutual Insurance company, which has promised to bury him decently.

It is not a man's duty, as a matter of course, to devote himself to the eradication of any, even the most enormous, wrong; he may still properly have other concerns to engage him; but it is his duty, at least, to wash his hands of it, and, if he gives it no thought longer, not to give it practically his support. If I devote myself to other pursuits and contemplations, I must first see, at least, that I do not pursue them sitting upon another man's shoulders. I must get off him first, that he may pursue his contemplations too. See what gross inconsistency is tolerated. I have heard some of my townsmen say, "I should like to have them order me out to help put down an insurrection of the slaves, or to march to Mexico;—see if I would go"; and yet these very men have each, directly by their allegiance, and so indirectly, at least, by their money, furnished a substitute. The soldier is applauded who refuses to serve in an unjust war by those who do not refuse to sustain the unjust government which makes the war; is applauded by those whose own act and authority he disregards and sets at naught; as if the state were penitent to that degree that it hired one to scourge it while it sinned, but not to that degree that it left off sinning for a moment. Thus, under the name of Order and Civil Government, we are all made at last to pay homage to and support our own meanness. After the first blush of sin

13

comes its indifference; and from immoral it becomes, as it were, *unmoral*, and not quite unnecessary to that life which we have made.

The broadest and most prevalent error requires the most disinterested   14
virtue to sustain it. The slight reproach to which the virtue of patriotism is commonly liable, the noble are most likely to incur. Those who, while they disapprove of the character and measures of a government, yield to it their allegiance and support are undoubtedly its most conscientious supporters, and so frequently the most serious obstacles to reform. Some are petitioning the State to dissolve the Union, to disregard the requisitions of the President. Why do they not dissolve it themselves—the union between themselves and the State—and refuse to pay their quota into its treasury? Do not they stand in the same relation to the State that the State does to the Union? And have not the same reasons prevented the State from resisting the Union which have prevented them from resisting the State?

How can a man be satisfied to entertain an opinion merely, and enjoy   15
it? Is there any enjoyment in it, if his opinion is that he is aggrieved? If you are cheated out of a single dollar by your neighbor, you do not rest satisfied with knowing that you are cheated, or with saying that you are cheated, or even with petitioning him to pay you your due; but you take effectual steps at once to obtain the full amount, and see that you are never cheated again. Action from principle, the perception and the performance of right, changes things and relations; it is essentially revolutionary, and does not consist wholly with anything which was. It not only divides States and churches, it divides families; ay, it divides the *individual*, separating the diabolical in him from the divine.

Unjust laws exist: shall we be content to obey them, or shall we   16
endeavor to amend them, and obey them until we have succeeded, or shall we transgress them at once? Men generally, under such a government as this, think that they ought to wait until they have persuaded the majority to alter them. They think that, if they should resist, the remedy would be worse than the evil. But it is the fault of the government itself that the remedy *is* worse than the evil. *It* makes it worse. Why is it not more apt to anticipate and provide for reform? Why does it not cherish its wise minority? Why does it cry and resist before it is hurt? Why does it not encourage its citizens to be on the alert to point out its faults, and *do* better than it would have them? Why does it always crucify Christ, and excommunicate Copernicus and Luther, and pronounce Washington and Franklin rebels?

One would think, that a deliberate and practical denial of its au-   17
thority was the only offence never contemplated by government; else, why has it not assigned its definite, its suitable and proportionate, penalty? If a man who has no property refuses but once to earn nine shillings for the State, he is put in prison for a period unlimited by any law that I know, and determined only by the discretion of those who placed him there; but if he

should steal ninety times nine shillings from the State, he is soon permitted to go at large again.

If the injustice is part of the necessary friction of the machine of government, let it go, let it go: perchance it will wear smoothly—certainly the machine will wear out. If the injustice has a spring, or a pulley, or a rope, or a crank, exclusively for itself, then perhaps you may consider whether the remedy will not be worse than the evil; but if it is of such a nature that it requires you to be the agent of injustice to another, then, I say, break the law. Let your life be a counter friction to stop the machine. What I have to do is to see, at any rate, that I do not lend myself to the wrong which I condemn.

As for adopting the ways which the State has provided for remedying the evil, I know not of such ways. They take too much time, and a man's life will be gone. I have other affairs to attend to. I came into this world, not chiefly to make this a good place to live in, but to live in it, be it good or bad. A man has not everything to do, but something; and because he cannot do *everything*, it is not necessary that he should do *something* wrong. It is not my business to be petitioning the Governor or the Legislature any more than it is theirs to petition me; and if they should not hear my petition, what should I do then? But in this case the State has provided no way: its very Constitution is the evil. This may seem to be harsh and stubborn and unconciliatory; but it is to treat with the utmost kindness and consideration the only spirit that can appreciate or deserves it. So is all change for the better, like birth and death, which convulse the body.

I do not hesitate to say, that those who call themselves Abolitionists should at once effectually withdraw their support, both in person and property, from the government of Massachusetts, and not wait till they constitute a majority of one, before they suffer the right to prevail through them. I think that it is enough if they have God on their side, without waiting for that other one. Moreover, any man more right than his neighbors constitutes a majority of one already.

I meet the American government, or its representative, the State government, directly, and face to face, once a year—no more—in the person of its tax-gatherer; this is the only mode in which a man situated as I am necessarily meets it; and it then says distinctly, Recognize me; and the simplest, the most effectual, and, in the present posture of affairs, the indispensablest mode of treating with it on this head, of expressing your little satisfaction with and love for it, is to deny it then. My civil neighbor, the tax-gatherer, is the very man I have to deal with—for it is, after all, with men and not with parchment that I quarrel—and he has voluntarily chosen to be an agent of the government. How shall he ever know well what he is and does as an officer of the government, or as a man, until he is obliged to consider whether he shall treat me, his neighbor, for whom he has respect, as a neighbor and well-disposed man, or as a maniac and disturber of the

18

19

20

21

peace, and see if he can get over this obstruction to his neighborliness without a ruder and more impetuous thought or speech corresponding with his action. I know this well, that if one thousand, if one hundred, if ten men whom I could name—if ten *honest* men only—ay, if *one* HONEST man, in this State of Massachusetts, *ceasing to hold slaves*, were actually to withdraw from this copartnership, and be locked up in the county jail therefore, it would be the abolition of slavery in America. For it matters not how small the beginning may seem to be: what is once well done is done forever. But we love better to talk about it: that we say is our mission. Reform keeps many scores of newspapers in its service, but not one man. If my esteemed neighbor, the State's ambassador,[8] who will devote his days to the settlement of the question of human rights in the Council Chamber, instead of being threatened with the prisons of Carolina, were to sit down the prisoner of Massachusetts, that State which is so anxious to foist the sin of slavery upon her sister—though at present she can discover only an act of inhospitality to be the ground of a quarrel with her—the Legislature would not wholly waive the subject the following winter.

Under a government which imprisons any unjustly, the true place for a just man is also a prison. The proper place to-day, the only place which Massachusetts has provided for her freer and less desponding spirits, is in her prisons, to be put out and locked out of the State by her own act, as they have already put themselves out by their principles. It is there that the fugitive slave, and the Mexican prisoner on parole, and the Indian come to plead the wrongs of his race should find them; on that separate, but more free and honorable, ground, where the State places those who are not *with* her, but *against* her—the only house in a slave State in which a free man can abide with honor. If any think that their influence would be lost there, and their voices no longer afflict the ear of the State, that they would not be as an enemy within its walls, they do not know by how much truth is stronger than error, nor how much more eloquently and effectively he can combat injustice who has experienced a little in his own person. Cast your whole vote, not a strip of paper merely, but your whole influence. A minority is powerless while it conforms to the majority; it is not even a minority then; but it is irresistible when it clogs by its whole weight. If the alternative is to keep all just men in prison, or give up war and slavery, the State will not hesitate which to choose. If a thousand men were not to pay their tax-bills this year, that would not be a violent and bloody measure, as it would be to pay them, and enable the State to commit violence and shed innocent blood. This is, in fact, the definition of a peaceable revolution, if any such is

22

---

[8]In 1844, Samuel Hoar, the statesman of Concord, was sent to Charleston, South Carolina, on behalf of African-American seamen from Massachusetts threatened with arrest and slavery on entering the port, and was rudely expelled from Charleston.

possible. If the tax-gatherer, or any public officer, asks me, as one has done, "But what shall I do?" my answer is, "If you really wish to do anything, resign your office." When the subject has refused allegiance, and the officer has resigned his office, then the revolution is accomplished. But even suppose blood should flow. Is there not a sort of blood shed when the conscience is wounded? Through this wound a man's real manhood and immortality flow out, and he bleeds to an everlasting death. I see this blood flowing now.

I have contemplated the imprisonment of the offender, rather than the seizure of his goods—though both will serve the same purpose—because they who assert the purest right, and consequently are most dangerous to a corrupt State, commonly have not spent much time in accumulating property. To such the State renders comparatively small service, and a slight tax is wont to appear exorbitant, particularly if they are obliged to earn it by special labor with their hands. If there were one who lived wholly without the use of money, the State itself would hesitate to demand it of him. But the rich man—not to make any invidious comparison—is always sold to the institution which makes him rich. Absolutely speaking, the more money, the less virtue; for money comes between a man and his objects, and obtains them for him; and it was certainly no great virtue to obtain it. It puts to rest many questions which he would otherwise be taxed to answer; while the only new question which it puts is the hard but superfluous one, how to spend it. Thus his moral ground is taken from under his feet. The opportunities of living are diminished in proportion as what are called the "means" are increased. The best thing a man can do for his culture when he is rich is to endeavor to carry out those schemes which he entertained when he was poor. Christ answered the Herodians according to their condition. "Show me the tribute-money," said he;—and one took a penny out of his pocket;—if you use money which has the image of Caesar on it, and which he has made current and valuable, that is, *if you are men of the State*, and gladly enjoy the advantages of Caesar's government, then pay him back some of his own when he demands it. "Render therefore to Caesar that which is Caesar's, and to God those things which are God's"—leaving them no wiser than before as to which was which; for they did not wish to know. 23

When I converse with the freest of my neighbors, I perceive that, whatever they may say about the magnitude and seriousness of the question, and their regard for the public tranquillity, the long and the short of the matter is, that they cannot spare the protection of the existing government, and they dread the consequences to their property and families of disobedience to it. For my own part, I should not like to think that I ever rely on the protection of the State. But, if I deny the authority of the State when it presents its tax-bill, it will soon take and waste all my property, and so harass me and my children without end. This is hard. This makes it impossible for a man to live honestly, and at the same time comfortably, in 24 outward respects. It will not be worth the while to accumulate property; that would be sure to go again. You must hire or squat somewhere, and raise but a small crop, and eat that soon. You must live within yourself, and depend upon yourself always tucked up and ready for a start, and not have many affairs. A man may grow rich in Turkey even, if he will be in all respects a good subject of the Turkish government. Confucius said: "If a state is governed by the principles of reason, poverty and misery are subjects of shame; if a state is not governed by the principles of reason, riches and honors are the subjects of shame." No: until I want the protection of Massachusetts to be extended to me in some distant Southern port, where my liberty is endangered, or until I am bent solely on building up an estate at home by peaceful enterprise, I can afford to refuse allegiance to Massachusetts, and her right to my property and life. It costs me less in every sense to incur the penalty of disobedience to the State than it would to obey. I should feel as if I were worth less in that case.

Some years ago, the State met me in behalf of the Church, and commanded me to pay a certain sum toward the support of a clergyman whose preaching my father attended, but never I myself. "Pay," it said, "or be locked up in the jail." I declined to pay.[9] But, unfortunately, another man saw fit to pay it. I did not see why the schoolmaster should be taxed to support the priest, and not the priest the schoolmaster; for I was not the State's schoolmaster, but I supported myself by voluntary subscription. I did not see why the lyceum should not present its tax-bill, and have the State to back its demand, as well as the Church. However, at the request of the selectmen, I condescended to make some such statement as this in writing:—"Know all men by these presents, that I, Henry Thoreau, do not wish to be regarded as a member of any incorporated society which I have not joined." This I gave to the town clerk; and he has it. The State, having thus learned that I did not wish to be regarded as a member of that church, has never made a like demand on me since; though it said that it must adhere to its original presumption that time. If I had known how to name them, I should then have signed off in detail from all the societies which I never signed on to; but I did not know where to find a complete list.

I have paid no poll-tax for six years. I was put into a jail once on this account, for one night; and, as I stood considering the walls of solid stone, two or three feet thick, the door of wood and iron, a foot thick, and the iron grating which strained the light, I could not help being struck with the foolishness of that institution which treated me as if I were mere flesh and blood and bones to be locked up. I wondered that it should have concluded at length that this was the best use it could put me to, and had never

25

26

---

[9]Thoreau's first act on returning to Concord after leaving college was to "sign off" from the Church.

thought to avail itself of my services in some way. I saw that, if there was a wall of stone between me and my townsmen, there was a still more difficult one to climb or break through before they could get to be as free as I was. I did not for a moment feel confined, and the walls seemed a great waste of stone and mortar. I felt as if I alone of all my townsmen had paid my tax. They plainly did not know how to treat me, but behaved like persons who are underbred. In every threat and in every compliment there was a blunder; for they thought that my chief desire was to stand the other side of that stone wall. I could not but smile to see how industriously they locked the door on my meditations, which followed them out again without let or hindrance, and *they* were really all that was dangerous. As they could not reach me, they had resolved to punish my body; just as boys, if they cannot come at some person against whom they have a spite, will abuse his dog. I saw that the State was half-witted, that it was timid as a lone woman with her silver spoons, and that it did not know its friends from its foes, and I lost all my remaining respect for it, and pitied it.

Thus the State never intentionally confronts a man's sense, intellec-   27
tual or moral, but only his body, his senses. It is not armed with superior wit or honesty, but with superior physical strength. I was not born to be forced. I will breathe after my own fashion. Let us see who is the strongest. What force has a multitude? They only can force me who obey a higher law than I. They force me to become like themselves. I do not hear of *men* being *forced* to live this way or that by masses of men. What sort of life were that to live? When I meet a government which says to me, "Your money or your life," why should I be in haste to give it my money? It may be in a great strait, and not know what to do: I cannot help that. It must help itself; do as I do. It is not worth the while to snivel about it. I am not responsible for the successful working of the machinery of society. I am not the son of the engineer. I perceive that, when an acorn and a chestnut fall side by side, the one does not remain inert to make way for the other, but both obey their own laws, and spring and grow and flourish as best they can, till one, perchance, overshadows and destroys the other. If a plant cannot live according to its nature, it dies; and so a man.

The night in prison was novel and interesting enough. The prisoners   28
in their shirt-sleeves were enjoying a chat and the evening air in the doorway, when I entered. But the jailer said, "Come, boys, it is time to lock up"; and so they dispersed, and I heard the sound of their steps returning into the hollow apartments. My room-mate was introduced to me by the jailer as "a first-rate fellow and a clever man." When the door was locked, he showed me where to hang my hat, and how he managed matters there. The rooms were whitewashed once a month; and this one, at least, was the whitest, most simply furnished, and probably the neatest apartment in the town. He naturally wanted to know where I came from, and what brought me there; and, when I had told him, I asked him in my turn how he came

there, presuming him to be an honest man, of course; and, as the world goes, I believe he was. "Why," said he, "they accuse me of burning a barn; but I never did it." As near as I could discover, he had probably gone to bed in a barn when drunk, and smoked his pipe there; and so a barn was burnt. He had the reputation of being a clever man, had been there some three months waiting for his trial to come on, and would have to wait as much longer; but he was quite domesticated and contented, since he got his board for nothing; and thought that he was well treated.

He occupied one window, and I the other; and I saw that if one stayed there long, his principal business would be to look out the window. I had soon read all the tracts that were left there, and examined where former prisoners had broken out, and where a grate had been sawed off, and heard the history of the various occupants of that room; for I found that even here there was a history and a gossip which never circulated beyond the walls of the jail. Probably this is the only house in the town where verses are composed, which are afterward printed in a circular form, but not published. I was shown quite a long list of verses which were composed by some young men who had been detected in an attempt to escape, who avenged themselves by singing them. 29

I pumped my fellow-prisoner as dry as I could, for fear I should never see him again; but at length he showed me which was my bed, and left me to blow out the lamp. 30

It was like travelling into a far country, such as I had never expected to behold, to lie there for one night. It seemed to me that I never had heard the town clock strike before, nor the evening sounds of the village; for we slept with the windows open, which were inside the grating. It was to see my native village in the light of the Middle Ages, and our Concord was turned into a Rhine stream, and visions of knights and castles passed before me. They were the voices of old burghers that I heard in the streets. I was an involuntary spectator and auditor of whatever was done and said in the kitchen of the adjacent village inn—a wholly new and rare experience to me. It was a closer view of my native town. I was fairly inside of it. I never had seen its institutions before. This is one of its peculiar institutions; for it is a shire town. I began to comprehend what its inhabitants were about. 31

In the morning, our breakfasts were put through the hole in the door, in small oblong-square tin pans, made to fit, and holding a pint of chocolate, with brown bread, and an iron spoon. When they called for the vessels again, I was green enough to return what bread I had left; but my comrade seized it, and said that I should lay that up for lunch or dinner. Soon after he was let out to work at haying in a neighboring field, whither he went every day, and would not be back till noon; so he bade me good-day, saying that he doubted if he should see me again. 32

When I came out of prison—for some one interfered, and paid that tax—I did not perceive that great changes had taken place on the common, 33 such as he observed who went in a youth and emerged a tottering and gray-headed man; and yet a change had to my eyes come over the scene—the town, and State, and country—greater than any that mere time could effect. I saw yet more distinctly the State in which I lived. I saw to what extent the people among whom I lived could be trusted as good neighbors and friends; that their friendship was for summer weather only; that they did not greatly propose to do right; that they were a distinct race from me by their prejudices and superstitions, as the Chinamen and Malays are; that in their sacrifices to humanity they ran no risks, not even to their property; that after all they were not so noble but they treated the thief as he had treated them, and hoped, by a certain outward observance and a few prayers, and by walking in a particular straight though useless path from time to time, to save their souls. This may be to judge my neighbors harshly; for I believe that many of them are not aware that they have such an institution as the jail in their village.

It was formerly the custom in our village, when a poor debtor came   34
out of jail, for his acquaintances to salute him, looking through their fingers, which were crossed to represent the grating of a jail window, "How do ye do?" My neighbors did not thus salute me, but first looked at me, and then at one another, as if I had returned from a long journey. I was put into jail as I was going to the shoemaker's to get a shoe which was mended. When I was let out the next morning, I preceeded to finish my errand, and, having put on my mended shoe, joined a huckleberry party, who were impatient to put themselves under my conduct; and in half an hour—for the horse was soon tackled—was in the midst of a huckleberry field, on one of our highest hills, two miles off, and then the State was nowhere to be seen.

This is the whole history of "My Prisons."   35

I have never declined paying the highway tax, because I am as desirous   36
of being a good neighbor as I am of being a bad subject; and as for supporting schools, I am doing my part to educate my fellow-countrymen now. It is for no particular item in the tax-bill that I refuse to pay it. I simply wish to refuse allegiance to the State, to withdraw and stand aloof from it effectually. I do not care to trace the course of my dollar, if I could, till it buys a man or a musket to shoot one with—the dollar is innocent—but I am concerned to trace the effects of my allegiance. In fact, I quietly declare war with the State, after my fashion, though I will still make what use and get what advantage of her I can, as is usual in such cases.

If others pay the tax which is demanded of me, from a sympathy with   37
the State, they do but what they have already done in their own case, or rather they abet injustice to a greater extent than the State requires. If they pay the tax from a mistaken interest in the individual taxed, to save his property, or prevent his going to jail, it is because they have not considered wisely how far they let their private feelings interfere with the public good.

This, then, is my position at present. But one cannot be too much on   38 his guard in such a case, lest his action be biased by obstinacy or an undue regard for the opinions of men. Let him see that he does only what belongs to himself and to the hour.

I think sometimes, Why, this people mean well, they are only igno- 39 rant; they would do better if they knew how: why give your neighbors this pain to treat you as they are not inclined to? But I think again, This is no reason why I should do as they do, or permit others to suffer much greater pain of a different kind. Again, I sometimes say to myself, When many millions of men, without heat, without ill will, without personal feeling of any kind, demand of you a few shillings only, without the possibility, such is their constitution, of retracting or altering their present demand, and without the possibility, on your side, of appeal to any other millions, why expose yourself to this overwhelming brute force? You do not resist cold and hunger, the winds and the waves, thus obstinately; you quietly submit to a thousand similar necessities. You do not put your head into the fire. But just in proportion as I regard this as not wholly a brute force, but partly a human force, and consider that I have relations to those millions as to so many millions of men, and not of mere brute or inanimate things, I see that appeal is possible, first and instantaneously, from them to the Maker of them, and, secondly, from them to themselves. But if I put my head deliberately into the fire, there is no appeal to fire or to the Maker of fire, and I have only myself to blame. If I could convince myself that I have any right to be satisfied with men as they are, and to treat them accordingly, and not according, in some respects, to my requisitions and expectations of what they and I ought to be, then, like a good Mussulman and fatalist, I should endeavor to be satisfied with things as they are, and say it is the will of God. And, above all, there is this difference between resisting this and a purely brute or natural force, that I can resist this with some effect; but I cannot expect, like Orpheus, to change the nature of the rocks and trees and beasts.

I do not wish to quarrel with any man or nation. I do not wish to split 40 hairs, to make fine distinctions, or set myself up as better than my neighbors. I seek rather, I may say, even an excuse for conforming the laws of the land. I am but too ready to conform to them. Indeed, I have reason to suspect myself on this head; and each year, as the tax-gatherer comes round, I find myself disposed to review the acts and positions of the general and State governments, and the spirit of the people, to discover a pretext for conformity.

We must affect our country as our parents,
And if at any time we alienate
Our love or industry from doing it honor,
We must respect effects and teach the soul
Matter of conscience and religion,
And not desire of rule or benefit.

I believe that the State will soon be able to take all my work of this sort out of my hands, and then I shall be no better a patriot than my fellow-countrymen. Seen from a lower point of view, the Constitution, with all its faults, is very good; the law and the courts are very respectable; even this State and this American government are, in many respects, very admirable, and rare things, to be thankful for, such as a great many have described them; but seen from a point of view a little higher, they are what I have described them; seen from a higher still, and the highest, who shall say what they are, or that they are worth looking at or thinking of at all?

However, the government does not concern me much, and I shall   41
bestow the fewest possible thoughts on it. It is not many moments that I live under a government, even in this world. If a man is thought-free, fancy-free, imagination-free, that which *is not* never for a long time appearing *to be* to him, unwise rulers or reformers cannot fatally interrupt him.

I know that most men think differently from myself; but those whose   42
lives are by profession devoted to the study of these or kindred subjects content me as little as any. Statesmen and legislators, standing so completely within the institution, never distinctly and nakedly behold it. They speak of moving society, but have no resting-place without it. They may be men of a certain experience and discrimination, and have no doubt invented ingenious and even useful systems, for which we sincerely thank them; but all their wit and usefulness lie within certain not very wide limits. They are wont to forget that the world is not governed by policy and expediency. Webster never goes behind government, and so cannot speak with authority about it. His words are wisdom to those legislators who contemplate no essential reform in the existing government; but for thinkers, and those who legislate for all time, he never once glances at the subject. I know of those whose serene and wise speculations on this theme would soon reveal the limits of his mind's range and hospitality. Yet, compared with the cheap professions of most reformers, and the still cheaper wisdom and eloquence of politicians in general, his are almost the only sensible and valuable words, and we thank Heaven for him. Comparatively, he is always strong, original, and, above all, practical. Still, his quality is not wisdom, but prudence. The lawyer's truth is not Truth, but consistency or a consistent expediency. Truth is always in harmony with herself, and is not concerned chiefly to reveal the justice that may consist with wrong-doing. He well deserves to be called, as he has been called, the Defender of the Constitution. There are really no blows to be given by him but defensive ones. He is not a leader, but a follower. His leaders are the men of '87. "I have never made an effort," he says, "and never propose to make an effort; I have never countenanced an effort, and never mean to countenance an effort, to disturb the arrangement as originally made, by which the various States came into the Union." Still thinking of the sanction which the Constitution gives to slavery, he says, "Because it was a part of the original compact—let it stand." Notwithstand-

ing his special acuteness and ability, he is unable to take a fact out of its merely political relations, and behold it as it lies absolutely to be disposed of by the intellect—what, for instance, it behooves a man to do here in America today with regard to slavery—but ventures, or is driven, to make such desperate answer as the following, while professing to speak absolutely and as a private man—from which what new and similar code of social duties might be inferred? "The manner," says he, "in which the governments of those States where slavery exists are to regulate it is for their own consideration, under their responsibility to their constituents, to the general laws of propriety, humanity, and justice, and to God. Associations formed elsewhere, springing from a feeling of humanity, or any other cause, have nothing whatever to do with it. They have never received any encouragement from me, and they never will."[10]

They who know of no purer sources of truth, who have traced up its   43
stream no higher, stand, and wisely stand, by the Bible and the Constitution, and drink at it there with reverence and humility; but they who behold where it comes trickling into this lake or that pool, gird up their loins once more, and continue their pilgrimage toward its fountainhead.

No man with a genius for legislation has appeared in America. They   44
are rare in the history of the world. There are orators, politicians, and eloquent men, by the thousand; but the speaker has not yet opened his mouth to speak who is capable of settling the much-vexed questions of the day. We love eloquence for its own sake, and not for any truth which it may utter, or any heroism it may inspire. Our legislators have not yet learned the comparative value of free trade and of freedom, of union, and of rectitude, to a nation. They have no genius or talent for comparatively humble questions of taxation and finance, commerce and manufactures and agriculture. If we were left solely to the wordy wit of legislators in Congress for our guidance, uncorrected by the seasonable experience and the effectual complaints of the people, America would not long retain her rank among the nations. For eighteen hundred years, though perchance I have no right to say it, the New Testament has been written; yet where is the legislator who has wisdom and practical talent enough to avail himself of the light which it sheds on the science of legislation?

The authority of government, even such as I am willing to submit to—   45
for I will cheerfully obey those who know and can do better than I, and in many things even those who neither know nor can do so well—is still an impure one: to be strictly just, it must have the sanction and consent of the governed. It can have no pure right over my person and property but what I concede to it. The progress from an absolute to a limited monarchy, from a limited monarchy to a democracy, is a progress toward a true respect for

---

[10]These extracts have been inserted since the lecture was read. [Author's note.]

the individual. Even the Chinese philosopher was wise enough to regard the individual as the basis of the empire. Is a democracy, such as we know it, the last improvement possible in government? Is it not possible to take a step further towards recognizing and organizing the rights of man? There will never be a really free and enlightened State until the State comes to recognize the individual as a higher and independent power, from which all its own power and authority are derived, and treats him accordingly. I please myself with imagining a State at least which can afford to be just to all men, and to treat the individual with respect as a neighbor; which even would not think it inconsistent with its own repose if a few were to live aloof from it, not meddling with it, nor embraced by it, who fulfilled all the duties of neighbors and fellow-men. A State which bore this kind of fruit, and suffered it to drop off as fast as it ripened, would prepare the way for a still more perfect and glorious State, which also I have imagined, but not yet anywhere seen.

Questions for Study and Discussion

1. What, according to Thoreau, is the purpose of government? What does he believe government should do? What does he think government can do? What does he believe government can't do?

2. Why was Thoreau jailed? Even though jailed, why did he consider himself free?

3. What, according to Thoreau, should people do about laws they consider unjust? What other alternatives are available? Do governments have a conscience? Should they have a conscience?

4. What is Thoreau's tone in this essay? Who is his audience? What is his attitude toward his audience?

5. What is Thoreau's purpose in this essay? Is he merely trying to rationalize his own behavior or does he have a deeper purpose?

6. On what grounds does Thoreau find fault with Daniel Webster? Do you agree with his assessment?

7. What types of evidence does Thoreau use both to support and to document his claims?

Writing Topics

1. Thoreau wrote, "Under a government which imprisons any unjustly, the true place for a just man is also a prison." Using examples from recent history, argue for or against the validity of Thoreau's statement.

2. Write an essay in which you attempt to reconcile individual conscience with majority rule.

3. Read "Letter from Birmingham Jail" by Martin Luther King, Jr. (pp. 703–17), and write an essay in which you discuss the influences of Thoreau's "Civil Disobedience" on King's thinking.

ELIZABETH CADY STANTON

Elizabeth Cady Stanton (1815–1902), American reformer and leader of the women's rights movement, was born in Johnstown, New York. She was admitted to the Johnstown Academy, an all-male institution, by special arrangement. Stanton excelled in Greek and went on to study at the Emma Willard Academy in Troy, New York, graduating in 1832. Emma Willard was the best school Stanton could attend; all other degree-granting institutions at the time excluded women. After college Stanton studied law with her father, but again, because of her sex, was not able to gain admission to the bar.

Influenced by the legal restrictions placed upon women and the discriminations shown against them, Stanton also showed early interest in the temperance and antislavery movements. In 1840 she married Henry Brewster Stanton, an abolitionist and journalist, but in a not uncharacteristic fashion refused to "obey" him or be referred to as Mrs. Stanton. After a brief period in which the couple lived in Boston, they moved to Seneca Falls, New York, where in July of 1848 the Seneca Falls Convention, which she helped to organize, was held. At the convention, generally regarded as the beginning of the women's rights movement, Elizabeth Cady Stanton read her "Declaration of Sentiments," a list of grievances against existing laws and customs that restricted the rights of all women. Because of her pioneering work and tireless efforts on behalf of women, Stanton was elected president of the National American Woman Suffrage Association in 1890.

Declaration of Sentiments and Resolutions

Adopted by the Seneca Falls Convention,
July 19–20, 1848

When, in the course of human events, it becomes necessary for one 1 portion of the family of man to assume among the people of the earth a position different from that which they have hitherto occupied, but one to which the laws of nature and of nature's God entitle them, a decent respect to the opinions of mankind requires that they should declare the causes that impel them to such a course.

We hold these truths to be self-evident: that all men and women are 2 created equal; that they are endowed by their Creator with certain inalienable rights; that among these are life, liberty, and the pursuit of happiness; that to secure these rights governments are instituted, deriving their just powers from the consent of the governed. Whenever any form of government becomes destructive of these ends, it is the right of those who suffer from it to refuse allegiance to it, and to insist upon the institution of a new government, laying its foundation on such principles, and organizing its powers in such form, as to them shall seem most likely to effect their safety and happiness. Prudence, indeed, will dictate that governments long established should not be changed for light and transient causes; and accordingly all experience hath shown that mankind are more disposed to suffer, while evils are sufferable, than to right themselves by abolishing the forms to which they are accustomed. But when a long train of abuses and usurpations, pursuing invariably the same object, evinces a design to reduce them under absolute despotism, it is their duty to throw off such government, and to provide new guards for their future security. Such has been the patient sufferance of the women under this government, and such is now the necessity which constrains them to demand the equal station to which they are entitled.

The history of mankind is a history of repeated injuries and usurpa- 3 tions on the part of man toward woman, having in direct object the establishment of an absolute tyranny over her. To prove this, let facts be submitted to a candid world.

He has never permitted her to exercise her inalienable right to the 4 elective franchise.

He has compelled her to submit to laws, in the formation of which she 5 had no voice.

He has withheld from her rights which are given to the most ignorant 6 and degraded men—both natives and foreigners.

Having deprived her of this first right of a citizen, the elective fran- 7 chise, thereby leaving her without representation in the halls of legislation, he has oppressed her on all sides.

He has made her, if married, in the eye of the law, civilly dead. 8

He has taken from her all right in property, even to the wages she 9 earns.

He has made her, morally, an irresponsible being, as she can commit 10 many crimes with impunity, provided they be done in the presence of her husband. In the covenant of marriage, she is compelled to promise obedience to her husband, he becoming to all intents and purposes, her master—the law giving him the power to deprive her of her liberty, and to administer chastisement.

He has so framed the laws of divorce, as to what shall be the proper 11 causes, and in case of separation, to whom the guardianship of the children shall be given, as to be wholly regardless of the happiness of women—the law, in all cases, going upon a false supposition of the supremacy of man, and giving all power into his hands.

After depriving her of all rights as a married woman, if single, and the 12 owner of property, he has taxed her to support a government which recognizes her only when her property can be made profitable to it.

He has monopolized nearly all the profitable employments, and from 13 those she is permitted to follow, she receives but a scanty remuneration. He closes against her all the avenues to wealth and distinction which he considers most honorable to himself. As a teacher of theology, medicine, or law, she is not known.

He has denied her the facilities for obtaining a thorough education, all colleges being closed against her. 14

He allows her in Church, as well as State, but a subordinate position, claiming Apostolic authority for her exclusion from the ministry, and, with some exceptions, from any public participation in the affairs of the Church. 15

He has created a false public sentiment by giving to the world a different code of morals for men and women, by which moral delinquencies which exclude women from society, are not only tolerated, but deemed of little account in man. 16

He has usurped the prerogative of Jehovah himself, claiming it as his right to assign for her a sphere of action, when that belongs to her conscience and to her God. 17

He has endeavored, in every way that he could, to destroy her confidence in her own powers, to lessen her self-respect, and to make her willing to lead a dependent and abject life. 18

Now, in view of this entire disfranchisement of one-half the people of this country, their social and religious degradation—in view of the unjust laws above mentioned, and because women do feel themselves aggrieved, oppressed, and fraudulently deprived of their most sacred rights, we insist that they have immediate admission to all the rights and privileges which belong to them as citizens of the United States. 19

In entering upon the great work before us, we anticipate no small amount of misconception, misrepresentation, and ridicule; but we shall use every instrumentality within our power to effect our object. We shall employ agents, circulate tracts, petition the State and National legislatures, and endeavor to enlist the pulpit and the press in our behalf. We hope this Convention will be followed by a series of Conventions embracing every part of the country. 20

[The following resolutions were discussed by Lucretia Mott, Thomas and Mary Ann McClintock, Amy Post, Catharine A. F. Stebbins, and others, and were adopted:] 21

WHEREAS, the great precept of nature is conceded to be, that "man shall pursue his own true and substantial happiness." Blackstone[1] in his Commentaries remarks, that this law of Nature being coeval[2] with mankind, and 22

---

[1]Sir William Blackstone (1723–1780): The most influential of English scholars of the law. His *Commentaries of the Laws of England* (4 vols., 1765–1769) form the basis of the study of law in England.

[2]coeval: Existing simultaneously.

dictated by God himself, is of course superior in obligation to any other. It is binding over all the globe, in all countries and at all times; no human laws are of any validity if contrary to this, and such of them as are valid, derive all their force, and all their validity, and all their authority, mediately and immediately, from this original; therefore,

Resolved, That such laws as conflict, in any way, with the true and substantial happiness of woman, are contrary to the great precept of nature and of no validity, for this is "superior in obligation to any other." [23]

Resolved, That all laws which prevent woman from occupying such a station in society as her conscience shall dictate, or which place her in a position inferior to that of man, are contrary to the great precept of nature, and therefore of no force or authority. [24]

Resolved, That woman is man's equal—was intended to be so by the Creator, and the highest good of the race demands that she should be recognized as such. [25]

Resolved, That the women of this country ought to be enlightened in regard to the laws under which they live, that they may no longer publish their degradation by declaring themselves satisfied with their present position, nor their ignorance, by asserting that they have all the rights they want. [26]

Resolved, That inasmuch as man, while claiming for himself intellectual superiority, does accord to woman moral superiority, it is preeminently his duty to encourage her to speak and teach, as she has an opportunity, in all religious assemblies. [27]

Resolved, That the same amount of virtue, delicacy, and refinement of behavior that is required of woman in the social state, should also be required of man, and the same transgressions should be visited with equal severity on both man and woman. [28]

Resolved, That the objection of indelicacy and impropriety, which is so often brought against woman when she addresses a public audience, comes with a very ill-grace from those who encourage, by their attendance, her appearance on the stage, in the concert, or in feats of the circus. [29]

Resolved, That woman has too long rested satisfied in the circumscribed limits which corrupt customs and a perverted application of the Scriptures have marked out for her, and that it is time she should move in the enlarged sphere which her great Creator has assigned her. [30]

Resolved, That it is the duty of the women of this country to secure to themselves their sacred right to the elective franchise. [31]

Resolved, That the equality of human rights results necessarily from the fact of the identity of the race in capabilities and responsibilities. [32]

Resolved, therefore, That, being invested by the Creator with the same capabilities, and the same consciousness of responsibility for their exercise, it is demonstrably the right and duty of woman, equally with man, to promote every righteous cause by every righteous means; and especially in regard to the great subjects of morals and religion, it is self-evidently her right to participate with her brother in teaching them, both in private and in public, by writing and by speaking, by any instrumentalities proper to be used, and in any assemblies proper to be held; and this being a self-evident truth growing out of the divinely implanted principles of human nature, any custom or authority adverse to it, whether modern or wearing the hoary sanction of antiquity, is to be regarded as a self-evident falsehood, and at war with mankind.

[At the last session Lucretia Mott[3] offered and spoke to the following   34
resolution:]

Resolved, That the speedy success of our cause depends upon the   35
zealous and untiring efforts of both men and women, for the overthrow of the monopoly of the pulpit, and for the securing to woman an equal participation with men in the various trades, professions, and commerce.

Questions for Study and Discussion

1. The opening paragraphs of the Seneca Falls declaration closely parallel those of the Declaration of Independence. Why do you suppose Stanton chose to start in this manner?
2. What is a parody? Is Stanton's essay a parody of the Declaration of Independence? Why or why not?
3. What is it that Elizabeth Cady Stanton and the other women at the Seneca Falls convention want?
4. What is the "elective franchise"? Why is it so fundamental to Stanton's argument?
5. What does Stanton mean when she says, "He has made her, if married, in the eye of the law, civilly dead"?
6. In paragraphs 4–18 Stanton catalogs the abuses women suffer. Who is the "He" referred to in each of the statements? What is the rhetorical effect of listing these abuses and starting each one with similar phrasing?
7. At what audience is Stanton's declaration aimed? What in the declaration itself led you to this conclusion?
8. What is the function of the resolutions that conclude the declaration? What would have been gained or lost if Stanton had concluded the declaration with paragraph 20?
9. Is there anything in the style, tone, or voice of this document that would lead you to call it "feminine" or "female"? Explain.

---

[3]Lucretia Mott (1793–1880): One of the founders of the 1848 convention at which these resolutions were presented. She is one of the earliest and most important of the feminists who struggled to proclaim their rights. She was also a prominent abolitionist.

Writing Topics

1. Write a report updating Stanton's declaration. What complaints have been resolved? Which still need to be redressed? What new complaints have been voiced by women in the last twenty years?

2. Write an essay in which you compare and contrast the Declaration of Independence with Stanton's declaration. You should consider such things as purpose, audience, and style.

CHIEF SEATTLE

Born around 1786, Seattle was chief of the Suquamish Indians and leader of other tribes in the area around Puget Sound. He was a loyal friend of the white settlers who in the early nineteenth century were coming to the region in increasing numbers. In 1853, during the administration of President Franklin Pierce, the region was organized as the Washington Territory, with Isaac Stevens as governor. The next year Stevens, on behalf of the federal government, offered to buy two million acres of land from Seattle's people, and the Indians agreed. In later years, the settlers named their growing city after him, though Seattle consented to this reluctantly, believing that after death his spirit would be disturbed every time his name was mentioned. He died in 1866.

The following is Seattle's reply to Governor Stevens's offer. Though the great Indian relocations and massacres that were to begin in the 1860s were still in the future, and Indians were still the chief inhabitants of nearly half of the continent, Seattle clearly understood what was to come. His words are a prophecy—and a warning.

My People

Yonder sky that has wept tears upon my people for centuries untold,   1
and which to us appears changeless and eternal, may change. Today is fair.
Tomorrow may be overcast with clouds. My words are like the stars that
never change. Whatever Seattle says the great chief at Washington can rely
upon with as much certainty as he can upon the return of the sun or the
seasons. The White Chief says that Big Chief at Washington sends us
greetings of friendship and goodwill. That is kind of him for we know he has
little need of our friendship in return. His people are many. They are like
the grass that covers vast prairies. My people are few. They resemble the
scattering trees of a storm-swept plain. The great, and—I presume—good,
White Chief sends us word that he wishes to buy our lands but is willing to
allow us enough to live comfortably. This indeed appears just, even generous, for the Red Man no longer has rights that he need respect, and the
offer may be wise also, as we are no longer in need of an extensive country. . . . I will not dwell on, nor mourn over, our untimely decay, nor
reproach our paleface brothers with hastening it, as we too may have been
somewhat to blame.

Youth is impulsive. When our young men grow angry at some real or   2
imaginary wrong, and disfigure their faces with black paint, it denotes that
their hearts are black, and then they are often cruel and relentless, and our
old men and old women are unable to restrain them. Thus it has ever been.
Thus it was when the white men first began to push our forefathers further

westward. But let us hope that the hostilities between us may never return. We would have everything to lose and nothing to gain. Revenge by young men is considered gain, even at the cost of their own lives, but old men who stay at home in times of war, and mothers who have sons to lose, know better.

Our good father at Washington—for I presume he is now our father as well as yours, since King George has moved his boundaries further north— our great good father, I say, sends us word that if we do as he desires he will protect us. His brave warriors will be to us a bristling wall of strength, and his wonderful ships of war will fill our harbors so that our ancient enemies far to the northward—the Hydas and Tsimpsians—will cease to frighten our women, children, and old men. Then in reality will he be our father and we his children. But can that ever be? Your God is not our God! Your God loves your people and hates mine. He folds his strong and protecting arms lovingly about the paleface and leads him by the hand as a father leads his infant son—but He has forsaken His red children—if they really are his. Our God, the Great Spirit, seems also to have forsaken us. Your God makes your people wax strong every day. Soon they will fill the land. Our people are ebbing away like a rapidly receding tide that will never return. The white man's God cannot love our people or He would protect them. They seem to be orphans who can look nowhere for help. How then can we be brothers? How can your God become our God and renew our prosperity and awaken in us dreams of returning greatness? If we have a common heavenly father He must be partial—for He came to his paleface children. We never saw Him. He gave you laws but He had no word for His red children whose teeming multitudes once filled this vast continent as stars fill the firmament. No; we are two distinct races with separate origins and separate destinies. There is little in common between us.

To us the ashes of our ancestors are sacred and their resting place is hallowed ground. You wander far from the graves of your ancestors and seemingly without regret. Your religion was written upon tables of stone by the iron finger of your God so that you could not forget. The Red Man could never comprehend nor remember it. Our religion is the traditions of our ancestors—the dreams of our old men, given them in solemn hours of night by the Great Spirit; and the visions of our sachems[1]; and it is written in the hearts of our people.

Your dead cease to love you and the land of their nativity as soon as they pass the portals of the tomb and wander way beyond the stars. They are soon forgotten and never return. Our dead never forget the beautiful world that gave them being.

Day and night cannot dwell together. The Red Man has ever fled the approach of the White Man, as the morning mist flees before the morning

---

[1]Indian chiefs.

sun. However, your proposition seems fair and I think that my people will accept it and will retire to the reservation you offer them. Then we will dwell apart in peace, for the words of the Great White Chief seem to be the words of nature speaking to my people out of dense darkness.

It matters little where we pass the remnant of our days. They will not   7
be many. A few more moons; a few more winters—and not one of the descendants of the mighty hosts that once moved over this broad land or lived in happy homes, protected by the Great Spirit, will remain to mourn over the graves of a people once more powerful and hopeful than yours. But why should I mourn at the untimely fate of my people? Tribe follows tribe, and nation follows nation, like the waves of the sea. It is the order of nature, and regret is useless. Your time of decay may be distant, but it will surely come, for even the White Man whose God walked and talked with him as friend with friend, cannot be exempt from the common destiny. We may be brothers after all. We will see.

We will ponder your proposition, and when we decide we will let you   8
know. But should we accept it, I here and now make this condition that we will not be denied the privilege without molestation of visiting at any time the tombs of our ancestors, friends and children. Every part of this soil is sacred in the estimation of my people. Every hillside, every valley, every plain and grove, has been hallowed by some sad or happy event in days long vanished. . . . The very dust upon which you now stand responds more lovingly to their footsteps than to yours, because it is rich with the blood of our ancestors and our bare feet are conscious of the sympathetic touch. . . . Even the little children who lived here and rejoiced here for a brief season will love these somber solitudes and at eventide they greet shadowy return- ing spirits. And when the last Red Man shall have perished, and the memory of my tribe shall have become a myth among the White Men, these shores will swarm with the invisible dead of my tribe, and when your children's children think themselves alone in the field, the store, the shop, upon the highway, or in the silence of the pathless woods, they will not be alone. . . . At night when the streets of your cities and villages are silent and you think them deserted, they will throng with the returning hosts that once filled and still love this beautiful land. The White Man will never be alone.

Let him be just and deal kindly with my people, for the dead are not   9
powerless. Dead, did I say? There is not death, only a change of worlds.

Questions for Study and Discussion

1. What are Chief Seattle's purposes in his speech? Whom is it ad- dressed to?

2. What condition does Seattle demand before yielding the land to the U.S. government? How does he prepare for this condition in his speech?

3. What is Seattle's attitude toward the white men, their president, and their god? How do you know? Seattle refers to the president as the Indians' "father." What does this signify? Why might Seattle presume that the White Chief is good as well as great?

4. What, for you, is the most powerful part of the speech? What gives it its power? Did anything in his speech surprise you? If so, why?

5. What differences between red men and white men does Seattle describe? Why do you think he chooses to mention those particular differences? What other differences might he have included, and why do you think he didn't?

6. Chief Seattle's address is rich in figures of speech, beginning with "My words are like the stars that never change." What areas of knowledge and experience does he continually draw on for his analogies and metaphors? Give examples.

Writing Topics

1. Despite his obvious regret, Chief Seattle worked out an accommodation with the more powerful forces of the United States. If you were in his position, would you have done the same or would you have led your people to fight for its land and independence? Write an essay in which you explain your choice.

2. Throughout his speech, Chief Seattle quietly registers a complaint that was to become a battle cry in later years. This sentiment can be summed up by his pessimistic view, "not one of the descendants of the mighty hosts that once moved over this broad land or lived in happy homes, protected by the Great Spirit, will remain to mourn over the graves of a people once more powerful and hopeful than yours." Write an essay in which you explain what in the history of the American Indians may have led Chief Seattle to make this prediction, and what later events seemed almost to fulfill it. Use library resources to support your answer.

MARTIN LUTHER KING, JR.

Martin Luther King, Jr., was born in 1929 in Atlanta, Georgia. The son of a Baptist minister, he was himself ordained at the age of eighteen and went on to study at Morehouse College, Crozer Theological Seminary, Boston University, and Chicago Theological Seminary. He first came to prominence in 1955, in Montgomery, Alabama, when he led a successful boycott against the city's segregated bus system. As the first president of the Southern Christian Leadership Conference, King promoted a policy of massive but nonviolent resistance to racial injustice, and in 1964 he was awarded the Nobel Peace Prize. He was assassinated in Memphis, Tennessee, in 1968.

Dr. King dated his landmark letter from Birmingham jail April 16, 1963. He appended the following note to the published version:

> This response to a published statement by eight fellow clergymen from Alabama (Bishop C. C. J. Carpenter, Bishop Joseph A. Durick, Rabbi Hilton L. Grafman, Bishop Paul Hardin, Bishop Holan B. Harmon, the Reverend George M. Murray, the Reverend Edward V. Ramage and the Reverend Earl Stallings) was composed under somewhat constricting circumstances. Begun on the margins of the newspaper in which the statement appeared while I was in jail, the letter was continued on scraps of writing paper supplied by a friendly Negro trusty, and concluded on a pad my attorneys were eventually permitted to leave me. Although the text remains in substance unaltered, I have indulged in the author's prerogative of polishing it for publication.

Letter from Birmingham Jail

My Dear Fellow Clergymen:

While confined here in the Birmingham city jail, I came across your recent statement calling my present activities "unwise and untimely." Seldom do I pause to answer criticism of my work and ideas. If I sought to answer all the criticisms that cross my desk, my secretaries would have little time for anything other than such correspondence in the course of the day, and I would have no time for constructive work. But since I feel that you are men of genuine good will and that your criticisms are sincerely set forth, I want to try to answer your statement in what I hope will be patient and reasonable terms.

I think I should indicate why I am here in Birmingham, since you have been influenced by the view which argues against "outsiders coming in." I have the honor of serving as president of the Southern Christian Leadership Conference, an organization operating in every southern state, with headquarters in Atlanta, Georgia. We have some eighty-five affiliated organizations across the South, and one of them is the Alabama Christian Movement for Human Rights. Frequently we share staff, educational, and financial resources with our affiliates. Several months ago the affiliate here in Birmingham asked us to be on call to engage in a nonviolent direct-action program if such were deemed necessary. We readily consented, and when the hour came we lived up to our promise. So I, along with several members of my staff, am here because I was invited here. I am here because I have organizational ties here.

But more basically, I am in Birmingham because injustice is here. Just as the prophets of the eighth century B.C. left their villages and carried their "thus saith the Lord" far beyond the boundaries of their home towns, and just as the Apostle Paul left his village of Tarsus and carried the gospel of Jesus Christ to the far corners of the Greco-Roman world, so am I compelled to carry the gospel of freedom beyond my own home town. Like Paul, I must constantly respond to the Macedonian call for aid.

Moreover, I am cognizant of the interrelatedness of all communities and states. I cannot sit idly by in Atlanta and not be concerned about what happens in Birmingham. Injustice anywhere is a threat to justice everywhere. We are caught in an inescapable network of mutuality, tied in a single garment of destiny. Whatever affects one directly, affects all indirectly. Never again can we afford to live with the narrow, provincial, "outside agitator" idea. Anyone who lives inside the United States can never be considered an outsider anywhere within its bounds.

You deplore the demonstrations taking place in Birmingham. But your statement, I am sorry to say, fails to express a similar concern for the conditions that brought about the demonstrations. I am sure that none of you would want to rest content with the superficial kind of social analysis that deals merely with effects and does not grapple with underlying causes. It is unfortunate that demonstrations are taking place in Birmingham, but it is even more unfortunate that the city's white power structure left the Negro community with no alternative.

In any nonviolent campaign there are four basic steps: collection of the facts to determine whether injustices exist; negotiation; self-purification; and direct action. We have gone through all these steps in Birmingham. There can be no gainsaying the fact that racial injustice engulfs this community. Birmingham is probably the most thoroughly segregated city in the United States. Its ugly record of brutality is widely known. Negroes have experienced grossly unjust treatment in courts. There have been more unsolved bombings of Negro homes and churches in Birmingham than in any other city in the nation. These are the hard, brutal facts of the case. On the basis of these conditions, Negro leaders sought to negotiate with the city fathers. But the latter consistently refused to engage in good-faith negotiation.

Then, last September, came the opportunity to talk with leaders of Birmingham's economic community. In the course of the negotiations, certain promises were made by the merchants—for example, to remove the stores' humiliating racial signs. On the basis of these promises, the Reverend Fred Shuttlesworth and the leaders of the Alabama Christian Movement for Human Rights agreed to a moratorium on all demonstrations. As the weeks and months went by, we realized that we were the victims of a broken promise. A few signs, briefly removed, returned; the others remained.

As in so many past experiences, our hopes had been blasted, and the shadow of deep disappointment settled upon us. We had no alternative except to prepare for direct action, whereby we would present our very bodies as means of laying our case before the conscience of the local and the national community. Mindful of the difficulties involved, we decided to undertake a process of self-purification. We began a series of workshops on nonviolence, and we repeatedly asked ourselves: "Are you able to accept blows without retaliating?" "Are you able to endure the ordeal of jail?" We decided to schedule our direct-action program for the Easter season, realizing that except for Christmas, this is the main shopping period of the year. Knowing that a strong economic-withdrawal program would be the by-product of direct action, we felt that this would be the best time to bring pressure to bear on the merchants for the needed change.

Then it occurred to us that Birmingham's mayoral election was coming up in March, and we speedily decided to postpone action until after election day. When we discovered that the Commissioner of Public Safety, Eugene "Bull" Connor, had piled up enough votes to be in the run-off, we decided again to postpone action until the day after the run-off so that the demonstrations could not be used to cloud the issues. Like many others, we waited to see Mr. Connor defeated, and to this end we endured postponement after postponement. Having aided in this community need, we felt that our direct-action program could be delayed no longer.

You may well ask, "Why direct action? Why sit-ins, marches, and so forth? Isn't negotiation a better path?" You are quite right in calling for negotiation. Indeed, this is the very purpose of direct action. Nonviolent direct action seeks to create such a crisis and foster such a tension that a community which has constantly refused to negotiate is forced to confront the issue. It seeks so to dramatize the issue that it can no longer be ignored. My citing the creation of tension as part of the work of the nonviolent-resister may sound rather shocking. But I must confess that I am not afraid of the word "tension." I have earnestly opposed violent tension, but there is a type of constructive, nonviolent tension which is necessary for growth. Just as Socrates[1] felt that it was necessary to create a tension in the mind so that individuals could rise from the bondage of myths and half-truths to the unfettered realm of creative analysis and objective appraisal, so must we see the need for nonviolent gadflies to create the kind of tension in society that will help men rise from the dark depths of prejudice and racism to the majestic heights of understanding and brotherhood.

The purpose of our direct-action program is to create a situation so   11
crisis-packed that it will inevitably open the door to negotiation. I therefore concur with you in your call for negotiation. Too long has our beloved Southland been bogged down in a tragic effort to live in monologue rather than dialogue.

One of the basic points in your statement is that the action that I and   12
my associates have taken in Birmingham is untimely. Some have asked: "Why didn't you give the new city administration time to act?" The only answer that I can give to this query is that the new Birmingham administration must be prodded about as much as the outgoing one, before it will act. We are sadly mistaken if we feel that the election of Albert Boutwell as mayor will bring the millennium to Birmingham. While Mr. Boutwell is a much more gentle person than Mr. Connor, they are both segregationists, dedicated to maintenance of the status quo. I have hoped that Mr. Boutwell will be reasonable enough to see the futility of massive resistance to desegregation. But he will not see this without pressure from devotees of civil rights. My friends, I must say to you that we have not made a single gain in civil rights without determined legal and nonviolent pressure. Lamentably, it is an historical fact that privileged groups seldom give up their privileges voluntarily. Individuals may see the moral light and voluntarily give up their unjust posture; but, as Reinhold Niebuhr[2] has reminded us, groups tend to be more immoral than individuals.

We know through painful experience that freedom is never voluntarily   13
given by the oppressor; it must be demanded by the oppressed. Frankly, I have yet to engage in a direct-action campaign that was "well timed" in the view of those who have not suffered unduly from the disease of segregation. For years now I have heard the word "Wait!" It rings in the ear of every Negro with piercing familiarity. This "Wait" has almost always meant "Never." We must come to see, with one of our distinguished jurists, that "justice too long delayed is justice denied."

We have waited for more than 340 years for our constitutional and   14
God-given rights. The nations of Asia and Africa are moving with jetlike

---

[1]The greatest of the ancient Greek philosphers, Socrates was sentenced to death because he persisted in raising difficult questions of authority.

[2]Niebuhr (1892–1971), an American theologian, attempted to establish a practical code of social ethics based in religious conviction.

speed toward gaining political independence, but we still creep at horse-and-buggy pace toward gaining a cup of coffee at a lunch counter. Perhaps it is easy for those who have never felt the stinging darts of segregation to say, "Wait." But when you have seen vicious mobs lynch your mothers and fathers at will and drown your sisters and brothers at whim; when you have seen hate-filled policemen curse, kick, and even kill your black brothers and sisters; when you see the vast majority of your twenty million Negro brothers smothering in an airtight cage of poverty in the midst of an affluent society; when you suddenly find your tongue twisted and your speech stammering as you seek to explain to your six-year-old daughter why she can't go to the public amusement park that has just been advertised on television, and see tears welling up in her eyes when she is told that Funtown is closed to colored children, and see ominous clouds of inferiority beginning to form in her little mental sky, and see her beginning to distort her personality by developing an unconscious bitterness toward white people; when you have to concoct an answer for a five-year-old son who is asking, "Daddy, why do white people treat colored people so mean?"; when you take a cross-country drive and find it necessary to sleep night after night in the uncomfortable corners of your automobile because no motel will accept you; when you are humiliated day in and day out by nagging signs reading "white" and "colored"; when your first name becomes "nigger," your middle name becomes "boy" (however old you are) and your last name becomes "John," and your wife and mother are never given the respected title "Mrs."; when you are harried by day and haunted by night by the fact that you are a Negro, living constantly at tiptoe stance, never quite knowing what to expect next, and are plagued with inner fears and outer resentments; when you are forever fighting a degenerating sense of "nobodiness"—then you will understand why we find it difficult to wait. There comes a time when the cup of endurance runs over, and men are no longer willing to be plunged into the abyss of despair. I hope, sirs, you can understand our legitimate and unavoidable impatience.

You express a great deal of anxiety over our willingness to break laws. 15 This is certainly a legitimate concern. Since we so diligently urge people to obey the Supreme Court's decision of 1954 outlawing segregation in the public schools, at first glance it may seem rather paradoxical for us con-sciously to break laws. One may well ask: "How can you advocate breaking some laws and obeying others?" The answer lies in the fact that there are two types of laws: just and unjust. I would be the first to advocate obeying just laws. One has not only a legal but a moral responsibility to obey just laws. Conversely, one has a moral responsibility to disobey unjust laws. I would agree with St. Augustine[3] that "an unjust law is no law at all."

[3]An early bishop of the Christian church, St. Augustine (354–430) is considered the founder of theology.

Now, what is the difference between the two? How does one determine   16
whether a law is just or unjust? A just law is a manmade code that squares
with the moral law or the law of God. An unjust law is a code that is out of
harmony with the moral law. To put it in the terms of St. Thomas Aquinas[4]:
An unjust law is a human law that is not rooted in eternal law and natural
law. Any law that uplifts human personality is just. Any law that degrades
human personality is unjust. All segregation statutes are unjust because
segregation distorts the soul and damages the personality. It gives the
segregator a false sense of superiority and the segregated a false sense of
inferiority. Segregation, to use the terminology of the Jewish philosopher
Martin Buber, substitutes an "I-it" relationship for an "I-thou" relationship
and ends up relegating persons to the status of things. Hence segregation is
not only politically, economically, and sociologically unsound, it is morally
wrong and sinful. Paul Tillich[5] has said that sin is separation. Is not
segregation an existential expression of man's tragic separation, his awful
estrangement, his terrible sinfulness? Thus it is that I can urge men to obey
the 1954 decision of the Supreme Court, for it is morally right; and I can
urge them to disobey segregation ordinances, for they are morally wrong.

Let us consider a more concrete example of just and unjust laws. An   17
unjust law is a code that a numerical or power majority group compels a
minority group to obey but does not make binding on itself. This is
difference made legal. By the same token, a just law is a code that a majority
compels a minority to follow and that it is willing to follow itself. This is
sameness made legal.

Let me give another explanation. A law is unjust if it is inflicted on a   18
minority that, as a result of being denied the right to vote, had no part in
enacting or devising the law. Who can say that the legislature of Alabama
which set up that state's segregation laws was democratically elected?
Throughout Alabama all sorts of devious methods are used to prevent
Negroes from becoming registered voters, and there are some counties in
which, even though Negroes constitute a majority of the population, not a
single Negro is registered. Can any law enacted under such circumstances
be considered democratically structured?

Sometimes a law is just on its face and unjust in its application. For   19
instance, I have been arrested on a charge of parading without a permit.
Now, there is nothing wrong in having an ordinance which requires a
permit for a parade. But such an ordinance becomes unjust when it is used
to maintain segregation and to deny citizens the First Amendment privilege
of peaceful assembly and protest.

---

[4]The wide-embracing Christian teachings of medieval philosopher St. Thomas Aquinas
(1225–1274) have been applied to every realm of human activity.

[5]Tillich (1886–1965) and Buber (1878–1965) are both important figures in twentieth-
century religious thought.

I hope you are able to see the distinction I am trying to point out. In 20 no sense do I advocate evading or defying the law, as would the rabid segregationist. That would lead to anarchy. One who breaks an unjust law must do so openly, lovingly, and with a willingness to accept the penalty. I submit that an individual who breaks a law that conscience tells him is unjust, and who willingly accepts the penalty of imprisonment in order to arouse the conscience of the community over its injustice, is in reality expressing the highest respect for law.

Of course, there is nothing new about this kind of civil disobedience. 21 It was evidenced sublimely in the refusal of Shadrach, Meshach, and Abednego to obey the laws of Nebuchadnezzar,[6] on the ground that a higher moral law was at stake. It was practiced superbly by the early Christians, who were willing to face hungry lions and the excruciating pain of chopping blocks rather than submit to certain unjust laws of the Roman Empire. To a degree, academic freedom is a reality today because Socrates practiced civil disobedience. In our own nation, the Boston Tea Party represented a massive act of civil disobedience.

We should never forget that everything Adolf Hitler did in Germany 22 was "legal" and everything the Hungarian freedom fighters[7] did in Hungary was "illegal." It was "illegal" to aid and comfort a Jew in Hitler's Germany. Even so, I am sure that, had I lived in Germany at the time, I would have aided and comforted my Jewish brothers. If today I lived in a Communist country where certain principles dear to the Christian faith are suppressed, I would openly advocate disobeying that country's antireligious laws.

I must make two honest confessions to you, my Christian and Jewish 23 brothers. First, I must confess that over the past few years I have been gravely disappointed with the white moderate. I have almost reached the regrettable conclusion that the Negro's great stumbling block in his stride toward freedom is not the White Citizen's Counciler[8] or the Ku Klux Klanner, but the white moderate, who is more devoted to "order" than to justice; who prefers a negative peace which is the absence of tension to a positive peace which is the presence of justice; who constantly says, "I agree with you in the goal you seek, but I cannot agree with your methods of direct action"; who paternalistically believes he can set the timetable for another man's freedom; who lives by a mythical concept of time and who constantly advises the Negro to wait for a "more convenient season." Shallow understanding from people of good will is more frustrating than

---

[6]When Shadrach, Meshach, and Abednego refused to worship an idol, King Nebuchadnezzar had them cast into a roaring furnace; they were saved by God. [See Daniel 1:7–3:30]

[7]In 1956 Hungarian nationalists revolted against Communist rule, but were quickly put down with a violent show of Soviet force.

[8]Such councils were organized in 1954 to oppose school desegregation.

absolute misunderstanding from people of ill will. Lukewarm acceptance is much more bewildering than outright rejection.

I had hoped that the white moderate would understand that law and order exist for the purpose of establishing justice and that when they fail in this purpose they become the dangerously structured dams that block the flow of social progress. I had hoped that the white moderate would understand that the present tension in the South is a necessary phase of the transition from an obnoxious negative peace, in which the Negro passively accepted his unjust plight, to a substantive and positive peace, in which all men will respect the dignity and worth of human personality. Actually, we who engage in nonviolent direct action are not the creators of tension. We merely bring to the surface the hidden tension that is already alive. We bring it out in the open, where it can be seen and dealt with. Like a boil that can never be cured so long as it is covered up but must be opened with all its ugliness to the natural medicines of air and light, injustice must be exposed, with all the tension its exposure creates, to the light of human conscience and the air of national opinion, before it can be cured.

In your statement you assert that our actions, even though peaceful, must be condemned because they precipitate violence. But is this a logical assertion? Isn't this like condemning a robbed man because his possession of money precipitated the evil act of robbery? Isn't this like condemning Socrates because his unswerving commitment to truth and his philosophical inquiries precipitated the act by the misguided populace in which they made him drink hemlock? Isn't this like condemning Jesus because his unique God-consciousness and never-ceasing devotion to God's will precipitated the evil act of crucifixion? We must come to see that, as the federal courts have consistently affirmed, it is wrong to urge an individual to cease his efforts to gain his basic constitutional rights because the quest may precipitate violence. Society must protect the robbed and punish the robber.

I had also hoped that the white moderate would reject the myth concerning time in relation to the struggle for freedom. I have just received a letter from a white brother in Texas. He writes: "All Christians know that the colored people will receive equal rights eventually, but it is possible that you are in too great a religious hurry. It has taken Christianity almost two thousand years to accomplish what it has. The teachings of Christ take time to come to earth." Such an attitude stems from a tragic misconception of time, from the strangely irrational notion that there is something in the very flow of time that will inevitably cure all ills. Actually, time itself is neutral; it can be used either destructively or constructively. More and more I feel that the people of ill will have used time much more effectively than have the people of good will. We will have to repent in this generation not merely for the hateful words and actions of the bad people, but for the appalling silence of the good people. Human progress never rolls in on wheels of inevitability; it comes through the tireless efforts of men willing to be co-workers with God, and without this hard work, time itself becomes an ally

24

25

26

of the forces of social stagnation. We must use time creatively, in the knowledge that the time is always ripe to do right. Now is the time to make real the promise of democracy and transform our pending national elegy into a creative psalm of brotherhood. Now is the time to lift our national policy from the quicksand of racial injustice to the solid rock of human dignity.

You speak of our activity in Birmingham as extreme. At first I was 27 rather disappointed that fellow clergymen would see my nonviolent efforts as those of an extremist. I began thinking about the fact that I stand in the middle of two opposing forces in the Negro community. One is a force of complacency, made up in part of Negroes who, as a result of long years of oppression, are so drained of self-respect and a sense of "somebodiness" that they have adjusted to segregation; and in part of a few middle-class Negroes who, because of a degree of academic and economic security and because in some ways they profit by segregation, have become insensitive to the problems of the masses. The other force is one of bitterness and hatred, and it comes perilously close to advocating violence. It is expressed in the various black nationalist groups that are springing up across the nation, the largest and best-known being Elijah Muhammad's Muslim movement. Nourished by the Negro's frustration over the continued existence of racial discrimination, this movement is made up of people who have lost faith in America, who have absolutely repudiated Christianity, and who have concluded that the white man is an incorrigible "devil."

I have tried to stand between these two forces, saying that we need 28 emulate neither the "do-nothingism" of the complacent nor the hatred and despair of the black nationalist. For there is the more excellent way of love and nonviolent protest. I am grateful to God that, through the influence of the Negro church, the way of nonviolence became an integral part of our struggle.

If this philosophy had not emerged, by now many streets of the South 29 would, I am convinced, be flowing with blood. And I am further convinced that if our white brothers dismiss as "rabble-rousers" and "outside agitors" those of us who employ nonviolent direct action, and if they refuse to support our nonviolent efforts, millions of Negroes will, out of frustration and despair, seek solace and security in black-nationalist ideologies—a development that would inevitably lead to a frightening racial nightmare.

Oppressed people cannot remain oppressed forever. The yearning for 30 freedom eventually manifests itself, and that is what has happened to the American Negro. Something within has reminded him of his birthright of freedom, and something without has reminded him that it can be gained. Consciously or unconsciously, he has been caught up by the *Zeitgeist*,[9] and with his black brothers of Africa and his brown and yellow brothers of Asia,

---

[9]*Zeitgeist*: German word for "the spirit of the times."

South America, and the Caribbean, the United States Negro is moving with a sense of great urgency toward the promised land of racial justice. If one recognizes this vital urge that has engulfed the Negro community, one should readily understand why public demonstrations are taking place. The Negro has many pent-up resentments and latent frustrations, and he must release them. So let him march; let him make prayer pilgrimages to the city hall; let him go on freedom rides—and try to understand why he must do so. If his repressed emotions are not released in nonviolent ways, they will seek expression through violence; this is not a threat but a fact of history. So I have not said to my people, "Get rid of your discontent." Rather, I have tried to say that this normal and healthy discontent can be channeled into the creative outlet of nonviolent direct action. And now this approach is being termed extremist.

But though I was initially disappointed at being categorized as an extremist, as I continued to think about the matter I gradually gained a measure of satisfaction from the label. Was not Jesus an extremist for love: "Love your enemies, bless them that curse you, do good to them that hate you, and pray for them which despitefully use you, and persecute you." Was not Amos an extremist for justice: "Let justice roll down like waters and righteousness like an ever-flowing stream." Was not Paul an extremist for the Christian gospel: "I bear in my body the marks of the Lord Jesus." Was not Martin Luther an extremist: "Here I stand; I cannot do otherwise, so help me God." And John Bunyan: "I will stay in jail to the end of my days before I make a butchery of my conscience." And Abraham Lincoln: "This nation cannot survive half slave and half free." And Thomas Jefferson: "We hold these truths to be self-evident, that all men are created equal. . . ." So the question is not whether we will be extremists, but what kind of extremists we will be. Will we be extremists for hate or for love? Will we be extremists for the preservation of injustice or for the extension of justice? In that dramatic scene on Calvary's hill three men were crucified. We must never forget that all three were crucified for the same crime—the crime of extremism. Two were extremists for immorality, and thus fell below their environment. The other, Jesus Christ, was an extremist for love, truth, and goodness, and thereby rose above his environment. Perhaps the South, the nation, and the world are in dire need of creative extremists.

I had hoped that the white moderate would see this need. Perhaps I was too optimistic; perhaps I expected too much. I suppose I should have realized that few members of the oppressor race can understand the deep groans and passionate yearnings of the oppressed race, and still fewer have the vision to see that injustice must be rooted out by strong, persistent, and determined action. I am thankful, however, that some of our white brothers in the South have grasped the meaning of this social revolution and committed themselves to it. They are still all too few in quantity, but they are big in quality. Some—such as Ralph McGill, Lillian Smith, Harry

Golden, James McBride Dabbs, Ann Braden, and Sarah Patton Boyle—have written about our struggle in eloquent and prophetic terms. Others have marched with us down nameless streets of the South. They have languished in filthy, roach-infested jails, suffering the abuse and brutality of policemen who view them as "dirty nigger-lovers." Unlike so many of their moderate brothers and sisters, they have recognized the urgency of the moment and sensed the need for powerful "action" antidotes to combat the disease of segregation.

Let me take note of my other major disappointment. I have been so 33 greatly disappointed with the white church and its leadership. Of course, there are some notable exceptions. I am not unmindful of the fact that each of you has taken some significant stands on this issue. I commend you, Reverend Stallings, for your Christian stand on this past Sunday, in welcoming Negroes to your worship service on a nonsegregated basis. I commend the Catholic leaders of this state for integrating Spring Hill College several years ago.

But despite these notable exceptions, I must honestly reiterate that I 34 have been disappointed with the church. I do not say this as one of those negative critics who can always find something wrong with the church. I say this as a minister of the gospel, who loves the church; who was nurtured in its bosom; who has been sustained by its spiritual blessings and who will remain true to it as long as the cord of life shall lengthen.

When I was suddenly catapulted into the leadership of the bus protest 35 in Montgomery, Alabama, a few years ago, I felt we would be supported by the white church. I felt that the white ministers, priests, and rabbis of the South would be among our strongest allies. Instead, some have been outright opponents, refusing to understand the freedom movement and misrepresenting its leaders; all too many others have been more cautious than courageous and have remained silent behind the anesthetizing security of stained-glass windows.

In spite of my shattered dreams, I came to Birmingham with the hope 36 that the white religious leadership of this community would see the justice of our cause and, with deep moral concern, would serve as the channel through which our just grievances could reach the power structure. I had hoped that each of you would understand. But again I have been disappointed. . . .

There was a time when the church was very powerful—in the time 37 when the early Christians rejoiced at being deemed worthy to suffer for what they believed. In those days the church was not merely a thermometer that recorded the ideas and principles of popular opinion; it was a thermostat that transformed the mores of society. Whenever the early Christians entered a town, the people in power became disturbed and immediately sought to convict the Christians for being "disturbers of the peace" and "outside agitators." But the Christians pressed on, in the conviction that they were "a colony of heaven," called to obey God rather than man. Small in number, they were big in commitment. They were too God-intoxicated to be "astronomically intimidated." By their effort and example they brought an end to such ancient evils as infanticide and gladitorial contests.

Things are different now. So often the contemporary church is a weak, ineffectual voice with an uncertain sound. So often it is an arch-defender of the status quo. Far from being disturbed by the presence of the church, the power structure of the average community is consoled by the church's silent—and often even vocal—sanction of things as they are.   38

But the judgment of God is upon the church as never before. If today's church does not recapture the sacrificial spirit of the early church, it will lose its authenticity, forfeit the loyalty of millions, and be dismissed as an irrelevant social club with no meaning for the twentieth century. Every day I meet young people whose disappointment with the church has turned into outright disgust.   39

Perhaps I have once again been too optimistic. Is organized religion too inextricably bound to the status quo to save our nation and the world? Perhaps I must turn my faith to the inner spiritual church, the church within the church, as the true *ekklesia*[10] and the hope of the world. But again I am thankful to God that some noble souls from the ranks of organized religion have broken loose from the paralyzing chains of conformity and joined us as active partners in the struggle for freedom. They have left their secure congregations and walked the streets of Albany, Georgia, with us. They have gone down the highways of the South on torturous rides for freedom. Yes, they have gone to jail with us. Some have been dismissed from their churches, have lost the support of their bishops and fellow ministers. But they have acted in the faith that right defeated is stronger than evil triumphant. Their witness has been the spiritual salt that has preserved the true meaning of the gospel in these troubled times. They have carved a tunnel of hope through the dark mountain of disappointment.   40

I hope the church as a whole will meet the challenge of this decisive hour. But even if the church does not come to the aid of justice, I have no despair about the future. I have no fear about the outcome of our struggle in Birmingham, even if our motives are at present misunderstood. We will reach the goal of freedom in Birmingham and all over the nation, because the goal of America is freedom. Abused and scorned though we may be, our destiny is tied up with America's destiny. Before the pilgrims landed at Plymouth, we were here. Before the pen of Jefferson etched the majestic words of the Declaration of Independence across the pages of history, we   41

---

[10]*ekklesia*: word referring to the early Church and its spirit; from the Greek New Testament.

were here. For more than two centuries our forebears labored in this country without wages; they made cotton king; they built the homes of their masters while suffering gross injustice and shameful humiliation—and yet out of a bottomless vitality they continued to thrive and develop. If the inexpressible cruelties of slavery could not stop us, the opposition we now face will surely fail. We will win our freedom because the sacred heritage of our nation and the eternal will of God are embodied in our echoing demands.

42   Before closing I feel impelled to mention one other point in your statement that has troubled me profoundly. You warmly commended the Birmingham police force for keeping "order" and "preventing violence." I doubt that you would have so warmly commended the police force if you had seen its dogs sinking their teeth into unarmed, nonviolent Negroes. I doubt that you would so quickly commend the policemen if you were to observe their ugly and inhumane treatment of Negroes here in the city jail; if you were to watch them push and curse old Negro women and young Negro girls; if you were to see them slap and kick old Negro men and young boys; if you were to observe them, as they did on two occasions, refuse to give us food because we wanted to sing our grace together. I cannot join you in your praise of the Birmingham police department.

43   It is true that the police have exercised a degree of discipline in handling the demonstrators. In this sense they have conducted themselves rather "nonviolently" in public. But for what purpose? To preserve the evil system of segregation. Over the past few years I have consistently preached that nonviolence demands that the means we use must be as pure as the ends we seek. I have tried to make clear that it is wrong to use immoral means to attain moral ends. But now I must affirm that it is just as wrong, or perhaps even more so, to use moral means to preserve immoral ends. Perhaps Mr. Connor and his policemen have been rather nonviolent in public, as was Chief Pritchett in Albany, Georgia, but they have used the moral means of nonviolence to maintain the immoral end of racial injustice. As T. S. Eliot has said, "The last temptation is the greatest treason: To do the right deed for the wrong reason."

44   I wish you had commended the Negro sit-inners and demonstrators of Birmingham for their sublime courage, their willingness to suffer, and their amazing discipline in the midst of great provocation. One day the South will recognize its real heroes. They will be the James Merediths,[11] with the noble sense of purpose that enables them to face jeering and hostile mobs, and with the agonizing loneliness that characterizes the life of the pioneer. They will be old, oppressed, battered Negro women, symbolized in a

---

[11]In 1961 James Meredith became the first black student to enroll at the University of Mississippi, sparking considerable controversy and confrontation.

seventy-two-year-old woman in Montgomery, Alabama, who rose up with a sense of dignity and with her people decided not to ride segregated buses, and who responded with ungrammatical profundity to one who inquired about her weariness: "My feets is tired, but my soul is at rest." They will be the young high school and college students, the young ministers of the gospel and a host of their elders, courageously and nonviolently sitting in at lunch counters and willingly going to jail for conscience' sake. One day the South will know that when these disinherited children of God sat down at lunch counters, they were in reality standing up for what is best in the American dream and for the most sacred values in our Judaeo-Christian heritage, thereby bringing our nation back to those great wells of democracy which were dug deep by the founding fathers in their formulation of the Constitution and the Declaration of Independence.

Never before have I written so long a letter. I'm afraid it is much too   45
long to take your precious time. I can assure you that it would have been much shorter if I had been writing from a comfortable desk, but what else can one do when he is alone in a narrow jail cell, other than write long letters, think long thoughts, and pray long prayers?

If I have said anything in this letter that overstates the truth and   46
indicates an unreasonable impatience, I beg you to forgive me. If I have said anything that understates the truth and indicates my having a patience that allows me to settle for anything less than brotherhood, I beg God to forgive me.

I hope this letter finds you strong in the faith. I also hope that   47
circumstances will soon make it possible for me to meet each of you, not as an integrationist or a civil-rights leader but as a fellow clergyman and a Christian brother. Let us all hope that the dark clouds of racial prejudice will soon pass away and the deep fog of misunderstanding will be lifted from our fear-drenched communities, and in some not too distant tomorrow the radiant stars of love and brotherhood will shine over our great nation with all their scintillating beauty.

Yours for the cause of Peace and Brotherhood,

MARTIN LUTHER KING, JR.

Questions for Study and Discussion

1. Why did King write this letter? What was he doing in Birmingham? What kinds of "direct action" did he take there and why? What did he do that caused him to be jailed?

2. King says that he "stands in the middle of two opposing forces in the Negro community." What are those forces and why does he see himself between them?

3. What does King find wrong with the contemporary church as opposed to the early Christian church?

4. What specific objections to his activities have been presented in the statement that King is responding to? How does he answer each objection?

5. What does King call upon the clergy to do? What actions does he wish them to take and what beliefs to hold?

6. King says that he advocates nonviolent resistance. What does he mean? In his letter he notes that the Birmingham Police Department has been praised for its nonviolent response to demonstrations. What is King's response to this claim?

7. King's letter was written in response to a published statement by eight fellow clergymen. While these men are his primary audience, he would appear to have a secondary audience as well. What is that audience? How does King show himself to be a man of reason and thoughtfulness in his letter of response?

Writing Topics

1. Write an essay in which you discuss how Martin Luther King's actions and his "Letter from Birmingham Jail" both exemplify Thoreau's principle of civil disobedience (pp. 675–92).

2. King advocates nonviolent resistance as a way of confronting oppression. What other means of confronting oppression were available to him? What are the strengths and weaknesses of those alternatives? Write an essay in which you assess the effectiveness of nonviolent resistance in the light of its alternatives.

W. H. AUDEN

Wystan Hugh Auden was born in York, England, in 1907, and was educated at Oxford University. While a student at Christ Church College there, he began to write the poems that brought him attention as an original, modern voice in English letters. During the 1930s, Auden developed his special kind of direct, often political poetry and also wrote plays, a movie script, and books that grew out of journeys to Iceland and China with such friends and fellow writers as Louis MacNeice and Christopher Isherwood. At the end of the thirties, he left England for the United States, later to become an American citizen. As he grew older, his poetry became more introspective, less "public" and political. He died in 1973.

Many countries have monuments dedicated to their "unknown soldier," a soldier killed on the battlefield who symbolizes the ideals of national service and sacrifice. "The Unknown Citizen" suggests what might be written on a monument for a symbolic civilian, who represents his society's peacetime values.

The Unknown Citizen

(To JS/07/M/378
This Marble Monument
Is Erected by the State)

He was found by the Bureau of Statistics to be
One against whom there was no official complaint,
And all the reports on his conduct agree
That, in the modern sense of an old-fashioned word, he was a saint,
For in everything he did he served the Greater Community.   5
Except for the War till the day he retired
He worked in a factory and never got fired,
But satisfied his employers, Fudge Motors Inc.
Yet he wasn't a scab or odd in his views,
For his Union reports that he paid his dues,   10
(Our report on his Union shows it was sound)
And our Social Psychology workers found
That he was popular with his mates and liked a drink.
The Press are convinced that he bought a paper every day

718

And that his reactions to advertisements were normal in every way.   15
Policies taken out in his name prove that he was fully insured,
And his Health-card shows he was once in hospital but left it cured.
Both Producers Research and High-Grade Living declare
He was fully sensible to the advantages of the Instalment Plan
And had everything necessary to the Modern Man,   20
A phonograph, a radio, a car and a frigidaire.
Our researchers into Public Opinion are content
That he held the proper opinions for the time of year;
When there was peace, he was for peace; when there was war, he went.
He was married and added five children to the population,   25
Which our Eugenist says was the right number for a parent of his
    generation,
And our teachers report that he never interfered with their education.
Was he free? Was he happy? The question is absurd:
Had anything been wrong, we should certainly have heard.

Questions for Study and Discussion

1. Do the words in this poem literally express Auden's own views? What makes you think so? If not, whose views are they meant to express?

2. Why do you think Auden presents this poem as an inscription on a public monument? What is the advantage of this choice? Why would a society erect a monument to its "unknown citizen"?

3. What does the poem tell us about the unknown citizen? What doesn't it tell us? What do its inclusions and omissions reveal about the state's official attitudes and values? How do these attitudes and values compare with Auden's? How do you know?

4. Look at the inscription following the title. What can you say about its content and style? How does it affect your understanding of the poem?

5. Comment on Auden's use of capitalization, citing examples from the poem. How does it affect the poem's meaning?

6. How do you think Auden meant readers to respond to this poem? Cite evidence from the poem to support your answer. How do you respond to it? Why do you respond that way?

Writing Topics

1. Auden wrote his poem in 1939. Using whatever information you think relevant, write an essay in which you describe the "unknown citizen" of today.

2. Suppose that in the year 2000 the state were to erect a monument to you, and that you could write the inscription yourself. What would you want your monument to say? Write your own inscription, limiting yourself to 500 words.

3. The United States government relies heavily on statistical information about its citizens, information that depersonalizes them in various ways. What sort of information does the government collect? What are the advantages and uses of having such information? What are the disadvantages and abuses? What information—to your knowledge—has the government collected about you? Write an essay in which you discuss the pros or the cons or both of extensive information-gathering by the government.

CHARLOTTE PERKINS GILMAN

Charlotte Perkins Gilman (1860–1935) was a reformer and feminist who was born in Hartford, Connecticut. In addition to her distinguished career as a writer of stories, poetry, and nonfiction, and a lecturer on the labor movement and feminism, she edited the *Forerunner*, a liberal journal. Suffering from an incurable disease, Perkins Gilman died by her own hand. *Women and Economics* (1898) is considered to be her most important work. However, the reemergence of the feminist movement brought "The Yellow Wallpaper" into a prominence it hardly enjoyed when it was written.

Referred to by one critic as a "literary masterpiece" and by another as a story to "freeze our . . . blood," "The Yellow Wallpaper" is drawn from Perkins Gilman's own life. In it she makes the reader witness to a woman's mental breakdown with vivid and frightening detail.

The Yellow Wallpaper

It is very seldom that mere ordinary people like John and myself secure ancestral halls for the summer. 1

A colonial mansion, a hereditary estate, I would say a haunted house, and reach the height of romantic felicity—but that would be asking too much of fate! 2

Still I will proudly declare that there is something queer about it. 3

Else, why should it be let so cheaply? And why have stood so long untenanted? 4

John laughs at me, of course, but one expects that in marriage. 5

John is practical in the extreme. He has no patience with faith, an intense horror of superstition, and he scoffs openly at any talk of things not to be felt and seen and put down in figures. 6

John is a physician, and *perhaps*—(I would not say it to a living soul, of course, but this is dead paper and a great relief to my mind)—*perhaps* that is one reason I do not get well faster. 7

You see he does not believe I am sick! 8

And what can one do? 9

If a physician of high standing, and one's own husband, assures friends and relatives that there is really nothing the matter with one but temporary nervous depression—a slight hysterical tendency—what is one to do? 10

My brother is also a physician, and also of high standing, and he says the same thing. 11

So I take phosphates or phospites—whichever it is, and tonics, and journeys, and air, and exercise, and am absolutely forbidden to "work" until I am well again. 12

Personally, I disagree with their ideas.   13

Personally, I believe that congenial work, with excitement and change,   14
would do me good.

But what is one to do?   15

I did write for a while in spite of them; but it *does* exhaust me a good   16
deal—having to be so sly about it, or else meet with heavy opposition.

I sometimes fancy that in my condition if I had less opposition and   17
more society and stimulus—but John says the very worst thing I can do is to
think about my condition, and I confess it always makes me feel bad.

So I will let it alone and talk about the house.   18

The most beautiful place! It is quite alone, standing well back from the   19
road, quite three miles from the village. It makes me think of English places
that you read about, for there are hedges and walls and gates that lock, and
lots of separate little houses for the gardeners and people.

There is a *delicious* garden! I never saw such a garden—large and   20
shady, full of box-bordered paths, and lined with long grape-covered arbors
with seats under them.

There were greenhouses, too, but they are all broken now.   21

There was some legal trouble, I believe, something about the heirs and   22
coheirs; anyhow, the place has been empty for years.

That spoils my ghostliness, I am afraid, but I don't care—there is   23
something strange about the house—I can feel it.

I even said so to John one moonlight evening, but he said what I felt   24
was a *draught*, and shut the window.

I get unreasonably angry with John sometimes. I'm sure I never used   25
to be so sensitive. I think it is due to this nervous condition.

But John says if I feel so, I shall neglect proper self-control; so I take   26
pains to control myself—before him, at least, and that makes me very tired.

I don't like our room a bit. I wanted one downstairs that opened on   27
the piazza and had roses all over the window, and such pretty old-fashioned
chintz hangings! but John would not hear of it.

He said there was only one window and not room for two beds, and   28
no near room for him if he took another.

He is very careful and loving, and hardly lets me stir without special   29
direction.

I have a schedule prescription for each hour in the day; he takes all   30
care from me, and so I feel basely ungrateful not to value it more.

He said we came here solely on my account, that I was to have perfect   31
rest and all the air I could get. "Your exercise depends on your strength, my
dear," said he, "and your food somewhat on your appetite; but air you can
absorb all the time." So we took the nursery at the top of the house.

It is a big, airy room, the whole floor nearly, with windows that look   32
all ways, and air and sunshine galore. It was nursery first and then playroom and gymnasium, I should judge; for the windows are barred for little

children, and there are rings and things in the walls.

The paint and paper look as if a boys' school had used it. It is stripped 33
off—the paper—in great patches all around the head of my bed, about as far
as I can reach, and in a great place on the other side of the room low down. I
never saw a worse paper in my life.

One of those sprawling flamboyant patterns committing every artistic 34
sin.

It is dull enough to confuse the eye in following, pronounced enough 35
to constantly irritate and provoke study, and when you follow the lame
uncertain curves for a little distance they suddenly commit suicide—plunge
off at outrageous angles, destroy themselves in unheard of contradictions.

The color is repellent, almost revolting; a smouldering unclean yellow, 36
strangely faded by the slow-turning sunlight.

It is a dull yet lurid orange in some places, a sickly sulphur tint in 37
others.

No wonder the children hated it! I should hate it myself if I had to live 38
in this room long.

There comes John, and I must put this away,—he hates to have me 39
write a word.

We have been here two weeks, and I haven't felt like writing before, 40
since that first day.

I am sitting by the window now, up in this atrocious nursery, and 41
there is nothing to hinder my writing as much as I please, save lack of
strength.

John is away all day, and even some nights when his cases are serious. 42

I am glad my case is not serious! 43

But these nervous troubles are dreadfully depressing. 44

John does not know how much I really suffer. He knows there is no 45
reason to suffer, and that satisfies him.

Of course it is only nervousness. It does weigh on me so not to do my 46
duty in any way!

I meant to be such a help to John, such a real rest and comfort, and 47
here I am a comparative burden already!

Nobody would believe what an effort it is to do what little I am able,— 48
to dress and entertain, and order things.

It is fortunate Mary is so good with the baby. Such a dear baby! 49

And yet I *cannot* be with him, it makes me so nervous. 50

I suppose John never was nervous in his life. He laughs at me so about 51
this wall-paper!

At first he meant to repaper the room, but afterwards he said that I 52
was letting it get the better of me, and that nothing was worse for a nervous
patient than to give way to such fancies.

He said that after the wall-paper was changed it would be the heavy 53 bedstead, and then the barred windows, and then that gate at the head of the stairs, and so on.

"You know the place is doing you good," he said, "and really, dear, I   54 don't care to renovate the house just for a three months' rental."

"Then do let us go downstairs," I said, "there are such pretty rooms   55 there."

Then he took me in his arms and called me a blessed little goose, and   56 said he would go down to the cellar, if I wished, and have it whitewashed into the bargain.

But he is right enough about the beds and windows and things.   57

It is an airy and comfortable room as any one need wish, and, of   58 course, I would not be so silly as to make him uncomfortable just for a whim.

I'm really getting quite fond of the big room, all but that horrid paper.   59

Out of one window I can see the garden, those mysterious deepshaded   60 arbors, the riotous old-fashioned flowers, and bushes and gnarly trees.

Out of another I get a lovely view of the bay and a little private wharf   61 belonging to the estate. There is a beautiful shaded lane that runs down there from the house. I always fancy I see people walking in these numerous paths and arbors, but John has cautioned me not to give way to fancy in the least. He says that with my imaginative power and habit of story-making, a nervous weakness like mine is sure to lead to all manner of excited fancies, and that I ought to use my will and good sense to check the tendency. So I try.

I think sometimes that if I were only well enough to write a little it   62 would relieve the press of ideas and rest me.

But I find I get pretty tired when I try.   63

It is so discouraging not to have any advice and companionship about   64 my work. When I get really well, John says we will ask Cousin Henry and Julia down for a long visit; but he says he would as soon put fireworks in my pillow-case as to let me have those stimulating people about now.

I wish I could get well faster.   65

But I must not think about that. This paper looks to me as if it *knew*   66 what a vicious influence it had!

There is a recurrent spot where the pattern lolls like a broken neck   67 and two bulbous eyes stare at you upside down.

I get positively angry with the impertinence of it and the everlasting-   68 ness. Up and down and sideways they crawl, and those absurd, unblinking eyes are everywhere. There is one place where two breaths didn't match, and the eyes go all up and down the line, one a little higher than the other.

I never saw so much expression in an inanimate thing before, and we   69 all know how much expression they have! I used to lie awake as a child and get more entertainment and terror out of blank walls and plain furniture than most children could find in a toy-store.

I remember what a kindly wink the knobs of our big, old bureau used to have, and there was one chair that always seemed like a strong friend. 70

I used to feel that if any of the other things looked too fierce I could always hop into that chair and be safe. 71

The furniture in this room is no worse than inharmonious, however, for we had to bring it all from downstairs. I suppose when this was used as a playroom they had to take the nursery things out, and no wonder! I never saw such ravages as the children have made here. 72

The wall-paper, as I said before, is torn off in spots, and it sticketh closer than a brother—they must have had perseverance as well as hatred. 73

Then the floor is scratched and gouged and splintered, the plaster itself is dug out here and there, and this great heavy bed which is all we found in the room, looks as if it had been through the wars. 74

But I don't mind it a bit—only the paper. 75

There comes John's sister. Such a dear girl as she is, and so careful of me! I must not let her find me writing. 76

She is a perfect and enthusiastic housekeeper, and hopes for no better profession. I verily believe she thinks it is the writing which made me sick! 77

But I can write when she is out, and see her a long way off from these windows. 78

There is one that commands the road, a lovely shaded winding road, and one that just looks off over the country. A lovely country, too, full of great elms and velvet meadows. 79

This wall-paper has a kind of sub-pattern in a different shade, a particularly irritating one, for you can only see it in certain lights, and not clearly then. 80

But in the places where it isn't faded and where the sun is just so—I can see a strange, provoking, formless sort of figure, that seems to skulk about behind that silly and conspicuous front design. 81

There's sister on the stairs! 82

Well, the Fourth of July is over! The people are all gone and I am tired out. John thought it might do me good to see a little company, so we just had mother and Nellie and the children down for a week. 83

Of course I didn't do a thing. Jennie sees to everything now. 84

But it tired me all the same. 85

John says if I don't pick up faster he shall send me to Weir Mitchell in the fall. 86

But I don't want to go there at all. I had a friend who was in his hands once, and she says he is just like John and my brother, only more so! 87

Besides, it is such an undertaking to go so far. 88

I don't feel as if it was worth while to turn my hand over for anything, 89
and I'm getting dreadfully fretful and querulous.

I cry at nothing, and cry most of the time. 90

Of course I don't when John is here, or anybody else, but when I am 91
alone.

And I am alone a good deal just now. John is kept in town very often 92
by serious cases, and Jennie is good and lets me alone when I want her to.

So I walk a little in the garden or down that lovely lane, sit on the 93
porch under the roses, and lie down up here a good deal.

I'm getting really fond of the room in spite of the wall-paper. Perhaps 94
because of the wall-paper.

It dwells in my mind so! 95

I lie here on this great immovable bed—it is nailed down, I believe— 96
and follow that pattern about by the hour. It is as good as gymnastics, I
assure you. I start, we'll say, at the bottom, down in the corner over there
where it has not been touched, and I determine for the thousandth time
that I *will* follow that pointless pattern to some sort of a conclusion.

I know a little of the principle of design, and I know this thing was not 97
arranged on any laws of radiation, or alternation, or repetition, or symmetry, or anything else that I ever heard of.

It is repeated, of course, by the breadths, but not otherwise. 98

Looked at in one way each breadth stands alone, the bloated curves 99
and flourishes—a kind of "debased Romanesque" with *delirium tremens*—go
waddling up and down in isolated columns of fatuity.

But, on the other hand, they connect diagonally, and the sprawling 100
outlines run off in great slanting waves of optic horror, like a lot of
wallowing seaweeds in full chase.

The whole thing goes horizontally, too, at least it seems so, and I 101
exhaust myself in trying to distinguish the order of its going in that
direction.

They have used a horizontal breadth for a frieze, and that adds 102
wonderfully to the confusion.

There is one end of the room where it is almost intact, and there, 103
when the crosslights fade and the low sun shines directly upon it, I can
almost fancy radiation after all,—the interminable grotesques seem to form
around a common centre and rush off in headlong plunges of equal distraction.

It makes me tired to follow it. I will take a nap I guess. 104

I don't know why I should write this. 105

I don't want to. 106

I don't feel able.   107

And I know John would think it absurd. But I *must* say what I feel and   108
think in some way—it is such a relief!

But the effort is getting to be greater than the relief.   109

Half the time now I am awfully lazy, and lie down ever so much.   110

John says I mustn't lose my strength, and has me take cod liver oil and   111
lots of tonics and things, to say nothing of ale and wine and rare meat.

Dear John! He loves me very dearly, and hates to have me sick. I tried   112
to have a real earnest reasonable talk with him the other day, and tell him
how I wish he would let me go and make a visit to Cousin Henry and Julia.

But he said I wasn't able to go, nor able to stand it after I got there;   113
and I did not make out a very good case for myself, for I was crying before I
had finished.

It is getting to be a great effort for me to think straight. Just this   114
nervous weakness I suppose.

And dear John gathered me up in his arms, and just carried me   115
upstairs and laid me on the bed, and sat by me and read to me till it tired
my head.

He said I was his darling and his comfort and all he had, and that I   116
must take care of myself for his sake, and keep well.

He says no one but myself can help me out of it, that I must use my   117
will and self-control and not let any silly fancies run away with me.

There's one comfort, the baby is well and happy, and does not have to   118
occupy this nursery with the horrid wall-paper.

If we had not used it, that blessed child would have! What a fortunate   119
escape! Why, I wouldn't have a child of mine, an impressionable little thing,
live in such a room for worlds.

I never thought of it before, but it is lucky that John kept me here after   120
all, I can stand it so much easier than a baby, you see.

Of course I never mention it to them any more—I am too wise,—but I   121
keep watch of it all the same.

There are things in that paper that nobody knows but me, or ever   122
will.

Behind that outside pattern the dim shapes get clearer every day.   123

It is always the same shape, only very numerous.   124

And it is like a woman stooping down and creeping about behind that   125
pattern. I don't like it a bit. I wonder—I begin to think—I wish John would
take me away from here!

It is so hard to talk with John about my case, because he is so wise,   126
and because he loves me so.

But I tried it last night.   127

It was moonlight. The moon shines in all around just as the sun does.   128

I hate to see it sometimes, it creeps so slowly, and always comes in by   129
one window or another.

John was asleep and I hated to waken him, so I kept still and watched   130
the moonlight on that undulating wall-paper till I felt creepy.

The faint figure behind seemed to shake the pattern, just as if she   131
wanted to get out.

I got up softly and went to feel and see if the paper *did* move, and   132
when I came back John was awake.

"What is it, little girl?" he said. "Don't go walking about like that—   133
you'll get cold."

I thought it was a good time to talk, so I told him that I really was not   134
gaining here, and that I wished he would take me away.

"Why darling!" said he, "our lease will be up in three weeks, and I   135
can't see how to leave before.

"The repairs are not done at home, and I cannot possibly leave town   136
just now. Of course if you were in any danger, I could and would, but you
really are better, dear, whether you can see it or not. I am a doctor, dear,
and I know. You are gaining flesh and color, your appetite is better, I feel
really much easier about you."

"I don't weigh a bit more," said I, "nor as much; and my appetite may   137
be better in the evening when you are here, but it is worse in the morning
when you are away!"

"Bless her little heart!" said he with a big hug, "she shall be as sick as   138
she pleases! But now let's improve the shining hours by going to sleep, and
talk about it in the morning!"

"And you won't go away?" I asked gloomily.   139

"Why, how can I, dear? It is only three weeks more and then we will   140
take a nice little trip of a few days while Jennie is getting the house ready.
Really dear you are better!"

"Better in body perhaps—" I began, and stopped short, for he sat up   141
straight and looked at me with such a stern, reproachful look that I could
not say another word.

"My darling," said he, "I beg of you, for my sake and for our child's   142
sake, as well as for your own, that you will never for one instant let that idea
enter your mind! There is nothing so dangerous, so fascinating, to a
temperament like yours. It is a false and foolish fancy. Can you not trust me
as a physician when I tell you so?"

So of course I said no more on that score, and we went to sleep before   143
long. He thought I was asleep first, but I wasn't, and lay there for hours
trying to decide whether that front pattern and the back pattern really did
move together or separately.

On a pattern like this, by daylight, there is a lack of sequence, a   144
defiance of law, that is a constant irritant to a normal mind.

The color is hideous enough, and unreliable enough, and infuriating 145
enough, but the pattern is torturing.

You think you have mastered it, but just as you get well underway in 146
following, it turns a back-somersault and there you are. It slaps you in the
face, knocks you down, and tramples upon you. It is like a bad dream.

The outside pattern is a florid arabesque, reminding one of a fungus. If 147
you can imagine a toadstool in joints, an interminable string of toadstools,
budding and sprouting in endless convolutions—why, that is something
like it.

That is, sometimes! 148

There is one marked peculiarity about this paper, a thing nobody 149
seems to notice but myself, and that is that it changes as the light changes.

When the sun shoots in through the east window—I always watch for 150
that first long, straight ray—it changes so quickly that I never can quite
believe it.

That is why I watch it always. 151

By moonlight—the moon shines in all night when there is a moon—I 152
wouldn't know it was the same paper.

At night in any kind of light, in twilight, candle light, lamplight, and 153
worst of all by moonlight, it becomes bars! The outside pattern I mean, and
the woman behind it is as plain as can be.

I didn't realize for a long time what the thing was that showed behind, 154
that dim sub-pattern, but now I am quite sure it is a woman.

By daylight she is subdued, quiet. I fancy it is the pattern that keeps 155
her so still. It is so puzzling. It keeps me quiet by the hour.

I lie down ever so much now. John says it is good for me, and to sleep 156
all I can.

Indeed he started the habit by making me lie down for an hour after 157
each meal.

It is a very bad habit I am convinced, for you see I don't sleep. 158

And that cultivates deceit, for I don't tell them I'm awake—O no! 159

The fact is I am getting a little afraid of John. 160

He seems very queer sometimes, and even Jennie has an inexplicable 161
look.

It strikes me occasionally, just as a scientific hypothesis,—that perhaps 162
it is the paper!

I have watched John when he did not know I was looking, and come 163
into the room suddenly on the most innocent excuses, and I've caught him
several times *looking at the paper!* And Jennie too. I caught Jennie with her
hand on it once.

She didn't know I was in the room, and when I asked her in a quiet, a 164
very quiet voice, with the most restrained manner possible, what she was
doing with the paper—she turned around as if she had been caught stealing,
and looked quite angry—asked me why I should frighten her so!

Then she said that the paper stained everything it touched, that she 165 had found yellow smooches on all my clothes and John's, and she wished we would be more careful!

Did not that sound innocent? But I know she was studying that 166 pattern, and I am determined that nobody shall find it out but myself!

Life is very much more exciting now than it used to be. You see I have 167 something more to expect, to look forward to, to watch. I really do eat better, and am more quiet than I was.

John is so pleased to see me improve! He laughed a little the other day, 168 and said I seemed to be flourishing in spite of my wall-paper.

I turned it off with a laugh. I had no intention of telling him it was 169 *because* of the wall-paper—he would make fun of me. He might even want to take me away.

I don't want to leave now until I have found it out. There is a week 170 more, and I think that will be enough.

I'm feeling ever so much better! I don't sleep much at night, for it is so 171 interesting to watch developments; but I sleep a good deal in the daytime.

In the daytime it is tiresome and perplexing. 172

There are always new shoots on the fungus, and new shades of yellow 173 all over it. I cannot keep count of them, though I have tried conscientiously.

It is the strangest yellow, that wall-paper! It makes me think of all the 174 yellow things I ever saw—not beautiful ones like buttercups, but old foul, bad yellow things.

But there is something else about that paper—the smell! I noticed it 175 the moment we came into the room, but with so much air and sun it was not bad. Now we have had a week of fog and rain, and whether the windows are open or not, the smell is here.

It creeps all over the house. 176

I find it hovering in the dining-room, skulking in the parlor, hiding in 177 the hall, lying in wait for me on the stairs.

It gets into my hair. 178

Even when I go to ride, if I turn my head suddenly and surprise it— 179 there is that smell!

Such a peculiar odor, too! I have spent hours in trying to analyze it, to 180 find what it smelled like.

It is not bad—at first, and very gentle, but quite the subtlest, most 181 enduring odor I ever met.

In this damp weather it is awful, I wake up in the night and find it 182 hanging over me.

It used to disturb me at first. I thought seriously of burning the 183 house—to reach the smell.

But now I am used to it. The only thing I can think of that it is like is 184 the *color* of the paper! A yellow smell.

There is a very funny mark on this wall, low down, near the mop-board. A streak that runs round the room. It goes behind every piece of furniture, except the bed, a long, straight, even *smooch*, as if it had been rubbed over and over. 185

I wonder how it was done and who did it, and what they did it for. Round and round and round—round and round and round—it makes me dizzy! 186

I really have discovered something at last. 187

Through watching so much at night, when it changes so, I have finally found out. 188

The front pattern *does* move—and no wonder! The woman behind shakes it! 189

Sometimes I think there are a great many women behind, and some-times only one, and she crawls around fast, and her crawling shakes it all over. 190

Then in the very bright spots she keeps still, and in the very shady spots she just takes hold of the bars and shakes them hard. 191

And she is all the time trying to climb through. But nobody could climb through that pattern—it strangles so; I think that is why it has so many heads. 192

They get through, and then the pattern strangles them off and turns them upside down, and makes their eyes white! 193

If those heads were covered or taken off it would not be half so bad. 194

I think that woman gets out in the daytime! 195

And I'll tell you why—privately—I've seen her! 196

I can see her out of every one of my windows! 197

It is the same woman, I know, for she is always creeping, and most women do not creep by daylight. 198

I see her on that long road under the trees, creeping along, and when a carriage comes she hides under the blackberry vines. 199

I don't blame her a bit. It must be very humiliating to be caught creeping by daylight! 200

I always lock the door when I creep by daylight. I can't do it at night, for I know John would suspect something at once. 201

And John is so queer now, that I don't want to irritate him. I wish he would take another room! Besides, I don't want anybody to get that woman out at night but myself. 202

I often wonder if I could see her out of all the windows at once. 203

But, turn as fast as I can, I can only see out of one at one time. 204

And though I always see her, she *may* be able to creep faster than I can turn! 205

I have watched her sometimes away off in the open country, creeping as fast as a cloud shadow in a high wind. 206

If only that top pattern could be gotten off from the under one! I mean to try it, little by little. 207

I have found out another funny thing, but I shan't tell it this time! It does not do to trust people too much. 208

There are only two more days to get this paper off, and I believe John is beginning to notice. I don't like the look in his eyes. 209

And I heard him ask Jennie a lot of professional questions about me. She had a very good report to give. 210

She said I slept a good deal in the daytime. 211

John knows I don't sleep very well at night, for all I'm so quiet! 212

He asked me all sorts of questions, too, and pretended to be very loving and kind. 213

As if I couldn't see through him! 214

Still, I don't wonder he acts so, sleeping under this paper for three months. 215

It only interests me, but I feel sure John and Jennie are secretly affected by it. 216

Hurrah! This is the last day, but it is enough. John to stay in town over night, and won't be out until this evening. 217

Jennie wanted to sleep with me—the sly thing! but I told her I should undoubtedly rest better for a night all alone. 218

That was clever, for really I wasn't alone a bit! As soon as it was moonlight and that poor thing began to crawl and shake the pattern, I got up and ran to help her. 219

I pulled and she shook, I shook and she pulled, and before morning we had peeled off yards of that paper. 220

A strip about as high as my head and half around the room. 221

And then when the sun came and that awful pattern began to laugh at me, I declared I would finish it to-day! 222

We go away to-morrow, and they are moving all my furniture down again to leave things as they were before. 223

Jennie looked at the wall in amazement, but I told her merrily that I did it out of pure spite at the vicious thing. 224

She laughed and said she wouldn't mind doing it herself, but I must not get tired. 225

How she betrayed herself that time! 226

But I am here, and no person touches this paper but me,—not *alive!* 227

She tried to get me out of the room—it was too patent! But I said it was 228 so quiet and empty and clean now that I believed I would lie down again and sleep all I could; and not to wake me even for dinner—I would call when I woke.

So now she is gone, and the servants are gone, and the things are gone, and there is nothing left but that great bedstead nailed down, with the canvas mattress we found on it. 229

We shall sleep downstairs to-night, and take the boat home to-morrow. 230

I quite enjoy the room, now it is bare again. 231

How those children did tear about here! 232

This bedstead is fairly gnawed! 233

But I must get to work. 234

I have locked the door and thrown the key down into the front path. 235

I don't want to go out, and I don't want to have anybody come in, till John comes. 236

I want to astonish him. 237

I've got a rope up here that even Jennie did not find. If that woman does get out, and tries to get away, I can tie her! 238

But I forgot I could not reach far without anything to stand on! 239

This bed will *not* move! 240

I tried to lift and push it until I was lame, and then I got so angry I bit off a little piece at one corner—but it hurt my teeth. 241

Then I peeled off all the paper I could reach standing on the floor. It sticks horribly and the pattern just enjoys it! All those strangled heads and bulbous eyes and waddling fungus growths just shriek with derision! 242

I am getting angry enough to do something desperate. To jump out of the window would be admirable exercise, but the bars are too strong even to try. 243

Besides I wouldn't do it. Of course not. I know well enough that a step like that is improper and might be misconstrued. 244

I don't like to *look* out of the windows even—there are so many of those creeping women, and they creep so fast. 245

I wonder if they all come out of that wall-paper as I did! 246

But I am securely fastened now by my well-hidden rope—you don't get *me* out in the road there! 247

I suppose I shall have to get back behind the pattern when it comes night, and that is hard! 248

It is so pleasant to be out in this great room and creep around as I please! 249

I don't want to go outside. I won't, even if Jennie asks me to. 250

For outside you have to creep on the ground, and everything is green instead of yellow. 251

But here I can creep smoothly on the floor, and my shoulder just fits in that long smooch around the wall, so I cannot lose my way. 252

Why there's John at the door! 253

It is no use, young man, you can't open it!   254

How he does call and pound!   255

Now he's crying for an axe.   256

It would be a shame to break down that beautiful door!   257

"John dear!" said I in the gentlest voice, "the key is down by the front   258
steps, under a plantain leaf!"

That silenced him for a few moments.   259

Then he said—very quietly indeed, "Open the door, my darling!"   260

"I can't," said I. "The key is down by the front door under a plantain   261
leaf!"

And then I said it again, several times, very gently and slowly, and   262
said it so often that he had to go and see, and he got it of course, and came
in. He stopped short by the door.

"What is the matter?" he cried. "For God's sake, what are you doing!"   263

I kept on creeping just the same, but I looked at him over my shoulder.   264

"I've got out at last," said I, "in spite of you and Jane. And I've pulled   265
off most of the paper, so you can't put me back!"

Now why should that man have fainted? But he did, and right across   266
my path by the wall, so that I had to creep over him every time!

Questions for Study and Discussion

1. What sorts of activities make the heroine tired?

2. How is the paper a metaphor for the woman's life? for the life of all women of her time? What is the significance of the paper's having a "front pattern" and a "back pattern"?

3. How does the wife's attitude toward her husband change during the story? What words does she use to describe him early and then later?

4. The husband "knows there is no reason to suffer." Is he right? What is really wrong with his wife?

5. Based on clues from the story, how would you contrast the husband's image of his wife with what you learn about her?

6. What are some of the ways the author makes the wife's illness real for us? Cite examples of figures of speech, diction, and pace.

7. Why do the women in the wallpaper "creep"?

8. What are the similarities between the wife's attitudes toward her writing and toward the wallpaper?

9. How does her attitude toward the room change? What does this change signify? Why is she afraid to go out of the house in the end? Does she achieve any kind of victory?

Writing Topics

1. In the story we learn that the wife has recently had a baby. Today her "condition" might be diagnosed as postpartum depression. However, the author

wishes to make the point that the wife is also the victim of misunderstanding and the unrealistic expectations of an insensitive husband. Look up "postpartum depression" in your encyclopedia. How well does it explain the wife's symptoms? How are you inclined to explain the wife's illness? Does a hormonal explanation strengthen or weaken the point of Perkins Gilman's story or does it have no effect at all?

2. Charlotte Perkins Gilman was born before married women in this country could own their own property, and she died only shortly after they won the legal right to vote. Read more about the life of the author and her other works of fiction. Are all her heroines similarly doomed? What role model did she provide to women of her time? What other role models does she offer through her fiction?

Contemporary Issues

JONATHAN KOZOL

Born in 1936, Jonathan Kozol received his B.A. from Harvard in 1958. He has taught at Yale University and the University of Massachusetts as well as in the Boston and Newton, Massachusetts, public schools and is considered to be in the forefront in the move for educational reform. Kozol has received fellowships from the Guggenheim, Ford, and Rockefeller foundations to support his writing and research, and the National Book Award for *Death at an Early Age: The Destruction of the Hearts and Minds of Negro Children in the Boston Public Schools* (1967). Kozol's other books include *The Night Is Dark and I Am Far Away from Home* (1975), *Children of the Revolution* (1978), *Prisoners of Silence: Breaking the Bonds of Adult Illiteracy in the United States* (1979), *On Being a Teacher* (1981), *Illiterate America* (1985), and *Rachel and Her Children: Homeless Families in America* (1986).

The following selection is from *Illiterate America*, Kozol's magnum opus on illiteracy in which he advocates and outlines a grass-roots solution to the problem. In "The Human Cost of an Illiterate Society," Kozol attempts to convince readers of the seriousness of the homeless problem using an unexpected argument. Unlike other writers who advocate affordable housing as a solution to the problem of homelessness, Kozol suggests that illiteracy is the chief obstacle facing many people without homes.

The Human Cost of an Illiterate Society

PRECAUTIONS. READ BEFORE USING.
Poison: Contains sodium hydroxide (caustic soda-lye).
Corrosive: Causes severe eye and skin damage, may cause blindness.
Harmful or fatal if swallowed.
If swallowed, give large quantities of milk or water.
Do not induce vomiting.
Important: Keep water out of can at all times to
prevent contents from violently erupting . . .
                                        —*warning on a can of Drano*

We are speaking here no longer of the dangers faced by passengers on   1
Eastern Airlines or the dollar costs incurred by U.S. corporations and
taxpayers. We are speaking now of human suffering and of the ethical
dilemmas that are faced by a society that looks upon such suffering with
qualified concern but does not take those actions which its wealth and
ingenuity would seemingly demand.

Questions of literacy, in Socrates' belief, must at length be judged as   2
matters of morality. Socrates could not have had in mind the moral compromise peculiar to a nation like our own. Some of our Founding Fathers did,
however, have this question in their minds. One of the wisest of those
Founding Fathers (one who may not have been most compassionate but
surely was more prescient than some of his peers) recognized the special
dangers that illiteracy would pose to basic equity in the political construction that he helped to shape.

"A people who mean to be their own governors," James Madison   3
wrote, "must arm themselves with the power knowledge gives. A popular
government without popular information or the means of acquiring it, is
but a prologue to a farce or a tragedy, or perhaps both."

Tragedy looms larger than farce in the United States today. Illiterate   4
citizens seldom vote. Those who do are forced to cast a vote of questionable
worth. They cannot make informed decisions based on serious print information. Sometimes they can be alerted to their interests by aggressive voter
education. More frequently, they vote for a face, a smile, or a style, not for a
mind or character or body of beliefs.

The number of illiterate adults exceeds by 16 million the entire vote   5
cast for the winner in the 1980 presidential contest. If even one third of all
illiterates could vote, and read enough and do sufficient math to vote in
their self-interest, Ronald Reagan would not likely have been chosen president. There is, of course, no way to know for sure. We do know this:
Democracy is a mendacious term when used by those who are prepared to
countenance the forced exclusion of one third of our electorate. So long as
60 million people are denied significant participation, the government is
neither of, nor for, nor by, the people. It is a government, at best, of those
two thirds whose wealth, skin color, or parental privilege allows them
opportunity to profit from the provocation and instruction of the written
word.

The undermining of democracy in the United States is one "expense"   6
that sensitive Americans can easily deplore because it represents a contradiction that endangers citizens of all political positions. The human price is
not so obvious at first.

Since I first immersed myself within this work I have often had the   7
following dream: I find that I am in a railroad station or a large department
store within a city that is utterly unknown to me and where I cannot
understand the printed words. None of the signs or symbols is familiar.

Everything looks strange: like mirror writing of some kind. Gradually I understand that I am in the Soviet Union. All the letters on the walls around me are Cyrillic. I look for my pocket dictionary but I find that it has been mislaid. Where have I left it? Then I recall that I forgot to bring it with me when I packed my bags in Boston. I struggle to remember the name of my hotel. I try to ask somebody for directions. One person stops and looks at me in a peculiar way. I lose the nerve to ask. At last I reach into my wallet for an ID card. The card is missing. Have I lost it? Then I remember that my card was confiscated for some reason, many years before. Around this point, I wake up in a panic.

This panic is not so different from the misery that millions of adult illiterates experience each day within the course of their routine existence in the U.S.A. 8

Illiterates cannot read the menu in a restaurant. 9

They cannot read the cost of items on the menu in the *window* of the restaurant before they enter. 10

Illiterates cannot read the letters that their children bring home from their teachers. They cannot study school department circulars that tell them of the courses that their children must be taking if they hope to pass the SAT exams. They cannot help with homework. They cannot write a letter to the teacher. They are afraid to visit in the classroom. They do not want to humiliate their child or themselves. 11

Illiterates cannot read instructions on a bottle of prescription medicine. They cannot find out when a medicine is past the year of safe consumption; nor can they read of allergenic risks, warnings to diabetics, or the potential sedative effect of certain kinds of nonprescription pills. They cannot observe preventive health care admonitions. They cannot read about "the seven warning signs of cancer" or the indications of blood-sugar fluctuations or the risks of eating certain foods that aggravate the likelihood of cardiac arrest. 12

Illiterates live, in more than literal ways, an uninsured existence. They cannot understand the written details on a health insurance form. They cannot read the waivers that they sign preceding surgical procedures. Several women I have known in Boston have entered a slum hospital with the intention of obtaining a tubal ligation and have emerged a few days later after having been subjected to a hysterectomy. Unaware of their rights, incognizant of jargon, intimidated by the unfamiliar air of fear and atmosphere of ether that so many of us find oppressive in the confines even of the most attractive and expensive medical facilities, they have signed their names to documents they could not read and which nobody, in the hectic situation that prevails so often in those overcrowded hospitals that serve the urban poor, had even bothered to explain. 13

Childbirth might seem to be the last inalienable right of any female citizen within a civilized society. Illiterate mothers, as we shall see, already 14 have been cheated of the power to protect their progeny against the likelihood of demolition in deficient public schools and, as a result, against the verbal servitude within which they themselves exist. Surgical denial of the right to bear that child in the first place represents an ultimate denial, an unspeakable metaphor, a final darkness that denies even the twilight gleamings of our own humanity. What greater violation of our biological, our biblical, our spiritual humanity could possibly exist than that which takes place nightly, perhaps hourly these days, within such overburdened and benighted institutions as the Boston City Hospital? Illiteracy has many costs; few are so irreversible as this.

Even the roof above one's head, the gas or other fuel for heating that   15 protects the residents of northern city slums against the threat of illness in the winter months become uncertain guarantees. Illiterates cannot read the lease that they must sign to live in an apartment which, too often, they cannot afford. They cannot manage checking accounts and therefore seldom pay for anything by mail. Hours and entire days of difficult travel (and the cost of bus or other public transit) must be added to the real cost of whatever they consume. Loss of interest on the checking accounts they do not have, and could not manage if they did, must be regarded as another of the excess costs paid by the citizen who is excluded from the common instruments of commerce in a numerate society.

"I couldn't understand the bills," a woman in Washington, D.C.,   16 reports, "and then I couldn't write the checks to pay them. We signed things. We didn't know what they were."

Illiterates cannot read the notices that they receive from welfare offices   17 or from the IRS. They must depend on word-of-mouth instruction from the welfare worker—or from other persons whom they have good reason to mistrust. They do not know what rights they have, what deadlines and requirements they face, what options they might choose to exercise. They are half-citizens. Their rights exist in print but not in fact.

Illiterates cannot look up numbers in a telephone directory. Even if   18 they can find the names of friends, few possess the sorting skills to make use of the yellow pages; categories are bewildering and trade names are beyond decoding capabilities for millions of nonreaders. Even the emergency numbers listed on the first page of the phone book—"Ambulance," "Police," and "Fire"—are too frequently beyond the recognition of nonreaders.

Many illiterates cannot read the admonition on a pack of cigarettes.   19 Neither the Surgeon General's warning nor its reproduction on the package can alert them to the risks. Although most people learn by word of mouth that smoking is related to a number of grave physical disorders, they do not get the chance to read the detailed stories which can document this danger with the vividness that turns concern into determination to resist. They can see the handsome cowboy or the slim Virginia lady lighting up a filter cigarette; they cannot heed the words that tell them that this product is (not "may be") dangerous to their health. Sixty million men and women are condemned to be the unalerted, high-risk candidates for cancer.

Illiterates do not buy "no-name" products in the supermarkets. They   20
must depend on photographs or the familiar logos that are printed on the packages of brand-name groceries. The poorest people, therefore, are denied the benefits of the least costly products.

Illiterates depend almost entirely upon label recognition. Many labels,   21
however, are not easy to distinguish. Dozens of different kinds of Campbell's soup appear identical to the nonreader. The purchaser who cannot read and does not dare to ask for help, out of the fear of being stigmatized (a fear which is unfortuntely realistic), frequently comes home with something which she never wanted and her family never tasted.

Illiterates cannot read instructions on a pack of frozen food. Packages   22
sometimes provide an illustration to explain the cooking preparations; but illustrations are of little help to someone who must "boil water, drop the food—*within* its plastic wrapper—in the boiling water, wait for it to simmer, instantly remove."

Even when labels are seemingly clear, they may be easily mistaken. A   23
woman in Detroit brought home a gallon of Crisco for her children's dinner. She thought that she had bought the chicken that was pictured on the label. She had enough Crisco now to last a year—but no more money to go back and buy the food for dinner.

Recipes provided on the packages of certain staples sometimes tempt a   24
semiliterate person to prepare a meal her children have not tasted. The longing to vary the uniform and often starchy content of low-budget meals provided to the family that relies on food stamps commonly leads to ruinous results. Scarce funds have been wasted and the food must be thrown out. The same applies to distribution of food-surplus produce in emergency conditions. Government inducements to poor people to "explore the ways" by which to make a tasty meal from tasteless noodles, surplus cheese, and powdered milk are useless to nonreaders. Intended as benevolent advice, such recommendations mock reality and foster deeper feelings of resentment and of inability to cope. (Those, on the other hand, who cautiously refrain from "innovative" recipes in preparation of their children's meals must suffer the opprobrium of "laziness," "lack of imagination . . .").

Illiterates cannot travel freely. When they attempt to do so, they   25
encounter risks that few of us can dream of. They cannot read traffic signs and, while they often learn to recognize and to decipher symbols, they cannot manage street names which they haven't seen before. The same is true for bus and subway stops. While ingenuity can sometimes help a man or woman to discern directions from familiar landmarks, buildings, cemeteries, churches, and the like, most illiterates are virtually immobilized. They seldom wander past the streets and neighborhoods they know. Geographical paralysis becomes a bitter metaphor for their entire existence.

They are immobilized in almost every sense we can imagine. They can't move up. They can't move out. They cannot see beyond. Illiterates may take an oral test for drivers' permits in most sections of America. It is a questionable concession. Where will they go? How will they get there? How will they get home? Could it be that some of us might like it better if they stayed where they belong?

Travel is only one of many instances of circumscribed existence.   26
Choice, in almost all its facets, is diminished in the life of an illiterate adult. Even the printed TV schedule, which provides most people with the luxury of preselection, does not belong within the arsenal of options in illiterate existence. One consequence is that the viewer watches only what appears at moments when he happens to have time to turn the switch. Another consequence, a lot more common, is that the TV set remains in operation night and day. Whatever the program offered at the hour when he walks into the room will be the nutriment that he accepts and swallows. Thus, to passivity, is added frequency—indeed, almost uninterrupted continuity. Freedom to select is no more possible here than in the choice of home or surgery or food.

"You don't choose," said one illiterate woman. "You take your wishes   27
from somebody else." Whether in perusal of a menu, selection of highways, purchase of groceries, or determination of affordable enjoyment, illiterate Americans must trust somebody else: a friend, a relative, a stranger on the street, a grocery clerk, a TV copywriter.

"All of our mail we get, it's hard for her to read. Settin' down and   28
writing a letter, she can't do it. Like if we get a bill . . . we take it over to my sister-in-law . . . My sister-in-law reads it."

Billing agencies harass poor people for the payment of the bills for   29
purchases that might have taken place six months before. Utility companies offer an agreement for a staggered payment schedule on a bill past due. "You have to trust them," one man said. Precisely for this reason, you end up by trusting no one and suspecting everyone of possible deceit. A submerged sense of distrust becomes the corollary to a constant need to trust. "They are cheating me . . . I have been tricked . . . I do not know . . ."

Not knowing: This is a familiar theme. Not knowing the right word for   30
the right thing at the right time is one form of subjugation. Not knowing the world that lies concealed behind those words is a more terrifying feeling. The longitude and latitude of one's existence are beyond all easy apprehension. Even the hard, cold stars within the firmament above one's head begin to mock the possibilities for self-location. Where am I? Where did I come from? Where will I go?

"I've lost a lot of jobs," one man explains. "Today, even if you're a   31
janitor, there's still reading and writing . . . They leave a note saying, 'Go to room so-and-so . . . ' You can't do it. You can't read it. You don't know."

"The hardest thing about it is that I've been places where I didn't   32
know where I was. You don't know where you are . . . You're lost."

"Like I said: I have two kids. What do I do if one of my kids starts 33
choking? I go running to the phone . . . I can't look up the hospital phone
number. That's if we're at home. Out on the street, I can't read the sign. I
get to a pay phone. 'Okay, tell us where you are. We'll send an ambulance.' I
look at the street sign. Right there, I can't tell you what it says. I'd have to
spell it out, letter for letter. By that time, one of my kids would be dead . . .
These are the kinds of fears you go with, every single day . . . "

"Reading directions, I suffer with. I work with chemicals . . . That's 34
scary to begin with . . . "

"You sit down. They throw the menu in front of you. Where do you go 35
from there! Nine times out of ten you say, 'Go ahead. Pick out something for
the both of us.' I've eaten some weird things, let me tell you!"

Menus. Chemicals. A child choking while his mother searches for a 36
word she does not know to find assistance that will come too late. Another
mother speaks about the inability to help her kids to read: "I can't read to
them. Of course that's leaving them out of something they should have. Oh,
it matters. You *believe* it matters! I ordered all these books. The kids belong
to a book club. Donny wanted me to read a book to him. I told Donny: 'I
can't read.' He said: 'Mommy, you sit down. I'll read it to you.' I tried it one
day, reading from the pictures. Donny looked at me. He said, 'Mommy,
that's not right.' He's only five. He knew I couldn't read . . . "

A landlord tells a woman that her lease allows him to evict her if her 37
baby cries and causes inconvenience to her neighbors. The consequence of
challenging his words conveys a danger which appears, unlikely as it seems,
even more alarming than the danger of eviction. Once she admits that she
can't read, in the desire to maneuver for the time in which to call a friend,
she will have defined herself in terms of an explicit impotence that she
cannot endure. Capitulation in this case is preferable to self-humiliation.
Resisting the definition of oneself in terms of what one cannot do, what
others take for granted, represents a need so great that other imperatives
(even one so urgent as the need to keep one's home in winter's cold)
evaporate and fall away in face of fear. Even the loss of home and shelter, in
this case, is not so terrifying as the loss of self.

"I come out of school. I was sixteen. They had their meetings. The 38
directors meet. They said that I was wasting their school paper. I was
wasting pencils . . . "

Another illiterate, looking back, believes she was not worthy of her 39
teacher's time. She believes that it was wrong of her to take up space within
her school. She believes that it was right to leave in order that somebody
more deserving could receive her place.

Children choke. Their mother chokes another way: on more than 40
chicken bones.

People eat what others order, know what others tell them, struggle not 41
to see themselves as they believe the world perceives them. A man in
California speaks about his own loss of identity, of self-location, definition:

"I stood at the bottom of the ramp. My car had broke down on the   42
freeway. There was a phone. I asked for the police. They was nice. They said
to tell them where I was. I looked up at the signs. There was one that I had
seen before. I read it to them: ONE WAY STREET. They thought it was a joke. I
told them I couldn't read. There was other signs above the ramp. They told
me to try. I looked around for somebody to help. All the cars was going by
real fast. I couldn't make them understand that I was lost. The cop was nice.
He told me: 'Try once more.' I did my best. I couldn't read. I only knew the
sign above my head. The cop was trying to be nice. He knew that I was
trapped. 'I can't send out a car to you if you can't tell me where you are.' I
felt afraid. I nearly cried. I'm forty-eight years old. I only said: 'I'm on a one-
way street . . .' "

Perhaps we might slow down a moment here and look at the realities   43
described above. This is the nation that we live in. This is a society that
most of us did not create but which our President and other leaders have
been willing to sustain by virtue of malign neglect. Do we possess the
character and courage to address a problem which so many nations, poorer
than our own, have found it natural to correct?

The answers to these questions represent a reasonable test of our   44
belief in the democracy to which we have been asked in public school to
swear allegiance.

Questions for Study and Discussion

1. Why has Kozol chosen to begin his essay with the warning label from a
Drano can? How does it work to set the tone for the rest of his essay?

2. What kinds of evidence does Kozol use to support his argument?
Which kinds of evidence did you find most convincing? Explain.

3. Reread paragraph 5. What does Kozol say is one consequence of
illiteracy?

4. In your own words, exactly what is the cost to America of an illiterate
society?

5. Does Kozol make a rational or emotional appeal to the reader by his
use of examples? Support your answer by citing some of Kozol's examples from
the text.

6. What does the essay imply about an illiterate's ability to verbalize and
remember? How does Kozol characterize the illiterates he speaks of?

7. Was there anything in Kozol's essay to make readers appreciate their
advantage in being able to read? Explain.

Writing Topics

1. Kozol offers no solutions for the illiteracy problem. In an essay, discuss
what is currently being done and what steps need to be taken to reduce
illiteracy.

2. Interview a professor on your campus who teaches freshman English or who is a faculty adviser to freshmen. How serious is the problem of freshman illiteracy on your campus? How do illiterate students graduate from high school and go on to college? What is being done about illiteracy at your school? What more can be done?

THOMAS J. MAIN

Thomas J. Main was born in 1955 and graduated from the University of Chicago and the John F. Kennedy School of Government at Harvard. After trying his hand as a reporter and freelance writer, Main returned to Princeton University to study politics. Main's essays have appeared in *The New York Times, Public Interest,* and the *Wall Street Journal.*

In the following essay, which first appeared in the May 1988 issue of *Commentary,* Main attempts to get a handle on the problem of homelessness in America. His analysis gives us insights into the size of the problem, some of its probable causes, and possible solutions.

What We Know about the Homeless

In April 1986, Joyce Brown, a former New Jersey secretary (who also 1 calls herself Billie Boggs), had a fight with her sisters with whom she was then living—and hopped on a bus to New York City. Something happened, and she ended up living near the hot-air vent of Swensen's restaurant at Second Avenue and Sixty-fifth Street. She stayed there for a year, during which time her hair became tangled and matted; she insulted passers-by (especially black men, at whom she hurled racial epithets, although she herself is black); she burned the money she was given by sympathetic observers; and she relieved herself on the streets.

Eventually she came to the attention of Project Help, a mobile psychi- 2 atric unit that monitors mentally ill homeless people in lower Manhattan. Until recently, Project Help would not involuntarily transport a "street person" to a hospital unless he was an immediate danger to himself or others, and it interpreted that criterion strictly. When the Koch administration decided to apply a less strict interpretation—on the grounds that living on the street is dangerous for the mentally ill even if not immediately so— Joyce Brown became the first person removed from the streets to Bellevue Hospital for psychiatric evaluation. She was diagnosed as a chronic schizophrenic, and the city held her in the hospital for twelve weeks, during which time her doctors attempted to obtain permission to have her medicated. But with the aid of Robert Levey, a lawyer from the New York Civil

Liberties Union (NYCLU), Miss Brown not only avoided medication but successfully litigated for her release.

At this point, under the guidance of Levey and NYCLU president   3 Norman Siegel, Miss Brown declared that she had been "appointed the homeless spokesperson." After shopping trips to Saks Fifth Avenue, Lord & Taylor, and Bloomingdale's, and dinner at Windows on the World, Miss Brown and her lawyers hit the lecture circuit. She spoke at New York University Law School and at the Cardozo Law School, she was interviewed on "60 Minutes" and "Donahue," and she received half-a-dozen book and film proposals. Then, on February 18, 1988, Miss Brown, Levey, and Siegel all participated in the Harvard Law School Forum on "The Homeless Crisis: A Street View."

Levey (describing himself as a kind of "warm-up act . . . at a rock   4 concert") spoke first. He wanted, he said, only to raise some questions, of which the key one was why our society had decided to make Joyce Brown into a celebrity. Was it because we wanted to sweep the problem under the rug by focusing on the fate of a single individual who had successfully challenged the city and gotten off the streets? This seemed an odd question and a still odder answer since it was precisely Levey and his colleagues at the NYCLU who had made Joyce Brown a celebrity; and the last thing in the world they had in mind was to sweep the problem of homelessness under the rug.

At length, Miss Brown herself spoke. Her speech was slurred, and she   5 dropped a few lines from her prepared statement, but she certainly gave a creditable performance. The first part of her talk sounded very much as if it had been stitched together out of slogans made familiar by advocates for the homeless: homelessness is caused by policies that help the rich and not the poor; it will be solved only by building low-income public housing; etc. Of her stay in the hospital she said, "I was a political prisoner."

Much more interesting was what Miss Brown called "my street view"   6 of homeless life. She said nothing about her history either of heroin and cocaine abuse or of mental illness. According to her, she had had only two problems in being homeless. The first was police harassment. She claimed that at some point she had been beaten with night sticks and kicked by several police officers. Project Help also had degraded and humiliated her and had denied her what she called "my right to live on the street." Never, she said, had Project Help been of any use, except to offer her a sandwich.

Her second problem was that, obviously, she had been unable to find   7 an apartment, which was why she had ended up on the streets. With no place of her own and since there are no public toilets, she had to use the streets as a bathroom. She did not explain why she did not return to live with her sisters in New Jersey, who had been looking for her during the year she was living on the streets. Moreover, if she had been eager all along to come indoors, what was the point of fighting tooth and nail for the right to live on the streets?

Joyce Brown's claim that she had been beaten by the police also presented difficulties. She provided no details of the event. When she was asked during the question period if she intended to press charges against the police for their abuse, her response was, "Everyone knows New York City cops are killers." 8

Another difficulty was her complaint of being degraded by Project Help. It is true that for most of the time she was on the streets, outreach workers only offered her sandwiches. The reason for this was that Miss Brown spurned all other help. Project Help workers kept regular tabs on her; they coaxed her to accept further services, such as transportation to washroom facilities and a women's shelter. Miss Brown refused every time. 9

In other words, until the city decided to bring her inside against her will, Project Help was following exactly the policy that her lawyers told the Harvard audience ought to be followed in these cases: the city kept an eye on her, offered whatever services she would accept, and tried to win her confidence. It was only after months of such attempts that this approach was abandoned. 10

Joyce Brown ended her talk, received applause, and sat down. Norman Siegel then rose to speak. He too claimed that homelessness was essentially a housing problem, or rather that it was an issue of economic justice and equality and in no sense a mental-health issue, still less a matter of public order or law enforcement. The main cause of homelessness was the construction of high-rise developments for the rich and the destruction of the single-room-occupancy hotels (SROs) that many poor people once lived in. Allowing landlords to warehouse apartments, failing to require developers to build low-income housing, and the unwillingness of the city to redevelop the abandoned apartments it had seized—these were the real problems. 11

As Siegel saw it, the only way to deal with these problems was by radical political action. Just as law students from Harvard had gone to the South during the 1960s to organize and register blacks as part of a progressive political movement, so in the late 1980s lawyers should go to the bus terminals and park benches of America's cities and organize for economic justice. Homeless people needed "guerrilla legal tactics" in order to win, though "non-legal solutions" pressed forward "in a harassing way," were also important. 12

Whatever else one may say of the approach that Siegel and Levey put forward at the Harvard Law School Forum, it is very close to the position taken by most advocates and researchers on the homeless. Writers like Jonathan Kozol in his new book, *Rachel and Her Children: Homeless Families in America*; activists like Mitch Snyder of Communities for Creative Non- 13

Violence (CCNV) and Robert Hayes of Coalition for the Homeless; and research centers like New York's Community Service Society all agree with Joyce Brown's lawyers in their general analysis of the problem.

The thrust of this analysis is as follows: 14

1. Homelessness is a huge problem and it is getting worse. The size of the homeless population is at least two to three million (a figure originally advanced by CCNV in 1982), perhaps as large as four million, and growing.

2. Homelessness is simply or primarily a housing issue. As Kozol puts it, "The cause of homelessness is lack of housing" due to federal cutbacks and urban redevelopment.

3. Mental illness and other disabilities, such as alcoholism, while frequent among the homeless, have been greatly exaggerated. About one-third of the homeless are members of homeless families, who are neither mentally ill nor otherwise disabled.

4. Radical tactics and objectives are necessary if the problem is ever to be solved. Homelessness is a systemic problem, caused by the structure of the economy and society in general. As such it cannot be effectively addressed either by the charity of the welfare state or by benefits conferred at the whim of legislatures. What is needed is the enactment of a constitutional "right to shelter" that would be enforceable through the courts.

Let us take up these claims one by one, especially as they relate to the   15
Joyce Brown case.

First, as to the size of the homeless population. The CCNV estimate   16
of two to three million as of 1982 was based on an unsystematic telephone survey of shelter providers and advocates. It was never clear just how CCNV went from these local to its national estimates, or even exactly how CCNV defined homelessness.

To try to get things straight, the Department of Housing and Urban   17
Development (HUD) conducted its own survey, released in 1984, which concluded that, as of 1983, there were about 250,000 to 350,000 homeless people in America.

The HUD report was widely attacked. Mitch Snyder of CCNV   18
declared that the officials who had inspired it reminded him "of nothing so much as a school of piranha, circling, waiting to tear the last ounce of flesh." Various methodological critiques were also brought against the report, but their validity remained uncertain in the absence of an independent cross-check of its methods.

Such an independent cross-check was finally completed in 1986 by   19
Richard B. Freeman and Brian Hall of Harvard University in their Report of the National Bureau of Economic Research, "Permanent Homelessness in America?" The bottom line of the Freeman-Hall study was that "the much-maligned" HUD figure of 250,000–350,000 was "roughly correct." Freeman

and Hall's exact estimate for 1983 was 279,000 (and Freeman estimates that as of 1988 the number has jumped to about 400,000). Further, the key data on which they based their numbers were confirmed by surveys of homeless people done by other researchers using several different methods in Boston, Chicago, Nashville, Washington, D.C., Phoenix, Pittsburgh, and Los Angeles. I myself have also confirmed these findings in a survey of homeless people in San Diego.

To cite only the example of Chicago: CCNV had reported one   20
estimate of 250,000; later, Coalition for the Homeless cut this by a factor of ten, to 25,000. Neither of these estimates was based on systematic scientific research, nor was either organization willing to say exactly how they were arrived at. Then after two surveys of his own, Peter Rossi of the University of Massachusetts released his conclusions: in the winter of 1986 there were about 2,020 homeless people in Chicago (give or take about 275).

These studies, all independent of one another, using various method-   21
ologies, and all arriving at approximately the same conclusions, reinforce one basic point: the estimate circulated by advocacy groups of between two and three (and even up to four) million homeless people is about ten times too high.

When confronted with this evidence, Jonathan Kozol and the others   22
frequently argue (although without ever withdrawing their own claims) that, in Kozol's words, "Whether the number is one million or four million or the administration's estimate of less than a million, there are too many homeless people in America." Or as Chester Hartman, a housing analyst at the Institute for Policy Studies, testified before Congress during its hearings on the HUD report, "the real issue is that in a society with the wealth of the United States, there should not be a single involuntary homeless person."

Now, it is undoubtedly true that homelessness is a tragedy no matter   23
how few or how many people it touches, and it is also true that 400,000 is a large number. But such statements as Kozol's and Hartman's will not do. It is as though someone were to claim that the unemployment rate is 60 percent and then, upon being informed that the real rate is closer to 6 percent, were to respond: "No matter whether the rate is 60 percent or 6 percent, too many people are unemployed. The real issue is that in a society this wealthy not a single person should be involuntarily unemployed."

One final point on the size of the homeless population. Surveys done   24
in Nashville and Boston, and shelter counts in New York, suggest that the growth of the homeless population has leveled off. One should therefore be very skeptical about recent claims by the National Coalition for the Homeless and the U.S. Conference of Mayors that the number of people on the streets has grown by 25 percent over the last year. Homelessness undoubtedly did increase throughout the early 1980s, but it may by now have reached its peak.

What about the cause of homelessness? Is it, as Kozol says, lack of 25
housing? Before we can evaluate this claim, we have to reacquaint ourselves
with a few basic facts.

First, it is indeed true that New York (to take a city with an especially 26
large homeless population, and which is the subject of Kozol's recent book)
faces serious housing problems. Between 1981 and 1984 the number of
apartments renting for under two hundred dollars a month dropped from
437,000 to 256,000. As single-room-occupancy hotels have been torn down
for development, thousands of dwelling units for the poor have vanished.

Yet the fact is that, as in most other cities, the housing stock in New 27
York is so large (about 1.8 million rental units), and the number of homeless
families is so "small" (about five thousand at any given point and about
twelve thousand in the course of a year) relative to that stock, that a simple
"lack" of housing cannot be the trouble. The real trouble is that the current
housing market is prevented from making a rational allocation of such
housing as exists. For the housing market could easily meet the demand that
a few thousand homeless families impose on it if it were allowed to, and it
could do so in a manner consistent with current standards of decency and
fairness.

Again, the Freeman and Hall study throws light on the subject. They 28
report that for the United States as a whole there was no dramatic decline
in the number of "affordable" units (i.e., those renting for under $200 in
real terms) during the recent increase in homelessness between 1979 and
1983. In central cities, as the case of New York shows, the number of such
units did decline during this period (by about 5.4 percent according to
Freeman and Hall), but this decline is in itself too small to have caused
homelessness. Nor is it correct that the number of public-housing units
declined during this same period. In fact, public housing units actually
increased from 1,178,000 in 1979 to 1,250,000 in 1983.

What did happen, however, was a sharp rise in the number of people 29
looking for such units. Between 1979 and 1983 the number of poor unattached individuals increased by about 21 percent and the number of poor
families by 45 percent.

Yet this increase need not, in itself, have led to homelessness. In an 30
open market, landlords and perhaps some developers would have responded to the new demand by providing more cheap housing. Through
some combination of dividing up old units, renovating abandoned buildings, renting out space formerly used as garages and basements and the like,
those newly-poor renters could have had their demand met. Admittedly
such accommodations would have been of inferior quality, but they would
have prevented homelessness.

This demand was never met because housing regulations in New York 31
(and some other cities) made it difficult for the market to adjust. For

example, New York offered a bonus of $6,000 to landlords who would put up homeless families. There were few takers, even when the bonus was raised to $9,700. One reason seems to be that participating landlords would have had to spend more than the bonus to bring their buildings up to the required standard.

That homelessness is not due to a lack of housing is also shown by the 32 fact that most homeless families in New York *do* manage to find a place to stay fairly soon after they enter the shelter system. Half leave the system within two to five months, and two-thirds leave within a year. Writers like Kozol who think that most families in welfare hotels are in effect permanently homeless are focusing on the long-term stayers and missing the majority who do leave after several months. In other words, homeless families simply need more assistance in finding housing more quickly in the stock that already exists.

Since advocates for the homeless claim that homelessness is entirely or 33 primarily caused by a housing shortage, they typically deemphasize the role that disabilities like mental illness, alcoholism, and drug abuse play in the plight of the homeless. This is the theme sounded by Peter Marcuse, a professor of urban affairs at Columbia University. Marcuse cautions against "blaming the victim," a tendency which (according to him) holds that "The homeless are not like you and me. There is something wrong with them or they wouldn't be homeless." We should, as Louisa Stark, president of Coalition for the Homeless puts it, "Blame the System, Not Its Victims."

To get a sense of how valid such claims are, we have to distinguish for 34 the moment between homeless individuals and homeless families. This approach is controversial. Indeed, one reason that disability among the homeless is sometimes thought to be less of a factor than is popularly supposed is that many of the homeless are members of homeless families. Since these families—especially the children—have much lower rates of mental illness and other disabilities than homeless individuals do, amalgamating the two groups brings the disability rate down. At the same time, however, it conceals the true dimension of disability among homeless individuals. The best way to proceed, therefore, is first to consider individuals and families separately and then to reaggregate them for the total picture.

In some journalistic accounts of homelessness during the mid to late 35 1970s, all homeless individuals were assumed to be mentally ill. It was thought that most such mentally ill homeless individuals had once been patients in mental hospitals before they were "deinstitutionalized."

It is clear, however, that deinstitutionalization—if by this is meant the 36 policy of reducing the number of patients in mental hospitals with an eye to having them cared for by community mental-health centers—cannot explain the plight of *today's* homeless, because this policy was implemented mostly during the 1960s. Very few homeless people today came to the streets or shelters *directly* from mental hospitals. (In the Freeman and Hall study the number of such people was only 1 percent of the sample.)

On the other hand, while few of the homeless are direct victims of deinstitutionalization, we learn from Freeman and Hall that more than ninety thousand of the people on the streets today would have been in mental hospitals in the days before the policy of deinstitutionalization came into being. Almost all surveys indicate that between a quarter and a third of the homeless are indeed mentally ill. For example, the Freeman and Hall study found 33 percent of its sample to be mentally ill. Rossi, in a survey of eighteen studies of homeless individuals, found that the average rate of chronic mental illness was 36.5 percent.

According to some writers, these findings demonstrate that the perception of the homeless as being mentally ill is merely a stereotype. Thus Louisa Stark tells us that "Although only one-third of homeless people nationwide are mentally disabled, since the early 1980s homelessness has become synonymous in the public mind with mental illness. What we have done, then, is taken one stigmatized illness, alcoholism, and replaced it with another, mental illness, as a stereotype for the homeless." Peter Marcuse presents the other side of this observation when he remarks that "most of the mentally ill are not homeless. More mentally ill are housed than homeless."

But neither of these superficially correct observations can break the link between mental illness and homelessness. For a rate of mental illness of 33 percent is very high. In the general population, according to Freeman and Hall, the rate is less than 2 percent, and it is not much more than that even among the dependent poor: Rossi has found that among individuals receiving General Relief in Chicago the rate of previous hospitalization for mental illness is between 3 and 4 percent.

Further, to say that the majority of the mentally ill are housed and that therefore mental illness is not a key factor in the current homeless problem is like saying that during the 1930s the majority of Americans were employed and that therefore the Depression had nothing to do with unemployment.

Yet those researchers who stress that the majority of the homeless are not mentally ill are making an important point. Just as it is misleading to assume that homelessness is *simply* a housing problem (although it is partly that), so too is it misleading to assume that homelessness is *entirely* a problem of mental illness (although it is partly that, too). There are several other groups among homeless individuals with different problems of their own.

The most obvious are alcoholics and hard-drug abusers. Freeman and Hall report that 29 percent of their sample suffered from alcohol abuse (the rate for the general population is 13 percent), and they found a rate of hard-drug abuse of 14 percent (the rate for the general population is less than 1 percent). My own guess is that something like a fifth to a third of homeless individuals suffer from some combination of these disabilities.

Mental illness, alcoholism, and drug abuse are all regarded as   43
quasimedical problems. But of course straightforward medical or physical problems can be disabling, too. Indeed, such disabilities turn out to be characteristic of significant percentages of homeless individuals. For example, 36 percent of Rossi's Chicago sample reported "fair" or "poor" health (a level of self-reported ill health roughly twice that of the general population); 28 percent reported a hospital stay of more than twenty-four hours in the last year; and 28 percent were unable to work for health reasons. Also, a survey of over eight thousand clients in New York's shelters for individuals (conducted in 1984 by Stephen Crystal and Mervyn Goldstein, then of New York City's Human Resources Administration) found almost two-fifths had a current medical problem.

It is difficult to extrapolate from these numbers to a hard estimate of   44
physical disability among the homeless. But a safe guess is that about 25 to 30 percent of homeless individuals suffer from such problems.

In addition to such strictly or quasi-medical difficulties, there are   45
problems of a qualitatively different type that can be contributing factors to a spell of homelessness. Thus 41 percent of Rossi's sample had been in jail for periods of longer than forty-eight hours, 28 percent had at some point been convicted by a court and given probation, and 17 percent had felony convictions behind them. And Freeman and Hall found 39 percent of their sample had at some point been in jail.

One objection to regarding a criminal record as a disability charac-   46
teristic of a subpopulation of the homeless is that such a history might be considered a result rather than a precipitating or contributing cause of homelessness. My experience in San Diego suggests that many homeless people are frequently convicted of misdemeanors like jay-walking or littering as a form of harassment by police. Yet Freeman and Hall found that 61 percent of the time spent in jail by their sample was before the subjects became homeless. This indicates that being convicted of a crime can indeed be a contributing cause of homelessness. Moreover, it is unlikely that minor police harassment can account for a felony conviction rate of 17 percent.

What, then, is the overall picture of disability among homeless individ-   47
uals? First, these data—dramatic as they are—do not support the idea that homelessness is some "special" problem quite unlike any other social problem. The disabilities involved are not unique to the homeless; they are found among the extremely poor and the underclass in general. In this sense, those who caution against "stereotyping" the homeless have a point.

However, a point which these data highlight with at least equal force   48
is that homeless individuals are much more disabled than the general

population or even than the poor in general. Somewhere between 70 and 80 percent of homeless individuals suffer from one or more major disability. Thus Rossi found that 82 percent of his survey had *at least one* of the following disabilities: poor or fair health; previous mental hospitalization; previous stay in a detoxification unit; clinically high scores on psychological tests for depression or psychotic thinking; sentence(s) by a court.

Similarly, the Crystal and Goldstein study of New York's shelters for singles found that 74.9 percent of the men and 70.4 percent of the women suffered from *at least one* of the following disabilities: hard-drug abuse; alcoholism; jail record; less than an eighth-grade education; never employed; physical/medical problems; psychiatric problems; over sixty-five years old. 49

The homeless, then, are *not* "just like you and me" and most of them *do* have "something wrong with them" which contributes to their being homeless. (We should also keep in mind, however, the approximately 20 to 30 percent of the homeless who are relatively able and who have been described in other studies by Crystal as "economic-only" clients.) 50

When advocates for the homeless are confronted with figures like the above, they often choose to shift attention away from homeless individuals to homeless families. For example, a recent publication of the National Coalition for the Homeless argues: 51

> not only is homelessness increasing in numbers, it is also broadening in reach. The old stereotype of the single, male alcoholic—the so called "skid-row derelict"—no longer applies. Increasingly, the ranks of the homeless poor are comprised of families, children, ethnic and racial minorities, the elderly, and the disabled. The face of America's homeless now mirrors the face of America's poor: skid row has become more democratic. Perhaps the starkest indication of this diversity is the fact that, today, the fastest growing segment of the homeless population consists of families with children. In some areas, families with children comprise the majority of the homeless . . . families with children now account for about 30 percent of the homeless population.

Kozol and other advocates also claim that the rate of disabilities like drug abuse and mental illness among such families is very low. Although "Many homeless *individuals* may have been residents of such [mental] institutions," writes Kozol, "in cities like New York . . . where nearly half the homeless are small children, with an average age of six, such suppositions [of former mental hospitalization] obviously make little sense." 52

There are two questions here: (1) Just how many homeless family members are there and what percentage of the total homeless population do they represent? (2) What are the rates of disability among homeless family members? 53

As to the question of numbers, the Freeman and Hall study again 54
provides the best source. They estimate that in 1983 there were 32,000
homeless family members, and that in 1985 there were 46,000 such people.

Right away, we can see from the Freeman-Hall data that Kozol is 55
exaggerating wildly when he tells us that 500,000 children are currently
homeless. Since only 46,000 members of families were homeless in 1985 (this
includes *both* adults and children), homeless families would have had to
grow by more than ten times in three years for Kozol's figure even to
approach reality—not to mention that there are in fact no more than a *total*
of 400,000 homeless people in 1988. The truth is that the widely circulated
estimate that families with children represent 30 percent of the total
homeless population is more than twice too high.

So far as the question of disability goes, we know roughly what the 56
rates are among homeless individuals, but at this point we do not know
enough to conclude either that homeless families suffer from no more
disabilities than do other poor families, or that in fact they do have special
problems which contribute to their being homeless. Such studies as we do
have suggest that the rate of disabilities among such families may be
significant. But until better information is available on this subject, we have
to regard the confident pronouncements of advocates that homeless families
are simply victims of a tight housing market as being largely conjectural.

What are we to make of the advocates' interpretation of the politics of 57
homelessness? It is important to understand that they see homelessness not
as an aberration or a failing but as a natural outcome of the ordinary
workings of social policy and the economy in general. As Mitch Snyder of
CCNV writes (in collaboration with Mary Ellen Hombs):

> We live in a disposable society, a throwaway culture. The homeless are our
> human refuse, remnants of a culture that assigns a pathologically high value
> to independence and productivity. America is a land where you *are* what you
> consume and produce. The homeless are simply surplus souls in a system
> firmly rooted in competition and self-interest, in which only the "strongest"
> (i.e., those who fit most snugly within the confines of a purely arbitrary norm)
> will survive.

Similar sentiments are expressed by Robert Hayes of Coalition for the 58
Homeless ("the homeless are indeed the most egregious symbol of a cruel
economy, an unresponsive government, a festering value system") and by
Peter Marcuse of Columbia ("homelessness in the midst of plenty may
shock people into the realization that homelessness exists not because the
system is failing to work as it should, but because the system *is* working as it
must").

Yet it ought to be obvious that homelessness cannot be the result of "a 59 festering value system," or "free-market capitalism," or "a system firmly rooted in competition and self-interest," or any other long-term systemic feature of American society, for the simple reason that all these have remained more or less what they always have been, and so cannot explain the rise of homelessness *now.*

Advocates seem to recognize this at some level, since, after having 60 made sweeping pronouncements against American society in general, they usually concentrate their fire on the Reagan administration's social and economic policies. But while poverty did increase during the Reagan years, the Reagan administration can hardly be blamed either for deinstitutionalization or for the housing policies—such as rent control and byzantine regulations—which in cities like New York have undoubtedly exacerbated this situation.

To sum up: homelessness is a much *smaller* problem, in terms of the 61 number of people affected by it, than is commonly thought, but it is also much more *intractable* than advocates understand. This intractability stems from the fact that the great majority of homeless individuals, and possibly some significant proportion of homeless families, are afflicted with behavioral or medical disabilities or both. Dealing with such problems requires a willingness to assert *authority*—for example, in refusing to allow people like Joyce Brown to live on the streets—as much as it requires an expenditure of resources. Nonetheless, an important part of the problem is economic, and can best be addressed not by building more public housing but by raising the income of the extremely poor and removing regulations which block the allocation of housing to them.

In short, a reformist agenda—one aimed at enabling our mental- 62 health system to treat people who need treatment, at reducing extreme poverty through income supports, and at allowing housing markets to function—can go a long way toward the elimination of homelessness.

This agenda is a far cry from the radical systemic measures such as a 63 constitutional "right to shelter," or the "guerilla legal tactics" and the "harassing" techniques recommended by Joyce Brown's lawyers and other activists in the field. But it has the virtue of being based on a truthful diagnosis rather than on wild and tendentious analyses which, by simultaneously exaggerating the dimensions of the problem and underplaying its difficulties, make it harder rather than easier to help the homeless at all. In taking up the case of Joyce Brown, and in securing her release, the NYCLU lawyers may have furthered the "delegitimation" (as Peter Marcuse calls it) of a social system they consider evil. But as for Joyce Brown herself, only a short time after her appearance at Harvard, she was found begging on the streets and hurling abuse at passers-by who refused to give her money.

Questions for Study and Discussion

1. What rationale could a lawyer offer in his fight to prevent a diagnosed schizophrenic from being mediated?

2. Joyce Brown disdained any attempt to help her while she was on the streets. How does she defend her "right" to live there? Does she ever contradict her point of view? On what grounds does she object to Project Help's actions? Do you agree with her objections? Why or why not?

3. How has Main organized his essay? How do Main's individual arguments resemble the overall structure of the essay?

4. What strategy does Main use to argue his thesis? Is he convincing? Explain.

5. In paragraph 58, Main quotes Peter Marcuse. How do you interpret Marcuse's words? Do you think there always will be homelessness under our current system?

6. Main argues that homelessness does not result from the lack of affordable housing. What argument does he offer to support this point of view? How convincing is he? Would landlords and developers accommodate the needs of the homeless? Why?

Writing Topics

1. Main quotes Kozol, the author of another essay (pp. 737–44) in this section. Read Kozol's essay on illiteracy. Compare and contrast the way the two authors present their arguments. How is the tone similar or different? Why do you think Main quotes Kozol? Given his views, how might each of the two authors address each other's topic?

2. Although it is clearly not their fault, children who have AIDS are being blackballed from schools in some communities. How is this attitude toward children with AIDS similar to and different from society's attitude toward the homeless? What does it say about American society?

ANNA QUINDLEN

Following a career as a reporter for *The New York Times*, Anna Quindlen began in the early eighties to write the enormously popular column, "Life in the Thirties," also for *The Times*. In a warm, and witty style Quindlen shared her reflections on the pleasures and pitfalls of a "thirty-something" career woman, wife, and mother, from dealing with a son's fear of the bogeyman to a woman's need for solitude. In 1989, at the imminent arrival of her third child, Quindlen informed readers that she was leaving her job to stay at home and work on her first novel. Less than a year later, Quindlen was back at her desk at *The Times* with a new column, "Public and Private." As its title suggests, Quindlen's column is about issues that arise further from home, such as "women in battle," and "the plight of the homeless," to describe the ways these issues are experienced in the everyday life of a woman.

In "Abortion Is Too Complex to Feel All One Way About," taken from one of her earlier columns, Quindlen shares her dilemma over whether or not abortion should be a matter of choice for women. Quindlen argues that for "thoughtful" people, those who have pondered the arguments on both sides of the issue, there are no easy answers.

Abortion Is Too Complex to Feel All One Way About

It was always the look on their faces that told me first. I was the 1
freshman dormitory counselor and they were the freshmen at a women's college where everyone was smart. One of them could come into my room, a golden girl, a valedictorian, an 800 verbal score on the SAT's, and her eyes would be empty, seeing only a busted future, the devastation of her life as she knew it. She had failed biology, messed up the math; she was pregnant.

That was when I became pro-choice. 2

It was the look in his eyes that I will always remember, too. They were 3
as black as the bottom of a well, and in them for a few minutes I thought I saw myself the way I had always wished to be—clear, simple, elemental, at peace. My child looked at me and I looked back at him in the delivery room, and I realized that out of a sea of infinite possibilities it had come down to this: a specific person born on the hottest day of the year, conceived on a Christmas Eve, made by his father and me miraculously from scratch.

Once I believed that there was a little blob of formless protoplasm in   4
there and a gynecologist went after it with a surgical instrument, and that
was that. Then I got pregnant myself—eagerly, intentionally, by the right
man, at the right time—and I began to doubt. My abdomen still flat, my
stomach roiling with morning sickness, I felt not that I had protoplasm
inside but instead a complete human being in miniature to whom I could
talk, sing, make promises. Neither of these views was accurate; instead, I
think, the reality is something in the middle. And that is where I find
myself now, in the middle, hating the idea of abortions, hating the idea of
having them outlawed.

For I know it is the right thing in some times and places. I remember   5
sitting in a shabby clinic far uptown with one of those freshmen, only three
months after the Supreme Court had made what we were doing possible,
and watching with wonder as the lovely first love she had had with a nice
boy unraveled over the space of an hour as they waited for her to be called,
degenerated into sniping and silences. I remember a year or two later seeing
them pass on campus and not even acknowledge one another because their
conjoining had caused them so much pain, and I shuddered to think of
them married, with a small psyche in their unready and unwilling hands.

I've met 14-year-olds who were pregnant and said they could not have   6
abortions because of their religion, and I see in their eyes the shadows of 22-
year-olds I've talked to who lost their kids to foster care because they hit
them or used drugs or simply had no money for food and shelter. I read not
long ago about a teen-ager who said she meant to have an abortion but she
spent the money on clothes instead; now she has a baby who turns out to be
a lot more trouble than a toy. The people who hand out those execrable
little pictures of dismembered fetuses at abortion clinics seem to forget the
extraordinary pain children may endure after they are born when they are
unwanted, even hated or simply tolerated.

I believe that in a contest between the living and the almost living, the   7
latter must, if necessary, give way to the will of the former. That is what the
fetus is to me, the almost living. Yet these questions began to plague me—
and, I've discovered, a good many other women—after I became pregnant.
But they became even more acute after I had my second child, mainly
because he is so different from his brother. On two random nights 18
months apart the same two people managed to conceive, and on one
occasion the tumult within turned itself into a curly-haired brunet with
merry black eyes who walked and talked late and loved the whole world,
and on another it became a blond with hazel Asian eyes and a pug nose
who tried to conquer the world almost as soon as he entered it.

If we were to have an abortion next time for some reason or another,   8
which infinite possibility becomes, not a reality, but a nullity? The girl with
the blue eyes? The improbable redhead? The natural athlete? The thinker?
My husband, ever at the heart of the matter, put it another way. Knowing

that he is finding two children somewhat more overwhelming than he expected, I asked if he would want me to have an abortion if I accidentally became pregnant again right away. "And waste a perfectly good human being?" he said.

Coming to this quandary has been difficult for me. In fact, I believe the issue of abortion is difficult for all thoughtful people. I don't know anyone who has had an abortion who has not been haunted by it. If there is one thing I find intolerable about most of the so-called right-to-lifers, it is that they try to portray abortion rights as something that feminists thought up on a slow Saturday over a light lunch. That is nonsense. I also know that some people who support abortion rights are most comfortable with a monolithic position because it seems the strongest front against the smug and sometimes violent opposition.

But I don't feel all one way about abortion anymore, and I don't think it serves a just cause to pretend that many of us do. For years I believed that a woman's right to choose was absolute, but now I wonder. Do I, with a stable home and marriage and sufficient stamina and money, have the right to choose abortion because a pregnancy is inconvenient right now? Legally I do have that right; legally I want always to have that right. It is the morality of exercising it under those circumstances that makes me wonder.

Technology has foiled us. The second trimester has become a time of resurrection; a fetus at six months can be one woman's late abortion, another's premature, viable child. Photographers now have film of embryos the size of a grape, oddly human, flexing their fingers, sucking their thumbs. Women have amniocentesis to find out whether they are carrying a child with birth defects that they may choose to abort. Before the procedure, they must have a sonogram, one of those fuzzy black-and-white photos like a love song heard through static on the radio, which shows someone is in there.

I have taped on my VCR a public-television program in which somehow, inexplicably, a film is shown of a fetus in utero scratching its face, seemingly putting up a tiny hand to shield itself from the camera's eye. It would make a potent weapon in the arsenal of the antiabortionists. I grow sentimental about it as it floats in the salt water; part fish, part human being. It is almost living, but not quite. It has almost turned my heart around, but not quite turned my head.

Questions for Study and Discussion

1. Quindlan begins her essay with two stories. How effective is this beginning for her essay? Would another beginning have been better? Why or why not?

2. Make a list of the things Quindlen "believes" or "thinks" to be true. What do they have in common? Make another list of the things she is uncertain about? What do they have in common?

3. After reading Quindlen's essay, what precisely would you say is the "quandary" she faces?

4. Quindlen bases her questioning of abortion on feelings she experienced only after she had children of her own. In your opinion is this a strength or a weakness in her argument? Explain.

5. Quindlen refers to the "pro-choicers," the "right-to-lifers," and the "thoughtful." What distinguishes them according to Quindlen? What seems to be her attitude toward the people in each group? In which group does she include herself?

6. Who is Quindlen writing for? What risk did she take in writing this essay for that audience? Why do you suppose she took that risk?

Writing Topics

1. As you might expect, Quindlen's essay on abortion generated more mail than any other essay she had written for *The New York Times*. Write your own letter to the editor in response to her essay.

2. Write an essay in which you defend one side of a controversial issue—for example, abortion, euthanasia, or the distribution of condoms to college students. What kinds of examples will you use to argue your position? Who will your audience be? How easy or difficult is it for you to be "thoughtful" about an emotionally charged issue?

LEWIS H. VAN DUSEN, JR.

Born in 1910, Lewis H. Van Dusen, Jr., is a lawyer who graduated from Harvard and was a Rhodes Scholar. Van Dusen now practices law in Philadelphia and was once Chancellor to the Philadelphia Bar Association. His strong concern for legal ethics is apparent in his role in the American Bar Association where he is chairman of the Committee on Ethics and Professional Responsibility and a member of the Committee on the Federal Judiciary. Van Dusen's writing on the nature of democracy is more than armchair intellectualism: for his service as an Army officer during World War II, he was decorated with the Purple Heart, the Bronze Star, the Legion of Merit, the Legion of Honor, and (from France), the Croix de Guerre.

In the following essay, first published in February 1969 in the *American Bar Association Journal*, Van Dusen does the unexpected and "attacks" Henry David Thoreau, among others, to argue that civil disobedience is not a true and appropriate expression of democracy.

Civil Disobedience: Destroyer of Democracy

As Charles E. Wyzanski, Chief Judge of the United States District   1
Court in Boston, wrote in the February 1968, *Atlantic*: "Disobedience is a long step from dissent. Civil disobedience involves a deliberate and punishable breach of legal duty." Protesters might prefer a different definition. They would rather say that civil disobedience is the peaceable resistance of conscience.

The philosophy of civil disobedience was not developed in our Ameri-   2
can democracy, but in the very first democracy of Athens. It was expressed by the poet Sophocles and the philosopher Socrates. In Sophocles's tragedy, Antigone chose to obey her conscience and violate the state edict against providing burial for her brother, who had been decreed a traitor. When the dictator Creon found out that Antigone had buried her fallen brother, he confronted her and reminded her that there was a mandatory death penalty for this deliberate disobedience of the state law. Antigone nobly replied, "Nor did I think your orders were so strong that you, a mortal man, could overrun the gods' unwritten and unfailing laws."

Reprinted with permission from the February 1969 issue of the *ABA Journal, The Lawyer's Magazine*, published by the American Bar Association.

Conscience motivated Antigone. She was not testing the validity of   3
the law in the hope that eventually she would be sustained. Appealing to
the judgment of the community, she explained her action to the chorus. She
was not secret and surreptitious—the interment of her brother was open
and public. She was not violent; she did not trespass on another citizen's
rights. And finally, she accepted without resistance the death sentence—the
penalty for violation. By voluntarily accepting the law's sanctions, she was
not a revolutionary denying the authority of the state. Antigone's behavior
exemplifies the classic case of civil disobedience.

Socrates believed that reason could dictate a conscientious disobe-   4
dience of state law, but he also believed that he had to accept the legal
sanctions of the state. In Plato's *Crito*, Socrates from his hanging basket
accepted the death penalty for his teaching of religion to youths contrary to
state laws.

The sage of Walden, Henry David Thoreau, took this philosophy of   5
nonviolence and developed it into a strategy for solving society's injustices.
First enunciating it in protest against the Mexican War, he then turned it to
use against slavery. For refusing to pay taxes that would help pay the
enforcers of the fugitive slave law, he went to prison. In Thoreau's words, "If
the alternative is to keep all just men in prison or to give up slavery, the state
will not hesitate which to choose."

Sixty years later, Gandhi took Thoreau's civil disobedience as his   6
strategy to wrest Indian independence from England. The famous salt
march against a British imperial tax is his best-known example of protest.

But the conscientious law breaking of Socrates, Gandhi and Thoreau   7
is to be distinguished from the conscientious law testing of Martin Luther
King, Jr., who was not a civil disobedient. The civil disobedient withholds
taxes or violates state laws knowing he is legally wrong, but believing he is
morally right. While he wrapped himself in the mantle of Gandhi and
Thoreau, Dr. King led his followers in violation of state laws he believed
were contrary to the Federal Constitution. But since Supreme Court decisions in the end generally upheld his many actions, he should not be
considered a true civil disobedient.

The civil disobedience of Antigone is like that of the pacifist who   8
withholds paying the percentage of his taxes that goes to the Defense
Department, or the Quaker who travels against State Department regulations to Hanoi to distribute medical supplies, or the Vietnam war protestor
who tears up his draft card. This civil disobedient has been nonviolent in
his defiance of the law; he has been unfurtive in his violation; he has been
submissive to the penalties of the law. He has neither evaded the law nor
interfered with another's rights. He has been neither a rioter nor a revolutionary. The thrust of his cause has not been the might of coercion but the
martyrdom of conscience.

Was the Boston Tea Party Civil Disobedience?

Those who justify violence and radical action as being in the tradition   9
of our Revolution show a misunderstanding of the philosophy of democracy.

James Farmer, former head of the Congress of Racial Equality, in   10
defense of the mass action confrontation method, has told of a famous
organized demonstration that took place in opposition to political and
economic discrimination. The protesters beat back and scattered the law
enforcers and then proceeded to loot and destroy private property. Mr.
Farmer then said he was talking about the Boston Tea Party and implied
that violence as a method for redress of grievances was an American
tradition and a legacy of our revolutionary heritage. While it is true that
there is no more sacred document than our Declaration of Independence,
Jefferson's "inherent right of rebellion" was predicated on the tyrannical
denial of democratic means. If there is no popular assembly to provide an
adjustment of ills, and if there is no court system to dispose of injustices,
then there is, indeed, a right to rebel.

The seventeenth century's John Locke, the philosophical father of the   11
Declaration of Independence, wrote in his *Second Treatise on Civil Govern-*
ment: "Wherever law ends, tyranny begins . . . and the people are absolved
from any further obedience. Governments are dissolved from within when
the legislative [chamber] is altered. When the government [becomes] . . .
arbitrary disposers of lives, liberties and fortunes of the people, such
revolutions happen. . . . "

But there are some sophisticated proponents of the revolutionary   12
redress of grievances who say that the test of the need for radical action
is not the unavailability of democratic institutions but the ineffectuality
of those institutions to remove blatant social inequalities. If social injustice exists, they say, concerted disobedience is required against the
constituted government, whether it be totalitarian or democratic in structure.

Of course, only the most bigoted chauvinist would claim that Amer-   13
ica is without some glaring faults. But there has never been a utopian
society on earth and there never will be unless human nature is remade.
Since inequities will mar even the best-framed democracies, the injustice
rationale would allow a free right of civil resistance to be available always as
a shortcut alternative to the democratic way of petition, debate and assembly. The lesson of history is that civil insurgency spawns far more injustices
than it removes. The Jeffersons, Washingtons and Adamses resisted tyranny
with the aim of promoting the procedures of democracy. They would never
have resisted a democratic government with the risk of promoting the
techniques of tyranny.

Legitimate Pressures and Illegitimate Results

There are many civil rights leaders who show impatience with the   14
process of democracy. They rely on the sit-in, boycott or mass picketing to
gain speedier solutions to the problems that face every citizen. But we must
realize that the legitimate pressures that won concessions in the past can
easily escalate into the illegitimate power plays that might extort demands
in the future. The victories of these civil rights leaders must not shake our
confidence in the democratic procedures, as the pressures of demonstration
are desirable only if they take place within the limits allowed by law. Civil
rights gains should continue to be won by the persuasion of Congress and
other legislative bodies and by the decision of courts. Any illegal entreaty
for the rights of some can be an injury to the rights of others, for mass
demonstrations often trigger violence.

Those who advocate taking the law into their own hands should   15
reflect that when they are disobeying what they consider to be an immoral
law, they are deciding on a possibly immoral course. Their answer is that the
process for democratic relief is too slow, that only mass confrontation can
bring immediate action, and that any injuries are the inevitable cost of the
pursuit of justice. Their answer is, simply put, that the end justifies the
means. It is this justification of any form of demonstration as a form of
dissent that threatens to destroy a society built on the rule of law.

Our Bill of Rights guarantees wide opportunities to use mass meet-   16
ings, public parades and organized demonstrations to stimulate sentiment,
to dramatize issues and to cause change. The Washington freedom march of
1963 was such a call for action. But the rights of free expression cannot be
mere force cloaked in the garb of free speech. As the courts have decreed in
labor cases, free assembly does not mean mass picketing or sit-down strikes.
These rights are subject to limitations of time and place so as to secure the
rights of others. When militant students storm a college president's office to
achieve demands, when certain groups plan rush-hour car stalling to protest
discrimination in employment, these are not dissent, but a denial of rights
to others. Neither is it the lawful use of mass protest, but rather the unlawful
use of mob power.

Justice Black, one of the foremost advocates and defenders of the right   17
of protest and dissent, has said:

> . . . Experience demonstrates that it is not a far step from what to many seems
> to be the earnest, honest, patriotic, kind-spirited multitude of today, to the
> fanatical, threatening, lawless mob of tomorrow. And the crowds that press in
> the streets for noble goals today can be supplanted tomorrow by street mobs
> pressuring the courts for precisely opposite ends.

Society must censure those demonstrators who would trespass on the   18
public peace, as it must condemn those rioters whose pillage would destroy

the public peace. But more ambivalent is society's posture toward the civil disobedient. Unlike the rioter, the true civil disobedient commits no violence. Unlike the mob demonstrator, he commits no trespass on other's rights. The civil disobedient, while deliberately violating a law, shows an oblique respect for the law by voluntarily submitting to its sanctions. He neither resists arrest nor evades punishment. Thus, he breaches the law but not the peace.

But civil disobedience, whatever the ethical rationalization, is still an assault on our democratic society, an affront to our legal order and an attack on our constitutional government. To indulge civil disobedience is to invite anarchy, and the permissive arbitrariness of anarchy is hardly less tolerable than the repressive arbitrariness of tyranny. Too often the license of liberty is followed by the loss of liberty, because into the desert of anarchy comes the man on horseback, a Mussolini or a Hitler. 19

Violations of Law Subvert Democracy

Law violations, even for ends recognized as laudable, are not only assaults on the rule of law, but subversions of the democratic process. The disobedient act of conscience does not ennoble democracy; it erodes it. 20

First, it courts violence, and even the most careful and limited use of nonviolent acts of disobedience may help sow the dragon-teeth of civil riot. Civil disobedience is the progenitor of disorder, and disorder is the sire of violence. 21

Second, the concept of civil disobedience does not invite principles of general applicability. If the children of light are morally privileged to resist particular laws on grounds of conscience, so are the children of darkness. Former Deputy Attorney General Burke Marshall said: "If the decision to break the law really turned on individual conscience, it is hard to see in law how [the civil rights leader] is better off than former Governor Ross Barnett of Mississippi who also believed deeply in his cause and was willing to go to jail." 22

Third, even the most noble act of civil disobedience assaults the rule of law. Although limited as to method, motive and objective, it has the effect of inducing others to engage in different forms of law breaking characterized by methods unsanctioned and condemned by classic theories of law violation. Unfortunately, the most patent lesson of civil disobedience is not so much nonviolence of action as defiance of authority. 23

Finally, the greatest danger in condoning civil disobedience as a permissible strategy for hastening change is that it undermines our democratic processes. To adopt the techniques of civil disobedience is to assume that representative government does not work. To resist the decisions of courts and the laws of elected assemblies is to say that democracy has failed. 24

There is no man who is above the law, and there is no man who has a   25
right to break the law. Civil disobedience is not above the law, but against
the law. When the civil disobedient disobeys one law, he invariably subverts
all law. When the civil disobedient says that he is above the law, he is saying
that democracy is beneath him. His disobedience shows a distrust for the
democratic system. He is merely saying that since democracy does not work,
why should he help make it work. Thoreau expressed well the civil disobedient's disdain for democracy:

> As for adopting the ways which the state has provided for remedying the evil,
> I know not of such ways. They take too much time and a man's life will be
> gone. I have other affairs to attend to. I came into this world not chiefly to
> make this a good place to live in, but to live in it, be it good or bad.

Thoreau's position is not only morally irresponsible but politically   26
reprehensible. When citizens in a democracy are called on to make a
profession of faith, the civil disobedients offer only a confession of failure.
Tragically, when civil disobedients for lack of faith abstain from democratic
involvement, they help attain their own gloomy prediction. They help
create the social and political basis for their own despair. By foreseeing
failure, they help forge it. If citizens rely on antidemocratic means of protest,
they will help bring about the undemocratic result of an authoritarian or
anarchic state.

How far demonstrations properly can be employed to produce political   27
and social change is a pressing question, particularly in view of the provocations accompanying the National Democratic Convention in Chicago last
August and the reaction of the police to them. A line must be drawn by the
judiciary between the demands of those who seek absolute order, which can
lead only to a dictatorship, and those who seek absolute freedom, which
can lead only to anarchy. The line, wherever it is drawn by our courts,
should be respected on the college campus, on the streets and elsewhere.

Undue provocation will inevitably result in overreaction, human   28
emotions being what they are. Violence will follow. This cycle undermines
the very democracy it is designed to preserve. The lesson of the past is that
democracies will fall if violence, including the intentional provocations that
will lead to violence, replaces democratic procedures, as in Athens, Rome
and the Weimar Republic. This lesson must be constantly explained by the
legal profession.

We should heed the words of William James: 29

> Democracy is still upon its trial. The civic genius of our people is its only
> bulwark and . . . neither battleships nor public libraries nor great newspapers
> nor booming stocks: neither mechanical invention nor political adroitness,
> nor churches nor universities nor civil service examinations can save us from
> degeneration if the inner mystery be lost.

That mystery, at once the secret and the glory of our English-speaking race, consists of nothing but two habits. . . . One of them is habit of trained and disciplined good temper towards the opposite party when it fairly wins its innings. The other is that of fierce and merciless resentment toward every man or set of men who break the public peace. (James, *Pragmatism* 1907, pages 127–128)

Questions for Study and Discussion

1. What characteristics distinguish "true civil disobedients"?
2. By what means can injustice properly be addressed under a democracy? Under what single circumstance does Van Dusen find civil disobedience permissible?
3. Van Dusen spends most of his essay distinguishing between "authentic" and "inauthentic" civil disobedience. Why do you suppose he makes this distinction if he intends to argue that all civil disobedience is a threat to democracy?
4. Van Dusen refers to Henry David Thoreau's position on civil disobedience as "morally irresponsible" and "politically reprehensible." What was the effect on you of reading this description? What other surprising references did Van Dusen include in his essay? How did they affect your overall appreciation of his argument?
5. According to Van Dusen, what is the fundamental irony in taking the law into one's own hands?
6. Van Dusen does not use "legalese" in his argument. Instead, he sounds like an attorney arguing in front of a jury made up of the general public. Would you describe his tone as pedantic, self-righteous, concerned, or something else? How does he use diction to persuade his audience of the truth of his position?
7. According to Van Dusen, in what ways does violating the law erode democracy? Do you agree with all his arguments? Why or why not?
8. What prophecy does Van Dusen make at the end of his essay?

Writing Topics

1. In his essay Van Dusen says that "the concept of civil disobedience does not invite principles of general applicability." Explain what he means by this statement. Do you agree with him? How might some civil libertarians argue against Van Dusen?
2. Obviously Van Dusen is familiar with Henry David Thoreau's essay on civil disobedience (pp. 675–92). Read it yourself, if you haven't already. Then, point for point, write Thoreau's response to Van Dusen's argument.

3. College campuses have traditionally been the scenes of protest in the United States. Often, protests involve issues that seem to have little to do with campus life. Talk to students on your campus who have participated in campus protests. How do they justify their activities? What reasons do they give for protesting issues outside the control of the school administration? What conclusions can you draw about the role of student protest on college campuses?

JAMES RACHELS

Suppose that someone is dying and is experiencing great pain which no medicine can relieve. Is it better to keep that person alive as long as possible, despite the suffering, or to end the suffering quickly through euthanasia? Active euthanasia, or "mercy killing," is legally considered murder, but passive euthanasia—withholding treatment that would keep the patient alive—is not; indeed, it is even endorsed by the American Medical Association. James Rachels, a professor of philosophy who is particularly concerned with ethical issues, disputes this position. Born in 1941 in Columbus, Georgia, Rachels earned degrees at Mercer University and the University of California, and has taught at the University of Miami, Coral Gables, since 1972. He is the editor of *Moral Problems*, a reader in the ethical dimensions of contemporary social issues, and the author of *The Elements of Moral Philosophy* (1986) and *The End of Life: Euthanasia and Mortality* (1986).

"Active and Passive Euthanasia" was first published in the *New England Journal of Medicine* in 1975, and has since been often reprinted and widely discussed. Arguing that mercy killing is morally no worse than allowing people to die, Rachels challenges doctors—and indeed all of us—to reconsider some basic assumptions.

Active and Passive Euthanasia

The distinction between active and passive euthanasia is thought to be crucial for medical ethics. The idea is that it is permissible, at least in some cases, to withhold treatment and allow a patient to die, but it is never permissible to take any direct action designed to kill the patient. This doctrine seems to be accepted by most doctors, and it is endorsed in a statement adopted by the House of Delegates of the American Medical Association on December 4, 1973:

> The intentional termination of the life of one human being by another—mercy killing—is contrary to that for which the medical profession stands and is contrary to the policy of the American Medical Association.
>
> The cessation of the employment of extraordinary means to prolong the life of the body when there is irrefutable evidence that biological death is imminent is the decision of the patient and/or his immediate family. The advice and judgment of the physician should be freely available to the patient and/or his immediate family.

However, a strong case can be made against this doctrine. In what follows I will set out some of the relevant arguments, and urge doctors to reconsider their views on this matter.

To begin with a familiar type of situation, a patient who is dying of incurable cancer of the throat is in terrible pain, which can no longer be satisfactorily alleviated. He is certain to die within a few days, even if present treatment is continued, but he does not want to go on living for those days since the pain is unbearable. So he asks the doctor for an end to it, and his family joins in the request.

Suppose the doctor agrees to withhold treatment, as the conventional doctrine says he may. The justification for his doing so is that the patient is in terrible agony, and since he is going to die anyway, it would be wrong to prolong his suffering needlessly. But now notice this. If one simply withholds treatment, it may take the patient longer to die, and so he may suffer more than he would if more direct action were taken and a lethal injection given. This fact provides strong reason for thinking that, once the initial decision not to prolong his agony has been made, active euthanasia is actually preferable to passive euthanasia, rather than the reverse. To say otherwise is to endorse the option that leads to more suffering rather than less, and is contrary to the humanitarian impulse that prompts the decision not to prolong his life in the first place.

Part of my point is that the process of being "allowed to die" can be relatively slow and painful, whereas being given a lethal injection is relatively quick and painless. Let me give a different sort of example. In the United States about one in 600 babies is born with Down's syndrome. Most of these babies are otherwise healthy—that is, with only the usual pediatric care, they will proceed to an otherwise normal infancy. Some, however, are born with congenital defects such as intestinal obstructions that require operations if they are to live. Sometimes, the parents and the doctor will decide not to operate, and let the infant die. Anthony Shaw describes what happens then:

> . . . When surgery is denied [the doctor] must try to keep the infant from suffering while natural forces sap the baby's life away. As a surgeon whose natural inclination is to use the scalpel to fight off death, standing by and watching a salvageable baby die is the most emotionally exhausting experience I know. It is easy at a conference, in a theoretical discussion, to decide that such infants should be allowed to die. It is altogether different to stand by in the nursery and watch as dehydration and infection wither a tiny being over hours and days. This is a terrible ordeal for me and the hospital staff—much more so than for the parents who never set foot in the nursery.[1]

---

[1]A. Shaw, "Doctor, Do We Have a Choice?" *The New York Times Magazine*, January 30, 1972, p. 54. (Author's note.)

I can understand why some people are opposed to all euthanasia, and insist that such infants must be allowed to live. I think I can also understand why other people favor destroying these babies quickly and painlessly. But why should anyone favor letting "dehydration and infection wither a tiny being over hours and days?" The doctrine that says that a baby may be allowed to dehydrate and wither, but may not be given an injection that would end its life without suffering, seems so patently cruel as to require no further refutation. The strong language is not intended to offend, but only to put the point in the clearest possible way.

My second argument is that the conventional doctrine leads to deci- 5 sions concerning life and death made on irrelevant grounds.

Consider again the case of the infants with Down's syndrome who 6 need operations for congenital defects unrelated to the syndrome to live. Sometimes, there is no operation, and the baby dies, but when there is no such defect, the baby lives on. Now, an operation such as that to remove an intestinal obstruction is not prohibitively difficult. The reason why such operations are not performed in these cases is, clearly, that the child has Down's syndrome and the parents and doctor judge that because of that fact it is better for the child to die.

But notice that this situation is absurd, no matter what view one takes 7 of the lives and potentials of such babies. If the life of such an infant is worth preserving, what does it matter if it needs a simple operation? Or, if one thinks it better that such a baby should not live on, what difference does it make that it happens to have an unobstructed intestinal tract? In either case, the matter of life and death is being decided on irrelevant grounds. It is the Down's syndrome, and not the intestines, that is the issue. The matter should be decided, if at all, on that basis, and not be allowed to depend on the essentially irrelevant question of whether the intestinal tract is blocked.

What makes this situation possible, of course, is the idea that when 8 there is an intestinal blockage, one can "let the baby die," but when there is no such defect there is nothing that can be done, for one must not "kill" it. The fact that this idea leads to such results as deciding life or death on irrelevant grounds is another good reason why the doctrine should be rejected.

One reason why so many people think that there is an important 9 moral difference between active and passive euthanasia is that they think killing someone is morally worse than letting someone die. But is it? Is killing, in itself, worse than letting die? To investigate this issue, two cases may be considered that are exactly alike except that one involves killing whereas the other involves letting someone die. Then, it can be asked whether this difference makes any difference to the moral assessments. It is important that the cases be exactly alike, except for this one difference, since otherwise one cannot be confident that it is this difference and not some other that accounts for any variation in the assessments of the two cases. So, let us consider this pair of cases:

In the first, Smith stands to gain a large inheritance if anything should happen to his six-year-old cousin. One evening while the child is taking his bath, Smith sneaks into the bathroom and drowns the child, and then arranges things so that it will look like an accident. 10

In the second, Jones also stands to gain if anything should happen to his six-year-old cousin. Like Smith, Jones sneaks in planning to drown the child in his bath. However, just as he enters the bathroom Jones sees the child slip and hit his head, and fall face down in the water. Jones is delighted; he stands by, ready to push the child's head back under if it is necessary, but it is not necessary. With only a little thrashing about, the child drowns all by himself, "accidentally," as Jones watches and does nothing. 11

Now Smith killed the child, whereas Jones "merely" let the child die. That is the only difference between them. Did either man behave better, from a moral point of view? If the difference between killing and letting die were in itself a morally important matter, one should say that Jones's behavior was less reprehensible than Smith's. But does one really want to say that? I think not. In the first place, both men acted from the same motive, personal gain, and both had exactly the same end in view when they acted. It may be inferred from Smith's conduct that he is a bad man, although that judgment may be withdrawn or modified if certain further facts are learned about him—for example, that he is mentally deranged. But would not the very same thing be inferred about Jones from his conduct? And would not the same further considerations also be relevant to any modification of this judgment? Moreover, suppose Jones pleaded, in his own defense, "After all, I didn't do anything except just stand there and watch the child drown. I didn't kill him; I only let him die." Again, if letting die were in itself less bad than killing, this defense should have at least some weight. But it does not. Such a "defense" can only be regarded as a grotesque perversion of moral reasoning. Morally speaking, it is no defense at all. 12

Now, it may be pointed out, quite properly, that the cases of euthanasia with which doctors are concerned are not like this at all. They do not involve personal gain or the destruction of normal healthy children. Doctors are concerned only with cases in which the patient's life is of no further use to him, or in which the patient's life has become or will soon become a terrible burden. However, the point is the same in these cases: the bare difference between killing and letting die does not, in itself, make a moral difference. If a doctor lets a patient die, for humane reasons, he is in the same moral position as if he had given the patient a lethal injection for humane reasons. If his decision was wrong—if, for example, the patient's illness was in fact curable—the decision would be equally regrettable no 13 matter which method was used to carry it out. And if the doctor's decision was the right one, the method used is not in itself important.

The AMA policy statement isolates the crucial issue very well; the crucial issue is "the intentional termination of the life of one human being by another." But after identifying this issue, and forbidding "mercy killing," the statement goes on to deny that the cessation of treatment is the intentional termination of a life. This is where the mistake comes in, for what is the cessation of treatment, in these circumstances, if it is not "the intentional termination of the life of one human being by another"? Of course it is exactly that, and if it were not, there would be no point to it. 14

Many people will find this judgment hard to accept. One reason, I think, is that it is very easy to conflate the question of whether killing is, in itself, worse than letting die, with the very different question of whether most actual cases of killing are more reprehensible than most actual cases of letting die. Most actual cases of killing are clearly terrible (think, for example, of all the murders reported in the newspapers), and one hears of such cases every day. On the other hand, one hardly ever hears of a case of letting die, except for the actions of doctors who are motivated by humanitarian reasons. So one learns to think of killing in a much worse light than of letting die. But this does not mean that there is something about killing that makes it in itself worse than letting die, for it is not the bare difference between killing and letting die that makes the difference in these cases. Rather, the other factors—the murderer's motive of personal gain, for example, contrasted with the doctor's humanitarian motivation—account for different reactions to the different cases. 15

I have argued that killing is not in itself any worse than letting die; if my contention is right, it follows that active euthanasia is not any worse than passive euthanasia. What arguments can be given on the other side? The most common, I believe, is the following: 16

"The important difference between active and passive euthanasia is that, in passive euthanasia, the doctor does not do anything to bring about the patient's death. The doctor does nothing, and the patient dies of whatever ills already afflict him. In active euthanasia, however, the doctor does something to bring about the patient's death: he kills him. The doctor who gives the patient with cancer a lethal injection has himself caused his patient's death; whereas if he merely ceases treatment, the cancer is the cause of the death." 17

A number of points need to be made here. The first is that it is not exactly correct to say that in passive euthanasia the doctor does nothing, for he does do one thing that is very important: he lets the patient die. "Letting someone die" is certainly different, in some respects, from other types of action—mainly in that it is a kind of action that one may perform by way of not performing certain other actions. For example, one may let a patient die by way of not giving medication, just as one may insult someone 18 by way of not shaking his hand. But for any purpose of moral assessment, it is a type of action nonetheless. The decision to let a patient die is subject to moral appraisal in the same way that a decision to kill him would be subject to moral appraisal: it may be assessed as wise or unwise, compassionate or sadistic, right or wrong. If a doctor deliberately let a patient die who was suffering from a routinely curable illness, the doctor would certainly be to blame for what he had done, just as he would be to blame if he had needlessly killed the patient. Charges against him would then be appropriate. If so, it would be no defense at all for him to insist that he didn't "do anything." He would have done something very serious indeed, for he let his patient die.

Fixing the cause of death may be very important from a legal point of view, for it may determine whether criminal charges are brought against the doctor. But I do not think that this notion can be used to show a moral difference between active and passive euthanasia. The reason why it is considered bad to be the cause of someone's death is that death is regarded as a great evil—and so it is. However, if it has been decided that euthanasia—even passive euthanasia—is desirable in a given case, it has also been decided that in this instance death is no greater an evil than the patient's continued existence. And if this is true, the usual reason for not wanting to be the cause of someone's death simply does not apply.   19

Finally, doctors may think that all of this is only of academic interest—the sort of thing that philosophers may worry about but that has no practical bearing on their own work. After all, doctors must be concerned about the legal consequences of what they do, and active euthanasia is clearly forbidden by the law. But even so, doctors should also be concerned with the fact that the law is forcing upon them a moral doctrine that may well be indefensible, and has a considerable effect on their practices. Of course, most doctors are not now in the position of being coerced in this matter, for they do not regard themselves as merely going along with what the law requires. Rather, in statements such as the AMA policy statement that I have quoted, they are endorsing this doctrine as a central point of medical ethics. In that statement, active euthanasia is condemned not merely as illegal but as "contrary to that for which the medical profession stands," whereas passive euthanasia is approved. However, the preceding considerations suggest that there is really no moral difference between the two, considered in themselves (there may be important moral differences in some cases in their *consequences*, but, as I pointed out, these differences may make active euthanasia, and not passive euthanasia, the morally preferable option). So, whereas doctors may have to discriminate between active and passive euthanasia to satisfy the law, they should not do any more than that. In particular, they should not give the distinction any added authority and weight by writing it into official statements of medical ethics.   20

Questions for Study and Discussion

1. What is Rachels's thesis? Is he in favor of euthanasia? Support your answer.

2. According to Rachels, what is the difference between active and passive euthanasia? Which is generally considered more ethical? Which is more humane in Rachels's view? What do you think?

3. Is the example in paragraph 4 and the following discussion relevant to Rachels's thesis? Why does he include it?

4. What is the purpose of the hypothetical case involving Smith and Jones? Why do you think Rachels invented an example instead of drawing it from real life? What are the example's advantages and its limitations?

5. What was Rachels's purpose in writing this article? Who are his expected readers? How can you tell? Why is the article relevant to other readers?

Writing Topics

1. Are there any circumstances in which you might wish for euthanasia? If so, what are the circumstances and what would be your reasons? If not, what are your objections to euthanasia? Write an essay in which you explain your position.

2. As doctors have discovered means of prolonging the lives of terminally ill people, the debate over euthanasia has intensified. Some terminally ill people have taken their lives and their deaths into their own hands. This of course amounts to suicide and is prohibited by law. It is defended, however, under the banner of "death and dignity." Research the issues involved and discuss the pros and cons of euthanasia, taking medical, legal, and moral considerations into account.

3. As Rachels's article shows, the law often intervenes in moral questions. Do you think this is a proper function of the law? When, if ever, should we seek to legislate morality? How effective is such legislation? How should we respond when the law compels us to act against our moral sense? Write an essay in which you address one or more of these questions.

SHIRLEY JACKSON

Shirley Jackson (1919–1965), a novelist and writer of short stories, is considered a master of Gothic horror and the occult. The settings of her stories, in contemporary, familiar surroundings make them more immediate and hence more frightening. "The Lottery," for instance, which was first published in 1948 in *The New Yorker*, is set in a small New England town in the present. In fact, it was written while Jackson was living in Bennington, Vermont. The story generated more mail than anything published in the magazine until then. According to one critic, "The Lottery" embodied Jackson's belief that "humankind is more evil than good."

Her husband, Stanley Edgar Hyman, said critics who saw in Jackson's stories a playing out of her own neurotic fantasies, misunderstood her work: "They are a sensitive and faithful anatomy of our times, fitting symbols of the concentration camp and the bomb." Among her many other works are *We Have Always Lived in a Castle* (1953) and *The Haunting of Hill House* (1959). "The Lottery" tells the story of a town that conducts a cruel, annual ritual made crueller for being repeated even though no one remembers why it is being done.

The Lottery

The morning of June 27th was clear and sunny, with the fresh warmth   1
of a full-summer day; the flowers were blossoming profusely and the grass was richly green. The people of the village began to gather in the square, between the post office and the bank, around ten o'clock; in some towns there were so many people that the lottery took two days and had to be started on June 26th, but in this village, where there were only about three hundred people, the whole lottery took less than two hours, so it could begin at ten o'clock in the morning and still be through in time to allow the villagers to get home for noon dinner.

The children assembled first, of course. School was recently over for   2
the summer, and the feeling of liberty sat uneasily on most of them; they tended to gather together quietly for a while before they broke into boisterous play, and their talk was still of the classroom and the teacher, of books and reprimands. Bobby Martin had already stuffed his pockets full of stones, and the other boys soon followed his example, selecting the smooth-

est and roundest stones; Bobby and Harry Jones and Dickie Delacroix—the villagers pronounced this name "Dellacroy"—eventually made a great pile of stones in one corner of the square and guarded it against the raids of the other boys. The girls stood aside, talking among themselves, looking over their shoulders at the boys, and the very small children rolled in the dust or clung to the hands of their older brothers or sisters.

Soon the men began to gather, surveying their own children, speaking of planting and rain, tractors and taxes. They stood together, away from the pile of stones in the corner, and their jokes were quiet and they smiled rather than laughed. The women, wearing faded house dresses and sweaters, came shortly after their menfolk. They greeted one another and exchanged bits of gossip as they went to join their husbands. Soon the women, standing by their husbands, began to call to their children, and the children came reluctantly, having to be called four or five times. Bobby Martin ducked under his mother's grasping hand and ran, laughing, back to the pile of stones. His father spoke up sharply, and Bobby came quickly and took his place between his father and his oldest brother. 3

The lottery was conducted—as were the square dances, the teen-age club, the Halloween program—by Mr. Summers, who had time and energy to devote to civic activities. He was a round-faced, jovial man and he ran the coal business, and people were sorry for him, because he had no children and his wife was a scold. When he arrived in the square, carrying the black wooden box, there was a murmur of conversation among the villagers, and he waved and called, "Little late today, folks." The postmaster, Mr. Graves, followed him, carrying a three-legged stool, and the stool was put in the center of the square and Mr. Summers set the black box down on it. The villagers kept their distance, leaving a space between themselves and the stool, and when Mr. Summers said, "Some of you fellows want to give me a hand?" there was a hesitation before two men, Mr. Martin and his oldest son, Baxter, came forward to hold the box steady on the stool while Mr. Summers stirred up the papers inside it. 4

The original paraphernalia for the lottery had been lost long ago, and the black box now resting on the stool had been put into use even before Old Man Warner, the oldest man in town, was born. Mr. Summers spoke frequently to the villagers about making a new box, but no one liked to upset even as much tradition as was represented by the black box. There was a story that the present box had been made with some pieces of the box that had preceded it, the one that had been constructed when the first people settled down to make a village here. Every year, after the lottery, Mr. Summers began talking again about a new box, but every year the subject was allowed to fade off without anything being done. The black box grew shabbier each year; by now it was no longer completely black but splintered badly along one side to show the original wood color, and in some places faded or stained. 5

Mr. Martin and his oldest son, Baxter, held the black box securely on   6
the stool until Mr. Summers had stirred the papers thoroughly with his
hand. Because so much of the ritual had been forgotten or discarded, Mr.
Summers had been successful in having slips of paper substituted for the
chips of wood that had been used for generations. Chips of wood, Mr.
Summers had argued, had been all very well when the village was tiny, but
now that the population was more than three hundred and likely to keep on
growing, it was necessary to use something that would fit more easily into
the black box. The night before the lottery, Mr. Summers and Mr. Graves
made up the slips of paper and put them in the box, and it was then taken
to the safe of Mr. Summers' coal company and locked up until Mr. Summers was ready to take it to the square next morning. The rest of the year,
the box was put away, sometimes one place, sometimes another; it had
spent one year in Mr. Graves's barn and another year underfoot in the post
office, and sometimes it was set on a shelf in the Martin grocery and left
there.

There was a great deal of fussing to be done before Mr. Summers   7
declared the lottery open. There were the lists to make up—of heads of
families, heads of households in each family, members of each household in
each family. There was the proper swearing-in of Mr. Summers by the
postmaster, as the official of the lottery; at one time, some people remembered, there had been a recital of some sort, performed by the official of the
lottery, a perfunctory, tuneless chant that had been rattled off duly each
year; some people believed that the official of the lottery used to stand just
so when he said or sang it, others believed that he was supposed to walk
among the people, but years and years ago this part of the ritual had been
allowed to lapse. There had been, also, a ritual salute, which the official of
the lottery had had to use in addressing each person who came up to draw
from the box, but this also had changed with time, until now it was felt
necessary only for the official to speak to each person approaching. Mr.
Summers was very good at all this; in his clean white shirt and blue jeans,
with one hand resting carelessly on the black box, he seemed very proper
and important as he talked interminably to Mr. Graves and the Martins.

Just as Mr. Summers finally left off talking and turned to the assem-   8
bled villagers, Mrs. Hutchinson came hurriedly along the path to the
square, her sweater thrown over her shoulders, and slid into place in the
back of the crowd. "Clean forgot what day it was," she said to Mrs.
Delacroix, who stood next to her, and they both laughed softly. "Thought
my old man was out back stacking wood," Mrs. Hutchinson went on, "and
then I looked out the window and the kids were gone, and then I remembered it was the twenty-seventh and came a-running." She dried her hands
on her apron, and Mrs. Delacroix said, "You're in time, though. They're
still talking away up there."

Mrs. Hutchinson craned her neck to see through the crowd and found 9
her husband and children standing near the front. She tapped Mrs. Delacroix on the arm as a farewell and began to make her way through the
crowd. The people separated good-humoredly to let her through; two or
three people said, in voices just loud enough to be heard across the crowd,
"Here comes your Missus, Hutchinson," and "Bill, she made it after all."
Mrs. Hutchinson reached her husband, and Mr. Summers, who had been
waiting, said cheerfully, "Thought we were going to have to get on without
you, Tessie." Mrs. Hutchinson said, grinning, "Wouldn't have me leave
m'dishes in the sink, now, would you, Joe?" and soft laughter ran through
the crowd as the people stirred back into position after Mrs. Hutchinson's
arrival.

"Well, now," Mr. Summers said soberly, "guess we better get started, 10
get this over with, so's we can go back to work. Anybody ain't here?"

"Dunbar," several people said. "Dunbar, Dunbar." 11

Mr. Summers consulted his list. "Clyde Dunbar," he said. "That's 12
right. He's broke his leg, hasn't he? Who's drawing for him?"

"Me, I guess," a woman said, and Mr. Summers turned to look at her. 13
"Wife draws for her husband," Mr. Summers said. "Don't you have a grown
boy to do it for you, Janey?" Although Mr. Summers and everyone else in
the village knew the answer perfectly well, it was the business of the official
of the lottery to ask such questions formally. Mr. Summers waited with an
expression of polite interest while Mrs. Dunbar answered.

"Horace's not but sixteen yet," Mrs. Dunbar said regretfully. "Guess I 14
gotta fill in for the old man this year."

"Right," Mr. Summers said. He made a note on the list he was 15
holding. Then he asked, "Watson boy drawing this year?"

A tall boy in the crowd raised his hand. "Here," he said. "I'm drawing 16
for m'mother and me." He blinked his eyes nervously and ducked his head
as several voices in the crowd said things like "Good fellow, Jack," and
"Glad to see your mother's got a man to do it."

"Well," Mr. Summers said, "guess that's everyone. Old Man Warner 17
make it?"

"Here," a voice said, and Mr. Summers nodded. 18

A sudden hush fell on the crowd as Mr. Summers cleared his throat 19
and looked at the list. "All ready?" he called. "Now, I'll read the names—
heads of families first—and the men come up and take a paper out of the
box. Keep the paper folded in your hand without looking at it until
everyone has had a turn. Everything clear?"

The people had done it so many times that they only half listened to 20
the directions; most of them were quiet, wetting their lips, not looking
around. Then Mr. Summers raised one hand high and said, "Adams." A
man disengaged himself from the crowd and came forward. "Hi, Steve,"

Mr. Summers said, and Mr. Adams said, "Hi, Joe." They grinned at one another humorlessly and nervously. Then Mr. Adams reached into the black box and took out a folded paper. He held it firmly by one corner as he turned and went hastily back to his place in the crowd, where he stood a little apart from his family, not looking down at his hand.

"Allen," Mr. Summers said. "Anderson . . . Bentham." 21

"Seems like there's no time at all between lotteries any more," Mrs. 22
Delacroix said to Mrs. Graves in the back row. "Seems like we got through with the last one only last week."

"Time sure goes fast," Mrs. Graves said. 23

"Clark . . . Delacroix." 24

"There goes my old man," Mrs. Delacroix said. She held her breath 25
while her husband went forward.

"Dunbar," Mr. Summers said, and Mrs. Dunbar went steadily to the 26
box while one of the women said, "Go on, Janey," and another said, "There she goes."

"We're next," Mrs. Graves said. She watched while Mr. Graves came 27
around from the side of the box, greeted Mr. Summers gravely, and selected a slip of paper from the box. By now, all through the crowd there were men holding the small folded papers in their large hands, turning them over and over nervously. Mrs. Dunbar and her two sons stood together, Mrs. Dunbar holding the slip of paper.

"Harburt . . . Hutchinson." 28

"Get up there, Bill," Mrs. Hutchinson said, and the people near her 29
laughed.

"Jones." 30

"They do say," Mr. Adams said to Old Man Warner, who stood next 31
to him, "that over in the north village they're talking of giving up the lottery."

Old Man Warner snorted. "Pack of crazy fools," he said. "Listening to 32
the young folks, nothing's good enough for *them*. Next thing you know, they'll be wanting to go back to living in caves, nobody work any more, live *that* way for a while. Used to be a saying about 'Lottery in June, corn be heavy soon.' First thing you know, we'd all be eating stewed chickweed and acorns. There's *always* been a lottery," he added petulantly. "Bad enough to see young Joe Summers up there joking with everybody."

"Some places have already quit lotteries," Mrs. Adams said. 33

"Nothing but trouble in *that*," Old Man Warner said stoutly. "Pack of 34
young fools."

"Martin." And Bobby Martin watched his father go forward. "Over- 35
dyke . . . Percy."

"I wish they'd hurry," Mrs. Dunbar said to her older son. "I wish 36
they'd hurry."

"They're almost through," her son said. 37

"You get ready to run tell Dad," Mrs. Dunbar said.   38

Mr. Summers called his own name and then stepped forward precisely   39
and selected a slip from the box. Then he called, "Warner."

"Seventy-seventh year I been in the lottery," Old Man Warner said as   40
he went through the crowd. "Seventy-seventh time."

"Watson." The tall boy came awkwardly through the crowd. Someone   41
said, "Don't be nervous, Jack," and Mr. Summers said, "Take your time, son."

"Zanini."   42

After that, there was a long pause, a breathless pause, until Mr.   43
Summers, holding his slip of paper in the air, said, "All right, fellows." For a
minute, no one moved, and then all the slips of paper were opened.
Suddenly, all the women began to speak at once, saying, "Who is it?"
"Who's got it?" "Is it the Dunbars?" "Is it the Watsons?" Then the voices
began to say, "It's Hutchinson. It's Bill," "Bill Hutchinson's got it."

"Go tell your father," Mrs. Dunbar said to her older son.   44

People began to look around to see the Hutchinsons. Bill Hutchinson   45
was standing quiet, staring down at the paper in his hand. Suddenly, Tessie
Hutchinson shouted to Mr. Summers, "You didn't give him time enough to
take any paper he wanted. I saw you. It wasn't fair."

"Be a good sport, Tessie," Mrs. Delacroix called, and Mrs. Graves   46
said, "All of us took the same chance."

"Shut up, Tessie," Bill Hutchinson said.   47

"Well, everyone," Mr. Summers said, "that was done pretty fast, and   48
now we've got to be hurrying a little more to get done in time." He
consulted his next list. "Bill," he said, "you draw for the Hutchinson family.
You got any other households in the Hutchinsons?"

"There's Don and Eva," Mrs. Hutchinson yelled. "Make *them* take   49
their chance!"

"Daughters draw with their husbands' families, Tessie," Mr. Summers   50
said gently. "You know that as well as anyone else."

"It wasn't *fair*," Tessie said.   51

"I guess not, Joe," Bill Hutchinson said regretfully. "My daughter   52
draws with her husband's family, that's only fair. And I've got no other
family except the kids."

"Then, as far as drawing for families is concerned, it's you," Mr.   53
Summers said in explanation, "and as far as drawing for households is
concerned, that's you, too. Right?"

"Right," Bill Hutchinson said.   54

"How many kids, Bill?" Mr. Summers asked formally.   55

"Three," Bill Hutchinson said. "There's Bill, Jr., and Nancy, and little   56
Dave. And Tessie and me."

"All right, then," Mr. Summers said, "Harry, you got their tickets   57
back?"

Mr. Graves nodded and held up the slips of paper. "Put them in the   58
box, then," Mr. Summers directed. "Take Bill's and put it in."

"I think we ought to start over," Mrs. Hutchinson said, as quietly as   59
she could. "I tell you it wasn't *fair*. You didn't give him time enough to
choose. *Everybody* saw that."

Mr. Graves had selected the five slips and put them in the box, and he   60
dropped all the papers but those onto the ground, where the breeze caught
them and lifted them off.

"Listen, everybody," Mrs. Hutchinson was saying to the people   61
around her.

"Ready, Bill?" Mr. Summers asked, and Bill Hutchinson, with one   62
quick glance around at his wife and children, nodded.

"Remember," Mr. Summers said, "take the slips and keep them folded   63
until each person has taken one. Harry, you help little Dave." Mr. Graves
took the hand of the little boy, who came willingly with him up to the box.
"Take a paper out of the box, Davy," Mr. Summers said. Davy put his hand
into the box and laughed. "Take just *one* paper," Mr. Summers said. "Harry,
you hold it for him." Mr. Graves took the child's hand and removed the
folded paper from the tight fist and held it while little Dave stood next to
him and looked up at him wonderingly.

"Nancy next," Mr. Summers said. Nancy was twelve, and her school   64
friends breathed heavily as she went forward, switching her skirt, and took
a slip daintily from the box. "Bill, Jr.," Mr. Summers said, and Billy, his face
red and his feet over-large, nearly knocked the box over as he got a paper
out. "Tessie," Mr. Summers said. She hesitated for a minute, looking
around defiantly, and then set her lips and went up to the box. She
snatched a paper out and held it behind her.

"Bill," Mr. Summers said, and Bill Hutchinson reached into the box   65
and felt around, bringing his hand out at last with the slip of paper in it.

The crowd was quiet. A girl whispered, "I hope it's not Nancy," and   66
the sound of the whisper reached the edges of the crowd.

"It's not the way it used to be," Old Man Warner said clearly. "People   67
ain't the way they used to be."

"All right," Mr. Summers said. "Open the papers. Harry, you open   68
little Dave's."

Mr. Graves opened the slip of paper and there was a general sigh   69
through the crowd as he held it up and everyone could see that it was blank.
Nancy and Bill, Jr., opened theirs at the same time, and both beamed and
laughed, turning around to the crowd and holding their slips of paper above
their heads.

"Tessie," Mr. Summers said. There was a pause, and then Mr. Sum-   70
mers looked at Bill Hutchinson, and Bill unfolded his paper and showed it.
It was blank.

"It's Tessie," Mr. Summers said, and his voice was hushed. "Show us   71
her paper, Bill."

Bill Hutchinson went over to his wife and forced the slip of paper out   72
of her hand. It had a black spot on it, the black spot Mr. Summers had
made the night before with the heavy pencil in the coal-company office. Bill
Hutchinson held it up, and there was a stir in the crowd.

"All right, folks," Mr. Summers said. "Let's finish quickly."   73

Although the villagers had forgotten the ritual and lost the original   74
black box, they still remembered to use stones. The pile of stones the boys
had made earlier was ready; there were stones on the ground with the
blowing scraps of paper that had come out of the box. Mrs. Delacroix
selected a stone so large she had to pick it up with both hands and turned to
Mrs. Dunbar. "Come on," she said. "Hurry up."

Mrs. Dunbar had small stones in both hands, and she said, gasping for   75
breath, "I can't run at all. You'll have to go ahead and I'll catch up with you."

The children had stones already, and someone gave Davy Hutchinson   76
a few pebbles.

Tessie Hutchinson was in the center of a cleared space by now, and she   77
held her hands out desperately as the villagers moved in on her. "It isn't
fair," she said. A stone hit her on the side of the head.

Old Man Warner was saying, "Come on, come on, everyone." Steve   78
Adams was in the front of the crowd of villagers, with Mrs. Graves beside
him.

"It isn't fair, it isn't right," Mrs. Hutchinson screamed, and then they   79
were upon her.

Questions for Study and Discussion

1. At what point in the story do you first begin to suspect that something
terrible is going to happen? When do you figure out what it is?

2. What kinds of details does the author use in her story to create a sense
of normality? to create a sense of horror? Support your answer with examples.

3. Describe the ritual in your own words. What is the terrible irony of
this ritual? What other ironies are there in the story?

4. What different attitudes toward the ritual are expressed by Old Man
Warner, Tessie, Mr. Summers, Nancy's friend. Did those attitudes remain fixed
or did they change? Explain. Which person do you think speaks for most of the
town?

5. How believable is Jackson's story? What effect does that believability
have on the impact of the story?

6. The townspeople continue to live in their town knowing that yearly
they risk either killing each other or being killed. Why do they stay? What point
about society is Jackson trying to make in her story?

Writing Topics

1. What do you know about "scapegoat" rituals such as the one depicted in Jackson's story? What is a scapegoat? What was the intention of these rituals? Do some research to find out more about them. In what kinds of cultures were they practiced? Have any of these cultures survived into the present?

2. Consider some of the religious or fraternal rituals you, your community, or your friends observe. During which rituals are you or your friends aware of the meaning each time you participate? Which rituals have you repeated without thought to their meaning? Are you surprised at your answers? In what way do your answers enhance or detract from your understanding of Jackson's story?

Glossary

Abstract: *See Concrete/Abstract.*

Action is the series of events in a narrative. It is also called the story line. See also *Plot.*

Alliteration: See *Sound.*

Allusion is a passing reference to a person, place, or thing. Often drawn from history, the Bible, mythology, or literature, allusions are an economical way for a writer to convey the essence of an idea, atmosphere, emotion, or historical era. Some examples of allusion are "The scandal was his Watergate," "He saw himself as a modern Job," and "The campaign ended not with a bang but a whimper." An allusion should be familiar to the reader; if it is not, it will neither add to the meaning of a text nor enrich an emotion.

Analogy is a special form of comparison in which the writer explains something unfamiliar by comparing it to something familiar: "A transmission line is simply a pipeline for electricity. In the case of a water pipeline, more water will flow through the pipe as water pressure increases. The same is true of electricity in a transmission line."

787

Analysis is a type of exposition in which the writer considers a subject in terms of its parts or elements. For example, one may analyze a movie by considering its subject, its plot, its dialogue, its acting, its camera work, and its set. See also *Cause and Effect, Classification, Process Analysis.*

Anecdote. An anecdote is a brief story told to illustrate a concept or support a point. Anecdotes are often used to open essays because of the inherent interest of a story.

Antagonist. An antagonist is a character who struggles against the central character, or protagonist, in a conflict. Chillingworth in *The Scarlet Letter* is a villainous antagonist; Jim in *The Adventures of Huckleberry Finn*, a virtuous antagonist. See also *Protagonist.*

Aphorism. An aphorism is a short, concise statement embodying a general truth.

Appropriateness: See *Diction.*

Argument is one of the four basic forms of discourse. (Narration, description, and exposition are the other three.) To argue is to attempt to persuade a reader to agree with a point of view or to pursue a particular course of action by appealing to the reader's rational or intellectual faculties. See also *Deduction, Induction, Logical Fallacies*, and *Persuasion.*

Assonance: See *Sound.*

Assumptions are things one believes to be true, whether or not their truth can be proven. All writing includes many unstated assumptions as well as some that are stated, and an active reader seeks to discover what those assumptions are and to decide whether they are acceptable.

Attitude is the view or opinion of a person; in writing, the author's attitude is reflected in its tone. See also *Tone.*

Audience is the expected readership for a piece of writing. For example, the readers of a national weekly newsmagazine come from all walks of life and have diverse interests, opinions, and educational backgrounds. In contrast, the readership for an organic chemistry journal is made up of people whose interests and education are quite specialized.

Cause and Effect is a form of analysis that answers the question *why*. It explains the reasons for an occurrence or the consequences of an action. Determining causes and effects is usually thought-provoking and quite complex.

One reason for this is that there are two types of causes: (1) *immediate causes*, which are readily apparent because they are closest to the effect, and (2) *ultimate causes*, which are somewhat removed, not so apparent, or perhaps even obscure. Furthermore, ultimate causes may bring about effects which themselves become causes, thus creating what is called a *causal chain*. For example, the immediate cause of a flood may be the collapse of a dam, and the ultimate cause might be an engineering error. An intermediate cause, however, might be faulty construction of the dam owing to corruption in the building trades.

Character. A character is a person in a story. Characters are generally regarded as being one of two types: flat or round. A flat character is one who exhibits a single trait, such as the devoted husband, the kind grandmother, or the shrewd businessman; such a character is stereotypic, unwavering, and thoroughly predictable. A round character, on the other hand, displays various traits and is complex and at times unpredictable—in short, very much like most of us. The chief character in a story is often called the *protagonist*, whereas the character or characters who oppose the protagonist are the *antagonists*.

Classification, sometimes called classification and division, is a form of exposition. When classifying, the writer sorts and arranges people, places, or things into categories according to their differing characteristics. When dividing, the writer creates new, smaller categories within a large category, usually for purposes of classification. For example, a writer might divide the large category *books* into several smaller ones: textbooks, novels, biographies, reference books, and so on. Then specific books could be classified by assigning them to these categories.

Cliché. A cliché is a trite or hackneyed expression, common in everyday speech but avoided in most serious writing.

Climax. In a work of fiction or drama, the climax is the point of highest tension, sometimes identical with the turning point of the narrative.

Coherence is a quality of good writing that results when all sentences, paragraphs, and longer divisions of an essay are naturally connected. Coherent writing is achieved through (1) a logically organized sequence of ideas, (2) the repetition of key words and ideas, (3) a pace suitable for the topic and the reader, and (4) the use of transitional words and expressions. See also *Organization, Transitions.*

Colloquial Expressions: See *Diction.*

Comparison and Contrast is a form of exposition in which the writer points out the similarities and differences between two or more subjects in the same class or category. The function of any comparison and contrast is to clarify—to reach some conclusion about the items being compared and contrasted. The writer's purpose may be simply to inform, or to make readers aware of similarities or differences that are interesting and significant in themselves. Or, the writer may explain something unfamiliar by comparing it to something very familiar, perhaps explaining squash by comparing it to tennis. Finally, the writer can point out the superiority of one thing by contrasting it with another—for example, showing that one product is the best by contrasting it with all its competitors.

Conclusion. The conclusion of an essay is the sentences or paragraphs that sum up the main points and suggest their significance or in some other way bring the essay to a satisfying end. See also *Introduction*.

Concrete/Abstract. A concrete word names a specific object, person, place, or action: *bicycle, milkshake, building, book, John F. Kennedy, Chicago,* or *hiking*. An abstract word, in contrast, refers to general qualities, conditions, ideas, actions, or relationships which cannot be directly perceived by the senses: *bravery, dedication, excellence, anxiety, stress, thinking,* or *hatred*. Although writers must use both concrete and abstract language, good writers avoid too many abstract words. Instead, they rely on concrete words to define and illustrate abstractions.

Conflict in a story is the clash of opposing characters, events, and ideas. A resolution of the conflict is necessary in order for the story to conclude.

Connotation/Denotation refer to the meanings of words. Denotation is the literal meaning of a word. Connotation, on the other hand, is the implied or suggested meaning of a word, including its emotional associations. For example, the denotation of *lamb* is "a young sheep." The connotations of lamb are numerous: *gentle, docile, weak, peaceful, blessed, sacrificial, blood, spring, frisky, pure, innocent,* and so on. Good writers are sensitive to both the denotations and connotations of words.

Consonance: See *Sound*.

Contrast: See *Comparison and Contrast*.

Deduction is a method of reasoning from the general to the particular. The most common form of deductive reasoning is the *syllogism*, a three-part argument that moves from a general statement (major premise) and a specific statement (minor premise) to a logical conclusion, as in the following example:

   a. All women are mortal. (major premise)
   b. Judy is a woman. (minor premise)
   c. Therefore, Judy is mortal. (conclusion)

The conclusion to a deductive argument is persuasive only when both premises are true and the form of the syllogism is correct. Then it is said that the argument is sound.

Definition is a statement of the meaning of a word, or of an idea or even an experience. A definition may be brief or extended, the latter requiring a paragraph of an essay or even an entire essay. There are two basic types of brief definitions, each useful in its own way. The first method is to give a *synonym*, a word that has nearly the same meaning as the word you wish to define: *dictionary* for *lexicon*, *nervousness* for *anxiety*. No two words ever have exactly the same meaning, but you can, nevertheless, pair a familiar word with an unfamiliar one and thereby clarify your meaning. The other way to define quickly, often with a single sentence, is to give a *formal definition*; that is, to place the term to be defined in a general class and then to distinguish it from other members of that class by describing its particular characteristics. For example:

WORD	CLASS	CHARACTERISTICS
A *canoe*	is a *small boat*	that has *curved sides* and *pointed ends* and is *narrow, made of lightweight materials*, and *propelled by paddles*.
A *rowboat*	is a *small boat*	that has a *shallow draft* and usually a *flat* or *rounded bottom*, a *squared-off* or *V-shaped stern*, and *oarlocks* for the *oars with which it is propelled*.

Denotation: See *Connotation/Denotation*.

Denouement is the resolution or conclusion of a narrative.

Description is one of the four basic forms of discourse. (Narration, exposition, and argument are the other three.) To describe is to give a verbal picture of a person, a place, or a thing. Even an idea or a state of mind can be made vividly concrete, as in, "The old woman was as silent as a ghost." Although descriptive writing can stand alone, description is often used with other rhetorical strategies; for instance, description can make examples more interesting, explain the complexities of a process, or clarify a definition or comparison. A good writer selects and arranges descriptive details to create a *dominant impression* that reinforces the point or the atmosphere of a piece of writing.

Objective description emphasizes the *object* itself and is factual without resorting to such scientific extremes that the reader cannot understand the facts. *Subjective* or *impressionistic description*, on the other hand, emphasizes the *observer* and gives a personal interpretation of the subject matter through language rich in modifiers and figures of speech.

Dialogue is the conversation that is recorded in a piece of writing. Through dialogue writers reveal important aspects of characters' personalities as well as events in the plot.

Diction refers to a writer's choice and use of words. Good diction is precise and appropriate—the words mean exactly what the writer intends and are well suited to the writer's subject, intended audience, and purpose in writing. There are three main levels of diction, each with its own uses: formal, for grand occasions; colloquial, or conversational, especially for dialogue; and informal, for most essay writing. See also *Connotation/Denotation*, *Concrete/Abstract*, *Specific/General*.

Discourse, Forms of. The four traditional forms of discourse, often called "rhetorical modes," are narration, description, exposition, and argument. Depending on the purpose, a writer may use one or more than one of these forms in a piece of writing. For more information see *Argument*, *Description*, *Exposition*, and *Narration*.

Division: See *Classification*.

Dominant Impression: See *Description*.

Draft. A draft is a version of a piece of writing at a particular stage in the writing process. The first version produced is usually called the rough draft or first draft and is a writer's beginning attempt to give overall shape to his or her ideas. Subsequent versions are called revised drafts. The copy presented for publication is the final draft.

Editing. During the editing stage of the writing process, the writer makes his or her prose conform to the conventions of the language. This includes making final improvements in sentence structure and diction and proofreading for wordiness and errors in grammar, usage, spelling, and punctuation. After editing, the writer is ready to type a final copy.

Effect: See *Cause and Effect*.

Emphasis is the placement of important ideas and words within sentences and longer units of writing so that they have the greatest impact. In general, the end has the most impact, and the beginning nearly as much; the middle has the least. See also *Organization*.

Essay. An essay, traditionally, is a piece of nonfiction prose, usually fairly brief, in which the writer explores his or her ideas on a subject. Essays come in many forms including personal narratives and scientific and theoretical inquiries, as well as critical, humorous, and argumentative pieces. The word *essay* presently is used fairly loosely to include not only personal writing but most short nonfiction prose pieces.

Evaluation of a piece of writing is the assessment of its effectiveness or merit. In evaluating a piece of writing, one should ask the following questions: What does the writer have to say? Are the writer's ideas challenging or thought-provoking? What is the writer's purpose? Is it a worthwhile purpose? Does the writer achieve the purpose? Is the writer's information sufficient and accurate? What are the strengths of the essay? What are its weaknesses? Depending on the type of writing and the purpose, more specific questions can also be asked. For example, with an argument one could ask: Does the writer follow the principles of logical thinking? Is the writer's evidence convincing?

Evidence is the data on which a judgment or argument is based or by which proof or probability is established. Evidence usually takes the form of statistics, facts, names, examples, illustrations, and opinions of authorities, and always involves a clear indication of its relevance to the point at issue.

Example. An example is a person, place, or thing used to represent a group or explain a general statement. Many entries in this glossary contain examples used in both ways. Examples enable writers to show and not simply to tell readers what they mean. The terms *example* and *illustration* are sometimes used interchangeably. See also *Specific/General*.

Exposition is one of the four basic forms of discourse. (Narration, description, and argument are the other three.) The purpose of exposition is to clarify, explain, and inform. The methods of exposition are analysis, definition, classification, comparison and contrast, cause and effect, and process analysis. For a discussion of each of these methods of exposition, see *Analysis, Cause and Effect, Classification, Comparison and Contrast, Definition*, and *Process Analysis*.

Fallacy: See *Logical Fallacies*.

Figures of Speech are words and phrases that are used in an imaginative rather than literal way. Figurative language makes writing vivid and interesting and therefore more memorable. The most common figures of speech are:

Simile. An explicit comparison introduced by *like* or *as*: "The fighter's hands were like stone."

Metaphor. An implied comparison that uses one thing as the equivalent of another: "All the world's a stage."

Personification. The attributing of human traits to an inanimate object: "The engine coughed and then stopped."

Hyperbole. A deliberate exaggeration or overstatement: "I am so hungry I could eat a horse."

Metonymy. A type of comparison in which the name of one thing is used to represent another, as in the words *White House* used to represent the president of the United States.

   Synecdoche. Another comparison in which a part stands for the whole, as in the word *crown* used to represent a king or the word *sail* to represent a ship.

   See also *Symbol.*

Focus. Focus is the limitation that a writer gives his or her subject. The writer's task is to select a manageable topic given the constraints of time, space, and purpose. For example, within the general subject of sports, a writer could focus on government support of amateur athletes or narrow the focus further to government support of Olympic athletes.

General: See *Specific/General.*

Genre. A genre is a type or form of literary writing, such as poetry, fiction, or the essay; the term is also used to refer to more specific literary forms, such as an epic poem, novel, or detective story.

Hyperbole: See *Figures of Speech.*

Illustration: See *Example.*

Imagery is the verbal representation of a sensory experience: sight, hearing, touch, smell, taste, even the sensations one feels inside one's own body. Writers use imagery to create details in their descriptions. Effective images can make writing come alive and enable the reader to experience vicariously what is being described.

Induction is a method of reasoning that moves from particular examples to a general statement. In doing so, the writer makes what is known as an *inductive leap* from the evidence to the generalization, which can never offer the absolute certainty of deductive reasoning. For example, after examining enrollment statistics, we can conclude that students do not like to take courses offered early in the morning or late in the afternoon. See also *Argument.*

Introduction. The introduction of an essay consists of the sentences or paragraphs in which the author captures the reader's interest and prepares for what is to come. An introduction normally identifies the topic, indicates what purpose the essay is to serve, and often states or implies the thesis. See also *Conclusion.*

Irony is the use of language to suggest other than its literal meaning. *Verbal irony* uses words to suggest something different from their literal meaning. For example, when Jonathan Swift writes in *A Modern Proposal* that Ireland's population problem should be solved through cannibalism, he means that almost any other solution would be preferable. *Dramatic irony*, in literature, presents words or actions that are appropriate in an unexpected way. For example, Oedipus promises to find and punish the wrongdoer who has brought disaster on Thebes, then discovers that the criminal is himself. *Irony of situation* involves a state of affairs the opposite of what one would expect: a pious man is revealed as a hypocrite, or an athlete dies young.

Jargon refers to specialized terms associated with a particular field of knowledge. Also, it sometimes means pseudotechnical language used to impress readers.

Logic, in writing, is the orderly, coherent presentation of a subject. As a subdivision of philosophy, logic is both the study and the method of correct reasoning, using the techniques of deduction or induction to arrive at conclusions.

Logical Fallacies are errors in reasoning that render an argument invalid. Some of the more common logical fallacies are:

Oversimplification. The tendency to provide simple solutions to complex problems: "The way to solve the problem of our high national debt is to raise taxes."

Non sequitur ("It does not follow"). An inference or conclusion that does not follow from the premises or evidence: "He was a brilliant basketball player; therefore, he will be an outstanding Supreme Court justice."

Post hoc, ergo propter hoc ("After this, therefore because of this"). Confusing chance or coincidence with causation. Because one event comes after another one, it does not necessarily mean that the first event caused the second: "I know I caught my cold at the hockey game, because I didn't have it before I went there."

Begging the question. Assuming in a premise that which needs to be proved: "Government management of a rail system is an economic evil because it is socialistic."

Either/or thinking. The tendency to see an issue as having only two sides: "America—love it or leave it."

Metaphor: See *Figures of Speech.*

Meter: See *Sound.*

Metonymy: See *Figures of Speech.*

Modes, Rhetorical: See *Discourse, Forms of.*

Mood is the emotional effect or feeling that a literary work evokes in the reader.

Narration is one of the four basic forms of discourse. (Description, exposition, and argument are the other three.) To narrate is to tell a story, to tell what happened. Whenever you relate an incident or use an anecdote to make a point, you use narration. In its broadest sense, narration includes all writing that provides an account of an event or a series of events.

Objective/Subjective. Objective writing is impersonal in tone and relies chiefly on facts and logical argument. Subjective writing refers to the author's personal feelings and conveys his or her emotional response to the subject. A writer may modulate between the two within the same essay, according to his or her purpose, but one or the other is usually made to dominate.

Opinion. An opinion is a belief or conclusion not substantiated by positive knowledge or proof. An opinion reveals personal feelings or attitudes or states a position. Opinion should not be confused with argument.

Organization is the plan or scheme by which the contents of a piece of writing are arranged. Some often-used plans of organization are *chronological order*, which relates people and events to each other in terms of time, for example, as one event coming before another, or two conditions existing simultaneously; *spatial order*, which relates objects and events in space, for example, from far to near or from top to bottom; *climactic order*, which presents ideas and evidence in order of increasing importance, power, or magnitude to heighten emphasis; and its opposite, *anticlimactic order*.

Paradox. A paradox is a self-contradictory statement that yet has truth in it, for example: "Less is more."

Paragraph. The paragraph, the single most important unit of thought in an essay, is a series of closely related sentences. These sentences adequately develop the central or controlling idea of the paragraph. This central or controlling idea, usually stated in a topic sentence, is necessarily related to the purpose of the whole composition. A well-written paragraph has several distinguishing characteristics: a clearly stated or implied topic sentence, adequate development, unity, coherence, and an appropriate organizational strategy.

Parallelism. Parallel structure is the repetition of word order or form either within a single sentence or in several sentences that develop the same central idea. As a rhetorical device, parallelism can aid coherence and add emphasis. Roosevelt's statement, "I see one third of the nation ill-housed, ill-clad, and ill-nourished," illustrates effective parallelism.

Persona, or speaker, is the "voice" you can imagine uttering the words of a piece of writing. Sometimes the speaker is recognizably the same as the author, especially in nonfiction prose. Often, however, the speaker is a partly or wholly fictional creation, as in short stories, novels, poems, and some essays.

Personification: See *Figures of Speech.*

Persuasion is the effort to make one's audience agree with one's thesis or point of view and thus accept a belief or take a particular action. There are two main kinds of persuasion: the appeal to reason (see *Argument*) and the appeal to an audience's emotions; both kinds are often blended in the same piece of writing.

Plot is the sequence or pattern of events in a short story, novel, film, or play. The chief elements of plot are its *action,* the actual event or events; *conflict,* the struggle between opposing characters or forces; the *climax,* the turning point of the story; and the *denouement,* the final resolution or outcome of the story.

Poetry is a rhythmical, imaginative, and intense form of expression. Poetry achieves its intensity by not only saying things in the fewest possible words but also in relying more heavily than other forms of literature on such language devices as metaphor, symbol, connotation, allusion, sound repetition, and imagery.

Point of View, as a technical term in writing, refers to the grammatical person of the speaker in a piece of writing. For example, a first-person point of view uses the pronoun *I* and is commonly found in autobiography and the personal essay; a third-person point of view uses the pronouns *he, she,* or *it* and is commonly found in objective writing. Both are used in the short story to characterize the narrator, the one who tells the story. The narrator may be *omniscient*—that is, telling the actions of all the characters whenever and wherever they take place, and reporting the characters' thoughts and attitudes as well. A less knowing narrator, such as a character in the story, is said to have a *limited,* or restricted, point of view.

Prewriting. Prewriting is a name applied to all the activities that take place before a writer actually starts a rough draft. During the prewriting stage of the writing process, the writer will select a subject area, focus on a particular topic, collect information and make notes, brainstorm for ideas, discover connections between pieces of information, determine a thesis and purpose, rehearse portions of the writing in the mind and/or on paper, and make a scratch outline.

Process Analysis answers the question *how* and explains how something works or gives step-by-step directions for doing something. There are two types of process analysis: directional and informational. The *directional* type provides instructions on how to do something. These instructions can be as brief as the directions for making instant coffee printed on a label or as complex as the directions in a manual for building your own home computer. The purpose of directional process analysis is simple: the reader can follow the directions and achieve the desired results. The *informational* type of process analysis, on the other hand, tells how something works, how something is made, or how something occurred. You would use informational process analysis if you wanted to explain to a reader how the human heart functions, how hailstones are formed, how an atomic bomb works, how iron ore is made into steel, how you selected the college you are attending, or how the Salk polio vaccine was developed. Rather than giving specific directions, the informational type of process analysis has the purpose of explaining and informing.

Protagonist. The protagonist is the central character in the conflict of a story. He or she may be either a sympathetic character (Hester Prynne in *The Scarlet Letter*) or an unsympathetic one (Captain Ahab in *Moby-Dick*).

Publication. The publication stage of the writing process is when the writer shares his or her writing with the intended audience. Publication can take the form of a typed or oral presentation, a dittoed or photocopied copy, or a commercially printed rendition. What's important is that the writer's words are read in what amounts to the final form.

Purpose. The writer's purpose is what he or she wants to accomplish in a particular piece of writing. Sometimes the writer may state the purpose openly, but sometimes the purpose must be inferred from the written work itself.

Revision. During the revision stage of the writing process, the writer determines what in the draft needs to be developed or clarified so that the essay says what the writer intends it to say. Often the writer needs to revise several times before the essay is "right." Comments from peer evaluators can be invaluable in helping writers determine what sorts of changes need to be made. Such changes can include adding material, deleting material, changing the order of presentation, and substituting new material for old.

Rhetoric is the effective use of language, traditionally the art of persuasion, though the term is now generally applied to all purposes and kinds of writing.

Rhyme: See *Sound.*

Rhythm: See *Sound.*

Satire is a literary composition, in prose or poetry, in which human follies, vices, or institutions are held up to scorn.

Setting is the time and place in which the action of a narrative occurs. Many critics also include in their notion of setting such elements as the occupations and life-styles of characters as well as the religious, moral, and social environment in which they live.

Short Story. The short story, as the name implies, is a brief fictional narrative in prose. Short stories range in length from about 500 words (a short short story) to about 15,000–20,000 words (a long short story or novella).

Simile: See *Figures of Speech.*

Sound. Writers of prose and especially of poetry pay careful attention to the sounds as well as the meanings of words. Whether we read a piece aloud or simply "hear" what we read in our mind's ear, we are most likely to notice the following sound features of the language:

Rhythm. In language, the *rhythm* is mainly a pattern of stressed and unstressed syllables. The rhythm of prose is irregular, but prose writers sometimes cluster stressed syllables for emphasis: "Théy sháll nót páss." Much poetry is written in highly regular rhythms called *meters*, in which a pattern of stressed and unstressed syllables is set and held to: "Th' ĕxpénse | ŏf spír | ĭt iń | ă wáste | ŏf sháme." Even nonmetrical poetry may sometimes use regular rhythms, as in this line by Walt Whitman: "I célĕbráte mўsélf aňd síng mўsélf."

Assonance, Consonance, and Rhyme. The repetition of a consonant is called *consonance*, and the repetition of a vowel is called *assonance*. The following line of poetry uses consonance of *l* and *d*, and assonance of *o*: "Roll on, thou deep and dark blue ocean—roll!" When two nearby words begin with the same sound, like *deep* and *dark* above, that sound pattern is called *alliteration*. And when two words end with whole syllables that sound the same, and one of those syllables is stressed, the result is called *rhyme*, as in strong/along and station/gravitation.

Specific/General. General words name groups or classes of objects, qualities, or actions. Specific words, on the other hand, name individual objects, qualities, or actions within a class or group. To some extent the terms *general* and *specific* are relative. For example, *dessert* is a class of things. *Pie*, however, is more specific than *dessert* but more general than *pecan pie* or *chocolate cream pie*. Good writing judiciously balances the general with the specific. Writing with too many general words is likely to be dull and lifeless. General words do not create vivid responses in the reader's mind as concrete specific words can. On the other hand, writing that relies exclusively on specific words may lack focus and direction, the control that more general statements provide. See also *Example*.

Style is the individual manner in which a writer expresses his or her ideas. Style is created by the author's particular selection of words, construction of sentences, and arrangement of ideas. A skillful writer adapts his or her style to the purpose and audience at hand. Some useful adjectives for describing styles include literary or journalistic, ornamental or economical, personal or impersonal, formal or chatty, among others. But these labels are very general, and an accurate stylistic description or analysis of a particular author or piece of writing requires consideration of sentence length and structure, diction, figures of speech, and the like.

Subjective: See *Objective/Subjective*.

Symbol: A symbol is a person, place, or thing that represents something beyond itself. For example, the eagle is a symbol of the United States, and the cross a symbol of Christianity.

Synecdoche: See *Figures of Speech*.

Theme is the central idea in a piece of writing. In fiction, poetry, and drama, the theme may not be stated directly, but it is then presented through the characters, actions, and images of the work. In nonfiction prose the theme is often stated explicitly in a thesis statement. See also *Thesis*.

Thesis. The thesis of an essay is its main idea, the point it is trying to make. The thesis is often expressed in a one- or two-sentence statement, although sometimes it is implied or suggested rather than stated directly. The thesis statement controls and directs the content of the essay. Everything that the writer says must be logically related to the thesis. Some therefore prefer to call the thesis the *controlling idea*.

Tone. Comparable to "tone of voice" in conversation, the tone of a written work reflects the author's attitude toward the subject and audience. For example, the tone of a work might be described by such terms as friendly, serious, distant, angry, cheerful, bitter, cynical, enthusiastic, morbid, resentful, warm, playful, and so forth.

Transitions are words or phrases that link sentences, paragraphs, and larger units of a composition to achieve coherence. These devices include connecting words and phrases like *moreover*, *therefore*, and *on the other hand*, and the repetition of key words and ideas.

Unity. A well-written essay should be unified; that is, everything in it should be related to its thesis, or main idea. The first requirement for unity is that the thesis itself be clear, either through a direct statement, called the thesis statement, or by implication. The second requirement is that there be no digressions, no discussion or information that is not shown to be logically related to the thesis. A unified essay stays within the limits of its thesis.

Writing Process. The writing process consists of five major stages: prewriting, writing drafts, revision, editing, and publication. The process is not inflexible, but there is no mistaking the fact that most writers follow some version of it most of the time. Although orderly in its basic components and sequence of activities, the writing process is nonetheless continuous, creative, and unique to each individual writer. See also *Prewriting, Draft, Revision, Editing,* and *Publication.*

Index of Authors and Titles